Cases on Web 2.0 in Developing Countries:

Studies on Implementation, Application, and Use

Nahed Amin Azab
American University in Cairo, Egypt

Information Science
REFERENCE

Managing Director:	Lindsay Johnston
Editorial Director:	Joel Gamon
Book Production Manager:	Jennifer Yoder
Publishing Systems Analyst:	Adrienne Freeland
Development Editor:	Austin DeMarco
Assistant Acquisitions Editor:	Kayla Wolfe
Typesetter:	Lisandro Gonzalez
Cover Design:	Nick Newcomer

Published in the United States of America by
Information Science Reference (an imprint of IGI Global)
701 E. Chocolate Avenue
Hershey PA 17033
Tel: 717-533-8845
Fax: 717-533-8661
E-mail: cust@igi-global.com
Web site: http://www.igi-global.com

Library of Congress Cataloging-in-Publication Data

Cases on Web 2.0 in developing countries : studies on implementation, application, and use / Nahed Amin Azab, editor.
    pages cm
  Includes bibliographical references and index.
  Summary: "This book investigates the perception of the value of Web 2.0, the adoption and application of its technologies, as well as the different approaches and innovations necessary for the implementation of Web applications in developing countries"--Provided by publisher.
   ISBN 978-1-4666-2515-0 (hbk.) -- ISBN (invalid) 978-1-4666-2516-7 (ebook) -- ISBN (invalid) 978-1-4666-2517-4 (print & perpetual access) 1. Web 2.0. 2. Internet--Social aspects. 3. Online social networks. I. Azab, Nahed Amin, 1961-
  TK5105.88817.C37 2012
  006.7'54--dc23
                                2012033663

British Cataloguing in Publication Data
A Cataloguing in Publication record for this book is available from the British Library.

This book is dedicated to the soul of my beloved mother, Fatma Ahmed Mostafa (1938 – 2012). Her unconditional love and support were always the cornerstone of any achievement I reached.

List of Reviewers

Hesham Abdel Salam, *Cairo University, Egypt*
Geetha Abeseingh, *Middlesex University, UK*
Maged Ali, *Brunel University, UK*
Mariam F. Alkazemi, *University of Florida, USA*
Said Assar, *Telecom Business School, France*
Mirjana Pejic Bach, *University of Zagreb, Croatia*
Ahmed El Ragal, *German University in Cairo, Egypt*
Hoda Hosny, *American University in Cairo, Egypt*
Damián Keller, *Federal University of Acre, Brazil*
Nermine Khalifa, *Arab Academy for Science and Technology, Egypt*
Dimitris Kotzinos, *Technical Educational Institution of Serres, Greece*
Edward Ku, *National Kaohsiung University of Hospitality and Tourism, China*
Zaigham Mahmood, *University of Derby, UK*
Evandro M. Miletto, *Federal Institute of Rio Grande do Sul, Brazil*
Maha Mourad, *American University in Cairo, Egypt*
Marcelo Soares Pimenta, *Federal University of Rio Grande do Sul, Brazil*
Dina Rateb, *American University in Cairo, Egypt*
Carla Ruiz, *University of Valencia, Spain*
Omneya Yacout, *Alexandria University, Egypt*
Abou Bakr Zade, *Middlesex University, UK*

Table of Contents

Detailed Table of Contents

Nahed Azab, American University in Cairo, Egypt
Nermine Khalifa, Arab Academy for Science and Technology, Egypt

This chapter investigates the role of Web 2.0 technologies in supporting entrepreneurs. Web 2.0 provides a convenient tool for entrepreneurs to market their products or services, and to build communities around their brands. Through reviewing the literature related to Web 2.0 and its value for entrepreneurs as well as the entailed challenges, a research is performed to explore the use of Web 2.0 by Egyptian Internet entrepreneurs who operate their business either traditionally or virtually. The objective of the chapter is to portray the present situation of the Web 2.0's exploitation of Web 2.0 and the authors' perceptions regarding the value and challenges towards this emerging technology.

Caitlin M. Bentley, Royal Holloway University of London, UK

This chapter addresses online tools for collaboration among civil society organizations. It demonstrates the stages and requirements for designing and implementing an online collaboration tool for inter-organizational communication among 17 civil society organizations in five West African nations. The chapter aims to present the lessons learned from such initiatives, providing an invaluable resource by highlighting the critical factors that should be considered when leading projects within similar contexts.

Chapter 3

The Conceptualization of a Research Model for the Measurement of

Yfantis Vasileios, University of the West of Scotland, UK
Abel Usoro, University of the West of Scotland, UK
Tseles Dimitrios, Technological Education Institute of Piraeus, Greece

The authors discuss the value of Web 2.0 by governments in developing countries. They argue that for governments to incorporate Web 2.0, they should consider both technological and human dimensions. The chapter's objective is to suggest a framework for measuring electronic government 2.0's readiness derived from the technology acceptance model, theory of planned behavior, and indexes from the United Nation's database. The implications of the proposed model are presented pinpointing its potential for South Sudan as a case study.

Chapter 4

Robert A. Cropf, Saint Louis University, USA
Mamoun Benmamoun, Saint Louis University, USA
Morris Kalliny, Saint Louis University, USA

The chapter addresses the relationship between Web 2.0 and democracy pinpointing on the power of Web 2.0 in changing the political climate in some Arab countries, referred to as the Arab Spring. However, Arab Spring countries still did not reach institutionalized democracy. The objective of this chapter is to highlight the preconditions for successful e-democracy implementation through Web 2.0 tools. Through applying the path dependency model—that stresses the existence of political and economic institutions as well as supporting culture and norms in using technology—on four Arab countries, the authors highlight the political environment in these countries that affects the influence of Web 2.0 in realizing e-democracy.

Chapter 5

Web 2.0 Goes Mobile: Motivations and Barriers of Mobile Social Networks

Carla Ruiz-Mafé, University of Valencia, Spain
Silvia Sanz-Blas, University of Valencia, Spain
José Martí-Parreño, European University of Madrid, Spain

The authors investigate several issues related to the use of mobile social networking applications in both developed and developing countries. After reviewing previous research that identifies the key drivers and barriers of the adoption of mobile social networks, the authors suggest a model for social network adoption through mobile devices, and test this model through conducting a research on a sample of students in a Spanish university. Hence, the chapter attempts to highlight the perception of users towards this technology, and analyze their behavior of mobile social networks.

Chapter 6

Leonor Barroca, The Open University, UK
Itana M. S. Gimenes, Universidade Estadual de Maringá, Brazil

This chapter highlights the importance of learning from the best practices of distant education in developed countries, and means to apply them in other context in the developing world, taking into consideration the local dimension. The authors conducted a research to study their experience of incorporating Web 2.0 in postgraduate courses in The Open University (OU) in the UK, and its applicability on Brazilian distant learning education. The chapter emphasizes the importance of distant education in Brazil, and presents an overview of the postgraduate education in the UK and Brazil, comparing both systems. The chapter objective is to introduce OU experience and induce guidance from it to assess the possibility to adopt it in a Brazilian context pinpointing the underpinning opportunities and barriers, and critical success factors.

Chapter 7

Jacques Bughin, McKinsey and Company, Belgium, ECARES, ULB,
ECORE (UCL, ULB), Brussels & KUL, Belgium

The author investigates the use of Web 2.0 in organizations in developing economies through a survey on a sample of 3600 enterprises in 60 countries that represents enterprises in both developed an developing countries. The chapter analyzes several aspects concerning Web 2.0 in companies in the developing world such as extent of internal and external use, implemented activities, performance, and tendency and ability of business process change.

Chapter 8

Agus Mutohar, The University of Texas at Austin, USA
Joan E. Hughes, The University of Texas at Austin, USA

This chapter addresses the role of information and communication technology in general, and Web 2.0 in particular, to improve education in Indonesia. A review was conducted on related research, NGO studies, and education policies of Indonesian Government analyzing the context of the study from both macro and micro perspectives. The objective of the chapter is to shed light on the education laws and policies in Indonesia, the initiatives undertaken to incorporate Web 2.0 in both primary and secondary education, and the numerous challenges limiting Web 2.0 adoption. Based on the research findings, the authors introduce a number of recommendations suggesting effective strategies to reinforce the integration of Web 2.0 in educational programs to enrich learning content and practice.

Chapter 9

Sergio Ricardo Mazini, São Paulo State University, Brazil
José Alcides Gobbo, Jr., São Paulo State University, Brazil

The chapter discusses the value of users' input in the innovation aspect, which support organizations in gaining an edge over their competitors. The chapter emphasizes the importance of innovation and user involvement in the product development process, and introduces different models of open innovations in relation with the extent of user's role at different levels throughout the entire product life cycle. The chapter's objective is to develop a framework for user involvement in organizational innovation encompassing the various stages of the innovation process. The framework was applied on a case study of a Brazilian automotive company to assess the degree and means of contribution in a company's innovative process.

Chapter 10

Mariam F. Alkazemi, University of Florida, USA
Brian J. Bowe, Michigan State University, USA
Robin Blom, Michigan State University, USA

This chapter describes the role social media plays in authoritarian regimes to attempt to fill the gap in free expression. Through selecting the Egyptian Revolution in 2011 as a case study, the authors analyze the messages posted on Facebook by activists of one of the major Egyptian opposition groups, 6th Youth Movement, just before, during, and after the revolution. The goal of the chapter is to describe the content exchanged during that period to understand how this technology was effective for activists and opposition groups aiming to reach democracy in their societies.

Chapter 11

Marcelo S. Pimenta, Federal University of Rio Grande do Sul (UFRGS), Brazil
Evandro M. Miletto, Federal Institute of Rio Grande do Sul (IFRS), Brazil
Damián Keller, Federal University of Acre (UFAC), Brazil
Luciano V. Flores, Federal University of Rio Grande do Sul (UFRGS), Brazil
Guilherme G. Testa, Federal University of Rio Grande do Sul (UFRGS), Brazil

This chapter demonstrates how Web 2.0 features enable music creation by non-professionals of online communities. The authors argue that Web 2.0 applications can assist music amateurs in improving music skills without prior musical knowledge. The chapter aims to develop and test a Web 2.0 application that encourages user engagement and collaboration in music creation that fits the multi-cultural Brazilian nature characterized by a combination flexibility, improvisation, openness for diverse ideas, and criticism.

Chapter 12

Using Social Media Technology to Improve Collaboration: A Case Study of
Micro-Blogging Adoption in a South African Financial Services Company 313

Garron Stevenson, University of Cape Town, South Africa
Jean-Paul Van Belle, University of Cape Town, South Africa

The authors shed light on the use of micro-blogging technology for fostering internal cooperation among employees in an organization. A study was conducted on the IT department of a South African financial services company to investigate the use and perception of employees towards a micro-blogging application. Data was gathered through a survey and an analysis of the messages posted on this platform during a period of one month. The chapter goal is to assess the effectiveness of micro-blogging in increasing the level of informal collaboration among teams in organizations. The benefits reaped were demonstrated as well as the barriers the users faced. The authors conclude by presenting recommendations to increase the usefulness of micro-blogging in internal collaborative activities and solutions to reduce the underlying impediments.

Chapter 13

Web 2.0 as a Foundation for Social Media Marketing: Global Perspectives
and the Local Case of Croatia.. 342

Vedran Podobnik, University of Zagreb, Croatia
Daniel Ackerman, iSTUDIO, Croatia
Tomislav Grubisic, iSTUDIO, Croatia
Ignac Lovrek, University of Zagreb, Croatia

This chapter shows how social networks have a great impact on social media marketing that relies on content generated by consumers. This approach serves in spreading brand awareness through viral marketing. The chapter discusses the effect of social networks on Internet marketing in general, with special emphasis on the Croatian environment. The objective of the chapter is to describe the features and use of social networks in marketing activities through introducing some enabling tools of three recognized social media platforms. Several Croatian case studies using these applications were presented pinpointing their efficiency in building online communities for marketing purpose.

Chapter 14

Virtual Collaborative Learning: Opportunities and Challenges of Web
2.0-Based E-Learning Arrangements for Developing Countries...................... 380

Wissam Tawileh, Technische Universität Dresden, Germany
Helena Bukvova, Technische Universität Dresden, Germany
Eric Schoop, Technische Universität Dresden, Germany

The authors address the use of Web 2.0 in electronic learning, and how it can improve the educational process in developing countries through providing access to educational material, and opportunities to interact and exchange views within a collaborative environment. The authors draw from their long and rich experience in teaching based on a Virtual Collaborative Learning (VCL) approach. This arrangement was offered to higher education students from a number of developed and developing countries. The chapter aims to show the ability of Web 2.0 in addressing several societal issues in developing countries, as well as the underpinning challenges in adopting VCL methods within a development context.

Chapter 15

Nuddy Pillay, Manukau Institute of Technology, New Zealand

This chapter focuses on the factors that influence the effective use of Web 2.0 by students for learning activities. Even though Web 2.0 applications were embedded in numerous educational experiences, the author claims that they did not reap the expected outcomes. This triggers the need to investigate the drivers that have an impact on the students to embrace this technology in participating successfully throughout their learning process. The chapter's main goal is to analyze the use and usefulness of Web 2.0 in education, as well as the associated challenges of applying this technology especially on different developing environments where students come from diverse backgrounds. To realize the chapter objective, a study was conducted to assess the effect of the use of a blog—by students of different age ranges and ethnic origins, in a course offered at an institution of higher learning—in smoothing the communication between students as well as between students and instructors.

Chapter 16

Alessia D'Andrea, IRPPS-CNR, Italy
Fernando Ferri, IRPPS-CNR, Italy
Patrizia Grifoni, IRPPS-CNR, Italy

The authors in this chapter address the importance of Web 2.0 technologies in improving health services in Africa. As declared by the authors, information and communication technology in general, and Web 2.0 in particular, has a significant impact on health in three main applications: electronic medical records, telemedicine, and e-commerce of health products. The chapter objective is to portray electronic health readiness in Africa presenting different initiatives undertaken in Africa in electronic health application, and the barriers that limit electronic health implementation in Africa.

Foreword

The content of this book is timely and highly valuable due to the growing importance of the Web 2.0 business economy and its implications on individuals, organizations, and societies in an ever-growing competitive global marketplace. Today, the outreach realized through information and communication technology is magnified based on state-of-the-art tools and techniques in both the marketspace and marketplace. Time and distance barriers are gradually diminishing, providing an invaluable strength to network effects and its multiple and associated influence on different constituents. Web 2.0 clearly represents the impact that collaboration and teamwork can achieve. It is the most recent evolution of the information and communication technology industry caused by the growing role of the Internet as a platform for business and societal development. The role of people in such a platform is integral in its effectiveness and success. How people contribute, collaborate, compete, and capitalize on information and communication technology is a prerequisite to the realization of the potentials of Web 2.0. The different online models available vary in their success; however, they are all changing, learning, and adapting, and are on course to enable a growing market of users worldwide to benefit from as well as grow and excel given the potential benefits expected from the digital economy.

Web 2.0 is gradually contributing to the massive knowledge repository that is growing online and made accessible to over two billion Internet users worldwide. Blogs, Wikis, enterprise applications, and social networking are all contributing to a flat platform for collaboration and knowledge exchange that help in smoothing all the barriers while supporting in developing, implementing, and institutionalizing cutting-edge applications that can have positive impact on the individual, organizational, and societal levels. It is a great pleasure to see the publication of this book, which sees the production of 16 different chapters reflecting applications, tools, models, cases, and processes related to Web 2.0 from around the world with many lessons learned for future research and implementation. The content of these chapters is important for different constituents of the Web 2.0 ecosystem linking industry, business, and academia as well as blending educational content with business and industry needs demonstrated in real-life market practices and emerging concepts and trends. Web 2.0 is all about creating value and demonstrating how businesses and customers interact, which automatically provides a venue for emerging business models that are adaptable to market changes and transformations. In many ways, Web 2.0 is a demonstration of what Alvin Toffler called in the 1980s "prosumers," where each one is a mix of do-it-yourself producer blended with his natural setting as a consumer.

User-generated information and knowledge is at the core of Web 2.0 leading to changes in market forces, educational platform, and industry interactions amongst other collaborative settings. Individuals previously known as observers are nowadays actively engaged individuals. Groups online learn from each other and extend the collaboration irrespective of the geographic location, which at a minimal cost, if any, scales up the outcome and expectations of Web 2.0. For a few decades, the literature addressing the potential of online collaboration in developing and emerging economies had witnessed minimal coverage. This book provides a new direction of the potential of Web 2.0 in transforming developing economies and societies amongst others. This has been already realized in the case of a few companies in the emerging world but also in the socioeconomic and political platform. It is clearly demonstrated in the transformation taking place in a number of countries in the Middle East, such as Egypt, with a clear and effective role being played by Web 2.0.

The book combines a variety of chapters that address opportunities for entrepreneurs created through technology applications; platforms for civil society collaboration; eGovernment application; societal transformation; social networking; educational development; corporate performance; innovation; social marketing; eLearning; and eHealth. One of the most important aspects of the book is its broad coverage of challenges and opportunities involved from around the world. Some of the elements addressed reflect the business thinking, strategies, and implementation tools and techniques that can help Web 2.0 have its potential impact on society. While information was power in the past, sharing it today makes its holder more powerful and increasingly profitable. Web 2.0 is a platform for scalability, diversity, and inclusion. The inputs accumulated are usually a reflection of different yet collaborative analysis of ideas and issues that are of growing interest to a large global population. The Internet generation, irrespective of age, background, and expertise, blends different experiences leading to an outcome that is at the core of Web 2.0 and expected to yield exponential growth in the years to come as the technology and its acceptance among a wider community is well diffused and properly utilized.

Communication and internetworking have always been the mechanism for knowledge transfer and exchange across time. Today, Web 2.0 is providing a newly innovative technique to address that knowledge component, create it, amend it, adapt it, and adapt it in a way that can cater for the changes taking place on a constant basis. People are building new ways of connections that are timely, efficient, and effective. The clusters of people created through Web 2.0 are linking expertise that otherwise might not have connected to each other. In addition, such connection is being made faster, easier, and less costly leapfrogging most, if not all, other communication channels. The more platforms created through Web 2.0 becomes mature, the more benefits and rewards the beneficiaries across different constituents will feel from the opportunities presented. The world is becoming all about competition in a timely fashion. Time to react is minimized, and Web 2.0 extends the competitive knowledge advantage with the possibility for reaching out to different constituents and delivers the expected outcome in a mobile and remote way. Viral growth of Web 2.0 will increase in the years to come to address different sectors and industries. This book demonstrates through its different chapters the extent of the effect that Web 2.0 could have on business and industry in the years to come. In addition, the value the different users will be able to generate by sharing and exchanging basic information and knowledge will be shared by a growing group of people and the acceleration and speed of the impact will be constantly growing as more people become increasingly interested in collaborative tools, techniques, and applications that are enabled through Web 2.0. All these elements will not only help create the expected ecosystem but also improve and leverage the competencies of its different stakeholders. Web 2.0 is a reflection of an invaluable mindset that will have remarkable impact on different sectors in the years to come as we move into the next decade of the 21st century, and that is innovation and creativity. Web 2.0 is all about innovative tools, innovative communication, innovation collaboration, and innovative thinking, and this book provides an important contribution to the growing literature addressing innovation and creativity aspects such as Web 2.0. I would like to seize this opportunity and thank the editor, authors, reviewers, and everyone that was associated in the preparation and publication of this book for their invaluable contribution to the body of knowledge of emerging and innovative information and communication technology tools and applications.

Sherif Kamel
The American University in Cairo, Egypt

Sherif Kamel *is Founding Dean of the School of Business at the American University in Cairo and Professor of Management Information Systems. Before joining AUC, he was Director of the Regional IT Institute (1992-2001) and managed the training department of the Cabinet of Egypt Information and Decision Support Centre (1987-1992). He holds a PhD in Information Systems from the London School of Economics and Political Science, an MBA and a BA in Business Administration from the American University in Cairo. His research and teaching interests include management of information technology, information technology transfer to developing nations, electronic business, and decision support systems. His work is broadly published in IS and management journals and books.*

He is the Associate Editor of the Journal of Cases on Information Technology and Journal of IT for Development. He is a member of the World Bank Knowledge Advisory Commission, board member in the Association of African Business Schools, and founding member of the Internet Society of Egypt. He was VP for communications and member of the Executive Council of the Information Resources Management Association (2002-2007), member of the board of trustees of the Information Technology Institute (2005-2011) and the Sadat Academy for Management Sciences (2007-2011). Kamel is an Eisenhower Fellow (2005). Kamel is an advocate of diversity, empowerment, and inclusion.

Preface

The potential of Information and Communication Technology (ICT) for developing countries has been raised since the 1990s. Research has shown that investing in ICT returns a number of economic benefits such as increasing productivity, saving costs, introducing new economic opportunities, creating a variety of jobs, fostering innovation, and boosting economic trade and collaboration. Additionally, ICT has started garnering more interest among politicians, researchers, and economists, particularly after the United Nations' Millennium Plan, where ICT's role was clearly perceived. Such a plan aims to reach eight main goals referred to as "Millennium Development Goals" (MDGs). It is generally agreed that ICT is one of the main enablers of realizing socio-economic development, which in turn contributes to attaining MDGs. There is a common agreement that in today's knowledge-driven economy, development is not possible without ICT. Therefore, access to ICT should be evenly available among societies and countries worldwide because the digital divide cannot be regarded merely as a technical divide, but rather one that reflects a gap in all aspects of life. The remarkable advancement in technology during the past few decades has had a strong impact on minimizing the digital divide; for example, the development of mobile innovative applications and broadband Internet—part of wireless technologies enhancement—has facilitated access to knowledge to an extent that could not have been possible, especially in rural areas of developing countries. In terms of the effect of mobile penetration on the economy, the World Bank Group declared that a 10 percent increase in mobile phones leads to a 0.6 percent growth in GDP (Navas-Sabater, 2006).

Moreover, the growing acceptance and adoption of Web 2.0 applications represents another major factor in bridging the digital divide. People in developing countries are encouraged to use social networks, blogs, wikis, and other Web 2.0 tools, since they foster the concepts of openness, collaboration, and participation. Web 2.0 has redefined the notion of development. Referring to this as "development 2.0," Richard Heeks (2008) sees that this second wave of the Web has changed the function of ICT from "a tool for development" to a "platform for that development." Seeing as Web 2.0 technology allows for user engagement and participation, it enables people in developing countries to be active producers and innovators rather than passive recipients for others in developed countries. This fact highlights the value of empowerment and inclusion that has resulted from user-generated content. Even though Web 2.0 is enabled by a relatively simple technical platform, it represents a societal transformation that calls for different social behaviors and allows creation and sharing of information in a manner that had not occurred before. If well exploited, Web 2.0 can have a positive impact on several areas of society such as education, businesses, politics, and the public sector.

Aside from the fact that ICT in general has had a great impact on the above sectors in developing countries, Web 2.0 has added more functionalities and value to each of these vital areas in any society. In education, it has further fostered the sense of collaboration: an integral element in creating an effective e-learning environment; it enables learners to discuss, argue, negotiate, express themselves, and create rich and diverse content that reflects their knowledge and beliefs. This potential is even effective in most developing countries with youth who are not able to enroll in schools or universities, or those who cannot completely benefit from traditional education systems in their societies that sometimes restrict their interaction and participation in class. Concerning businesses, Web 2.0 continues to present a valuable opportunity to conduct several marketing activities, customer communication, and customer support at lower costs and with higher exposure. In addition, it strengthens the culture of participation not only with customers, partners, and suppliers, but also internally among employees within the same organization. Web 2.0 also diminishes the boundary between internal issues in organizations and their surrounding external environment since it allows for more openness, hence leading to a reinforcement of the culture of learning and innovation. The different tools provided by Web 2.0 enable small businesses and entrepreneurs in developing countries to develop trust through building intimacy with the business and the product or service. The possibility of empowering customers and offering them the opportunity to express their opinions also has more influence on consumers' decision-making—which is now shaped by customers' reviews and ratings—than do traditional media and old marketing techniques.

Furthermore, the role of several Web 2.0 applications in assisting developing countries to change their political status-quo has become a reality, especially during and in the wake of the Arab Spring. Facebook, Twitter, YouTube, and blogs were the main channels for expressing and exchanging political views in Arab Spring countries, where authoritarian regimes had previously posed strong restrictions on freedom of speech and civic engagement and participation. In Egypt in particular, these tools served in mobilizing people, coordinating between protestors, and documenting and publishing facts that occurred on the ground during the 18 days of the revolution (Azab, 2012). Web 2.0 further confirms the concept of the "public sphere" as highlighted by Jürgen Habermas (1974): "a place where communities could jointly form public opinions in an environment removed from the government or economy." As for e-government attempts to transform the public sector during the first wave of the Web, most initiatives have failed to reap the expected benefits or solve prevalent problems in the public sector. One of the main challenges for government lies in the absence of a dialogue with citizens. Attaining healthy dialogues with its citizens enables government to know their thoughts and opinions, and to engage them in public policy making. This helps overcome bureaucratic approaches in making decisions that lack social involvement, a phenomenon that still exists in most developing countries. Web 2.0 can support governments in addressing this challenge since it provides a platform for mashable services and better communication, leading in turn to a more responsive and transparent government. Gartner (2007) declares that 79 percent of social networking activities surrounding the US Government lead to cost reduction and positive strategic outcomes. Web 2.0 technology facilitates the availability and accessibility of information, and the participation of citizens in the decision making process...or at the very least contributes in raising the level of collective consciousness.

The abovementioned benefits of Web 2.0 apply to all societies worldwide and to developing countries in particular, but cannot be reached smoothly. There are keystone challenges that need to be addressed carefully to exploit the features of this technology. Since the power of Web 2.0 lies in user participation, it is not sufficient to provide the technology required for creating digital content and services. More importantly, it is the users' recognition of the value of this technology in the first place that would encourage them to incorporate it within their professional and societal behaviors, and not merely for leisure and personal communication. This objective may face difficulty as it sometimes contradicts with specific culture circles in some developing countries where there is a tendency to resist transparency and openness. In addition, several authorities, businesses, and institutions in the developing world remain skeptical about losing control over content generation or decision-making, which are two of the most apparent outcomes of adopting Web 2.0. These challenges need to be considered thoroughly on a long-term basis because they entail cultural and institutional changes that would not be possible to effectively implement through one-off projects or initiatives. Sustainable and scalable projects would be more appropriate to assist governments, organizations, and individuals throughout a complete process to accept Web 2.0 tools and integrate them in their daily activities. Moreover, since the content available on social media is produced by non-professional users, concerns are often triggered about the credibility, quality, and accountability of the material published. A major risk that relates to this is the possibility of publishing destructive ideas through newly discovered Web 2.0 channels, especially in developing countries where several segments of the society are not privileged with adequate standards of education necessary for them to analyze critically diversified—and sometimes contradicting—views. Furthermore, security and privacy issues cause a common concern associated with social networks' implementation; users fear that their personal data would be exposed. This matter is further intensified because there is a probability that data protection policies will be changed over time in Web 2.0 applications.

Evidently, Web 2.0 presents an opportunity for advancement in several areas in developing countries. However, desired outcomes cannot take place without first ensuring that a number of enabling conditions are satisfied. It is necessary to always consider and revise the link between Web 2.0 initiatives and socio-economic development. Web 2.0 implementers should also benefit from the lessons learned from development 1.0 projects that highlighted the importance of sustainability and the significance of continuous evaluation. Most of the developments on the past ICT were conducted on a pilot scale without a wide vision—bearing in mind all resources required—that ensures enough continuity and scalability to cause a remarkable effect on people's lives. Eventually, Web 2.0 implementation does not occur in isolation; on the contrary, it is ultimately based on user engagement and participation. Therefore, in-depth studies should be undertaken to identify the best applications, stages, policies, functions, and skills relevant to each project's context, taking into consideration specific issues such as the capability, beliefs, and culture of the people involved. Moreover, other environmental factors should be investigated: social, economic, institutional, and political structures, as well as government policies (e.g., public private partnership, market competition, decision-making and control, etc.). Finally, policy makers and researchers should place special emphasis on prior Web 2.0 literature and practices that share similar problems and solutions. This will guide them to address challenges, avoid pitfalls, and shape effective strategies. As highlighted by Batchelor (2003) from InfoDev: "The possibility to replicate and scale up successful projects will not fully materialize until the knowledge accumulated from IT for development projects (successful and unsuccessful) is widely documented and shared."

The *Cases on Web 2.0 in Developing Countries: Studies on Implementation, Application, and Use,* hence, provides a valuable contribution to different research areas in information systems management, electronic commerce, and ICT development. The book presents several issues related to Web 2.0 such as cases, strategies, policies, concepts and models, critical success factors, challenges and opportunities, and drivers for adopting Web 2.0 technologies over both micro and macro scales. These issues cover a variety of sectors including politics, education, health, government, and business. Therefore, this book will offer guidelines to professionals for future implementation of Web 2.0 projects in developing countries, merging both theoretical and practical perspectives. It will also assist scholars and students, since it combines a body of knowledge about several Web 2.0 concepts and their adoption in a number of developing countries including Egypt, Indonesia, Brazil, Morocco, Bahrain, Croatia, Libya, West African Countries, South Sudan, and South Africa.

Nahed Amin Azab
American University in Cairo, Egypt

REFERENCES

Azab, N. (2012). The role of the internet in shaping the political process in Egypt. *International Journal of E-Politics, 3*(2), 30–49. doi:10.4018/jep.2012040103

Batchelor, S., Evangelista, S., Hearn, S., Peirce, M., Sugden, S., & Webb, M. (2003). *ICT for development: Contributing to the millennium development goals: Lessons learned from seventeen infoDev projects*. Retrieved from http://www.infodev.org/en/Publication.19.html

Gartner. (2007). *Web 2.0 in government: Blessing or curse?* Retrieved from http://wiki.dbast.com/images/8/8a/Web_2-0_in_Government-_Blessing_or_Curse.pdf

Habermas, J. (1974). *The public sphere: In the information society reader*. New York, NY: Routledge.

Heeks, R. (2008). ICT4D 2.0: The next phase of applying ICT for international development. *IEEE Computer, 41*(6), 26-33. Retrieved from http://research.microsoft.com/en-us/um/people/cutrell/heeks-ictd%20two-point-zero.pdf

Navas-Sabater, J. (2006). Gender and ICT: Role of the world bank group. In *Proceedings of PREM Learning Week, Global Information and Communication Technologies Department (GICT)*. New York, NY: The World Bank Group.

Acknowledgment

My deepest appreciation to all those who contributed to this book throughout its different stages of preparation. In particular, I would like to thank the IGI Global team for their continuous and efficient administrative support: Hannah Abelbeck, Austin DeMarco, Jan Travers, and Erika Carter under the leadership of Mehdi Khoshrow-Pour.

Special recognition is in order to the authors who dedicated—with passion—precious time to share their cases, research, and findings in the chapters of the book, and furthermore, who tolerated the requested corrections to improve the quality of the material. In my opinion, generosity with knowledge is the utmost one could give. I would also like to acknowledge the authors who allocated additional time and effort to review manuscripts in the double-blind review process. Appreciation also goes to all reviewers who provided constructive and helpful input that definitely enriched the book's content.

In addition, I cannot overlook the guidance extended to me by Dr. Sherif Kamel, who was kind enough to share his previous experience in producing similar projects.

Warm gratitude goes to my father for his sincere prayers and encouragement, and to my dear friend Ola for caring, as a friend would. My beloved husband and best friend, Ahmed, my son, Nabil, and my daughter, Farah, kept pushing and helping me throughout this demanding project until it materialised, so thank you wholeheartedly. Without you I couldn't have gotten there.

Nahed Amin Azab
American University in Cairo, Egypt

Chapter 1
Web 2.0 and Opportunities for Entrepreneurs:
How Egyptian Entrepreneurs Perceive and Exploit Web 2.0 Technologies

Nahed Azab
American University in Cairo, Egypt

Nermine Khalifa
Arab Academy for Science and Technology, Egypt

EXECUTIVE SUMMARY

The increasing value of Web 2.0 applications and their effects on consumers and organizations are frequently attracting academic and professional communities. A new set of new technologies, called Web 2.0, offers new opportunities, and blurs the boundaries between online and offline activities, opening a new era characterized by: openness, collaboration, and participation. It presents a new affordable channel for entrepreneurs in different sectors to market and build communities, and to receive a direct feedback about their products and services.

DOI: 10.4018/978-1-4666-2515-0.ch001

Even though entrepreneurship in general and their use of Web 2.0 in particular are relatively new concepts especially in developing countries, entrepreneurship has gained a special interest in Egypt due to the success realized by some youth entrepreneurs who consider the Internet and different Web 2.0 applications as an integral aspect in their daily lives. Hence, the present chapter investigates opportunities for small businesses in the Web 2.0 era. In-depth semi-structured interviews were arranged with a number of Egyptian entrepreneurs who started their business. The research conducted revealed that Web 2.0 adoption by Egyptian entrepreneurs is affected by three main factors: age of entrepreneur, date of establishment of the company, and nature of the business: traditional or virtual. It was concluded also that Egyptian entrepreneurs are still at an early stage in using Web 2.0 since a large number of the sample used in this research are still reluctant to consider incorporating this technology in their working practice. For those already embracing Web 2.0, they limit such use on social media only without considering other applications (such as podcasts, really simple syndication, blogs, wikis, etc.), and they do not have clear objectives and strategies that govern such use. Findings of this study can provide helpful guidelines for small businesses to begin using and leveraging Web 2.0. This chapter provides a valuable contribution to the field of entrepreneurship and electronic business research. Specifically, the chapter highlights the applicability of Web 2.0 in entrepreneurial activities in developing countries: an area of research yet unexplored.

INTRODUCTION

Web 2.0 is currently drawing the attention of public communities (Constantinides & Fountain, 2008; Stobbe, 2010). It has been among the topics of interest in the news media. It started when *The Economist*'s front page had the title "Power at Last," publishing a special report entitled "Consumer Power." In addition, *Time Magazine* selected "You" as Person of the Year in December 2006 (Constantinides & Fountain, 2008; Stobbe, 2010). Both publications were highlighting the power of Web 2.0 in providing the platform for the communication and collaboration of millions of Internet users affecting their social and professional daily lives. This is considered a revolution than the first wave of the Internet where users were recipients of multimedia content (reading, listening, observing) rather than generating it (Blinn, et al., 2009; McAfee, 2006a; O'Reilly, 2005). Since then, the interest in Web 2.0 publications is usually directed towards its customer behavioral change and on the consequent challenges encountering strategists and marketers (Urban, 2003; McKinsey, 2007).

Web 2.0 applications, referred as Social media—characterized by "participation, openness, conversation, community, and connectedness" (SpannerWorks, 2007)— have not only changed individuals and groups' attitudes but has also transformed the balance of power in the marketplaces, shifting the power from the seller to the consumer; hence, creating a more impartial relationship among both parties (Jones, 2010). Through 'a mouse click,' today's online buyer has a wide exposure to a huge information and knowledge reservoir providing unlimited options (Constantinides & Fountain, 2008).

Using Web 2.0, the perception of identity through consumption (Trentmann, 2006) is further strengthened. In this new era of technology, customers are becoming "prosumers" (Toffler, 1984; Tapscott & Williams, 2006) capable of connecting online with other peers (which they trust more than media and advertising) to form a mass response to businesses nurturing "the politics of consumption" (Jones, 2010). Such fact highlights the integral role Web 2.0 plays in the functioning and delivery of marketing and entrepreneurship (Jones, 2010). Small businesses can use social media applications that provide a cheap and convenient communication channel with customers for different marketing and sales purposes, such as creating new or improving existing products and services, providing better support to increase customer satisfaction, having access to an additional sales' outlet, and targeting new customers (Lee, et al., 2008).

The main reason that encourages businesses to deploy Web 2.0 tools is their wide adoption by Internet users. Social media has become a habit not only by young generations but also by upper age range people. Such growing popularity with Web 2.0 over time gives a strong indication that it will gain more importance in the future (Stobbe, 2010). As Mashable Social Media (2012) reported in its latest statistics, from the 845 million Facebook active users worldwide, 68% are older than 34 years old.

Due to the benefits of Web 2.0 and its value on business strategy and marketing, many companies in the developed world adopted such technology (Constantinides & Fountain, 2008). Other businesses are reluctant to embrace Web 2.0 tools since they present a relatively new concept for businesses, and still have various meanings related to different academic disciplines (Yourdon, 2006; Clarke, 2008). There is also a fear that it could be "the latest hype that will dash hopes just as rapidly as was the case, for instance, when the bubble burst in the days of the new economy" (Stobbe, 2010). Such situation is evidently more apparent in developing countries since developed ones were always the pioneers in Internet economy.

Web 2.0 area of research is gradually raising interest among researchers and academics (Karger & Quan, 2005; Deshpande & Jadad, 2006; Boll, 2007), but unfortunately there is no common research direction in the academic literature (Constantinides & Fountain, 2008). Clarke (2008) asserts that there is a scarcity in research papers in Web 2.0, and that most contributions are mainly press articles or speeches in conferences rather than reviewed academic studies considering in-depth investigation, analysis, and conclusions. Therefore, there is a need for an extensive research in Web 2.0 concept. This chapter extends the line of research and knowledge in the relationship between Web 2.0 and entrepreneurship. It attempts hence to fill a research gap since it aims to present Web 2.0 meaning from different perspectives identifying the technological and commercial foundations of this new trend of online applications. It highlights also the opportunities Web 2.0 applications present for entrepreneurs, and their potential for change to add value to their business, as well as the challenges that could arise from their use. The chapter then investigates the adoption of Web 2.0 technology by Egyptian entrepreneurs, the way they perceive it, the main drivers, the implications it might be for small businesses, and also the barriers that limit or sometimes drive them to avoid using Web social media. In addition, the chapter portrays Internet marketing environment within a local context over different sectors including product and service providers. Findings are discussed in the light of the relevant literature leading to the authors' reflection on the entire research. Through highlighting best practices, and existing challenges and drawbacks, this chapter serves in assisting prospective or current entrepreneurs in using Web 2.0 in their business.

BACKGROUND

This section starts by explaining several concepts related to Web 2.0 followed by an overview of entrepreneurship as addressed in the literature. Next, a special focus on the importance of Web 2.0 for entrepreneurs is discussed, the value it could create to entrepreneurs, and the undermining challenges identified by prior research.

What is Web 2.0?

Web 2.0 was first introduced by O'Reilly (2005) as "business revolution in the computer industry caused by the move to the Internet as platform." It is mainly about considering users as content generators through a number of Web-based software applications such as, blogs, Social networks, content communities, forums/bulletin boards, and content aggregators (Constantinides & Fountain, 2008). Asynchronous JavaScript and XML (AJAX), Really Simple Syndication (RSS), or ATOM Syndicat Format (ASF) are among the different technologies that support the creation of Web 2.0 applications (Alby, 2007).

A controversy about Web 2.0 still exists lacking a common agreement about its meaning since it is concerned with different disciplines. The term was discussed in business management (Blinn, et al., 2009; Jones & Iredale, 2009; Peris, et al., 2011) and in social sciences (Beer & Burrows, 2007; Parameswaran & Whinston, 2007; Beer, 2008; Snee, 2008). Constantinides and Fountain (2008) suggest a description of Web 2.0 that summarize its main aspects as being "Web 2.0 is a collection of open-source, interactive and user-controlled online applications expanding the experiences, knowledge and market power of the users as participants in business and social processes. Web 2.0 applications support the creation of informal users' networks facilitating the flow of ideas and knowledge by allowing the efficient generation, dissemination, sharing, and editing/refining of informational content." User participation in the Web 2.0 world can be classified into several functions: Authoring (editing and publishing), Sharing of information and knowledge, Collaboration and Networking, and Scoring related to users' ratings (Pleil, 2006).

A number of research agree on common key issues undermining Web 2.0 (Daconta, et al., 2003; Shirky, 2003; Anderson, 2004; O'Reilly, 2005): (1) online applications based on service-based and open-source solutions; (2) continuous and incremental improvement and development of software applications through producing beta versions to consolidate on the users' collective intelligence; (3) new business models and innovative ways to reach individual customers interested in low-volume products.

The above Web 2.0 issues have an apparent effect on four main dimensions: (1) Technological, developing new technologies that enable more dynamic data processing and automation to allow an efficient compilation, dissemination, and exchange of information; (2) Sociological, capability to build virtual communities relying on network externalities; (3) Economical, based on richness of information and shortage of time since there is an information download created by 'prosumers' or 'Pro-Ams' (Leadbeater & Miller, 2004) representing users between professionals and amateurs influencing the society and the economy by creating useful content; and (4) Legal, governing such phenomenon to protect intellectual property, information sharing, or social concerns related to Web accessibility (Lee, et al., 2008).

Perspectives about Entrepreneurs

There is a body of knowledge in the literature about entrepreneurship. When attempting to describe them, Czarniawska and Wolff (1991) portray them as "the makers of new worlds." Bolton and Thompson (2004) see an entrepreneur as a person capable of choosing the right people, building a strong team, and accomplishing his objective in an efficient and quick manner. When identifying entrepreneur's main job in relation with scientific innovation, Schumpeter (1947) notes that "the inventor produces ideas, the entrepreneur 'gets things done' … an idea of scientific principle is not, by itself, of any importance for economic practice."

Cunningham and Lischeron (1991) classify six views in the literature that define entrepreneurship based on two distinct approaches: personal qualifications or re-evaluation and adaptation ability in organizations. Doyle et al. (2002) refer entrepreneurship to two research categories: demographics or personal characteristics. Few scholars criticize the second view arguing that personal traits were not sufficiently tested particularly in the case of entrepreneurship, and that they cannot be assessed in isolation of the environment (Robinson, et al., 1991). In addition, Gartner (1989) concludes that compiled studies undertaken in entrepreneurs' personality described a 'psychological profile' encompassing a number of contradictory characteristics that cannot exist in one person. However, most research gave a specific emphasis on entrepreneurial personality with its different aspects such as Barbosa et al. (2007), Becherer and Maurer (1999), Busenitz (1999), Rauch and Frese (2007), and Sambasivan et al. (2009). A number of studies agree that personality of entrepreneurs depends on the degree and type of performance to be examined (Rauch & Frese, 2007). Hence, as Cunningham and Lischeron (1991) propose: one cannot study entrepreneurship without considering three interrelated dimensions over time: the entrepreneur, the venture, and the environment.

In the last decade, researchers were interested in investigating the tendency towards opportunity recognition. Most studies confirmed that entrepreneurs have the ability to spot opportunities more than others, which makes them the best candidates for starting businesses (Baron & Ensley, 2006; Casson & Wadeson, 2007). Entrepreneurial process towards opportunity entails two main stages: exploration of an opportunity, and exploiting it after accumulating sufficient knowledge about its viability (Choi, et al., 2008). An entrepreneur should determine the appropriate time frame of each stage to reach a balance between an early start of exploiting an opportunity (which would lead to a first mover advantage) versus delaying such stage to allow for acquiring knowledge to reduce ignorance.

Web 2.0 for Entrepreneurs

Before the existence of the Web in 1994, the Internet was not useful for entrepreneurs and small businesses because it was slow and was rarely used by both businesses and customers. Since the starting of the Internet and until 1984, there were only around 1000 hosts connected to the Internet (Frana, 2004) in contrast with hundreds of millions in the present. The creation of the Web presented an opportunity for entrepreneurs to display their products or services' catalogs and everything about their business online through informational websites. Orders at that time were placed through postal mail or over the phone (Lee, et al., 2008). It was a paradigm shift because it allowed small businesses to have the same exposure and reach by customers as large enterprises locally and internationally (Evans & Wurster, 1999;

Friedman, 2007). Later, e-commerce enabled committing full transactions through ordering and paying online; which helped small business to compete with large ones. The above features of the first wave of the Web known as Web 1.0 allowed entrepreneurs and small businesses to use the Internet for different activities such as, posting information, selling directly to customers, building relationships with them, and conducting business with other companies (Lee, et al., 2008).

Despite the importance of Web 1.0 for entrepreneurs, the communication between them and their customers is only one way through posting content to customers without real interactivity with them, or also between customers themselves. Consumers are able to contact businesses only through e-mails by visiting their websites. This does not ensure a sustainable dialogue between them that could assist entrepreneurs in attracting customers to express their true opinions about the products and services offered (Lee, et al., 2008). E-mails allow for communication within limited groups of accounts, and are always viewed by customers as a "deluge of information that can only be handled with difficulty" (Stobbe, 2010). Furthermore, when examining customers' behaviors on organizations' websites, it is not guaranteed that customers keep accessing the websites regularly (Bakos, 1991). Such fact limits the effect of the electronic marketplace since its success relies mainly on the traffic on businesses' websites and their abilities to attract customers (European Commission, 2004; Moor, 2003).

Web 2.0 applications provided a solution to the above problems that existed in Web 1.0. Being described as an environment for user participation, openness, and social networks (Musser, et al., 2006), Web 2.0 applications allow for two-way communication and reinforce the sense of participation among consumers. User involvement and participation proved to be the main factors that attract customers to be in continuous relationships with organizations (Salam, et al., 2008). Moreover, in the case of Facebook and Twitter for example, since consumers are continuously accessing them, this offers a convenient and efficient mean for entrepreneurs to stay in contact with their customers (Stobbe, 2010). Entrepreneurs and small businesses do not have to depend on traditional media to market their products, reach their customers, and communicate with them. They can rely on social networks, blogs, podcasts, and other applications, and cope with this fast changing platform in targeting diverse individual and combined tastes and requirements (Jones, 2010).

Evidently, Web 2.0 technologies are efficient for businesses in general providing more flexibility and responsiveness (Jones, 2010), but the authors argue that they are particularly compatible with the needs and characteristics of entrepreneurs. Usually, entrepreneurs are restricted with a limited budget, specifically in their starting phases, which makes them more encouraged to use Web 2.0 since its adoption is coupled with low investment costs (Stobbe, 2010) reducing the cost of marketing and communication (Jones, 2010). Also, as described in the previous section, since entrepreneurs in general have the tendency to spot opportunities, they could be the best candidates to use Web 2.0 either to exploit its capabilities in communicating with customers—being among the early movers to adopt such technology—or to rely on it in facilitating and speeding up the process of acquiring knowledge. In addition, the fast, efficient, and nature of Web 2.0 is completely relevant to entrepreneurs who aims always to "get things done" and to be a good decision maker in an efficient and quick manner. Moreover, since using Web 2.0 applications provide different applications that could be tailored to the needs of users, it offers a flexible mean for entrepreneurs who seek always innovative ways to conduct their business, and to make different trials in marketing and communicating with their customers, and in learning from their experiences. Since most entrepreneurs are in evolutionary phases, listening to their customers and obtaining their feedback through fostering crowdsourcing (Howe, 2009) would assist them in improving and in continuously refining their business models. As Web 2.0 brings a radical change in a company's business processes and in its relation with its customers, it is definitely accompanied with risks that arise as a result of this degree of change. Entrepreneurs, who are risk takers by nature, could be willing to embrace Web 2.0 technologies more than other well-established and large businesses. As Salam et al. (2008) note, ICT and small businesses will continuously develop and for those who will withstand the risk underlying such adoption, will have an early movers' edge over their competitors (Bakos, 1991).

Furthermore, as trust is considered a core element in building and sustaining a customer relationship management (Jones, 2010), entrepreneurs should focus more than other businesses on developing trust with consumers. Consumers prefer usually to deal with large and known organizations rather than with entrepreneurs still building a reputation, especially for those operating only virtually. Web 2.0 provides a channel to reinforce trust through building intimacy with the business and the product or service. In fact, social media proved to be more influential on customer behavior than traditional media and old marketing approaches because they depend on customers' empowerment and feedback (Gillin, 2007). In addition, consumers are increasingly distrusting traditional marketers. As Deloitte Touche USA reported, 62 percent of consumers access consumers' online reviews, and 80 percent revealed that such reviews have an influence on their buying decisions (Constantinides & Fountain, 2008). The first step for companies to opt into this relatively new environment is usually through establishing their own channels on YouTube, and developing a Facebook page. They use these applications to post images, news, and videos to promote their business (Stobbe, 2010).

There are a number of marketing activities that could be performed by entrepreneurs and small-businesses through the use of Web 2.0 tools. Jones (2010) summarizes them into the following: (1) promote their business offerings; (2) communicate with publics and stakeholders; (3) brand, distribute, position, segment, and target their products and services; (4) disseminate knowledge and communications; (5) differentiate their offerings from their competitors; (6) raise their profile; (7) research and better understand the markets in which they operate; (8) open possibilities for building a networked business environment with other businesses; (9) create customer interest; (10) grow their business; (11) co-create value; (12) reinforce crowdsourcing; and (13) gather customer feedback.

Web 2.0 Value Creation

Realizing a competitive advantage from an Internet business can be reached through adding value (Porter, 2001). In particular, determining the value of using Web 2.0 would guide businesses to develop and would lead to standardizing and reaching a common ground about expected outcomes (Jones, 2010). Web 2.0 media can help create additional value and wealth. It can lead to improvements in efficiencies and productivity. It was confirmed by several researchers that Web 2.0 creates value for businesses (Prahalad & Ramaswarmy, 2000; Bjerke & Hultman, 2002; Vargo, et al., 2008) through affecting consumer behavior strengthening the development of 'prosumers' (Toffler, 1984; Tapscott & Williams, 2006). For entrepreneurs, Web 2.0 enables them to enhance service quality: a key to success for them (Jones, 2010). For individuals and small businesses, Web 2.0 represents a new era for them to collaborate in production and to contribute largely to wider economic systems (Tapscott & Williams, 2006).

Constantinides and Fountain (2008) suggest that businesses can create value from Web 2.0 through three means: (1) conducting public relations using social media either by advertising in the most used search engines and popular blogs, and approaching online influencers (such as bloggers, podcasters) and raise their awareness about their products or services, and their promotional campaigns. This provides an efficient way of reaching a company's target segment with a much lower costs than using traditional media; (2) searching for, monitoring, and learning from customers' posts about a company and its products in blogs, podcasts, and social networks (Vargo & Lusch, 2004). It facilitates the acquisition of plenty and valuable customers' feedback in an easier and cheaper method than offline marketing research methods (such as, surveys or focus groups); and (3) strategizing on Web 2.0 to perform personalized direct marketing, and to build a community around a company's product or service.

In the same line of thought, Parise and Guinan (2008) confirm that in order to realize value from Web 2.0 adoption organizations should change their approach to allow for more control to consumers, which affects an organization's value proposition. Through interviewing more than 30 interviews with key employees in different areas in a number of organizations, they recommend four important concepts for organizations to derive value from Web 2.0 applications: (1) engage customers in marketing activities: (such as, product development, learning consumers' behavior in much faster and cheaper than traditional marketing techniques, assessing the effectiveness of marketing campaigns, etc.) through building online communities; (2) encourage members to participate in online communities: by using an easy to use system for communication, and by providing both monetary and non-monitory incentives; (3) monitor online content about the organization generated by customers: due to the credibility of customers' opinions regardless of any underlying risk. Organizations should search regularly for any relevant content in bookmarks and tags, ranking and social shopping websites, influencers' blogs, or other popular online communities; and (4) test continuously all online communications exploiting the different features of the digital media (audios, videos, interactivity options, images, etc.).

In an attempt to capture all Web 2.0 successful business models, Kim (2008) defines four types of business models based on two main processes: Production (P) and Filtering (F). These four models are illustrated in Figure 1: (1) Model 1: limited P and limited F (such as, Encyclopedia), where both processes are performed by a small group of employees in an organization, which ensures a high quality outcome, but restricts engagement and participation. Such model is similar to Web 1.0 models; (2) Model 2: open P and open F (such as, a Meta blog), which is the

Figure 1. Web 2.0 business models based on the production/filtering (P/F) model (adopted from Kim, 2008)

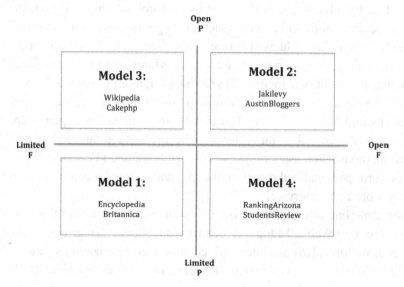

opposite of the previous model where everyone can do both processes, which does not guarantee a quality. In a Meta blog (i.e., a blog of blogs), users can create a blog and can rank any other blog at the same time; (3) Model 3: open P and Limited F (such as, wikis), where the production is performed by the mass, and the filtering process is undertaken by a limited number of corresponding professionals, which ensures the high quality of the outcome; (4) Model 4: limited P and open F (such as, students' reviews), allowing for a restricted number of experts to publish content, and enabling the public to vote, which encourage mass participation.

Tapscott and Williams (2006) argue that the features of Web 2.0 Internet economy or "Wikinomics"—such as openness, sharing, peering, and global thinking—can assist organizations in realizing success since they provide seven new business models superior than traditional ones: (1) Peer pioneers: that relies on voluntary mass production among communities of individuals; (2) Ideagoras: where organizations can consider the Internet as an environment for generating new ideas and innovations and not restrict such activities on their internal talent; (3) Prosumers: a new concept enabling consumers to have an input on organizations' designs and products; (4) New Alexandrian: promoting the notion of "Science 2.0" or collaborative science, through open knowledge development through publishing and sharing scientific material; (5) Platforms for participation: through aggregation, remixing, and filtering of online content referred as "mashups"; (6) Global plant floor: where companies embrace a new model that crosses national boundaries, and allows for exploitation of global resources and proficiencies; and (7) Wiki workplace: facilitating the link and participation among an organization's employees in virtual teams.

The literature above shows clearly that to create value from Web 2.0, there should be essentially an organizational cultural based on collaboration, transparency, acceptance of control among companies and consumers. In addition, management should evaluate different business models to choose the best production/filtering framework, the most appropriate tool and the right time to implement it. It is also important to conduct a continuous learning process from best practices as well as a company's prior experimentations in order to reach the best solution relevant to a local context. Furthermore, marketers should regularly strive to create new ways for approaching and attracting customers to participate in online social media, and to merge them with real world communities, especially in developing countries where online communication is still not sufficient to build trust among consumers. The keyword here lies in the ability for organization to be 'agile' to develop through spotting new technologies and check their potential in adding value. Finally, organizations should appreciate and encourage the concept of crowdsourcing, content aggregation, monitoring their online existence, and the possibility of expanding globally.

Challenges in using Web 2.0

Even though there are a number of approaches that enable Web 2.0 to add value to businesses, it is not guaranteed that such technology would always reach success. As Jones (2010) declares: "Web 2.0 can add value, be of no value and can also destroy value." Evidently, the features of Web 2.0 attracted businesses to have a presence on Twitter, blogs and Facebook, but this underlies several risks (Walker, 2010) usually due to non-technical barriers and challenges (Blinn, et al., 2009).

In the case of Small and Medium Enterprises (SMEs), they use the Internet for different purposes: information research, communication via electronic mail, and sales and customer services through a company's website (Blinn, et al., 2009). However, SMEs' use of Web 2.0 applications is still very limited (DeSaulles, 2008). Only few entrepreneurs acknowledge the benefits of Web 2.0 for their business (Peris, et al., 2011; Stobbe, 2010). In fact, entrepreneurs and SMEs are reluctant to embrace Web 2.0 not only for external communications but also internally (Kautz, 2010). The main barrier to implementation lies in the organizations' culture that is not willing to accept the major shift in the working behavior that result from such adoption (McKinsey, 2008; Raabe, 2007). As an example, a study conducted by Forrester Research—on knowledge workers in US companies—revealed that 60 percent of employees do not feel any value added from using Web 2.0 tools in their daily work (Forrester Consulting, 2009). In addition, since only 40 percent of new enterprises survive for ten years, the management style of SMEs is based on a survival strategy, and is concerned with a short-term perspective due to limited resources (Levy & Powell, 2005). This applies also on the use of Information Technology (IT), which is focused on the day-to-day operation. Also, the fact that entrepreneurs' personality is the leading factor in affecting the organization's strategy being usually the main decision maker (Masurel, et al., 2003; Burns, 2001), and that SMEs do not generally have a separate IT department or IT professional; thus, most of them do not use IT extensively due to their limited IT competencies, and their inability to spot opportunities that could arise from IT adoption (Levy & Powell, 2005; Street & Cameron, 2007). Even for businesses interested in communicating with their customers, they lack the sustainability of maintaining an open discourse with their them. They start their Web 2.0 existence by setting a profile on Facebook and posting images, press releases, and videos, but fail to be engaged continuously with their customers, hence, the "dialogue character of the medium Web 2.0 is neglected" (Stobbe, 2010).

Web 2.0 challenges are not only limited to the culture of management and employees in any organization, they also extend to cover the customers' culture. Even though Twitter has gained popularity among users for its ability to broadcast important political and social news and events, customers are not always attracted to organizations' tweets to check them regularly (Stobbe, 2010). Although there is a high expectation of interactivity and responsiveness through Web 2.0 applications, prosumers are still reluctant to be exposed unless they receive a value-added from such privacy invasion Clarke (2008). In addition, Stobbe (2010) affirms that customers' interest varies in communicating with businesses over the Internet depending on each business sector. For example, technology related products and fan communities (such as, sporting products, cars, and some food categories) are more eligible for fostering communications with customers than other segments such as financial services. Furthermore, one cannot deny the fact that the majority of Web 2.0 users read only posted content, and only 30 percent of the respondents are actually contributing in composing and spreading online material (Busemann & Christoph, 2009). This represents a challenge for entrepreneurs since it is difficult to receive a feedback from a large number of customers since most of them are passive users.

Entrepreneurs should also consider that online customers' reviews could be sometimes damaging the organization's reputation through posting negative reviews about a company's products, strategy, and services (Peris, et al., 2011). Such possibility is valid even if companies do not participate in the Web 2.0 World, customers' posts and reviews can still be available in the Web 2.0 world. Hence, entrepreneurs should continuously monitor any information especially manipulated ones in the virtual world and take the correct measures towards this risk (Stobbe, 2010). Negative comments can be spread rapidly on the Internet and can even be transferred through other conventional media and disseminated further (Stobbe, 2010). This is particularly crucial due to the increasing mistrust of customers in traditional marketing techniques, paying more attention to other customers' reviews, and their prior communication and transactions with product or service providers. In fact, Web 2.0 induced more complexity to the customer decision-making process since its influence is beyond marketers' control, unlike the first wave of the Internet that allowed them to approach customers through a mix of online marketing techniques (Constantinides, 2004).

One important consequence of posting user-generated content (such as videos, images, and music) is that it could lead to public confusion because it blurs the boundaries between facts, fictions, and advertising, and represents copyrights' infringement (Keen, 2007; Keegan, 2007; Wilson, 2007). Constantinides and Fountain (2008) and Perise et al. (2008) pinpoint also that users, being publishers, would constitute a threat to professional artists and would cause an absence of control and accountability on the material published. Moreover, it poses a concern about the quality of the information presented, which could be recorded in an inaccurate or inappropriate way for a certain segment of customers, or sometimes not targeting the right audience (OECD, 2007).

Whilst Web 2.0 provides a great chance for entrepreneurs to know their customers and to interact with them, it could also raise concerns about security and privacy issues related to data protection and consumer rights (Blinn, et al., 2009; Burg & Pitcher, 2006; Menn, 2010). Social networking changed the boundaries between private and personal information since they produce an enormous relational and complex personal data (Gates, 2007). The online world still cannot mimic the analog world in enabling a person to apply a "fine-grained access control" on his personal data to a certain group of people. The possibility of a personal information public disclosure represents a threat to the development and continuity of several social, political, and economic initiatives in the Web 2.0 World (Gates, 2007). In addition, the fact that personal information is stored in social networks raises a question about the probability of changing the privacy policies on these applications (Needle, 2010).

A final challenge to Web 2.0 adoption is referred to the lack of rigorous measurements of the effect of Web 2.0 initiatives on organizational business performance. The absence of such evaluation could demotivate organizations to embrace this technology. According to a study by emarketer.com (2010), less than 20 percent of the decision makers worldwide assess the return on investment of their Web 2.0 projects, and they use general measurements (such as Web traffic or the quality of communication with customers) not catered for each project in particular (Stobbe, 2010). Even though the effect of Web 2.0 was remarkable in increasing employees' motivation and collaboration, it is less perceived in boosting sales (Leibhammer & Weber, 2008). Probably, setting standard Web 2.0 measurements will require several more years, since Web 2.0 is a relatively new concept still under experimentation, and not widespread among organizations worldwide.

METHODOLOGY

In the beginning, a research was undertaken to identify two categories of Egyptian entrepreneurs: those operating from physical stores or offices, and others relying on the Internet to conduct their business virtually. It was taken into consideration to select businesses across multiple industries including services (e.g., consultancy, insurance, real estate, equipment maintenance, and interior design) and products (e.g., open houses for clothes, production and customization of T-shirts, food catering, confectionaries, restaurants, silver jewelries, books, electric equipment, furniture production, marble manufacturing, and production). In addition to the coverage of a diversity of sectors, the authors considered different age ranges of entrepreneurs, and new and relatively old founded companies. 21 in-depth interviews with these entrepreneurs were performed: 14 with traditional entrepreneurs and 7 with Internet ones. The researchers prepared a list of questions (see Appendix A) as guidelines for the interviewees, but allowed space for them to listen to their views, and to obtain deep insights about several issues related to their use of the Internet in general, and Web 2.0 applications in particular.

FINDINGS AND DISCUSSION

Since e-business concept is relatively new in Egypt, most websites and Web 2.0 applications adopted were launched recently, only when the Internet in Egypt started to create a critical mass capable of using and accepting this technology. Although the Internet started in Egypt since 1993 (Azab, 2012), and users were exponentially increasing since that date, they remained representing a small percentage of the population. Only recently this percentage started to be noticed and reached around 38 percent of the population (MCIT, 2012), and Egyptians started to perceive the importance of the Internet after Egypt's revolution, especially social networks applications (Azab, 2012). Evidently this figure is low compared to its corresponding in developed countries, but was sufficient to attract few Internet entrepreneurs to think seriously of starting projects to serve this sector, and other entrepreneurs in traditional businesses to penetrate that medium assuming the past growth pattern will be maintained or even exceeded in the future.

The research findings cover several points: the factors affecting Web 2.0 adoption, how entrepreneurs perception use Web 2.0 applications, drivers for having a website or a Web 2.0 presence, their perceptions towards Web 2.0 and ways to measure its effectiveness.

Factors affecting Web 2.0 Adoption

It was concluded from the interviews conducted that the use of Web 2.0 applications is affected by three main dimensions: (1) the age of the entrepreneur; (2) the date of establishment of each company; and (3) the nature of business whether it is a traditional or an Internet one.

Young entrepreneurs are more willing and already using Web 2.0 applications especially social networks since it is a natural behavior for them being familiar with such applications in their personal lives. As one of the young interviewees who opened a pretzel outlet declared: "I spend usually from 4 to 5 hours on Facebook and Twitter every day." In addition, young entrepreneurs have the ability to connect with the Internet different communities and business networks, and to integrate their Internet initiatives with the physical business world. A silver-making entrepreneur revealed that: "the Internet enabled me to have access to a wide network of event organizers and exhibitors, which opened an efficient channel for promoting and selling my products." As for older entrepreneurs, besides being difficult for them to accept change that could occur through the use of Web 2.0 adoption, their knowledge of the Internet is minimal, and only restricted to searching for information and communicating with their customers through emails, without considering the Internet as an integral element in their business. While interviewing older entrepreneurs, all of them admitted that they are very late in catching the Web 2.0 era. An entrepreneur who founded a real estate agency stated: "the market has completely changed, customers used to buy newspapers everyday to look for available flats and apartments, nowadays, they review newspapers only once a week. Unfortunately, more recent real estate companies exploited the opportunities offered by the Internet and realized a great success because a large sector of our target customers are continuously available on the Internet."

Furthermore, relatively new organizations are more likely to adopt Web 2.0 than well-established ones. This could be due to the fact that old organizations are more structured with rigid business processes and policies that limit their tendency to change the way they conduct business. This is contrary to new organizations operating in a more flexible approach. However, the acceptance of Web 2.0 in new organizations is not embedded in their business processes and not standardized; it is only based on a personal desire since entrepreneurs themselves are the representatives in these applications communicating with their customers in an ad-hoc manner. A restaurant owner showed the interviewer his blackberry being the fast and only tool of communication with customers: "I am always connected and monitoring all complaints and comments through my device, and I respond with a maximum of 15 minutes especially on Twitter and Facebook."

The third element that have an impact on the use of Web 2.0 is the type of business; virtual businesses tend to rely more on Web 2.0 applications especially Facebook. Since the Internet facilitates the start of new businesses due to the low startup cost, Internet entrepreneurs usually have a limited budget, which encourages them to use the affordable Web 2.0 applications in their marketing activities as opposed to the high overheads in using other traditional marketing channels. As mentioned by a silver-making entrepreneurs who has only an online existence: "I started with my partner 2 years ago with a startup capital of only L.E. 400 (less than $30) divided equally among us." Since Internet entrepreneurs do not have a place to meet their customers, they try to build trust through social networks to compensate the absence of the face-to-face interaction. For example, even though there are a number of ads on Facebook about cupcakes' sellers, the most popular cupcakes' seller has a physical shop, as declared by its owner: "I have a competitive advantage over all competitors since I'm the only one having a place where my customers meet me (I'm always present at my 2 shops every single day), and see my fresh cakes."

Types and Functions of Web 2.0 Applications Used

As for Web 2.0 applications that are adopted by entrepreneurs, it was found that all entrepreneurs use only Facebook and Twitter, and sometimes YouTube. The majority of them are not aware of other Web 2.0 applications such as, podcasts, blogs, Wikis, etc., or sometimes do not know that they could be relevant and beneficial to their business. One entrepreneur said that: "it is too early to consider other applications because Egyptian Internet users will not be attracted to tools other than social networks for the next coming years." It was also concluded that all interviewees do not differentiate between Facebook and Twitter and they use both of them in delivering the same message. Only one entrepreneur thinks that: "Twitter expresses a more intimate feeling." The interviews revealed also that there are different ways to approach customers through social networks depending on each industry, a service or product sector, and whether the entrepreneur is a direct seller or an intermediary, and an Internet business or a traditional one. For example, traditional businesses use social networks to show their products, and to advertise for events and promotions to attract customers to visit their stores, or for online ordering or reservation in the case of restaurants. This is seen clearly in the food and beverage sector, where Facebook and Twitter announce for discounts on restaurants for a limited period of time. A cupcake entrepreneur undertook a successful initiative when a customer decided to propose to his girlfriend in the store. A video was posted on YouTube showing him offering his girlfriend an engagement ring inside a cake especially made for this occasion. The video became very popular reaching more than 10,000 views. For Internet entrepreneurs, a group buying website started a competition among its Facebook members to choose every day's winner of the best bowl of salad encouraging members to post the salad that they prepare. The timing of the competition was correctly chosen during the entire month of Ramadan (the fasting month for Muslims) where Egyptians are usually interested in preparing new food recipes. A t-shirt manufacturer entrepreneur uses Facebook to allow for customers to design their own T-shirts. After taking votes from the members of his fan page (who reached 120,000 presently), the best design is to be announced and produced in large quantities publishing the name of the winner and offering him/her a T-shirt for free or for a discounted price.

Drivers for Launching a Website/Social Network Existence

When entrepreneurs were asked about their Internet existence, some of them started by having a website, and others created first a Facebook group or a Twitter profile. Some of them have either a website or only an existence on social networks, and others have both. Many entrepreneurs who have a website were attracted to social networks because they are not satisfied with the content and design of the websites of their companies. For those who do not have a website, they prefer to promote their business through social networks because it is cheaper than establishing a website especially in the beginning of their career path. Some Internet entrepreneurs selling products use Facebook in particular to build a customer base that guarantees the sustainability of their business before opening a physical store. All entrepreneurs having a Facebook group appreciate the services this application offers such as, promoting their group, placing their ads for their predefined customers' segments, and presenting monthly detailed statistics about the usage traffic on their page: visits, like, shares, etc. They asserted also that most sales are usually generated from Facebook members more than Twitter followers, and that broadcasting Facebook messages is very efficient: "80% received likes even before having a Facebook group."

Measurements and Perceptions of Web 2.0 Benefits

In addition to the number of likes, the interviewees measure their success on Web 2.0 applications through the number of shares, visits, and comments on Facebook, the number of followers on Twitter, and the number of views for videos posted on YouTube. An entrepreneur pinpointed that it is not only a matter of numbers; measurements should reflect real customers: "my 7000 followers on Twitter are reflected in my business return on investment because they are real ones that I know by name, and with whom I meet and love to chat with at my store. My philosophy is not only to sell my product, but to also build intimacy with my customers." As for the benefits that entrepreneurs perceive in social network sites, they stated several ones: "an efficient tool to promote my business," "a channel for building strong relationships, and to listen carefully to customers' feedback," "increase my organization's transparency," and "improve customer service with minimal cost." Traditional entrepreneurs see that it is important to show their products both virtually and physically. An interior design entrepreneur stated that: "I created a Facebook page to show my design for brand awareness, but most frequently, I go to my clients' places to show them more designs, to take the required measurements, and to interact physically with them to build more trust, and to understand more their tastes and needs."

For entrepreneurs who do not have a Web 2.0 existence, most of them admitted that this is a deficiency in the way they are doing their business. A Marble manufacturer declared: "it would be great to show the large variety of marble types that we sell." Another one owning a consultancy agency believes that: "having a dynamic Facebook page would generate cold requests (contrary to warm ones that are initiated through word of mouth)." One interviewee who runs a company responsible for selling, installing, and maintaining elevators explained that his company faces a fierce competition, but unfortunately the majority of competitors do not provide the same safety measures as his company, which makes their prices cheaper: "We would like to use Facebook to inform our targeted customers how our service is different."

Web 2.0 Challenges and Future Plans

Despite their recognition of the value of Web 2.0 applications, interviewees expressed that the main impediments to exploiting Web 2.0 features are lack of time for them to understand how to use Web 2.0 correctly and for being prepared to change their way of approaching customers, and to assign a well-trained employee to be responsible for communicating and responding to customers' inquiries and comments in a standard and professional manner. Another common challenge for open-days' entrepreneurs is their insistence on the privacy aspect; they usually invite their customers to their houses to see their products, and do not prefer to be exposed except for the customers they already know. They rely on sending mobile text messages whenever they plan for an event. They did not even welcome the suggestion to create a closed Facebook group only for their customers because they feel more comfortable to communicate with their customers through mobiles only. Open-days' entrepreneurs declared also that they could be found on some bazaars Facebook pages when they sometimes participate in bazaars outside their houses. For food catering, they are reluctant to use Web 2.0 because they do not prefer that their plates would be seen by their competitors. Being exposed to competitors is not only considered by non-Web 2.0 adopters, but also by entrepreneurs who use Facebook efficiently. For example in different sectors such as, clothing, silver jewelries, and interior design, there is a fierce competition over social networks, and usually designs can be copied.

Whilst there exist many challenges, all entrepreneurs using Web 2.0 were planning to continue in this direction but giving more emphasis on improving their existence and widening their messages with their customers to be seen globally, and to assess their success through a continuous evaluation of pre-defined Web 2.0 metrics. For those who still did not embrace such technology, most of them were determined to consider integrating Web 2.0 in their working environment in the near future.

Table 1 summarizes the main research findings. It presents common issues among Egyptian entrepreneurs as well as differences among them based on the three main elements that affect Web 2.0 adoption: age of entrepreneur, date of establishment of the company, and type of the business: traditional or virtual.

Table 1. Summary of main findings

	Differences			Similarities
	Age	Date of Establish-ment	Type of Business (Traditional/Pure Play)	
Website existence	Older entrepreneurs.		Traditional.	
Website's value proposition				Not satisfied with each company's Website.
Website's update				No updates.
Started first a website or a Web 2.0 application?	- Youth entrepreneurs: Web 2.0. - Older entrepreneurs: website.	- New organizations: Web 2.0. - Old organizations: website.	- Virtual: Web 2.0. - Traditional: website.	
Type of Web 2.0 application	Youth entrepreneurs: Twitter, YouTube.			Facebook.
Perception towards Web 2.0				Very useful (promote business; build strong relationships with customers; receive customer feedback; increase transparency; cheap approach to improve customer service).
Actual use of Web 2.0	- Youth entrepreneurs: continuous communication with customers; more interest in receiving reviews; quick learning by experience.		- Virtual: launch competitions; encourage customization and participation through continuous innovative ideas; get access to relevant business networks. - Traditional: Announce for events to be performed in physical stores and companies; publish previous physical events.	Awareness about products/services.
Web 2.0 measurements				- Facebook: likes, shares, comments. - Twitter: number of followers.
Measuring Web 2.0 value creation				No

continued on following page

Table 1. Continued

	Differences			Similarities
Continuous Web 2.0 evaluation	Youth: yes.		Virtual: yes.	
Integration with other marketing media				No
Web 2.0 challenges	- Youth entrepreneurs: company is presented only by owner. - Older entrepreneurs: privacy; lack of technical skills.	- New organizations: lack of business structure; company is presented only by owner; limited resources. - Old organizations: less flexibility and difficult to change working practices.	- Traditional: privacy; lack of technical skills. - Virtual: fierce competition, exposed to competitors; culture of consumers; expensive ads on Facebook.	- Allocate sufficient time. - Negative reviews. - Instability in Egyptian environment.
Response to customers on Web 2.0 tools	Youth entrepreneurs: quick and effective.		Virtual: quick and effective; special focus on providing a superior customer service.	
Future plans in using Web 2.0	- Youth entrepreneurs: allocating more interest; planning to widen exposure locally and globally. - Older entrepreneurs: less determined in Web 2.0 engagement.		- Virtual: Youth: allocating more interest; planning to widen exposure. - Traditional: less determined in Web 2.0 engagement.	

RESEARCH LIMITATIONS

Even though the study produced valuable findings that would contribute to the research area of Web 2.0 and entrepreneurship, it entails one important limitation concerning the sample size. The sample used in the empirical research for Internet entrepreneurs is very small (only 7 entrepreneurs). Normally, such small sample cannot represent a population in a certain context. However, as an exception, this thought cannot be applicable in case the topic under study addresses Internet entrepreneurs in Egypt. Since e-commerce is at an early stage in Egypt—since only 0.44 percent of Internet users conduct online transactions (Axelrod, et al., 2010)—there is still a limited number of popular local e-business websites.

Evidently, the number of traditional entrepreneurs in Egypt exceeds that of Internet ones, but the authors preferred to limit the interviews with traditional entrepreneurs to 14 to better conduct an adequate comparison with Internet ones. Moreover, since the concept of entrepreneurship in general is new to the Egyptian market, only few names could be considered as 'entrepreneurs.' Despite the small sample used in the research, the authors attempted to cover as much as possible different industrial sectors.

RECOMMENDATIONS FOR FURTHER RESEARCH

As Constantinides and Fountain (2008) advise, from the academic as well as the practical point of view, there should be more emphasis on framing and assessing the real value of Web 2.0 in business. This chapter attempts to provide a contribution in this direction. Going forward, the descriptive study provided paves the way for more research venues. Some suggestions are summarized into the following:

- Conduct a detailed analysis in identifying and classifying the different types of Web 2.0 applications from both technical and business perspectives. This will set the basis for a systematic comprehension and use of this technology for different business objectives.
- Assess the influence of these Web 2.0 tools on consumer behavior and decision-making patterns to assist marketers, entrepreneurs, and small businesses to use them efficiently.
- Develop a framework that portrays all possible functions and use of Web 2.0 applications depending on the nature and size of business. Such framework requires considering the special dynamic characteristics of small businesses, and recommending relevant approaches to apply Web 2.0 different tools on several practical cases and situations catered specifically for them.
- Carry out a survey on a large sample of entrepreneurs to examine quantitatively the weight of several factors (such as, age of entrepreneur and organization, personal qualifications and perception towards technology, business size and sector, and virtual vs. traditional organization) on affecting Web 2.0 adoption.

CONCLUSION

This research highlighted several aspects related to entrepreneurship and the use of Web 2.0 technology. Even though application of Web 2.0 in marketing is still at an early stage, its potential in realizing value to companies is perceived both by academics and practitioners (Peris, et al., 2011). Web 2.0 tools are used primarily in direct and one-to-one marketing and in communicating with customers, and can open also a space for further innovation and collaboration (Stobbe, 2010). Entrepreneurs and small businesses are increasingly embracing Web 2.0 applications (e.g., social networks, Wikis, blogs, etc.) changing the scope and nature of communication with their customers and other stakeholders, and emphasizing the concept of partnership where all participants can contribute and feel they can make a difference, which leads to more brand credibility (Jones, 2010). Web 2.0 adds a new "uncontrollable element" that affects customer decision-making, which could raise interest among marketers who are aware of the decreasing effect of traditional marketing approaches on consumer behavior and conversion rate (Constantinides & Fountain, 2008).

This research builds on the recommendation of Jones (2010) calling for "a more grounded, empirically informed, evidence-based case study analysis of specific small business practice of using Web 2.0" as the optimum approach for evaluating its influence. It is particularly necessary also to determine the cause of the modest usage of Web 2.0 by small businesses compared to their remarkable adoption of the Internet in general (Blinn, et al., 2009). Hence, the purpose of our research was to investigate several issues related to Web 2.0 and its use, value, and challenges for entrepreneurs. After reviewing these aspects in the literature, this study aimed to learn from entrepreneurs in different industries to pinpoint their perception towards Web 2.0 and the way they use it in their marketing and communication activities. Through conducting 21 in-depth interviews with a sample representing Egyptian entrepreneurs, it was concluded that Web 2.0 acceptance is affected by three main factors: age of the entrepreneur, date of establishment of the organization, and the nature of business whether it is a traditional or a virtual one. Interviews revealed also that entrepreneurs are currently presenting themselves externally with profiles in social networks only; either because they are not aware of other Web 2.0 applications and their potential or because they believe that Egyptian Internet users are still not prepared to be engaged in other tools, especially that social networks have gained more interest after the Egyptian revolution in January 2011. Usually the content presented on these channels is in the form of recycled information that was created for traditional communication.

Egyptian entrepreneurs are continuously thriving for innovative ideas to attract and keep consumers to their virtual environment; they always try to understand their target customers and develop several tactics to reach them, depending on each business sector. While most entrepreneurs acknowledge the features of social networks, few of them are exploiting them successfully. The main Web 2.0 challenges that Egyptian entrepreneurs expressed are their inability to cope with this new communication platform that provokes a major change in their working habits, especially in case they are satisfied with their existing working activities. Others were concerned with being exposed easily to their competitors where ideas can be imitated, or with the availability of extra time to understand more this technology and allocate the required time and resources to realize more value from using it. It was deduced that interacting with customers in an ad-hoc manner from the part of each entrepreneur is a common behavior among all interviewees adopting social network sites.

Finally, all indications show that Web 2.0—the second wave of the Internet's evolution—will continue gaining more interests among businesses and consumers (Constantinides & Fountain, 2008). Stobbe (2010) affirms that Web 2.0 will be always associated with organizations' working practices. Small business should understand the new change such technology triggers in producing and distributing information, and incorporate new marketing strategies accordingly (Jones, 2010). A successful marketing strategy should be a multi-channeled one integrating the different today's customer touch points (Weinberg, et al., 2007). The study conducted revealed that Egyptian entrepreneurs are not completely aware of the concepts, features, and effect Web 2.0 could do to their business. Moreover, they are still struggling in setting the right marketing mix to realize benefits. In addition, they measure their success on Web 2.0 based on their increasing popularity on social media (e.g., number of likes, shares, comments, etc.) without conducting a detailed analysis to evaluate how their social media practices are reflected in their bottom line, and identifying the most effective tool that has the highest return and the reasons leading to its success.

Egyptian entrepreneurs should exploit efficiently the new shapes of interactive and one-to-one marketing imposed by Web 2.0. They should also learn how to co-exist and address a powerful customer who is not only influenced by traditional push marketing approaches as before, but also appreciating his value in participating and committing change in the business marketing process (Constantinides & Fountain, 2008). The fact that their strategies, products, and marketing campaigns are exposed and evaluated by the public, and can even affect their reputation even if they do decide not to create their online existence, dictates that they do not have a choice but to be engaged in this new environment even at least through monitoring how prosumers portray them in the virtual world (Stobbe, 2010). Presenting a credible image and managing reputation in the Web 2.0 environment requires working skills such as, diplomacy, flexibility, and confidence: "questioning and challenging perceived wisdom and ways of thinking are key requisites in the new world of entrepreneurial marketing and social media" (Jones, 2010). It is also important to exploit Web 2.0 features to facilitate one-to-one marketing to send the right message to each customer; whilst consuming is planned as a cooperative project, it is usually done on a personal basis (Jones, 2010).

Based on the interviews conducted, the majority of entrepreneurs think that the main driver for them to turn to social media was simply because it is agreed that this is the modern way of representing themselves in this trendy and promising landscape, but they still do not have clear objectives or analyses of their presence in these applications. Such unplanned behavior does not leave a space for a rigorous study of the effect of any resulting change before any unexpected undesirable incident happens (Jones, 2010) such as, resistance to change (Raabe, 2007), privacy concerns (Walker, 2010; Palmer, 2010), etc. Despite these negative signals, it is essential for entrepreneurs to look to Web 2.0 as a challenge rather than a threat, and consider it as a new component in their marketing strategy. Even though the adoption rate of Web 2.0 among Egyptian entrepreneurs is still modest, many of them plan to tap into this technology and have high expectations towards it.

Regarding the main pillars for Web 2.0 success, this research results are in-line with prior research (e.g., Gilden, 2006; Gillin, 2007; Parise & Guinan, 2008). It was concluded that successful cases are the ones who were able to facilitate user-generated content, provide support to customers, convey a trustworthy image, gain and retain customers through offering them the right incentives, understand the power of the reviews on affecting their decisions, and engage into a learning process through continuous experimentation and evaluation. The point is to understand how Web 2.0 is transferring the market structure, and how to deal with such change. As highlighted by Tapscott and Williams (2006) in their landmark book *Wikinomics*: "whenever such a shift occurs, there are always realignments of competitive advantage and new measures of success and value. To succeed in this new world, it will not be enough—indeed, it will be counterproductive—simply to intensify current policies, management strategies, and curricular approaches. Remaining innovative requires us to understand both the shifts and the new strategy agenda that follows. We must collaborate or perish across borders, cultures, disciplines, and firms, and increasingly with masses of people at one time."

As such, the research performed poses some interesting questions: would Egyptian entrepreneurs address the challenges involved in Web 2.0 adoption? Would they be capable of integrating Web 2.0 with other traditional marketing channels? Could they standardize their Web 2.0 existence and responses, and understand the particular features and functions of each Web 2.0 tool to exploit it effectively? How to measure different Web 2.0 benefits (e.g., improve communication and the quality of information exchanged, modernize business processes, enhance and promote products and services, etc.)? How to apply Web 2.0 to add value in which product/service or stage of the customer life cycle: awareness, learning, purchase, and post-sales service? How to assess and deal with Web 2.0 acceptance by both employees and customers?

These key questions and issues should be addressed by Egyptian entrepreneurs to be among the leaders in gaining a competitive advantage through embracing Web 2.0 technologies. Web 2.0 is only a new set of applications that can be effective in case entrepreneurs exploit them correctly.

REFERENCES

Alby, T. (2007). *Web 2.0: Concepts, applications, technologies*. München, Germany: Hanser.

Anderson, C. (2006). *The long tail: Why the future of business is selling less of more*. New York, NY: Hyperion.

Axelrod, M., Brockman, S., Doumet, F., & Zahr, S. (2010). *E-commerce in Egypt*. Philadelphia, PA: Wharton School. Retrieved from http://knowledge.wharton.upenn.edu/arabic/article.cfm?articleid=1209

Azab, N. (2012). The role of the internet in shaping the political process in Egypt. *International Journal of E-Politics, 3*(2), 30–49. doi:10.4018/jep.2012040103

Bakos, J. Y. (1991). A strategic analysis of electronic marketplaces. *Management Information Systems Quarterly, 15*(3), 295–310. doi:10.2307/249641

Barbosa, S., Gerhardt, M., & Kickul, J. (2007). The role of cognitive style and risk preference on entrepreneurial self-efficacy and entrepreneurial intentions. *Journal of Leadership & Organizational Studies, 13*(4), 86–104. doi:10.1177/107179190 70130041001

Baron, R., & Ensley, M. (2006). Opportunity recognition as the detection of meaningful patterns: Evidence from comparisons of novice and experienced entrepreneurs. *Management Science, 52*(9), 1331–1344. doi:10.1287/mnsc.1060.0538

Becherer, R., & Maurer, J. (1999). The proactive personality disposition and entrepreneurial behaviour among small company presidents. *Journal of Small Business Management, 38*, 28–36.

Beer, D. (2008). Making friends with Jarvis Cocker: Music culture in the context of web 2.0. *Cultural Sociology, 2*(2), 222–241. doi:10.1177/1749975508091034

Beer, D., & Burrows, R. (2007). Sociology and, of and in web 2.0: Some initial considerations. *Sociological Research Online*. Retrieved from http://www.socresonline.org.uk/12/5/17.html

Bettelheim, B. (1986). *The informed heart*. Harmondsworth, UK: Penguin.

Bjerke, B., & Hultman, C. M. (2002). *Entrepreneurial marketing: The growth of small firms in the new economic era.* Cheltenham, UK: Edward Elgar.

Blinn, N., Lindermann, N., & Nüttgens, M. (2009). Web 2.0 in SME networks - A design science approach considering multi-perspective requirements. In *Proceedings of the Fifteenth AMCIS.* San Francisco, CA: AMCIS.

Boll, S. (2007). MultiTube: Where web 2.0 and multimedia could meet. *IEEE MultiMedia, 14*(1), 9–13. doi:10.1109/MMUL.2007.17

Bolton, B., & Thompson, J. (2004). *Entrepreneurs: Talent, temperament, technique* (2nd ed.). London, UK: Elsevier.

Burg, T. N., & Pircher, R. (2006). Social software in unternehmen. *Wissensmanagement, 8,* 26–28.

Burns, P. (2001). *Entrepreneurship and small business.* Hampshire, UK: Palgrave.

Busemann, K., & Christoph, G. (2009). Results of the ARD/ZDF online Study 2009 - Web 2.0: Popular communities among young users. *Media Perspectives, 7,* 356.

Busenitz. (1999). Entrepreneurial risk and strategic decision making: It's a matter of perspective. *Journal of Applied Behavioral Science, 35*(3), 325-340.

Casson, M., & Wadeson, N. (2006). The discovery of opportunities: Extending the economic theory of the entrepreneur. *Small Business Economics, 28*(4), 285–300. doi:10.1007/s11187-006-9037-7

Choi, Y., Lévesque, M., & Shepherd, D. (2008). When should entrepreneurs expedite or delay opportunity exploitation? *Journal of Business Venturing, 23*(3), 333–355. doi:10.1016/j.jbusvent.2006.11.001

Clarke, R. (2008). Web 2.0 as syndication. *Journal of Theoretical and Applied Electronic Commerce Research, 3*(2), 30–43. doi:10.4067/S0718-18762008000100004

Constantinides, E. (2004). Influencing the online consumer's behaviour: The web experience. *Journal of Internet Research, 14*(2), 111–126. doi:10.1108/10662240410530835

Constantinides, E., & Fountain, S. (2008). Web 2.0: Conceptual foundations and marketing issues. *Journal of Direct. Data and Digital Marketing Practice, 9*(3), 231–244. doi:10.1057/palgrave.dddmp.4350098

Cunningham, J., & Lischeron, J. (1991). Defining entrepreneurship. *Journal of Small Business Management, 29*(1), 45–61.

Czarniawska, B., & Wolff, R. (1991). Leaders, managers, entrepreneurs on and off the organizational stage. *Organization Studies, 12*(4), 529–546. doi:10.1177/017084069101200404

Daconta, M. (2003). *The semantic web: A guide to the future of XML, web services, and knowledge management*. New York, NY: John Wiley & Sons Inc.

De Saulles, M. (2008b). Never too small to join the party. *Information World Review*. Retrieved from http://www.iwr.co.uk/informationworld-review/features/2225252/never-small-join-party

Deshpande, A., & Jadad, A. (2006). Web 2.0: Could it help move the health system into the 21st century. *Journal of Men's Health & Gender, 3*(4), 332–336. doi:10.1016/j.jmhg.2006.09.004

Doyle, W., Fisher, R., & Young, J. (2002). Entrepreneurs: Relationships between cognitive style and entrepreneurial drive. *Journal of Small Business and Entrepreneurship, 16*(2), 2–20.

E-Marketer.com. (2010). *Website*. Retrieved from http://www.emarketer.com/Article.aspx?R=1007506

European Commission. (2004). *Five-year assessment of the European Union research framework programmes 1999-2003*. Retrieved from http://ec.europa.eu/research/reports/2004/pdf/fya_en.pdf

Evans, P., & Wurster, T. (1999). *Blown to bits: How the new economics of information transforms strategy*. Boston, MA: Harvard Business School Press.

Forrester Consulting. (2009). *Building the future of collaboration*. Retrieved from http://wwwimages.adobe.com/www.adobe.com/content/dam/Adobe/en/products/acrobat/pdfs/Building_The_Future_Of_Collaboration.pdf

Frana, P. (2004). Before the web there was gopher. *IEEE Annals of the History of Computing, 26*(1), 20–41. doi:10.1109/MAHC.2004.1278848

Friedman, T. (2007). *The world is flat: A brief history of the twenty-first century*. New York, NY: Picador.

Gartner, W. (1989). Some suggestions for research on entrepreneurial traits and characteristics, entrepreneurship. *Theory into Practice, 14*(1), 27–38.

Gates, C. (2007). Access control requirements for web 2.0 security and privacy. In *Proceedings of the IEEE Web, Web 2.0 Security and Privacy Workshop*. IEEE Press. Retrieved from http://w2spconf.com/2007/papers/paper-205-z_708.pdf

Gilden, J. (2006). Travel websites gain visitors by offering more than low prices. *Los Angeles Times*, 22 January 2006

Gillin, P. (2007). *The new influencers: A marketer's guide to the new social media*. San Francisco, CA: Quill DriverBooks\Word Dancer Press.

Howe, J. (2009). *Crowdsourcing: Why the power of the crowd is driving the future of business*. New York, NY: Crown Business.

Jones, B. (2010). Entrepreneurial marketing and the web 2.0 interface. *Journal of Research in Marketing and Entrepreneurship*, *12*(2), 143–152. doi:10.1108/14715201011090602

Jones, B., & Iredale, N. (2009). Entrepreneurship education and web 2.0. *Journal of Research in Marketing and Entrepreneurship*, *11*(1), 66–77. doi:10.1108/14715200911014158

Karger, D., & Quan, D. (2005). What would it mean to blog on the semantic web. *Web Semantics: Science. Services and Agents*, *3*(2-3), 147–157. doi:10.1016/j.websem.2005.06.002

Kautz, K. (2010). Participatory design activities and agile software development. In J. Pries-Heje et al. (Eds.), *Human Benefit through the Diffusion Information Systems Design Science Research, IFIP AICT 318*, (303–316). Berlin, Germany: Springer.

Keegan, V. (2007, July 5). Amateurs can be good and bad news. *The Guardian*.

Keen, A. (2007). *The cult of the amateur: How today's internet is killing our culture*. New York, NY: Doubleday/Random House.

Kim, T. (2008). *MEconomy*. New York, NY: Hanbit Media, Inc.

Leadbeater, C., & Miller, P. (2004). *The pro-am revolution: How enthusiasts are changing our economy and society*. London, UK: Demos. Retrieved from http://www.demos.co.uk/publications/proameconomy/

Lee, S., DeWester, D., & Park, S. (2008). Web 2.0 and opportunities for small businesses. *Service Business*, *2*, 335–345. doi:10.1007/s11628-008-0043-5

Leibhammer, J., & Weber, J. (2008). Enterprise 2.0: Analysis to state and prospects of the German economy. *BITKOM Federal Association for Information Technology*. Retrieved from http://www.bitkom.org/files/documents/BITKOM-Studie_Enterprise_2Punkt0.pdf

Levy, M., & Powell, P. (2005). *Strategies for growth in SMEs – The role of information and information systems*. Oxford, UK: Elsevier.

Mashable Social Media. (2012). *Website.* Retrieved from http://mashable. com/2012/03/09/social-media-demographics/

Masurel, E., van Montfort, K., & Lentink, R. (2003). *SME: Innovation and the crucial role of the entrepreneur.* Amsterdam, The Netherlands: University of Amsterdam.

McAfee, A. P. (2006). Enterprise 2.0: The drawn of emergent collaboration. *Sloan Management Review, 47*(3), 21–28.

MCIT. (2012, April). *ICT indicators in brief – April 2012 – Monthly issue.* Retrieved from http://mcit.gov.eg/Upcont/Documents/Publications_2052012000_Eng.pdf

McKinsey. (2007). How business are using web 2.0: A McKinsey global survey. *The McKinsey Quarterly.* Retrieved from http://www.mckinseyquarterly.com/Marketing/ How_businesses_are_using_Web_20_A_McKinsey_Global_Survey_1913_abstract

McKinsey. (2008). Building the web 2.0 enterprise: McKinsey global survey results. *The McKinsey Quarterly.* Retrieved from http://www.mckinseyquarterly.com

Menn, J. (2010, July 29). Virtually insecure. *Financial Times,* p. 9.

Moor, J. (2003). *The second superpower rears its beautiful head.* Boston, MA: Harvard Law School.

Musser, J., O'Reilly, T., & O'Reilly Radar Team. (2006). Web 2.0 principles and best practices. In *O'Reilly Radar,* (p. 101). New York, NY: O'Reilly Media.

Needle, D. (2010). Web 2.0 privacy and security issues won't go away. *IT Business Edge, eSecurity Planet: Internet Security for IT Pros.* Retrieved from http://www. esecurityplanet.com/trends/article.php/3878546/Web-20-Privacy-and-Security-Issues-Wont-Go-Away.htm

O'Reilly, T. (2005). *What is web 2.0 – Design patterns and business models for the next generation of software.* Retrieved from http://www.oreillynet.com/pub/a/ oreilly/tim/news/2005/09/30/what-is-web-20.html

OECD. (2007). *Participative web and user created content: Web 2.0, wikis and social networking.* Paris, France: OECD.

Palmer, M. (2010, May 13). European officials call changes to Facebook settings 'unacceptable'. *Financial Times,* p. 17.

Parameswaran, M., & Whinston, A. (2007). Research issues in social computing. *Journal of the Association for Information Systems, 8*(6), 336–350.

Parise, S., & Guinan, P. (2008). Marketing using web 2.0. In *Proceedings of the 41st Hawaii International Conference on System Sciences*. IEEE Press.

Peris, M., Sperling, A., Blinn, N., Nüttgens, M., & Gehrke, N. (2011). Participatory design of web 2.0 applications in SME networks. In *Proceedings of the 24th Bled eConference eFuture: Creating Solutions for the Individual, Organisations and Society*. Bled, Slovenia: IEEE.

Pleil, T. (2006). *Social software in editorial marketing*. Retrieved from http://thomaspleil.files.wordpress.com/2006/09/pleil-medien-2-0.pdf

Porter, M. (2001). Strategy and the internet. *Harvard Business Review*. Retrieved from http://hbswk.hbs.edu/item/2165.html

Prahalad, C. K., & Ramaswarmy, V. (2000). Co-opting customer competence. *Harvard Business Review, 78*(1), 79–87.

Raabe, A. (2007). *Social software in unternehmen: Wikis and weblogs for knowledge management and communication*. Saarbrücken, Germany: VDM Verlag.

Rauch, A., & Frese, M. (2007). Born to be an entrepreneur? Revisiting the personality approach to entrepreneurship. In Baum, J., Frese, M., & Baron, R. (Eds.), *The Psychology of Entrepreneurship: The Organizational Frontiers* (pp. 41–65). Mahwah, NJ: Lawrence Erlbaum Associates Publishers.

Robinson, P., Stimpson, D., Huefner, J., & Hunt, H. (1991). An attitude approach to the prediction of entrepreneurship. *Entrepreneurship Theory & Practice, 15*(4), 13–30.

Salam, M., Steenkamp, A., & khoury, F. (2008). The evolution of small and medium enterprise in digital business ecosystem. In *Proceedings of the Information and Communication Technologies: From Theory to Applications, 2008*. Damascus, Syria: ICTTA.

Sambasivan, M., Abdul, M., & Yusop, Y. (2009). Impact of personal qualities and management skills of entrepreneurs on venture performance in Malaysia: Opportunity recognition skills as a mediating factor. *Technovation, 29*(11), 798–805. doi:10.1016/j.technovation.2009.04.002

Schumpeter, J. (1947). The creative response in economic history. *The Journal of Economic History, 7*(2), 149–159.

Shirkey, C. (2003). *Power laws, weblogs, and inequality, networks, economics, and culture mailing list*. Retrieved from http://www.shirky.com/writings/power-law_weblog.html

Snee, H. (2008). Web 2.0 as a social science research tool. *The British Library*. Retrieved from www.bl.uk/reshelp/bldept/socsci/socint/web2/web2.pdf

SpannerWorks. (2007). *What is social media*. Retrieved from www.spannerworks. com/ebooks

Stobbe, A. (2010). *Enterprise 2.0: How companies are tapping the benefits of web 2.0*. Berlin, Germany: Deutsche Bank Research.

Street, C. T., & Cameron, A. F. (2007). External relationships and the small business: A review of small business alliance and network research. *Journal of Small Business Management, 45*(2), 239–266.

Tapscott, D., & Williams, A. D. (2006). *Wikinomics: How mass collaboration changes everything*. London, UK: Portfolio Hardcover.

Toffler, A. (1984). *The third wave*. New York, NY: Bantam.

Trentmann, F. (2006). *The making of the consumer: Knowledge, power and identity in the modern world*. Oxford, UK: Berg.

Urban, G. (2003). *Customer advocacy: Is it for you?* Cambridge, UK: MIT Sloan School of Management.

Vargo, S. L., & Lusch, R. F. (2004). Evolving to a new dominant logic for marketing. *Journal of Marketing, 68*(1), 1–17. doi:10.1509/jmkg.68.1.1.24036

Vargo, S. L., Maglio, P. P., & Akaka, M. A. (2008). On value and value co-creation: A service systems and service logic perspective. *European Management Journal, 26*(3), 145–152. doi:10.1016/j.emj.2008.04.003

Walker, P. (2010, May 15). Facebook loses friends as privacy campaign grows. *The Guardian*, p. 7.

Weinberg, B., Parise, S., & Guinan, P. J. (2007). Multichannel marketing: mindset and program development. *Business Horizons, 50*(5), 385–394. doi:10.1016/j. bushor.2007.04.002

Wilson, A. N. (2007, June 8). The internet is destroying the world as we know it. *Daily Mail Online*.

Yourdon, E. (2006). Creating business value with web 2.0. *Cutter IT Journal, 19*(10), 3–5.

Chapter 2
Designing and Implementing Online Collaboration Tools in West Africa

Caitlin M. Bentley
Royal Holloway University of London, UK

EXECUTIVE SUMMARY

This chapter explores how the Web 2.0 principle of the Web as a platform was applied in the context of a development aid-funded project aimed to enhance online collaboration capacities of 17 Civil Society Organisations (CSOs) in five West African Nations. The main issues confronted in the project related to the linear project design and a misconceptualisation of technology as an input, thus separating the design and implementation processes from the ultimate collaboration aims that are desired outcomes. It is therefore argued that technology-mediated collaboration initiatives within development cooperation contexts can draw from underlying Web 2.0 principles, but that these principles could more usefully be linked to development concepts in order to further enable critical reflection by primary stakeholders, so as to include them in all aspects of technology design. By focusing less on technology provision and more on the capacity of users to assess their own emergent needs has potentially more important long-term collaboration impacts.

DOI: 10.4018/978-1-4666-2515-0.ch002

INTRODUCTION

In 2004 and 2005, directors from 17 CSOs in five West African nations—Ghana, Mali, Niger, Senegal, and Togo—were brought together by a Canadian international development organisation, Crossroads International, for regional workshops. Following the workshops, the CSOs voiced a strong desire to continue to meet with each other and to begin collaborating at a networked level. They wanted to share knowledge, resources and coordinate their efforts, thus creating common strategies for cross-cutting sectoral and regional issues. In 2006, Crossroads launched an experimental project in order to explore distance-based means for the CSOs to continue to build these collaborative relationships. The project's objectives were: 1) to identify the connectivity, equipment, and skills necessary to participate in technology mediated means of collaboration; and 2) to guide the participating organisations through a pilot project experience, in order to identify the learning and results attributable to the project (Crossroads International, 2006).

As many of the CSOs were not connected to the Internet prior to this initiative, we had the opportunity to explore whether technology could play an incubation role for emerging collaboration networks. O'Reilly (2005) lists the first core Web 2.0 principle as "The Web as Platform." One way of envisioning this principle is to think of the Web as an interactional performance. Instead of approaching the Web in terms of what users can *get* from it, rather, consider what users can *do* with the Web. This change is commonly presented as a paradigm shift from the dichotomous depiction of a transmission-based Web 1.0 (*e.g.* reading) to an interactive Web 2.0 (*e.g.* reading and writing) (Levy, 2009; O'Reilly, 2005; Thompson, 2008). In this sense, we hoped to create a collaboration platform that could be used for a variety of collaboration outcomes.

This chapter begins by exploring how inter-organisational collaboration tends to be envisaged by CSOs, and subsequently what constitutes appropriate Information and Communications Technologies (ICTs) for use within CSO collaboration networks. Following this, I explain how the project was carried out and discuss the results we obtained, in order to highlight the difficulties we faced in marrying the cultural, communicative, and technological factors that varied considerably across the CSOs. The remaining sections investigate the reasons why we had difficulty achieving our objectives, followed by an analysis of how similar initiatives could build upon or improve the notions we explored. The ultimate goal for online collaboration initiatives is not to create the 'killer app,' but to explore how the principle of creating a space on the Web for people to take and *do* however they please can be taken advantage of in the context of development. This chapter therefore has the following objectives:

- To explore concepts related to inter-organisational collaboration, and appropriate technology within development cooperation project-based work.
- To justify the approach that I took in carrying out the design and implementation of an online collaboration platform with 17 CSOs in West Africa.
- To question the conceptual role of ICTs as a means for inter-organisational collaboration in our project and to provide suggestions to overcome the difficulties we faced.

BACKGROUND

West African nations share similar 'development' challenges including political instability, poor governance, environmental crisis and disaster vulnerability, food insecurity, gender inequality, lack of institutional and technical capacity, poor health systems, and infectious diseases. Poverty remains one of the greatest challenges for these countries as on average 69 percent of their populations live off of less than 2 USA dollars per day (World Bank, 2012). The West African CSOs seek to address these challenges by carrying out activities related to the themes of gender inequality, community economic development, food security, and/or HIV/AIDs. The majority of the CSOs focus heavily on one of the stated thematic areas in each respective country whilst approaches differ amongst them (see Table 1).

Table 1. CSOs by country, sector, and development approach

	No. of CSOs	Sector	Development Approach
Ghana	4	HIV/Aids (1)	- Health service provision - Income-generating activities
		Gender Inequality (3)	- Income-generating activities (1) - Advocacy and research (2) - Training and education (2)
Mali	4	Community Economic Development (4)	- Income-generating activities (3) - Training and education (2)
Niger	3	Food Security (3)	- Income-generating activities (2) - Advocacy network (1) - Training and education (2)
Senegal	4	Gender Inequality (4)	- Advocacy network (1) - Communications (1) - Income-generating activities (2) - Training and education (2)
Togo	2	Gender Inequality (1)	- Advocacy and training
		HIV/AIDS (1)	- Health service provision

Source: Author

Crossroads initiated the collaboration project under discussion in 2005, and funding was sought from the Canadian International Development Agency (CIDA). In 2007, I became coordinator of the project and was based in the Crossroads office in Montreal, Canada. Five interns, financed by Netcorps Canada were recruited to work with between two and four partners in each country. This research project has the approval of the ethics board at Concordia University, Canada, and all partners and staff who provided interview data have granted their informed consent. The next section explores how and why collaboration is pursued as a means to overcome some of these common 'development' challenges.

THEORETICAL PERSPECTIVES

The purposes of inter-organisational collaboration in CSO development work depends on how collaboration is conceptualised, the first section therefore explores what means and objectives are often promoted in this context. Following this, I examine ideas about appropriateness of Information and Communications Technologies (ICTs) as a means to support collaboration between CSOs.

Shades of Collaboration

The concept of collaboration is not easily defined, especially within international development, and terms like 'networks' and 'partnerships' are popular. I will therefore briefly explore the historical context and purpose of collaboration in these veins, but will then zoom out to consider how collaboration is conceptualised in other areas, in particular from a Web 2.0 perspective.

The ways collaboration is conceptualised in international development is linked to the transformation of roles of CSOs in the 'North' and in the 'South,' where the end of the Cold War marked a shift in the nature of Northern CSO development work. Their role shifted from being primary implementers of development into one readily equipped to strengthen civil societies, and contribute to global governance (van Rooy, 2000). As their roles were changing, they began seeking Southern counterparts to work with (Lewis, 1998), and they began forming their relationships under the pretense of partnerships. In this scenario, Northern CSOs act as donors, assisting Southern CSOs through financing and capacity building. Funding relationships heavily influence the nature of collaboration in these types of relationships, as development aid nurtures financial and intellectual dependence (Maina, 2009, p. 166). Bierkart (2008), however, acknowledges that sustained capacity building can contribute positively to the strengthening of Southern CSOs, but this should go hand in hand with the building of strategic horizontal alliances—or alliances with other similar organisations. Likewise, Lewis (1998) gives precedence to South-South learning as means to make collaboration more relevant to local contexts.

Indeed, Korten (1990) rightly points out that CSOs often come to realise that their interventions are not sustainable without donor support, or that unless they combine their efforts with other organisations the reach of their initiatives is narrowed to a selective few. His argument is that CSOs must be able to link their initiatives into wider national or international development systems, and in order to do so, CSOs will need to change restrictive systems. These conditions have led to collaboration framed as inter-organisational networking, which relies less on the notion of funding arrangements and more on collaboration as a means to achieve systemic change. Nevertheless, Northern organisations still often have important and influential facilitation and financing roles even within Southern networks.

Regional and international networks usually concentrate on thematic or global issues, with some of the most successful examples stemming from Latin America (Clark, 2003). Their advancement over the past 20 years from practice-based sharing to policy-oriented initiatives indicates possible network pathways of progression. In other words, whilst the end game may be systemic change, starting with collaborative learning is potentially one way to eventually achieve it. CSO networking in Africa, however, is susceptible to being a donor-driven endeavour, and practice-based CSOs—those focusing more on implementation rather than advocacy roles—tend to be weakly connected (Clark, 1997). This was admittedly the case in our project, as the initiative was financed through Crossroads, and the majority of the CSOs were interested in sharing good practices.

Exploring the concept of practice-based networking, Wenger's (1998) Community of Practice (CoP) model accounts for how groups of people that have shared commitment or passion for a domain of practice pursue common interests through joint activities. Through participation in a CoP, members contribute their knowledge and skills and in exchange learn from other members (Lave & Wenger, 1991). Collaboration in this sense is strongly connected to mutual learning, thus forming a basis for collective action and the achievement of mutual goals. Vernooy *et al.'s* (2010) experience setting up centres of excellence in natural resource management in Asia highlights also the dimension of building critical reflection into the CoP model as a means for effective collaborative learning.

As CoPs often involve the coming together of separated individuals or organisational representatives, electronic communication has become an important feature in CSO networks, but Web 2.0 technologies have not been explored in this context in detail. In 2007, Web 2.0 tools were beginning to demonstrate their utility for online collaboration. For example, Nardi, Schiano, and Gumbrecht's (2004) study revealed that blogs were facilitating conversations that permeated across online spaces (thus being quite social in nature). Twitter was also demonstrating how conversations unfold, connecting diverse users over the Web. Twitter users were not only sharing information, but were using this platform to connect with others with similar intentions (Java, Song, & Finin, 2007). Likewise social tagging also presented a means for users to share and connect through serendipitous browsing (Bentley & Labelle, 2008). The common thread is that these social computing devices may precipitate serendipitous collaboration, where (potentially ad hoc) networks develop based on the users' interests and capacities to connect with others. Many of these serendipitous benefits, rely on design patterns focused on creating wide network effects and harnessing the long tail of collective intelligence (Alexander, Ishikawa, & Silverstein, 1977).

The Web 2.0 notion of collaboration as an emergent process has potential for international development networks. For example, many of our CSOs were engaged in numerous networks already, and sometimes they had multiple partnership arrangements. The CSOs were frequently time constrained, yet dynamic and opportunistic. We were curious to see whether we could address emergent collaboration needs in a flexible manner. Curtis and Lawson's (2001) concept of tele-mentoring, for instance, was interesting to us for this reason. By taking collaboration activities that normally occur in private spaces—like mentorship regularly conducted over telephone or email—and shifting these processes into open spaces enables others to browse and learn from the interaction, so that individuals can selectively network based on their own needs for collaboration. The next section explores what might be considered 'appropriate' as a means to support this idea.

Defining Appropriate Online Collaboration Tools

When the project was initially conceived, it was presumed that appropriate technologies existed that could simply be purchased and implemented. This was before it was well understood that most out-of-the-box software is not usually designed with developing country contexts in mind. This mindset originates from a belief that Western technology can merely be transferred to developing countries (McGowan & Wigand, 1984). Limited resources to maintain and replenish technology, degradation caused by environmental conditions, different modes of thinking and acting, language, literacy and culture have all demonstrated severe problems in this way of thinking (Sadowsky, 2012). In dealing with these difficulties, discourse surrounding what constitutes appropriate technology beginning with Schumacher's (1973) observations, led to views of appropriateness based on technical elements such as affordability, sustainability, and functionality of technology (van Reijswoud, 2009).

Discourse surrounding the distinctiveness of user-requirements in developing countries has also contributed to ideas about appropriateness. Comprehending user-requirements is a complex task, and designers should not assume qualities or attitudes of users in developing countries (Deardon, 2008). Brown's (2002) study in South Africa, for example, demonstrated that perceived ease-of-use was shown to be strongly affected by personal valuations of self-efficacy and computer anxiety. Regardless of whether participants found a website to be useful, perceived ease-of-use was more likely to predict whether or not they would use the service. The ability of users to contextualise and reflect on online content in relation to their regular learning and knowledge practices is key (Schneckenberg, 2009). Pitula and Dysart-Gale (2010) provide a sophisticated example of just how distinctive learning and knowledge practices were in a developing country, relating how the morality-based culture of the users affected the use and comprehension of a database system. Their study demonstrates the necessity of designers to get involved in a co-construction process, which is mindful of the interrelationships between practice and technology—often involving negotiation, education, and compromise.

It follows that once the social-embedded qualities of technology design and use are acknowledged, cultural and ideological values come into play. Walsham (2002) illustrates that culture can be seen as a dynamic construct in cross-cultural collaboration. This means that although some aspects of culture such as attitudes and behaviours are relatively stable, as organisations begin to collaborate with each other, shared culture tends to emerge over time. So the implication on technology design and use is what Avgerou (2010, p. 5) calls a hybridisation of artefacts, people and institutions that is "mutually re-constituted through technology innovation and the cultures that influence them." Appropriateness, in our case, should therefore also include a means to incorporate the formulation of design aspects amidst a backdrop that expresses mutual objectives of collaboration and the processes intended to expose the cultural and ideological values that impact knowledge sharing and practice.

One last aspect of appropriate technology is whether to commit to equitable software development models such as open source software development. Smith and Elder (2010, p. 69) argue that "building openness into polices and technologies will result in greater opportunities for developing countries to transform into equitable and sustainable knowledge societies." Many benefits such as no software licensing fees, lower server and maintenance fees, and the possibility to extend and customise software are advantageous to CSOs, especially when there is an underlying pressure on CSOs funded by public donor agencies that want to show that they are spending money responsibly. There are also many difficulties with open source solutions relating to overall low adoption rates, and unexpected challenges that tend to crop up (van Reijswoud & de Jager, 2008). Multiple open source content management systems seem to compete with each other, making it rather difficult at times to lead to productive discussions about how to improve standard features.

CSOs typically find open source solutions rather user-unfriendly and find it difficult to engage with technical jargon frequently encountered in open source communities (Schout, 2012). We generally confronted issues in design and implementation stemming from many of these dimensions, and trying to prepare for challenges was not an easy task either. The following section explains why.

PROJECT DESIGN AND RESULTS

There were two broad project objectives: 1) identify the connectivity, equipment, and skills necessary to participate in technology mediated means of collaboration, specifically synchronous and asynchronous online collaboration tools; and 2) guide the participating CSOs through a pilot project experience in order to identify the learning and results attributable to the project of the project. Based on my understanding of online collaboration and technology design in developing countries, I split the project into three phases, a learning phase, an acquisition/implementation phase, and an evaluation phase.

Learning Phase

The learning phase was primarily intended to address the first project objective, so at the end of this phase we would have a clear idea of the materials and services that needed to be acquired, and to have constructed an initial interpretation of the joint user-requirements of the CSOs. Activity theory (Engeström, 1987)—the idea that human activity is situated within a complex social practice system—was used as a framework for analysis during the learning phase, and to help define user-requirements for the design of the collaborative platform (Jonassen & Rohrer-Murphy, 1999). Activity theory was advantageous because none of the partners had much experience collaborating online other than through email-based discussion, and so it was necessary to consider how their offline experiences could be usefully supported by online contexts, which activity theory can cope with because of the way it positions tools in relation to other aspects, such as organisational customs and tasks, that work together to affect the desired outcome (Redmiles, 2002), and also because it frames learning as a social interaction (Vygotsky, 1978). The learning phase was split into different aspects reflecting individual, organisational and environmental elements, and the interns were provided with focus group and interview data collection tools, as well as a set of guiding research questions to investigate the various aspects the activity system. Dada's (2006) e-readiness framework was also useful for structuring the analysis of the interview data and organisational inventories that were collected by the interns, because it includes not only institutional elements as with activity theory, but helped us to critically reflect on environmental factors that contribute to the availability of affordable Internet connections.

Once the analyses were complete, the results were synthesised and discussed with CSO directors and Crossroads management to decide how to continue. Tension surfaced surrounding the sustainability of faster, more reliable Internet connections because of the sheer expense. Negotiations settled on justifying the extra costs by resultant savings in telephone communications and travel. In all of the countries except Togo, opening up of markets has seen an increase in Internet Service Providers (ISP), thus pushing down prices; however, the expense is still extremely prohibitive for small organisations, and they would not be able to cover the added cost without the financial support from Crossroads. For example, in Dakar, Senegal in 2009, a 512 kB/s ADSL connection cost about half as much as a 384 kB/s Wimax connection in Mali. Many ADSL connections were highly unstable, and so Wimax connections tended to offer the most reliable service. In Niger, however, a 512 kB/s Wimax connection cost approximately a half million CFA (about $1000 USD at the time). In order to afford such an expense we had to split up the connection to three organisations leaving them with only 170 kB/s each. In the end, we negotiated with the CSOs that inclusion was important to ensure that all of the organisations could have similar opportunity and representation within the CSO network.

Once we had a clear picture of the connectivity affordances, we carried out the activity analyses. One thing that I had not anticipated was the research skills needed by the interns to carry out essentially ethnographic research in order to gather rich data required by an activity theory analysis. I conducted a training session before they left Canada to introduce the rationale of the learning phase, as well as how the project would progress. I gave the interns quite a bit of leeway to follow their instincts so that they could learn flexibly, but this proved to be quite challenging for them, even with the provision of standard data collection tools. It was also the first internship abroad for many of them, so they were also undergoing personal transformations.

Three out of five interns were successful in accomplishing their tasks, but of the three that were successful, only one was capable of deeply and richly reporting on the particular organisational contexts that the workers were embedded in. The information that was reported was therefore mostly factual (*e.g.* Hala shares a desk with Tati and they both work as project managers). In addition, getting even a superficial report from the interns took a significant amount of time, and many of them surpassed reporting deadlines due to the availability of staff. For activity theory to shed light on the dynamics of internal organisational behaviour, a detailed description of specific collaboration activities amidst a general organisational, and

Table 2. Results and indicators of the learning phase

Results of the Learning Phase	Indicators
Identification of hardware and services needed	- 12 out of 17 CSOs had improved Internet connectivity, and 7 of these did not have any prior Internet connection at their organisation. - All 17 CSOs received additional hardware, Web cams and microphones. - 10 out of 17 established relationships with IT technicians to maintain equipment and provide support.
Appropriate technologies identified	- Two complementary online collaboration tools selected: Web conferencing and a community collaboration platform.
Skill development needs identified	- Identification of at least one staff member per CSO to receive training, and profiles of their experience.

Source: Author

environmental backdrop is necessary. The lack of engagement in the daily practice of organisations by the interns served to be problematic for the design of the collaboration platform as well. See Table 2 for a summary of overall results of the learning phase.

In order to select online collaboration tools, we focused on three practical problems and one request that were repeatedly voiced by the CSOs. The consistent request was for voice communication whilst being able to look at documents under discussion simultaneously. The three practical problems stemmed from the limited experience with Web-based applications of the CSOs, as many organisations were getting Internet connections for the first time. Prior to this, they would send one of their staff members to collect email at a cyber-cafe, return to the organisation to write and compile responses, and return to the cafe, sometimes numerous times during the day. Many staff struggled with managing email, finding messages, and responding to emails in a timely manner. Another major difficulty was keeping track of shared document versions and losing information due to file corruption and viruses. Language was also a major consideration as we had partners who communicated in either English or French but not both. Above all else, the CSOs wanted our key design requirements to reflect simplicity and ease of use.

To address the synchronous communication request, we decided to experiment with a Web-conference application designed to operate on-low bandwidth Internet connections. For the practical communication and collaboration problems, we evaluated a number of online community tools and ultimately decided to customise the Drupal (http://drupal.org) open-source content management system. The goal of the design was to simplify the process of communicating and collaborating by attempting to streamline document sharing and messaging whilst simultaneously embedding online interaction within an open collaborative environment. The following section outlines how we constructed this design and tried to implement it.

Implementation Phase

This chapter relates specifically to Web 2.0 applications in developing countries, therefore my discussion of the implementation phase focuses on the design and implementation of the Web 2.0 inspired asynchronous platform. Further explanations on the entire project and complete discussion of why we chose certain tools over others can be found in Bentley (2009). The objectives of the implementation phase were to acquire the selected tools, and to support the CSOs to begin using them.

We had initially hoped to involve the CSOs in a truly participative manner to steer the development of the platform, but because of project time constraints, we were only able to involve them consultatively (see Iivari, 2010). The project team met each week to set out tasks for the week, and to critically reflect on progress iteratively in an action research cycle (Reason & Bradbury, 2007). As a team, we developed trainings and learning opportunities to enable the CSO workers to explore authentic tasks whilst familiarising themselves with the technical environments (Bentley, 2008). To evaluate the tool design, we were collecting requests and complaints in a type of bug-tracking system, and usability tests combined with observations of the interns throughout the action research cycle also served as a formative evaluation of the tool.

We chose to use Drupal to build a user-group centric system, because it provides an adequate level of flexibility in the way that application developers can fashion customised types of content. We were ultimately able to determine what information and actions are possible within a 'group,' and CSOs could have the freedom to create groups and organise communications among group members in a flexible manner autonomously. For example, some CSOs wanted to share information with other CSOs based on a topic, others for project work, and some wanted it for internal communication purposes. Groups could therefore be created for any of these purposes. Moreover, opting for an open source solution enables the customisation required for dynamic design requirements, and so although we began with an initial design that was perhaps more consultative than participative, there was still the possibility to make changes as the project progressed.

For simplicity's sake, all of the content items that belong to a group appear on the same page in order to increase findability. In addition, all of the actions that a group member can take, *i.e.* post a message, task, or document, can be found in the right-hand side menu. Figure 1 displays a screenshot of the home-screen. Another important feature was email notifications to limit the necessity for users in developing countries to load the website every time they wanted to consult a new message.

Ironically, manipulating the Drupal modules to work together seamlessly, whilst attempting to embody simplicity took a great deal of expertise, testing, and most of all, time. We hired a programmer in December of 2007 and the initial milestone

Figure 1. A screenshot of the Drupal platform, source: http://cciextranet.concoctions.ca

deadline was January 11, 2008 in order to launch the website whilst the interns were still in the field. As can be expected with most software development projects, the initial release was not entirely functional and required much further development in order for it to be moderately usable. Unfortunately, the usable release was only ready by mid-March—only two weeks before most of the interns were due to return to Canada. At that time as well, the website was not available in both English and French, and a bilingual version had not been required in the first iteration of the software development because we wanted a fast prototype to begin testing and experimenting with as soon as possible. As a result, we made the decision to offer the website only in English at the start because the intern in Ghana had chosen to extend her placement. See Table 3 for a summary of the results of the implementation phase.

Because we had suffered serious delays with the platform development, the project was extended until the end of September 2009. We were left with approximately 6 months to complete trainings and experiment with the platform *in situ*.

Table 3. Results of the implementation phase

Results of the Implementation Phase	Indicators
Appropriate technologies acquired and available	- Purchase of perpetual licenses of a Web-conferencing application (now discontinued but still available through our own hosting arrangement). - Development of a bilingual community platform.
Skill formation guidance and training	- At least one staff member per organisation (27 total) received weekly training and guidance on the use of the tools.

Source: Author

We also received notice that we could extend the volunteers' internship contracts for up to three months; only the volunteer in Ghana decided to extend her contract, but for only one month. We later recruited additional volunteers but also experienced problems getting them into the field before the end of the project, only one additional support person was sent to Niger, and we hired one local staff member to take on a similar role in Togo.

What we learned about our design during the implementation phase was that two of the important design features backfired. The first were the email notifications because it was generally too confusing that emails come from the system and not the sender. The second was the organisation and filtering of information. Whilst we wanted to limit the need for users to search around for information, users often complained about the inability to organise messages, tasks, and documents into conceptual themes. In terms of usability, we found that information organisation for user-comprehension was very important; however, the capacity of users to organise information was generally fairly low indicating that whilst skills are developing, it might be useful to delegate the task of organising to a more experienced user, essentially providing models for less experienced users.

Evaluation Phase

The objective of the evaluation phase was to carry out pilot collaboration projects in order to assess learning and the effectiveness of the technologies as a means for inter-organisational collaboration.

Considering the interns had all returned to Canada before getting to this phase, it was a great challenge to coordinate and support the efforts of the 17 CSOs on my own. During the months of May and June 2009, I met with each of the CSOs individually to discuss the next steps of the project and to detect where their interests lay with respect to attempting to pilot the tools. In some cases, I began to notice that the employees with whom I was meeting were not the directors, and they had not been involved in the inception of the project. These employees therefore had trouble contributing to the discussions about how to pilot the tools and did not have many ideas about how their organisation had intended to benefit from inter-organisational collaboration.

By the end of June, we had but one pilot project planned involving only three partners, and no in-field support. In an attempt to organise a pilot project that all could be involved in, I organised a virtual meeting for all of the West African partners so that they could speak to each other in an informal social setting, exchange ideas about themed discussions, and hear about each others' current work. Although most partners came to the meeting and indicated that they valued the exchange, it was clear that although there was some overlap in interest, there was not an overarching topic that all were interested in pursuing. There was a lack of initiative to take the pilot project process any further than surface discussion.

Although it was rather simple for the partners to identify basic goals and opportunities for collaboration that the CSOs wanted to pursue, generally, these did not translate easily into the use of the collaboration platform. One explanation was that the CSOs felt most comfortable collaborating with those they knew well (for example, other CSOs within their own country), but in these cases, technology was not a desirable alternative to face-to-face or telephone communication. A second reason was the clear preference for voice communication over written communication. Emails and document sharing were weakly associated with informal collaboration patterns. The platform was therefore used limitedly due to the nascent nature of collaborative relationships. There was, however, an expressed expectation that these relationships would evolve over time, where document sharing and messaging would eventually become useful. See Table 4 for a summary of the results of the evaluation phase.

Furthermore, I travelled to West Africa to visit each CSO in Senegal, Mali, Togo, and Ghana, in order to carry out an evaluation of the tools, and to documented experiences and projects that were similar to organisations in other countries. In this way, I could suggest opportunities to further connect CSOs between sectors and countries to encourage the expansion of existing relationships. A realisation in the field was that the CSOs preferred that Crossroads maintain its role as an organiser of collaborative efforts, instead of taking initiative themselves. This reflects how communication with Crossroads increased significantly, and that the openness to flexibly choose how to use the collaboration platform was not of great value to them.

Another discovery was that whilst the focus of this project was to improve inter-organisational collaboration, the majority of our partners stated that the greatest benefit of this project was the increased access to the Internet. Many of our partners

Table 4. Results of the evaluation phase

Results of the Evaluation Phase	Indicators
Pilot experiences to assess the utility of the technologies	- Purchase of perpetual licenses of a Web-conferencing application (now discontinued but still available through our own hosting arrangement). - Development of a bilingual community platform.
Skill formation guidance and training	- At least one staff member per organisation received weekly training and guidance on the use of the tools.

Source: Author

felt they were wasting precious time by taking trips to an Internet cafe, and they now feel as though they are able to complete their work more efficiently, having greater access to information and communication resources.

Broadly speaking, the most significant lesson that we learned is that for group learning and collaboration to occur, social relationships were pivotal for the development of communal trust and objectives to emerge. In reality, it takes time for relationships to develop. I question the aptness of our community platform for this reason as well. Having focused on user preferences and practical technological communication issues, we neglected to understand just how important it was for these social relationships to form as a means to better identify design requirements. We did, however, experience success in this domain, but mainly through the Web-conferencing tool. Many relationships did form through training and experimentation, and now, all of the CSOs are connected to each other via Skype, and some of the CSOs have contributed to the construction of a Google Site to share social economy learning resources. Ultimately, most organisations were able to build on their relationships with each other, by finding appropriate ways to communicate and collaborate with each other after the project's termination. The emergent outcomes of our shared experiences bring about important considerations of what we considered success in the first place.

CRITICAL FACTORS

Upon examining the overall impact and effectiveness of this project, I question three aspects: the first relates to how technology was conceptualised as an input, the second reflects on our notion of collaboration, and the last explores how similar projects could be improved upon in the future.

(Re)Conceptualising Online Collaboration Technologies

The overarching difficulty that we experienced deals with how collaboration technology was conceptualised in the first place—technology is an input that can be acquired and implemented. This perspective is illustrated by the linear project cycle of selection, training, and then application. Upon reflection, we did try to overcome the underlying philosophy by re-positioning the rationale of the analyses, trying to build in consultation and responsiveness into the tool design process, and prioritising self-regulated learning strategies when providing guidance and training. What was missing, however, were overt discussions amongst CSOs concerning why these strategies are important. Pitula and Dysart-Gale's (2010) database example shows that even after tailoring technology to its users, they were still not inputting relevant information necessary for higher-level decision-making by their supervisors. What ended up working for them was conducting workshops to discuss the purposes and reasons for knowledge sharing from the perspective of the workers, in contrast to the use of this information by other actors. Eventually, the workers began to understand how the information could be used in other ways than how is reflected by their own tendencies to share, thus they began to see the value in changing their own practice. The point is that even customising and adapting software alone will not necessarily bring about changes in the ways that people use technology.

In our project, there was also a need to address the culture of volunteer-driven technology projects, as the CSOs had grown accustomed to receiving technical trainings in passive roles, perhaps because interns often report running out of time before returning home, having to squeeze a month's worth of learning into three hours. According to the intern evaluation reports, the employees also preferred to be directed with setting learning goals and strategies, and they did not enjoy working through complex and ill-structured tasks. They lost motivation fairly quickly and after a period did not attend planned training sessions. Another frequent occurrence was that executive directors were often those that had the most developed collaboration skills overall, and were more capable of seeing potential opportunities for collaborating with other organisations; however, they would often have to delegate the task of learning how to use the technical tools to staff members due to their busy schedules. In this case, defining personal learning objectives, and working towards them is almost always an externally motivated venture and often leads to disinterest. When there is a disconnect between personal motivation and the project objectives, the practical use of technology is lost track of and eventually abandoned (Unwin, 2009).

Both of these examples highlight that objectifying technology has a negative impact on both learning how to use it and incorporating it into real-world practice. There is a need to confront underlying philosophical hurdles that translate into mindsets about the roles of technology and participants. Perhaps these tensions could be eased by building in dialog not only surrounding knowledge sharing practice, but about roles of learners as well.

Distinguishing between "Online" and "Open" Collaboration

There was also a disjoint between our conceptualisation of collaboration and how successful CSO networks tend to operate. Development networks tend not to explicitly focus on serendipitous benefits of open collaboration, although discourse surrounding the benefits and challenges of openness in development is growing in wider debates (see Buskens, 2011; Gigler, Custer, & Rahemtulla, 2011; Smith & Elder, 2010). CSO development networks have capitalised on the use of online technology to grow networks, to represent marginalised perspectives, and to gain global influence (Clark, 2003). The Social Watch network, for example, evolved over a period of four years, as NGO alliances converged on a shared vision (val Relsen, 2012). They grew their success through the construction of formalised governance structures, and regularly reflected on their progress, whilst ensuring that they openly and transparently capitalised and supported the abilities of their networked organisations. Similarly, Vernooy's (2010, p. 145) exploration of collaborative learning in Asia corroborates that "careful preparation, a strong team, clear and shared goals, good technical and financial support, ongoing and systematic monitoring, involving students as much as possible, and continuous focus on learning-by-doing have been important in keeping things going on track."

Our project model was not a good fit for meeting the needs of an evolving collaboration network initiative, and this reflection is consistent with those listed above (see also Brunello, 2010). Our experience clearly demonstrates that without clear learning goals attached to collaboration objectives, technology training was virtually meaningless, but that defining these takes a great amount of relationship-building, negotiation, learning, and reflection. Although collaboration was the intended outcome, we did not plan for it. The serendipitous qualities of open collaboration, implies that excessive planning can focus attention too heavily on identified objectives. Likewise, there is the possibility that no over-arching common objectives exist, thus excluding the interests of the under-represented (Nieusma, 2004). The design decision to prioritise flexibility was therefore fitting because of the minimal existing South-South collaboration amongst the CSOs. We had hoped that eventually, the benefits of open collaboration might provide an incentive to use the platform regularly. Instead, we should have focused more on discussing collaboration opportunities and the values of openness. When technical issues cropped up relating to language, usability, and software bugs that the CSOs were generally unwilling to invest time to help remedy, and the benefits of the flexible design were overshadowed. The overall expectation was for technology 'to just work' and so the idea of technology as a 'work in progress' is very upsetting to inexperienced users who are unable to cope with unexpected problems, which is consistent with Brown's (2002) findings. In this sense, our failure stemmed from our rapid design, and our inability to expose the value of choice in how and with whom to collaborate amongst the CSOs. I am not convinced that open collaboration is not valuable, but we needed to be clearer about why we were working in that way, and we could have usefully been more goal-oriented in the beginning stages to start off.

If we had instead concentrated our efforts on supporting the understanding and formation of open collaboration skills rather than the platform itself, perhaps we would have seen greater participation in all aspects of the project. Cogburn (2004, p. 29), however, reported on "collaboration technology readiness" in an online network of CSOs, mentioning that as more advanced technologies were introduced by members, they were rarely taken up. He suggests that there are significant power dynamics at play that affect how technologies are used by networks as well. For this reason, there is also a need to consider who prioritises the need for open collaboration and why. The following section therefore considers the element of development approach within development aid funded programmes as a means to explore this dimension.

Open Collaboration and Development Aid-Funded Projects

Finally, the problems we faced involving the conceptualisation of technology and the project model are difficult to address without considering the development aid context. The outputs and outcomes of the project were planned at the outset of the project with very little leeway to modify once the contract has been negotiated. Capacity building is the dominant development approach that Canadian NGOs funded by CIDA tend to enact (Angeles & Gurstein, 2000), but in this case, there was more pressure to produce the outputs of the project for which the disbursement of the allocated funds hinged. The rationale being that capacity development will also naturally follow once the technology is in place, and if the technology is not acquired before the termination of the project, then the funds are revoked. Additionally, potential for open collaboration was not a convincing development impact in comparison to actual collaboration outcomes, and because there are also issues with the tendency of capacity development issues led by Northern organisations to be interpreted as paternalistic (Lewis, 1998), there is reason to question the relevance of the project design.

Kleine's (2010) Choice Framework has been used to analyse the development impact of ICT4D initiatives where technology has often contributed to unintended consequences, or does not achieve what was sought out. The Choice Framework is based on Sen's (2001) capability approach, which sees development as freedom, in that people should have the freedom to choose the life they have come to value. Kleine's (2010) framework establishes a means to systematically map outcomes that individuals wish for themselves, linking these to structure (available opportunities), agency (ability to act), and choice (ability to choose how to act within a given structure). Kleine (2010) suggests that the Choice Framework could also be used for project planning by essentially working backwards. The difference, for example, between this approach and a capacity building framework is the element of choice. In a capacity development framework, skills might be the primary outcome. Whereas choice is the primary outcome in the capability approach. Technology is also seen to provide certain opportunities, and so in this sense, it becomes clearer that although the opportunities are increased through the Web as a platform principle, the value of expanding opportunities is diminished if individuals neither have the ability to use the platform, nor would choose to use it. There is an assumed interrelationship between structure, agency, and choice. Designing the project by considering these interrelationships provides a basis to prioritise choice, and thus in this case, open collaboration.

Although it is doubtful that the CSOs would be able to go through the process of mapping out all of their potential and hoped for outcomes, especially for participants with little to no previous Internet culture and/or experience, beginning the process might at least begin the project in terms of a dialectical process rather than a linear one. Oosterlaken (2009) argues for the inclusion of designers in this process, implying that they would also have a role in educating and innovating within this process.

FUTURE RESEARCH DIRECTIONS

The Web as a platform is indeed an intriguing concept for development, but CSOs are consistently burdened by the task of experimenting with new technologies. Resource-constrained CSOs find it challenging to risk dedicating resources to experimentation and they lack knowledge and skill to carry out software development. Supporting the availability of common extendible and flexible open collaboration tools targeted specifically towards CSOs can potentially ease some of this frustration, whilst aligning with CSO ethics and values (see Hartung, Anokwa, Brunette, & Lerer, 2010 for an example of such an initiative). One way to support this would be to infuse on-going joint technology funds that enable open source modular development that all CSOs could gain access to.

In relation to development, there is also a need to better understand the opportunities that technologies can enable. For example, what does openness bring to collaboration? We were not very successful in promoting the value of openness, so the best collaboration outcomes transpired from close, trusting relationships leading to intentional collaboration. There is a need to further delineate how open collaboration can build on experience, or how open culture can add value to inter-organisational collaboration. The value of openness will largely depend on the expansion of the platform concept, which up until now has mostly been about Web-based platforming. There have been successful forays into mobile application development and online services, but rarely, if any, that do both integratively. Statistics indicate that a significant proportion of mobile users access social network sites like Facebook primarily through their mobiles (Rao, 2011), but it is not sufficiently clear how users are interacting with Facebook on mobiles. How do devices change the user's ability to interact with platform-based services? Openness could contribute if users are opportunistically connected, socially and informationally, to resources based on their existing use patterns. Meaning that the device or service should not negatively affect opportunities to connect to information and people.

A last issue is that when donors invest resources in assisting CSOs to connect to the Internet and build communications capacities, Mawdsley *et al.* (2002) observe that it logically follows that CSOs can then more readily, frequently, and immediately communicate with donors. This might ultimately distract them from communicating with their constituents who for the most part are not connected in the same way. Understanding how constituents can be brought into online collaboration processes must also be considered. Successful applications of citizen monitoring, crowdsourcing, and SMS systems have contributed new ways to help CSOs engage with their constituents (Ashley, Corbett, Jones, Garside, & Rambaldi, 2009), but it is not clear how practice-based networks of CSOs would be able to incorporate another communicative dimension into their collaborative activities. Separating these activities may cause even more frustration for over-burdened CSOs.

CONCLUSION

In conclusion, for the West African CSOs, the process of designing and implementing the collaboration platform challenged them to take on different collaboration roles both in their relationship to volunteers and to other CSOs. The incompatibility of time constrained project work and the resulting technology design process left much to be desired, ultimately leading to the demise of the website. The experiment itself, however, has led to significant changes in the ways that the CSOs communicate and collaborate at a distance due in part to increased Internet connectivity, relationship building, and experience. In order to assess the value of unplanned outcomes related to collaboration capacity building, and to better define desirable outcomes in the future, I suggest that open collaboration project planning should consider the interrelationships between technology, collaboration outcomes, and the inclusion of participants in a dialectical design process.

REFERENCES

Alexander, C., Ishikawa, S., & Silverstein, M. (1977). *A pattern language: Towns, buildings, construction.* Oxford, UK: Oxford University Press.

Angeles, L., & Gurstein, P. (2000). Planning for participatory capacity development: The challenges of participation and north-south partnership in capacity building projects. *Canadian Journal of Development Studies, 21*(1). doi:10.1080/0225518 9.2000.9669926

Ashley, H., Corbett, J., Jones, D., Garside, B., & Rambaldi, G. (2009). Change at hand: Web 2.0 for development. *Participatory Learning and Action, 59*(1), 8–20.

Avgerou, C. (2010). Discourses on ICT and development. *Information Technologies & International Development, 6*(3), 1–18.

Bentley, C. M. (2008). Strategies to encourage local ownership of online collaboration technologies in West Africa. In N. Whitton & M. McPherson (Eds.), *ALT-C 2008: Rethinking the Digital Divide, the 15th Association for Learning Technology Conference*. Leeds, UK: ALT-C.

Bentley, C. M. (2009). *Using technology to enhance collaborative partnerships in West Africa: A project implementation by Canadian Crossroads International.* (Unpublished Master Internship Report). Concordia University. Montreal, Canada.

Bentley, C. M., & Labelle, P. (2008). A comparison of social tagging designs and user participation. In J. Greenberg & W. Klas (Eds.), *International Conference on Dublin Core and Metadata Applications: Metadata for Semantic and Social Applications,* (p. 205). Berlin, Germany: Universitätsverlag Göttingen.

Biekart, K. (2008). Learning from Latin America: Recent trends in European NGO policymaking. In Bebbington, A., Hickey, S., & Mitlin, D. C. (Eds.), *Can NGOs make a Difference? The Challenge of Development Alternatives* (pp. 71–89). London, UK: Zed Books.

Brown, I. T. J. (2002). Individual and technological factors affecting perceived ease of use of web-based learning technologies in a developing country. *The Electronic Journal on Information Systems in Developing Countries, 9*(5), 1–15.

Buskens, I. (2011). The importance of intent: Reflecting on open development for women's empowerment. *Information Technologies & International Development, 7*(1), 71–76.

Clark, J. (1997). The state, popular participation and the voluntary sector. In Hulme, D., & Edwards, M. (Eds.), *NGOs, States and Donors: Too Close for Comfort (International Political Economy)*. Basingstoke, UK: Palgrave Macmillan. doi:10.1016/0305-750X(94)00147-Q

Clark, J. (2003). *Globalizing civic engagement: Civil society and transnational action*. London, UK: Earthscan.

Cogburn, D. (2004). Diversity matters, even at a distance: Evaluating the impact of computer-mediated communication on civil society participation in the world summit on the information society. *Information Technologies and International Development, 1*(3-4), 14–40. doi:10.1162/1544752043557404

Crossroads International. (2006). *West African communications capacity building project*. Toronto, Canada: Gardner.

Curtis, D., & Lawson, M. (2001). Exploring collaborative online learning. *Journal of Asynchronous Learning Networks, 5*(1), 21–34.

Dada, D. (2006). e-Readiness for developing countries: Moving the focus from the environment to the users. *The Electronic Journal of Information Systems in Developing Countries, 27*(6), 1–14.

Dearden, A. (2008). User-centered design considered harmful1 (with apologies to Edsger Dijkstra, Niklaus Wirth, and Don Norman). *Information Technologies & International Development, 4*(3), 7–12. doi:10.1162/itid.2008.00013

Engeström, Y. (1987). *Learning by expanding: An activity theoretical approach to developmental research*. (F. Seeger, Trans.). Retrieved August 8, 2012, from http://lchc.ucsd.edu/MCA/Paper/Engestrom/expanding/toc.htm

Gigler, B.-S., Custer, S., & Rahemtulla, H. (2011). *Realizing the vision of open government data*. Washington, DC: Open Development Technology Alliance.

Hartung, C., Anokwa, Y., Brunette, W., & Lerer, A. (2010). Open data kit: Tools to build information services for developing regions. In *Proceedings of the International Conference on Information and Communication Technologies and Development - ICTD 2010*. London, UK: ICTD.

Iivari, J. (2010). Varieties of user centredness: An analysis of four systems development methods. *Information Systems Journal, 21*, 125–153. doi:10.1111/j.1365-2575.2010.00351.x

Java, A., Song, X., & Finin, T. (2007). Why we Twitter: Understanding microblogging usage and communities. In *Proceedings of the Joint 9th WEBKDD and 1st SNA-KDD Workshop 2007*. San Jose, CA: WEBKDD.

Jonassen, D. H., & Rohrer-Murphy, L. (1999). Activity theory as a framework for designing constructivist learning environments. *Educational Technology Research and Development, 47*(1), 61–79. doi:10.1007/BF02299477

Kleine, D. (2010). ICT4what? Using the choice framework to operationalise the capability approach to development. *Journal of International Development, 22,* 674–692. doi:10.1002/jid.1719

Korten, D. C. (1990). *Getting to the 21st century: Voluntary action and the global agenda.* West Hartford, CT: Kumarian Press.

Lave, J., & Wenger, E. (1991). *Situated learning: Legitimate peripheral participation.* Cambridge, UK: Cambridge University Press. doi:10.1017/CBO9780511815355

Levy, M. (2009). WEB 2.0 implications on knowledge management. *Journal of Knowledge Management, 13*(1), 120–134. doi:10.1108/13673270910931215

Lewis, D. (1998). Development NGOs and the challenge of partnership: Changing relations between north and south. *Social Policy and Administration, 32*(5), 501–512. doi:10.1111/1467-9515.00111

Maina, W. (2009). Kenya: The state, donors and the politics of democratization. In van Rooy, A. (Ed.), *Civil Society and the Aid Industry* (pp. 134–167). London, UK: Earthscan Publications Ltd.

Mawdsley, E., Townsend, J., Porter, G., & Oakley, P. (2002). *Knowledge, power and development agendas: NGOs north and south.* Oxford, UK: INTRAC.

McGowan, P. J., Wigand, R. T., & Betz, M. J. (Eds.). (1984). *Appropriate technology: Choice and development.* Durham, NC: Duke University Press.

Nardi, B. A., Schiano, D. J., & Gumbrecht, M. (2004). Blogging as social activity, or, would you let 900 million people read your diary? In *Proceedings of the 2004 ACM Conference on Computer Supported Cooperative Work,* (pp. 222-231). Chicago, IL: ACM Press.

Nieusma, D. (2004). Alternative design scholarship: Working toward appropriate design. *Design Issues, 20*(3), 13–24. doi:10.1162/0747936041423280

O'Reilly, T. (2005). *What is web 2.0: Design patterns and business models for the next generation of software.* Retrieved August 8, 2012, from http://oreilly.com/web2/archive/what-is-web-20.html

Oosterlaken, I. (2009). Design for development: A capability approach. *Design Issues, 25*(4), 91–102. doi:10.1162/desi.2009.25.4.91

Pitula, K., & Dysart-Gale, D. (2010). Expanding the boundaries of HCI: A case study in requirements engineering for ICT4D. *Information Technologies & International Development, 6*(1), 78–93.

Rao, M. (2011). *Mobile Africa report 2011: Regional hubs of excellence and innovation.* Retrieved August 8, 2012, from http://www.mobilemonday.net/reports/MobileAfrica_2011.pdf

Reason, P., & Bradbury, H. (Eds.). (2007). *The SAGE handbook of action research.* London, UK: Sage.

Redmiles, D. (2002). Introduction to the special issue on activity theory and the practice of design. *Computer Supported Cooperative Work, 11,* 1–11. doi:10.1023/A:1015215726353

Sadowsky, G. (Ed.). (2012). *Accelerating development using the web: Empowering poor and marginalized populations.* Retrieved August 8, 2012, from http://public.webfoundation.org/2012/02/wf_study.pdf

Schneckenberg, D. (2009). Web 2.0 and the empowerment of the knowledge worker. *Journal of Knowledge Management, 13*(6), 509–520. doi:10.1108/13673270910997150

Schout, L. (2011). Foss and civil society organisations (CSO): Why civil society is not embracing FOSS. *i4donline.net.* Retrieved September 23, 2011, from http://www.i4donline.net/oct04/civil.asp

Schumacher, E. F. (1973). *Small is beautiful: Economics as if people mattered.* New York, NY: Harper & Row.

Sen, A. (2001). *Development as freedom.* Oxford, UK: Oxford University Press.

Smith, M., & Elder, L. (2010). Open ICT ecosystems transforming the developing world. *Information Technologies & International Development, 6*(1), 65–71.

Thompson, M. (2008). ICT and development studies: Towards development 2.0. *Journal of International Development, 20,* 821–835. doi:10.1002/jid.1498

Unwin, T. (Ed.). (2009). *ICT4D: Information and communication technology for development.* Cambridge, UK: Cambridge University Press.

val Relsen, M. (2012). *The lion's teeth - THE 'prehistory' of social watch.* Retrieved August 8, 2012 from http://www.socialwatch.org/node/79

van Reijswoud, V. (2009). Appropriate ICT as a tool to increase effectiveness in ICT4D: Theoretical considerations and illustrating cases. *The Electronic Journal of Information Systems in Developing Countries, 38*(9), 1–18.

van Reijswoud, V., & de Jager, A. (2008). *Free and open source software for development: Exploring expectations, achievements and the future.* Monza, Italy: Polimetrica.

van Rooy, A. (2000). Good news! You may be out of a job reflections on the past and future 50 years for northern NGOs. *Development in Practice, 10*(3), 300–318. doi:10.1080/09614520050116479

Vernooy, R. (2010). *Collaborative learning in practice: Examples from natural resource management in Asia*. Ottawa, Canada: International Development Research Centre. doi:10.1017/UPO9788175968639

Vygotsky, L. (1978). *Mind in society: The development of higher psychological processes*. Boston, MA: Harvard University Press.

Walsham, G. (2002). Cross-cultural software production and use: A structurational analysis. *Management Information Systems Quarterly, 26*(4), 359–380. doi:10.2307/4132313

Wenger, E. (1998). *Communities of practice: Learning, meaning, and identity*. Cambridge, UK: Cambridge University Press.

World Bank. (2012). *Poverty headcount ratio at $2 a day (PPP) (% of population)*. Retrieved August 8, 2012, from http://data.worldbank.org/indicator/SI.POV.2DAY

ADDITIONAL READING

Bjørn, P. (2009). Virtual team collaboration: Building shared meaning, resolving breakdowns and creating translucence. *Information Systems Journal, 19*, 227–253. doi:10.1111/j.1365-2575.2007.00281.x

Brown, I. T. J. (2002). Individual and technological factors affecting perceived ease of use of web-based learning technologies in a developing country. *The Electronic Journal on Information Systems in Developing Countries, 9*(5), 1–15.

Brown, J. S., Collins, A., & Duguid, P. (1989). Situated cognition and the culture of learning. *Educational Researcher, 18*(1), 32–42.

Brunello, P. (2010). ICT for education projects: A look from behind the scenes. *Information Technology for Development, 16*(3), 232–239. doi:10.1080/0268110 2.2010.497275

Buskens, I. (2011). The importance of intent: Reflecting on open development for women's empowerment. *Information Technologies & International Development, 7*(1), 71–76.

Curtis, D., & Lawson, M. (2001). Exploring collaborative online learning. *Journal of Asynchronous Learning Networks, 5*(1), 21–34.

Dada, D. (2006b). e-Readiness for developing countries: Moving the focus from the environment to the users. *The Electronic Journal of Information Systems in Developing Countries, 27*(6), 1–14.

Dearden, A. (2008). User-centered design considered harmful (with apologies to Edsger Dijkstra, Niklaus Wirth, and Don Norman). *Information Technologies & International Development, 4*(3), 7–12. doi:10.1162/itid.2008.00013

Ferguson, J., Huysman, M., & Soekijad, M. (2010). Knowledge management in practice: Pitfalls and potentials for development. *World Development, 38*(12), 1797–1810. doi:10.1016/j.worlddev.2010.05.004

Flynn, D. (1998). Constructing user requirements: A social process for a social context. *Information Systems Journal, 8*, 53–83. doi:10.1046/j.1365-2575.1998.00004.x

Graham, M., & Haarstad, H. (2011). Transparency and development: Ethical consumption through web 2.0 and the internet of things. *Information Technologies & International Development, 7*(1), 1–18.

Heeks, R. (2010). Do information and communication technologies (ICTs) contribute to development? *Journal of International Development, 22*, 625–640. doi:10.1002/jid.1716

Iivari, J. (2010). Varieties of user-centredness: An analysis of four systems development methods. *Information Systems Journal, 21*, 125–153. doi:10.1111/j.1365-2575.2010.00351.x

Jonassen, D. H., & Rohrer-Murphy, L. (1999). Activity theory as a framework for designing constructivist learning environments. *Educational Technology Research and Development, 47*(1), 61–79. doi:10.1007/BF02299477

Joyes, G., & Chen, Z. (2007). Researching a participatory design for learning process in an intercultural context. *International Journal of Education and Development using Information and Communication Technology, 3*(3), 78–88.

Kleine, D. (2010). ICT4what? Using the choice framework to operationalise the capability approach to development. *Journal of International Development, 22*, 674–692. doi:10.1002/jid.1719

Mawdsley, E., Townsend, J., Porter, G., & Oakley, P. (2002). *Knowledge, power and development agendas: NGOs north and south.* Oxford, UK: INTRAC.

O'Reilly, T. (2005). *What is web 2.0: Design patterns and business models for the next generation of software*. Retrieved August 8, 2012, from http://oreilly.com/web2/archive/what-is-web-20.html

Reason, P., & Bradbury, H. (Eds.). (2007). *The SAGE handbook of action research: Participative inquiry and practice*. London, UK: Sage.

Smith, M., & Elder, L. (2010). Open ICT ecosystems transforming the developing world. *Information Technologies & International Development, 6*(1), 65–71.

Smith, M., & Elder, L. (2011). Open development: A new theory for ICT4D. *Information Technologies & International Development, 7*(1), iii–ix.

Toyama, K. (2011). Technology as amplifier in international development. In *Proceedings of iConference 2011: Inspiration, Integrity, Intrepidity* (pp. 75–82). Seattle, WA: ACM.

Unwin, T. (Ed.). (2009). *ICT4D: Information and communication technology for development*. Cambridge, UK: Cambridge University Press.

van Reijswoud, V. (2009). Appropriate ICT as a tool to increase effectiveness in ICT4D: Theoretical considerations and illustrating cases. *The Electronic Journal of Information Systems in Developing Countries, 38*(9), 1–18.

van Reijswoud, V., & de Jager, A. (2008). *Free and open source software for development: Exploring expectations, achievements and the future*. Monza, Italy: Polimetrica.

Wenger, E., McDermott, R. A., & Snyder, W. (2002). *Cultivating communities of practice: A guide to managing knowledge*. Boston, MA: Harvard Business Press.

KEY TERMS AND DEFINITIONS

Collaboration: When two or more people interact for the purpose of knowledge sharing, exchange, support, or joint work efforts.

Consultative: A concept of participation whereby stakeholders are consulted to provide feedback, but the final decision-making power does not lie with the consulted stakeholders.

Development: A historically dependent term often used to describe processes through which people intentionally try to improve, in some way, shape, or form social, political, and/or economic conditions of humans. Key differences in interpretations relate to who is 'doing' development, why and for what purposes. In this chapter, I define development merely as a means to explain that development here refers to human development rather than software development.

ICT4D: Information and Communication Technologies for Development, refers to the use of ICTs for/and human development.

Online Collaboration: Can refer to any type of collaboration that occurs using at least one communication channel provided by digital technology.

Open Collaboration: Flexibility in opening up information and communication channels to include additional collaborators—inclusion sometimes serving as a goal rather than merely an outcome as well.

Participative: A form of participation that entirely involves stakeholders in a shared action and decision-making process, and where all stakeholders should theoretically have equal power to act and provide decision-making input.

Web 2.0 Principles: The underlying philosophy that guides thinking about Web 2.0 topics, and ultimately plays a part in defining Web 2.0.

Chapter 3

The Conceptualization of a Research Model for the Measurement of e-Government 2.0 Readiness in the Developing Countries

Yfantis Vasileios
University of the West of Scotland, UK

Abel Usoro
University of the West of Scotland, UK

Tseles Dimitrios
Technological Education Institute of Piraeus, Greece

EXECUTIVE SUMMARY

This chapter explores the potential of Web 2.0 utilization in developing countries through the concept of e-government. Successful implementation of the Web 2.0 concept has to combine both technological and human factors. Thus, this chapter proposes a conceptual model that will measure e-government 2.0 readiness. The conceptual model is based on a combination of the Technology Acceptance Model, Theory of Planned Behavior, and indexes from the United Nation's database. South Sudan is used at the end as a brief case study of the potential of e-Government 2.0. Future research should validate the empirical model. Meanwhile, the implications of the model are presented.

DOI: 10.4018/978-1-4666-2515-0.ch003

WEB 2.0 AND E-DEMOCRACY

Web 2.0 is commonly used by virtual communities to maintain their status and to implement the will of their members. Web 2.0 as a concept and a term originates from Tim O'Reilly (2003) who characterized the Web as a platform for software applications that focuses on the interaction between Internet users. Since then, Web 2.0 still continues to develop itself and adopts the state of the art technologies so as to take advantage and to meet the needs of the broadband world. Web 2.0 is not only a hardware and software conceptual model but it is based on the use of technology social purposes with associated advantages that meets the common needs of communities.

Teamwork (Rothwell, 2012) and democracy (Coleman & Shane, 2011) are the main pillars of Web 2.0. Teamwork refers to the work performed by a team or a community towards a common goal where each member of the team contributes in the working process. For instance, if a Facebook group exists that gathers electronic signatures to save the whales in Japan then each member of the group can be trying to persuade people outside of the community to sign an electronic form. In this case, teamwork operates in the Web 2.0 community in order to reach the common goal, which is the preservation of the life of the whales. Democracy is the second element of the Web 2.0 and it is implemented in various ways. The word democracy itself is of Greek origin and describes the unity of "demos" (people) and "kratos" (power). In other words, it is a philosophy that strongly supports the "power to the people" message where people vote equally for the future and take decisions upon common issues.

The electronic utilization of democracy is popular under the name of e-democracy (Insua, 2010) and it is present at the electronic community through various forms such as e-participation and e-voting. Governmental authorities all over the world consider e-democracy as one of the most important tools for national progress. Especially in the continents of Europe and USA, e-democracy seems to influence the local culture and people tend to show relatively less discrimination towards minorities and disabled people.

BACKGROUND OF E-GOVERNMENT 2.0

E-democracy is a concept that it is used further in governmental and political activities, especially in the implementation of e-government. E-government is defined as the use of information and communications technology to improve the governance (Gordon, 2002). The use of information technology improves the effectiveness and the efficiency of the governments. Depending on the government's transaction with third parties, the primary delivery models of e-government are (Yahehyirad, 2006):

a. **Government to Citizen (G2C):** Exchange of electronic information between the citizen and the government that includes electronic delivery of service (UNESCO, 2005).
b. **Government to Business (G2B):** Online noncommercial transaction between the government and the private sector.
c. **Government to Government (G2G):** Interaction involving the share of data and electronic information exchange between governmental departments (UNESCO, 2005).

In many countries, there are various applications for public services that can be implemented online, such as tax declaration, certificates of family status and driving licenses. Online transactions between the citizens and the public sector save the time of waiting on long queues in front of office front desks and during working hours. Citizens are able to get their requests fulfilled 24/7 because all the applications are stored in a server and often, even some back office functions like database actions are open to the citizens. Another important factor is the place of transaction because when using online services there is often no personal contact between citizens and the public servants. In this case citizens do not need to ask the public servants "to walk the extra mile" and help them with some documents or take other step of a procedure, which may oblige the citizens to pay the servants some amount as a reward. One additional factor is that the online share of information helps the government to save cost by offering a paperless way to deal with the public. The fact that less or no paper is required reduces the costs of buying paper or cartridges for printers. Despite the progressively successful route of e-government in a global level, there are still a few barriers that delay the e-government strategies. Three of them identified by Jason Baumgarten (2009) are:

a. Ineffective governance.
b. Lack of Web-related capabilities.
c. Reluctance to allow user participation in the creation of applications and content.

Governments have to tackle the last barrier by recognizing the current trend of social networks of human communities encouraged by social computing. The online participation of the citizen in the creation and sharing of contents in e-government defines an e-government approach towards the adoption of Web 2.0 concept. The user's participation in the creation of applications and content require teamwork, which is one of the Web 2.0's important elements.

Figure 1. Technology and social tools are important parts of e-government 2.0

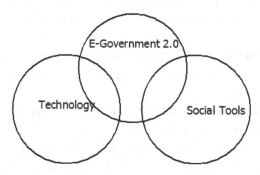

The application of Web 2.0 in government activities is often termed "Government 2.0," which the Australian Department of Finance and Deregulation describes as "not specifically about social networking or technology …. It represents a fundamental shift in the implementation of government—toward an open, collaborative, cooperative arrangement where there is (wherever possible) open consultation, open data, shared knowledge, mutual acknowledgment of expertise, mutual respect for shared values and an understanding of how to agree to disagree. Technology and social tools are an important part of this change but are essentially [just] an enabler in this process" (Government 2.0 Taskforce, 2009) (see Figure 1).

The concept of e-government 2.0 is already known to some non-African countries who use this concept in the governance of their nation. For instance, South Korea's website ePeople (www.epeople.go.kr) conducts surveys online and afterwards organizes discussions based on the result of voting as part of the surveys. In Greece, the governmental website Diavgeia (http://diavgeia.gov.gr) announces the plan for each new law and people comment on that by suggesting changes and improvements. Afterwards, a report is created based on the findings and the Greek parliament edits the suggestions before they end up in the final contents of new laws. In Denmark, the Ministry of Finance built a wiki that intends to create an integrated model, which encourages the public servants to improve their information technology infrastructure (Ostergaard & Hvass, 2008).

In the African continent where most of the developing countries are located, the concept of e-government is active but e-government 2.0 is still a theoretical concept that has not been implemented yet. In 2012, United Nations conducted a global e-government survey to show the status of e-government (United Nations, 2012). The top ranking countries in this report include Seychelles, Mauritius, and South Africa as can be seen in Table 1.

While Africa is considered a region with developing countries, we can notice that countries such as Seychelles and Mauritius have an e-government development index value higher than the world average in the year 2012. This fact defines Af-

Table 1. Top e-government ranked countries in Africa

		E-government development index	
Rank	**Country**	**2012**	**2010**
1	Seychelles	0.5192	0.4179
2	Mauritius	0.5066	0.4645
3	South Africa	0.4869	0.4306
4	Tunisia	0.4833	0.4826
5	Egypt	0.4611	0.4518
6	Cape Verde	0.4297	0.4054
7	Kenya	0.4212	0.3338
8	Morocco	0.4209	0.3287
9	Botswana	0.4186	0.3637
10	Namibia	0.3937	0.3314
	Regional average	0.2780	0.2733
	World Average	0.4882	0.4406

Source: Adapted from United Nations (2012)

rica as an interesting nation for research since there is a potential for the implementation of e-government in the African continent. Despite the information from this report that is useful for further research, it does not include the factor of Web 2.0, which is crucial since social networking has influenced the current status of the technology users. Thus, the question is to find a conceptual model that will lead us in the measurement of e-government 2.0 readiness in the developing countries. The measurement of e-government 2.0 readiness will show how ready the African continent is to adopt e-government 2.0.

PROPOSED RESEARCH MODEL

According to the definition of e-government 2.0 by the Australian Department of Finance and Deregulation, it is divided into factors that are related to technology and social tools. Thus, the requested information needs a conceptual model that will combine data based on both factors.

In 2005, the United Nations Department of Economic and Social Affairs issued the Global E-Government Readiness Report that captures the relationship of each country with the e-government concept. There are 3 crucial factors that define the final ranking for each country and show the level of willingness in order to adopt e-government:

- **Web measure index (Yayehyirad, 2006):** It is based upon a five stage model that represents the status of sophistication of a country's online presence. The first stage is Emerging Presence where the available governmental information is limited to the presence of websites with hyperlinks and few online forms. The second stage is the Enhanced Presence where more reports and laws exist online. Moreover, there is the option for the user to use a search engine so as to find the available online documents. The third stage is the Interactive presence. During this stage, the delivery of public information becomes interactive because the citizens are able to contact the public authorities via e-mail or other ways. The fourth stage is the Transactional Presence. During this stage, a two-way interaction between the government and the citizens is being implemented. The citizens are able to apply online for the issuing of ID cards or even paying the annual taxes. The last stage is the Networked Presence. It is a stage where a high amount of qualified and secured transactions with the government exist. At this stage too, there is a continuous discussion between the government and the citizens about the law environment. Moreover, the citizens can comment on governmental activities.
- **Telecommunications Infrastructure Index (Yayehyirad, 2006):** It is a combination of six indexes that are related to ICT infrastructural indicators. These indexes are: PCs per 1000 persons, Internet users per 1000 persons, telephone lines per 1000 persons, online population, mobile phones per 1000 persons, and TVs per 1000 persons.
- **Human Capital Index (Yayehyirad, 2006):** It is a human development index that includes the adult literacy rate and the combined primary, secondary, and tertiary gross enrolment.

These three indexes are useful to measure the e-government readiness but the element of Web 2.0 is missing. These three indexes include both social and technology elements. We can use two of the indexes that the United Nations used for the e-government readiness in 2005: Web Measure Index and Telecommunications Infrastructure Index. These indexes are associated with technology and we can find data from secondary research in the information pool of the United Nations or World Bank. The third index, Human Capital Index, is more appropriate to be a social tool for e-Government 2.0.

Based on these secondary research findings, the research model of e-government 2.0 is shown in Figure 2.

This secondary research model for e-government is suitable to measure the e-government readiness just like United Nation did in 2005 but it requires improve-

Figure 2. E-government 2.0 readiness research model

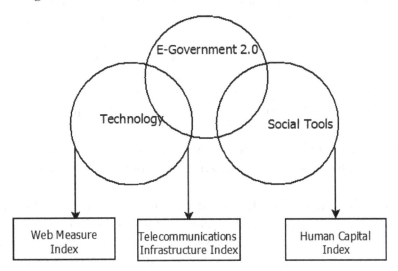

ment because a weak point exists. E-government 2.0 is an interactive process and the citizen's feedback to the technology and social factors is not depicted in this model. They are only indexes that can support the argument for e-government 2.0 based on the potentiality of the current infrastructure and not on the willingness of the citizen to adopt e-government 2.0.

The willingness of the citizen to adopt technology and socialize with the other members of the local community will transform this model into a working one to test the readiness of e-government 2.0 in the developing countries. The scope of this book chapter is to recommend a research model based on the authors' point of view and not to test the proposed model. However, any proposed improvement for the model will be accompanied by research hypotheses that would be helpful to test the model through a qualitative research.

The most known theoretical model to detect the potentiality of the people to adopt technology is the Technology Acceptance Model (Davis, 1989) which is known as TAM. It is an information systems theory that shows when users are dealing with a new system, if they are going to use it and in which way. The potential user of the new technology explores the technology's perceived usefulness and ease of use.

The perceived usefulness of the new technology is described by Davis as the degree to which a person believes that a specific system will improve his performance (Davis, 1989). This is a very important element for our research because e-government 2.0 will probably include new technologies or a new use of already known technologies. Therefore, it is a tool to predict the community's behavior towards the e-government 2.0 use. In this case, we adjust this sector into a hypothesis:

- **H₁:** There is a positive relationship between perceived usefulness of use of e-government 2.0 technologies and citizens' interaction with government.

The perceived ease of use of the new technology is described by Davis as the degree to which a person believes that the use of a specific system will be easy (Davis, 1989). Regarding e-government 2.0 technology, it is a tool to predict if the community expects the Web 2.0 technology to be easy. The hypothesis here would be:

- **H₂:** There is a positive relationship between perceived ease of use of e-government 2.0 technologies and citizens' interaction with government.

By embedding the TAM model into the existing conceptual model, the shape of the e-government 2.0 research model would be shown as in the Figure 3.

The two indexes of Web Measure and Telecommunications Infrastructure along with the TAM model contribute to the technological readiness of e-government 2.0.

Figure 3. E-government 2.0 readiness research model including technology acceptance model

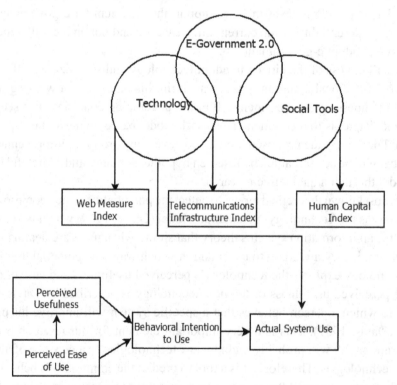

Thus, if researchers want to test the technological readiness of e-government 2.0 in the developing countries, they could collect secondary data from the two indexes and primary data from the TAM model's application through a survey.

The social readiness of e-government 2.0 could be measured with the use of a model that will predict the social behavior of the citizens towards the social networks. Theory of Planned Behavior (Ajzen, 1985) is a theoretical model that has been used to explain the attitude and predict the behavior of people towards advertising and healthcare. Therefore, the application of this model to understand the attitudes and predict the behavior towards social networks is an innovative approach of the topic.

The Theory of Planned Behavior is almost similar to the Theory of Reasoned Action (Ajzen & Fishbein, 1980). The Theory of Planned Behavior states that the individual behavior is influenced by behavioral intentions which is a combination of (a) individual's attitude towards the behavior, (b) the subjective norms of the performance of the behavior, and (c) the individual's perception of how easy the behavior can be performed (behavioral control) (Eagly & Chaiken, 1993). If researchers want to gather information by using this theoretical model then the three elements of the Theory of Planned Behavior will be adjusted to three hypotheses. These hypotheses would be useful for the prediction of the citizens' adoption of social networks into e-government:

- H_3: There is a positive (or negative) relationship between attitude to behavior and behavioral intention
- H_4: There is a positive or negative association between subjective norms and behavioral intention.
- H_5: There is a positive relationship between perceived behavioral control and behavioral intention.

The combination of the secondary data taken from the Human Capital index along with the primary data taken from the application of the Theory of Planned Behavior would lead to a measurement of the e-government 2.0 social readiness. The final shape of the research model for the detection of the e-government 2.0 readiness in shown in Figure 4.

The competitive advantage of the e-government 2.0 readiness research model is the fact that it combines both primary and secondary data that are associated with social and technological factors. Once validated in a future study, the implementation of this research model or an adjusted version of it (as a result of the validation process) in the developing countries should define the strategies that they should follow in order to improve their governmental activities.

Figure 4. E-government 2.0 readiness research model including technology acceptance model and the theory of planned behavior

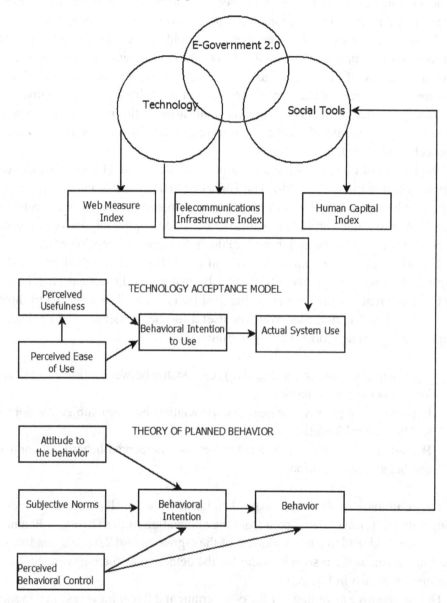

FUTURE IMPLEMENTATIONS OF E-GOVERNMENT 2.0 IN SOUTH SUDAN

A future study will use South Sudan as a case study to test the model developed in this chapter. Meanwhile, this part of chapter lays the groundwork for the case study by giving preliminary description of the country and explaining the justification of choosing it as a case study. South Sudan became an independent country in 9th July 2011. It is included into ten states and the country's overall population is 8,260,490 people. The capital of the country is Juba and the official language is English.

The fact that South Sudan is a recent nation means that the international presence of the country is limited in terms of collaborations with other countries. However, the country's effort to develop a new path in the potential national progress would trigger the interest for new political methods in terms of governance. Most of the countries that have an established political status and a long-term political system would be afraid to change its political culture. On the contrary, a new nation such as South Sudan would be open to experiment in political level, so the timing is perfect to experiment with an innovative model of e-government in order to maintain a strong political status in the content of Africa. This means that e-Government 2.0 would find a virgin framework to work and the proposed research model would be helpful so as to define the characteristics of that new framework.

The illiteracy rate of South Sudan is about 73%, which is a sign of digital divide and a disadvantage for the instant application of e-government 2.0 in the whole country. However, a long-term strategy for the application of e-government 2.0 would become true if the research model would be initially applied on mobile phone users. Mobile phone users are more familiar with technology and it is more possible to adopt an m-government model of e-government. An estimated population of one million people of South Sudan own a mobile phone and local telecom carriers such as Zain invested $110 million in fiber optics in 2011. Moreover Zain predicts that the population of mobile phones owners in South Sudan will grow to thirty six percent by 2016 with transactions of about $1.03 billion (Economic Times, 2012). There are no official statistics yet about the number of Internet users in South Sudan after becoming an independent nation. However it is estimated that in the whole Sudan (including South Sudan area) ten percent of the population has access on the Internet (Internet World Stats, 2012). The percentage is small but if the prediction for the increased mobile phone users becomes true then access on the Internet via phone would increase as well.

The overall budget of the country is estimated to be less than 1.5 billion dollars and most of it comes from the share of 50% from oil revenues. Fortunately, the region's Vice President, Riek Machar Teny, announced that South Sudan will mobilize 500 billion dollars' worth of investment for infrastructure development in the next 5 years. There is a strong interest from investors due to the country's wealth of oil and other natural resources. The political climate of the country is still suffering from the recent war between the southern and northern Sudan. The war ended recently but the country is in the progress of recovering from the war and trying to establish democracy and peace in this new country. So the question here is: what is the appropriate strategy to transform South Sudan from a disorganized country to a democratic nation?

The digital divide is really obvious in South Sudan but the development of the technological infrastructure is in progress and new investments are coming to the country. Thus while it would be difficult to use technology as a medium of democracy at the moment, the authorities of the country should plan now for the future. Web 2.0 as a philosophy features democracy and so it could be one of the most important tools for the democratization of the nation. Web 2.0 is mainly used in e-government strategies to encourage the citizens to participate in the country's decisions. Moreover, it lessens the bureaucracy and reduces the cost of interacting and getting services from the government. South Sudan authorities seem to realize the value of information and communication technologies and they try to popularize it through the World Wide Web. According to the official website of the Ministry of Telecommunication and Postal Services, "the Government recognizes the convergence of Information and Communication Technologies (ICT) and therefore will put in place appropriate mechanisms to ensure maximum synergy and harmonized policies, laws, and regulations within the ICT sector. The overall access to the basic telecommunication services by the majority of the Southern Sudanese as well as modern and state-of-the art services by the commercial enterprises and international organizations are key strategic priorities that the Government shall aim to achieve" (Yel, 2008).

It is obvious that the recommendation of a conceptual model that is based on e-government through Web 2.0 will benefit the country of South Sudan. In 2006 South Sudan's President, Salva Kiir, said: "Without proper training, implementation of e-government program can hit a wall but those trained will be able to train others from district to lower levels." It is important to say that South Sudan is located geographically in the center of Africa so the prospective development of the nation should benefit the other African countries as well.

CONCLUSION

The proposed research model will be very useful for the developing countries that intend to use both Web 2.0 and e-government as essential concepts so as to establish democracy in their region. The social and technological frameworks that this model uses include the embedded parts of e-Government 2.0: Social Tools and Technology.

The concept proposed by this chapter is yet to be empirically tested and also, since the developing nations and especially in Africa differ in terms of language and culture. Another option would be to use a different model that features these topics as well. For instance, instead of the TAM and TBT we could use the Unified Theory of Acceptance and Use of Technology (Venkatesh, 2003) which includes additional factors such as gender, age, experience, voluntariness. These issues will be addressed in a future research, which should use both published statistics and survey to validate the proposed research model. The findings of the future research should contribute to successful implementation of e-government 2.0 in developing countries.

REFERENCES

Ajzen, I. (1985). From intentions to actions: A theory of planned behavior. In Kuhl, J., & Beckmann, J. (Eds.), *Action Control: From Cognition to Behavior*. Berlin, Germany: Springer-Verlag. doi:10.1007/978-3-642-69746-3_2

Ajzen, I., & Fishbein, M. (1980). *Understanding attitudes and predicting social behavior*. Englewood Cliffs, NJ: Prentice-Hall.

All Africa. (2010). *Visit to juba bar where old and new mix*. Retrieved from http://allafrica.com/stories/201010251086.html

Australian Government. (2011). *Engage getting on with government 2.0*. Retrieved from http://www.finance.gov.au/publications/gov20taskforcereport/chapter1.htm

Baumgarten, J., & Chui, M. (2009). *E-government 2.0*. Retrieved from http://www.mckinseyquarterly.com/E-government_20_2408

Coleman, S., & Shane, P. (2011). *Connecting democracy: Online consultation and the flow of political communication*. Cambridge, MA: MIT Press.

Davis, F. D. (1989). Perceived usefulness, perceived ease of use, and user acceptance of information technology. *Management Information Systems Quarterly*, *13*(3), 319–340. doi:10.2307/249008

Eagly, A. H., & Chaiken, S. (1993). *The psychology of attitudes*. Fort Worth, TX: Harcourt Brace Jovanovich College Publishers.

Economic Times. (2012). *Zain and MTN target South Sudan as next mobile-money frontier*. Retrieved from http://articles.economictimes.indiatimes.com/2012-07-19/news/32747333_1_mobile-money-mobile-money-south-sudan

Gordon, F. T. (2002). *E-government – Introduction*. Retrieved from http://www.ercim.eu/publication/Ercim_News/enw48/intro.html

Insua, D. (2010). *E-democracy: A group decision and negotiation perspective.* Madrid, Spain: Springer.

Internet World Stats. (2012). *Africa internet stats.* Retrieved from http://www. internetworldstats.com/africa.htm

Laurie, M. (2011). *South Sudan launches electronic public finance management.* Retrieved from http://gbiportal.net/2011/07/08/south-sudan-launches-electronic-public-finance-management/

Mwanda, J. (2011). *New born South Sudan has ambitious goals.* Retrieved from http://globalgeopolitics.net/wordpress/2011/07/12/new-born-south-sudan-has-ambitious-goals/

National Informatics Centre & UNESCO. (2005). *E-government tool-kit for developing countries.* New Delhi, India: National Informatics Centre and UNESCO.

O'Reilly, T. (2005). *What is web 2.0.* Retrieved from http://oreilly.com/web2/archive/what-is-web-20.html

Ostergaard, S., & Hvass, M. (2008). eGovernment 2.0 – How can government benefit from web 2.0. *Journal of Systemics. Cybernetics and Informatics, 6*(6), 13–18.

Raaflaub, A. K., Ober, J., & Wallace, R. W. (2008). *Origins of democracy in ancient Greece.* Los Angeles, CA: University of California Press.

Rothwell, W. (2012). *Encyclopedia of human resource management, critical and emerging issues in human resources.* San Francisco, CA: John Wiley & Sons.

United Nations. (2010). *E-government survey 2010 leveraging e-government at a time of financial and economic crisis.* Retrieved from http://www2.unpan.org/egovkb/global_reports/10report.htm

United Nations. (2012) *E-government survey 2012, e-government for the people.* Retrieved from http://unpan1.un.org/intradoc/groups/public/documents/un/unpan048065.pdf

Venkatesh, V., Morris, M. G., Davis, G. B., & Davis, F. D. (2003). User acceptance of information technology: Toward a unified view. *Management Information Systems Quarterly, 27*(3), 425–478.

Yayehyirad, K. (2006). *E-government in Africa – Prospects, challenges and practices.* Retrieved from http://people.itu.int/~kitaw/egov/paper/E-Government_in_Africa.pdf

Yel, M. (2008). *Ministry of telecommunications & postal service - Telecommunications policy.* Retrieved from http://www.motps.goss.org/index.php?option=com_content&view=article&id=54&Itemid=56&lang=en

Zain Group & Telefonaktiebolaget LM Ericsson. (2009). *Economic impact of mobile communications in Sudan report.* Khartoum, Sudan: Zain Group.

Chapter 4
The Role of Web 2.0 in the Arab Spring

Robert A. Cropf
Saint Louis University, USA

Mamoun Benmamoun
Saint Louis University, USA

Morris Kalliny
Saint Louis University, USA

EXECUTIVE SUMMARY

The Arab Spring seemed to give a renewed sense of promise to proponents of Web 2.0 as a force for democratization. However, a year on, throughout the Arab world the prospects for democracy are still far from certain. Our conclusion, based on an examination of the events in four countries—Egypt, Morocco, Bahrain, and Libya—is that Web 2.0 collaborative tools are without parallel in their ability to mobilize vast numbers of the public. Unknown, however, is whether Web 2.0 can also assist in institutionalizing democracy throughout the Arab world. In this study, the authors adapt the path dependency model of Douglass North and others to explain why, despite the huge popularity of Web 2.0 in the region, the growth of Arab e-democracy will be slow and uncertain. Path dependency suggests that in order for e-democracy to eventually take root and thrive in the region, certain preconditions must be met.

DOI: 10.4018/978-1-4666-2515-0.ch004

INTRODUCTION

What are some of the necessary preconditions for making the transition to e-democracy, which is generally recognized as one of the chief pillars of e-government along with e-administration and e-service (Heeks, 2001; Dawes, 2002; Jansen, 2005)? In the aftermath of the successful attempt to topple Egypt's regime and the other events of the "Arab Spring," spurred by protesters using social media, there is an air of optimism surrounding the power of social media and Web 2.0 to facilitate political change. In this study, we suggest a path dependency model to explain the transition some countries make to e-democracy and apply this model to countries in the Middle East where social media have played an important role in recent political developments. In the path dependency model, successful transition to e-democracy is dependent on the existence of formal rules (i.e., political and economic institutions) and informal constraints (i.e., political culture and norms governing use of technology) of a polity.

We assert that Information and Communication Technology (ICT) can create opportunities for the development of genuine democracy, but in order for there to be a meaningful impact on actual governance and policymaking, favorable preconditions of formal and informal constraints also have to be met.

There is little doubt that globalization enabled by technology has had a significant impact on cultural values worldwide. The impact of globalization was made possible mainly by advances in technological innovation particularly in the area of global communication (Hill, 2011). One of the regions that has been significantly impacted by technology (in the sense that technology and globalization has brought significant political, social and cultural changes to it) is the Arab world. This revolution has been spurred by expanding broadcast technologies and increasing mobile phone usage to access Web 2.0.

Thomas (1998) contended that growing new broadcast technologies and the worldwide deregulation of the broadcast industry in the 1980s and 1990s have opened the door for globalization. Lueg and Finney (2007) argue that mobile phones are key instruments that bring people together and stimulate interactive communication during the process of consumer socialization and interpersonal communication. In a 2011 report by the Arab Advisors Group, 14 Arab countries mobile have high-speed networks. For example, the report indicates that there were 1.37 million 3G mobile subscriptions in Morocco and nearly 3 million subscriptions in Saudi Arabia at the end of 2010. It is estimated the Middle East has surged to become the second-fastest growing mobile phone market in the world with a penetration rate of more than 50% (Trading Media, 2010). This surge in mobile phone usage has also helped spur the explosive growth in social media as an expected 100 million Arab users will be attracted to social media by 2015 (Ghannam, 2011).

Traditionally slow to respond to globalization imperatives, the Arab world has indeed embraced the Internet Revolution and collaborative technologies. Yet, the adoption of these technologies in the policy process is highly unequal and biased. Assimilated largely by an educated middle class and youth, the Web 2.0 technologies such as blogs, YouTube, and social networking have been influential in the Arab Spring. They have been employed as medium of expression and collaboration between citizens, revitalizing the drive toward democracy. On the whole, Arab governments have not taken advantage of the Web 2.0 revolution to bolster collaboration with citizens, although e-government initiatives have grown across the Arab world. For example, by late 2010, many Arab governments, including Bahrain, Egypt, and Morocco, had an on-line presence. In addition, their attitude is still much driven by the same old cultural and political biases and security concerns that have stalled innovation in the Arab world (see Jabbra, 1989). Similarly, Arab industries still lag behind their western counterparts in adopting and diffusing Web 2.0 technologies. Although progress has been made, Arab businesses still have far to go to implement Web 2.0 technologies. Unless and until businesses and governments embrace Web 2.0 and, more importantly, also embrace the participatory ethos of the Arab spring social movements, there will be no e-democracy in the Arab world any time soon.

In the next section, we introduce the theory of path dependence, which underlies our analysis of the Arab Spring. The second section deals with media in the Arab world in the historical context. The Arab Spring brought to the forefront of the world's attention the powerful influence of mobile technology and Social Media; we examine this topic in the third section on new communications technology in the Arab world. In the fourth section, we examine the events of the Arab Spring from the perspective of the cases of Morocco, Egypt, Bahrain, and Libya, focusing on the role of Social Media in spurring the path toward democracy in each country. Finally, in the fifth section, we conclude our analysis of the role of Web 2.0 in the Arab Awakening and suggest that a path dependency approach requires a cautious optimism on the part of the observer regarding the Arab World's transition to democratic regimes.

ARAB SPRING AND WEB 2.0: USING PATH DEPENDENCE TO EXPLAIN THE ROLE OF SOCIAL MEDIA

The euphoria over the Arab Spring, which was spurred by protesters using social media, has renewed the sense of optimism surrounding the power of Web 2.0 to bring about change. However, the jury is still out with regards to the ability of Arab countries to make the transition to democracy as it is too early to judge the outcome of steps taken toward democracy. In this chapter, we draw on the work of Douglass North and others to develop a path dependent model that can help explain events in the Arab world and the role that Web 2.0 plays in those events. In our explanation, the successful transition to stable democracy is largely dependent on the formal rules (i.e., political and economic institutions) and informal constraints (i.e., political culture) of a society. Web 2.0 can aid in the development of genuine political democracy; however, it is unclear whether it will have as significant an impact on the actual day-to-day aspects of democratic government as it has had on effectively mobilizing opposition to repressive regimes, without, first, the necessary conditions of formal and informal constraints being met.

We begin our analysis by noting that democracies can be conceptualized in a variety of different ways. Three notable conceptions have been identified in the literature: aggregative, direct, and deliberative (Bohman & Rehg, 1997). Each one provides a useful lens with which to view the democratic character of the transition from authoritarianism to democracy and has implications for the role of Web 2.0 generally. As conceptual frameworks, these three different modes of democracy also illustrate the variety found in emerging Arab democracies.

Democracies are political systems that contain the rights, liberties, norms, and institutions needed to channel the formulation and exercise of public power (Dahl, 1971). As an ideal, democracy emphasizes the need to treat all citizens as free and equal. In sum, all those affected by a political decision have a say in how that decision is made in a democratic system of government. The values of freedom and political equality are embedded within the structure of democratic systems to a greater or lesser degree and operationalized in a variety of ways in accordance with the prevailing social norms. Thus in practice, the mechanisms responsible for the direct expression of these democratic values, along with the social understanding of these values, are specific to a given time and place. American democracy under the Articles of Confederation, for example, functioned differently than under the U.S. Constitution, even though both documents and their associated structures embody a similar understanding of core democratic values.

The implication is that democracies can vary significantly in the manner in which they seek to realize core democratic values and the interpretations citizens give these values. In aggregative democracy, for example, competition, bargaining, and efficiency characterize decision-making. Self-interested actors pursue their preferences, develop optimal strategies for achieving their goals, and seek out compromise through bargaining and negotiation. An aggregative view of democracy focuses on the way government enhances the efficiency of the delivery of public goods and services. In such a conception, citizens benefit from the efficiency gains and expanded choices brought about by democratic government.

Direct democracy, by contrast, stresses the importance of public participation and extols the value of the grassroots approach to governance. In this conception, citizens mobilize to stake their claim in the process and positions are legitimated, in part, through mass political movement. This is the model for the protest stage of the Arab democracy movement. This view of democracy recognizes the expanding access to information, opinions, and ideas brought about by social media and Web 2.0, which makes more information accessible to a greater number of people and without a centralized source controlling the content. As was shown by the events of the Arab Spring, the subsequent shift away from elite control over information and its dissemination is both empowering and potentially transformative.

Finally, a deliberative conception of democracy stresses the role that public discourse plays in steering policy decisions. In many ways, this conception represents a more mature system of democracy, one that has already incorporated the aggregative and direct approaches and augments them through deliberative structures such as the public sphere (Habermas, 1991). New technologies, such as blogs and wikis, give rise to new virtual communities and forms of political self-expression and engagement. In the ideal deliberative democracy, citizens engage in political discussion in order to develop deeper understandings of the ideas discussed with the objective of influencing policy-making.

To understand how and why these various modes of democracy take root, and how Web 2.0 can be used to help facilitate the transition in Arab countries, we use a model drawn from Douglass North's work on national economies. North stipulates the importance of formal rules and informal constraints in shaping economies in both developed and developing countries. Similarly, we argue preexisting political structures and the informal constraints of civic culture can impact the success of nascent Arab democracy efforts. In other research (see Cropf & Krummenacher, 2011) we use examples from countries around the world, to demonstrate how changes in either or both of these structures can alter the shape of technology efforts to bolster democracy in a given polity.

Adapting a path dependent approach to the events in the Arab sphere provides an advantage that is often lacking in much of the research—it highlights the historical nature of the changes produced by Web 2.0 in connection with traditional institutions and mechanisms of governance. As North astutely points out, "We cannot understand where we are going without an understanding of where we have been" (North, 2005, p. 51). However, more than merely recognizing the importance of history, is the fully fleshed-out understanding of path dependent relationships found in North's work, which can be summarized as the self-perpetuating nature of institutions and the organizations that have arisen around them. Thus, these same organizations and institutions will vigorously resist any change that can be perceived as threatening to their survival.

The findings of many of the authors in Cropf and Krummenacher (2011) confirm the validity of applying a path dependent model to e-government and the growth of democracy in the Arab world. Importantly, they confirm the notion that history and culture matter in building democratic institutions and fostering democratic norms. Nyirenda (2011) and Bwalya et al. (2011), for example, indicate a very strong correlation between the legacy of colonialism in sub-Saharan Africa (e.g., rent-seeking, weak civil society, etc.) and the failure to establish a solid foundation on which to build e-democracy (although some strides have been made toward e-administration in that region). Raman (2011) in her study of Banagalore, India, identifies some of the challenges faced by virtual public spheres in developing countries and how ICT can be used to empower ordinary citizens to participate in local governance, even though deep structural barriers persist. In Hacker and Morgan's (2011) study of the rise of social media and the development of virtual public spheres, they point out that the powerful in society tend to be early ICT adopters and thus have had a disproportionate effect on new social networks, particularly those that arise around new media, and can perpetuate existing social inequities.

As the evolution of Arab democracy proceeds, it is important for us to remember that while Web 2.0 truly marks a revolution in human communication, the deep channels of history and culture still serve to influence and direct human behavior in pathways that often run counter to progressive social and political change. An important example of the informal constraints that can either help or hinder democracies in their infancy is civil society. The London School's Centre for Civil Society defines civil society as "the arena of uncoerced, collective action around shared interests, purposes, and values. Therefore, as the arena of social life that consists primarily of voluntary relations and encompasses all forms of non-coerced individual participation in public life" (London School of Economics Centre for Civil Society, 2004, Definition of Civil Society section).

ICT has been criticized by some analysts as being disruptive of civil society (Heim, 1993; Fukuyama, 1999; Nie & Erbring, 2000). Technology, particularly social media, however, has its advocates who argue that the decentralized and non-hierarchical social interactions of Web 2.0 are more democratic than traditional, hierarchical broadcast technologies. They point to the use of social media in helping to topple repressive Arab regimes as the best example so far of the power of technology to effect social and political change.

Despite these changes, the virtual public sphere created by Web 2.0 still owes much to earlier versions of the public sphere. In our discussion, we therefore pay close attention to the traditional Arab public sphere as it has existed for centuries. Web 2.0 influences this traditional public sphere in many powerful, unforeseen ways, and this is the focus of our chapter.

E-GOVERNMENT AND E-GOVERNANCE

Before moving into our discussion of the role of Web 2.0 in the Arab Spring, there needs to be a discussion of how we use the terms, e-government and e-governance in this chapter. It is useful to begin by quoting Dawes' definition of e-government: E-government is the use of information technology to support government operations, engage citizens, and provide government services (2002). In the literature, however, there is no clear-cut distinction drawn between e-Government and e-Governance. For example, Heeks (2001) considers operations to improve government processes employing ICT to be e-administration, which he includes as one of the three pillars of e-Governance; the other two being connecting citizens (e-citizens and e-services); and building external interactions (e-society). Besides the semantic advantage of having a definition that distinguishes between e-government and e-governance, as Jansen suggests in his 2005 article, there may be a benefit in terms of helping to provide a clear assessment framework. In other words, he asserts that our current frameworks for understanding of e-government lack a clearly defined purpose.

In recognition of this, the authors put forth two separate definitions: one for e-government and another for e-governance. When we use the term, e-Government in this chapter we refer exclusively to what Dawes includes in her dimensions of e-services (the electronic delivery of government information, programs, and services often (but not exclusively) over the Internet), e-commerce (the electronic exchange of money for goods and services between government and citizens) and e-management (the use of information technology to improve the management of government). When we use e-Governance in the text, we will be referring to what Dawes calls e-democracy or "the use of electronic communications to increase citizen participation in the public decision-making process" (Dawes, 2002).

MEDIA IN THE ARAB WORLD: HISTORICAL CONTEXT

The landscape of Arab media has changed significantly in recent years and in order to understand the current state of the Arab media, we provide a quick review of the major historical eras and events that shaped the Arab media landscape in the past.

The independent Arab written press did not appear until mid-nineteenth century. It was then that the legal and political restraints on newspapers were removed and the formation of an independent press in Egypt, Syria, and Iraq could proceed un-hindered. In Egypt alone, this development led to the creation of over one hundred newspapers, which contributed significantly to the growth of the Arab free press movement (Andersen, 1992).

Another turning point for the Arab press came when Arab countries began seeking independence from foreign control in the second half of the 19ᵗʰ century. As a consequence of national liberation movements, the Arab press became one of the main tools used in fighting for national independence. This led to the Arab press being subjected to a brutal treatment by the colonial authorities; including the suspension or ban of newspapers. The reduction in the number of free and independent newspapers was a major setback for press freedom and expansion in the Arab world (Benmamoun, Kalliny, & Cropf, 2012).

Some of the Arab states such as Egypt managed to get their independence in the early 1950s. While one might expect that this would favor the Arab press by having got rid of foreign rule, this marked the end of the multiparty political system and the independent press in the majority of the Arab region giving a fatal blow to the free Arab press that would last a long time (Benmamoun, Kalliny, & Cropf, 2012). The press became a casualty of independence where new established Arab governments nationalized the press where journalists were often subject to censorship and legislation, which repressed independent criticism in the name of protecting the public order. Violators of such orders were severely punished. These policies led to regression for press freedom in the entire region by the 1960s and continuing throughout the 1980s, with the exception of Lebanon (Essoulami, 2006; Kraidy & Khalil, 2009).

As a result of these actions, Arab media were reduced to a small number of state owned and controlled media outlets. No wonder the Reporters without Borders' Report for 2010 placed the majority of the Arab countries at the bottom (Syria 173, Sudan 172, Yemen 170, Tunisia 164, Libya 160, and Saudi Arabia 157) regarding freedom of the press (http://en.rsf.org/press-freedom-index-2010,1034.html). Therefore, over the years, the media's role in the Arab world has been confined to reinforcing the existing cultural values and keeping traditions and the status quo. The tight government control over Arab media has eliminated any mass media forum that could be used to challenge old ideas and communicate new ones (Kraidy & Khalil, 2009). This caused a severe stagnation in Arab media and limited its impact by not allowing it to grow, expand, or experience the freedom it needed to move forward.

A new era in the Arab press started when the Emir of Qatar, Sheikh Hamad Bin Khalifa provided a grant of about 150 million U.S. dollars to establish the Al-Jazeera television satellite network channel, which started broadcasting in late 1996. Al-Jazeera started a new revolution in the Arab world by providing a new form of reporting. Fandy (2007) stated that:

Both governments and ordinary people in Washington and London and all over the world consider Al-Jazeera to be synonymous with the broader Arab media. The channel's willingness and boldness to broadcast dissenting views, including call-in shows, created controversies throughout the Arab region and fascinated millions. The nature of Al-Jazeera programs diverging from the well known traditional way of reporting and entertaining in the Arab world caused loud cries across the region where Saudi Arabia responded by recalling its ambassador from Qatar where the station is located in 2002 over content viewed as damaging to the kingdom, Jordan recalled its ambassador in 2002 in response to perceived insults against the Hashemite ruling family (p. 1).

The birth of Al-Jazeera marked a milestone in the media history of the Arab World (Kraidy & Khalil, 2009; Lavine, Sweeney, & Wagner, 1999). Thus, transforming the Arab media world from a largely state-run affair to a predominately private one (Benmamoun, Kalliny, & Cropf, 2012).

The tremendous success and acceptance of television channels such as Al-Jazeera prompted the introduction of many independent television channels that appealed to diverse market segments including news, entertainment, sports, children, etc. (Benmamoun, Kalliny, & Cropf, 2012). These changes not only acted as a catalyst for the increase of Arab media outlets but also helped make some of them very large (Benmamoun, Kalliny, & Cropf, 2012). This media expansion and growth makes the impact of the Arab media significant and far-reaching. Therefore, Arab media are not only becoming more sophisticated but are also launching programs in Arabic, English, Farsi and Urdu.

NEW COMMUNICATIONS TECHNOLOGY IN THE ARAB WORLD

Mobile Phones

Lueg and Finney (2007) argued that mobile phones are key instruments that bring people together and stimulate interactive communication during the process of consumer socialization and interpersonal communication. There are 1.6 billion mobile phones owned globally (Luck & Mathews, 2010). Mobile phones can be considered one of the most influential technological innovations introduced to the Arab world, as they have allowed millions of Arabs to go from no phones at all to a mobile phone entirely skipping the landline phone technology. According to the report, there were 1.37 million 3G mobile subscriptions in Morocco by end of 2010, and close to 3 million subscriptions in Saudi Arabia.

The Middle East is estimated to have surged to becoming the second-fastest growing mobile phone market in the world with a penetration rate of more than 50% (Trading Media, 2010). Open Arab Internet (2009) reported that there are 176 million cell phone users in the Arab world. There are 41 million mobile subscribers in Saudi Arabia alone representing an increase of 162% since January of 2009. This number far exceeds the 25 million people living in the Kingdom indicating multiple lines for some users. Having multiple lines per user was not limited to just Saudi Arabia but various other Arab countries. Figures reported for United Arab Emirates showed the number of mobile phone subscribers in the country stood at 7.6 million at the end of 2008—a ratio as high as 173 to each 100 people. Qatar came second, with a ratio of a 150.4 mobile phone per 100 people followed by Bahrain with 148.2 for every one hundred people (Olwan, 2008). The low cost of mobile phone lines made it possible for people to obtain multiple lines to use for various purposes. In 2012, a mobile phone line in Egypt would cost a mere one Egyptian pound, which translates to about 20 U.S. cents. At first, individuals had either to purchase two handset phones at the same time to use both lines or had to switch between the two lines based on which one they wanted to use. However, recent technology has given users the ability to use two lines on the same handset (German, 2006).

Internet in the Arab World

Internet technology represents the fastest diffusion of global technology in history. It took only four years to reach a critical mass of 50 million users from the time it was commercialized. According to Wheeler (2004) the Internet grew to 600 million users and more than 171 million host computers in 25 years.

The first connection to the Internet in the Arab world dates back to Tunisia being the first Arab country to link to the Internet in 1991. Kuwait came next in 1992, followed by Egypt and the UAE establishing links to the Internet in 1993. Jordan soon followed in 1994, while Syria and Saudi Arabia were the slowest Arab states to allow public access to the Internet with regular access not becoming available until the late 1990s.. Once Internet access was made officially available in Saudi Arabia, the Kingdom witnessed the largest and fastest growth in Internet user population than any other Arab country (Wheeler, 2004). According to the Internet World Stats Usage and Population Statistics (2011), there are more than 60 million Arabic Internet users today.

The Arab Advisors Group (2010) found the Internet in Egypt was the most common source amongst respondents for getting daily and global news (69.7%), getting information (97.6%), and looking for job vacancies (57.1%). The survey also revealed that the peak time for browsing the Internet for entertainment and personal issues amongst respondents is at nighttime (after 9 PM). The survey also found that international users have the largest share of email and search services where 85.8% of respondents who have an email account use Yahoo, and 99.0% of respondents who use search engines use Google. The Yahoo accounts can be explained by the Arab population's desire to chat using the Yahoo account to connect with others around the globe.

Sakr (2007) concluded from various studies that the Arab population uses the Internet for the following:

facilitate and extend social contacts through e-mail and chat; obtain news from reliable non-local sources; discuss almost everything under the sun, especially topics in the realms of religion, politics and relations between the sexes that have traditionally been taboo; enjoy entertainment, especially in the form of music downloads, sports, and games; and take moral guidance from what is perceived as contemporary Islamic perspective on modern life, including how to live as a Muslim woman in the modern world. Sites are also used to answer questions about fashion, family, food, relationships, sex life and work, and to provide match-making services and business information (p. 70).

The explosive growth in the Internet has given rise to the growth of e-government in the Arab world. By late 2010, 15 Arab countries had electronic government portals including Algeria, Bahrain, Egypt, Jordan, Kuwait, Lebanon, Mauritania, Morocco, Oman, Qatar, Saudi Arabia, Syria, Tunisia, UAE, and Yemen, according to the Arab Advisor's Group (2011). The Internet has, therefore, become an important force for the Arab population where information is obtained and an important source of communication for the entire region.

Social Media Usage in the Arab World

The popularity of social media to connect with friends and family, as well as advertise and create an on-line presence, is not restricted to the United States. The Nielsen Company, in a 2010 study on social network usage across 10 countries, reported that people around the world spend an average time of about five and a half hours a month on social media. Generation Y spends more than 70 hours per week engaging in new media and has pioneered the growth of MySpace, Facebook, and YouTube (Goetz & Barger, 2008). In the following sections, we examine how the various social media outlets are being used in the Arab world.

Facebook

Facebook is a service that links social networks and connects people via exchanges of email, short message service, economic exchanges, blogs, chat forums, photos and audio file exchanges. As a result of its large menu of services, Facebook is the most popular social networking website worldwide (Nielsen Company, 2010). In its short time, the impact of Facebook has been significant and far-reaching. Over 600 million people use Facebook with 70 translations available on the site according to Facebook's official press information website. However, 70 percent of the total Facebook users are outside the United States.

The growth in Facebook usage in the Arab world has been rapid. For example, the number increased by 1 million each month from June to August in 2010, with Egypt alone adding more than 600,000 users (Ghannom, 2011). As of April 2011, Trust Metrics (2011) reported that during 2010, the number of Facebook users in the Arab world increased by 78% from 11.9 million to 21.3 million. Despite the common preconception that it is mostly teen agers that use social media sites. People over 25 years old comprise about 70 percent of Facebook users in the Arab region (Huffington Post, 2011). Facebook has become a powerful force in the Arab world to deal with sensitive issues such as political and religious views. Indeed, it was one of the, if not the main, tools of communication during the recent Arab revolutions. The importance of Facebook was such that the Egyptian government blocked the site during the revolution in an unsuccessful attempt to halt the protest movement. The power of social media was further increased by the large volume of people who have joined it to get information, communicate with others and be in touch with what was happening during the Arab revolutions.

YouTube

YouTube is another social media outlet that Arab countries are using to communicate with the world. Because the Arab world has been fairly isolated for so long, as in the case of Facebook, the Arab population uses YouTube to express itself and present its views to the world (Benmamoun, Kalliny, & Cropf, 2012).

The most notable illustration of this trend is Queen Rania Al-Abdullah of Jordan using the YouTube website to broadcast segments focusing on fighting prejudice, promoting greater understanding between cultures, and promoting education (Benmamoun, Kalliny, & Cropf, 2012). Her efforts on YouTube to bridge the cultural gap between Arabs and non Arab communities and promote social issues has won her the first ever YouTube Visionary Award (http://www.youtube.com/watch?v=-Z-aQAEA7U8).

Twitter

Twitter, another important social media outlet, launched its Arabic interface in 2011 (Ghannam, 2011). The Washington Post reported that Twitter was probably the most effective social media used to get information from Iran to rest of the world about what was happening with the re-election of President Mahmoud Ahmadinejad (Morozov, 2009). People in Egypt regularly report irregularities of their government and women can anonymously report mistreatment via Twitter.

Blogs

Another example of social media that has grown significantly in the Arab world is blogging. It is estimated that there are almost 40,000 Arabic blogs on the Internet (Trust Metrics, 2011). Blogging has given the Arab population a tremendous amount of freedom to express their opinions, share their ideas, and reach the outside world with ideas that have been traditionally confined to their close-knit communities. Blogging has also allowed the Arab population to challenge the political and religious establishments. For example, bloggers in Lebanon played an important role in repealing legislation that would have limited online freedom of expression and they are also serving as watchdogs on the official Arab press or government press (Ghannam, 2011). This has not come without cost to bloggers, as some of them have been jailed (BBC News, 2007) for insulting Islam and government leaders. Blogging has also opened up a door for females to express their opinion, which is usually discouraged in Arab culture.

Satellite TV

The Arab world has been fairly closed to the outside world before the 1990s. Free To Air networks (FTA), however, have changed the media landscape in the Arab world forever. The introduction of this technology to the Arab world initially required a large investment; however, the situation has changed significantly in the last five years. Currently, a person needs only about a $150 or less to obtain a receiver and dish in order to have a working connection to satellite networks.

It is estimated that there are more than 400 Arab television channels (Forrester, 2009) in the region. The number of FTA satellite TV channels grew by 270 percent between January 2004 and August 2007 (Ameinfo.com, 2007). Legalizing ownership of satellite dishes and access to satellite networks by many Arab states resulted in the introduction of hundreds of independent and privately owned TV channels covering a wide range of issues (Koranteng, 1997; Sakr, 2001).

FTA networks have provided tremendous new opportunities for local and international advertisers to take advantage of, compared to previous years when airtime allocated to advertising on government owned television stations was very limited and commercial television was virtually unknown to the Arab consumer (Kraidy, 2002).

SOCIAL MEDIA AND THE PATH TOWARD DEMOCRACY: THE CASES OF MOROCCO, EGYPT, BAHRAIN, AND LIBYA

By means of four case studies, we shed light on the role of Web 2.0 in the Arab Spring. This section provides an analytical review of the complex, but close interplay between Web 2.0 and social and political engagements in the embattled regimes across the Middle East and North Africa, particularly Bahrain, Egypt, Morocco, and Libya. An essential starting point is a review of the information technologies that have helped to shape and set the stage for the Arab awakening. This review will look closely at the international and domestic factors and conditions that have facilitated or constrained the effect of Web 2.0 on Arab societies, particularly the demographics, and the social dynamics of the protests in each country. The four countries were selected for three reasons:

1. In all cases, information technology and social networking have played a significant role in the uprisings and civil engagements that swept the region.
2. The uprisings in these countries have some similarities, but each country has its own unique social, economic, and political characteristics and each rebellion has been manifested differently and in various forms (civil war in Libya, mass uprisings in Egypt, civil disobedience in Syria, demonstrations in Morocco, etc.). In addition, each one has a received different response from authorities ranging from mutual conciliation to downright suppression.
3. Each country has embraced information technology to varying degrees.
4. The political systems in these countries are different in the sense that some are republics (e.g. Egypt and Libya) while others are monarchies (e.g. Bahrain and Morocco).

Morocco's Youth Movement and Web 2.0 Collaborative Tools

In 1999, King Hassan II, who reigned over the 300-year-old Moroccan (Sunni) Alawite dynasty for 38 years, was succeeded by his son King Mohamed VI. The 48-year-old king has so far succeeded in prolonging the relative stability of the monarchy in a region that is witnessing a historic and overwhelming popular uprising and in an era when regimes in Tunisia, Libya, and Egypt succumbed to popular revolts.

Though the monarch wields wide powers, Morocco has been adopting a multiparty system of governance since the country's independence in 1956. In addition, the monarchy allowed some of its bitter opponents, including moderate Islamists and Socialists, to join the political process. Also the participation of women in the political process has been noteworthy, particularly after the introduction of the gender quota in 2002 which enables women lawmakers to hold 11% of the seats in Morocco's parliament, one of the highest rates of women' participation in the Arab world and Africa.

Contrary to other embattled Arab leaders, King Mohammed VI reacted to the pro-democracy demonstrations, which erupted in Morocco in Feb 20, 2011, with new constitutional reforms. The amended constitution was reportedly approved by 98.49% of voters (BBC, 2011) and was hailed by many western governments.

Both the protests and the reform have been aided by a massive media campaign, which included traditional communication media and Web 2.0 including political blogs, Facebook, Twitter, and YouTube. The majority of stakeholders, including the government, political parties, "February 20th movement[1]," religious groups, and other activists used these media in their campaign to propagate their respective agenda and participate in the ongoing public debate.

Web 2.0 has been, however, the medium of choice of the youth movement in Morocco due in large part to its relative affordability, widespread accessibility, exponential growth and less control by government. Indeed, and most importantly for this chapter, "[i]nternet access in Morocco is, for the most part, open and unrestricted" (OpenNet Initiative, 2011). This Internet policy might, among other reasons and technical complexities, be explained by the government's attempt to project an image of a modern and democratic country on the international scene.

In contrast, the regime has kept tighter control over traditional media, although it relatively tolerated and expanded the free press and opposing views on issues within the "proper" boundaries, particularly those affecting religion, the territorial integrity of the Kingdom and the institution of the monarchy. Nevertheless, the print media broke, on several occasions, these "taboos" and wound up confronting the Moroccan judicial system. This confrontation caused some journalists to suffer censorship, heavy fines, and/or imprisonments. According to the nonprofit advocacy group Reporters without Borders:

Morocco's drop (-8 places) [in RSF's 2010 World Press Freedom Index] reflects the authorities' tension over issues relating to press freedom, evident since early 2009. The sentencing of a journalist to one year in prison without possibility of parole (he will serve eight months), the arbitrary closing down of a newspaper, the financial ruin of another newspaper, orchestrated by the authorities, etc.—all practices which explain Morocco's fall in the Index rankings (2010, p. 12).

At times, the government, keen to establish and preserve the outward appearance of progressivism and openness, refrains from pursuing widely criticized alleged violations or releases, or reduces the sentences of some political detainees.

Additionally, traditional media, particularly newspapers, have been in large part financially dependent on government subsidy and ideologically associated with traditional political parties (Press Reference, 2012). These subsidies and ideological affiliations undermine the integrity and independence of Moroccan journalism and raises genuine concerns about their political agenda. For instance, the top largest Moroccan daily newspapers in terms of circulation such as Al Ittihad, Al Ichtiraki, Al Alam, and Le Matin du Sahara et du Maghreb are the voices of the country's two biggest political parties (the Socialist Union of Popular Forces and the nationalist Istiqlal party) and the Moroccan monarchy, respectively. Moreover, official media and televised coverage of major national events including the recent demonstrations has been overwhelmingly pro-government. This might explain why many Moroccans are relatively alienated by the apparent bias of the traditional media. According to UNESCO Institute for Statistics, Morocco published an average of 350,000 daily newspapers in 2003 with an average circulation of 11.74 per 1,000 inhabitants (see Table 1).

On the other hand, the Internet and, more recently, Web 2.0 have enjoyed exponential growth since the country deregulated the telecommunications industry in 1996. Over a short period, access to Morocco's Internet and mobile services skyrocketed (see Table 2). According to the National Telecoms Regulation Agency (ANRT), the number of Internet subscribers has jumped from 168,000 in 2005 to 835,000 in 2009 with most connected via High-speed (ADSL) and 3G Internet services (Jankari, 2009). The number of Internet users has also been on the rise. In 2004, Morocco had only 3,500,000 Internet users with 12 percent Internet penetration (Moroccan Ministry of Industry, Trade, and New Technologies, 2010). Four years later, 10,300,000 Moroccans were using the Internet with 34 percent Internet penetration (Moroccan Ministry of Industry, Trade, and New Technologies, 2010). Not only has the number of Internet subscribers and users increased, but also the number of blogs and active Facebook users. As of 2008, Morocco had around 30,000 blogs (OpenNet Initiative, 2009).

It seems, then, that the rapid dissemination of new communication technology has provided the Moroccan youth with an immediate alternative to the state-controlled

Table 1. Daily newspapers: total average circulation in selected countries, 2003

	Total average circulation	Total average circulation per 1,000 inhabitants
Lebanon	215000	54.88139365
Morocco	350000	11.73678457
South Africa	1286000	27.31012318

Source: UNESCO Institute for Statistics, October 2011

Table 2. Morocco internet and mobile indicators, 2009

	2006	2009
Fixed broadband Internet subscribers	391,857	475,767
Fixed broadband Internet subscribers (per 100 people)	1.28	1.50
Internet users	6,100,000	10,300,000
Internet users (per 100 people)	19.87	32.56
Mobile cellular subscriptions	16,004,731	25,310,760
Mobile cellular subscriptions (per 100 people)	52.13	80.01

Source: World Bank's World Development Indicators, 2011

and ideological mainstream media. Indeed, social media-driven political activism has been a principal agent of political change in Morocco. Social media have provided the traditionally marginalized a venue to express themselves and organize protests; reporting stories of corruption, oppression, police brutality, and to freely discuss and debate issues deemed taboo by traditional media. For instance, according to *The National*, "[e]ducated, often multilingual and sometimes expatriate, prominent bloggers such as 'Larbi' and 'Ibn Kafka'—both pseudonyms—are increasingly driving debate of sensitive topics largely avoided by mainstream media" (Thorne, 2009).

Ultimately, both the government and political parties started to take serious notice of how social media is empowering Moroccan discontent and threatening the old guard. For example, there is the case of Oussama el-Khlifi, who had given up on the Socialist Union of Popular Forces to organize, via Facebook, the February 20 movement and demonstrations. As the movement start gaining momentum, the "traditional opposition parties that initially shunned the upstart movement jumped in, trying to ride the wave churned up by the young" (*New York Times,* March 17, 2011).

As of 2011, Morocco has an estimated population of almost 31 million, with a median age of 26.9 years (CIA World Factbook, 2011). The youthfulness of Moroccan population is another reason for the growth and intensity of social media activism in Morocco. For instance, Morocco ranked 35th worldwide with 3,905,080 Facebook users, 42 percent of whom are in the 18-24 age range and 24 percent are in the 25-34 age range (Socialbakers, 2011a). Although Moroccan males are still the primary Facebook users (69% participation), Moroccan females are getting more active online (38% participation) (Socialbakers, 2011a). Ethnically, Arab-Berber constitutes 99.1% of the Moroccan population (CIA World Factbook, 2011). Although, the Islamic faith and intermarriage has lessened the ethnic divide between Arabs and Berber (both Sunni Muslims) in Morocco, a sizeable Berber youth took to the Internet to defend their linguistic and cultural rights. Eventually, pressure from women and ethnic rights groups has led to a greater recognition of the Berber (Amazigh) culture and more language and gender equality.

Indeed, Web 2.0 has created the necessary conditions, which have enabled the political system in Morocco to move, albeit timidly, from the path dominated by traditional political and social forces. In what many observers believe to be a significant shift in the Moroccan political system, and in the wake of pro-democracy protests in spring of 2011, a new constitution, curbing the King's political power, establishing stronger separation of powers, and recognizing ethnic and religious diversity, was overwhelmingly approved in a 2011 referendum. In addition, for the first time, a religious-based party, Morocco's moderate Islamist Justice and Development Party (PJD), leads a government after winning the majority of the parliamentary election in November 25, 2011. Do these developments reflect a mere adaptation of traditional institutions, particularly the King, to exogenous shocks (i.e. Arab Spring) and endogenous institutional changes (i.e. emergence of various movements including Islamists, youth, feminist, and ethnic), which, ultimately, strengthens the dominant path? This would suggest a return to path dependency. Or do they constitute a conjuncture, effectively establishing a new path? It is still early to fully comprehend the trajectory of political changes in Morocco. In the meantime, political reforms in Morocco seem incremental in their formulation and implications and they have not radically deviated from the existing path. The King of Morocco still wield significant powers and political reforms fall short of full constitutional monarchy. In addition, King Muhammad the VI's political reforms and popularity have "slowed the momentum of opposition protests" (King, 2011, p. 7). Nonetheless, there is an emerging consensus that Web 2.0 has helped pave the way toward democratic progress in Morocco. In the words of Ahmed Benchemsi, a Moroccan journalist, "This movement has already achieved freedom of speech for the average man and woman in the street, and there is no way back on that […] That's all we have granted for now, but this is the starting point for democratic change (McTighe, 2011).

Web 2.0 and Democratization in Egypt

Although, there are some similarities in the e-democratization process between Egypt and Morocco, the social-political dynamics and the historical and geopolitical profiles are considerably different between the two states. In addition, so are the political outcomes. As suggested by the path dependency model, they are, as Volker Perthes argued, "to a large extent shaped by the agendas and strategies of political actors in addition to being influenced by global and regional structures and developments, and by constraints that limit the capabilities of individual states" (2004, p. 1).

In this complex environment where the regime, the religious forces, the military, and social and professional elites have long shaped the power structure in Egypt, a new leaderless and heterogeneous youth coalition emerged crystallizing in the popular uprising that ended Egypt's autocratic regime. New media, particularly Web 2.0 and pan-Arab satellite channels, played a significant role in the regime change.

In Egypt, Pan-Arabism has been interwoven with domestic developments and networking readiness to produce the conditions that brought down the regime of the 82-years old and ailing President Hosni Mubarak who ruled Egypt for nearly three decades. The 2010 Jasmine Revolution in Tunisia helped to "provoke" events in Egypt and "resurrected a new sense of pan-Arabism based on the struggle for social justice and freedom" (Andoni, 2011). Even before that, specifically in November 2010, demonstrations and riots took place in several cities protesting Egypt's parliamentary elections that were marred by widespread manipulations and rampant vote rigging and overshadowed by the prospect of power inheritance. At the time, however, these protests did not threaten the ruling establishment. In fact, the ruling National Democratic Party dismissed the protests and continued to manipulate the election to preserve its hold on political power and to weaken the regime's fierce rival, the Muslim Brotherhood and El Wafd Party. Ironically, these policies have set the stage for the emergence of a social movement to take on the ruling party as the power and standing of the opposition wanes. Egyptian civil society was at what social scientists term a tipping point (Gladwell, 2000). Although, the fall of the Tunisian regime was the spark, the breaking of the fear barrier from repression was the vital precondition for the uprising. The fact that people could voice their opinions and discontent with state policies using social media, without being identified, has gradually helped to break the long-held fear.

In this volatile environment, social media have given Egyptian youth the opportunity to escape not only the regime's grip on traditional media, but also the unpopular opposition's newspapers that "failed to win the trust of their audience" (Fandy, 2007, p. 132). Egypt's educated youth has taken advantage of the country's growing access to new technologies. It is estimated that almost one third of Arabic-speaking blogs are in Egypt (Hroub, 2009). In addition, Egypt ranks 22nd in Facebook usage worldwide with 8,887,300 Facebook users, 40 percent of whom are in the 18-24 age group and 28 percent are in the 25-34 age group (Socialbakers, 2011b). As the like-minded youth movement in Tunisia succeeded in toppling the Tunisian Regime, the youth movement in Egypt became more daring. During the uprising that began on January 25, 2011, men and women of all classes and ages, and groups of different religions and ideologies joined forces against Mubarak's regime. Importantly, although not receiving the support of the powerful military establishment, they at least benefited from the military's relative neutrality. Social media were also backed by broadcasting from popular international radio and TV stations

The spectacular political use of Web 2.0 collaboration tools took the Egyptian government so much by surprise that they decided to shut down the Internet throughout Egypt. However, the government was forced to relent because of the harmful effects of the shut down on the national economy. This one act clearly indicates the advent of the new age of social media politics. In the words of Campbell, the "Egyptian Revolution was to social media's coming of age as television was to JFK's assassination coverage; radio to the 1955 failed Hungarian revolution; newspapers to World War II and house-to-house messages passed along the barricades of the French Revolution" (p. 364).

Ultimately, Web 2.0 has provided the stimulus and created the necessary conditions, which has enabled the resurgence of opposition movements in Egypt vying to fill the power vacuum left by Mubarak's overthrow. Chief among them is the Muslim Brotherhood, which scored significant victories in Parliamentary and presidential elections. Whether the Muslim Brotherhood would be able to layout a new political path remains to be seen. There are still traditional forces in Egypt, particularly the secular Military and the remnants of Mubarak's defunct ruling National Democratic Party (NDP), that work against large-scale change. Although at present Egyptian President Mohamed Morsi of the Muslim Brotherhood seems to achieve dominance over his rivals, the political scene in Egypt since the fall of Mubarak displays a level of uncertainty capable of swinging the balance of power back and forth between those battling for path stability and those battling for new path in Egypt's political system.

Web 2.0 and the Fall of Gaddafi's Regime in Libya

Compared to Morocco and Egypt, the Libyan case is all the more interesting in that the violent fall of the 41-year Gaddafi's regime has been the product of domestic unrest and foreign intervention. Additionally, Libya is a north-African and non-monarchical country that belongs to the set of oil-rich Arab states. However, unlike other oil-rich Arab countries, Libya's Internet readiness has been very modest and very recent, having started at the end of 1989 and not widely available until the early 2000s (Eid, 2012). As Table 3 shows, Libya's Internet penetration is still one of the lowest in the Middle East and North Africa (MENA) region. Yet in a span of 10 years, the number of Internet users has increased exponentially (see Table 4). The number of Internet users soared from 10,000 in 2000 to 353,900 in 2009. Considering the small size of the population in Libya, the growth of Internet users was large enough to provoke interest from Libyan opposition groups and uneasiness from the government. According to Eid (2012):

Table 3. Internet in the Middle East and North Africa (MENA), 2009

Country Name	Fixed broadband Internet subscribers	Fixed broadband Internet subscribers (per 100 people)	Internet users	Internet users (per 100 people)
Bahrain	165,000	14.11	649,300	55.52
UAE	690,424	9.95	3,777,900	54.45
Israel	1,850,000	24.71	3,700,000	49.43
Oman	41,114	1.52	1,236,658	45.60
Kuwait	45,000	1.70	1,100,000	41.57
Iran	400,000	0.55	27,914,700	38.17
Saudi Arabia	1,437,718	5.36	9,800,000	36.55
Tunisia	372,818	3.57	3,500,000	33.53
Morocco	475,767	1.50	10,300,000	32.56
Jordan	203,472	3.44	1,741,866	29.45
Qatar	129,907	8.13	399,000	24.97
Lebanon	222,000	5.29	1,000,000	23.83
Egypt	1,077,489	1.35	16,635,753	20.87
Syria	34,657	0.17	3,935,000	19.64
Algeria	818,000	2.34	4,700,000	13.45
West Bank and Gaza	233,000	5.76	356,000	8.80
Libya	10,000	0.16	353,900	5.65
Djibouti	5,285	0.61	25,900	2.97
Yemen, Rep.	--	--	420,000	1.80
Iraq	121	0.00	325,000	1.05

Source: World Bank's World Development Indicators, 2011

Table 4. Internet users in Libya, 2000-2009

	Internet users	Internet users (per 100 people)
2000	10,000	0.19
2001	20,000	0.38
2002	125,000	2.3
2003	160,000	2.89
2004	205,000	3.63
2005	232,044	4.02
2006	260,000	4.41
2007	291,300	4.84
2008	323,000	5.25
2009	353,900	5.65

Source: World Bank's World Development Indicators, 2011

The Role of Web 2.0 in the Arab Spring

The spread of Internet service provides Libyan dissidents scattered around the world with the opportunity to contact Libyan citizens and to strengthen their networks in the country. [...] The number of Libyan oppositional websites is even greater than that of foreign-based Saudi oppositional websites.

Politically, Libya has gone through exceptional circumstances and military confrontations during the longtime rule of Colonel Gaddafi. Domestically, his style of governance created an exceptional system, which he coined, in Arabic, "Jamahiriya," or state of the masses. This system, which he proclaimed to be "democratic," relied on a single political institution, the Popular Committee and Congress, "but few Libyans had any illusions as to its actual power" (Vandewalle, p. 50). There was no constitution or political parties and a strict ban on civil society. In practice, Colonel Gaddafi, his family, tribal entourage, and his feared Revolutionary Committee Movement wielded absolute control of the country's politics, intelligence services, and wealth. He manipulated the country's tribal structure to maintain power, lavishly rewarding loyal tribes and systematically depriving and silencing the rebellious tribes. Libya has been bitterly divided into two major parts: The western and southern part (Tripolitania, with Tripoli as the capital, and Fezzan) and the eastern part (Cyrenaica, with Benghazi as the Capital). The tribes in the western and southern part were pivotal in 1969 Gaddafi's coup against the Sanussi monarchy and remained loyal to him during his reign. Even when officers from the Warfalla tribe in eastern Tripolitania were implicated in a failed coup in 1993, Gaddafi's response was slow and careful (Niblock, 2001, p. 92). The eastern part, from which the Sanussi monarchy originated, has been historically hostile to Gaddafi's regime. It is no wonder then that elements in the latter part orchestrated the uprising that effectively ended Gaddafi's rule.

The Libyan leader's recent attempts at international openness did not result in a let up in his repression of domestic opponents. This has earned the regime Freedom House's label "the Worst of the Worst" in terms of political rights and civil liberties (Freedom House, 2012). Indeed, the Libyan regime controlled and exerted complete influence over what could be reported in print and broadcast media. BBC News (2011b) reported that, "Libya has a law forbidding group activity based on a political ideology opposed to Col Gaddafi's revolution. The regime has imprisoned hundreds of people for violating the law and sentenced some to death, Human Rights Watch says. Torture and disappearances have also been reported."

Consequently, people turned to foreign news media (particularly Al-Jazeera, Al Arabiya, and the BBC Arabic) and social media to voice their displeasure with the regime and report human rights violations in Libya. Gaddafi responded with censorship, filtration, manipulation, and intimidation. One tactic, according to Eid (2012), was "to force owners of Internet cafés to place stickers on computers that warn visitors from logging onto Web sites deemed oppositional." For instance, cyberdissident Abdel Razak Al Mansuri was sentenced to 18 months for posting an online article critical of Libyan authorities' social and human right policies.

These tactics did not deter Libyans' online activism, however. This could be explained by the success of social media in shielding individual identities and of the Internet in providing tools to circumvent governmental interference. According to Dabarah (2009), Libyans have been using alternative technologies to evade government Internet filtration. In addition, the success of Libyans' online brethren in neighboring Tunisia and Egypt bolstered Libyan online activism. They were effective in posting--through YouTube, Twitter, Facebook, blogs, and other Web 2.0 collaboration tools—real-time accounts, filmed videos, emotional stories, and reports—that succeeded in presenting an anti-Gaddafi agenda around which domestic and international opinion could form. Mekay (2011) of the *New York Times* reported, that popular sites such as libyaFeb17.com, Almanara and Libya Alyoum, "are widely credited with spurring support for the protests among Libyans abroad, especially in the United States and Europe."

In sum, the path dependency model predicts that Libya will have a difficult time in transitioning to e-democracy. While social media statistics attest to the power of Web 2.0 collaboration tools in mobilizing the masses and influencing domestic and international opinion, it is too early to judge whether the fall of Gaddafi will lead to the embrace of democratic institutions including e-democracy. Only time will tell whether the next regime will lift Internet filtering on content that is critical to the government and embrace Web 2.0 collaboration tools to engage citizens and strengthen democracy.

Protests in Bahrain: Role of Web 2.0

Amid growing Sunni-Shi'a divide in the Middle East and a worsening of the relationship between predominantly Shia Iran and predominantly Sunni Saudi Arabia, Bahrainis took to the streets on February 16, 2011 calling for social justice and the end of sectarian discrimination. As in Egypt, the street protest in Bahrain started with a social media campaign, converged on the capital, and was also commonly called the "Day of Rage." In the run-up to the protest, the minority Sunni government in Bahrain offered financial incentives and political concessions to appease Bahrain's Shiite majority (Al-Jazeera English, 2011). When that failed, Bahrain's security forces violently suppressed the Shiite-led protests causing some deaths.

Unlike protests in Morocco, Tunisia, Yemen, and Egypt, however, the Bahraini "Day of Rage" has been largely viewed through sectarian lenses. The western news media largely framed the tension in Bahrain as a clash between the Shi'a majority and the Sunni minority (Council on Foreign Relations, 2011, p. 188).

The reform-minded and western-educated King of Bahrain, who succeeded his father in 1999, has undertaken several economic and political reforms in the past few years that helped to westernize Bahrain. This is reflected in the country's expanding financial sector, modern infrastructure, economic growth rates, and the huge inflow of capital. Politically, the king loosened the repressive policies he inherited from his father. He granted, for instance, amnesty to political dissidents and exiled opponents, abolished the 1974 State Security Law, advanced women's rights, issued a new Constitution, and established constitutional monarchy and a bicameral parliament.

While the reforms received international acclaim, there has been a growing dissatisfaction and feeling of discrimination from Shiite majority. In 2006, the Islamic National Accord Association (Al Wefaq), the country's main Shiite opposition political party, captured 43% of the seats in Bahrain's parliament. The sense of marginalization was further reinforced by the government policy of tajnis (naturalization) of Sunni immigrants. These conditions contributed to relatively violent protests in Shia villages in 2010 to which government responded with massive crackdown, "arresting 23 dissidents, including human rights workers and a well-known blogger, allegedly subjecting some to torture while in detention" (Council on Foreign Relations, 2011, p. 190).

The protests escalated in 2011 as the Arab Spring's social media contagion reached Bahrain. In fact, it was relatively easier for Bahrainis to organize protests online because of Bahrain's strong foundation in Web 2.0 technologies. As Table 3 shows, Bahrain has the highest Internet penetration in North Africa and is only second to Israel in terms of fixed broadband subscription in the entire Middle East.

In practice, however, the e-democratization process is limited by Internet filtering and government control of media content. For instance, Bahrain has a number of laws that restrict the broadcasting of all forms of anti-government content including the Internet, particularly the 2002 Press Law, the amendments to the Association Law and the counterterrorism bill (Karlekar & Marchant, 2007, p. 64). Reporters without Borders (2012) reported several instances in which the Bahraini government has tightened Internet control. For instance, Bahrain blocked access to several websites and social media tools and containing content critical of the regime (Reporters without Borders, 2012). Among these websites are the Arabic Network for Human Rights Information (http://www.anhri.net/en/) and Bahrain Centre for Human Rights (http://www.bahrainrights.org/en). Bahrain censored some YouTube videos (including applications for live streaming videos such as Bambuser), cell phone chat groups, Facebook pages, and Twitter accounts such as the Twitter account of the President of the Bahrain Human Rights Centre (Reporters without Borders, 2012). In addition to blocking access on the Internet, Bahrain attempted to interfere with Internet access in other ways such as slowing down individual's access to the network.

Yet, government control of social media and new technologies has been difficult to accomplish as users effectively circumvent Web censorship. For instance, in August 2006, Bahrain ordered all Internet Service Providers (ISPs) in the country to block Google Earth because the free service "allows users to see the lavish palaces and illegal coastal reclamations on land privately owned by members of the Al-Khalifa royal family" (Bahrain Center for Human Rights, 2012). Yet, the Google Earth images were soon in circulation anonymously by e-mails (Bahrain Center for Human Rights, 2012). The case of Bahrain once again shows the appropriateness of using the path dependency model, in which the transition to e-democracy encounters barriers, in the form of formal constraints, and the use of Web 2.0 collaborative tools is shaped by informal social and political norms.

CONCLUSION: WEB 2.0 AND THE ARAB AWAKENING

As the Bahrain case study above shows, we are indeed witnessing a social media race between governments and cyberactivists, whereby anti-government content is being circulated soon after being banned. With the thriving of Web 2.0 collaborative tools, authoritarian governments in the Arab world choose the nondemocratic route to crack down on the ease with which citizen circumvent Web censorship. For now, it looks as though they are losing the race. This is not a declaration that social media will bring about democracy. However, as Blogger Fahad Desmukh notes, "Internet alone will by no means bring down any government. But the continued repression of discussion on the Internet may certainly exacerbate the desire for change" (Choney, 2012).

Each of the four countries presents a unique set of circumstance but with some marked similarities. Morocco represents a stable monarchy that has actively embraced political reform and has an image of openness. Moroccans, however, perceive the traditional media as either being too close to the ruling establishment or ideologically affiliated with the mainstream political parties. The Internet and Web 2.0 are viewed as alternative sources of political information making a large impact in terms of paving the way toward democratic progress.

In Egypt, clearly the "poster child" for the effects of Web 2.0 on the Arab world, a unique set of pre-conditions, including Pan-Arabism, civil society, the military and other important institutions of Egyptian society, provided the critical ingredients and Web 2.0 served as catalyst for the uprising that ended nearly three decades of rule by President Mubarak (Benmamoun, Kalliny, & Cropf, 2012). The country's youth, who, as in the rest of the Arab world, embrace new technology, drove the social and political change. The regime tried to prevent the inevitable by shutting down access to the Internet, but quickly relented because of intense economic pressure from businesses. This led to the collapse of the Mubarak government within a matter of days.

While the other three governments can be considered authoritarian but with some relative openness, Libya was a genuine dictatorship with repressive policies (Benmamoun, Kalliny, & Cropf, 2012). Despite being relatively backward in its use of the Internet compared to the rest of the region, by the 2000s, its network penetration rapidly grew and provided a means to mobilize the opposition to Gaddafi. Again, the ability of Web 2.0 tools to connect internal enemies of the regime with international allies was key (Benmamoun, Kalliny, & Cropf, 2012). In technologically sophisticated Bahrain, protests coalesced around a social media campaign but failed to produce a change in the country's leadership.

The tension between technologically advanced youth and anti-democratic governments will persist going forward. No amount of e-government innovation will change this fundamental fact of Arab political life (Benmamoun, Kalliny, & Crop, 2012). Conservative political and social elements also dominate traditional media outlets that will act as barriers to long-lasting reforms. Finally, the formal rules and informal constraints of Arab society have been scarcely changed by the recent events. Thus, a path dependency approach suggests that it is too early to be optimistic regarding the scope of democratic change in the region. It is also likely that, for most countries in the region, aspirations for democracy will include the three conceptions of democracy discussed earlier in the chapter: aggregative, direct, and deliberative. Web 2.0 can provide valuable tools in implementing aspects of the three conceptions. The cultural change that is essential for permanent democracy remains the ultimate challenge in the region.

REFERENCES

Ameinfo.com. (2007). 370 sat channels in arab world. *Ameinfo.com*. Retrieved August 5, 2011, from http://www.ameinfo.com/134225.html

Andersen, A., & Di Domenico, L. (1992). Diet vs. shape content of popular male and female magazines: A dose-response relationship to the incidence of eating disorders? *The International Journal of Eating Disorders*, *11*(3), 283–287. doi:10.1002/1098-108X(199204)11:3<283::AID-EAT2260110313>3.0.CO;2-O

Andoni, L. (2011, February 11). The resurrection of pan-Arabism. *Al Jazeera English*. Retrieved September 10, 2011, from http://english.aljazeera.net/indepth/opinion/2011/02/201121115231647934.html

Arab Advisor Group. (2010, June 8). News release. *Arab Advisor Group*. Retrieved August 15, 2011, from http://www.tegaranet.com/BAF/Arab%20Advisors%20 press%20-%20FTA%20Satellite.pdf

Bahrain Center for Human Rights. (2012). Bahraini authorities block access to Google Earth and Google Video. *Bahrain Center for Human Rights*. Retrieved September 10, 2011, from http://www.bahrainrights.org/ref08080600

Benmamoun, M., Kalliny, M. A., & Cropf, R. (2012). The Arab spring, MNEs, and virtual public spheres. *Multinational Business Review, 20*(10), 26–43. doi:10.1108/15253831211217189

Bohman, J., & Rehg, W. (1997). *Deliberative democracy: Essays on reason and politics*. Cambridge, MA: The MIT Press.

Bwalya, K. J., Du Plessis, T., & Rensleigh, C. (2011). Setting the foundations for e-democracy in Botswana: An exploratory study of intervention. In *Information Communication Technologies and the Virtual Public Sphere: Impact of Network Structures on Civil Society*. Hershey, PA: IGI Global. doi:10.4018/978-1-60960-159-1.ch012

Choney, S. (2011, February 17). Bahrain Internet service starting to slow. *Technology on MSNBC*. Retrieved October 25, 2011, from http://technolog.msnbc.msn. com/_news/2011/02/17/6075162-bahrain-internet-service-starting-to-slow

Council on Foreign Relations. (2011). *The new Arab revolt: What happened, what it means, and what comes next*. New York, NY: Council on Foreign Relations Press.

Cropf, R., & Krummenacher, W. S. (Eds.). (2011). *Information communication technologies and the virtual public sphere: Impact of network structures on civil society*. Hershey, PA: IGI Global. doi:10.4018/978-1-60960-159-1

Dabarah, I. (2009, March 5). الإنترنت في ليبيا... الجميع يتمرّد على الحجب والرقابة مُستمرّة. *Elaph*. Retrieved September 10, 2011, from www.elaph.com/Web/Politics/2009/3/415948. htm

Dahl, R. (1971). *Polyarchy: Participation and opposition*. New Haven, CT: Yale University Press.

Dawes, S. S. (2002). The future of e-government. *Center for Technology in Government*. Retrieved August 13, 2012 from http://www.ctg.albany.edu/publications/ reports/future_of_egov

Eid, G. (2012). *Libya: The internet in a conflict zone: The internet in the Arab world a new space of repression?* Retrieved September 10, 2011, from www.anhri.net/en/reports/net2004/libya.shtml

Essoulami, S. (2006, January 7). The Arab press: Historical background. *AL-BAB*. Retrieved August 5, 2011, from http://www.al-bab.com/media/introduction.htm

Facebook. (2011). Statistics. *Facebook*. Retrieved September 20, 2011, from http://www.facebook.com/press/info.php?statistics

Fandy, M. (2007). *(Un)civil war of words: Media and politics in the Arab world.* Westport, CT: Academic Press.

Forrester, C. (2009, September/October). HDTV and the Mid-East. *International Broadcast Engineer*, 8-9.

Freedom House. (2011). Worst of the worst 2011: The world's most repressive societies. *Freedom in the World 2011*. Retrieved September 10, 2011, from www.freedomhouse.org/uploads/special_report/101.pdf

Fukuyama, F. (1999). *The great disruption: Human nature and the reconstitution of social order.* New York, NY: The Free Press.

German, K. (2006, August 8). Two numbers on the same cell phone. *CNET Reviews*. Retrieved August 15, 2011, from http://reviews.cnet.com/4520-11282_7-6625917-1.html

Ghanem, S., Kalliny, M., & Elghoul, S. (2010). The impact of technology on the Arab culture. In *Proceedings of the Academy of Marketing Science Cultural Perspectives in Marketing.* Academy of Marketing Science.

Ghannam, J. (2011). Social media in the Arab world: Leading up to the uprisings of 2011. *The Center for International Media Assistance.* Retrieved August 5, 2011, from http://cima.ned.org/sites/default/files/CIMA-Arab_Social_Media-Report_1.pdf

Gladwell, M. (2000). *The tipping point: How little things can make a big difference.* Boston, MA: Little Brown.

Goetz, J., & Barger, C. (2008). Harnessing the media revolution to engage the youth market. *Journal of Integrated Marketing Communications.* Retrieved from http://jimc.medill.northwestern.edu/archives/2008/EngageYouthMarket.pdf

Habermas, J. (1991). *The structural transformation of the public sphere.* Cambridge, MA: The MIT Press.

Hacker, K. L., & Morgan, E. L. (2011). Issues of digital disempowerment and new media networking (NMN) in relation to e-government. In *Information Communication Technologies and the Virtual Public Sphere: Impact of Network Structures on Civil Society*. Hershey, PA: IGI Global. doi:10.4018/978-1-60960-159-1.ch005

Heeks, R. (2001). Understanding e-governance for development. *Institute for Development Policy and Management*. Retrieved August 11, 2012 from http://unpan1.un.org/intradoc/groups/public/documents/NISPAcee/UNPAN015484.pdf

Heim, M. (1993). *The metaphysics of virtual reality*. Oxford, UK: Oxford University Press.

Hill, C. (2011). *Global business today*. Boston, MA: Irwin/McGraw-Hill.

Hroub, K. (2009). *Internet freedom in the Arab world: Its impact, state controls, Islamisation and the overestimation of it all*. Retrieved September 10, 2011, from www.iemed.org/anuari/2009/aarticles/a267.pdf

Huffington Post. (2010, November 24). *Facebook, Twitter and the search for peace in the Middle East*. Retrieved August 5, 2011, from http://www.huffingtonpost.com/arianna-huffington/facebook-twitter-and-the-_b_788378.html?ir=Technology

Internet World Stats. (2011). *World stats usage and population statistics*. Retrieved August 5, 2010, from http://www.internetworldstats.com/stats19.htm

Jabbra, J. (1989). *Bureaucracy and development in the Arab world*. New York, NY: E. J. Brill. doi:10.1177/002190968902400101

Jankari, R. (2009, July 23). *Morocco's information technology market expands*. *Magharebia.com*. Retrieved September 10, 2011, from http://www.magharebia.com/cocoon/awi/xhtml1/en_GB/features/awi/features/2009/07/23/feature-03

Jansen, A. (2005). *Assessing e-government progress– Why and what*. Retrieved August 12, 2012 from http://www.afin.uio.no/om_enheten/folk/ansatte/jansen.html

Karlekar, K. D., & Marchant, E. (2009). *Freedom of the press 2008: A global survey of media independence*. New York, NY: Freedom House.

King, S. J. (2011). *The constitutional monarchy option in Morocco and Bahrain*. Retrieved August 18, 2012 from http://www.mei.edu/sites/default/files/publications/King_0.pdf

King, S. J. (2011). The constitutional monarchy option in Morocco and Bahrain. *Middle East Institute 2011*. Retrieved August 5, 2012, from http://www.mei.edu/sites/default/files/publications/King_0.pdf

Koranteng, J. (1997). Saudi ban on dishes doesn't stop viewing. *Advertising Age International, 16.*

Kraidy, M. (2002). Arab satellite television between regionalization and globalization. *Global Media Journal, 1*(1). Retrieved August 5, 2011, from http://lass.calumet. purdue.edu/cca/gmj/fa02/gmj-fa02-kraidy.htm

Kraidy, M. (2010). *Reality television and Arab politics: Contention in public life.* Cambridge, UK: Cambridge University Press.

Kraidy, M., & Khalil, J. F. (2009). *Arab television industries.* Basingstoke, UK: Palgrave Macmillan.

Lavine, H., Sweeney, D., & Wagner, S. H. (1999). Depicting women as sex objects in television advertising: Effects on body dissatisfaction. *Personality and Social Psychology Bulletin, 25*(8), 1049–1058. doi:10.1177/01461672992511012

London School of Economics Centre for Civil Society. (2004). *What is civil society?* Retrieved from http://www.lse.ac.uk/collections/CCS/what_is_civil_society.htm

Luck, E., & Mathews, S. (2010). What advertisers need to know about the iygeneration: An Australian perspective. *Journal of Promotion Management, 16,* 134–147. doi:10.1080/10496490903574559

Lueg, J. E., & Finney, R. Z. (2007). Interpersonal communication in the consumer socialization process: Scale development and validation. *Journal of Marketing Theory and Practice, 15*(1), 25–39. doi:10.2753/MTP1069-6679150102

McTighe, K. (2011, May 11). Moroccan youth demands action, not words. *The New York Times.* Retrieved September 10, 2011, from http://www.nytimes.com/2011/05/12/ world/middleeast/ 12iht-M12-MOROCCO-MOVEMENT.html?pagewanted=all

Mekay, E. (2011, February 23). One Libyan battle is fought in social and news media. *The New York Times.* Retrieved September 10, 2011, from http://www.nytimes. com/2011/02/24/world/middleeast/24iht-m24libya.html?_r=1

Moroccan Ministry of Industry, Trade, and New Technologies. (2010, June 21). *Digital Morocco 2013.* Retrieved September 10, 2011, from www.egov.ma/SiteCollectionDocuments/Morocco%20Digital.pdf

Morozov, E. (2009, June 17). Iran elections: A Twitter revolution? *The Washington Post.* Retrieved August 5, 2010, from http://www.washingtonpost.com/wp-dyn/ content/discussion/2009/06/17/DI20090

Nielsen Company. (2010). *Global audience spends two hours more a month on social networks than last year*. Retrieved August 5, 2011, from http://blog.nielsen. com/nielsenwire/global/ global-audience-spends-two-hours-more-a-month-on-social-networks-than-last-year/

News, B. B. C. (2007, February 22). Egypt blogger jailed for 'insult'. *BBC News*. Retrieved August 5, 2011, from http://news.bbc.co.uk/2/hi/6385849.stm

News, B. B. C. (2011, June 27). Profile: Muammar Gaddafi. *BBC News*. Retrieved September 10, 2011, from http://www.bbc.co.uk/news/world-africa-12488278

Niblock, T. (2001). *Pariah states and sanctions in the Middle East: Iraq, Libya, Sudan*. Boulder, CO: Lynne Rienner Publishers.

Nie, N., & Lutz, E. (2000). Internet and society: A preliminary report. *Stanford University*. Retrieved August 5, 2011, from http://www.bsos.umd.edu/socy/alan/webuse/handouts/Nie%20and%20Erbring-Internet%20and%20Society%20a%20Preliminary%20Report.pdf

North, D. C. (2005). *Understanding the process of economic change*. Princeton, NJ: Princeton University Press.

Olwan, R. (2011, February 11). *UAE has highest mobile penetration in GCC*. Retrieved August 5, 2011, from http://www.olwan.org/index.php?option=com_content&view=article&id=80%3Auae-has-highest-mobile-penetration-in-gcc-&Itemid=210

Open Arab Internet. (2011). Facts and numbers. *Open Arab Internet*. Retrieved September 10, 2011, from http://old.openarab.net/en/node/1614

OpenNet Initiative. (2009, August 6). Morocco | OpenNet initiative. *OpenNet Initiative*. Retrieved September 10, 2011, from http://opennet.net/research/profiles/morocco

Perthes, V. (2004). *Arab elites: Negotiating the politics of change*. Boulder, CO: Lynne Rienner Publishers.

Press Reference. (2011). *Morocco press, media, TV, radio, newspapers*. Retrieved September 10, 2011, from http://www.pressreference.com/Ma-No/Morocco.html

Raman, V. V. (2011). Habermas, networks and virtual public spheres: A blended deliberative model from developing countries. In *Information Communication Technologies and the Virtual Public Sphere: Impact of Network Structures on Civil Society*. Hershey, PA: IGI Global. doi:10.4018/978-1-60960-159-1.ch004

Reporters without Borders. (2010, October 20). *Europe falls from its pedestal, no respite in the dictatorships: 2010 world press freedom index*. Retrieved September 10, 2011, from www.rsf.org/IMG/CLASSEMENT_2011/GB/C_GENERAL_GB.pdf

Reporters without Borders. (2011). Countries under surveillance: Bahraïn. *Reporters without Borders*. Retrieved September 10, 2011, from http://en.rsf.org/surveillance-bahrain,39748.html

Sakr, N. (2001). *Satellite realms: Transnational television, globalization and the Middle East*. New York, NY: Tauris.

Sakr, N. (2007). *Arab media and political renewal community, legitimacy and public life*. London, UK: Tauris.

Schemm, P. (2012). *Morocco*: *Islamist justice and development party leads government*. Retrieved August 18, 2012 from http://www.huffingtonpost.com/2012/01/03/morocco-islamist-justice-and-development_n_1181086.html

Socialbakers. (2011a). Morocco Facebook statistics, penetration, demography. *Socialbakers*. Retrieved September 10, 2011, from http://www.socialbakers.com/facebook-statistics/morocco

Socialbakers. (2011b). Egypt Facebook statistics, penetration, demography. *Socialbakers*. Retrieved September 10, 2011, from http://www.socialbakers.com/facebook-statistics/egypt

Thomas, J. B., Peters, C. O., & Tolson, H. (2007). An exploratory investigation of the virtual community myspace.com: What are consumers saying about fashion? *Journal of Fashion Marketing and Management, 11*(4), 587–603. doi:10.1108/13612020710824625

Thorne, J. (2009, August 6). Moroccan dissent alive on Twitter. *The National*. Retrieved September 10, 2011, from http://www.thenational.ae/news/worldwide/africa/moroccan-dissent-alive-on-twitter

Trading Media. (2010). *The evolution of mobile phones in Saudi Arabia (present & future)*. Retrieved August 5, 2010, from http://bayazidt.wordpress.com/com-546-papers/ the-evolution-of-mobile-phones-in-saudi-arabia-present-future/

Trust Metrics. (2011). *Online advertising, blogging, and social networking growing in the Arab world*. Retrieved August 5, 2010, from http://trustmetrics.com/blog/2011/04/online-advertising-blogging-and-social-networking-growing-in-the-arab-world/

Tryhorn, C. (2009, March 2). Mobile phone use passes milestone as UN report reveals global growth. *The Guardian*. Retrieved August 5, 2011, from http://www.guardian.co.uk/technology/2009/mar/03/mobile-phones1

Twitter. (2011). *Twitter is the best way to discover what's new in your world*. Retrieved August 5, 2010, from http://twitter.com/about

Vandewalle, D. J. (2008). *Libya since 1969: Qadhafi's revolution revisited*. New York, NY: Palgrave Macmillan.

Wheeler, D. (2004*). The internet in the Arab world: Digital divides and cultural connections*. Retrieved August 5, 2010, from http://www.riifs.org/guest/lecture_text/Internet_n_arabworld_all_txt.htm

ENDNOTES

[1]	A Moroccan youth movement that initiated and led calls for pro-democracy protests on February 9, 2011.

Chapter 5
Web 2.0 Goes Mobile:
Motivations and Barriers of Mobile Social Networks Use in Spain

Carla Ruiz-Mafé
University of Valencia, Spain

Silvia Sanz-Blas
University of Valencia, Spain

José Martí-Parreño
European University of Madrid, Spain

EXECUTIVE SUMMARY

Mobile social networking sites have become one of the fastest growing Web 2.0 services worldwide both in developing and developed countries and have a major interest for the information systems research community. This chapter aims to give managers and students insight into the mobile social networking industry and the different drivers and barriers to mobile social networking sites adoption. The chapter's specific goals are to: (i) Identify consumer segments more likely to adopt mobile social networking services; (ii) Analyze the perceived benefits and barriers that encourage/discourage the adoption of mobile social networking services; (iii) Provide empirical research on the Spanish market that analyses the influence of uses and gratifications in attitude and usage behavior of mobile social networks; (iv) Provide future trends on the mobile social networking services industry and use the study's findings to develop strategies for managers of developing countries on how to maximize the rate of mobile social networking adoption.

DOI: 10.4018/978-1-4666-2515-0.ch005

The chapter is divided into three parts. In the first section, the authors include the literature review on key drivers of consumer adoption of mobile social networks and present a conceptual model, focusing on the rationale of the constructs used. In the second part, methodology design using a sample of 220 Spanish teenagers is presented and validated. Finally, the results are presented and implications for developing countries are discussed.

INTRODUCTION

Social networking sites (SNS) provide services that allow people with common interests to create their communities online. These services offer functions for contact and information exchange among users, which include sharing photos or videos, personal blogs, group discussion, real-time messaging or e-mails, thereby enhancing social interaction (Hsiao, 2011; Wang et al., 2010). With social networks, consumers can access not only the opinions of close friends, relatives and work colleagues but also those of anyone in the world who has used a given product or service.

Social networking sites (SNS) have become one of the fastest growing Web 2.0 services worldwide both in developing and developed countries (Boyd and Ellison, 2007). By way of illustration, Facebook which began in early 2004 as a Harvard-only SNS, expanded later to include high school students, professionals in side corporate networks and everyone and reached over 600 million users at the beginning of 2011, which accounts for nearly 10% of the world population. The economic impact of SNSs on economic markets is also increasing, i.e. Facebook's market value has been set at about 50 billion dollars with a forecast of one billion users by 2012 (ABC, 2011). SNS have grown differently in different countries, while initially MySpace attracted the majority of media attention in the U.S. and abroad, other SNSs were proliferating and growing in popularity worldwide. Friendster gained attraction in the Pacific Islands while Orkut became the premier SNS in developing countries such as Brazil and India (Madhavan, 2007), Mixi attained widespread adoption in Japan, LunarStormtook off in Sweden, Dutch users embraced Hyves, Grono captured Poland, Hi5 was adopted in smaller countries in Latin America, South America, and Europe, and Bebo became very popular in the United Kingdom, New Zealand, and Australia. Additionally, other communication services began implementing SNS features. The Chinese QQ instant messaging service became the largest SNS worldwide when it added profiles and made friends visible (McLeod, 2006), while the forum tool Cyworld cornered the Korean market by introducing home pages and buddies (Ewers, 2006). Although SNSs like QQ, Orkut, and Live Spaces are just as large as, if not larger than, MySpace, they receive little coverage in U.S. and English-speaking media, making it difficult to track their trajectories.

The benefits of social network use extend not only to participants but also to companies that, through the comments left on the sites, can find out about the tastes, desires and needs of the users of these networks, their consumption behavior, the levels of satisfaction/dissatisfaction with the products and services purchased or used (Casaló et al., 2008; Royo and Casamassima, 2011). Mobile social networking sites are also a way of developing closer relations with customers and encouraging satisfaction and brand loyalty. Research made by Okazaki (2012) in Japan showed that SNS engagement influences on positive word of mouth on mobile social networking.

We can state that smartphones – enhanced mobile phones devices that allow consumers accessing to data services like email, games, videos or mobile applications through Mobile Internet- are playing a strategic role in accessing Web 2.0 applications such as social networking sites. Kaplan (2012) define mobile social media as a group of mobile marketing applications that allow the creation and exchange of user-generated content. The audience for mobile social networking in the EU5 region (France, Germany, Italy, Spain and UK) grew 44 percent last year with 55.1 million mobile users in the EU5 accessing social networking sites or blogs via their mobile devices in September 2011 (Comscore, 2011). The same is true for developing areas such as Africa where mobile social networking sites access is growing at very high rates (Opera, 2008). Mobile phones increase the availability, frequency and speed of communication (Scharl et al., 2005). The ubiquity of mobile communications - anytime, everywhere- can encourage marketers to use social networks in their advertising campaigns. From a consumer's perspective the unique characteristics of mobile phones, such as ubiquity, increase the likelihood of using social networks because now the consumer can access his profile and functionalities of the network – chat, pictures and video uploading, tagging, and so on- anytime, anywhere.

This chapter is focused in the Spanish market. Spain has been chosen because despite its medium B2C Internet adoption rate, the percentage of mobile social networking users is noteworthy. This case of study can be used as a reference framework comparison with developing countries because of their mobile penetration rates are higher than and PCs and laptops as well as social network suscribers. It should be noted that in Spain, the social networking phenomenon attracts 84% of Spanish Internet users and is present in the daily activity of many Internet users with 61% of them claiming to consult such sites every day in 2010 (AIMC, 2011). Facebook (75% penetration) is the most popular social networking site in Spain followed by Tuenti (33% penetration) and Twitter (25% penetration) (Ocionetworks, 2011). SNSs are becoming increasingly popular among young users. As stated in Sánchez and Álvaro (2011) more than 79 per cent of adolescents in Spain have joined these SNSs, and 40 per cent of them visit the sites daily. According to Socialbakers (April, 2012), Facebook's student audience skews towards younger Internet users: 58% are 34 or younger, while only 6% are 55 or older. Smartphones are playing an increasing role as a platform to access these social media in Spain. So 23.1% of Internet users accessed social media through mobile phones in 2010 representing a 272% increase of such activity in the period 2009-2010 and a 320% increase if we focus on younger audiences. Mobile social media users play an active role accessing their online profiles on a daily (44%) or a weekly basis (79%) (Zenithmedia, 2011). These users represent a new consumer who is not just exposed to advertising but also listening, talking, recommending and influencing other consumers about brands, products and services.

There is no doubt that the Spanish mobile phone market has enormous potential and is moving towards a new business model where users can enjoy a wide variety of services like social networking sites with a growing level of signification. In this context, mobile Internet navigation has a high potential determined by the low participation of people who connect to Internet through this type of equipment (23%), despite the flexibility this service provides. That is why it is very important to understand the key drivers of mobile social networking adoption.

Social networks, as advanced Web 2.0 applications, have become a major interest for the information systems research community (Shin, 2010). Prior studies emphasizes that attitude to use is a key factor in analysis of technology adoption behavior (Davis et al., 1989; Kuo and Yeng, 2009; Liao et al., 2007; Lu et al., 2009). Furthermore, perceived risk has been identified as a significant predictor of consumer predisposition towards the use of mobile Internet services (Cheong and Park, 2005; Luarn and Lin, 2005; Ruiz et al., 2009) as the risk associated to possible losses stemming from use is greater than in traditional environments. Consequently, it is fundamental for managers to know about the barriers to mobile social network acceptance with a view to developing strategies that enable increased use and recommendation to other consumers.

In contrast to the possible drawbacks, participation in social networks has many advantages with regard to covering entertainment, sociability and status needs. Studies on social network use motivations are based on Uses and gratifications Theory (Anderson and Meyer, 1975; Katz et al., 1974; Krotz and Eastman, 1999; Mcquail, 1995; Rubin, 1979). This theory has been considered as one of the most influential in the study of mass media since, unlike other approaches or theories; it has enabled better understanding of the needs covered by the content of the communication and the gratifications for mass media audiences, including the mobile audience.

Even though the literature on the adoption and the use of Web 2.0 is quite extensive, few studies have explored the factors influencing consumer behavior towards mobile social networks. This study offers an insight into mobile social networking in Spain, which has not previously been investigated.

It should also be noted that few studies have been carried out on young adolescents. Various studies state that young consumers are the greatest technophiles, the first to adopt mobile services and to make more active use of the mobile phone (Conecta, 2011; Zenith Media, 2011). Many studies regard these young people as digital natives because technology is an essential determinant of who they are and what they are like (Conecta, 2011). We also focused our research on teenagers because mobile phones are essential to many youth lifestyles and it has been noted that the improved capabilities of mobile phones as personal and portable multi-media devices have led mobile phones to become indispensable to young consumers, attracting marketers' attention (Grant and O'Donohoe, 2007). Mobile phones have become integrated into young people's everyday lives and are used to connect and synchronise peer networks (Oksman and Raitiainen, 2001; Skog, 2002). Being connected anytime, anywhere through mobile social networks can be seen as a great opportunity for marketers as mobile communications create new opportunities for marketers to advertise, build, and develop customer relationships, and receive direct response from customers (Soroa-Koury and Yang, 2010). As teenagers use mobile phones extensively they are expected to be the future focus of a great deal of mobile advertising campaigns on social networks due to their changing consumer behavior and media habits (Waldt et al., 2009).

In this chapter we define mobile social networking services as "social networking where one or more individuals who share similar interests or commonalities, are conversing and connecting with one another using the mobile phone".

The chapter aims to present an in-depth study of the motivators and barriers influencing mobile social networking services adoption. The chapter's specific goals are to:

1.   Identify consumer segments more likely to adopt mobile social networking services.
2.   Analyse the perceived benefits and barriers that encourage/discourage the adoption of mobile social networking services.
3.   Provide empirical research on the Spanish market that analyses the influence of uses and gratifications in: (i) attitude towards mobile social networking services and (ii) frequency of use of mobile social networks.
4.   Provide future trends on the mobile social networking services industry and use the study's findings to develop strategies for managers of developing countries on how to maximize the rate of mobile social networking adoption.

The chapter is divided into three parts. In the first section, we include the literature review on key drivers of consumer adoption of mobile social networks and we present a conceptual model, focusing on the rationale of the constructs used. In the second part, methodology design, sample and measures are presented and validated. Finally, the results are presented and implications for developing countries are discussed.

BACKGROUND: FACTORS INFLUENCING CONSUMER ADOPTION OF MOBILE SOCIAL NETWORKS

Past research has identified à number of consumer personal factors predetermining electronic services adoption by consumers. This section shows a description of the impact of demographics, attitude towards online networking services, perceived benefits (uses and gratifications) and barriers (perceived ease-of-use, lack of usefulness and perceived monetary cost) on mobile social networking services use.

Demographics

In the sphere of virtual environments men and women behave differently. It has been detected that men and women have different website use motivations, giving rise to different online use behavior (Citrin et al., 2003; Dholakia and Uusitalo, 2002). Socio-cultural pressure has made men generally more independent in their purchase decisions, whereas women place greater value on personal contact and social relations (Citrin et al, 2003). Society traditionally has fostered interdependence in social relationships between women, whereas men have been encouraged to develop individualism, even though this has meant they have had to suppress their affective and relational needs. These schemes of interdependence and separation influence not only the individual's personality but also his or her attitude and service use behaviour (Sánchez-Franco et al., 2009).

Men's motivations are usually mainly utilitarian (result orientated), whereas women's motivations are hedonic (process orientated) (Yang and Lee, 2010). Men's motivations, in general, show a greater degree of extrinsic orientation and their perception of the value of the process is based on the effects of its operation. Women perceive themselves as being less skilled in the use of new technologies, with lower levels of personal effectiveness/efficiency. This means they show greater levels of risk and experience greater stress and anxiety when using the system (Im et al., 2008). Furthermore, women, in general, make an exhaustive analysis of the information before using electronic services. Men analyse less information, avoiding peripheral indicators such as credibility and the attractiveness of the source or positive expectations about the future behavior of the online service provider (Sánchez-Franco et al., 2009). By way of illustration, in Spain, men access business, banks and sports mobile wap sites – utilitarian motivation- while women prefer social networking sites and video delivering services – hedonic motivation- (TNS, 2011). So it is of academic interest to study differences between men and women's attitudes and motivations when using mobile social networking sites.

Previous research carried out in developing countries shows gender influences on online services usage behavior (Shen et al., 2010; Sanz et al., 2011). Sanz et al.

(2011) show gender influences on Mexican consumers commitment towards tourism services. Research by Shen et al. (2010) highlighted important differences in SNS usage among Chinese consumers regarding gender. Their results demonstrated that the effects of attitude and positive emotions, on usage intention were more important for men, whereas the effects of social identity and negative emotions were more significant for women to collectively participate in social network-facilitated team collaboration.

Attitude

Attitude is an individual's positive or negative evaluation of a given object or behavior (Ajzen, 1991) and includes feelings or affective responses. It refers to the individual's general willingness to engage in a given behavior. This attitude is the result of individual beliefs concerning the behavior, the results of that behavior and the importance attached to such beliefs. Attitudes towards mobile applications and use of them to access social networks are not only the result of beliefs concerning the behavior, but are also determined by other variables that act on the individual-medium relationship such as use motivations, the opinions of other users or experience (Baron, 2006; Nysveen et al., 2005 a,b).

Social psychology literature clearly suggests that attitude has two components: affective and cognitive (Bagozzi and Burnkrant, 1985; Chaiken and Stangor, 1987; McGuire, 1985; Weiss and Cropanzano, 1996). The affective component in attitude refers to how much the person likes the object of his thoughts (McGuire, 1985) and measures the degree of emotional attraction to the object. The cognitive component refers to the individual's specific beliefs about the object (Bagozzi and Burnkrant, 1985) and consists in a value-based assessment, judgment, reception or perception of the object (Chaiken and Stangor, 1987). The cognitive dimension of attitude directly influences the individual's use and adoption of information systems, whereas the affective dimension has to be treated as a result variable in itself.

Perceived Benefits: Uses and Gratifications

Mobile social networks offer consumers a set of benefits which favour adoption, including: entertainment, socialization and to improve user's status. These motivations can be studied in the framework of Uses and gratifications Theory (Katz et al., 1974; McQuail, 1995). Uses and gratifications Theory enables examination of the medium's functions from the consumer perspective to discover what the medium is used for (McQuail, 1995) and, therefore, what needs and desires it is able to meet (Anderson and Meyer, 1975). The basic premise of this approach then, is that individuals expose themselves to the medium to satisfy a set of needs that motivate the audience to actively seek, in that medium, gratification of their specific needs (Anderson and Meyer, 1975; Katz et al., 1974).

Despite furthering study of communication media, this approach initially had a series of problems or limitations (Anderson and Meyer, 1975) since: (i) the conceptual framework was not fully defined and could even include more than one discipline (ii) the main concepts and terms lacked precision; (iii) the audience was considered an active user of the medium (always seeking an objective or a need); (iv) it did not take into account the possible conditioning factors of the environment and personal and/or social factors. These problems or limitations have been gradually overcome and the approach has become one of the most influential theories in the study of communication.

The uses and gratifications theory seeks to understand audience media uses in light of their social and psychological needs (Rubin, 1984). In its early stages, the Uses and gratifications Theory was applied to various mass media such as the press, radio or television (Rubin, 1984). It has recently been applied to interactive media such as Internet (Eighmey, 1997; Eighmey and McCord, 1998; Rafaeli, 1986; Parker and Plank, 2000; Roy, 2009; Stafford et al., 2004) and mobile phones (Leung and Wei, 2000; Ozcan and Kocak, 2003; Wei et al., 2010).

According to Katz et al. (1974), by consuming messages, receivers seek to satisfy four types of needs: (i) social and personal integration related to reinforcing the features of their personality and their personal relations; (ii) evasion or escape in relation to the desire for fun and entertainment; (iii) cognitive needs associated with satisfying information needs and (iv) affective-aesthetic needs, related to reinforcing emotional and pleasure experiences.

Focusing on the area of Internet, Stafford et al. (2004) identify three types of gratifications perceived by the audience: (i) content gratifications (provided by content: entertainment, information, etc...); (ii) gratifications associated to the process (navigation, experience with a new technology, etc...); and (iii) social gratifications (interpersonal communication and belonging to a social network). Rafaeli (1986) identifies a set of use motivations for online university bulletins associated with entertainment, recreation and fun. Subsequently, Eighmey (1997) and Eighmey and McCord (1998) studied commercial websites and identified the greatest navigation motivations as being personal importance, involvement with the information and value of the entertainment. Parker and Plank (2000) identified the need for company and socialisation, the need to learn and the need for relaxation and fun. Roy (2009) identifies six Internet use motivations: personal development, exhibition, ease of use, relaxation, job opportunities and global exchange of experiences.

If we focus on Web 2.0 services usage motivations, research carried out in markets with different development level show contrasting results, maybe due to cultural reasons. Research by Lim and Palacios-Marques (2011), show Koreans use Web 2.0 services mainly for social relationships, whereas the US uses them more for conducting their tasks. The Spanish showed a balanced and high level of usage for both kinds of activities.

The telephony has been found to involve intrinsic or social uses and gratifications (such as status, keeping in touch with family, overcoming loneliness, and entertainment or escapism) and instrumental or task-oriented uses (such as scheduling, ordering, and reassurance), regardless of whether it is fixed or wireless. The study by Leung and Wei (1998) applies the Uses and gratifications Theory framework to the context of pagers and identifies an additional motivation over other studies concerning the need to be fashionable. That is why adopters of certain innovations see them as symbols of status and social identity, helping them to reinforce their belonging to a group. Social networks are both a socialisation tool and an expression of identity. Social networks enable users to share photographs, project or manage their desired self-image and keep up-to-date with the latest trends in their environment. Leung and Wei (2000) further identified mobility and immediate access as two unique gratifications for mobile phone use. Furthermore, studies focusing on social networks report that members of virtual communities participate to satisfy three types of needs: (i) functional needs (to carry out certain activities), (ii) social needs (willingness to provide help and support, exchange ideas, etc...) and (iii) psychological needs (belonging to a community, membership, etc...).

Social Capital Theory can also provide a theoretical framework for the satisfaction of consumer needs in online social networks as web-based opinion platforms can be regarded as collective groups of consumers who participate by exchanging information in exchange for covering certain needs for affection, gratitude, socialisation, status etc. Users who participate in social networks can develop affective ties with other participants (Gruen et al., 2006) and this in turn influences their attitude. The exchange of information in social networks also modifies participants' attitudes (Söderlund and Rosengren, 2007). Thus, Lee et al. (2008) consider that negative comments from other users influence participants' attitudes. The study by Hsu and Lu (2004) demonstrates that social factors influence attitude towards the use of online games. Leung and Wei (1998) posit that the need to be fashionable is another motivation to use social networks.

The need for information is another important motivation to use electronic services. In a marketing context, informativeness is defined as the extent to which the advertising media provides users with resourceful and helpful information (Ko et al., 2005). In a mobile advertising context, informativeness can increase the perceived advertising value of mobile phones leading to favourable attitude formation (Bauer et al. 2005; Xu et al., 2009) and a positive attitude toward mobile advertising (Gao et al., 2010; Saadeghvaziri and Seyedjavadain, 2011). Bauer et al. (2005) found that mobile advertising messages delivering a high information value lead to a positive attitude towards mobile advertising - which in turn leads to the behavioural intention to use mobile advertising services. Tsang et al. (2004) also found informativeness positively correlated to the overall attitude toward mobile advertising.

This need for information can also be satisfied through mobile social networks particularly through the concept of ubiquity. From a Uses and gratifications framework, ubiquity has been defined as the usage flexibility of time and location of mobile phones and is a unique feature of mobile phones (Barnes and Huff, 2003). From a technological perspective, ubiquity has been conceptualized as one of the main characteristics of u-commerce, a new marketing context based on time and space transformations (Watson et al., 2002). In a mobile marketing context, ubiquity has been considered one of the main attributes of mobile marketing services, extending the time and space aspect of traditional mass media advertising (Muk, 2007; Watson et al., 2002) to deliver advertisements without limitations of time and space (Friman, 2010). Thus in a mobile social network context, ubiquity means being informed and sharing information with the network anytime, anywhere satisfying consumer needs in a time-space continuum. Bauer et al. (2005) found information needs – along with entertainment and social needs- to be a contributing factor of overall perceived usefulness of mobile marketing leading to a positive effect on attitude toward mobile marketing. Research done in developing countries like Iran (Saadeghvaziri and Hosseini, 2011) also shows informativeness as an important driver of mobile advertising services adoption.

Also according to Uses and gratifications Theory, individuals accept and interact daily with different technologies because of intrinsic and extrinsic motivations. Therefore, there is a set of consumers who use new technologies for motives other than utilitarian motives. In particular, they seek fun, escapism and spontaneity (Mathwick et al., 2002). They seek subjective, personal values that are not associated with performing a specific task (Dholakia and Uusitalo, 2002). This hedonic value increases when virtual environments stimulate consumer imagination. Research done by Chiu et al. (2011) focused on the Taiwanese market show that playfulness is critical for virtual community members' satisfaction and continuance intention. Waldt et al. (2009) also evidenced entertainment is correlated to African Young consumers' overall attitudes toward mobile advertising. These hedonic motivations have also been found when using other mobile services (Ha et al., 2007; Nysveen et al., 2005a,b; Saadeghvaziri and Hosseini, 2011). Currently, mobile phones are increasing their capability to deliver entertainment through more technological advanced devices like smartphones. These smartphones allow consumers not only download games and entertainment applications but also to play online with friends and acquaintances thereby meeting entertainment and sociability needs (chats, groups, teams). Ubiquity allows consumers to play these casual mobile social games during short times while waiting for their bus or during a coffee break. This is one of the causes that have led gaming to mainstream as any owner of a mobile phone has his own portable gaming device.

The influence of perceived entertainment on attitude towards technology use has been compared in previous studies. Nysveen et al. (2005a, b) demonstrate the influence of perceived entertainment on men's attitude to the use of mobile chat services. Ha et al. (2007) also show that perceived entertainment influences attitude towards use of interactive games.

MAIN BARRIERS TO ADOPTING MOBILE SOCIAL NETWORKS

Access to mobile social networks is an innovation and therefore, adoption depends on the profile of potential consumers, as not all consumers accept an innovation at the same moment in time. Despite the fact that use of mobile phones as a platform for accessing social networks is increasing, it does not show a comparable rate of growth to the use of online social networks. Thus although 84% of Internet users in Spain used social networks in 2010, only 23.1% of them accessed social networks through their mobile phones (Zenithmedia, 2011). Therefore, it is important to understand the barriers to the adoption of mobile social networking.

The main disadvantages of using a technology include the difficulty associated with its use and the lack of perceived usefulness. These consumer beliefs have been identified as significant predictors of the decision to use mobile services in developing countries such as Colombia (Ruiz et al., 2010).

Lack of Perceived Ease-of-Use

Perceived difficulty of use is defined as the degree to which the user expects that use of the technology will require effort (Davis et al. 1989). In the context of mobile social networking, this perceived difficulty is conceptualized as users' perception of their lack of knowledge about using their mobile phone to access the social network and whether access is difficult or impossible (for example due to the technological limitations of their mobile device). The effect of the perceived difficulty of use in the attitude is caused through two mechanisms: self-efficiency and instrumentality (Davis et al., 1989) thus the more complicated the interaction, the lower the sensation of personal effectiveness and control.

Perceived Usefulness

Perceived usefulness has been defined as consumer perception that the use of the technology in question will improve performance. In the context of our research it refers to "the perception that the use of the mobile phone as a platform for accessing social networks will improve user's performance". Both perceived difficulty of use and perceived usefulness exercise a joint influence on intention to use mobile services through attitude and in the case of perceived usefulness also directly influence intention (Davis et al., 1989). The relationship between perceived usefulness and attitude is justified by "expectation-value" models (Fishbein and Ajzen, 1975), so that attitude towards a behavior depends on the expected result. Consequently, consumer beliefs can be a barrier on the use of mobile social networks due to their influence on attitude towards such networks.

Perceived Financial Risk (Monetary Cost)

The concept of perceived risk suggests that consumer behavior involves a risk because the consumer cannot completely foresee the consequences of his or her behavior and those consequences may be disagreeable (Bauer, 1960). According to Forsythe and Shi (2003), the perceived risk of online shopping is the Internet user's expectation of loss in a given electronic transaction. Therefore, the perceived risk for the mobile social network user can be defined as the expectation of loss in the pursuit of a desired outcome from using mobile social networking services. Several studies have considered perceived risk as a multidimensional construct that subdivides into several losses or risk factors, which together, explain the overall risk associated with the use of a service. This paper focuses on the financial risk dimension as it has been cited as a major obstacle to the adoption of electronic services (Forsythe and Shi, 2003; Lee et al., 2005; Haneefa and Sumitha, 2011).

Financial risk is the potential monetary outlay associated with the initial purchase price as well as the subsequent maintenance cost of the product. Research carried out in Korea by Cheong and Park (2005) show the cost of using M-Internet to access social networks is twofold: initial investment in the device and the subscription charge. In developing a behavioural intention, customers compare service benefit and service cost. If the cost exceeds the benefit, they do not subscribe to the service. Preliminary studies (Cheong and Park, 2005; Ruiz et al., 2009) show that perceived cost has a negative influence on the decision to use mobile internet services. For that reason, perceived risk is expected to be a barrier on the use of the mobile as a platform for accessing social networks.

The conceptual model of mobile social networking adoption which will be contrasted in the Spanish market (see Figure 1) is an outcome of the literature review presented above.

Figure 1. Conceptual model

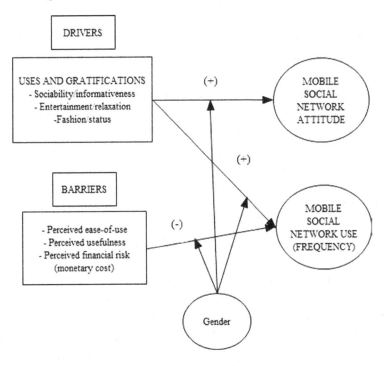

Our conceptual model integrates the main drivers and barriers influencing mobile social networks consumer behavior (consumer attitude and usage behaviour). If we focus on consumer drivers, mobile social networks provide entertainment, sociability and status gratifications that improve consumers' attitude towards them and boost consumers' use. Regarding the drawbacks of mobile social networks, the monetary cost of participating and consumer beliefs about the use of this technology (lack of simplicity and usefulness) have been identified as barriers that discourage consumers from using mobile social networks.

THE CASE STUDY: MOBILE SOCIAL NETWORKS USE IN SPAIN BY SPANISH TEENAGERS

Research Questions

After identifying the motivations and barriers of mobile social networking adoption, the second part of the chapter presents an empirical study of the Spanish market. The quantitative analysis provides answers to the following research questions:

a. How do gender influence mobile social networking behaviour among Spanish teenagers?

b. Are Spanish teenagers keen on mobile social networks?

c. What gratifications/benefits do mobile social networks deliver for Spanish teenagers?

d. What is the impact of main mobile social networks gratifications (socialization, entertainment and fashion) on Spanish teenagers' attitude and decision to use mobile social networking services?

e. What are the main perceived barriers to mobile social networking services adoption for Spanish teenagers?

Methodology

Survey respondents for this study were recruited from a Spanish High School during July 2011. The survey instrument was pre-tested with 9 focus groups to examine the dynamics of mobile networking services. Participants were teenagers (all of them owned a smartphone) with different levels of familiarity with mobile data services. The qualitative research, as with previous studies focused on mobile social networking in cultural environments different to that in Spain helped us to identify Spanish consumer standards of behavior and attitudes in the adoption of this type of services. Based on the information provided by focus group meetings the questionnaire was modified and finalized. A final sample of 220 secondary school students was used, Classes and participants in the test were randomly assigned, with ages ranging from 15 to 16 years. This age range was selected because most mobile phone market studies highlight young consumers as being more technophile, more active users, and among the first to adopt mobile services (Zenith Media, 2011). Moreover, a sample of students has been used in previous research on mobile applications (Gao et al., 2010; Haneefa and Sumitha, 2011; Kamran, 2010; Ozok and Wei, 2010; Yang and Lee, 2010). The questionnaire was self-administered but a researcher supervised the process in order to answer students' doubts about the questions.

In the quantitative analysis, we firstly analyze differences between men and women. Secondly, we used linear regression to empirically contrast the model proposed in Figure 1.

Demographic characteristics of the respondents are shown in Table 1. 61.8% of the respondents are men and 38.2% are women, and the sample is equally distributed between 15 and 16-year-old users in the penultimate and final year of compulsory secondary education. Interviewees very frequently access social networks (76.5%), and a significant percentage uses the application through their mobiles (66.3%). Tuenti (96% of cases) and Facebook (70% of cases) are the respondents' preferred

Table 1. Sample characteristics

	Variables	N= 220
Gender	Male	61.8%
	Female	38.2%
Age	15 years old	50.4%
	16 years old	49.6%
Social Network access	Facebook	70%
	Myspace	14.6%
	Tuenti	96%
	Twtter	24%
	Xing	2.7%
	Linkedin	2.1%
Frequency of network access	Very often	76.5%
	Quite often	17.1%
	Not very often	3.2%
	Hardly ever	3.2%
Mobile social network	I access	66.3%
	I don't access	33.7%

social networks (see Table 1), unlike most emerging Latin American countries where Facebook is the social network most frequently used by adolescents (Sánchez and Álvaro, 2011).

RESULTS

Attitudes towards Mobile Social Networks Use

Of the total respondents who use social networks through their mobile devices (146 individuals), 54.4% are men and 45.6% are women (see Table 2). In general, the interviewees show a very positive attitude towards the use of the mobile as a platform for accessing social networks (4.2 out of 5), although women like mobile access more than men (4.50 vs 4.05), and also consider it a good idea (4.59 vs 4.05), more interesting (4.34 vs 4.03), and more positive (4.28 vs 3.88).

Women show a more positive attitude towards mobile use for accessing their social network profile. Significant differences have been identified between men and women in relation to the activities engaged in during mobile social network access: reading and writing comments, uploading photos and videos and accessing

Table 2. Descriptive analysis of mobile social network users

		Mobile social network users (N= 146)				
		Average N= 146	Global average	MALE N= 79	FEMALE N= 67	Sig* Differences
Mobile social network attidtude	I like it	4.29	4.2	4.08	4.50	1268,000 (,079)
	I think it is interesting	4.17		4.05	4.34	
	I think it is a good idea	4.30		4.05	4.59	
	I think it is a positive thing	4.04		3.88	4.28	
Activities	Writing comments	3.84		3.51	4.30	1117.000 (.003)
	Reading comments	3.99		3.66	4.34	1200.500 (.012)
	Uploading photos	2.88		2.69	3.25	1276.000 (.051)
	Uploading videos	2.15		2.40	1.90	1286.000 (.046)
	Taking part in surveys	1.68		1.76	1.61	1611.500 (.997)
	Taking part in competitions and draws	1.80		1.92	1.69	1535.000 (.601)
	Looking for friends, acquaintances, classmates, etc.	3.07		3.08	3.15	1574.500 (.826)
	Searching for information (events, prices)	2.30		2.24	2.42	1488.000 (.460)
	Chatting	4.19		4.08	4.30	1430.000 (.241)
	Accessing the profiles of friends, acquaintances and work/class mates	3.84		3.66	4.15	1284.500 (.048)

* p<.01

the profiles of friends, acquaintances and study and work colleagues. Women show higher average values to men in relation to mobile network use for reading and writing comments (4.34 and 4.30 vs 3.66 and 3.51), uploading photos and accessing other profiles (3.25 and 4.15 vs 2.69 and 3.66). The non parametric Mann-Whitney test (see Table 2) confirms this result, identifying significant differences in all the aforementioned variables. These results show that women are more active and more curious than men when they access and use social networking sites.

No significant differences were found in the other activities analyzed, which show very similar values in both collectives. The results suggest that neither men nor women use mobile social networks to take part in surveys, competitions, draws or to seek information on events and prices. Mobile social networks are mainly used to chat with friends and acquaintances.

These results highlight the fact that for women the mobile is an important device in their lives that enables them, through access to social networks to exchange and share information and maintain social relationships with others anytime, anywhere.

Usage Motivations

To measure mobile social networks usage motivations, interviewees were asked to score the importance they attached to each of the motivations on a 5 point Likert where 1 equals "not important at all" and 5 "very important". Table 3 shows the average importance attached to each motivation. The 17 use motivations items were taken from the literature on the subject, based mainly on the works by Leung and Wei (2000) and Ozcan and Kocak (2003) on the uses and gratifications of mobile phone use, and on the works by Grant and O´Donohoe (2007) and Wei et al., (2010) studying the uses and gratifications of SMS use.

Table 3. Motivations for mobile social network use

Use motivations	Average (N=146)
1. To escape boredom	4.02
2. To contact/chat with my friends/acquaintances/relations	4.61
3. To notify, update friends/acquaintances/relations with the latest news	4.00
4. To pass the time	4.17
5. For entertainment	4.28
6. For fun	4.22
7. For relaxation	3.80
8. To maintain or improve relations with friends/acquaintances/relations	4.10
9. To feel closer, more involved in the lives of friends/acquaintances/relations	3.64
10. To keep in touch with people I don't see very often	4.44
11. So that others know that I care about them	3.25
12. To be always available for people who care about me	3.54
13. To greet friends/acquaintances/relations	4.10
14. To get to know new people	3.01
15. To be fashionable	2.50
16. To look stylish	2.26
17. To be up-to-date with the latest fashion	2.25

Table 3 shows that users access mobile social networks for hedonic and utilitarian motivations. This finding is consistent with studies in countries with different degrees of development such as Japan, USA, Taiwan and Korea (Lim and Palacios-Marques, 2011; Shang et al., 2011; Okazaki and Yagüe, 2012). Thus access to mobile social networking allows them to escape boredom (4.02), pass the time (4.17), entertain themselves (4.28) and have fun (4.22) and also keep in touch (4.44), chat to (4.61), greet (4.10), inform, maintain or improve relations with the people they are closest to and people they do not see very often (4.10). Therefore users find entertainment and social motivations in mobile social networking and thus reinforce social relationships with people around them.

However, they do not agree that they access mobile networking to be fashionable (2.50) or look stylish (2.26). Therefore there are no fashionable/status motivations for mobile social networking (2.25).

FACTORS INFLUENCING ATTITUDES TOWARDS MOBILE SOCIAL NETWORKS USAGE

The dimensions underlying the scale of mobile social network use motivations were identified by running a principal components factor analysis, after the appropriate tests to ensure that the data could be subjected to this type of analysis (see Table 4). Scale reliability was checked first, with the following results: (1) there was no need to eliminate items (2) Cronbach's alpha was 0.88.

After applying factor analysis to the set of 17 variables 3 factors were obtained which explain 61.5% of the variance. The condition required to retain a factor is that its eigen value be greater than 1. The composition of the factors is shown in Table 5, having assigned the variables to the factors with loading over 0.5 (following Hair et al., 1999).

The first factor, called relax/entertainment, explains 21.95% of the variance and comprises the variables: escape boredom; pass the time; entertain myself; have fun and relax.

Tabla 4. KMO and Bartlett's test

Kaiser-Meyer-Olkin measure of sampling adequacy	0.797
Correlation matrix determinant	0.0004
Bartlett's sphericity test	693.308
G.l.	136
Sig.	0.000

Table 5. Data on the rotated factor matrix for the three main factors

Study variables	Factor 1	Factor 2	Factor 3
1. To escape boredom	0,655		
2. To contact/chat with my friends/acquaintances/relations		0,87	
3. To notify, update friends/acquaintances/relations with the latest news		0,537	
4. To pass the time	0,724		
5. For entertainment	0,764		
6. For fun	0,689		
7. For relaxation	0,792		
8. To maintain or improve relations with friends/acquaintances/relations		0,561	
9. To feel closer, more involved in the lives of friends/acquaintances/relations		0,622	
10. To keep in touch with people I don't see very often		0,739	
11. So that others know that I care about them		0,637	
12. To be always available for people who care about me		0,610	
13. To greet friends/acquaintances/relations		0,740	
14. To get to know new people		0,746	
15. To be fashionable			0,791
16. To look stylish			0,819
17. To be up-to-date with the latest fashion			0,757
Cronbach's alpha for each factor	0,82	0,83	0,86

The second factor, called sociability/information, explains 21.04% of the variance and is made up of the following variables: keep in touch/chat with friends/acquaintances/relations; find out about/tell update myself/update friends/acquaintances/relations about the latest news; maintain or improve relations with friends/acquaintances/relations; feel closer to, more involved in the life of friends/acquaintances/relations; keep in touch with people I don't see very often; so others know that I care about them; be always available for the people who care about me; greet friends/acquaintances/relations; meet new people.

The third factor, with the name fashion/status, explains 18.48% of the variance and reflects the variables: be fashionable; look stylish; be up-to-date with the latest fashion.

Thus, users access mobile social networks to satisfy three types of needs: (i) functional/playfulness needs (engaging in certain activities such as uploading photos, taking part in games or sharing events) (ii) social needs (willingness to provide help and support, exchange ideas etc..) and (iii) identity needs (status symbol, belonging to a group). Thus the use of mobile social networks allows users to share photographs, project or manage desired images of them and be up to date with the latest trends in their environment.

After determining the main components or factors and having accepted the reliability of the underlying scales, their potential effects on attitude to mobile social networks was determined through multiple linear regressions (see Table 6). This analysis was carried out using the stepwise method, with attitude towards mobile social networks as dependent variable and the different factors or components previously obtained in the exploratory factor analysis as explanatory variables.

The results show (see Table 6) that two of the three factors analyzed have a positive and statistically significant effect ($p<0.05$) on attitude to the use of mobile social networks.

The factor with the greatest influence on attitude is relax/entertainment, and the second most important factor is sociability/information. The factor fashion/status was not found to be significant. These variables are largely able to explain attitude to mobile social networks use as the adjusted R^2 represents almost 50%.

The results highlight that hedonic motivations reinforce and improve individual attitudes to mobile social networks. If mobile network use is relaxing and pleasurable and provides pleasant experiences, then attitude towards their use becomes more positive.

FACTORS INFLUENCING FREQUENCY OF USE OF MOBILE SOCIAL NETWORKS

In order to analyze the effect of mobile social networks motivations on frequency of social network use, a multiple linear regression analysis was run again with frequency of mobile social networks use as the dependent variable (see Table 7).

Table 6. Regression analysis of use motivational factors to attitude to mobile social networks

Purchase motivations factors	Standardised Beta Coefficient	T Value	Sig.
Constant		3.111	0.003
Factor 1: relax/entertainment	0.361**	2.928	0.004
Factor 2: sociability/information	0.261**	2.725	0.042
Factor 3: fashion/status	0.046	0.424	0.673
R2: 0.69; adjusted R2: 0.49 Durbin Watson =1.589; F=10,473 (Signif. F = 0.000) *** = p<. 001; ** = p<. 01; * = p<. 05			

Source: Produced with SPSS v. 17.0. Stepwise regression analysis.

Table 7. Regression analysis of the use motivation factors to frequency of mobile social network use

Purchase motivations factors	Standardized Beta Coefficient	T Value	Sig.
Constant		3.816	0.000
Factor 1: relax/entertainment	0.203*	2.013	0.045
Factor 2: sociability/information	0.287*	2.493	0.014
Factor 3: fashion/status	0.049	0.501	0.617
R2: 0.35; adjusted R2: 0.29 Durbin Watson =1.939; F=8.505 (Signif. F = 0.000) *** = p<. 001; ** = p<. 01; * = p<. 05			

Source: Produced with SPSS v. 17.0. Stepwise regression analysis.

The results show again differences in the factors that are most significant for explaining frequency of mobile social networks use (see Table 7). While fashion/status motivations are irrelevant for explaining use behavior, relax/entertainment and socialization/information are important factors. In this case, socialization/information is the most relevant factor, followed by relax/entertainment. The value of adjusted R2 is not too high, which indicates that use behavior may be influenced by other factors not related to use gratifications such as personal factors and sociodemographic or attitudinal variables.

The results in this case show that utilitarian motivations lead to higher frequency use of mobile social networks. It would seem therefore that it is mainly the social component that awakes interest in ubiquitous access to the social network.

Barriers to Mobile Social Networks Adoption

If we focus on non-access motivations of teenagers who are not users of mobile social networks, it can be seen (see Table 8) that significant differences have been identified only in relation to non use of the mobile network because there is no flat rate and access is expensive. Women most often state that they do not use the service because of the associated cost. Research carried out in developing countries such as Pakistan (Kamran, 2010) also show the main barrier among youth is lack of low priced prepaid packages offered by the telecom operators.

No significant differences have been found in other motivations analyzed, as the values are very similar in both collectives. The results show that neither men nor women stop accessing mobile networks because they do not know the application, because access is difficult or because they are not interested in the service. However, both groups agree that they do not access because they do not have a data

Table 8. Descriptive analysis of non users of mobile social networks

		Non users of mobile social networks (n= 74)			
		Average N= 74	Male N= 47	Female N= 27	Sig* Differences
Non access Moti- vations	I don't know how to	1.88	2.10	1.52	306.000 (.108)
	I haven't got Internet on my mobile	3.79	3.67	4.00	331.000 (.305)
	Because it is difficult for me	2.88	2.92	2.52	334.000 (.355)
	Because I prefer to do it on the computer	3.75	3.70	3.66	364.500 (.680)
	Because I'm not interested in social networks	2.00	2.05	1.80	349.500 (.474)
	Because I can't do it on my mobile	3.10	3.16	3.14	385.500 (.960)
	Because I haven't got a flat rate and its expensive	3.69	3.40	4.38	260.500 (.024)

* $p < .05$

service on their mobile or because they prefer to access via a computer. Furthermore, they are not very sure that their mobile will permit them access to the service (see Table 8). These results suggest that both technological limitations (mobile Internet access is not possible through the device) and the limitations of the device itself (smaller screen than a computer, limited interface with smaller keys or a touch screen that does not always facilitate access to the different utilities, etc.) may be currently acting as important barriers to the adoption of mobile social networking.

CONCLUSIONS AND IMPLICATIONS FOR DEVELOPING COUNTRIES

Mobile phones have altered consumer behavior in social networks, promoting development thanks to improvements in the user interface, ubiquity (the power of the "here and now") and data flat rates. In the segment of adolescents, the mobile has become an essential element in their lives thanks to the gratifications of socialization, entertainment and information it provides them with.

In the near future, mobile devices will likely penetrate the world becoming the only means of communication that allows true global reach for customers in countries with different development levels and demographic groups. By helping social media shrug off its chains, mobile social media has the potential to bridge the gap between the virtual sphere and real life (Kaplan, 2012).

In developed countries such as Spain, Japan or the United States, the penetration of mobile phones and personal computers is just about equal, with 9 out of 10 Americans having access to both devices and with penetration rates higher than 100% in most European countries. In emerging markets such as the BRIC countries (Brazil, Russia, India, China), however, there are nearly four times as many mobile-phone subscriptions as PCs in use (1.65 billion vs. 0.43 billion). On a global scale, there are five billion mobile phone connections for 6.9 billion people, leading to an overall penetration rate of 70%. In several countries——including Hong Kong, Italy, and Germany——penetration rates exceed 100%, as many consumers own at least two mobile devices. According to the Pew Research Center, by 2020 a mobile device will be the primary Internet connection tool for most people around the world (Pew Research Center, 2012).

Companies from developing countries should turn to mobile devices if they are interested in reaching Generation Z or the Net Generation: customers born between 1990 and 2000. Teenagers are surrounded by their personal mobile devices most of the time, which makes nearly impossible to reach them through mass media. But the fact that social media have always been part of their lives——Facebook was founded in 2004, YouTube in 2005, and Twitter in 2006——makes them perfect candidates for mobile social media applications (Kaplan, 2012). Mobile social networks are likely to become the main channel of communication for most companies around the globe.

The influence of social networks in interpersonal relations and their growing use by consumers justifies the need to continue studying use behavior. Although there is now a significant body of literature on the use of social networks from a computer, there is scanty literature on their use from mobile devices. Media convergence is a reality nowadays and there is a need to know if consumers behave in the same way when a service is accessed from different platforms. The sacrifice of using a limited interface such as that of the mobile phone (as opposed to a desktop computer) can be recompensed by the immediacy and ubiquity offered by a mobile platform.

The main academic contribution of this chapter is that it will give managers and students insight into the mobile social networking industry and the different drivers and barriers to mobile social network adoption. In addition, these factors can be applied to the specific context of the Spanish market. Specifically, this study will improve managers' understanding of consumer demographics, task performed on mobile social networks, mobile social networks attitude, perceived benefits and barriers and their relation to the use of mobile social network services. The study can also contribute to further understanding of how to develop successful marketing strategies involving mobile social networks.

The results of this study show that most of the young people interviewed use social networks on a daily basis, preferably Tuenti and Facebook, and have a very positive attitude towards access from a mobile device. There is no doubt that for these young people, the mobile is more than just a means of communication, it has become part of their lives. Accessing social networks via the mobile phone strengthens users' social relations by increasing access to a platform that they access mainly to chat and to read and write comments to friends, acquaintances, relations and class/work mates. Access to these social networks from the mobile phone enables users to upload their profiles while they are on a trip or visiting a museum; they can make comments on their status and share information as it is happening; and it enables them to chat or speak to someone whenever and wherever they need to.

Relax/entertainment and social/informative are the main gratifications for teenagers to access a mobile social network, although the cost of the service is still an important barrier to access for some of these teenagers. Since these economic barriers may be even greater in developing countries, both advertisers and mobile telephony operators could consider the option of subsidizing this type of networks in order to facilitate access to as much of the population as possible. This is the case of services which have been used in the mobile phone industry for a long time (for example, free first minute of a call in exchange for listening to an advertisement before making the call. Some other brand sponsored strategies like branded content – broadly used in computer-Internet contexts- should also be explored. Consumers would partially overcome these economic limitations and advertisers would have a larger highly segmented audience with many opportunities for monetization (knowledge of the consumer, publicity, online sales, etc.). Apple, for example, has already developed its own social network, called Ping, around the world of music. It seems obvious that its aims include monetizing the network through downloads of music videos and songs from iTunes.

The importance of these motivations is also evident when analyzing their impact on attitude to the use of mobile social networks and frequency of use. Thus relax/entertainment motivations positively strengthen adolescents' attitudes towards mobile social network use. Research carried out in developing countries such as Taiwan (Chiu et al., 2011; Shang et al., 2011) also shows the influence of entertainment motivations on consumer social networking usage behavior. Socialization/information motivations are the main driver which led teenagers to access mobile social networking more frequently (daily use of the network). Socialization has been also highlighted in previous research (Lim and Daniel-Palacios, 2011) as the main motivation to access Web 2.0 services in Korea. The fact that the popular casual social game Farmville, played online through Facebook, already has a version for the mobile phone indicates the market opportunity that has been detected based on these entertainment and socialization motivations (as the game enables team playing and collaboration with friends and acquaintances). The advertising of the mobile version of the game itself highlights improved performance for players due to the fact that they can look after their farm more often at any time and place.

Implications for Developing Countries

This chapter can help managers in developing countries to develop effective strategies to attract mobile consumers and, therefore, to gain competitive advantages, taking the case of Spain as reference. Entertainment and socialization motivations detected when there are positive attitudes to mobile social networks use suggests that marketing actions should be based on entertainment and socialisation just like casual social games. These games enable brands to be included in a non intrusive way (for example, by product placement) providing important information in the context of the game. For example in the game Farmville, a user could use a given brand of fertiliser to obtain better results in a particular crop. In the educational version, governments in developing countries could use these simulations in mobile social networks to educate their citizens on a variety of matters (from agriculture to health or domestic economy) and facilitate a platform for contact and information exchange among those in the network. In particular by being directed at younger audiences, these mobile social entertainment networks can motivate and commit these publics through a device with an intrinsec attraction for them which in turn enables them to gain familiarity with collaborative online environments like those they will use when joining the labour market.

Managers in developing countries should take special care when using mobile social networks as a marketing tool because this study highlights that it is important not only to identify correctly the target public for the messages, but also to provide content with an advertising message that is suited to the motivations and needs (social and entertainment) of these users. This procedure could be applied in a developing country like India where social networking sites are developing fast and several global brands are taking advantage of the popularity of social networking sites (eMarketer, 2009). It is worth noting that in 2008 India became the world's largest market in terms of mobile phones net additions for the first time –ahead of China- with at least one-third of the population having a mobile phone (eMarketer, 2009). This growth may mean that social networking sites users could be moving rapidly to mobile access as is happening in some developing African countries like Egypt (Opera, 2008). In fact, Facebook was the second top-ten site accessed through mobile-browser Opera in India in June 2011 (Opera, 2011).

Advertising communications in mobile social networks should also be informative and so the content of the message to be transmitted in the social network must be as detailed as possible providing- where necessary- links to expand the information.

The mobile platform offers powerful tools (such as location-based services) which enable this information to be sent at the optimum time and place for the consumer.

Although the study has detected that attitudes towards mobile social networks are positive, companies must continue to strengthen them so that people continue to use them. In the case of mobile social networks, this could be achieved by strengthening perceived entertainment in the network; ensuring that the individual finds the search and information exchange process easy and working on aspects of profile design. It is important to adapt the profile to the mobile medium, making it easy to participate and locate content and comments. As well as text, images, photographs and videos must be offered to awaken users' interest and also offer them fun and entertainment. The success of a mobile application like Whatsapp is based precisely on ease of use when integrating the different contents that consumers want to share with other members of their mobile social network.

Limitations and Future Research Lines

The conclusions obtained bring up a series of limitations and make it possible to open up future lines of research.

In terms of the limitations of this study, the main limitation is the employment of a convenience sampling (students from a Spanish High School), which limits the generalization of the results obtained, although this technique has been widely used in research on mobile phone applications (Gao et al., 2010; Haneefa and Sumitha, 2011; Kamran, 2010; Ozok and Wei, 2010; Yang and Lee, 2010). As Oksman and Raitiainen (2001) and Skog (2002) suggest, teenagers are not homogeneous audiences for mobile phones. Factors such as social background, gender, urban/rural lifestyles, and technological literacy can widely vary their usage patterns and attitudes, so a main limitation of this study is that it focuses on just one homogeneous demographic group and cannot be generalized to other demographic or psychographic groups. Future research should address this limitation in order to generalize the findings of this study to a broader social group.

Another limitation is the speed of change in the area of study which restricts the validity of the results to a given moment in time, as increased experience of users with the medium affects their behavior. Also only one mobile device, the mobile phone has been analyzed. Increased use of other mobile Internet access devices, (tablets such as the iPad, for example) raises questions about how the characteristics of the type of device (for example, screen size) can affect attitude and frequency of use of social networks through the device.

As future lines of research we propose replicating the study with a sample of young adults (25-39) to compare results. It would also be interesting to propose a behavioral model that includes new personal factors of the consumer such as innovation or perceived control together with mobile social network use motivations in the intention to recommend their use to other people. At the level of marketing communications, it would be interesting to know about young adolescents' attitude and acceptance of advertising messages integrated in mobile social networks, analyzing both their antecedents (characteristics of the message) and the possible effects (opening, reading, resending). More in-depth qualitative understanding of factors is needed such as the emotions evoked by consumers when they are using this type of social network through their mobile phones and the effects these emotions have on the advertising messages received.

In order to validate these results in other socio-economic-cultural contexts it is also necessary to contrast this data with data from other developing companies or countries with emerging economies that may have particularly interesting opportunities in this new context of mobile social networks.

ACKNOWLEDGMENT

Carla Ruiz-Mafé and José Martí-Parreño acknowledge the financial support of the research project of the Valencian Regional Government (Generalitat Valenciana) (GV/2011-009).

REFERENCES

ABC. (2011). *Facebook estrena el año con otro record.* Retrieved September 20, 2011, from http://www.abc.es/20110107/medios-redes/abci-facebook-600millones-usuarios-201101071119.html

AIMC. (2011). *Navegantes en la Red. 13ª Encuesta a usuarios de Internet.* Retrieved June 20, 2011, from available in http://www.aimc.es

Ajzen, I. (1991). The theory of planned behavior. *Organizational Behavior and Human Decision Processes, 50*(2), 179–211. doi:10.1016/0749-5978(91)90020-T

Anderson, J. A., & Meyer, T. P. (1975). Functionalism and the mass media. *Journal of Broadcasting, 19*(1), 11–22. doi:10.1080/08838157509363766

Bagozzi, R. P., & Burnkrant, R. E. (1985). Attitude organization and the attitude–behavior relationship: A reply to Dillon and Kumar. *Journal of Personality and Social Psychology, 49*, 1–16. doi:10.1037/0022-3514.49.1.47

Barnes, S., & Huff, S. L. (2003). Rising Sun: i-mode and the wireless internet. *Communications of the ACM, 46*(11), 79–84.

Baron, S., Patterson, A., & Harris, K. (2006). Beyond technology acceptance: Understanding consumer practice. *International Journal of Service Industry Management, 17*(2), 111–135. doi:10.1108/09564230610656962

Bauer, H. H., Barnes, S. J., Reichardt, T., & Neumann, M. M. (2005). Driving consumer acceptance of mobile marketing: A theoretical framework and empirical study. *Journal of Electronic Commerce Research, 6*(3), 181–191.

Bauer, R. A. (1960). Consumer behavior as risk taking. In R. Hancock (Ed.), *Dynamic marketing for a changing world: Proceedings of 43rd Conference* (pp. 389-398). Chicago, IL: American Marketing Association.

Boyd, D. M., & Ellison, N. B. (2007). Social network sites: Definition, history, and scholarship. *Journal of Computer-Mediated Communication, 13*(1). Retrieved June 3, 2011, from http://jcmc.indiana.edu/vol13/issue1/boyd.ellison.html

Casaló, L., Flavián, C., & Guinalíu, M. (2011). Antecedents and consequences of consumer participation in online communities: The case of the travel sector. *International Journal of Electronic Commerce, 15*(2), 137–167. doi:10.2753/JEC1086-4415150205

Chaiken, S., & Stangor, C. (1987). Attitudes and attitude change. *Annual Review of Psychology, 38*, 575–630. doi:10.1146/annurev.ps.38.020187.003043

Chao, C. H., Wang, E., Shih, F., & Fan, Y. (2011). Understanding knowledge sharing in virtual communities. An integration of expectancy disconfirmation and justice theories. *Online Information Review, 35*(1), 134–153. doi:10.1108/14684521111113623

Cheong, J., & Park, M. C. (2005). Mobile Internet acceptance in Korea. *Internet Research, 15*(2), 125–140. doi:10.1108/10662240510590324

Citrin, A., Stern, D., Spangerberg, E., & Clark, M. (2003). Consumer need for tactile input. An Internet retailing challenge. *Journal of Business Research, 56*(11), 915–922. doi:10.1016/S0148-2963(01)00278-8

Comscore. (2011). *Mobile social networking audience grew 44 percent over past year in EU5*. Retrieved May 16, 2012, from http://www.comscore.com/Press_Events/Press_Releases/2011/11/Mobile_Social_Networking_Audience_Grew_44_Percent_Over_Past_Year_in_EU5

Conecta (2011). *6° observatorio de tendencias NOKIA: los jóvenes, los móviles y la tecnología*. Retrieved June 17, 2011, from http://www.conectarc.com/Articulos%20y%20Estudios/Highlights%206%BA%20Observatorio%20Final.pdf

Davis, F. D., Bagozzi, R. P., & Warshaw, P. R. (1989). User acceptance of computer technology: A comparison of two theoretical models. *Management Science, 35*, 982–1003. doi:10.1287/mnsc.35.8.982

Dholakia, R., & Uusitalo, O. (2002). Switching to electronic stores: Consumer characteristics and the perception of shopping benefits. *International Journal of Retail and Distribution Management, 30*(10), 459–469. doi:10.1108/09590550210445335

Eighmey, J. (1997). Profiling user responses to commercial web sites. *Journal of Advertising Research, 37*(May/June), 59–66.

Eighmey, J., & McCord, L. (1998). Adding value in the information age: Uses and gratifications of sites on the World Wide Web. *Journal of Business Research, 41*, 187–194. doi:10.1016/S0148-2963(97)00061-1

Ewers, J. (2006). Cyworld: Bigger than YouTube? *U.S. News & World Report*.

Fishbein, M., & Ajzen, I. (1975). *Belief, attitude, intention and behavior: An introduction to theory and research*. New York, NY: Addison-Wesley.

Forshyte, S., & Shi, B. (2003). Consumer patronage and risk perceptions in Internet shopping. *Journal of Business Research, 56*(11), 867–875. doi:10.1016/S0148-2963(01)00273-9

Friman, J. (2010). *Consumer attitudes toward mobile advertising*. Unpublished doctoral dissertation, Department of Marketing and Management, School of Economics, Aalto University.

Grant, I., & O'Donohoe, S. (2007). Why young consumers are not open to mobile marketing communication. *International Journal of Advertising, 26*(2), 223–246.

Gruen, T. W., Osmonbekov, T., & Czaplewski, A. J. (2006). eWOM: The impact of customer-to-customer online know-how exchange on customer value and loyalty. *Journal of Business Research, 59*, 449–456. doi:10.1016/j.jbusres.2005.10.004

Ha, I., Yoon, Y., & Choi, M. (2007). Determinants of adoption of mobile games under mobile broadband wireless access environment. *Information & Management, 44*, 276–286. doi:10.1016/j.im.2007.01.001

Hair, J. F., Anderson, R. E., Tatham, R. L., & Black, W. C. (1999). *Multivariate data analysis* (5th ed.). Englewood Cliffs, NJ: Prentice Hall.

Hsiao, J. (2010). Why internet users are willing to pay for social networking services? *Online Information Review, 35*(5), 770–788. doi:10.1108/14684521111176499

Hsu, C. H., & Lu, H. P. (2004). Why do people play on-line games? An extended TAM with social influences and flow experience. *Information & Management*, *41*(7), 853–868. doi:10.1016/j.im.2003.08.014

Im, I., Kim, Y., & Han, H. J. (2008). The effects of perceived risk and technology type on users' acceptance of technologies. *Information & Management*, *45*, 1–9. doi:10.1016/j.im.2007.03.005

ITU (International Telecommunication Union). (2011). *The world in 2011: ICT facts and figures*. Retrieved September 15, 2011, from http://www.itu.int/ITU-D/ict/material/FactsFigures2011.pdf

Kamran, S. (2010). Mobile phone: Calling and texting patterns of college in Pakistan. *International Journal of Business and Management*, *5*(4), 26–36.

Kaplan, A. (2012). If you love something, let it go mobile: Mobile marketing and mobile social media 4x4. *Business Horizons*, *55*, 129–139. doi:10.1016/j.bushor.2011.10.009

Katz, E., Blumler, J. G., & Gurevitch, M. (1974). Utilization of mass communication by the individual. In Blumler, J. G., & Katz, E. (Eds.), *The uses of mass communication: Current perspective on gratifications research* (pp. 19–34). Beverly Hills, CA: Sage.

Ko, H., Cho, C.-H., & Roberts, S. M. (2005). Internet uses and gratifications: A structural equation model of interactive advertising. *Journal of Advertising*, *34*, 57–70.

Krotz, F., & Eastman, S. T. (1999). Orientations toward television outside the home. *The Journal of Communication*, *49*(1), 5–27. doi:10.1111/j.1460-2466.1999.tb02779.x

Kuo, Y., & Yen, S. (2009). Towards an understanding of the behavioural intention to use 3G mobile value-added services. *Computers in Human Behavior*, *25*, 103–110. doi:10.1016/j.chb.2008.07.007

Lee, E., Kwon, K., & Schumann, D. (2005). Segmenting the non-adopter category in the diffusion of internet banking. *International Journal of Bank Marketing*, *23*(5), 414–437. doi:10.1108/02652320510612483

Lee, J., Park, D. H., & Han, I. (2008). The effect of negative online consumer reviews on product attitude: An information processing view. *Electronic Commerce Research and Applications*, *7*(3), 341–352. doi:10.1016/j.elerap.2007.05.004

Leung, L., & Wei, R. (1998). The gratifications of pager use: sociability, information-seeking, entertainment, usefulness and fashion and status. *Telematics and Informatics, 15*, 253–264. doi:10.1016/S0736-5853(98)00016-1

Leung, L., & Wei, R. (2000). More than just talk on the move: Uses and gratifications of the cellular phone. *Journalism & Mass Communication Quarterly, 77*(2), 308–320. doi:10.1177/107769900007700206

Liao, C., Tsou, C., & Huang, M. (2007). Factors influencing the usage of 3G mobile services in Taiwan. *Online Information Review, 31*(6), 759–774. doi:10.1108/14684520710841757

Lim, S., & Palacio-Marques, D. (2011). Culture and purpose of web 2.0 service adoption: A study in the USA, Korea and Spain. *The Service Industries Journal, 31*, 123–131. doi:10.1080/02642069.2010.485634

Lu, Y., Tao, Z., & Wang, B. (2009). Exploring Chinese users' acceptance of instant messaging using the theory of planned behavior, the technology acceptance model and the flow theory. *Computers in Human Behavior, 25*, 29–39. doi:10.1016/j.chb.2008.06.002

Luarn, P., & Lin, H. (2005). Toward an understanding of the behavioral intention to use mobile banking. *Computers in Human Behavior, 21*(6), 873–891. doi:10.1016/j.chb.2004.03.003

Madhavan, N. (2007). India gets more Net cool. *Hindustan Times*. Retrieved June 7, 2008, from http://www.hindustantimes.com/StoryPage/StoryPage.aspx?id=f2565bb8-663e-48c1-94eed99567577bdd

Mathwick, C. H., Malhotra, N., & Rigdon, E. (2002). The effect of dynamic retail experiences on experiential perceptions of value: An Internet and catalog comparison. *Journal of Retailing, 78*(1), 51–60. doi:10.1016/S0022-4359(01)00066-5

McGuire, W. J. (1985). Attitudes and attitude change. In Lindzey, G., & Aronson, E. (Eds.), *Handbook of social psychology* (*Vol. 19*, pp. 233–346). New York, NY: Random House.

McLeod, D. (2006). QQ attracting eyeballs. *Financial Mail* (South Africa). Retrieved July 30, 2007, from LexisNexis.

McQuail, D. (1995). *Mass communication theory*. Newbury Park, CA: Sage.

Muk, A. (2007). Consumer's intentions to opt in to SMS advertising. *International Journal of Advertising, 26*(2), 177–198.

Netsize. (2011). *The Netsize Guide 2010: Mobile renaissance.* Retrieved September 13, 2011, from http://www.netsize.com/Ressources_Guide.htm

Nysveen, H., Pedersen, P. E., & Thorbjornsen, H. (2005a). Explaining intention to use mobile chat services: moderating effects of gender. *Journal of Consumer Marketing, 22*(5), 247–256. doi:10.1108/07363760510611671

Nysveen, H., Pedersen, P. E., & Thorbjornsen, H. (2005b). Intentions to use mobile services: Antecedents and cross-service comparisons. *Academy of Marketing Science Journal, 33*(3), 330–346. doi:10.1177/0092070305276149

Ocio Networks. (2011). *Estudio de hábitos de Internet 2010.* Retrieved September 27, 2011, from http://www.dataprix.com/files/Informacion,%20consumo%20de%20medios%20y%20redes%20sociales.pdf

Okazaki, S., & Yague, M. J. (2012). Responses to an advergaming campaign on a mobile social networking site: An initial research report. *Computers in Human Behavior, 28*, 78–86. doi:10.1016/j.chb.2011.08.013

Oksman, V., & Raitiainen, T. (2001). *Perhaps it is a body part. How the mobile phone became an organic part of everyday lives of children and teenagers. Nodiska konferensen för medie-ock kommunikationfiorskning.* Island.

Özcan, Y. Z., & Kocak, A. (2003). A need or a status symbol? Uses of cellular telephone in Turkey. *European Journal of Communication, 18*(2), 241–254. doi:10.1177/0267323103018002004

Ozok, A. A., & Wei, J. (2010). An empirical comparison of consumer usability preferences in online shopping using stationary and mobile devices: Results from a college student population. *Electronic Commerce Research, 10*(2), 111–137. doi:10.1007/s10660-010-9048-y

Parker, B., & Plank, R. (2000). A uses and gratifications perspective on the Internet: As a new information source. *American Business Review, 18*(June), 43–49.

Pew Research Center. (2012). *The future of money: Smartphone swiping in the mobile age.* Retrieved May 17, 2012, from http://www.pewinternet.org/~/media//Files/Reports/2012/PIP_Future_of_Money.pdf

Rafaeli, S. (1986). The electronic bulletin board. A computer-driven mass-medium. *Computers and the Social Sciences, 2*, 123–131. doi:10.1177/089443938600200302

Rao, S., & Troshani, I. (2007). A conceptual framework and propositions for the acceptance of mobile services. *Journal of Theoretical and Applied Electronic Commerce Research, 2*(2), 61–73.

Roy, S. (2009). Internet uses and gratifications. A survey in the Indian context. *Computers in Human Behavior, 25*, 878–886. doi:10.1016/j.chb.2009.03.002

Royo-Vela, M., & Casamassima, P. (2011). The influence of belonging to virtual brand communities on consumers' affective commitment, satisfaction and word-of-mouth advertising: The ZARA case. *Online Information Review, 35*(4), 517–542. doi:10.1108/14684521111161918

Rubin, A. M. (1979). Television use by children and adolescents. *Human Communication Research, 5*, 109–120. doi:10.1111/j.1468-2958.1979.tb00626.x

Rubin, A. M. (1984). Ritualized and instrumental television viewing. *The Journal of Communication, 34*(3), 67–77. doi:10.1111/j.1460-2466.1984.tb02174.x

Ruiz, C., Sanz, S., Broz, A., & Marchuet, D. (2009). Mobile Internet adoption by Spanish consumers. In Head, M., & Li, E. (Eds.), *Mobile and ubiquitous commerce: Advanced e-business methods* (pp. 221–236). Hershey, PA: IGI Global. doi:10.4018/978-1-60566-366-1.ch012

Ruiz, C., Sanz, S., & Tavera, J. F. (2010). A comparative study of mobile messaging services acceptance to participate in television programmes. *Journal of Service Management, 21*(1), 69–102. doi:10.1108/09564231011025128

Saadeghvaziri, F., & Hosseini, H. K. (2011). Mobile advertising: An investigation of factors creating positive attitude in Iranian customers. *African Journal of Business Management, 5*, 394–404.

Saadeghvaziri, F., & Seyedjavadain, S. (2011). Attitude toward advertising: Mobile advertising vs advertising-in-general. *European Journal of Economics. Finance and Administrative Sciences, 28*, 104–114.

Sánchez, A., & Álvaro, A. (2011). *Hábitos de uso de los adolescentes españoles y de América Latina.* Retrieved February 17, 2011, from http://ticsyformacion.com/2011/09/05/uso-de-las-redes-sociales-por-adolescentes-espanoles-y-latino-americanos-socialmedia

Sanchez-Franco, M. J., Villarejo, A. F., & Martin, F. A. (2009). The moderating effect of gender on relationship quality and loyalty toward Internet service providers. *Information & Management, 46*(3), 196–202. doi:10.1016/j.im.2009.02.001

Sanz, S., Ruiz, C., Pérez, I., & Hernández, A. (2011). *Papel moderador del género en el análisis de la lealtad a webs turísticas que ofrecen alojamiento.* Paper presented at the Marketing Trends Conference, Paris.

Scharl, A., Dickinger, A., & Murphy, J. (2005). Diffusion and success factors of mobile marketing. *Electronic Commerce Research and Applications, 4*(2), 159–173. doi:10.1016/j.elerap.2004.10.006

Shang, S., Li, E., Wu, Y., & Hou, O. (2011). Understanding web 2.0 service models: A knowledge creating perspective. *Information & Management, 48*, 178–184. doi:10.1016/j.im.2011.01.005

Shen, A., Lee, M., Cheung, C., & Chen, H. (2010). Gender differences in intentional social action: We-intention to engage in social network-facilitated team collaboration. *Journal of Information Technology, 25*(2), 152–169. doi:10.1057/jit.2010.12

Shin, D. (2010). Analysis of online social networks: a cross- national study. *Online Information Review, 34*(3), 473–495. doi:10.1108/14684521011054080

Skog, B. (2002). Mobiles and the Norwegian teen: Identity, gender and class. In Katz, J. E., & Aakhus, M. (Eds.), *Perpetual contact*. New York, NY: Cambridge University Press.

Socialbakers (2011). *Facebook adoption high, ad rates low in Spain*. Retrieved February 5, 2012, from http://www.emarketer.com/Article.aspx?R=1009047&ecid=a6506033675d47f881651943c21c5ed4

Soderlund, M., & Rosegren, S. (2007). Receiving word-of-mouth from the service customer. An emotion-based effectiveness assessment. *Journal of Retailing and Consumer Services, 14*, 123–136. doi:10.1016/j.jretconser.2006.10.001

Soroa-Koury, S., & Yang, K. (2010). Factors affecting consumers' responses to mobile advertising. *Telematics and Informatics, 27*(1), 103–113. doi:10.1016/j.tele.2009.06.001

Stafford, T., Stafford, M., & Schkade, L. (2004). Determining uses and gratifications for the Internet. *Decision Sciences, 35*(2), 259–288. doi:10.1111/j.00117315.2004.02524.x

Tao, G., Sultan, F., & Rohm, A. J. (2010). Factors influencing Chinese youth consumers' acceptance of mobile marketing. *Journal of Consumer Marketing, 27*(7), 574–583. doi:10.1108/07363761011086326

TNS. (2011). *Mobile life 2011*. Retrieved October 3, 2011, from http://www.tnsglobal.com/research/key-insight-reports/D030D5468903455DA353587691807B5C.aspx

Tsang, M. M., Ho, S. C., & Liang, T. P. (2004). Consumer attitudes toward mobile advertising: An empirical study. *International Journal of Electronic Commerce, 8*(3), 65–78.

Waldt, D., Rebbello, T. M., & Brown, W. J. (2009). Attitude of young consumers toward SMS advertising. *African Journal of Business Management, 3*, 444–452.

Wang, S., Moon, S., Kwon, K., Evans, C., & Stefanone, M. (2010). Face off: Implications of visual cues on initiating friendship of Facebook. *Computers in Human Behavior, 26*(2), 226–234. doi:10.1016/j.chb.2009.10.001

Watson, R. T., Pitt, L. F., Berthon, P., & Zinkhan, G. M. (2002). U-Commerce: Expanding the universe of marketing. *Journal of the Academy of Marketing Science, 30*(4), 333–347. doi:10.1177/009207002236909

Wei, R., Xiaoming, H., & Pan, J. (2010). Examining user behavioural response to SMS ads: Implications for the evolution of the mobile phone as a bona-fide medium. *Telematics and Informatics, 27*, 32–41. doi:10.1016/j.tele.2009.03.005

Weiss, H. M., & Cropanzano, R. (1996). Affective events theory: A theoretical discussion of the structure, causes and consequences of affective experiences at work. In Staw, B. M., & Cummings, L. L. (Eds.), *Research in organizational behavior* (pp. 1–74). Greenwich, CT: JAI Press.

Xu, H., Oh, L. B., & Teo, H. H. (2009). Perceived effectiveness of text vs. multimedia location-based advertising messaging. *International Journal of Mobile Communications, 7*(2), 154–177. doi:10.1504/IJMC.2009.022440

Yang, K., & Lee, H. J. (2010). Gender differences in using mobile data services: Utilitarian and hedonic value approaches. *Journal of Research in Interactive Marketing, 4*(2), 142–156. doi:10.1108/17505931011051678

Zenith Media. (2010). *Panorama de medios en España 2009*. Madrid, Spain: Zenith Optimedia Group.

Zenith Media. (2011). *Móviles y publicidad. Percepciones, usos y tendencias*. Madrid, Spain: Zenith Optimedia Group.

KEY TERMS AND DEFINITIONS

Consumer Attitude: An individual's positive or negative evaluation of a given object or behavior (Ajzen, 1991) and includes feelings or affective responses. It refers to the individual's general willingness to engage in a given behavior.

Mobile Social Networking Sites: Social networking where one or more individuals who share similar interests or commonalities, are conversing and connecting with one another using the mobile phone.

Perceived Ease-of-Use: The degree to which the user expects that use of the technology will require effort (Davis et al. 1989). In the context of mobile social networking, this perceived difficulty is conceptualized as users' perception of their lack of knowledge about using their mobile phone to access the social network and whether access is difficult or impossible (for example due to the technological limitations of their mobile device).

Perceived Financial Risk (Monetary Cost): According to Forsythe and Shi (2003), the perceived risk of online shopping is the Internet user's expectation of loss in a given electronic transaction. Therefore, the perceived risk for the mobile social network user can be defined as the expectation of loss in the pursuit of a desired outcome from using mobile social networking services.

Perceived Usefulness: Consumer perception that the use of the technology in question will improve performance. In the context of our research it refers to "the perception that the use of the mobile phone as a platform for accessing social networks will improve user's performance".

Smartphones: Enhanced mobile phones devices that allow consumers accessing to data services like email, games, videos or mobile applications through Mobile Internet.

Social Networking Sites (SNS): Web 2.0 services that allow people with common interests to create their communities online. These services offer functions for contact and information exchange among users, which include sharing photos or videos, personal blogs, group discussion, real-time messaging or e-mails, thereby enhancing social interaction.

Uses and Gratifications Theory: This theory (Anderson and Meyer, 1975; Katz et al., 1974; Krotz and Eastman, 1999; Mcquail, 1995; Rubin, 1979) has been considered as one of the most influential in the study of mass media. Uses and gratifications Theory enables examination of the medium's functions from the consumer perspective to discover what the medium is used for (McQuail, 1995) and, therefore, what needs and desires it is able to meet (Anderson and Meyer, 1975). The basic premise of this approach then, is that individuals expose themselves to the medium to satisfy a set of needs that motivate the audience to actively seek, in that medium, gratification of their specific needs (Anderson and Meyer, 1975; Katz et al., 1974).

APPENDIX: QUESTIONNAIRE

1. What is your favourite online social network?					

2. How often do you access to your favourite social network? □ Very often □ Quite often □ Not very often □ Hardly ever

3. Have you ever accessed to your favourite social network using your mobile phone? □ YES □ NO

4. What do you think about the use of the mobile as a platform for accessing social networks?	Strongly disagree				Strongly agree
4.1. I like it	1	2	3	4	5
4.2. I think it is interesting	1	2	3	4	5
4.3. I think it is a good idea	1	2	3	4	5
4.4. I think it is a positive thing	1	2	3	4	5
5. What are the main activities you are engaged in when using mobile social networks?	Not important				Very important
5.1. Writing comments	1	2	3	4	5
5.2. Reading comments	1	2	3	4	5
5.3. Uploading photos	1	2	3	4	5
5.4. Uploading videos	1	2	3	4	5
5.5. Taking part in surveys	1	2	3	4	5
5.6. Taking part in competitions and draws	1	2	3	4	5
5.7. Looking for friends, acquaintances, classmates, etc.	1	2	3	4	5
5.8. Searching for information (events, prices)	1	2	3	4	5
5.9. Chatting	1	2	3	4	5
5.10. Accessing the profiles of friends, acquaintances and work/class mates	1	2	3	4	5
6. Why do you use mobile social networks?	Not important				Very important
6.1. To escape boredom	1	2	3	4	5
6.2. To contact/chat with my friends/acquaintances/relations	1	2	3	4	5
6.3. To notify, update friends/acquaintances/relations with the latest news	1	2	3	4	5
6.4. To pass the time	1	2	3	4	5
6.5. For entertainment	1	2	3	4	5
6.6. For fun	1	2	3	4	5
6.7. For relaxation	1	2	3	4	5
6.8. To maintain or improve relations with friends/acquaintances/relations	1	2	3	4	5
6.9. To feel closer, more involved in the lives of friends/acquaintances/ relations	1	2	3	4	5

continued on following page

6.10. To keep in touch with people I don't see very often	1	2	3	4	5
6.11. So that others know that I care about them	1	2	3	4	5
6.12. To be always available for people who care about me	1	2	3	4	5
6.13. To greet friends/acquaintances/relations	1	2	3	4	5
6.14. To get to know new people	1	2	3	4	5
6.15. To be fashionable	1	2	3	4	5
6.16. To look stylish	1	2	3	4	5
6.17. To be up-to-date with the latest fashion	1	2	3	4	5
7. Why don't you use mobile social networks?	Not important				Very important
7.1. I don't know how to	1	2	3	4	5
7.2. I haven't got Internet on my mobile	1	2	3	4	5
7.3. Because it is difficult for me	1	2	3	4	5
7.4. Because I prefer to do it on the computer	1	2	3	4	5
7.5. Because I'm not interested in social networks	1	2	3	4	5
7.6. Because I can't do it on my mobile	1	2	3	4	5
7.7. Because I haven't got a flat rate and its expensive	1	2	3	4	5
8. Gender □ Male □ Female					
9. Age					

Chapter 6
Computing Postgraduate Programmes in the UK and Brazil:
Learning from Experience in Distance Education with Web 2.0 Support

Leonor Barroca
The Open University, UK

Itana M. S. Gimenes
Universidade Estadual de Maringá, Brazil

EXECUTIVE SUMMARY

Education can benefit from experiences and collaborations across different countries and cultures. The authors carried out a study to analyse the experiences of the use of Web 2.0 tools in distance education in the UK and propose a set of lessons that can be applied in the Brazilian context. The recent economic growth in Brazil has resulted in a strong demand for further education. Distance education has emerged as a strong contestant to address this demand. The authors present, in this chapter, the case of the provision of postgraduate education for professionals at a distance. Distance education in Brazil is currently gathering support as it offers great potential to address the big geographic and social divides. However, there are many barriers and misconceptions that perpetuate a climate of distrust.

DOI: 10.4018/978-1-4666-2515-0.ch006

Their study draws a set of lessons learned focusing on the benefits that distance education can bring to the development of professional postgraduate education in technical and engineering areas, in the light of the experience of The Open University (OU) in the UK. They emphasise the support that Web 2.0 can bring to these experiences, but also draw attention to the quality that the production process plays in the learning experiences. These lessons address the following: support for skills development with Web 2.0 technologies, the role of the digital educator, open educational resources, open education and social dimension, and quality and pedagogy in the educational process.

INTRODUCTION

Education, in an era of globalization, can benefit from many opportunities for collaboration and mutual enrichment across experiences in different contexts. It is relevant to look at comparable situations in different countries, to understand important factors of success in a specific situation, and to discuss what can be learned, adapted, and applied elsewhere.

This chapter presents the results of a study of two countries, Brazil and the UK. This study was intended to understand their current situation in terms of postgraduate education, and what could be learned from experience in the development of distance education using Web 2.0 tools. Our case study presents a contribution to the future of postgraduate education for professionals at a distance in Brazil, in the context of the current high demand imposed by its fast economic growth.

Brazil is a country in rapid development but with strong regional inequalities. It has a population of 190,732,694[1], distributed in a geographically large area. Governmental efforts are making the access to the Internet widely spread. According to CGI.br[2], the Brazilian Web has been growing since mid 90s, both in the number of users and in the range of services and applications provided through the network. Internet usage by the Brazilian population has raised from 37 million users in 2005 to 65 million users in 2009. Current statistics indicate that 45% of the population have access to the Internet[3]. The Brazilian plan for postgraduate education 2011-2020 (MEC, 2010) has as one of its objectives to cope with the industry's demands for qualifications. A recent study carried out by Brasscom[4] (2011), pointed out a need of 78,000 professionals whereas the education sector will only provide half of this demand. Federal, state, and private universities provide full Internet support in their postgraduate education. Thus, this scenario creates a unique opportunity to explore how Web 2.0 technologies can support the promotion of postgraduate distance education in Computing in Brazil, learning from the experience in the UK.

The UK has extensive experience in distance education for the last 40 years, triggered by The Open University (OU)[5]. The OU is the biggest university in the UK, and the only one providing higher education entirely at a distance (except for full-time research students). It has a strong widening participation agenda, promoting social justice and equality of opportunity. Brazil has a more recent experience (Junior, 2009) with some positive steps being taken in public sector distance education with, for example, the creation of the Universidade Aberta do Brasil[6] (UAB) (Costa & Pimentel, 2009) in 2005. Even if growing quickly, distance education has not yet expanded to postgraduate programmes in Computing. There are also still some strong pockets of resistance, which view distance education as synonymous of lower quality (Porto & Berge, 2008; Sommer, 2010a), in particular at postgraduate level.

With the advances of Web 2.0 technologies (Conole & Alevizou, 2010), new pedagogical opportunities have been opened to distance education. In particular, the emergence of social and participatory media has started to challenge course designers to understand, and make the best use of, the way students communicate with others (Conole, 2011). These facilities, together with the widespread use of the technologies, many of which are available as open source tools, make Web 2.0 appealing to educators especially in developing countries.

This chapter starts by looking at the systems in the UK and Brazil for postgraduate education: regulation of curriculum and awards by governments and institutions, and the type of degrees offered. The following section discusses the situation of distance education in Brazil, and analyses the experience in the OU (UK) in particular, with design initiatives for distance education. We then present experiences in using Web 2.0 technologies in postgraduate distance education in Computing. The main contribution of this chapter is presented as a set of lessons from experience of both course design and use of Web 2.0 technologies. This is a contribution to a debate (Almeida, 2010) on the way forward for Computing postgraduate distance education in Brazil. We focus, in particular, on professional masters, which have a great potential for innovation, can provide significant social benefits and promote an improvement in the qualification of many professionals. We finally suggest future directions and conclude.

Throughout this chapter, we will be using the generic context of Computing postgraduate degrees, in particular those geared to the development of a professional body; most of the experiences observed in this research and presented here are, more specifically, from within Software Engineering (SE). Both authors have a long experience of postgraduate education: the first author at the OU and the second author in Brazil. This research was undertaken with the second author being immersed for one year in the context of the OU and results from extended participation, observation, and analysis. This experience underpins the discussion and recommendations of what can be learned from one context and applied in another.

THE BACKGROUND FOR POSTGRADUATE PROGRAMMES

This section sets up, for each of the two countries, the generic background in which higher education sits. We look at how curriculum and awards are regulated by government and other agencies, and the type of degrees offered. We can then highlight the major differences in order to further analyse their influence in distance learning practice with Web 2.0 support.

Postgraduate Degrees in Brazil

The Brazilian government's educational department, Ministério de Educação e Cultura (MEC), is responsible for the regulation of higher education provided by both public and private institutions. The Coordenação de Aperfeiçoamento de Pessoal de Nível Superior (CAPES) is the MEC's agency responsible for postgraduate programmes at national level. Postgraduate degrees are classified in *lato sensu*, and *stricto sensu*. The former are shorter programmes, typically one year and a half long, offered for professional training or updating, comparable to postgraduate diplomas in the UK. They are regulated nationally by the MEC, but once established they are not assessed regularly. *Stricto sensu* degrees consist of master and doctorate programmes and are nationally assessed for quality by CAPES. The assessment of postgraduate programmes is a major activity undertaken by CAPES; it consists of a very precise system for assessment and approval of new programme proposals. Existing programmes are assessed every three years and given a classification on a scale from 1 (one) to 7 (seven). Assessment is currently based on: research profiles of staff (20%), research profiles of student body (dissertations and publications) (30%), research publications (40%), and social integration/impact (10%). This determines the number of student grants and the annual funding to programmes according to the classification obtained by each programme.

For historical reasons, postgraduate programmes have been developed geared to the achievement of high academic standards establishing a well-defined research path towards a doctorate. Thus, they have become rather inflexible (Porto & Berge, 2008; Romizowski, 2005) as regards the demands of professional sectors (MEC, 2010). Recognition of this inflexibility has led to an increased interest in professional masters (Ribeiro, 2010); however, these have not yet been widely implemented. Professional masters are also strong contenders for distance education due to the type of people they attract; but, distance provision at this level has not happened yet in Brazil in the public higher education sector. Currently, there are professional masters in Computing in only six state institutions in Brazil. In contrast, there are 53 master (non-professional) and 23 doctorate programmes. Professional masters are fee-paying[7], have a different type of final dissertation, and are assessed, by CAPES.

The assessment criteria is similar to the one for academic masters but with different weights for each item: research profiles of staff (15 to 20%), research profiles of student body (dissertations and publications) (25 to 30%), research publications (30 to 35%), and social integration/impact (20 to 25%) (CAPES, 2010).

There is an ongoing debate about the status of professional masters, in particular: whether a dissertation from a professional master can be of the same standard of a dissertation from a non-professional master degree and how it should be assessed; whether or not public money should be spent on education that is going to benefit the private sector; and, whether the negative attitudes towards these masters, in particular from assessors, are justified (Agopyan & Lobo, 2007; Negret, 2008; Ribeiro, 2010; Spink, 1997). A recent assessment of postgraduate education in Brazil (Almeida, 2010) criticises the lack of diversity and flexibility of postgraduate courses. It proposes that master degrees as they exist (strongly research oriented) should disappear in favour of shorter, specialised professional masters that are not directly tied up with a doctorate, and are more widely available. This suggests an approximation between master's degrees in Brazil and those in the UK although the debate is only starting. This chapter contributes to this debate by discussing how Brazil can benefit from the experience with distance education in the UK, to make professional masters reach a wider audience.

Postgraduate Degrees in the UK

The UK higher education institutions are responsible for maintaining academic standards and quality (QAA, 2009). The Quality Assurance Agency for Higher Education (QAA) is an independent body responsible for checking that these responsibilities are met, making recommendations and sharing good practice. Within this remit, QAA provides an infrastructure that contains the following components:

- Framework for Higher Education Qualifications (QAA, 2008)
- Subject benchmarks (QAA, 2000, 2011)
- Guidance on programme specifications
- Good practice guidelines

The framework defines the qualifiers for each type of grade in higher education; subject benchmarks define the whole of the cognate area, abilities and skills expected of students in the area, principles of course design and learning, teaching and assessment issues. Guidelines for preparing programme specifications and guidelines on good practice in several areas of activity are also made available by QAA.

The subject benchmark does not impose restrictions on curricula other than in very generic terms. There is, therefore, a wide variation in postgraduate degrees in the UK (HEPI, 2010). Masters degrees are defined, in the qualifications framework, by a descriptor, which encompasses a wide variety: those with only taught courses, those following a programme of research, and those which are the majority, and that combine both courses and research. In computing, even for degrees with taught courses and a dissertation, the variety is wide. Computing attracts not only people from other disciplines, but also professionals with a need for ongoing development. Computing conversion masters became popular, from the 80s onwards, attracting undergraduates from other disciplines converting into Computing. However, this type of master has faced some criticism (CPHC, 2004) with the development of the qualifications frameworks, and the definition of standards required at master's level. This criticism triggered an effort into benchmarking masters in Computing. Recently, the QAA issued a benchmark for masters in Computing (QAA, 2011); this statement encompasses a wide range of degrees: those building on undergraduate honours degrees, professional programmes, interdisciplinary programmes, masters of research (MRes[8]) programmes, as well as "generalist" and "specialist" degrees. The benchmark also defines the learning outcomes in terms of generic subject knowledge, understanding, and skills at master's level in computing. In addition, it includes guidelines on teaching, learning, and assessment and a threshold level. However, these are general enough to allow for a great diversity of masters on offer, and conversion masters have not yet gone away.

Comparative Summary

Table 1 summarises the differences in postgraduate education in the two countries under: quality assessment, qualifications, awards, and fees.

DISTANCE EDUCATION INITIATIVES

Brazilian Context

Since the creation of UAB in 2005, a range of different distance education experiences started being reported (Litto & Marthos, 2006), research has been increasing, and, more recently, gathering greater interest. However, distance education in higher education in Brazil has followed a slower path than in some developing countries (Romizowski, 2005).

UAB does not offer its own courses; instead, it integrates all the different distance education offers from the public sector higher education institutions. According to INEP (2010), the number of undergraduate registrations in distance education has raised from 0.2% (of ~3,000,000) in 2001 to 14.1% (of ~5,000,000) in 2009. In

Table 1. Background comparison between UK and Brazil

	Brazil	**UK**
Quality assessment	Programmes assessed by CAPES. Assessment of masters and doctorates follow similar pattern.	Programmes assessed by institutions and by QAA. Assessment of research done separately from assessment of masters programmes by course.
Qualifications	Definitions centralised at governmental level; close link of all postgraduate qualifications with research. Professional masters defined, but still in small numbers, not well established, and generating still a considerable amount of controversy.	Nationally defined generic qualification frameworks, guidelines, and benchmarks. Variety of master degrees: by course, by research (MPhil[9]), specialist/generalist, interdisciplinary, professional.
Awards	Approval of new awards done centrally by CAPES. Strong homogeneity of awards both in terms of curriculum and structure.	Approval of new awards by institutions. Flexibility of institutions to define structure and curriculum.
Fees	State education is free including that at postgraduate level (masters and doctorates); professional masters are fee-paying.	Postgraduate degrees are fee-paying and there are no limits on fees.

addition, there is a high number of *lato sensu* courses not only in the public sector but also in the private sector. UAB leads a massive programme to qualify school teachers (Bof, 2004), and, more recently, a professional master programme in mathematics (PROFMAT)[10] dedicated to improving the level of school teachers. The new government (elected in 2011) restructured how distance education is dealt with making it a distributed responsibility of several subsections of the MEC covering different levels of education. CAPES accredits distance education courses, as part of its institutional or multi-institutional accreditation. *Stricto sensu* programmes are approved and assessed under the same system as the face-to-face ones.

There is now a wide variety of offerings and models of distance education (Moran, 2009). Most models require, at least partially, synchronous and/or physical attendance usually in local centres; there is no "entirely at a distance" initiative (MEC, 2007). This is seen as a way to guarantee quality. A common model for large groups is that of the class given at a distance (e.g. tele-conference or video); this model tends to perpetuate the idea of the teacher as the transmitter of knowledge rather than a facilitator for the learning process (Moran, 2009). Junior (2009), although identifying some success stories of distance education in Brazil, agrees that many of these initiatives still follow a traditional "broadcast" model of education.

Litto (2009) gives a snapshot of distance education and highlights the great potential it opens for a country where 40% of municipalities do not have a higher education institution. However, he identifies the conservative mentality of university staff that perpetuates the myth of poor quality in distance education as a major obstacle, together with the lack of references to the more recent literature on the subject, and the existence of a small number of institutions that provide poor quality distance education. This together with the inflexibility of bureaucracy and regulation justify the slow uptake of distance education in Brazil. Porto and Berge (2008) also identify some of the barriers to distance education in Brazil, amongst which is the "rigidity of Brazil's educational system, and [..] the growing centralized decision-making taking place in Brazil's education." They also identify the lack of an "academic tradition in e-learning pedagogy and delivery." Sommer (2010b) reflects on the polarization of the debate on distance education from the perspective of teacher training and raises some of the questions that could take this debate away from ideologies and party politics; namely, the nature of the educational experience, the relation between learning outcomes, skills development and quality assurance, and the role of the educator in a scenario of reflective practice and "learning to learn."

The debate is now stronger than ever and contributions to this debate from perspectives other than teacher training are needed in a path for a more mature and well-respected distance education system.

UK Experience

The OU has been a pioneer in distance education in the UK, and postgraduate programmes in computing have been offered there since 1984. Although many other higher education institutions have now adopted distance education, this chapter focuses on the OU, which is representative[11] in this area, and where one of the authors is based. Distance education in the UK is subject to the same quality processes as face-to-face education, and its accreditation is not differentiated from that of face-to-face offerings in higher education. Similarly, to what was discussed above, for new awards and curriculum, institutions in the UK have also flexibility in defining delivery, there are no governmental restrictions to distance education, and many institutions have now many offerings entirely at a distance.

The OU is entirely dedicated to distance education[12] and has developed its own model, called Supported Open Learning[13], as illustrated in Figure 1. By not requiring previous study ("open") the OU aims to reach those who had not followed a traditional educational path; it also aims at greater flexibility by letting students plan their study around their commitments and places. Students have the support of a tutor and of an online forum to help with study material, activities, and assignments have access to a regional centre with advisers, and network with other students at tutorials, day schools or through online conferencing, online social networks, informal study groups, and events. The model is also based on high-quality teaching materials.

Figure 1. OU's supported open learning

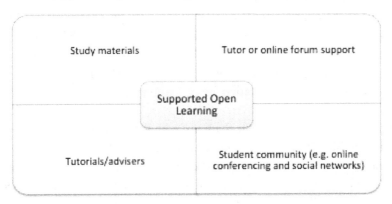

The quality processes in place are rigorous; tutors are supported in their work, they are monitored for quality of feedback to students and for accuracy in their marking, and their professional development is a serious concern for the OU. The model of distance education adopted by the OU was created forty years ago, when distance education was not a well-accepted practice. In addition, it was created for an institution entirely dedicated to distance education, which aimed to reach very large numbers of students. This has determined many aspects of the way it works now. Concerns with quality and equity with other institutions were very high in the agenda and the university had to fight for its acceptance; quality, therefore, permeates all its processes.

Many other universities in the UK offer now several postgraduate courses at a distance, in particular in the area of Computing and Software Engineering.

Course Design at the OU

Distance education requires an effort in curriculum and course design well above that of traditional education; in a traditional face-to-face setting, teaching strategies are easier to change dynamically as a result of teacher-student interactions. In distance education, the learning process and the supporting technologies need to be planned ahead and play a decisive role in the success of the learning experience. This is particularly relevant in a situation like Brazil where higher education follows a more traditional educational approach and concerns with distance pedagogy are not well established in the academic community (Porto & Berge, 2008).

At the OU, there is a robust and complex infrastructure both for the production and for the presentation of courses. Academics in the OU, for example, do not give lectures (in the traditional use of the term) at a distance; they are instead involved with the preparation of high quality materials that are the main vehicle for education in most of the courses; these consist of not only purpose-written educational materials, but also video, audio and other interactive materials. The production of a course is always done by a team and involves a large number of support staff. This includes, typically, a project manager, a designer, a software developer, a librarian, a student services representative, an educational technologist, and an external academic assessor.

Computing education has been changing with the development of new learning pedagogies (Seffah & Grogono, 2002). Denning (1992) did recognise already in 1992 the need to transform engineering education in universities from a broadcast mode where only good engineering concepts are taught, to one where students also acquire the skills to listen, reflect and become self-learners. In distance education, course design has to support explicitly the development of these skills. At the OU, every degree, and every module is designed based on a well-defined set of learning outcomes that comprise:

- **Knowledge and Understanding:** Content and subject matter of the course;
- **Cognitive Skills:** Analysis and synthesis of the course content;
- **Key Skills:** More general and concerns like ability to communicate, use relevant ICT and information literacy, or work with others; and,
- **Professional and Practical Skills:** Particular skills related to the subject area.

The design of a course assessment is dictated by what is generally required of each type of award (like a project with dissertation at the end) and from its learning outcomes; all skills are assessed to guarantee the achievement of the expected outcome. This is particularly relevant at a distance where the assessment also helps the students to pace their study and measure achievement.

Course design is important when using Web 2.0 tools so that they can be well integrated with the pedagogical objectives. The information literacy skills required and the technology and tool support to be used are part of the design of a module. In Computing, in particular, students will engage with techniques and tools specific to the discipline, on top of those incorporated in the design of the distance education. The design of the teaching module needs to make explicit decisions on how these tools will be made available, and how students can be supported in their use. The next section provides some examples of what is currently being used.

The OU has developed and refined its own course design processes. These have evolved with experience, with pedagogical practice, and with technological innovations. The OU is also heavily involved in research related to pedagogical theories and practice. Recently, OULDI[14] is a research initiative to develop a "methodology for learning design composed of tools, practice, and other innovation that both builds upon and contributes to existing academic and practitioner research." Tools being developed to support this initiative include CompendiumLD[15], to visualise course design, and Cloudworks[16], a social network "for sharing and discussing learning and teaching ideas and designs."

WEB 2.0 SUPPORT FOR COMPUTING POSTGRADUATE DISTANCE EDUCATION

It is now accepted that pedagogy and technology can head to a harmonious integration (Beetham & Sharpe, 2007). Currently available Web 2.0 tools can significantly improve production and access to information, as well as providing means to facilitate computer-mediated communication and collaboration amongst education players. Moreover, computer and network services are increasingly widely available in most people's daily life. This leads to a higher demand for mobility and digital media that support teaching and learning. In postgraduate computing, this is more the case, as students are familiar with the use of tools due to the technical character of the discipline.

This section looks at some experiences of using Web 2.0 in postgraduate courses and discusses some issues raised by their use. We use the categories for educational Web 2.0 activities presented in Crook et al. (2008): media sharing, media manipulation, conversational arenas, online games and virtual worlds, social networking, blogging, social bookmarking, recommender systems, collaborative editing, wikis, and syndication (RSS feeds).

The use of Web 2.0 technologies in OU courses is varied. Moodle (an OU customised version), and Elluminate[17] are universally used in existing programmes and courses. Students have access to *StudentHome* which is a gateway Moodle website that gives them amongst, many other facilities, access to a set of social Web 2.0 tools (e.g. forums, wikis, and blogs). Each OU module has its own Moodle website with access to the module's materials and assessment, access to online forums specific to the module, and an extensive set of resources, from library links, to virtual classroom sessions. Students are given access to Google Apps for Education[18] that include: email account, document creation, storage and sharing, and Web space.

Wikis and collaborative editing tools have been effective at supporting reflection, and collaboration; they can help students with teamwork, and in developing academic writing skills. We look, as an example, at one of the modules, Requirements for Business Systems, of the MSc in Software Engineering. This module adopts a well-accepted software requirements textbook; most of the modules in this programme have their teaching material entirely written by OU academics. It also provides research papers, and case studies. A study guide was written as the spine of the course. It takes students through the different topics and associated resources provided with the module. This guide supports students in their study through the acquisition of the required knowledge and skills, in their self-assessment (e.g. quizzes) and mandatory assignments. Course activities are planned by weeks of study in the course calendar. They include reading, group or individual tasks, and assignments that are submitted online. Forums are used for discussions and a wiki for online collaborative work. The wiki supports the collaborative development of a requirements specification document. Students are allocated to teams according to similar interests or geographical location. They define their specific roles in the team to collaboratively develop the requirements specification. Students are assessed both by the quality of the specification and their contribution to it. Collaborative work on the production of a requirements specification is a key skill in the module's learning outcomes. Therefore, student assignments and participation in team discussions are marked taking this into account. Students can use a personal journal tool, in the module website, to keep a record of their reflections or notes of their experiences on the collaborative activities. Reflection is seen as a strategy that facilitates learning through re-examination and re-interpretation of experience. It is central to effective learning and development. A student has also a personal calendar and a pointer to a set of structured resources with support material to access information. As stated in Schroeder et al. (2010a): "The scenario not only allowed students to learn the practice of wiki-based collaboration, but also contributed to a better understanding of the intricacies of identifying and negotiating systems requirements."

Another experiment with Web 2.0 for postgraduate Computing at the OU includes the Web 2.0 infrastructure to support research students entirely at a distance, for a Virtual MPhil (research degree) in Computing. A rich and flexible combination of synchronous, asynchronous, and immersive tools, was put together in order to foster an interactive online research community and promote the development of research skills at a distance. This includes a Moodle-based site integrated with an ePortfolio system, a synchronous virtual classroom system that uses Elluminate, and a purpose-built virtual campus in Second Life (Barroca, et al., 2010). Students have also the flexibility of using other popular freely available technologies, like free phone calls over the Internet (e.g. Skype or Google talk), or social networking tools. The structure developed to support these students is centred on research themes that include research students, supervisors, and their research collaborators. Students are encouraged to use the technology to develop a sense of belonging and to develop the skills that will make them independent researchers; they are given opportunities, as they would have in a face-to-face environment, such as to give presentations, get feedback, and access other researchers.

Other Web 2.0 tools have been used in education even if not specifically in the OU, or in postgraduate Computing (Fitzgerald, et al., 2009; Minocha, 2009); we describe a few cases of use in what follows.

There are many uses for blogs in education (Downes, 2009). They introduce a more interactive and lively version of what was previously done with personal Web pages. In Software Engineering, for example, blogs maintained by respected academics are effective at keeping a live running commentary on a specific area, and providing useful references, opinions, innovations and challenges (e.g. Thoughts on software and systems engineering[19] and Serendipity[20]). Blogs can be also an effective communication tool between educators and students. However, the effort and time required to maintain these blogs cannot be dismissed, mainly as this activity is not usually deserving of academic recognition (Weller, 2011).

Social bookmarking tools like BibSonomy[21] and delicious[22] are well accepted and have been increasingly applied in education, in particular, to support literature review, research groups, and the writing of final year projects and theses. For instance, library services, like those at the OU, do refer students to these tools to help them manage references[23]. Computing students, in particular, offer little resistance to the use of software tools, and should be encouraged from early on to use them.

Instant messaging tools such as Skype chat, Google talk, Messenger, and Twitter (conversational arenas) are already part of the everyday life of Computing educators and students. At the OU, for example, supervision sessions are often run using these tools. Microblogging tools like Twitter are also being reported; for example, Schroeder et al. (2010a) report the use of Twitter by an Engineering educator at a UK university to improve communication with students, and to make announcements.

Social networking tools like Facebook are now widely used and Universities have now set up presence there as well. At the OU, for example, several modules have their own Facebook group, and the Library maintains a regular presence with announcements, discussions, and references to interesting articles. Students use Facebook for socialization but it is not clear whether they are willing to mix tools used for social purposes with tools used for work or educational purposes. Conole et al. (2010) report evidence of the use of social networking in higher education, and Schroeder et al. (2010a) report the use of Facebook in a UK university to run induction for new students.

Academics and students have been largely using Web 2.0 tools to broadcast and share knowledge trough videos, audios, slides and texts (media sharing, manipulation, mash-ups, and recommender systems). Popular tools are Youtube, Flickr. and Slideshare. Students use such tools both to search for additional data, and informal knowledge. They need to develop skills to scrutinize information in order to use these tools effectively. At the OU, for example, students of a Digital Photography course make use of Flickr (Minocha & Kear, 2009) to present their course work and receive feedback from colleagues in the course.

Existing studies report the potential use of games in higher education (Freitas, 2010). They have been commonly used for professional training. However, Freitas (2010, p. 25) indicates that "while current research points to learner driven trends associated with games usage, many of the cutting edge examples of games use are in schools rather than in HE/FE, reflecting a broader uptake of game-based approaches amongst younger learners."

Given the context above described, Table 2 summarises learning experiences of Web 2.0 tools.

As Web 2.0 is being more widely used, research is also highlighting the challenges and risks of integrating its tools in the learning process (Conole, 2009). Schroeder et al. (2010a, 2010b) discuss the use of social software to education, by analysing several tools and evaluating how they contribute to the critical factors for a successful higher education experience as in Garrison et al. (1999, 2007); they use examples from UK higher education institutions. Under social software, they include tools in the categories of: conversational arenas, social networking, wikis, blogging, social bookmarking, and syndication. They identify strengths, weak-

Table 2. Summary of learning experiences in the use of Web 2.0 tools

Web 2.0 tools	Examples of application
VLEs, e.g. Moodle and Elluminate[24]	Act as the main gateway of interaction between institutions and students.
Wikis and collaborative editing tools, e.g. wikis in Moodle.	Support reflection, and collaboration; they can help students with teamwork, and in developing academic writing skills.
Blogs, e.g. Thoughts on software and systems engineering and Serendipity	Support teachers and groups to organize and disseminate knowledge in a more interactive and lively way than of what was previously done with personal Web pages.
Social bookmarking, e.g. BibSonomy and delicious	Support literature review, research groups, and the writing of final year projects and theses.
Instant messaging, e.g. Skype chat, Google talk, Messenger, and Twitter	Support supervision and communication with students and amongst students.
Social networks, e.g. Facebook, Google+, Cloudworks.	Support student integration.
Broadcast and Media sharing, e.g. Youtube, Flickr, and Slideshare	Search for additional data, and informal knowledge.
Virtual world, e.g. Second life	Provide a purpose-built virtual campus for students.
Games, e.g. SIMPLE, the SIMulated Professional Learning Environment[25]	Commonly used for professional training.

nesses, opportunities, and threats in a set of case studies, at both undergraduate and postgraduate level. A report of these case studies can be found in Minocha and Kear (2009). They identify concerns about security and privacy, as most tools are publicly available; they also mention anxieties created, by the use of these tools, on students who are required to accept a level of public exposure to which they are not necessarily used to. Moreover, they highlight a change of role for the educator: deciding on what level of involvement to have, accepting that extra effort may be required to set up, manage, moderate, but also adapting to a major change of attitude. The educator is no longer the "provider of information," but rather a facilitator or moderator with implications for their training needs.

LESSONS FROM EXPERIENCE IN COMPUTING POSTGRADUATE DISTANCE EDUCATION

The lack of experience of the Brazilian state sector in postgraduate computing distance education and the high demand for qualified IT professionals motivated the authors to learn from the experience in the UK, and formulate suggestions of what can be applied to the Brazilian scenario.

The debate is open now about the future of professional masters and the new Brazilian plan for postgraduate study (MEC, 2010) sets the background for that discussion. There is a strong concentration of professional masters in the southeast of the country (56%), and the private institutions offer 44.4% of all professional masters. They have grown in number between 2004 and 2009 of 104.2% for all curricular areas, and they are forecast to continue growing. The new plan puts a strong emphasis on the need to develop professional education and mentions specifically "critical spirit and reflection" as skills that should come out of that education. Amongst the main challenges for the next decade, the new plan identifies the expansion of professional education to take into account local, regional, and national needs and to promote sustainable development and social inclusion. The plan, however, does not make recommendations in relation to the mode of delivery.

Our take on the debate on the future of professional masters is that distance education and the use of Web 2.0 technologies open opportunities for innovation in the education of, and increase in the reach to, professionals in a country with considerable geographical and social inequalities.

In what follows we raise a series of issues that should be taken into account when thinking about implementing distance education professional postgraduate Computing degrees in Brazil. We separate them in two groups, those that can be facilitated by the use of Web 2.0 technologies, and those that have wider implications and for which technology is not the answer.

Web 2.0 Technologies

- **Support for Skills Development with Web 2.0 Technologies:** There is now a wide body of research on Web 2.0 technologies support for skills development. This literature should be taken into account when deciding which technologies to support and with what aims. There is, however, a need for more domain-specific evidence for the aspects of postgraduate computing that can be better supported through these technologies. Thus, Web 2.0 tools should not only be used for social integration but also to build knowledge in the specific subjects.

- **Tool Support:** There is a highly dynamic production of Web 2.0 tools, some are becoming widely accepted in the education area, whereas others are widely disseminated in the media but still have not found a systematic usage in courses. Course designers need to take reasoned decisions on what tools should be formally incorporated in a course and what tools students should be encouraged to try informally. Institutions need also to define strategies and the right balance between maintaining control over data and tools vs. open source adoption. Course design should consider the application of Web 2.0 tools taking into account benefits and risks.

- **Resources and Supporting Material:** Support materials need to be planned: existing books, study guides or purpose written material. A great amount of Open Educational Resources (OERs) (Conole, 2010) is now available from many different sources: MIT OpenCourseWare[26], OpenLearn[27], and iTunesU[28]. This can significantly improve dissemination of knowledge in emerging countries as well as reducing the cost of courses. UNESCO has a programme to disseminate OERs (UNESCO, 2011), and one of its recent forums, which took place in Brazil, focused on Latin America[29]. However, there are still few OERs in computing produced in Brazil (Santos, 2011).

- **The Role of the Digital Educator:** Digital educators should be well supported and be seen as highly qualified staff whose professional development should be a concern for their institution. Their activities will cover a wide range: from the production of digital content, to maintaining well-informed blogs and articulating professional and academic networks. This new type of intellectual production in the academic scenario needs to be recognized within institutions and nationally (Weller, 2011). Web 2.0 tools are available but educators need motivation and recognition for their good use.

- **Training of Digital Educators:** The role of distance education educators is fundamental for the success of the learning experience; it is necessary to promote their training for distance education and guarantee that workloads take into account the effort required with distance education. There is still scepticism in the advantages of Web 2.0 tools. Educators need both training in the tools and awareness of the improvements these tools can make to overcome the required learning curve.

Distance Learning Issues

- **Flexibility of Regulations:** Regulations of postgraduate education need to allow for greater flexibility in the creation and assessment of postgraduate degrees that are educationally innovative and fulfill professional needs; there is a need to rethink the link between these degrees and research-based ones.
- **Planning Ahead:** A process needs to be in place for the design of courses and modules; this process defines the workflow of activities to be undertaken, associated roles, tools, and support material.
- **Pedagogy:** Learning at a distance is challenging but it also offers new opportunities for interaction and experiences not necessarily present in a face-to-face setting. Delivering lectures at a distance in a broadcast mode is not necessarily the best way to teach; best pedagogic practices for distance education that are skills-centred, involve reflection, and collaboration, have been well researched and need to be taken into account.
- **Outcomes not Incomes:** The learning experience at a distance needs to be thought in terms of the learning outcomes (knowledge and skills) to be achieved from that experience and these should determine the assessment of learning. Reflection and collaboration are important skills that can be developed at a distance as long as this is planned and integrated in the learning experience.
- **Scale:** Distance education can scale, but this requires investment in infrastructures to support students, tutors, and assessment.
- **Quality:** Without processes that guarantee quality distance education will have no future; to survive it has to demonstrate that it can deliver high quality that competes in equal terms with face-to-face education.
- **Social Dimension:** Distance education programmes can be an important step for democratisation of education, and a means to achieve social and economical benefits for the nation. In the context of professional postgraduate computing, this requires recognition of the context of the profession and an understanding that professional masters will develop different skills to those leading to a research career.
- **Factors for Success:** Distance education initiatives and adoption of Web 2.0 technologies tend to appear in a bottom-up manner and resulting from individual's initiatives; for a wide success these initiatives need to be supported at different levels: institutional, professional, and governmental.

FUTURE RESEARCH DIRECTIONS

This chapter has looked at examples of distance education in higher education, and of application of Web 2.0 tools to support it. It reflected on the issues that should be taken into account when developing similar initiatives in a context like Brazil. From this research, two main areas of further research have been highlighted: one related to the lack of evidence of empirical data to support emerging ideas about the support offered by Web 2.0 tools; the other related to what is needed for a successful implementation of distance education in professional postgraduate Computing in Brazil. For the former, there is a clear need of research that provides feedback, with empirical data, on the application of Web 2.0 tools to support development of skills on domain-specific areas of computing education. For the latter, there are several more specific areas that need further research. These include the following:

- Development of Open Educational Resources (OERs) that are domain-specific and in the local language.
- Understanding of the economic models for distance education.
- Understanding of the relation between distance education and cultural specificities.
- Implications of a successful adoption of distance education, in particular, in an educational system in Brazil that is not strong in developing "learning to learn skills" such as the use of reflective learning, and student autonomy.

CONCLUSION

This chapter presents the results of a comparative study of the situation of postgraduate education in Computing in both the UK and Brazil. It surveyed Web 2.0 applications and their support in the delivery of distance education. Based on this study it has made a contribution to an ongoing debate on the future of postgraduate education in Brazil. There is a recognised need of a wider implementation of professional masters to fulfill market demands for the education of professionals in technical and engineering areas. Web 2.0 technologies have an important role to play in this implementation. However, other factors need also to be discussed, in particular, the current regulations for postgraduate education in Brazil that make professional masters inflexible and difficult to implement more widely.

This chapter has argued that professional masters, through distance education, can provide significant social benefits by reaching a wider population and breaching the many geographic and social inequalities. Distance education initiatives in Brazil are still fighting for credibility and recognition as equitable to traditional education. Quality processes need to be in place at all stages to guarantee success of any new initiatives. This chapter has contributed with some lessons in distance education, from the experience in the UK, which can be adapted to the specific cultural situation of Brazil. The chapter has highlighted the issues related to course design for distance learning, and the support that Web 2.0 technologies can provide, and potential for innovation in the educational experience.

REFERENCES

Agopyan, V., & Lobo, R. (2007). O futuro do mestrado profissional. *Revista Brasileira de Pós-Graduação, 4*(8), 293–302.

Almeida, M. H. (2010). A pós-graduação no Brasil: Onde está e para onde poderia ir. In CAPES (Ed.), *Plano Nacional de Postgraduação (PNGP) 2010-2020,* (vol. 2, pp. 17-28). Rio de Janeiro, Brasilia: Academic Press.

Barroca, L., Rapanotti, L., & Petre, M. (2010). *Developing research degrees online.* Paper presented at the ICERI (International Conference of Education, Reseach and Innovation). Rio de Janeiro, Brasilia.

Beetham, H., & Sharpe, R. (Eds.). (2007). *Rethinking pedagogy for a digital age.* Abingdon, UK: Routledge.

Bof, A. M. (2004). Distance learning for teacher training in Brazil. *International Review of Research in Open and Distance Learning, 5*(1), 1–14.

CAPES. (2010). *Ficha de avaliação do programa - Mestrado profissional.* Retrieved October 13, 2011, from http://www.fnmp.org.br/documentos/ficha-de-avaliacao-dos-mestrados-profissionais-2007-2009.pdf

Conole, G. (2009). Stepping over the edge: The implications of new technologies for education. In Lee, M. J. W., & McLoughlin, C. (Eds.), *Web 2.0-based e-learning: Applying social informatics for tertiary teaching.* Hershey, PA: IGI Global.

Conole, G. (2010). *Learning design – Making practice explicit.* Paper presented at the ConnectEd 2010: 2nd International Conference on Design Education. Rio de Janeiro, Brasilia.

Conole, G. (2011). *Designing for learning in an open world.* Retrieved July 19, 2011, from http://cloudworks.ac.uk/cloudscape/view/2155

Conole, G., & Alevizou, P. (2010). *A review of the use of web 2.0 tools in higher education.* Retrieved October 13, 2011, from http://oro.open.ac.uk/23154/

Costa, C. J. D., & Pimentel, N. M. (2009). The Brazilian open university system in the consolidation of the higher education distance learning offer in Brazil. *Educação Temática Digital, 10*(2), 71–90.

CPHC. (2004). *Towards benchmarking standards for taught masters degrees in computing*. London, UK: CPHC.

Crook, C. J. C., Fisher, T., Graber, R., Harrison, C., Lewin, C., et al. (2008). *Web 2.0 technologies for learning: the current landscape – Opportunities, challenges and tensions*. Retrieved September 12, 2011, from http://dera.ioe.ac.uk/1474/

Denning, P. (1992). Educaing a new engineer. *Communications of the ACM, 32*(12), 83–97.

Downes, S. (2009). Blogs in Learning. In Mishra, S. (Ed.), *STRIDE Handbook 8 - e-Learning* (pp. 88–91). New Delhi, India: Indira Gandhi National Open University.

Fitzgerald, R., Barrass, S., Campbell, J., Hinton, S., Ryan, Y., Whitelaw, M., et al. (2009). *Digital learning communities (DLC): Investigating the application of social software to support networked learning (CG6-36)*. Retrieved October 14, 2011, from http://eprints.qut.edu.au/18476/

Freitas, S. D. (2010). *Learning in immersive worlds: A review of game-based learning*. Retrieved from http://www.jisc.ac.uk/media/documents/programmes/elearninginnovation/gamingreport_v3.pdf

Garrison, D. R., Anderson, T., & Archer, W. (1999). Critical inquiry in a text-based environment: Computer conferencing in higher education. *The Internet and Higher Education, 2*(2-3), 87–105. doi:10.1016/S1096-7516(00)00016-6

Garrison, D. R., & Arbaud, J. B. (2007). Researching the community of inquiry framework: Review, issues, and future directions. *The Internet and Higher Education, 10*(3), 157–172. doi:10.1016/j.iheduc.2007.04.001

HEPI. (2010). *Postgraduate education in the United Kingdom*. Retrieved October 13, 2011, from http://www.hepi.ac.uk/466-1149/Postgraduate-Education-in-the-United-Kingdom.html

INEP. (2010). *Resumo técnico - Censo da Educação superior de 2009*. Retrieved October 17, 2011, from http://download.inep.gov.br/download/superior/censo/2009/resumo_tecnico2009.pdf

Junior, K. S. (2009). Distance education in Brazil: Paths, policies and perspective. *Educação Temática Digital, 10*(2), 16–36.

Litto, F. (2009). O retrato frente/verso da aprendizagem a distância no Brasil 2009. *Educação Temática e Digital, 10*(2), 108–122.

Litto, F., & Marthos, B. (Eds.). (2006). *Distance learning in Brazil: Best Practices 2006*. Rio de Janeiro, Brasilia: ABED.

MEC. (2007). *Referencias de qualidade para educação superior a distância*. Retrieved October 13, 2011, from http://www.educacaoadistancia.blog.br/arquivos/ REFERENCIAIS_DE_QUALIDADE_PARA_EDUCACAO_SUPERIOR_A_DIS-TANCIA.pdf

MEC. (2010). *Plano nacional de postgraduação (PNGP) 2011-2020*. Retrieved October 13, 2011, from http://www.capes.gov.br/sobre-a-capes/plano-nacional-de-pos-graduacao

Minocha, S. (2009). *A study of the effective use of social software by further and higher education in the UK to support student learning and teaching*. Retrieved October 21, 2011, from http://kn.open.ac.uk/public/workspace.cfm?wpid=8655

Minocha, S., & Kear, K. (2009). *Study of the effective use of social software to support student learning and engagement*. Retrieved October 13, 2011, from http:// www.jisc.ac.uk/whatwedo/projects/socialsoftware08.aspx#downloads

Moran, J. M. (2009). The models and the evaluation of higher distance education in Brazil. *Educação Temática Digital, 10*(2), 54–70.

Negret, F. (2008). A identidade e a importância dos mestrados profissionais no Brasil e algumas considerações para a sua avaliação. *Revista Brasileira de Pós-Graduação, 5*(10), 217–225.

Porto, S. C. S., & Berge, Z. L. (2008). Distance education and corporate training in Brazil: Regulations and interrelationships. *International Review of Research in Open and Distance Learning, 9*(2).

QAA. (2000). *Subject benchmark computing*. Retrieved October 13, 2011, from http://www.qaa.ac.uk/Publications/InformationAndGuidance/Documents/computing07.pdf

QAA. (2008). *The framework for higher education qualifications in England, Wales and Northern Ireland*. Retrieved October 13, 2011, from http://www.qaa.ac.uk/ Publications/InformationAndGuidance/Documents/FHEQ08.pdf

QAA. (2009). *An introduction to QAA*. Retrieved October 14, 2011, from http:// www.qaa.ac.uk/Publications/InformationAndGuidance/Documents/IntroQAA.pdf

QAA. (2011). *Subject benchmark statement masters degrees in computing*. Retrieved October 13, 2011, from http://www.qaa.ac.uk/Publications/CircularLetters/Documents/QAA386_Computing.pdf

Ribeiro, C. (2010). A universidade como disputa da reprodução social: Contribuição ao debate sobre os mestrados profissionais. *Revista Brasileira de Pós-Graduação, 7*(14), 433–450.

Romizowski, A. (2005). *A study of distance education public policy and practice in the higher education sectors of selected countries: Synthesis of key findings*. Johannesburg, South Africa: South African Council on Higher Education (CHE).

Santos, A. I. (2011). *Open educational resources in Brazil: State-of-the art, challenges and prospects for development and innovation*. Moscow, Russia: UNESCO Institute for Information Technology in Education.

Schroeder, A., Minocha, S., & Schneider, C. (2010a). Social software in higher education: The diversity of applications and their contributions to student's learning experiences. *Communications of the Association for Information Systems, 26*(1), 547–564.

Schroeder, A., Minocha, S., & Schneider, C. (2010b). The strengths, weaknesses, opportunities and threats of using social software in higher and further education teaching and learning. *Journal of Computer Assisted Learning, 26*(3), 159–174. doi:10.1111/j.1365-2729.2010.00347.x

Seffah, A., & Grogono, P. (2002). *Learner-centered software engineering education: From resources to skills and pedagogical patterns*. Paper presented at the 15th Conference on Software Engineering Education and Training (CSEE&T 2002). Rio de Janeiro, Brasilia.

Sommer, L. H. (2010a). Educação a distância: Problemas, perspectivas e possibilidades. *Em Aberto, 23*(84), 1–15.

Sommer, L. H. (2010b). Formação inicial de professores a distância: Questões para debate. *Em Aberto, 23*(84), 17–30.

Spink, P. (1997). A formação acadêmica e a ciência: Ampliando o debate sobre o mestrado profissional. *Revista de Administração Contemporânea, 1*(3), 163–169. doi:10.1590/S1415-65551997000300009

UNESCO. (2011). *Guidelines for open educational resources (OER) in higher education*. Retrieved from http://www.col.org/PublicationDocuments/Guidelines_OER_HE.pdf

Weller, M. (2011). *The digital scholar: How technology is transforming scholarly practice*. Basingstoke, UK: Bloomsbury Academic. doi:10.5040/9781849666275

ADDITIONAL READING

Almeida, M. H. T. D. (2010). A pós-graduação no Brasil: Onde está e para onde poderia ir. In CAPES (Ed.), *Plano Nacional de Postgraduação (PNGP) 2010-2020*, (vol. 2, pp. 17-28). Rio de Janeiro, Brasilia: Academic Press.

Beetham, H., & Sharpe, R. (Eds.). (2007). *Rethinking pedagogy for a digital age*. Abingdon, UK: Routledge.

Conole, G. (2011). *Designing for learning in an open world*. Retrieved July 19, 2011, from http://cloudworks.ac.uk/cloudscape/view/2155

Conole, G., & Alevizou, P. (2010). *A review of the use of web 2.0 tools in higher education*. Retrieved October 13, 2011, from http://oro.open.ac.uk/23154/

Crook, C. J. C., Fisher, T., Graber, R., Harrison, C., Lewin, C., et al. (2008). *Web 2.0 technologies for learning: the current landscape –Opportunities, challenges and tensions*. Retrieved September 12, 2011, from http://dera.ioe.ac.uk/1474/

Fitzgerald, R., Barrass, S., Campbell, J., Hinton, S., Ryan, Y., Whitelaw, M., et al. (2009). *Digital learning communities (DLC): Investigating the application of social software to support networked learning (CG6-36)*. Retrieved October 14, 2011, from http://eprints.qut.edu.au/18476/

Junior, K. S. (2009). Distance education in Brazil: Paths, policies and perspective. *Educação Temática Digital, 10*(2), 16–36.

Litto, F. (2009). O retrato frente/verso da aprendizagem a distância no Brasil 2009. *Educação Temática e Digital, 10*(2), 108–122.

Minocha, S., & Kear, K. (2009). *Study of the effective use of social software to support student learning and engagement*. Retrieved October 13, 2011, from http://www.jisc.ac.uk/whatwedo/projects/socialsoftware08.aspx#downloads

Ribeiro, C. (2010). A universidade como disputa da reprodução social: Contribuição ao debate sobre os mestrados profissionais. *Revista Brasileira de Pós-Graduação, 7*(14), 433–450.

Schroeder, A., Minocha, S., & Schneider, C. (2010b). The strengths, weaknesses, opportunities and threats of using social software in higher and further education teaching and learning. *Journal of Computer Assisted Learning, 26*(3), 159–174. doi:10.1111/j.1365-2729.2010.00347.x

KEY TERMS AND DEFINITIONS

Distance Education: Education delivery mode that does not assume the presence of the student in a face-to-face situation. It is associated with pedagogical and technological advances to support the learning experience to be of high quality.

Learning Outcomes: Statement of what is intended to have been learned at the end of a module or course. They include knowledge and understanding, and skills.

Professional Master: A postgraduate qualification at master's level that is directed to those practicing the profession.

ENDNOTES

1. http://www.ibge.gov.br/home/estatistica/populacao/censo2010/default.shtm.
2. A committee set up by government to coordinate and integrate Internet services in Brazil.
3. http://cetic.br/usuarios/tic/2011-total-brasil/. In the UK, in 2011, 77% of the households have Internet access (http://www.ons.gov.uk/ons/rel/rdit2/internet-access---households-and-individuals/2011/stb-internet-access-2011.html).
4. Brazilian Association of IT Companies, http://www.brasscom.org.br/.
5. www.open.ac.uk.
6. www.uab.capes.gov.br.
7. All other state education in Brazil is free, including masters and doctorates.
8. MRes is a master's degree by course preparing students for research and a route to PhD.
9. An MPhil is a degree by research usually lasting two years full-time and corresponding to the first two years of a doctorate.
10. www.profmat-sbm.org.br.
11. 9% market share of postgraduate IT and computing in the UK in 2009/10 and 46% of postgraduate IT and computing distance education students in 2010/11 (http://www.hesa.ac.uk).
12. The only students on campus are full-time PhD students.
13. http://www8.open.ac.uk/about/main/?samsredir=1308134592.
14. http://www.open.ac.uk/blogs/OULDI/.
15. http://compendiumld.open.ac.uk/.
16. http://cloudworks.ac.uk/.
17. Now under Blackboard Collaborate (http://www.blackboard.com/Platforms/Collaborate/).
18. http://www.google.com/apps/intl/en/edu/.
19. http://se9book.wordpress.com/.

20   http://www.easterbrook.ca/steve/.

21   http://www.bibsonomy.org/.

22   http://delicious.com/.

23   http://library.open.ac.uk/help/howto/manage_ref/index.cfm.

24   Not actually classified as Web 2.0 tools but is increasingly providing interactive and collaborative resources.

25   http://www.ukcle.ac.uk/projects/past-projects/tle/.

26   ocw.mit.edu.

27   openlearn.open.ac.uk/.

28   itunes.open.ac.uk/, itunes.stanford.edu, itunes.ox.ac.uk/.

29   http://www.unesco.org/new/en/communication-and-information/resources/news-and-in-focus-articles/all-news/news/brazil_hosts_latin_america_open_educational_resources_regional_forum/.

Chapter 7
Enterprise 2.0 Impact on Company Performance in Developing Countries

Jacques Bughin
*McKinsey and Company, Belgium, ECARES, ULB, ECORE (UCL, ULB),
Brussels & KUL, Belgium*

ABSTRACT

This chapter draws on findings from a unique global survey to analyze how Enterprise 2.0 has been adopted in developing economies and how much it contributes to individual company performance. Two results stand out. While the use of social technologies by companies is gaining momentum, adoption remains patchy and still lags in developed countries. Nevertheless, clear evidence exists that Enterprise 2.0 in developing countries, when used at scale, lifts company performance, especially when integrated into workflows and when companies redefine their processes and operating models through social technologies.

INTRODUCTION

Enterprise 2.0, the usage of Social Software in the enterprise, is a big chance (Koch, 2008)

To many people, the fact that three days after thousands of people demonstrated in the streets of Egypt to topple his regime, Hosny Mubarak took the unprecedented

DOI: 10.4018/978-1-4666-2515-0.ch007

step of shutting off the Internet is a testimony to the power of the Web as well as to the vast social capabilities of Web 2.0 technologies.

However, while Facebook and Twitter reach hundreds of millions of users, their incursion into the corporate sphere (often dubbed "Enterprise 2.0") is not as far-reaching as in the consumer space. In any case, their precise recipe for successful impact on organizational performance is poorly documented (see Kosalge & Tole, 2010). This chapter is an attempt to provide a statistically robust perspective as to how the set of Enterprise 2.0 technologies has so far been deployed and under what conditions they have or have not been able to improve the performance of companies in developing versus developed countries.

The chapter is structured as follows. After some literature background on Enterprise 2.0, it presents the methodology and sample of companies' use and leverage of Enterprise 2.0. Five important stylized facts emerging from the data are then discussed, confirming early conjectures in the literature, but also highlighting a lag in diffusion (and by implication, impact of Web 2.0 performance) among companies in developing versus developed countries. Finally, the inter-company differences in performance impact from Enterprise 2.0 are assessed via regression analysis; the latter confirms the importance of the scale of diffusion of social technologies in the enterprise as well as the integration of social technologies in workflows in driving performance impact. The concluding section synthesizes the crucial findings of a link between social technologies and organization performance—however, the magnitude of the effect remains on average small in developing countries. At current, only a small fringe of 5% of companies is already mastering the implementation and scale of Enterprise 2.0. This chapter calls for those to be taken as an important benchmark to be copied, if one wishes to observe a significant effect of Web 2.0 on organizations in developing countries.

BACKGROUND

Social Web-based technologies, from wikis and Wikipedia, from social networks and Facebook, to micro-blogging and Twitter, or video sharing such as YouTube, have all become mainstream in the consumer sphere, welcoming hundreds of millions of users worldwide.

While pervasive on the consumer side, these social technologies seem to have been much less successful in invading the enterprise sphere (Koushik, et al., 2009; Google, 2012). This is rather puzzling as one can easily imagine how crucial these technologies could be when used to improve company performance.

Literature Review

In the burgeoning literature on Enterprise 2.0, a few important stylized facts stand out concerning the use of social technologies and their impact on the performance of companies from developed countries. The first observation is that the global adoption and diffusion rates of social technologies are two to three times slower than for consumer adoption—here, considering only social networks (Chui, et al., 2009; McAfee, 2010).

The second stylized fact is that enterprise adoption exhibits a strong power-law distribution: only a few companies have widely adopted these technologies for use by their employees, while a long tail of businesses remains at a stage of minimal experimentation (Bughin, 2010b). The third stylized fact is that Enterprise 2.0 can successfully challenge business orthodoxies. This includes opening up the innovation process (Enkel, et al., 2009; Jayakhanthan & Sundarajan, 2012, Carboni, et al., 2012), leveraging social media in order to create a powerful buzz (Cooke & Buckley, 2008; Wright & Hinson, 2008; Mesgari & Basselier, 2011; Deloitte, 2012), delivering produsage with users and suppliers (Bruns, 2008; Chen, 2009; Liu & Liu, 2009), or using wikis for interactive information flows (Caby-Guillet, et al., 2009; Grace, 2009; Levy, 2009; Babushkina, 2011).

These effects in doing business should lead to a material impact on performance (see Zeiller & Schauer, 2011); for example, open innovation is usually deployed when the internal innovation process is unable to provide enough good ideas to feed the product pipeline, or when accelerated information flows tend to reduce companies' coordination costs as emphasized, e.g., by Williamson (2002).

Our fourth stylized fact is that the jury is still out as to as to the *statistical, global,* evidence of a link between Enterprise 2.0 and economic performance for enterprises. One line of research does not prove, but rather *states* reasons and hope as to why companies (should) invest in Enterprise 2.0. For example, recent research by McAfee (2010) states that 2 out of 3 organizations invest in the hope of extra revenue potential from Web 2.0, yet the author does not provide evidence of whether this hope has materialized by any means. Tapscott and Williams in their seminal book *Wikieconomics* (2006) were among the first to point out the large productivity gains potentially available from Enterprise 2.0 deployment. They quote case-study evidence that companies such as P&G, Dell, IBM, Cisco, and others have been reaping good benefits from using social technologies à la Enterprise 2.0. Yet, these case examples originate from high-profile global companies, and the question remains unanswered as to how representative they are for the average company (see Van Dijk & Nieborg, 2009).

Another recent line of research attempts to measure actual performance impact from Enterprise 2.0, but stops short of consensus evidence (Klososky, 2011). For example, Sadeghi et al. (2011) summarize both the capabilities and shortcomings of Enterprise 2.0 technologies, concluding that there is a lack of "generic and proven usage patterns" for impact on organizations. They also highlight some important shortcomings of each social technology applied to the enterprise, e.g., unknown data origin in RSS feed, time-wasting for social networks, limited search capabilities of blogs, spam spots for microblogging, etc. Macro-surveys looking systematically at the impact question are also plagued by methodology issues, i.e., the sample is not representative of the industry structure of economies (see the early study by the Economist Intelligence Unit in its report sponsored by Cisco, 2007, or more recent ones such as McAfee, 2010). Last but not least, these studies do not have a real focus on developing countries.

In a nutshell, the existing literature documents a mechanism of skewed diffusion in enterprise, but has yet to prove strong impact of this diffusion on organization performance. Lastly, the focus remains on companies in developed countries, at least when it comes to performance impact.

Research Objective and Methodology

This chapter fills the void by drawing on a 2011 survey conducted by the author and McKinsey colleagues, covering 3600 companies worldwide. The survey elicited information on the companies' adoption and use of Internet and social Web technologies, the impact of using these technologies on performance, and the mechanism at play in the link between usage and performance.

Sampling

At the outset, the survey addressed a completely random sample of 11,000 companies and achieved a return rate of 1/3 regarding Enterprise 2.0. The database, built in cooperation with TNS, was designed to reflect the economic structure of countries. As the database of companies is also used for a variety of other survey themes (e.g., companies' strategy process or involvement in cloud services), TNS requires that the survey companies are blind to the authors. We had the opportunity to select a random sample of companies willing to reveal their identity in order to ensure that companies answers match other public data (e.g., revenue, revenue growth, employment, etc.). The match was 98% correspondence. The answers are typically provided by at least a company manager, as the data to be collected is very comprehensive. TNS guarantees that respondents have been trained in filling in the questionnaire. There is also an incentive to answer adequately as outliers are removed, and only non-outlier respondents receive a comparison of insights among peers as a confidential file for their own use.

Developed vs. Developing Countries' Definitions

Note that the database covers more than 60 countries (e.g., Bughin, 2010). A specific feature of the database is that it allows comparisons of companies from the developing world with companies in the developed economies. Developed countries are here defined as *all* European countries, *North America*, and *other OECD countries*. The balance of countries makes up the developing countries, outside of India and China. India and China are both very active non-members of the OECD, and distinctive in that they are major economies with urban centers that behave more like developed countries. We have, however, removed them from the analysis in this chapter (Bughin & Manyika, 2007).

Further, since 2011 (the year for the data in this chapter), the survey allows major deep dives into how Enterprise 2.0 is transformative, e.g., by radically designing new, or amending old, business processes and functions, and organization structures. It also allows evaluation of Enterprise 2.0's impact on performance.

After data cleaning (e.g., to remove inconsistencies in answers through the years and non-answers), we thus have a sample of 800 companies located in developing countries against 2,200 in developed countries. The final responses were weighted by the relevant size of the economies in which companies make the bulk of their business. Country size is measured by its 2010 GDP, as provided by the World Bank.

To gauge further details of the survey, users are referred to a series of Web 2.0 surveys conducted by the author and published in, among other journals, the *McKinsey Quarterly* (Bughin & Maniyka, 2007; Bughin, et al., 2011) and other academic spheres (Bughin & Manyika, 2008; Bughin, 2010). For ease, an appendix provides a simplified version of the top 20 questions used for the analysis discussed in this chapter.

The reader will notice that our scope of the social technologies underpinning Enterprise 2.0 includes 11 technologies: social networks, wikis, microblogging, ratings, RSS feeds, mash-ups, podcasts, blogs, prediction markets, tagging, and video sharing. This set of technologies can be used only within the organization, or in relations with the suppliers or customers; furthermore, they can reside within the IT architecture of companies, or via other models, like the clouds, etc.

Note as well the limitations of the database. The survey is conducted online and thus eliminates all companies in developing countries without Internet connection. The survey focuses on a sample of large companies—in the sample, companies with more than 100 employees are over-represented by a factor of four. The answers here have been reweighted to adjust for the size distribution to the extent possible.

STATISTICAL EVIDENCE OF ENTERPRISE 2.0 IMPACT ON PERFORMANCE IN DEVELOPING COUNTRIES

This section provides a set of five empirical facts regarding Enterprise 2.0 in developing countries in comparison with developed countries, confirming the previously mentioned stylized facts highlighted from the literature. It also provides the first robust evidence, to our knowledge, of the (quite variable) effect of Enterprise 2.0 on organizations based in developing countries. Further, a statistical analysis has also been conducted to better gauge key drivers of this performance impact.

Highlights of Findings

In a nutshell, the stylized facts on usage of Enterprise 2.0 point to the following five findings:

1. Still limited usage of social technologies in companies based in developing countries. As a statistical example: to date, about 1.9 out of the 11 social technologies in the scope of the analysis are used within the average organization versus 3.1 in developed countries.
2. Emergence of networked Enterprise 2.0. Example: for those companies using Enterprise 2.0, as many use it to connect with their customers'/suppliers' ecosystems, as they do for their internal processes.
3. Enterprise 2.0 affects company performance. Example: average stated impact of about 3% on added value of companies using Enterprise 2.0 in developing countries.
4. Enterprise 2.0 affects company performance through process change: Example: Enterprise 2.0 has affected a dominant share of the developing-world companies in the survey in the process of innovation (61%), followed by competitive intelligence (55%).
5. Significant skewness in performance impact. Example: the Zipf power-law regression coefficient is 3.2 in developing economies versus 2.5 in developed countries.

Further, as unique to this 2011 survey sample, we also attempted to measure impact of Enterprise 2.0 on company performance. We found that:

6. Scale of diffusion, workflow integration, and collaboration outside of organization boundaries are the key predictors of performance impact. Example: doubling the proportion of customers able to perform external collaboration with the organization leads to a 1 point increase of added-value margin. The

last point, arising from the statistical analysis, demonstrates a significant bottom-line impact for organizations in developing countries. It shows that Enterprise 2.0 is not a fad, but a real enabler of company organization change, with significant competitive benefit.

Five Stylized Facts on Enterprise 2.0 Usage in Developing Countries[1]

Enterprise 2.0 Usage Not at Scale in Developing Countries

Figure 1 describes the usage, trials, and consideration of adoption for each of the 11 social technologies analyzed. About two-thirds of the respondents claim that their companies located in developing countries are deploying at least one of the 11 technologies analyzed.

Still, the range of technologies adopted remains rather narrow, with an average of only 1.9 out of 11 technologies being adopted (versus 3.2 for developed countries). In fact, only 3 technologies have been adopted by more than 20% of the companies (social networking, then video sharing, then blogs). For nearly all of the social

Figure 1. "Enterprise 2.0" technology adoption in developing countries

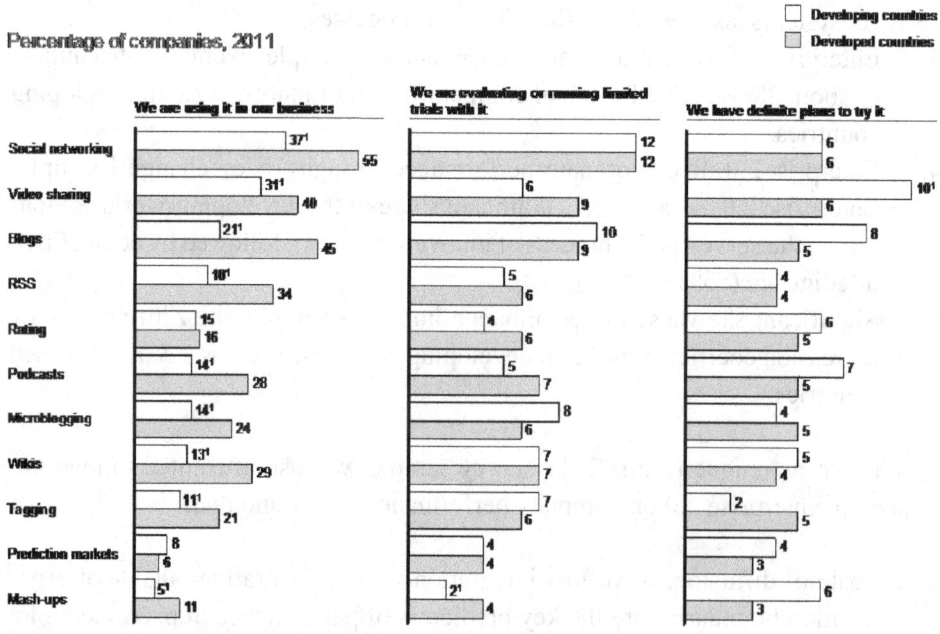

1 Statistically different at 5% between developed and developing countries

SOURCE: McKinsey Global web 2.0 survey, 2011; Author's computation

178

Enterprise 2.0 Impact on Company Performance in Developing Countries

Figure 2. "Enterprise 2.0" usage in developing countries

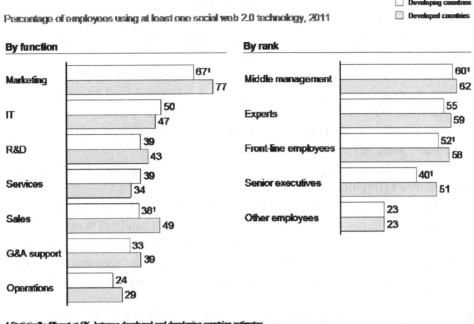

Percentage of employees using at least one social web 2.0 technology, 2011

☐ Developing countries
☐ Developed countries

1 Statistically different at 5% between developed and developing countries estimates

SOURCE: McKinsey Global web 2.0 survey, 2011; Author's computation

technologies analyzed (9 out of 11), adoption in developing countries lags developed countries, e.g., for the top 3 adopted in the developing countries: social networks (37% versus 55% in developed countries); video-sharing (31% versus 40%), blogs (21% versus 45%). Large gaps are noticeable for other social technologies, e.g., wikis (13% versus 29%) and RSS (18% versus 34%).

Even if the technology is being adopted in the enterprise, its use is limited. Figure 2 describes the use of the technologies by function and rank. Not surprisingly, the categories most amenable to Enterprise 2.0 technologies are in marketing as well as in IT functions. Usage adoption is higher for middle management than for executives. This pattern is the same whether one considers companies from developed or developing countries.

Except for the service function, Enterprise 2.0 is less diffused in developing than in developed countries. Further, a weighted average of usage among functions indicates that about 55% of employees claim to have used at least one of the technologies invested in by the enterprises. However, *none* of the Enterprise 2.0 technologies taken in isolation is being used by the majority of employees in a company. In fact, the technologies with more widespread use include social networks (41% of employees in companies vested in social networks), then wikis and video

179

sharing (29% of employees in vested companies), and finally, blogs (24% of employees in vested companies). All the other technologies are used by less than 20% of the employees, despite being made available by their employers. This fact was already spotted by Rask (2008), who identified a large difference in usage of Wikipedia between developing and developed countries.

All in all, then, multiplying the enterprise adoption rate with the employees' usage rate, the macro-picture is that employee usage of Enterprise 2.0 is still far from being at scale. Only 15% of employees from organizations in developing countries are using social networks in the enterprise, 9% video sharing, barely 6% blogs, and just 5% are using wikis.

These data imply a usage rate at about one-third the usage rate found in developed countries (Bughin, 2010).

In addition, these data do not compare well with consumer use of social Web tools. For example, in Latin America, our data suggest that barely 12% of employees are using social networks for enterprise purposes; this is to be compared with public Comscore data in 2011 indicating that the share of online-user consumers that uses social networks was close to 90% monthly, and still growing.

The Emergence of a Networked Enterprise in Developing Countries

When it comes to using these technologies *outside* of the inner circle of early-adopter enterprises, the share of enterprises using Enterprise 2.0 technologies in developing countries is actually at par with the share in developed countries.

The intent is to use social technologies rather extensively, not only for internal purposes (56%) but also for interfacing with customers (66%) and with suppliers (41%). However, there is gap *between intent and success*. While internal usage is visible for 55% of employees, only about 33% of customers are interfacing with social technologies and just 50% for suppliers.

Figure 3 clusters the data. Three clusters of roughly the same size emerge showing the main ways social Web 2.0 technologies interact with company boundaries. The largest segment is the one of non-adopters, that is 36% of companies in developing countries. The second reflects companies mostly interacting with employees internally (34%); the third (30%) concerns companies leveraging those technologies from interactions with customers, partners, and suppliers.

Visible Performance Effect of Developing Countries' Enterprise 2.0

Our survey asked whether Enterprise 2.0 might have already had some impact on the business system of companies in developing countries. Figure 4 summarizes

Enterprise 2.0 Impact on Company Performance in Developing Countries

Figure 3. "Enterprise 2.0" adoption purpose in developing countries

Percentage of enterprises, 2011

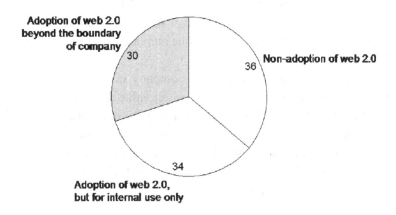

SOURCE: McKinsey Global web 2.0 survey, 2011; Author's computation

Figure 4. Stated Impact of "Enterprise 2.0" on Company Performance in Developing Countries

Percentage of metrics, 2011

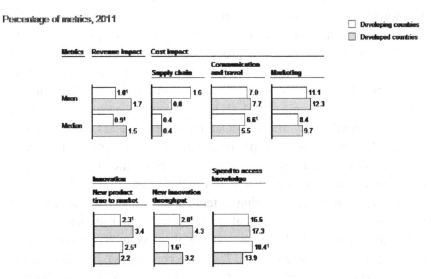

1 Statistically different at 5% between developed and developing countries estimates

SOURCE: McKinsey Global web 2.0 survey, 2011; Author's computation

the average (respectively, median) effect of these technologies on different metrics from revenue increases to innovation and cost efficiencies.

Note that impact is usually of the expected sign (cost decrease and revenue increase) and larger for companies in the developed countries, except, statistically, for the *median* effect on knowledge access speed, and communication/travel costs. In general, effects are significantly larger for these latter categories as well as for innovation, than direct impact on revenue increase and decrease in a company supply chain.

Using a pro-forma of the average company in our sample, the effect on the gross margin (60% of total revenue) and on value added (about 44% of revenue) is that current Enterprise 2.0 increases gross margin on average by 1.2% (1.1% at the median) and value added by 3.3% (2.6% at the median). These effects can be deemed to be small—but remember that they are in the context of limited usage diffusion. Scaling diffusion may have a significant effect on the performance metric, depending on diffusion elasticities. We return to this later.

Enterprise 2.0 Does Affect Business and Organizational Design in Developing Countries

In most cases, too, Enterprise 2.0 has an effect on processes and organization elements. We asked enterprises about current use of social technologies for eight generic business processes, from scanning the environment to assessing employee performance as well as for a set of organizational factors.

A minority (e.g., three companies out of ten, or 32%) is using Enterprise 2.0 with *no* process change; the balance delivers a mix of new and old processes (57%), and the rest (11%) goes for *entirely new* process designed via social Web 2.0 technologies. Of the processes with the largest process impact through Enterprise 2.0, the top contenders are idea generation (61%), then competitive scan (55%), compensation (35%), and strategic planning (30%). Of high relevance, one striking finding is that Enterprise 2.0 significantly affects human resource processes more in developing than in developing countries. In particular, the impact on the compensation and employee performance assessment processes is five times higher in companies located in developing countries than in developed ones.

Furthermore, companies adopting Enterprise 2.0 are also the ones to see major organizational changes in their typical operating and organizational design (Figure 5). The major changes, which companies strongly agree with, are to be found in: a) better data-centric decision making (37% of the companies); b) collaboration with vendors, customers, and employees (30%); and c) new flexible forms of organization (flatter hierarchy (31%) and more self-organized team units (30%).

Figure 5. Organizational impact of "enterprise 2.0" on developing countries

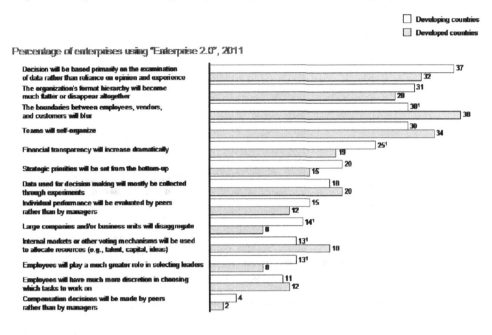

Percentage of enterprises using "Enterprise 2.0", 2011

1 Statistically different at 5% between developed and developing countries estimates at 5%

SOURCE: McKinsey Global web 2.0 survey, 2011; Author's computation

Three changes seem to be more prevalent in developing than in developed countries. The first is more financial transparency (25% of companies from developing countries adopting Enterprise 2.0 versus 19% in developed countries); employees' role in selecting leaders (13% versus 8%), and business unit disaggregation (14% versus 8%).

Power Law in Developing Countries' Enterprise 2.0

The world of Enterprise 2.0 is heavily concentrated, implying a form of strong power law. Let us define the degree of Enterprise 2.0 intensity for each company in our sample with a number scaled within the interval [0,1]—where 100% denotes an ideal company that has adopted *all* social technologies, each of which *all* its employees use at work, both internally and externally for third-party suppliers and customers. When the companies in the scope of analysis are ranked from high to low, and a log-log regression is run on the companies' Enterprise 2.0 intensity with their position rank, the resulting regression coefficient is the power coefficient of a so-called Zipf law, reflecting the fact that Enterprise 2.0 usage has only been extensively implemented by a happy few[2].

Figure 6. "Enterprise 2.0" usage power law in developing countries

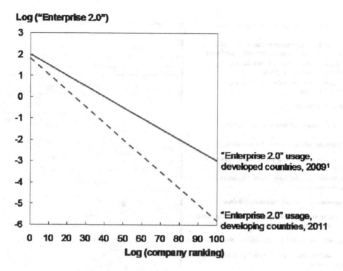

1 From Bughin (2010), The power law of enterprise 2.0, Encyclopedia of E-business development, IGI global, in Lee (ed.)

Figure 6 illustrates the regression results. The power coefficient of the Zipf law regression is estimated at 3.2 in absolute terms and is found to be highly significant. This stands for very high skewness, and statistically more so than for developed countries where the coefficient found was 2.5 in absolute terms (see Bughin, 2010b). As other benchmarks related to social online behavior in developed countries, Bughin (2010a) reported that social recommendations frequency on Amazon exhibits an exponent of the Zipf distribution of 1.5, edits frequency on Wikipedia, an exponent of 2.3, and crowd-working on Mechanical Turk and on Google mobile application posting an exponent at about 3. Hence, the power law arising from the use of specific social technologies in or outside the enterprise always implies less concentration in developed countries than what we are finding from Enterprise 2.0 usage in developing countries.

Drivers of Performance Impact of Enterprise 2.0

Besides the stylized facts, the originality of this research is to assess what drives difference of performance among companies. What indeed could make some companies lie in the head, while others are in the long tail of the performance distribution? This section uses statistical regression at company level to assess how Enterprise 2.0 parameters are actually tied to performance impact and tries to derive implications for pushing performance.

The findings in the following demonstrate that performance is materially enhanced when the majority of social technologies are used, when technologies are fully integrated into companies' workflows, and when the companies' collaborative approach spills over to the majority of suppliers and a large variety of customers. Such companies, as yet a clear minority in developing countries, offer clear benchmark cases to enhance the return on investment in social technologies in organizations.

Regression Model for Enterprise 2.0 Impact on Company Performance

An empirical regression model, of the form f, PERF = f(USAGE, SCOPE, CEXTENSION, SEXTENSION WORKFLOW, PROCESSES, ORG) has been constructed, where PERF is an indicator of performance, and f(.) is the functional form of the effects of the variables on performance, PERF.

Explanatory Variables

Explanatory variables included in the regression are of two natures, those from the stylized facts above, assumed to reflect an effect of Enterprise 2.0 on performance (symbol, PERF), and others used as control variables, e.g., size of companies, etc. The background of the set of variables included in performance is essentially from the stylized facts highlighted from the literature and from the descriptive statistics compiled from our survey. Hence, we assume that PERF should depend on:

a. Scale and scope, that is, intensity of usage within the enterprise (USAGE) as well as number of technologies (SCOPE) used. USAGE is the average of the 11 social technologies and is in the range of 0-100%. The average value of SCOPE is 15%; for USAGE, it is 16% among companies using Enterprise 2.0; and 9% for the total sample. Usage has been proven to be a major driver of performance impact, see among others, Bughin, Hung Byers, and Chui (2011), and Chui and Bughin (2010).

b. Level of extended enterprise, that is, share of customer participation and supply chain interaction (CEXTENSION and SEXTENSION, respectively). Both variables are within 0-100%. The average of CEXTENSION is 33%, and 50% for suppliers. This extent of collaboration has been shown to be a major driver of productivity by Carbone Contreras, Hernandez, and Gomez-Perez (2012).

c. Integration of tools into workflow (WORKFLOW). This variable varies between 0-100%, and is the sum of whether each social Web 2.0 technology used is or is not integrated into the workflow. The average of WORKFLOW is 18%. Tapscott and Williams (2006) were the first to highlight the importance of integration to workflow, and this relationship was empirically shown to be important by Bughin, Hung Byers, and Chui (2011).

d.   The extent to which processes and organization rules are adapted as Enterprise 2.0 spreads in a company (PROCESSES and ORG). This variable also falls within 0-100%, where 100% means all processes and organization structures are totally affected by Enterprise 2.0. The average value of PROCESSES is 24%, and 18% for ORG. McAfee (2009) explains why organizational changes are linked with company performance.

Finally, on top of using all the performance variables (SCALE, SCOPE, EXTEN-SION, WORKFLOW, PROCESSES, and ORG), we also use a few control variables such as firm size, firm continent location, and generic industry (NACE code level 2). Bughin (2010) shows that there is indeed some industry clustering in the use of social technologies (e.g., high-tech industries adopt faster than manufacturing), while both the report by McAfee and this chapter provide some evidence of difference among continents (e.g., Asia adopts faster than South America).

Dependent Variable and Functional Form

Two indicators of performance are used for PERF. The first is the value-added impact of Enterprise 2.0; which exhibits an average value of 3.3%. The second is the probability that the total company profit margin and market share alike have increased versus competitors (average = 11%), as our data surveys only collect binary impact on market share and profit.

We use a probit model for the regression analysis with probability impact, while we use a log transformation for the regression on value-added impact, given the power law nature of impact as highlighted above. we show the results in Figure 7 in linear form, though.

Regression Results

The regression only applies to companies that have invested in at least one social technology. Given that we also wanted to have all variables in the regression, the total regression sample is 312 companies for the first regression, and 246 for the second sample. We note that the sample for analysis is composed of firms with slightly higher revenue and slightly more Web 2.0 usage than the average, but in general, the sub-samples are in line with the total sample of companies.

The results are reported for the main variables in Figure 7. (Pseudo) R-squares are at about 38% and 11%, respectively, with the F-test on the significance of each model being highly significant (P=0.00). As expected, the first regression that directly measures Enterprise 2.0 impact is better described by the data. While not reported

Figure 7. Impact of "enterprise 2.0" with corporate performance on developing countries

Impact variables	Explanatory variables	Coefficients	Implied elasticity at the mean
	Constant	-0.07*	
	USAGE	0.11*	0.21*
	SCOPE	0.02*	0.11*
Value added "Enterprise 2.0" impact[1,2]	C. EXTENSION	0.06*	0.29*
	S. EXTENSION	-0.02	-0.10
	WORKFLOW	0.12*	0.23*
	PROCESS	0.03*	0.06*
	ORG	0.08*	0.15*
	Constant	-0.04*	
	USAGE	0.24*	0.45*
Company relative profit impact vs. competitor[3]	SCOPE	0.02	0.04
	C. EXTENSION	0.08*	0.39*
	S. EXTENSION	0.01	0.04
	WORKFLOW	0.08*	0.15*
	PROCESS	-0.02	-0.03
	ORG	0.13*	0.25*

1 In percent
2 Based on linear regression model
3 Probit regression model
Note: R-square for value added equation is 38%, pseudo R-square for relative profit is 13%; control variables is NACE 2 digit industry, company size
* statistically significant at 5%

SOURCE: McKinsey Global web 2.0 survey, 2011; Author's computation

here, statistical tests show no sign of multi-collinearity and misspecification in the regressions. Obviously, the regression results can pick up some omitted variables, and thus reported elasticities must be handled with caution.

We generally found statistically significant effects at many levels. First, the levels of usage and scope are statistically significant and positive in both regression types, confirming the importance of extensive diffusion as a requisite for performance. Second, the level of extension towards customers is positive in both equations, confirming the importance of collaboration with users for Enterprise 2.0. Extension towards suppliers is, however, *never* statistically significant. Third, the extent of workflow integration also positively affects performance, as does the proportion of organizational orthodoxies. Process has a conflicting effect depending on whether one looks at value-added impact or at the probability to generate a higher profit than competitors.

Finally, the implied elasticities seem to indicate that workflow integration, usage, and extension to customers/users are the most material factors for performance impact. For example, doubling usage can boost added-value impact by more than 20% at the mean. These quantification impacts are, to our knowledge, new results in the literature of Enterprise 2.0.

Simulations of Enterprise 2.0 Impact on Performance

Calibration

Using the results discussed previously, we now present some *calibrated case examples of the performance impact of social technologies.* Let us begin with the case of a company that we assume has invested in all social technologies (SCOPE= 1) but does not have any of his employees using them, and also has no integration whatsoever into production processes, workflows, etc. (all other variables set at zero). Such a company would generate a *negative* value added (-5% of total value added), as a result of investment waste and pressure from other companies leveraging Enterprise 2.0 for enhancing their competitive performance.

Let us contrast this case with a second one in which we assume the company has achieved average Enterprise 2.0 success, but also has fully adopted Enterprise 2.0 and uses it with its complete list of suppliers and customers. Such a company would generate an additional value added of 14% from Enterprise 2.0 and would have a 34% chance to grow company-wide profit versus average.

When the integration with a workflow and a complete change in operational and organization design is the goal, the impact on total value added will increase to 38%, accompanied by a mere 6% higher probability of more profit.

The above discussion shows that, beyond merely adopting social Web, Enterprise 2.0, technologies, what matters for companies is a) to stimulate employees and, even more so, customers to use these tools extensively, and b) to make sure that these tools are completely integrated into workflow and serve as levers to adapt the ways companies are run.

Four Types of Enterprise 2.0 Impact on Performance in Developing Countries

Let us remember also the current state of use of Enterprise 2.0 in developing countries. *The first segment,* and by far the largest, comprises companies that have not yet invested in Enterprise 2.0 or, if they have adopted it, have not yet boosted usage within the business. This segment still accounts for 45% of the companies. In accordance with the econometric model set forth above, these companies' financials are *suffering from a negative impact* of Enterprise 2.0, stemming from poor investment choices and/or loss of market share to other savvier companies.

The second segment, comprising 35% of the companies in the sample, is made up of experimenters that have adopted just two technologies and have established a niche (10%) of users. Furthermore, the companies in this segment have not yet extended the technologies beyond their own boundaries to customers or suppliers. Nor have they tried to integrate the technologies into the company eco-system. The effect of Enterprise 2.0 is just zero, no win, no loss. This segment does not yet see an impact from social technologies on their performance.

Unlike these first two segments, some companies are starting to see gains from Enterprise 2.0. However, within this remaining 20%, only a small slice of companies emerge as *an "Enterprise 2.0 success type."* Specifically, only 5% already makes use of the majority of Enterprise 2.0 solutions, having adopted more than 50% of the social technologies, which are also being used by more than 50% of their employees, integrated into workflows together with suppliers and a large variety of customers. These technologies have led to new forms of processes, especially concerning innovation (e.g., co-creation at the grassroots level and involving customers and suppliers), competitive intelligence (e.g., scanning competitors via direct social media, etc.). Such companies, as yet a clear minority, see significant impact of up to 10% in value-added upside impact, and double the probability of the current average of the sample of growing both profit and market share alike against competitors.

The remaining segment, 15% of the companies in our sample, resembles the average company archetype in developed regions (Europe and the US), with Enterprise 2.0 representing one set among several of IT investments, and delivering good, visible, but limited impact so far, i.e., 5% of the companies' value added.

FURTHER RESEARCH DIRECTIONS

The chapter has provided unique evidence that Enterprise 2.0 diffuses slowly within companies or organizations in developing countries. In addition, a large share of the companies in developing countries has yet to invest seriously in Enterprise 2.0, to see significant bottom-line impact. Yet bottom-line impact is prevalent and leads to significant return on investment in social technologies.

Clearly, we are just at the beginning of understanding social technologies' impact on organizational performance. Hence, one clear avenue of further research would be into confirmation of our findings through other samples, in particular, going beyond the limitations of the sample used in this chapter, e.g., focusing on smaller and medium-size companies rather than large corporations. The empirical model of Enterprise 2.0 impact should be backed up with a more comprehensive theory, so as to ensure adequate specification and minimize the risks of inaccurate specification.

Second, the so far limited adoption and diffusion of social technologies among employees calls for more work to understand the factors driving those adoption curves. Third, a truly small group (5% of the companies in the sample) is just doing a great job in leveraging Enterprise 2.0. One research task would be to study these companies in more detail, identify further companies, and understand their journey and how these companies organize themselves and challenge business orthodoxies to reap such large competitive benefits. Furthermore, it is clear that the organizational and process changes associated with Enterprise 2.0 are not one homogenous group and also merit further detailed research.

Much thus remains to be investigated, yet it holds out the important promise of increasing our knowledge of new ways for companies to continue their profit growth path and leverage the benefits of technology investments.

CONCLUSION

This chapter draws on a unique global survey to analyze how enterprise 2.0 has spurred advances in companies and organizations in the developing economies, and how it enhances related company performance.

While adoption of Web 2.0 technologies by businesses in developing countries is gaining momentum, adoption remains patchy and still significantly lags uptake in developed countries. There is, nevertheless, clear evidence that Enterprise 2.0 in developing countries, when used at scale, will positively affect company performance, especially when integrated into workflows and when companies modify their processes and operating models to leverage social technologies.

The hope is to see champions in developing countries showing the way.

ACKNOWLEDGMENT

The author thanks his colleagues at the McKinsey Global Institute, especially Dr. Michael Chui as well as Dr. James Manyika, for parallel research on the impact of technologies on company performance. The views expressed in this chapter are, however, solely the author's and do not necessarily represent those of any institution he is affiliated with.

REFERENCES

Babushkina, Y. (2011). Using web 2.0 for the information support of employees: The promise of web 2.0. *Journal of Scientific Information Processing, 38*(1).

Bruns, A. (2008). *Blogs, Wikipedia, Second Life and beyond: From production to produsage*. New York, NY: Peter Lang.

Bughin, J. (2010). The future of user participation. *McKinsey Technology Initiative Perspectives, 3*.

Bughin, J. (2010). The power law of enterprise 2.0. In In-Lee (Ed.), Encyclopedia of E-Business Development and Management in the Global Economy. Hershey, PA: IGI Global.

Bughin, J., Hung Byers, A., & Chui, M. (2011, November). How social technologies are extending the organization. *The McKinsey Quarterly*.

Bughin, J., & Manyika, J. (2007, December). How businesses are using web 2.0: A McKinsey global survey. *The McKinsey Quarterly*.

Bughin, J., & Manyika, J. (2008). Bubble or paradigm change? Assessing the global diffusion of Enterprise 2.0. In Koohang, A., Harman, K., & Britz, J. (Eds.), *Knowledge Management-Research and Applications*. Hershey, PA: IGI Global.

Caby-Guillet, L., Guesmi, S., & Maillard, A. (2009). Wiki professionnel et coopération en réseaux: Une étude explorative. *La Découverte – Réseaux, 154*, 195-227.

Carbone, F., Contreras, J., Hernandez, J., & Gomez-Perez, J. (2012). Open innovation in an enterprise 3.0 framework- 3 case studies. *Expert Systems with Applications: An International Journal, 39*(10).

Chen, T. F. (2009). Building a platform of business model 2.0 to creating real business value with web 2.0 for web information services industry. *International Journal of Electronic Business Management, 7*(3), 168–180.

Chui, M., & Bughin, J. (2010, December). The rise of the networked enterprise, web 2.0 finds its payday. *The McKinsey Quarterly*.

Chui, M., Miller, A., & Roberts, R. P. (2009). Six ways to make web 2.0 work. *McKinsey and Company*, 1-7.

Cooke, M., & Buckley, N. (2008). Web 2.0, social networks and the future of market research. *International Journal of Market Research, 50*, 267–292.

Economic Intelligence Unit. (2007). *Collaboration- Transforming the way business works. Report from the EIU*. Cisco Systems.

Elragal, A., & El-Telbany, O. (2012). Decision 2.0: An exploratory case study. [*th Hawaii International Conference on System Science*. IEEE Computer Society.]. *Proceedings of the, 2012*, 45.

Enkel, E., Gassmann, O., & Chesbrough, H. (2009). Open R&D and open innovation: Exploring the phenomenon. *R & D Management, 39*(4). doi:10.1111/j.1467-9310.2009.00570.x

Gaspoz, C. (2011). Prediction markets as web 2.0 tools for enterprise 2.0. In *Proceedings of the Seventeenth Americas Conference on Information Systems*. Detroit, MI: IEEE.

Google. (2012). *Customer perspective on the rela benefits delivered by Google. Google EVM Perspective Report*. Google.

Grace, T. P. L. (2009). Wikis as a knowledge management tool. *Journal of Knowledge Management, 13*(4), 64–74. doi:10.1108/13673270910971833

Jayakhanthan, R., & Sundarajan, D. (2012). Enterprise crowdsourcing solution for software development in an outsourcing organization. In *Proceedings of the 11ᵗʰ International Conference on Current Trends in Web Engineering*. Springer-Verlag.

Klososky, S. (2011). *Enterprise social technology: Harnessing the power*. New York, NY: GreenLeaf Book Group Press.

Kosalge, P., & Toole, O. (2010). Web 2.0 and business, ealy results on perception of web 2.0 and factors influencing its adoption. *Proceedings of AMCIS, 2010*, 1–10.

Koushik, S., Birkinshaw, J., & Crainer, S. (2009). Using web 2.0 to create management 2.0. *Business strategy. RE:view, 20*(2), 20–23.

Levy, M. (2009). WEB 2.0 implications on knowledge management. *Journal of Knowledge Management, 13*(1), 120–134. doi:10.1108/13673270910931215

Liu, C.-H., & Liu, H.-S. (2009). Increasing competitiveness of a firm and supply chain with web 2.0 initiatives. *International Journal of Electronic Business Management, 7*(4), 248–255.

McAfee. (2010). *Web 2.0: A complex balancing act – The first global study on web 2.0 usage, risks and best practices*. Retrieved from http://www.mcafee.com/us/resources/reports/rp-first-global-study-web-2.0-usage.pdf

McAfee, A. (2006). Enterprise 2.0: The dawn of emergent collaboration. *MIT Sloan Management Review, 47*(3), 21–28.

McAfee, A. P. (2009a, November). Shattering the myths about enterprise 2.0. *Harvard Business Review*. Retrieved from http://hbr.org/2009/11/shattering-the-myths-about-enterprise-20/ar/1

McAfee, A. P. (2009b). *Enterprise 2.0: New collaborative tools for your organization's toughest challenges*. Boston, MA: Harvard Business Review Publishing.

Mesgari, M., & Basselier, G. (2011). How online social networks create value for organizations: A resource based perspective. In *Proceedings of the Seventeenth Americas Conference on Information Systems*. Detroit, MI: IEEE.

Miller, M., Marks, A., & Decoulode, M. (2012). *Social software for business performance*. Retrieved from http://www.deloitte.com/assets/Dcom-UnitedStates/Local%20Assets/Documents/TMT_us_tmt/us_tmt_%20Social%20Software%20for%20Business_031011.pdf

Pélissié du Rausas, M., Manyika, J., Hazan, E., Bughin, J., Chui, M., & Said, R. (2011). *Internet matters: The net's sweeping impact on growth, jobs, and prosperity.* McKinsey Global Institute.

Rask, M. (2008). The reach and richness of Wikipedia: Is Wikipedia only for the rich countries. *First Monday, 13*(6).

Sadeghi, P., Kuzimsky, C., & Benyoucef, M. (2011). *Towards a readiness model for health 2.0.* Paper presented at MEDES Conference 11. San Francisco, CA.

Scarff, A. (2006). Advanced knowledge sharing with Intranet 2.0. *Knowledge Management Review, 9*(4).

Tapscott, D., & Williams, A. D. (2006). *Wikinomics: How mass collaboration changes everything.* New York, NY: Portfolio.

United Nations. (2011). *World economic situation and prospects 2011.* Retrieved from http://www.un.org/en/development/desa/policy/wesp/wesp_current/2011wesp_pre-release1.pdf

Van dijk, J., & Nieborg, N. (2009). Wikinomics and its discontents: A critical analysis of Web 2.0 business manifestos. *New Media & Society, 11*(4), 855–874.

Williamson, O. (2002). the theory of the firm as governance structure: from choice to contract. *The Journal of Economic Perspectives, 16*(3), 171–195. doi:10.1257/089533002760278776

Wright, N., & Hinson, T. (2008). How blogs and social media are changing public relations and the way it is practiced. *The Public Relations Journal, 2*(2).

Zeiller, M., & Schauer, B. (2011). *Adoption, motivation and success factors for team collaboration in SME's, mimeographed.* Burgenland, Austria: University of Applied Science.

ENDNOTES

[1] Note that the comparison with companies in developed countries has been tested in both directions and shown to be statistically significant at 5% risk (Is "risk" the right unit of measure for the statistical significance of the company comparisons in the developing vs. developed world?).

[2] For a tutorial on power law distributions, see http://en.wikipedia.org/wiki/Power_law. See also the application by the author in the article "The Power Law of Enterprise 2.0" available at http://en.wikipedia.org/wiki/Power_law.

APPENDIX

The current chapter draws on data from a major online survey conducted by the authors and McKinsey colleagues in the course of the spring of 2011. We have aggregated the data into three clusters: developed regions such as Europe and North America, developing economies, and China and India. The latter two were removed from the survey sample, leaving with data from about 800 respondents. The sample is mostly representative of large corporations, but it does still represent about 60% of the total added value activity of the various geographies analyzed. The survey covers the adoption and usage of Enterprise 2.0 technologies, their benefits, corporate performance, and the magnitude of the organizational and process changes that could result. A simplified version of the survey's top 20 questions, which were used for the analyses underlying this chapter, is provided below:

1. Is your company currently using any of the following social technologies or tools (Web 2.0)?

[Set rows as: Blogs, Prediction Markets, Mash-Ups, Podcasts, Video sharing, RSS, Social Networking, Wikis, Rating, Tagging, Micro-Blogging, Other; set glossary in pop-up window] [column heads: We're using it in our business; We're evaluating or running limited trials with it; We have definite plans to try it; We're considering it; We have not considered investing in it; We have tried it but no longer use it; Don't know]

2. To what extent, if at all, are social tools (Web 2.0) integrated into employees' day-to-day work activities?

[Not at all; A little; Somewhat; Very; Extremely; Don't Know/Not Applicable]

3. Who in your company is using social technologies (Web 2.0)? (Select all that apply)

Functions [Research and Development; Production/Operations; Marketing; Sales; Service; IT; Other General and Administrative]; employee type [Frontline Employees; Technical Experts (e.g., Researchers, Programmers); Middle Managers; Senior Executives (Vice President and above); Other Employees]

4. For which of the following purposes does your company use social tools or technologies?

[Internal Purposes; Customer-Related Purposes; Working with Partners, Suppliers, or Outside Experts; Don't Know]

5. In which of the following ways has the use of social technologies (Web 2.0) for internal purposes had a measurable effect on your company?

[Reducing time to market for products/services; Increasing revenue; Increasing the number of successful innovations; Increasing speed to access knowledge; No measurable effects/benefits]

6. [For each q5 answer] *Please estimate the percentage share of improvement attributable to your company's use of social technologies (Web 2.0).* [%; Don't know]
7. Which of the technologies or tools, if any, is your company using for each of the following process purposes?

[Developing strategy; Developing products or services; Internal recruiting and talent identification; Training; Managing knowledge; Fostering general collaboration across the company; Enhancing the company's culture]

8. What practices were most important for your company's success in using social technologies (Web 2.0)?

[Senior leaders role-modeling and/or championing the use of technology; Integrating the use of social technologies (Web 2.0) into employees' day-to-day work activities; Providing formal incentives (e.g., performance evaluation, pay); Providing informal incentives (e.g., reputation/fame, positive feedback); Allowing non-work uses (e.g., running club, pets, family); Other, please specify]

9. Please estimate the percentage of customers with whom your company interacts using social technologies (Web 2.0).
10. What practices were most important for your company's success in using social (Web 2.0) technologies for working with partners, suppliers, and external experts?

[Marketing social initiatives (Web 2.0) to partners, suppliers, and external experts; Providing formal incentives (e.g., monetary); Providing informal incentives (e.g., reputation/fame, positive feedback); Integrating social technologies (Web 2.0) with other modes of partner/supplier/expert interaction; Ensuring participation of leading partners/suppliers/external experts to gain critical mass; Other, please specify]:

11. Please estimate the percentage of business partners (e.g., suppliers, external experts) with whom your company interacts using social technologies (Web 2.0).

12. Approximately what share of your employees is using each of the following technologies or tools?

[1 to 10 percent, 11 to 30 percent, 31 to 50 percent, 51 percent or more, Don't know]

13. Which social technologies or tools (Web 2.0), if any, is your company using in each of the following processes?

[Developing strategic plan; Scanning external environment (e.g., consumer trends, competitors' conduct); Finding new ideas (e.g., for saving costs, for new products); Allocating resources (e.g., people, financial); Matching employees to tasks; Managing projects; Assessing employee performance; Determining compensation]

14. To what extent do you expect the use of social technologies and tools (Web 2.0) to change the ways in which your organization performs each of the following processes during the next three years?

[No change in process; Traditional process mixed with new process(es); Entirely new process; Don't know]

15. In an organization without any constraints related to social technologies (Web 2.0), which of the following changes in management processes and structure would be likeliest to happen over the next three to five years? (Select up to three)

[Large companies and/or business units will disaggregate; Employees will play a much greater role in selecting leaders; Strategic priorities will be set from the bottom up; Internal markets or other voting mechanisms will be used to allocate resources (e.g., talent, capital, ideas); Teams will self-organize; Individual performance will be evaluated by peers rather than by managers; Compensation decisions will be made by peers rather than by managers; The boundaries between employees, vendors, and customers will blur; Financial transparency will increase dramatically; The organization's formal hierarchy will become much flatter or disappear altogether; Employees will have much more discretion in choosing which tasks to work on; Decisions will be based primarily on the examination of data rather than reliance on opinion and experience; Data used for decision making will mostly be collected through experiments; None of the above]

16. How much do you agree or disagree with each of the following statements? [set as matrix, with columns as: Strongly Disagree, Disagree, No Opinion, Agree, Strongly Agree]

[My company has a policy for employees' participation in social media (e.g., social-networking sites); Some or all employees are allowed to speak on behalf of the company on external social-media platforms]

17. How many of your employees are allowed to speak on behalf of the company on external social media?

[10 or fewer; 11 to 50; 51 to 100; 101 to 500; More than 500]

18. How has your company's market share changed over the past 12 months?

[Lost market share and dropped below next competitor; Lost market share but did not drop below next competitor; No change in market share; Gained market share but did not increase above next competitor; Gained market share and increased above next competitor; Don't know/Prefer not to answer]

20. How would you describe your company's operating margins, compared with competitors, over the past 12 months?

[Much lower; Lower; About the Same; Higher; Much Higher; Don't Know/ Prefer not to Answer]

Chapter 8
Toward Web 2.0 Integration in Indonesian Education:
Challenges and Planning Strategies

Agus Mutohar
The University of Texas at Austin, USA

Joan E. Hughes
The University of Texas at Austin, USA

EXECUTIVE SUMMARY

Numerous efforts have been made to reform education to address globalization both in developed and developing countries. The integration of technology in education has been one vital reform effort in developing countries to prepare graduates for 21st century workplaces, which are digitally robust. Web 2.0 technologies are becoming prominent educational and workplace tools. This literature review of Indonesian government policies, NGO initiative reports, and contemporary research explores the integration of Web 2.0 in Indonesian education using an ecological perspective by introducing the Indonesian national educational policy and laws, describing national and non-government organizations' initiatives focused on Web 2.0 integration, identifying salient national and local challenges preventing Web 2.0 integration, and proposing strategies for future planning and research.

DOI: 10.4018/978-1-4666-2515-0.ch008

Challenges identified include lack of technological facilities, an absence of technology standards in education, a standardized testing culture, lack of coordination between government levels (national to local), lack of professional development, and a need for strong school technology leadership. The authors recommend Indonesia engage in comprehensive, visionary planning for Web 2.0 integration with strategies to meet local needs, invest in professional development and technology specialist positions, and advance mobile Web 2.0 computing and BYOT/D initiatives. Future research could examine how ecological factors at the national, provincial, and local levels coordinate to best establish Web 2.0 integration in education at the school level.

INTRODUCTION

In recent years, the integration of digital technology, especially Internet-based technologies, into education has become very important for both developed and developing countries. The earliest form of the Web, Web 1.0, was built through the use of Hypertext Markup Language (HTML) that coded Web pages for transmitting information from experts to the masses, who read or consumed the information. Web 2.0 technologies have been described as the next generation Web, one that organizes itself semantically through user and data connections with tags and linking. Web 2.0 re-characterizes the Internet as a participatory, collaborative, and distributed network of information, content creators, consumers, and organizing features. All users, who now form the center of the Web, materially participate in the generation of content. Such content can be expressed as original, remixes, or commentary and connections. Users also represent their identity(ies) through public or private profiles in the many formal and informal social spaces. Inter-technology data sharing enables distributed practices and collective intelligence to emerge as prominent (Anderson, 2007; Greenhow, Robelia, & Hughes, 2009; O'Reilly, 2005). Web 2.0 includes social media such as Facebook, Google+, Foursquare, and MySpace; bookmarking such as Diigo, Technocrati, Pinterest, and Digg; and other tools such as tagging tools and remixing tools. With the rapid development and dissemination of Web 2.0 tools, developing countries have considered incorporating Web 2.0 tools, such as Web blog, social media, and wiki, in education. Although there are many obstacles preventing integration of Web 2.0 such as lack of computers and Internet in schools, many developing countries still strive to integrate Web 2.0 tools in many ways with the support from governmental agencies and Non-Governmental Organizations (NGO).

Greenhow, Robelia, and Hughes (2009) state that Web 2.0 holds great promises and challenges for education. Thus, scholarship about Web 2.0 in developing countries is a worthwhile research topic because there will be different patterns in Web

2.0 integration in education between developed and developing countries. Research exploring the potential and challenges of Web 2.0 integration in developing countries is a pressing need. To date, there is a gap of research about Web 2.0 integration in education in developing countries. Current research focuses on policy preparation, such as the importance of careful planning in integrating technology in developing countries (Jhurree, 2005), which offers guidelines for technology integration for developing countries. Developing countries might need to embrace leapfrogging (Harkins, 2008) in order to implement Web 2.0 integration successfully. Leapfrogging is the strategy of jumping to the best innovation adoption condition by which time and costs are saved.

In developing countries like Indonesia, an adoption of technology in education can leverage large improvements in human development through education. Kim, Miranda, and Olaciregui (2008) describe possibilities of incorporating mobile technology to combat illiteracy in underserved area in Latin America. Kim et al. came to the conclusion that mobile devices can provide rich learning material for people in underserved area due to its low cost, portability, and versatile features. In addition, Perraton and Charlotte (2001) assert that the incorporation of new technologies such as Web 2.0 in education can bridge the gap between information rich countries and information poor countries such as the case of Finlandia in using Web (ENO—Environment Online) to raise environmental awareness among students in Finland schools and other schools around the World.

THEORETICAL FRAMEWORK

This chapter depicts Web 2.0 integration in primary and secondary education in the developing country, Indonesia, through a literature review of Indonesian government policies, NGO initiative reports, and contemporary research. We consulted government websites and archives, news reports, and associated NGO websites to obtain reports. We conducted literature searches within library databases (ERIC, Education Full Text, and PsycInfo) using keywords (Web 2.0, technology integration, developing country, Indonesia, Asia, South East Asia). We also identified pertinent articles within articles' reference lists. Conceptually, we employ an ecological system perspective (Bronfenbrenner, 1979; Zhao, 2003) to closely examine this complex topic. Our analysis identified national and local challenges from an ecological perspective (Bronfenbrenner, 1979). National challenges refer to the macrosystem: ideas, content, or actions reflective of the culture and its belief systems or ideologies. National and provincial policies are macrosystem elements. Local challenges align with Bronfenbrenner's exosystems—people, places, and actions that will indirectly impact the learner. Exosystem elements could involve teacher professional development and school policies. The microsystem involves the primary, immediate influences on the developing primary or secondary student, such as their home life or classroom experiences. When multiple microsystems come together to impact the learner, it reflects mesosystem elements. Mesosystem elements could involve a student's extracurricular and home activities. In this way, we identify best practices, challenges, and planning strategies regarding Web 2.0 implementation in ways that reveal the role and interrelationships between systemic levels—with a singular focus on how to best provide experiences for young learners to engage in 21st Century learning with Web 2.0 technologies. We close with recommendations and a futuristic outlook of Web 2.0 integration in Indonesian education.

BACKGROUND ON INDONESIAN GOVERNMENT AND LAWS

Indonesia has been recognized as a country since 1945. Indonesia is located in Southeast Asia and comprises of 13.466 islands and 33 provinces. This geographical condition becomes a challenge in establishing technology infrastructure. The Ministry of National Education (MoE) in Indonesia created *PUSTEKKOM* (i.e., Center of Technology Education) in 1987 as a unit to manage technology integration in education. Since then, *PUSTEKKOM* has introduced various technology integration initiatives to accelerate technology-based educational quality in Indonesia. *PUSTEKKOM* has created several technology integration initiatives such as TV education, radio education, e-books, and multimedia teaching resources.

The government of Indonesia through the Ministry of Education (MoE) has committed to advancing technologies for teaching and learning. The long-term national education plan from 2005 to 2025, as stated in the Ministry of Education's decree No. 25 year 2005, promotes the empowerment of technology use in education. The government believes that incorporation of technology in education will prepare students to be ready for today's and tomorrow's workplaces that necessitate technology literacy and other life skills such as collaboration.

In addition to the 2005-2025 long-term plan, the MoE sets short term plans that allow shallower forecasting, which is especially useful for educational technology since technologies reinvent themselves annually. The 2010-2015 plans purposely emphasize technology integration in education including Web 2.0 uses in education. In this, the MoE focuses on promoting technology use in teaching by providing technology infrastructure and teacher training. More recently, the national education decree No. 16 Year 2007 clearly mandates that every teacher must possess technology integration competency in teaching. The similar decree No 41 Year 2007 also requires teachers to incorporate technology in their curriculum.

The promise of Web 2.0 in Indonesian education is unequivocal for several reasons. First, compared to other Asian countries, the users of Internet in Indonesia are ranked number four after China, India, and Japan (Internet World Stats, 2011). Internet users in Indonesia are growing quickly due to the high access to hand-held devices, such as mobile phones. In 2011, the Internet users in Indonesia rose from 45 million to 55 million people (Jakarta Post, 2011). Nielsen (2011) revealed that 31% of Internet users access it from desktop computers, 29% from laptop computers, 78% from mobile phones, and 2% from tablet computers. From these data, mobile phones are the most popular device to access the Internet likely due to inexpensive mobile phone pricing and services. Second, Indonesia has an enormous number of social media users. Currently, Indonesian Facebook users are ranked number two with 36,568,620 users after United States (Social Bakers, 2011). In addition, Indonesia is also known to have a large number of users of other social media, such as Twitter. According to Sysomos, in 2010 the Twitter user in Indonesia is ranked number sixth worldwide (Evans, 2010).

THE STATUS OF WEB 2.0 IN INDONESIAN EDUCATION

Web 2.0 Initiatives by Government

There are very few government-sponsored initiatives specifically focused on Web 2.0 integration. The Ministry of Education (MoE) in Indonesia created a national scale initiative called *Jardiknas* (national education network), a national technology integration initiative that focuses on empowering school administration and providing online repositories on the Web. There are other government initiatives in technology integration in schools such as *e-dukasi.net*, which contains multimedia learning resources, and *Rumah Belajar* (house of learning) that provide downloadable learning materials, videos on demand, and online tutorials. While these initiatives use the Web, they do not promote or capitalize on Web 2.0 affordances for supporting teaching and learning. The initiatives still use Web as learning resources repository where students and teachers can download and upload learning material on the Web.

In 2009, the Ministry of Education initiated a Web 2.0 training program for primary and secondary teachers. In this program, trainers coached teachers on how to incorporate Web 2.0 tools in teaching. Web 2.0 tools such as Diigo, VoiceThread, Ning, Dimdim, Flickr, and Curriki were taught in the program. The intention behind the program was to harness potential of Web 2.0 for its ease of use, collaboration, and interactivity to support educational activities. Following the program, the government provided online tutorials for teachers to integrate those Web 2.0 tools in *PUSTEKKOM* website. However, in 2010 these tutorials that were hosted in the *PUSTEKKOM* website were shut down.

In 2008, The Ministry of Education, through *PUSTEKKOM*, created another program called SchoolNet to promote Web 2.0 uses in schools. SchoolNet provides both software and hardware for technology integration in schools, such as providing desktop computers and Internet access. Currently in 2011, MoE runs the SchoolNet program in all 33 provinces in Indonesia but only penetrates into 27% of secondary schools, 16.4% of middle schools, and 2.8% of elementary schools nationally. According to the report from *PUSTEKKOM*, students and teachers use the SchoolNet program in different ways such as looking up information related to assignments, uploading and downloading learning material online, communicating through email, blogging, and incorporating social media such as Facebook and Twitter in learning. Although this program has broader goals than only promoting Web 2.0 integration, some teachers use this opportunity to integrate Web 2.0 in their teaching. According to *PUSTEKKOM*, teachers have been using blogging platforms, such as Blogspot and Wordpress, and Facebook in teaching. For instance, teachers assign students to post their writings on the blog. However, there are very few teachers who use micro blogging platform such as Twitter. Wikipedia is also a favorite website for teachers when they look up information or assign students to find out information related to assignments. Although there is no clear statistics on the use of such Web 2.0 tools in teaching, the report reveals some early use of common Web 2.0 tools by teachers for teaching (Ministry of Education in Indonesia, 2011).

Web 2.0 Initiatives by Non-Government Organizations

Like other developing countries, Indonesia receives generous assistance through partnerships with non-government organizations to promote successful use of Web 2.0 in education. This section discusses several NGO-supported initiatives on Web 2.0 use in education.

Intel Teach Elements

Intel education has been an active NGO that specifically promotes technology integration and 21st century teaching. Intel education in cooperation with the Ministry of Education (MoE) has been implementing technology integration in education since 2007. Currently, Intel education promotes Web 2.0 online professional development for teachers through Intel Teach Elements. The program trains teachers to integrate Web 2.0 tools such as wiki, blog, and social media in teaching using a problem-based learning approach.

In Intel Teach Elements, teachers are taught two lessons that involve project based learning and assessment in 21st century skills. In the Project-Based Learning (PBL) lesson, teachers explore best practices of PBL and how to design and implement PBL in classrooms with Web 2.0 tools such as wiki and social networking sites. In the assessment in the 21st century lesson, teachers are taught strategies and methods to conduct assessments with Web 2.0. By the end of the course, Intel education in Indonesia awards three laptop computers for the teachers who create the best action plans for project based learning and assessment in their own classrooms. These action plans contain an introduction to the lesson, teaching strategies, and assessment using project based approach with Web 2.0 tools. This program is offered fully online which can be a challenge for teachers who do not have a sufficient Internet access.

Bridge

Bridge stands for Building Relationship through Intercultural Dialogue and Growing Engagement. The Bridge program is a partnership program between Australian and Indonesian schools. More than 30,000 Australian students and 90,000 Indonesian students participated in the program from 2008 to 2011. This program uses Web 2.0 tools for collaboration among students in the two countries. The Bridge program also initiates teacher exchange between the two countries. In order to run smooth collaboration, teachers were trained about project based learning and how to conduct online collaboration using Wikispaces.

This project mainly uses a wiki as a tool for collaboration among students; the wiki is hosted at http://indonesia.bridge.wikispaces.net/. Online collaboration activities about cultural understanding are provided in the website such as: culture and fashion, my story your story, let's celebrate, the language we use, and other topics. For instance, students collaborate in the "let's celebrate" topic to develop an understanding of each other's culture through a study of celebrations, ceremonies, festivals and rituals. Both students in Indonesia and Australia work to share their local ceremonies by using digital cameras with teachers' directions. After exploring the local ceremonies, students share the results on the wiki page. Students' work such as short stories, photos, recordings, and videos about local ceremonies are uploaded on the wiki. Both teachers in Indonesia and Australia facilitate peer assessment with student dyads of an Indonesian and Australian student. Finally, students pose questions through wiki discussions. Through these activities, students collaborate mainly through wiki, email, and synchronous collaboration using Web conferencing.

Thinkquest

In 2006, Oracle Education Foundation (OEF) in collaboration with the Ministry of Education in Indonesia, introduced Web-based learning collaboration called

Thinkquest: http://www.thinkquest.org/en/. Thinkquest is a Web-based learning environment where teachers and students engage in collaborative projects. Thinkquest opens opportunities for schools around the world to collaborate in real world projects.

According to the Oracle Education Foundation (OEF), Thinkquest leverages student development of 21st century skills, such as communication, critical thinking, technology skills, cross cultural understanding, teamwork, creativity, and self-direction. In addition to providing Web-based collaboration tools such as blogging, chatting, and email, Thinkquest provides an online library containing award winning learning projects in math, science and technology, social science, and many more. Thinkquest also hosts online teacher professional development in integrating Thinkquest into their lessons. In 2009, Thinkquest had been adopted as a Web-based learning environment in 7000 schools in West Java, Indonesia (Taqiyyah, 2009).

Every year OEF holds a competition among primary and secondary students to create Web-based, real world projects. Interestingly, two student groups from Indonesia became the first and second winner of annual Thinkquest competition in 2011. The first student group used the Web-based learning environment to promote "Algae's Power Cycle," a project promoting the use of algae for bio-Ethanol energy usage to reduce carbon emissions. The second group created a project called "Make Plastics and Paper Become the Earth's Friends," a project which discusses paper made from algae as an alternative to wood-based paper, biodegradable bio-plastic made from potatoes rather than petroleum, and other earth friendly alternatives to everyday materials (ThinkQuest, 2011).

SMILE (Stanford Mobile-Based Inquiry Learning Environment)

SMILE is an assessment maker that allows students to create their own questions based on their own learning in mobile devices. A SMILE team from Stanford University conducted a pilot study in Garut West Java, Indonesia in 2011. The SMILE team and teachers integrated SMILE in math teaching by allowing students to generate math questions for topics such as triangles, angle sum theorem, and fractions. There are five learning sequences during SMILE integration in math: "(1) device exploration; (2) prompting students for problems; (3) group collaboration and discussion; (4) inquiry generation and review; and (5) evaluation, reflection, repetition, and enrichments" (Buckner & Kim, 2012, p. 18). This type of mobile device application is beneficial to develop students' critical thinking and creativity in working with problems. The ability of the application to track on students' generated questions also allows teachers to differentiate instruction during the learning process as well as to recognize learning development.

Challenges of Integrating Web 2.0 in Indonesian Education

Although Web 2.0 initiatives exist in Indonesian education and there are a high number of social media users in Indonesia, widespread Web 2.0 integration in education remains challenging. Tondeur, van Keer, van Braak, and Valcke (2008) raise the issue of technology integration plans that do not really meet with teachers' or students' actual needs, current infrastructure, and effective implementation strategies. Instead, educational bureaucracies, who are unaware of the real needs of the institutions, drive planning decisions. Technology integration plans, especially those that include Web 2.0 integration as a goal, need to be based on the local educational institutions' needs. There is a large mismatch among national level policy makers, district administrators, and school teachers in the context of promoting Web 2.0 in Indonesian education. Our analysis identified national and local challenges from an ecological perspective (Bronfenbrenner, 1979) including macrosystem, exosystem, microsystem, and mesosystem elements.

National Macrosystem Challenges

Lack of Technology Facilities

Zakaria, Watson, and Edwards (2010) studied Web 2.0 use among Malaysian undergraduate students, and found that access to technology is one important factor in integrating Web 2.0 in teaching. A body of research about technology integration (Mumtaz, 2000; Pelgrum, 2001) also discusses that lack of access to computing resources can hinder technology integration in educational institutions.

A report on Web 2.0 integration in Indonesian education has found that access to technology resources remains problematic for accelerating Web 2.0 integration in Indonesian education. Jakaria (2007) conducted a study on technology integration in basic and secondary education in Indonesia. A large-scale quantitative study of 27 schools in 27 provinces was conducted to measure the availability of technology in school and teachers' mastery of technology use in schools. The study reported that 96% of schools had electricity. Telephone availability remained a problem in that only 18.64% of schools had cable telephones. Countrywide, elementary schools were least likely to have cable telephones. In terms of computer availability, 16.38% of schools did not have desktop computers and 63.28% of schools did not have laptop computers. In addition, 38% of schools across the country did not have computer laboratories. The study also yielded data that most schools have very minimum technology facilities. For instance, 64.69% of schools did not have an Internet connection. A similar study conducted by UNESCO Bangkok to evaluate "School Networking," a technology integration program for building technology infrastructure and training funded by Japanese Funds in Trust, reported a lack of technology resources in Indonesian education. The study reinforces that Indonesia still struggles with technology availability of resources in schools due to the lack of governmental budget and geographical challenges in that the country consists of 13.466 islands which raise challenges for building technology infrastructure (Unesco Bangkok, 2004).

Given the fact that technology infrastructure is still scarce in Indonesia, Web 2.0 technology integration remains a challenging goal. Moreover, it seems the Ministry of Education in Indonesia is not able to solve the problem of technology availability in the near future. It can be seen from the educational strategic planning 2010-2014, the Ministry of education states that by 2014 the government will be able to provide only 40% of elementary schools, 60% of middle schools, and 75% of high schools Internet access and technology availability (Nuh, 2010). Instead of focusing on building technology infrastructure, the government is still solving other significant problems such as reducing illiteracy and building schools.

An Absence of Technology Standards in Education

The education system in Indonesia envisions technology integration established in classrooms, and toward that goal, mandates that every teacher possess technology integration knowledge, although there is no specific inclusion of Web 2.0 practices. Several educational decrees, such as decree No 41 Year 2007 and No 1. 2010, specifically mention that teachers have to integrate technology in teaching. In addition, the South East Asian Ministers of Education Organization (SEAMEO) also reported that Indonesia holds a specific vision for technology integration in education. Using four stages of ICT integration—emerging, applying, infusing, and transforming—SEAMEO contends that the vision of technology integration in Indonesian education is the infusing stage (Southeast Asian Ministers, 2010). The Infusing stage requires that the country have a developed vision for national ICT in education and have technology infrastructure. Unfortunately, there is still large gap in availability of technology resources between urban and rural areas.

For those Indonesian schools that do have Internet and technological resources, meaningful technology integration in primary and secondary education classroom learning can be guided by standards. Yet, Indonesia has not created or adopted any standards that could be used by schools to guide attempts to integrate Web 2.0 in classrooms. The Ministry of Education needs to create actionable standards that correspond with the national vision, current technology trends that improve learning, and socio-cultural beliefs and ideologies (Lim & Hang, 2003). Creating technology standards is complex and requires careful planning and consultation with stakeholders, such as teachers. The decision makers across national, district, and school macrosystem and exosystem levels should take active roles in creating actionable standards.

Alternatively, the Ministry of Education could adopt technology integration standards from International Society Technology in Education (ISTE) for teachers, students, and administrators. These standards could be adjusted based on scalability of technology integration in Indonesia. For Web 2.0 integration, the Ministry of Education could discuss together with teachers how to best incorporate Web 2.0 tools in education using additional guidance from media literacy frameworks (e.g., Jenkins, 2006).

Standardized Testing Orientation

Since 1965, Indonesia has been regulating standardized testing, called *Ujian Nasional* or national examination, for elementary to high schools to examine the quality of national education on a yearly basis. This mandate was reconfirmed by national education decree No. 20 year 2003. There is no research or commentary from Indonesian or Asian researchers that examines the relationship between a standardized testing environment and establishing technology integration in schools. However, others argue that standardized testing undermines technology integration due to a tension between the perceived need to use technology for drill and practice quiz software to prepare students for testing and preferences to use technology to support student centered learning.

Standardized testing creates pressure for teachers to prepare students for the tests. In this environment, teachers enact activities that teach students how to pass examinations. Teachers provide students worksheets containing questions and answers for every lesson. This method is a panacea for standardized testing preparation because students are drilled by answering questions. However, this standardized testing environment overcomes teachers' teaching activities, reducing or shaping their attempts to integrate technology.

Keller and Bichelmeyer (2004) argue that standardized testing has hindered technology integration efforts when students and teachers are pressured to pass the test. Technology integration is likely to happen when students are actively engaged in an activity like problem-based, inquiry, and student-centered learning. However, standardized testing trumps such student-centered learning. From this view, there is a call for pedagogy reform that allows for technology integration with less emphasis on standardized testing formulas. The development of a holistic assessment which measures learning more comprehensively as opposed to only measuring cognitive performance, as measured by multiple-choice questions, will help schools integrate technology because learning experiences that happen during technology integration can be assessable and impact overall cognitive development.

Ineffective Coordination among Macrosystem and Exosystem Governmental Agencies

Technology integration efforts led at a national scale need to be initiated with top down efforts but only if they are followed by attention to local conditions for adoption (Fullan, 2007). The pivotal role of top down initiatives by governmental agencies is very important to make sure that technology integration is well implemented. National technology vision needs to be translated into actionable standards taking into account the local conditions. Thus, the need for effective, collaborative coordination among national to local governmental agencies is very crucial if any change will be achieved.

Like any other country, education in Indonesia is managed by the Ministry of Education bureau at the national level, and it has offices in every province, district, and sub district. A lack of coordination between those governmental agencies seems to undermine Web 2.0 integration efforts in Indonesia. For instance, the national level of Ministry of Education has a clear technology integration vision and plans including Web 2.0 integration. However, agencies in district levels cannot translate the initiatives locally for several reasons, such as a lack of capable leadership in understanding Web 2.0 integration (issue of leadership development and education) and a lack of human resources to implement Web 2.0 integration (issue of human resource infrastructure). Ineffective coordination also occurs during the process of planning and funding. Technology resources such as computing devices and Internet could be useless if teachers do not have enough knowledge regarding use in teaching. Jakaria (2007) reported that 22.03% of teachers from elementary to high schools did not have basic computer mastery. The government needs to simultaneously invest in technological infrastructure as well as professional learning and development for teachers, so that 100% of teachers have basic or mastery of digital technologies for education. In this way, the technological resources can be harnessed by teachers for learning purposes. Technology planning processes must interface from national to local conditions for planning successful technology integration. Thus, effective coordination among governmental agencies from national to local context is one of the keys to moving forward with Web 2.0 integration.

Local Exosystem Challenges

Lack of Professional Development

Professional development is one of the influential factors in achieving technology integration in a country. The existence of technology like Web 2.0 will have no meaning if teachers do not have knowledge of it or how to use it in teaching. Therefore, effective professional development must be developed, funded, and sustained by the government in order to help teachers feel comfortable using technology in teaching. However, traditional professional development such as one-shot workshops has little or no impact in modeling how to use technology in teaching (Fullan, 2007).

Rodriguez and Knuth (2000) state that effective professional development needs to have several components such as a clear connection to practice, opportunities for hands-on technology experience, peer collaboration, and an ongoing duration. As an illustration, the Indonesian government desires to have national scale professional development to infuse Web 2.0 tools in teaching. To be effective, according to Rodriguez and Knuth, the national professional development should connect to practice by matching institutional curriculum and standards. It would provide a theoretical foundation and practices for teachers that match the school curriculum and standards. Hands-on technology experiences provide teacher learners direct experience in using technology tools to practice, play, and envision possibilities for their use. Peer collaboration enables a school community(ies) consisting of teachers, students, administrators, and other stakeholders to work together during professional development, such as sharing best practices of Web 2.0 integration among teachers and even simply learning and sharing together. Finally, the effective professional development would involve an ongoing process, meaning there is a sustainability effort over time, a year or longer, made by government to help teachers become comfortable in integrating Web 2.0 in teaching.

However, most government-sponsored professional development still implements one-shot workshops. The Ministry of Education through the SchoolNet program offered several professional development sessions in different areas in the country. In these sessions, the representatives from *PUSTEKKOM* or Center of ICT in education traveled to the provinces to teach teachers how to integrate technology in teaching, such as Web 2.0 integration. Such professional development is not sustainable in terms of facilitating teachers' knowledge of Web 2.0 integration because it (a) may not match the school's needs, curriculum, and instructional approaches, (b) does not foster collaboration, and (c) is not ongoing.

Non-governmental organizations also tend to create one-shot professional development similar to governmental initiatives described above. Due to the absence of technology integration standards, non-governmental organizations' best solution is to create professional development based on other country's plans. Using best practices from developed countries may be not work well in a developing country like Indonesia. Thus, professional development must be based on the real conditions of the country. It will not work well to promote online professional development for teachers in integrating technology in classroom because it requires access to Internet to join in such online learning, which is often not available.

Need for Greater School Leadership

There is a body of research discussing the pivotal role of school leadership in the successful technology integration initiatives, like Web 2.0 integration, in schools. Changes of teaching practices with technology integration will not happen without high commitment from school leaders in creating technology integration visions and standards as well as creating school culture that supports technology integration (Yuen, Law, & Wong, 2003). Furthermore, Anderson and Dexter (2005) studied more than 800 schools to examine the role of school leaders and technology integration outcomes. They discovered that school leadership roles have a larger statistically significant influence on technology integration—higher than even technological hardware and software.

A lack of technology leadership in schools will reduce Web 2.0 integration in schools. In the Indonesian context, the school principals neither have clear visions of Web 2.0 integration nor have adequate knowledge to translate the governmental vision on Web 2.0 integration into actionable standards in school contexts. There is great need for schools principals who are able to create a positive culture for technology integration. Changes like pedagogical practice with technology integration will not occur without shared meaning across all school staff (Fullan, 2007). Shared meaning can be infused into technology integration practice if the school principal facilitates communication opportunities where teachers, principals, staff, parents, and students can discuss and map what needs to be done to create effective technology integration in schools. There is also an absence of human support for technology integration in schools. Most schools do not have technology specialists, and the rare technology specialists that do support schools must primarily focus on technical hardware and software support. In addition, technology specialist should have deep knowledge of instructional design in order to assist teachers to design Web 2.0 integration in their teaching.

Lack of infrastructure clearly prevents any technological use and therefore, is a very serious challenge. We feel lack of technology leadership to be the next most serious challenge. By focusing in tandem on infrastructure and leadership, a country develops the technical and intellectual capacity to grow.

Suggestions and Recommendations

The case of Web 2.0 integration in Indonesia is very complex and unique. Many reports cited in this chapter contend that there are several challenges in Web 2.0 integration, especially in consideration of the Indonesian education system. Therefore, we present several suggestions and recommendations.

Comprehensive Planning of Web 2.0 Integration

Comprehensive planning of Web 2.0 integration is a key to successful integration in schools. As technologies like Web 2.0 develop quickly and broadly, the government through the Ministry of Education and its agencies has to be able to create a national level technology integration vision that encompasses new technology in schools. A top down initiative of Web 2.0 integration made by national government, such as the development of a vision, plan, and goals, must be disseminated widely to the provincial and district levels with special consideration for meeting local needs. Furthermore, continuous monitoring and financial support of the initiatives both in national and local settings should be provided.

Professional Development and Institutional Support

A lack of technology mastery by teachers and institutional support reduces Web 2.0 integration. Thus, investment in professional development and support of technology specialists are needed. To create an efficient professional development with regard to budget efficiency, the government can train representative teachers and the principal from schools. Through facilitation from the school principal, trained teachers then would conduct peer training at the school level. This type of professional development also creates shared goals among teachers with regard to the integration of Web 2.0 in teaching. Dealing with the lack of institutional support, there should also be district or school-level technology specialists who provide leadership in translating national goals into actionable local initiatives that are supportable with local resources. Key teachers who have adequate background in technical knowledge could become mentors for other teachers in that district who desire to investigate a common problem-of-practice. Cultivating teachers' potential by creating teams for investigating Web 2.0 technology, pedagogy, and content will help teachers adapt Web integration in schools without requiring vast monetary resources for professional development.

Promoting the Use of Mobile Devices in Web 2.0 Integration

Although availability to desktop or laptop computers is still a significant challenge, there are tremendous opportunities for Web 2.0 use for learning, as described in the introduction, which can be supported through mobile devices. We suspect that the massive use of mobile devices by youth in Indonesia provides a natural potential in integrating Web 2.0 technology in teaching.

Research emphasizes the benefits of using mobile devices in classroom such as personalization of learning, flexibility in extending learning beyond classrooms, motivation improvement in students learning, and affordable use of mobile devices (So, Seow, & Looi, 2009; Swan, Van't Hooft, Kratcoski, & Unger, 2005). In addition, more specific research about the uses of mobile devices in education also reveals that mobile devices have the potential to support technology integration efforts (Thornton & Houser, 2005). Given these evidence-based practices, mobile devices, such as mobile phones that most students possess, could be harnessed in an educative way that resolves the lack of computer and Internet resources and leverages microsystem or mesosystem elements, namely youth's access to mobile phones at home and potentially at school.

We contend that mobile phones have potential due to their portability, low costs, and versatile features. The association of Indonesian mobile phones reported that in 2010, more than 80% of Indonesian citizens have mobile phones. Mobile phones are also ubiquitous among students although some schools still ban the use of mobile phones in schools. Students could purchase a mobile phone at a low price, around Rp. 400.000, about 40 USD. They also can purchase Internet access at about Rp. 20.000, about 2 USD. With these low costs, the benefits of using mobile devices could be harnessed to promote Web 2.0 integration. Moreover, it can be used for the province and districts that do not have wired Internet technology.

One of the examples of Web 2.0 integration using mobile device is using social networking communities like Elgg and Elgg Mobile. For instance, in a class in which students are learning about the characteristics of living things, as a group of four, students are assigned to identify the characteristics of living creatures such as plants and animals. Students work at home and at school for this assignment because it takes time to discover the development and characteristics of living creatures. To communicate students' findings, the teacher sets up a private Elgg group for the class so students can write their findings in the Elgg wall. Students can also ask their teachers questions through this Elgg group if issues arise during the project. By using mobile devices, students and teachers could engage in long-term inquiry projects that are supported by various mobile-accessible learning environments that allow learning in and outside the classroom.

Promoting BYOT/D (Bring Your Own Technology/Device)

Web 2.0 integration in Indonesian schools still face problems of technology availability. For this situation, Bring Your Own Technology (BYOT) or Bring Your Own Device (BYOD) can be a strategy for increased Web 2.0 integration. Teachers could ask students to bring their own devices to schools as a means of enacting Web 2.0 teaching in the classroom. Schools could provide some devices for students who do not have devices to bring from home. In this way, schools are alleviated from purchasing computers or providing digital technology devices for all students all the time. Both reduce required monetary resources. A large challenge in BYOT/D is changing restrictive attitudes towards students' use of their own technologies, such as the banning of mobile phones during school hours. In addition, schools need to give attention to developing an Acceptable Use Policy (AUP) governing the appropriate use of home-based devices to which parents and students would agree.

FUTURE RESEARCH DIRECTIONS

This chapter's focus was limited to understanding Web 2.0 integration in education with regards to Indonesian national policy, opportunities, and challenges. Given the findings and discussion, we recommend further research in the following areas:

- What school leader, teacher, student standards, and competencies should developing countries, like Indonesia, develop, adopt, and use to further Web 2.0 integration in education?
- What national strategies best serve Web 2.0 integration in schools?
- What local strategies best serve Web 2.0 integration in schools?
- How can mobile technologies support Web 2.0 integration?

These studies should consider local needs, resources, and limitations in capturing understandings of Web 2.0 uses in school contexts.

Studies should acknowledge the changing nature of Web 2.0 as there are constant developments in Web 2.0 technologies. Studies could be enacted to understand how such change in technology impacts the practice of Web 2.0 integration in education. Finally, studies should be conducted to understand national and local technology leadership initiatives to support Web 2.0 implementation. These studies could examine how leaders plan, implement, and monitor Web 2.0 technology integration and what are the leaders' roles in preparing teachers in Web 2.0 integration. Such studies would contribute to the dearth of studies on Web 2.0 integration and professional development in developing countries.

CONCLUSION

This chapter discusses Web 2.0 integration in Indonesian education from national perspective, namely national policy on Web 2.0 integration, opportunity, and challenges of Web 2.0 integration in education. A body of research cited in this chapter serves as a foundation to analyze opportunities and challenges of Web 2.0 integration in Indonesia and has led us to recommend national and local strategies to increase the likelihood that Web 2.0 technologies are considered a possibility for educational activities to support content area learning by primary and secondary students in Indonesia. While any nation-wide solution is complex, we suspect that a leapfrog move to embrace mobile technologies in schools, a large emphasis on leader and teacher development, and better coordination between national and local vision and goals will contribute toward the solution. The government has paid little attention in integrating Web 2.0 in education as many initiatives were implemented by non-governmental organizations. Thus, Web 2.0 integration in Indonesian education is piecemeal as there are no top down laws and visions from the national government.

REFERENCES

Anderson, P. (2007). *What is web 2.0? Ideas, technologies and implications for education*. London, UK: JISC Technology and Standards Watch. Retrieved from http://www.jisc.ac.uk/media/documents/techwatch/tsw0701b.pdf

Anderson, R. E., & Dexter, S. (2005). School technology leadership: An empirical investigation of prevalence and effect. *Educational Administration Quarterly, 41*(1), 49–82. doi:10.1177/0013161X04269517

Bronfenbrenner, U. (1979). *The ecology of human development: Experiments by nature and design*. Cambridge, MA: Harvard University Press.

Buckner, E., & Kim, P. (2012). *A pedagogical paradigm shift: The Stanford mobile inquiry-based learning environment project (SMILE)*. Retrieved from http://elizabethbuckner.files.wordpress.com/2012/02/smile-concept-paper.pdf

Evans, M. (2010). *Exploring the use of twitter around the world*. Retrieved September 7, 2011, from http://blog.sysomos.com/2010/01/14/exploring-the-use-of-twitter-around-the-world/

Fullan, M. (2007). *The new meaning of educational change* (4th ed.). New York, NY: Teachers College Press.

Greenhow, C., Robelia, B., & Hughes, J. E. (2009). Learning, teaching, and scholarship in a digital age: Web 2.0 and classroom research--What path should we take "now"? *Educational Researcher, 38*(4), 246–259. doi:10.3102/0013189X09336671

Harkins, A. M. (2008). Leapfrog principles and practices: Core components of education 3.0 and 4.0. *Futures Research Quarterly, 24*(1), 19–32.

Internet World Stats. (2011). *Internet usage in Asia*. Retrieved from http://www.internetworldstats.com/stats3.htm

Jakaria, Y. (2007). Studi pemetaan kemampuan teknologi informasi pendidikan dasar dan menengah di Indonesia. [Mapping of technology information in Indonesian basic and secondary education]. *Jurnal Pendidikan dan Kebudayaan, 66*(13), 488-506.

Jakarta Post. (2011, October 28). Internet users in Indonesia reaches 55 million people. *The Jakarta Post*. Retrieved from http://www.thejakartapost.com/news/2011/10/28/ internet-users-indonesia-reaches-55-million-people.html

Jenkins, H. (2006). *Confronting the challenges of participatory culture: Media education for the 21st century.* Chicago, IL: MacArthur Foundation. Retrieved from http://www.digitallearning.macfound.org/atf/cf/%7B7E45C7E0-A3E0-4B89-AC9C-E807E1B0AE4E%7D/JENKINS_WHITE_PAPER.PDF

Jhurree, V. (2005). Technology integration in education in developing countries: Guidelines to policy makers. *International Education Journal, 6*(4), 463–483.

Keller, J. B., & Bichelmeyer, B. A. (2004). What happens when accountability meets technology integration. *TechTrends, 48*, 17–24. doi:10.1007/BF02763351

Kim, P., Miranda, T., & Olaciregui, C. (2008). Pocket school: Exploring mobile technology as a sustainable literacy education option for underserved indigenous children in Latin America. *International Journal of Educational Development, 28*(4), 435–445. doi:10.1016/j.ijedudev.2007.11.002

Lim, C. P., & Hang, D. (2003). An activity theory approach to research of ICT integration in Singapore schools. *Computers & Education, 41*(1), 49–63. doi:10.1016/S0360-1315(03)00015-0

Ministry of Education in Indonesia. (2011). *Panduan SchoolNet*. Jakarta, Indonesia: Ministry of Education in Indonesia.

Mumtaz, S. (2000). Factors affecting teachers' use of information and communications technology: A review of the literature. *Journal of Information Technology for Teacher Education, 9*, 319–341. doi:10.1080/14759390000200096

Nielsen. (2011). *Surging internet usage in Southeast Asia reshaping the media landscape*. Retrieved from http://blog.nielsen.com/nielsenwire/global/ surging-internet-usage-in-southeast-asia-reshaping-the-media-landscape/

Nuh, M. (2010). *Rencana strategis kementrian pendidikan nasional*. Jakarta, Indonesia: Ministry of Education in Indonesia.

O'Reilly, T. (2005). *What is web 2.0?* Retrieved July 9, 2008, from http://www. oreillynet.com/pub/a/oreilly/tim/news/2005/09/30/what-is-web-20.html

Pelgrum, W. (2001). Obstacles to the integration of ICT in education: Results from a worldwide educational assessment. *Computers & Education, 37*, 163–178. doi:10.1016/S0360-1315(01)00045-8

Perraton, H., & Charlotte, C. (2001). Applying new technologies and cost-effective delivery system in basic education. *UNESCO.* Retrieved from http://www.unesco.org/education/wef/en-docs/findings/technofinal.pdf

Rodriguez, G., & Knuth, R. (2000). *Critical issue: Providing professional development for effective technology use.* Retrieved September 7, 2011, http://www.ncrel.org/sdrs/areas/issues/methods/technlgy/te1000.htm

Secretariat, S. E. A. M. E. O. (2010). *Report: Status of ICT integration in education in Southeast Asian countries.* Retrieved from http://www.seameo.org/images/stories/Publications/Project_Reports/SEAMEO_ICT-Integration-Education2010.pdf

So, H.-J., Seow, P., & Looi, C. K. (2009). Location matters: Leveraging knowledge building with mobile devices and Web 2.0 technology. *Interactive Learning Environments, 17*(4), 367–382. doi:10.1080/10494820903195389

Social Bakers. (2011). *Facebook statistics by country.* Retrieved September 8, 2011, http://www.socialbakers.com/facebook-statistics/

Swan, K., Van't Hooft, M., Kratcoski, A., & Unger, D. (2005). Uses and effects of mobile computing devices in K-8 classrooms. *Journal of Research on Technology in Education, 38*(1), 99–112.

Taqiyyah, B. (2009). Jaringan oracle thinkquest masuk ke 7000 sekolah di jabar. *Kompas.* Retrieved September 13, 2011, http://tekno.kompas.com/read/2009/06/26/20490652/Jaringan.Oracle.ThinkQuest.Masuk.ke.7000.Sekolah.di.Jabar

ThinkQuest. (2011). *Winners 2011 ThinkQuest projects event.* Retrieved October 1, 2011, from http://www.thinkquest.org/library/winners/2011_projects.html

Thornton, P., & Houser, C. (2005). Using mobile phones in English education in Japan. *Journal of Computer Assisted Learning, 21*(3), 217–228. doi:10.1111/j.1365-2729.2005.00129.x

Tondeur, J., van Keer, H., van Braak, J., & Valcke, M. (2008). ICT integration in the classroom: Challenging the potential of a school policy. *Computers & Education, 51*(1), 212–223. doi:10.1016/j.compedu.2007.05.003

Unesco Bangkok. (2004). *School networking: Lessons learned.* Retrieved from http://unesdoc.unesco.org/images/0013/001377/137741e.pdf

Yuen, A. H. K., Law, N., & Wong, K. C. (2003). ICT implementation and school leadership: Case studies of ICT integration in teaching and learning. *Journal of Educational Administration, 41*, 158–170. doi:10.1108/09578230310464666

Zakaria, M. H., Watson, J., & Edwards, S. L. (2010). Investigating the use of web 2.0 technology by Malaysian students. *Multicultural Education & Technology Journal, 4*(1), 17–29. doi:10.1108/17504971011034700

Zhao, Y., & Frank, K. A. (2003). Factors affecting technology uses in schools: An ecological perspective. *American Educational Research Journal, 40*(4), 803–840. doi:10.3102/00028312040004807

ADDITIONAL READING

Anderson, R. E., & Dexter, S. (2005). School technology leadership: An empirical investigation of prevalence and effect. *Educational Administration Quarterly, 41*(1), 49–82. doi:10.1177/0013161X04269517

Barell, J. (2006). *Problem-based learning: An inquiry approach* (2nd ed.). Thousand Oaks, CA: Corwin Press.

Barlow, T. (2008). Web 2.0: Creating a classroom without walls. *Teaching Science, 54*(1), 46–48.

Boss, S., Krauss, J., & Conery, L. (2008). *Reinventing project-based Learning: Your field guide to real-world projects in the digital age*. Eugene, OR: International Society for Technology in Education.

Collins, A., & Halverson, R. (2009). *Rethinking education in the age of technology: The digital revolution and schooling in America*. New York, NY: Teachers College Press.

Dede, C., Honan, J. P., & Peters, L. C. (2005). *Scaling up success: Lessons learned from technology-based educational improvement*. San Francisco, CA: Jossey-Bass.

Dede, C., Ketelhut, D. J., Whitehouse, P., Breit, L., & McCloskey, E. M. (2009). A research agenda for online teacher professional development. *Journal of Teacher Education, 60*(1), 8–19. doi:10.1177/0022487108327554

Dexter, S. (2011). School technology leadership: Artifacts in systems of practice. *Journal of School Leadership, 21*(2), 166–189.

Donnelly, D., McGarr, O., & O'Reilly, J. (2011). A framework for teachers' integration of ICT into their classroom practice. *Computers & Education, 57*(2), 1469–1483. doi:10.1016/j.compedu.2011.02.014

Donner, J. (2008). Research approaches to mobile use in the developing world: A review of the literature. *The Information Society, 24*(3), 140–159. doi:10.1080/01972240802019970

Ertmer, P. A. (1999). Addressing first- and second-order barriers to change: Strategies for technology integration. *Educational Technology Research and Development, 47*, 47–61. doi:10.1007/BF02299597

Fullan, M. (2007). *The new meaning of educational change* (4th ed.). New York, NY: Teachers College Press.

Fullan, M. (2010). *All systems go: The change imperative for whole system reform.* Thousand Oaks, CA: Corwin Press.

Greenhow, C., Robelia, B., & Hughes, J. E. (2009). Learning, teaching, and scholarship in a digital age. *Educational Researcher, 38*(4), 246–259. doi:10.3102/0013189X09336671

Hughes, J. E., Guion, J. M., Bruce, K. A., Horton, L. R., & Prescott, A. (2011). A framework for action: Intervening to increase adoption of transformative web 2.0 learning resources. *Educational Technology, 51*(2), 53–61.

Jacobs, H. H. (2010). *Curriculum 21: Essential education for a changing world.* Arlington, VA: Association for Supervision & Curriculum Development.

Lei, J., & Zhao, Y. (2007). Technology uses and student achievement: A longitudinal study. *Computers & Education, 49*(2), 284–296. doi:10.1016/j.compedu.2005.06.013

Leonard, L. J., & Leonard, P. (2006). Leadership for technology Integration. *The Alberta Journal of Educational Research, 52*(4), 212.

Lewis, T. (2000). Technology education and developing countries. *International Journal of Technology and Design Education, 10*(2), 163–179. doi:10.1023/A:1008967718978

Luckin, R., Clark, W., Graber, R., Logan, K., Mee, A., & Oliver, M. (2009). Do web 2.0 tools really open the door to learning? Practices, perceptions and profiles of 11-16-year-old students. *Learning, Media and Technology, 34*(2), 87–104. doi:10.1080/17439880902921949

Ormiston, M. (2010). *Creating a digital-rich classroom: Teaching and learning in a web 2.0 world.* Bloomington, IN: Solution Tree.

Papa, R. P. (2010). *Technology leadership for school improvement*. Thousand Oaks, CA: Sage.

Project, N. (2009). *National educational technology standards for administrators*. Eugene, OR: International Society for Technology in Education.

Schrum, L. M., & Levin, B. B. (2009). *Leading 21st-century schools: Harnessing technology for engagement and achievement*. Thousand Oaks, CA: Corwin Press.

So, H.-J., Seow, P., & Looi, C. K. (2009). Location matters: leveraging knowledge building with mobile devices and Web 2.0 technology. *Interactive Learning Environments*, *17*(4), 367–382. doi:10.1080/10494820903195389

Solomon, G., & Schrum, L. (2007). *Web 2.0: New tools, new schools*. Eugene, OR: International Society for Technology in Education.

Wallace, R. M. (2004). A framework for understanding teaching with the Internet. *American Educational Research Journal*, *41*(2), 447–488. doi:10.3102/00028312041002447

Zhao, Y., & Frank, K. A. (2003). Factors affecting technology uses in schools: An ecological perspective. *American Educational Research Journal*, *40*(4), 807–840. doi:10.3102/00028312040004807

Zhao, Y., Pugh, K., Sheldon, S., & Byers, J. L. (2002). Conditions for classroom technology innovations. *Teachers College Record*, *104*(3), 482–515. doi:10.1111/1467-9620.00170

KEY TERMS AND DEFINITIONS

Bookmarking: Bookmarking is the collection of Web-based tools that allow users to organize, store, and manage online resources. There are many bookmarking tools such as Diigo, Evernote, and Google bookmark.

Mobile Devices: Mobile device is a mini device that allows people to do computing activities such as accessing data and sending information to others. In this study, mobile device refers to cell phone that can be used to access Internet and support Web 2.0 applications.

Professional Development: Professional development is an activity to improve knowledge, skills, and attitudes. The professional development mentioned in this chapter is related to activities provided for teachers to improve skills in technology integration for teaching purposes.

Pustekkom: *Pustekkom* stands for *Pusat Teknologi informasi dan Komunikasi Pendidikan* (i.e., Center of Technology Education) is a unit under Ministry of Education that manages technology integration in education in Indonesia.

Social Networking: Social networking is the collection of Web-based tools that allow users to communicate and exchange information. The examples of social networking sites are Facebook and Twitter.

Technology Integration: Technology integration is the process of incorporating technologies into educational activities such as classroom instruction, administrations, and so on. However, technology integration in this chapter refers to the use of technology for classroom instruction that specifically discusses the use of Web 2.0 for teaching.

Technology Leadership: Technology leadership is a specific behavior belongs to person who promotes and influences others to incorporate technology in educational activities.

Technology Standards: Technology standards are the standards that define measurable behaviors of technology use. There are a lot of technology standards created by both government and non-governmental agencies such as technology standards for teachers and administrators.

Technology Vision: A technology vision is an image or statement of the future and often involves a set of goals about integrating technology into education that help organizations or countries reach their future goals.

Students-Centered Learning: Students centered learning is a learning environment in which students are actively engaged in learning activities based on their interests. In this environment, teachers act as facilitators who help students learn based on their needs, abilities, and learning style.

Web 2.0: Web 2.0 refers to Web applications that let users participate and collaborate within Web based environment. The nature of interactivity and open source such as social networking sites and blogs make Web 2.0 useful to be used in educational activities to promote collaboration and other skills among students.

Chapter 9

Users' Involvement in the Innovation Process through Web 2.0:
A Framework for Involvement Analysis in a Brazilian Automotive Company

Sergio Ricardo Mazini
São Paulo State University, Brazil

José Alcides Gobbo Jr.
São Paulo State University, Brazil

EXECUTIVE SUMMARY

Organizations are inserted into a competitive environment in which innovation is an essential factor in gaining temporary competitive advantages. The search for external sources of knowledge, which can contribute to the innovation process, has become a constant among the organizations. One of the actors involved in this search is users, who often play an important role in the development of new products. This chapter develops a framework for the analysis of users' involvement in the innovation process through Web 2.0. The research method used a unique case study conducted in a Brazilian automotive company that developed a project of a concept car involving users through Web 2.0. The presented study case was analyzed according to the framework.

DOI: 10.4018/978-1-4666-2515-0.ch009

The obtained result shows that users can contribute not only with idea generation, but also with involvement in the innovation process, depending on which steps of the New Product Development (NPD) process they take part in. Moreover, increasingly users' development, participation, and collaboration are essential factors in this process.

INTRODUCTION

External sources of knowledge and information are factors considered relevant in innovation activities and new product and service development. The open innovation (Chesbrough, 2003) has become an effective concept to provide the search of external resources. The concept suggests an approach for the innovation, through the collaboration of several actors in the value chain for the search of new knowledge and technologies. Ryzhkova (2009) argues that is a relatively new concept, which has attracted the attention of academics and practitioners. Generally, the paradigm of the open innovation suggests that companies search partnerships and the involvement of other actors (usually, external) that can contribute to the innovation process (Rossi, 2009). The ability to identify and involve customers during the innovation process can be considered an important factor for the development of innovative activities of a company (Lettl, 2006).

New information and communication technologies are contributing to the customers' participation in all steps of the product development process, which allows the improvement not only in costs and time, but also, projecting what the customers really want (Mattos & Laurindo, 2008). The innovation tools, based on Web technology, can simplify integration with customers and also, knowledge absorption, facilitating the interaction between company and customers (Prandelli, et al., 2006).

This research is limited to the exploration of different types of Web-based collaboration with users for the purpose of innovating. The focal point of this chapter is the exploration of Web based user innovation methods, from the companies' perspective, aiming to address organizational and management issues of collaboration with users. From the standpoint of management practice, the goal is to contribute to a better understanding of organizational and management challenges arising from the implementation of toolkits for innovation through the Web. From the standpoint of management research, the exploration of tools for user innovation, as methods of practicing open innovation, will help to improve the concept.

Additionally, it is described and analyzed a unique case study of a Brazilian automotive company, which adopted Web 2.0 for user innovation. This case represents a paradigm shift in the automotive sector, because no auto manufacturer has "opened" the development process of a car so far (Wentz, 2010). It is a common sense, that the auto companies use the Internet to organize their hundreds of suppliers, but not to design their cars. Gladwell (2010) suggests that the articulation of a coherent philosophy of auto design cannot be conducted by an open network system without a system of organizational leadership and control. The study will help to understand how to involve users in the process of innovation with Web 2.0 toolkits, as well as, the impact that the adoption of the method of user innovation has had on the company.

The literature has also shown the possibility of a successful involvement of users through the Web 2.0 in the efforts of companies' innovation (Piller & Ihl, 2009). Fredberg *et al.* (2008) suggests that the advent of new collaborative technologies, specifically the use of Web 2.0, lead to the need for reevaluation of existing models and their analysis based on the new practices. In order to benefit from user innovation, companies must respond to the new challenges, to modify their existing practices and to develop a specific set of skills (Piller & Ihl, 2009). Thus, this context opened up a gap in the theory to an effective analysis of this type of involvement.

OPEN INNOVATION

The open innovation model was proposed for the management of innovation and is based on the necessities of the companies to open up their innovation processes and to combine internal and external development of technology for the value creation in business. The term open innovation was firstly proposed by Chesbrough (2003), and it refers to the organizations capacity of searching ideas, information and knowledge outside the organizational environment. For Chesbrough (2003), the innovation processes of companies that are intensive in technology are changing from the "closed innovation" for the "open innovation" model. The open innovation emphasizes the importance of the use of external knowledge for the best development of the innovation process.

In the previous paradigm of closed innovation, the companies adopted the philosophy that an innovation to succeed needs control. In other words, the companies must generate their own idea and then develop them for the market. In the end of 20th Century, however, a combination of factors changed. Maybe the main factor was the increase in the number and mobility of the knowledge workers, bringing an amazing difficulty to the companies to control their original ideas. Other important factor was the crescent availability of private *venture capital*, which has helped to finance new companies and their efforts in commercialize ideas that were coming up outside the corporative research laboratories (Chesbrough, 2003). In the open innovation model, the companies commercialize their own ideas as well as the ideas

Figure 1. The open innovation model (Chesbrough, 2003)

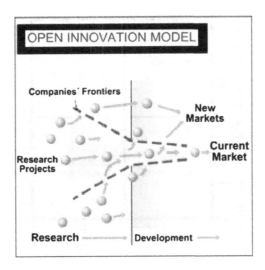

of other companies and seek for bringing the internal ideas to the market for the development of external ways to business (Chesbrough, 2003).

Figure 1 shows that the research projects are not restricted to the company's frontiers and, many of them, being conducted by external agents to the company. In this moment, the interaction with the external agents to the company is a constant. A great number of studies (Christensen, et al., 2005; Dogson, et al., 2006; Gassmann, 2006; Vanhaverbeke, 2006) are adopting this term to describe the phenomenon where the companies depend more and more on external sources of innovation and show the importance to investigate how the companies can implement the open innovation, emphasizing the importance of having the "suitable conditions" (in terms of strategy of the company, capacities, organizational factors, management tools, etc.) to implement an open approach successfully.

The first models of open innovation have been seen and studied in the development of Open Source Software (OSS) and were subsequently transferred to the more general practices (West & Gallagher, 2006). Today, open innovation is becoming a paradigm that connects the various parts of management research. The term is still being debated, and many authors agree that it has a much wider application than originally proposed by Chesbrough (e.g. Piller & Walcher, 2006). The literature discusses a wide range of topics such as: the concept of open innovation, business models, organizational design and boundary limits of the firm, leadership and culture, tools and technologies, Intellectual Property (IP), patenting and ownership, and industrial dynamics manufacturing. The research field is expanding in many directions and the ongoing discussions cover a variety of areas connected by the general purpose of understanding how companies can be more innovative.

Figure 2. The four ways of open innovation (Lazzarotti & Manzini, 2009)

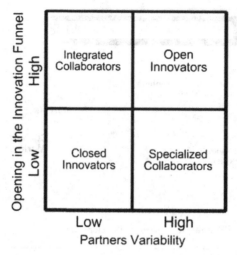

Lazzarotti and Manzini (2009) identify two variables that represent the opening level of the innovation process and of products development in a company: the number and kinds of partners which the company collaborates and the number and kind of innovation process steps that the company opens to external collaborations. The Figure 2 illustrates the authors' thoughts.

According to Lazzarotti and Manzini (2009), the closed innovators model corresponds to the companies that access external sources of knowledge only for a specific moment of the innovation funnel. The specialized collaborators model corresponds to the companies that are able to work with several kinds of partners but concentrate their collaborations in one point of the innovation funnel. Yet the integrated collaborator model corresponds to the companies that open all their innovation processes but the contributions are only from a few partners and, finally, the open innovators model corresponds to the companies that are really able to manage a wide set of technological relationships and that involve a vast set of different partners.

Chiaroni *et al.* (2011) proposes a theoretical framework to enable companies to dynamically deploy the new emerging paradigm of open innovation, as shown in Figure 3.

In the dimensions of open innovation, it is possible to identify two conceptually distinctions:

- Open innovation from outside to inside, e.g., *outside-in*, in which the practice to utilize the findings of others, involves the opening and establishment of

Figure 3. Theoretical framework for deployment of open innovation (Chiaroni, et al., 2011)

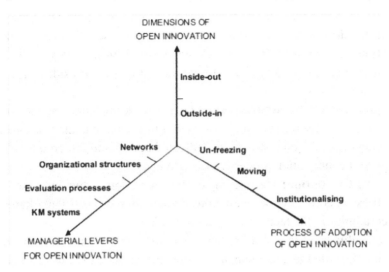

relations with the external organization in order to access their knowledge and skills to improve the company's innovation performance.

- Open innovation from inside to outside, e.g., *inside-out*, which suggests that, instead of relying entirely on internal paths to market, companies can look to outside organizations with business models that are more suitable for the commercialization of a particular technology.

In the adoption process of open innovation, it is possible to identify three phases through which organizations pass:

- The first phase involves the creation of a sense of urgency for change, creating an administrative coalition to defend change, in creation and communication of the new vision to both internal and external stakeholders.
- In the second phase, the concerns are with the actual implementation of change, driven by the creation of new procedures and standards of behavior compatible with the new vision, possibly acting on budget constraints, goals, schedules, and reward systems.
- The third phase involves the institutionalization of the new order, through the consolidation of the improvements made in the previous step, preventing a slide back to the previous situation.

In the managerial levels of open innovation, one can identify four main points that the implementation of open innovation has an impact:

- **Relationship Networks:** Implies an extensive use of interorganizational relations, in the generation of external ideas from a variety of innovation sources and, new ideas to the internal market that are outside to the current company´s business model.
- **Organizational Structures:** The success of knowledge management acquired externally requires the development of complementary networks and internal organizational structures dedicated access and integration of knowledge in the innovation process of the company.
- **Process Evaluation:** The opening of the innovation system increases the difficulties generated by the evaluation of innovation projects that often involve uncertainties in the techniques and the market.
- **Knowledge Management Systems:** Finally, managers may be forced to engage in knowledge management systems to facilitate the introduction of the new paradigm of innovation management.

Accordingly to Muller *et al.* (2012), the first step for companies who wish to adopt the process of open innovation is to evaluate each stage of the innovation process and to consider which methods of open innovation will be best applied to the company's growth objectives. Furthermore, the author also suggests that companies should approach external partners to get access to complementary knowledge. A central part of the innovation process is, also, the organization of searches for new ideas that have commercial potential (Laursen & Salter, 2006). So far, researchers have explored these issues in general and have concluded that a change of closed to open innovation will inevitably occur. However, how this will occur is less clear.

Open innovation is a paradigm that assumes that companies can and should use external ideas. There are many ways to practice the concept, and between these, user involvement is of a primary concern. Collaborating with users can be a valuable resource to access external knowledge. However, while collaboration with users can be a promising strategy, it also has its risks and limitations (Dahlander, 2006; Braun & Herstatt, 2008). After presenting the open innovation concept, the next step discusses the importance and mechanisms to involve customers in the innovation process, considering, above all, those that involve users along the process of New Product Development (NPD).

USERS' INVOLVEMENT IN INNOVATION PROCESS AND NPD

The change of innovation from directed by the manufacturer to the user-driven innovation has been identified several decades ago, when the influential role of users in the process of developing new products became evident, thanks to the influential work of von Hippel (1986). Accordingly to von Hippel (2007), economic actors are defined in terms of the manner in which they expect to appropriate the benefit of a certain innovation. Therefore, "users" are firms or individual consumers that expect to benefit from the use of a product or service. In contrast, "manufacturers" expect to benefit from selling a product or service. The user innovation and manufacturer innovation are the two general functional relationships. Users are unique, because they benefit directly from innovations. All others (considered here as "manufacturers") must sell the products and services to users directly or indirectly, in order to be profitable. User innovations are not necessarily innovations by end users or consumers. An innovation is a user innovation when the developer expects to benefit, by using it. An innovation is a manufacturer innovation when the developer expects to benefit from the sale of this (Franke, 2009). Thus, users can also be innovative companies if they play the role of product users.

The active role of consumers has been studied in the literature on innovation management in recent decades. Research has shown that many commercially successful products and processes are originally results of innovative users rather than manufacturers. The seminal work of von Hippel (1986) on lead users has shown their importance as a source of innovation and has been followed by other researchers (Olson & Bakke, 2001; Lilien, et al., 2002; Bonner & Walker, 2004).

Figure 4. The roles of leading users throughout the product development cycle (adapted from Moore, 1991)

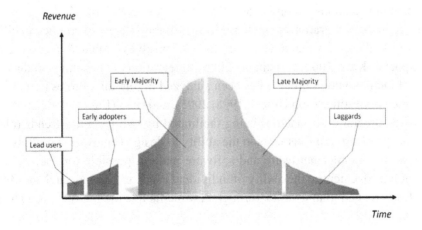

Accordingly to Moore (1991) five main segments are recognized in the technology adoption life cycle: innovators; early adopters; early and late majority; and laggards. Lead users especially express their value for companies that operate in fast-paced and turbulent markets as they move ahead of the market with their specific needs (Figure 4).

Develop an accurate understanding of user needs is neither easy nor free of cost, and the traditional approach is coming under increasing scrutiny as user needs change more rapidly, and firms increasingly seek to serve "individual markets" (von Hippel & Katz, 2002). Several authors argue that an over reliance on consumer feedback negatively impacts the degree of product innovation (Bennett & Cooper, 1981; Christensen, 1997; Christensen & Bower, 1996; Augusto & Coelho, 2009). The assumption is that consumers or users are generally unaware of how their needs will evolve and how certain technologies can impact the satisfaction of their needs (Augusto & Coelho, 2009). Users and consumers are usually not able to articulate their need for truly innovative products because their thinking is shaped by the actual products on the market (Grunert, et al., 2008).

Despite the great sophistication in market research methods, it remains difficult to understand customer needs. Very often, customers have very heterogeneous preferences. Von Hippel and his team revealed that user needs are extremely difficult to understand, because they often involve consumer's tacit knowledge, which is revealed only through learning-by-doing (von Hippel, 1998). Von Hippel (1998) describes this quality of customer information such as stickiness. The stickiness of a given unit of knowledge or, information, is defined as the incremental expenditure necessary to transfer this unit from one place to another, in order to be accessed by the recipient. When this expenditure is low, the stickiness of information is low; also, when this expenditure is high, the stickiness of information is high. Consequently, the customer information is more difficult to move (von Hippel, 1998). For this reason, many companies began to appreciate the deep integration of users in product development, in order to exploit their tacit knowledge.

The degree of integration has increased, towards the delivery of product specification for virtual users, which develop products themselves (Dahan & Hauser, 2002; von Hippel & Katz, 2002; Gassmann, 2006). Integration of consumers in the early stages of the innovation process has been analyzed in relation to roles (Brockhoff, 2003), the possibilities (von Hippel, 1998, 2005), and risks (Enkel, et al., 2005). An increasing integration of users is being facilitated by two technical trends related to: (1) the growing improvements in the ability to design (innovation toolkits) that advances in computer hardware and software make it possible for users, (2) the constant improvement in the ability of individual users, to combine and coordinate their efforts related to innovation through new media like the Internet (von Hippel,

2004). Thus, user innovation is not a new paradigm, but its importance is increasing due to cost reduction of interaction with the new communication technologies.

With the high market uncertainties of radical innovations, firms need to involve users as a source of knowledge related to the market. According Lettl (2007), two potential barriers related to users account for this. First, cognitive limitations may prevent users from delivering a value input (barriers of not knowing). Second, users may be unwilling to contribute to radical innovation projects (barrier of not wanting). A review of empirical studies reveals that some users are involved in innovation processes by acting as inventors and (co)developers. Computer users, who are using and redefining the open-source software, are the most visible and recent innovators (Shapiro, 2000; Braun & Herstatt, 2008). Information and communication technologies have enabled the sharing of software almost costless and led to global and virtual innovation communities (Tietz, et al., 2006).

In his book, *The Sources of Innovation*, von Hippel (1988) describes the importance of the interaction with customers in the NPD. Users that participate in the innovation process can develop exactly what they want, and interact with the company to deal with their agents. In this context, von Hippel (1986) defines a special category of users called leader users and that differentiate themselves from the common users in two aspects: they seek for their necessities for months and years before the costumers´ mass and, they are motivated and engaged in the effort for innovation.

The process of generating new products and services can be supported by leading users, as they reveal themselves as a source of knowledge and ideas about the products and services (Inauen & Wicki, 2011). Procter and Gamble, as an example, migrated part of their research and development (R&D) function to the concept of connect and develop (C&D) model that is based on external sources of ideas, which have involvement of lead users (Hennala, et al., 2011). Another example is Apple with its iPhone, where thousands of external software developers have developed applications for the product, turning it into a commercial success that became the center of a thriving business (Boudreau & Lakhani, 2009).

The customers can be involved not only in the ideas generation for new products, but also in the co-creation with the companies, in final tests of products and providing support to final users. According to Nambisam (2002), there is a variety of roles that the customers can play in product innovation and value creation. Table 1 describes the roles of customers in NPD.

The development of innovations by users, provided by the information and communication technologies, result in the existence of several kinds of relationships among companies and customers, which the consumers have different roles in the innovation process.

Table 1. Customer's role in the NPD (Nambisam, 2002)

Customer as a resource	Ideation	• Customers' appropriation as innovation source • Selection of innovative customers • Necessity of several incentives to the customers • Infrastructure to capture the customers' knowledge • Differentiated roles of existent and potential customers.
Customer as a co-creator	Design and Development	• Development in a wide range of design and development tasks • Context nature of new development process: industrial/consumption products. • Adjustment with internal teams of NPD process. • Uncertainties Management of the projects. • Reinforcement of the customers' knowledge in products/technologies.
Customer as an user	Products Test Products Support	• Scheduled Activities. • Assure the customers' diversities. • Continuous Activities. • Infrastructure to bear the interaction among customers.

Accordingly, to Piller and Ihl (2009), three ways of customers' participation in the NPD can help to understand the different roles that customers have to collaborate with the companies:

- **Design for Consumers (Mode 1):** In a first contact, the products are made according to the consumers' preferences. The company uses information acquired through several ways, such as feedback of sales and groups that search for the consumers' necessities.
- **Design with Consumers (Mode 2):** Besides the acquired information (Mode 1), solutions and different concepts for consumers are also sought, so that they can react in proposing other solutions of design.
- **Design by Consumers (Mode 3):** In this mode, the consumers are involved in the design and development of products. Usually, the company offers technological mechanisms for the interaction with the consumer.

The customer's focus seems to promote the advantage of new products in terms of reliability, quality, and exclusivity. Moreover, if the customers not only describe their needs, but also try to come up with solutions that satisfy these needs, the companies will get insights on the direct demands of the consumer market (Lüthje & Herstatt, 2004). The marketing literature also discusses about the value co-production through the consumers' involvement in the NPD processes. Lusch (2007) classifies the co-production in three perspectives: "to market" which the involvement, interaction

Figure 5. Collaboration mechanisms based on the Internet (Sawhney, et al., 2005)

Applicability to Stage of New Product Development Process

	Front-end (Ideation and Concept)	Back-end (Product Design and Testing)
Deep/ High Richness	Suggestion Box Advisory panels Virtual communities Web-based idea markets	Toolkits for users innovation Open-source mechanisms Web-based patent markets
Broad/ High Reach	Online survey Market intelligence services Web-based conjoint analysis Listening in techniques	Mass customization of the product Web-based prototyping Virtual product testing Virtual market testing

(Left axis label: **Nature of Collaboration**)

and worry about the consumers that do not present relevance in the development of new products, "market(ing) to" which the interaction and the involvement with the consumers are not part of the company´s strategy and are seen as resources and "market(ing) with" which the consumer is considered a partner that interacts with the company and takes part in the process of value co-production. Santos and Brasil (2010), in turn, describe three variables to be considered for the consumers´ involvement in the NPD processes: the involvement ways of the consumers, the process steps of development, and the involvement intensity.

Many companies seek for the customers´ knowledge to help and support the innovation process in the products development. The new information and communication technologies have created new opportunities for the integration with the customers. The tools based on Web 2.0 can simplify the integration with the customers and the absorption of the knowledge in a low cost (Prandelli, et al., 2006). The collaboration mechanisms based on the Internet can be mapped for the use in the new development process of products in two important dimensions—the nature of the customers´ involvement that is needed, and the stage in NPD which the customer is involved. The Figure 5 shows the variety of mechanisms based on the Internet classified in both dimensions: front-end and back-end (Sawhney, et al., 2005). Figure 5 shows the two main variables in the collaboration mechanisms based on the Internet: the first one is the collaboration nature and, the second one is the development phase of the product (front-end and back-end). According to these variables, some mechanisms and tools are more adequate than others.

The progress of NPD refers to the stage, in which customer inputs enter in the development process, i.e., the consumer input enters in the beginning of the front-end process (ideas generation and development concepts) or, if enter later in the back-end process (product design and testing).

Front-End Phase of Consumer Innovation

In the early stages of the NPD, generate ideas and select the best are the main activities. The process of idea generation is more open and creative than selection. Thus, two activities can be differentiated according to the different degrees of freedom. About the degrees of collaboration, both tasks are performed between the company and individual consumers without the collaboration of other consumers who characterize them as dyadic interactions. The task of generating and selecting ideas can be attributed to consumers through idea competitions (Piller & Walcher, 2006; Terwiesch & Xu, 2008) and screening of ideas (Toubia & Flowers, 2007), respectively. The mechanism of competition (companies offer rewards to winners) can also be seen as a powerful tool to motivate customers to transfer their innovative ideas. Moreover, this competitive mechanism can help to identify lead users in order to drive the integration of them in the later stage of the NPD (Piller & Ihl, 2009). As suggested by Toubia and Flores (2007), the next task of selecting ideas can also be delivered to consumers through idea screening.

In the network configuration, consumers perform similar tasks of idea generation and idea selection. Consumer communities are recognized as important sources of innovation, because they allow consumers collaboration that generates abundant and valuable innovations (e.g., Shah & Franke, 2003). As consumers communities differ in their objectives in relation of entry to NPD, Piller and IHL (2009) distinguish between communities that are concerned with the generation of new ideas and concepts (Sawhney & Prandelli, 2000) and discussion forums with related products, in which customers mainly exchange use experiences (Piller & Ihl, 2009). As communities of consumers differ in their objectives in relation to NPD entry, Piller and IHL (2009) distinguish between communities that are concerned with the generation of new ideas and concepts (Sawhney & Prandelli, 2000) and discussion forums with related products, in which, customers mainly exchange use experiences (Piller & Ihl, 2009).

The Back-End Phase of Consumer Innovation

The back-end of NPD requires more sophisticated inputs of consumers. Thus, in a dyadic interaction, companies, often, provide consumers with interactive platforms, called toolkits for open innovation (von Hippel & Katz, 2002; Franke & Piller, 2003). A toolkit is a development environment where users can find a solution according to your needs using the solution space available. The first revolutionary experience with toolkits for user innovation occurred in the semiconductor business in early 1980. The toolkits for designing integrated circuits transformed industry and led to a massive growth of the market between the 1980s and early 21st century (von Hippel, 2002).

Toolkits are differentiated into two types, according to the degrees of freedom that the solution space provides to customers: toolkits for user innovation and user toolkits for co-design and customization (Franke & Schreier, 2002, Piller & Ihl, 2009). The solution space of toolkits for user innovation is almost unlimited. One example is the solution information provided in the form of software or programming languages. In contrast, toolkit for user customization provides a solution space which is limited to a predefined set of components, such as a set of Lego bricks. The main function of these toolkits is to individualize and adapt the product to specific user needs.

Collaboration within networks of consumer's communities can continue to contribute to the degree of development of customer solutions. Piller and Ihl (2009) define this type of innovation in the consumer as peer production. In opposition to consumer communities that focus on the front-end activities of the idea generation and concept development, peer-based production activities usually extends from the back end of the NPD, where many users are working on the collective production and product development. The development of Open Source Software (OSS) is a recognized type of user innovation.

Piller and Ihl (2009) argue that different types of user innovation are used by companies when deciding on a particular approach to customer collaboration, which could be more advantageous in a given context. For example, the choice between strong and stable relationships with consumers or, the weak links, allowing the flexibility and dynamism that can be done deliberately using one or another method of the consumer innovation. Furthermore, these methods force companies to build capacity and infrastructure, which allow consumers to develop innovation activities.

Currently, absorbing the external knowledge to the organization can become an important factor for the creation of successful innovations. In the open innovation era, researchers question themselves about a more active engagement of the customers for the development of new products than the traditional market researches allow, and according to Füller and Matzler (2007), the customers can be virtually integrated into the innovation process of the companies through the new interaction tools that allow the companies to get valuable contributions of the customers through Internet.

User Involvement throughout Web 2.0

A type of structure for user innovation and their corresponding tools are the Web-based tools. Currently, there are a variety of innovation tools used by Web-based companies in different industries that can serve as inspiration for the development and testing of new services and business models. A number of innovation tools are used in the phases of exploration (front-end) and exploitation (back-end) of the innovation process. These collaboration tools with users are classified according to reach (reaching many users and generating a broad knowledge) or depth (reaching a few selected users and generating a detailed knowledge and deep).

In the early stages of NPD as ideation and concept development, tools such as virtual communities are more appropriate because they allow a greater participation of users to post their ideas and also to comment or vote on the ideas of other users. Already in the design and testing phases, the toolkits are an alternative for users to develop prototypes and new products. With toolkits, users can create a preliminary design, simulation or prototype and to evolve the development of new products in their own environment. Experiences in fields where toolkits have been pioneers show that, the developments of customized products begin much more quickly and at lower cost.

Perhaps no word in technology has generated so much discussion in management circles as "Web 2.0" (Cunningham & Wilkins, 2009). However, what is Web 2.0 and why do organizations should care about it? The second generation of Web emphasizes the construction of a common, open and friendly space to competitive intelligence, focused on data capital offered by multiple users with simple tools and shared across multiple interfaces (i.e., facilitating collaboration) (Hung, et al., 2008).

Web 2.0 tools are very simple to provide, require no maintenance and have very low costs. With Web 2.0 applications, firms can enter the "collective" in a much larger scale than had already occurred (Bonabeau, 2009). Therefore, Web 2.0 can provide to companies and users the effective ways to accomplish user innovation. Bernoff and Li (2008) argue that increased levels of social participation between consumers and the available sophisticated technology, allow organizations to place their social applications on equality with other business projects. There are thousands of Web 2.0 applications and specialized sites. The most typical classes are the different types of social networks, business networks, collaborative encyclopedias, enterprise 2.0, and many other specialized sites (See Lai & Turban, 2008, for examples).

Janzik and Herstatt (2008) argues that the motivation of members to participate is one of the most critical success factors to online communities. This determines the quality and quantity of ideas, as well as the selection and modification of the contributions. Reward mechanisms can be introduced to encourage more competent users to compete in solving problems in specific innovation markets with base on Internet (Nalebuff & Ayres, 2003; Sawhney, et al., 2005). Bretschneider *et al.* (2008) believes that the motivation of members to contribute requires incentives and a more appropriate approach to the involvement of users.

In order to benefit from innovation activities on the Web, a company needs to develop or acquire certain skills. Piller and Ihl (2009) proposed the need for three types of managerial skills in order to successfully manage open innovation practices. After a process of solving problems, they argue the need to: 1) disclosure competence: the competence to disclose the company's problems and to establish an interaction with users, 2) appropriation competence: the competence to capture and protect user-generated knowledge, and 3) assimilation competence: the competence to assimilate and integrate the knowledge generated by the user in the innovation process of the company. Moreover, the advent of relatively recent Web innovation tools makes many managers unaware and skeptical of these tools and corresponding skills. There are a number of management challenges to overcome before being able to benefit from the innovation generated by the user through innovation tools on the Web.

FRAMEWORK PROPOSAL FOR USER INVOLVEMENT

Based on the systematization of the literature presented and on the analysis of the case study presented in this work, it was developed a framework for the involvement analysis and users´ collaboration in the innovation process, through Web 2.0. The framework has as a basis the development process of new products (front-end and back-end) and it is divided in three dimensions: (1) user´s involvement ways; (2) participation level; and (3) Web 2.0 tools. The Table 2 illustrates the dimensions of the framework and the authors that are reference in the subject. In relation to the first dimension of the proposed framework, which refers to modes of user involvement, were referenced authors that distinguished by clarity and objectivity to address the major forms and stages of involvement of users in the innovation process. In

Table 2. Dimensions and references of the proposed framework

Dimensions of the framework	References
Users´ involvement ways	Nambisam, 2002; Lüthje & Herstatt, 2004; Lusch, 2007; Piller & Ihl, 2009; Lazzarotti & Manzini, 2009; Santos & Brasil, 2010
Users´ participation level	Füller & Matzler, 2007; Santos & Brasil, 2010
Web 2.0 Tools	Dahan & Hauser, 2002; Sawhney, et al., 2005; Prandelli, et al., 2006; Mattos & Laurindo, 2008

relation to the second dimension of the proposed framework, which refers to the level of participation of users, authors who were referenced have distinguished by approach to new ways of participation of users, such as the Internet, and also the intensity of these interactions. Finally, the last framework dimension refers to Web 2.0 tools. Authors were referenced by their explanation of digital media usage in various stages of NPD and innovation process.

- **User Involvement Modes:** The first dimension of the framework refers to the users´ involvement modes, according to the NPD phases. The development of innovation with users, promoted by the information technology, resulted in the existence of several kinds of relationships between users and companies. Users play different roles in the innovation process according to the stage in which they are involved.

The first mode of users´ involvement (Mode 1) limits to the generation and idea selection phase, which correspond to the front-end phase of the NPD. According to Nambisan (2002), the ideation phase is where the company will understand that its users are potential sources of innovation and can contribute to the innovation process through the generation and ideas selection. In this users´ involvement mode the organizations need to comprehend some necessary changes such as: Get the establishment of a connection with users; Identify the creation of several appropriate incentives with the objective of making the ideas contribution, agile; Capture the customers´ knowledge and needs.

The second mode of user involvement (Mode 2) passes by the front-end phase and gets to some back-end phases (design and development) where the company will understand that its users are potential sources to co-creation along with the organization and that can contribute with the innovation process through the creation of new designs and prototypes. Comparing to the first way of involvement, the interaction between users and the company tend to be much more intensive and frequent. In this user involvement mode, the organizations need to comprehend some necessary changes such as: new mechanisms to monitor and control the quality of development and project efficiency; necessity of a deeper technological and product knowledge; improved adjustment of internal teams of P&D with users.

The third mode of user involvement (Mode 3) passes by the front-end and back-end phase where the company will understand that its users are able to contribute with all the development phases of new products (idea generation, idea selection, design, tests, release). Comparing to the first and second involvement modes, the interaction between users and company´s tend to be much more intensive and frequent. In this mode of user involvement, organizations need to comprehend some necessary changes such as: the infrastructure to bear the interaction between the company and the users can have a high cost and end up limiting the interaction; a company also needs to identify who are its lead users, that are able to contribute to the process. The three modes of user involvement in NPD can help to understand the different roles that users play when they collaborate with the companies (Piller & Ihl, 2009).

- **Participation Level:** The second dimension of the framework refers to the participation level of the user during the development process of new products. In the first involvement mode, the level of participation is low because users are involved only in the initial phases (front-end). In addition, in the second involvement mode the participation level can be considered average, because users interact until the design and product development phases (back-end). In the last users´ involvement mode, the participation level is considered high, because users participate in all the front-end and back-end phases.

A central matter is how to identify users that can be motivated to participate and, to collaborate in the innovation process. The utilization of on-line communities, where users interact with others, tends to have an increased level of participation of users. The users´ individual necessities can be not so interesting for the organizations, but lead users, in particular, can have very distinctive necessities in relation to basic users and customers. Instead of trying to satisfy the necessity of a specific customer, it is economically more viable for the organization to identify necessities, product combinations, from several customers' points of view. It is possible to accomplish it, through the support and motivation of customers, to use their collective creativity to innovate together (Antikainen, et al., 2010).

Some factors that can motivate the users´ to collaborate to the innovation process of organizations are (Antikainen, et al., 2010): interesting goals and a clear purpose; an open and constructive environment; Influence in the development of new products and services; new points of view and synergy; efficiency sense; to be fun; rewards of participation and victories; cooperation sense; community and similarity sense.

- **Web 2.0 Tools:** The third dimension of the framework refers to some tools of social media, existent in Web 2.0 and, that can be used according to the development stage of new products, services, and processes.

According to the users´ involvement modes, some tools are more appropriate than others. In the first user involvement mode, tools such as Blog, YouTube, Twitter, and other social networks features are more appropriate because they allow larger participation of users "to post" their ideas and also "to comment" or "to vote" on

Figure 6. Framework for the analysis of the users' involvement in the innovation process through Web 2.0

DIMENSIONS	Development Phases of New Products				
	Front-end		Back-end		
	Ideas Generation	Ideas Selection	Design	Test	Release
Involvement Ways					
Participation Level					
Web 2.0 Tools					

other users' ideas. In the second user involvement mode, tools such as Forums and Online Communities allow a better organization of the discussions through subjects or topics, where the discussion of concepts and new technologies happen, which promotes a better engagement by those users. At the last user involvement mode, toolkits provide to users tools for the development of prototypes, new designs, creation, and test. It is necessary, increased engagement of specialists and technological resources due to those tools.

The social media, used in user's involvement modes, need to be evaluated through two main variables:

- **Engagement:** how easy is the engagement for users through the collaboration technologies for sharing knowledge and expressing their opinions and ideas?
- **Control:** how much control will be in users' and other stakeholders' hands and, what are the difficulties for the company to decentralize that control?

The three dimensions of the framework, for the analysis of user's involvement in the innovation process through Web 2.0 are illustrated in the Figure 6.

The framework includes key-factors analysis, as the opening of the innovation process of the organizations. In which stages will user's involvement happen?

- What types of modes users will be involved in the process?
- What is the level of freedom and engagement that the users will have?
- Which means will be utilized for the users' involvement?

For the application of the framework, it is recommended that organization, firstly, identify in which stages of the process of NPD, users will be involved. Then, it is recommended to identify in the first dimension of the structure proposal, what mode of users' involvement to be adopted: if the users will be only resources for the generation and selection of new ideas (Mode 1); if users, besides contributing to the generation and selection of new ideas, will also participate, giving their opinions during the prototyping and new product design creation, proposing other solutions (Mode 2); or, if users will have conditions to create their own prototypes and design for new products (Mode 3). to identify in the first dimension of the framework proposal, what users' involvement way to be adopted: if the users will be only resources for the generation and selection of new ideas (mode 1); if the users,

Subsequently, it is identified, in the second dimension of the framework, the participation level of users in the process. As moving forward in users' involvement, from Mode 1 to Mode 3, the participation level of users in NPD tends to increase. It can be noted, in this stage of the framework, which the lead users' identification and participation help in the collaboration and engagement process of other users.

Finally, at the third dimension of the framework, is necessary to determine, among the existent social media tools in Web 2.0, which will contribute the most at each step of the users' involvement process. For mode 1 of users' involvement, tools such as weblogs, Twitter, YouTube are indicated for the ideas generation and selection because of the easiness and agility in the posting. In addition, in the Mode 2 of users' involvement, tools such as forums and communities facilitate the necessary interaction for the ideas discussion, prototypes or even the products design. In the Mode 3 of users' involvement, tools such as toolkits promote the necessary resources for the prototypes creation and new products design and, in the products release phase, social networks such as Facebook, Orkut, and Twitter can contribute to the release and propagation of them. The intrinsic logic in the framework is to organize, sequentially, the key-factors of the opening of the innovation process and to manage the necessary actions to implement it.

RESEARCH METHOD

Exploratory research was conducted with the objective of capturing user's interaction in the innovation process and the development of new products through Web 2.0. The exploratory nature is justified, because there is a lack of researches about this subject that considers the interaction customer-company through the Internet (especially, when refer to emerging economy scenario).

In developed countries, empirical studies have shown that users often play a dominant role in the invention of new products. This was demonstrated in the study of Chesbrough and Crowther (2006) which investigated 12 industry segments such as aerospace and chemical. Vanhaverbeke (2006) and van der Meer (2007) also investigated open innovation in companies in developed countries with heterogeneous sectors (e.g. food and beverages; chemicals; machinery and equipment). A field, where promising approaches can be obtained is the experience of building networks in the context of a developing country. In other words, the context for the development of an innovative network is unfavorable and tends to exaggerate the involved problems. This is becoming an interesting field for exploring more general issues around the design and implementation of such networks (Morris, et al., 2008).

Case study was used in the empirical part of this research. Primary and secondary data was used for the data collection stage. According to Yin (2003), the use of several sources of evidence allows the researcher to dedicate himself to wide diversity of questions, such as historical, behavioral, and attitude. The criteria for choosing this study case, was due to its uniqueness, which demonstrates a paradigm shift in the automotive sector.

The case study was conducted from 2010 to 2011, whereas, in retrospect, the period from 2009 to 2011. The first unit of analysis was Agência, the digital media agency that turned the site operational and conducted the interaction between users and the project development team in Auto company´s concept car. The agency and the auto company were given fake names to preserve their image and to give more freedom for the researcher's analysis. The second unit of analysis was the automotive company itself, leading activities related to the selection and operationalization of the ideas generated at the site. Non-structured interviews were taken with the leaders of the project in both organizations, in order to understand the innovation process and the status of the development of the concept. In addition, written material and presentations were provided. The material was transcribed and analyzed in the framework context. In addition, secondary data was collected from several other sources, such as books, magazines, besides the access to the website about the project that makes possible the interaction (user-company) as the Web platform.

THE AUTO COMPANY PROJECT

The automotive company site was started in August 2009, asking for ideas. In the site appears the invitation: "The auto company invites you to create a car. A car to call your own." The auto company gathered ideas from consumers through social media to an idealization and creation of a concept car (Concept Car III) that was presented at the 2010 São Paulo International Auto Show in São Paulo, Brazil. The auto company is a large global corporation with origin in Italy, and businesses ranging from cars to tractor manufacturing plants spread across several countries.

The auto company is the largest automaker in Brazil with 24.8% market share, and the fifth largest advertiser in the country, spending approximately US$ 80 million per year (Wentz, 2010). Brazil was chosen for this project because it is a digitally sophisticated and innovative market, and the largest for the Italian company. The project also reflects the optimism of the Brazilians, supported by a market that grew 5% in 2010 to nearly 3 million vehicles (Wentz, 2010).

The first experience of Auto Company in the user's involvement through the Web began in 2006 when the business unit completed 30 years in Brazil. The company had prepared a campaign to celebrate its presence in the country. The slogan was "Auto Company 30 years, inviting you to think about the future," people were asked to think about the future, with the main protagonists being children and young people. Through the Internet, they participated in an interactive way of a survey research that sought to identify what the Brazilian Internet users from different regions, ages, and social classes were expecting for the next 30 years.

Auto company presented at the 2006 Sao Paulo International Auto Show, the Concept Car I (FCC I), being the first car entirely designed by the Auto Company Style Centre in Brazil. The design studies continued, but with the goal of creating an ecologically sustainable vehicle, which would provide driving pleasure. The result of this development was the Concept Car II (FCC II), another concept car presented at the 2008 São Paulo International Auto Show. Developed in Brazil, the FCC II was built with environmentally sustainable components. It was the first experience in the adoption and development of new technologies and mobility solutions with reusable and clean alternative materials. The concept cars are the basis for applications of technology, testing new concepts and materials that could be applied in series production cars.

The auto company had already detected the involvement of users in the projects of FCC I and FCC II through the Internet, however the turning point in the direction of Web tools occurred with the launch of Auto Company´s Line Car, whose market launch was preceded by the release of an Internet blog, with updates on the release of the vehicle and as a diary where users could leave their first impressions. In 2008, the Style Center asked to the communication area of the company, to establish a blog on the Internet so that users could participate in creating the next project of a concept car (FCC III).

The digital media agency (Agência) which managed the contents of the Auto Company´s site was observing projects that had used concepts of co-creation, crowdsourcing, and open innovation. They proposed the collaborative involvement of users' thought Web 2.0, as mean to create a concept car. Auto Company decided to evaluate the proposal, which led to the formation of a cross-functional team involving the internal areas: Style Center, Communication, Engineering, and Media agencies (Agência and Mídia). The multi-functional group was tasked to assess and discuss the ideas and other technical issues of the project.

Traditionally, auto manufacturers have always been closed in new product development and direct interaction with customers. Previous experiments of the Auto Company, apparently, assisted in moving to a more open model. Auto Company realized a workshop with representatives from all functional areas of the company, including the participation of the company's president, to create a development framework, in order that project phases could come along with the development of the prototype. Therefore, a key question was asked to motivate people and to give direction to what would be the input for the construction of the car.

Thus, Auto Company decided by the involvement of users through the Web, to design the Concept Car III for the 2010 São Paulo International Auto Show. With the project, it was planned to use the media and social networks as a communication channel with users to work collaboratively from car design to marketing communications. Agência (based in São Paulo) which had worked together in the design of the Auto Company Line Car Blog was chosen to lead the project site.

Agência was responsible for the development of the Web collaborative platform, and was also responsible for the operational management of the site and all digital communications strategy. The site was open to any type of user profile, from consumers to academics, to be given the most diverse ideas, techniques or not. It fell to Auto Company, and not the Agência, to organize a process of evaluation and selection of ideas and topics proposed by users thought the Internet.

The site was organized in the form of votes on ideas and incorporating various elements of media and social networking, including Twitter and Facebook. In the two subsequent weeks to 3rd of August, 2009 (the day of the launch on the Internet), the site had received 67,000 visitors, who submitted 1,700 ideas, and more than 40,000 comments related to the project were posted on Twitter.

The site, which originally had been released only in Portuguese, received up to 20% of traffic from outside Brazil. An English version was released on August 21, 2009, followed soon after by versions in French, Spanish, and Italian (Wentz, 2010). The posts were comments on the site, mostly in Portuguese, but they could

Table 3. Project numbers (as of March 2012)

Aspects of the project	Quantity
Posted Comments	17,682
Sent ideas	10,666
Registered participants	17,758
Unique visitors	2,313,914

be translated into other languages with one click. On October 27, 2009, the project had already received over 6,800 ideas and 9,600 participants, in addition to its more than 1,100 Twitter followers (Ong, 2009). In total, more than 10,000 ideas were submitted, 12,000 comments were posted, 17,000 registered participants and 2.1 million unique hits, as shown in Table 3. The countries that most accessed the site of the project were: Brazil, Spain, France, USA and Argentina. There were also unusual accesses in countries as Kazakhstan, Burkina Faso, Laos, and Namibia.

"We invited Brazilian consumers to invent the concept car that Auto Company will display at the auto show in October 2010," said Vice President of Agência in the interview. Even if the concept car will never be built for the mass market, the suggested characteristics can be incorporated into vehicles of Auto Company (Wentz, 2010). According to the respondent, concepts such as crowdsourcing and community involvement to make the best products and services had been implemented to a limited extent, particularly at Starbucks and Dell. In the case of the project, the role of users would go far beyond. Not only would these make recommendations on design, functionality, and other aspects of the car, but also on the current marketing strategy and communications.

Users have submitted ideas for the car design, which were studied by the group of NPD from Auto Company. Subsequently, users were asked for ideas for marketing and branding. The site is organized as a social networking site, with photos and comments from users, and a Twitter feed in the sidebar. The ideas are divided into categories such as design, materials, safety and infotainment, and also classified by the latest, most voted, and more discussed. Any user could participate with ideas, however, the team kept a closer communication with the lead users (identified by the quantity and popularity in suggested ideas).

In September 2009, Auto Company changed the positioning, asking users to more technical ideas. After this stage, teams of engineering and styling of Auto Company consolidated the technical design, which was published on the site in a form of open-source software in the beginning of 2010. In March of 2010, the discussion began to turn towards the development of a brand and marketing campaign before the Auto Show. At another stage, the Auto Company car dealers were involved.

The management team of site content (Agência and Mídia), which was formed by automotive journalists, initially grouped the ideas into predefined categories so that discussions were made by subjects, which would facilitate the progress of the weekly work of the multifunctional group. The suggestions were grouped into 21 questions, to users' answers. This process helped in the initial development of the car, through the enhancement of the discussions, the construction of the concept design of the vehicle and the actions on the site. The more technical issues were being evaluated, in terms of feasibility, by the Engineering team of Auto Company.

The internal processes of Auto Company were also changed with this project, especially regarding how decisions and approvals on the stages of the project would be conducted. The area of Product Development carried out the screening of ideas (possibly relying on the help of suppliers), and selected those that could potentially be used in future projects and applied in the mass production of vehicles.

The project covered the following aspects in the development process:

- **Mapping Scenarios:** In this phase, was explored the current issues that could inspire and guide the search of ideas for the concept car;
- **Key Question:** Definition of a key question that could orient the general development of the project;
- **Exploration of Concepts Ideas:** Based on the key question, a series of new questions were formulated to guide the open exchange of references between the project development team and users;
- **Briefing:** The best ideas and references were being incorporated into the composition of the preliminary design of the concept car;
- **Collective Design:** At this time, the cross-functional team fosters collective participation for users to choose solutions for the concept car according to the briefing;
- **The Concept Car:** The FCC III was developed from the proposed briefing together with the solutions proposed by the users;
- **Creative Commons Licenses:** Suggested ideas then turn into specifications for the concept car, which, through Creative Commons licenses, become free for use by any individuals or manufacturers.

Besides the appealing to consumers and users to participate via print ads, portals, Facebook and Auto Company's database, the firm turned to universities to get the participation of engineering and communication schools. The ideas generated by this project are protected by Creative Commons licenses and vary from the simple distribution of the car's manual in flash drive, even the most absurd, as the use of waste as a source of propulsion. As an example, we can highlight the idea posted in the use of glass lenses *transitions* in the material of the windshield. The Creative Commons licenses are more flexible in relation to copyright. Instead of "all rights reserved," for example that happens in movies, Creative Commons works with the concept of "some rights reserved," and the author is no longer the sole owner of the idea (Ong, 2009). Following, will be analyzed through the theoretical framework, the results obtained in the study case of the involvement of users (through the Web 2.0) in the innovation process.

ANALYSIS OF THE AUTO COMPANY PROJECT

This case study analysis along with the review concepts of the previous literature resulted in an analysis of the different users´ involvement modes through the Web 2.0 tools in the innovation process and NPD. According to the customer's roles in the NPD, proposed by Nambisan (2002), it was identified in the project that the Internet users had an active participation as resources in the ideas generation and selection and as co-creators in the design and development of the automobile assembler new car concept. The interaction with the development team of the auto company was through the Web 2.0 tools available in the project website: forums, pools, voting, and videos.

Three types of users´ involvement are differentiated through the Web 2.0 tools, as proposed by Piller and Ihl (2009). The project is fitted in the user´s involvement mode 2 (Design with users). The company can acquire information and ideas from the Internet users and also show solutions and different concepts to the consumers, which could then interact proposing other solutions to the automobile assembler. The users could submit their ideas, participate in discussions, or even follow the making of the project through videos.

The project is part of Mode 2, because they have an active role, but to a lesser degree than in Mode 3 (Design by users). As previously discussed, companies need to acquire new competencies as they move up in the modes of involvement of users. Therefore, it is implied that Auto Company has also developed skills in the activities of Mode 1 (Design for users), while moving up the stairs toward the activities of Mode 2 (Design with users). However, Auto Company has not reached the third mode of engagement (Design by users).

User's participation level in the NPD process was very high and it happened through the collaboration tools available through Internet. The users also had a high level of freedom to suggest the ideas or even to vote and express their opinions. As proposed by Lazzarotti and Manzini (2009), besides the number and type of partnerships, which the companies collaborate, other important variable is the number and type of phases of the innovation process that the company opens to the external collaboration. In this case, the auto company was concerned to not involve users in all the development phases, promoting the necessary follow-up through videos that were posted in the website. The project fits in the open innovators model.

In an analysis of the case, it is observed that the involvement of users was done through the project site (a site with social networking features), where users were registered and, during the generation of ideas. The ideas were posted and received a classification by keywords (tagging). In order to encourage the participation of users, in the selection phase and evaluation of ideas, the site has a special link with issues facing the automotive environment that inspires users for suggesting new ideas. Moreover, the ideas submitted by users received points, thus forming a ranking of most active users on the site, and those ideas, went to evaluation by a multi-functional team.

Users had an active participation in the generation, selection of ideas, as co-creators of the concept car design and in the evaluation concerning the same. The interactions were made, mainly, through the project website and the embedded Web 2.0 tools (blogs, forums, polls, videos, etc.). In the step of defining the design for the concept car, the discussions were conducted through the forums and later were voted the attributes of the design posted by the multi-functional development team of Auto Company. At the time of vehicle launch, users participated, giving suggestions for the promotional campaign of the concept car.

In the front-end stage of development of the concept car, the forums were used, due to the ease of organizing discussions in topics about the design of the vehicle and, voting polls have served as a test of the suggested design chosen for the car concept. In the back end stage, the site was used for the dissemination of the attributes chosen by Internet users to the concept car. Twitter and Facebook were used to advertise the concept car before its launch at the Motor Show. In the vehicle launch were used videos on YouTube.

Web 2.0 tools available in the project were indispensable for the involvement of users in several phases of the car construction, mainly, in the front-end phases where ideas and concepts were collected for the prototypes creation, which was subsequently presented to the Internet users by the automobile assembler. Tools such as forums, pools, voting, videos and the own website, created an environment as a social network where the Internet users create a profile and manage to collaborate with the other users, whether commenting their ideas or even voting in the best suggestions. This infrastructure helped to make the project collaborative and participatory. Other important factor was the constant activations through the website and social networks, such as Twitter and Facebook, with the purpose to involve and motivate the users´ participation.

CONCLUSION

Increasingly, organizations are seeking for external sources of knowledge for use in their innovation process. In this context, users are a key part in the innovation process. Web 2.0 technologies and tools are essential for user involvement to be carried out in a large scale and without boundaries.

The Auto Company´s project is a pioneer in the automotive industry and showed the users´ involvement in several innovation process stages, such as the ideas generation and selection, prototypes analysis and evaluation. All this involvement was possible due to the website developed for the Project, which used several Web 2.0 embedded technologies and tools.

User's involvement mode requires more and more virtual resources as moving upwards to the Mode 3 of Piller and Ihl (2009). Other relevant matter is the way that users are involved and kept in the project. Further studies are needed on how to keep the participants motivated at the same time, and how to select the best ideas without dismissing the potentially radical ideas.

The organizations involved in the project needed to restructure themselves, in order to manage the interaction with the Internet users in several car development phases. The company innovation process also needs to be mature enough, to be able to implement the new paradigm of the open innovation, in which new competences and knowledge are integrated to the current ones. The contribution for the success of this innovative project came from the participatory environment, the culture of focus on the innovation process, and the use of new technologies.

The authors expect that this study will motivate future researchers about this subject, and that they will add to the theoretical body of open innovation. Additionally, the results here presented could help managers to improve their products development practices through the interaction with consumers.

REFERENCES

Antikainen, M., Mäkipää, M., & Ahonen, M. (2010). Motivating and supporting collaboration in open innovation. *European Journal of Innovation Management*, *13*(1), 100–119. doi:10.1108/14601061011013258

Augusto, M., & Coelho, F. (2009). Market orientation and new-to-the-world products: Exploring the moderating effects of innovativeness, competitive strength, and environmental forces. *Industrial Marketing Management*, *38*, 94–108. doi:10.1016/j.indmarman.2007.09.007

Bennett, R. C., & Cooper, R. G. (1981). Beyond the marketing concept. *Business Horizons*, *22*(3), 76–83. doi:10.1016/0007-6813(79)90088-0

Bernoff, J., & Li, C. (2008). Harnessing the power of the oh-so-social web. *MIT Sloan Management Review*, *49*(3), 36–42.

Bonabeau, E. (2009). Decisions 2.0: The power of collective intelligence. *MIT Sloan Management Review*, *50*(2), 45–52.

Bonner, J. M., & Walker, O. C. Jr. (2004). Selecting influential business-to-business customers in new product development: Relational embeddedness and knowledge heterogeneity considerations. *Journal of Product Innovation Management, 21*(3), 55–69. doi:10.1111/j.0737-6782.2004.00067.x

Boudreau, K., & Lakhani, K. R. (2009). How to manage outside innovation. *MIT Sloan Management Review, 50*(4).

Braun, V., & Herstatt, C. (2008). The freedom-fighters: How incumbent corporations are attempting to control user-innovation. *International Journal of Innovation Management, 12*(3), 543–572. doi:10.1142/S1363919608002059

Bretschneider, U., Huber, M., Leimeister, J. M., & Krcmar, H. (2008). Community for innovations: Developing an integrated concept for open innovation. In *Proceedings of the IFIP 8.6 Conference*. Madrid, Spain: IFIP.

Brockhoff, K. (2003). Customers' perspectives of involvement in new product development. *International Journal of Technology Management, 26*(5/6), 464–481. doi:10.1504/IJTM.2003.003418

Chesbrough, H., & Crowther, A. K. (2006). Beyond high-tech: Early adopters of open innovation in other industries. *R & D Management, 36*(3), 229–236. doi:10.1111/j.1467-9310.2006.00428.x

Chesbrough, H. W. (2003). The era of open innovation. *MIT Sloan Management Review, 44*(3), 35–41.

Chiaroni, D., Chiesa, V., & Frattini, F. (2011). The open innovation journey: How firms dynamically implement the emerging innovation management paradigm. *Technovation, 31*, 34–43. doi:10.1016/j.technovation.2009.08.007

Christensen, C. M. (1997). *The innovators dilemma: When new technologies cause great firms to fail*. Cambridge, MA: Harvard Business School Press.

Christensen, C. M., & Bower, J. L. (1996). Customer power, strategic investment, and the failure of leading firms. *Strategic Management Journal, 17*(3), 197–218. doi:10.1002/(SICI)1097-0266(199603)17:3<197::AID-SMJ804>3.0.CO;2-U

Christensen, J. F., Olesen, M. H., & Kjaer, J. S. (2005). The industrial dynamics of open innovation: Evidence from the transformation of consumer electronics. *Research Policy, 34*(10), 1533–1549. doi:10.1016/j.respol.2005.07.002

Cunningham, P., & Wilkins, J. A. (2009). A walk in the cloud. *Information Management Journal, 43*(1), 22–30.

Dahan, E., & Hauser, Jr. (2002). The virtual customer. *Journal of Product Innovation Management, 19*, 332–353. doi:10.1016/S0737-6782(02)00151-0

Dahlander, L. (2006). *Managing beyond firm boundaries: Leveraging user innovation networks*. Gothenburg, Sweden: Chalmers University of Technology.

Dogson, M., Gann, D., & Salter, A. (2006). The role of technology in the shift towards open innovation: The case of Procter & Gamble. *R & D Management, 36*(3), 333–346. doi:10.1111/j.1467-9310.2006.00429.x

Enkel, E., Kausch, C., & Gassmann, O. (2005). Managing the risk of customer integration. *European Management Journal, 23*(2), 203–213. doi:10.1016/j.emj.2005.02.005

Franke, N. (2009). How can users' creativity be implemented in new products and services? In *Proceedings of the European Conference on Innovation*. Lund, Sweden: Lund University.

Franke, N., & Schreier, M. (2002). Entrepreneurial opportunities with toolkits for user innovation and design. *International Journal on Media Management, 4*(4), 225–234. doi:10.1080/14241270209390004

Fredberg, T., Elmquist, M., & Ollila, S. (2008). *Managing open innovation – Present findings and future directions. VINNOVA Report VR 2008, n.02, VINNOVA*. Stockholm, Sweden: Swedish Governmental Agency for Innovation Systems.

Füller, J., & Matzler, K. (2007). Virtual product experience and customer participation – A chance for customer-centered, really new products. *Technovation, 27*, 378–387. doi:10.1016/j.technovation.2006.09.005

Gassmann, O. (2006). Opening up the innovation process: Towards an agenda. *R & D Management, 36*(3), 223–228. doi:10.1111/j.1467-9310.2006.00437.x

Gladwell, M. (2010). A small change: Why the revolution will not be tweeted. *The New Yorker*. Retrieved from http://www.newyorker.com/reporting/2010/10/04/101004fa_fact_gladwell?currentPage=all

Grunert, K. G., Jensen, B. B., Sonne, A. M., Brunsø, K., Byrne, D. V., & Clausen, C. (2008). User-oriented innovation in the food sector: Relevant streams of research and an agenda for future work. *Trends in Food Science & Technology, 19*, 590–602. doi:10.1016/j.tifs.2008.03.008

Hennala, L., Parjanen, S., & Uotila, T. (2011). Challenges of multi-actor involvement in the public sector front-end innovation processes: Constructing an open innovation model for developing well-being services. *European Journal of Innovation Management, 14*(3). doi:10.1108/14601061111148843

Hung, C. L., Chou, J. C.-L., & Shu, K. Y. (2008). Searching for lead users in the context of web 2.0. In *Proceedings of the 2008 IEEE ICMIT*, (pp. 344-349). IEEE Press.

Inauen, M., & Wicki, S. A. (2011). The impact of outside-in open innovation on innovation performance. *European Journal of Innovation Management, 14*(4). doi:10.1108/14601061111174934

Janzik, L., & Herstatt, C. (2008). Innovation communities: Motivation and incentives for community members to contribute. In *Proceedings of the 2008 IEEE ICMIT*, (pp. 350-355). IEEE Press.

Lai, L. S. L., & Turban, E. (2008). Groups formation and operations in the web 2.0 environment and social networks. *Group Decision and Negotiation, 17*, 387–402. doi:10.1007/s10726-008-9113-2

Laursen, K., & Salter, S. (2006). Open for innovation: The role of openness in explaining innovation performance among UK manufacturing firms. *Strategic Management Journal, 27*, 131–150. doi:10.1002/smj.507

Lazzarotti, V., & Manzini, R. (2009). Different modes of open innovation: A theoretical framework and an empirical study. *International Journal of Innovation Management, 13*(4), 615–636. doi:10.1142/S1363919609002443

Lettl, C. (2007). User involvement competence for radical innovation. *Journal of Engineering and Technology Management, 24*, 53–75. doi:10.1016/j.jengtecman.2007.01.004

Lettl, C., Herstatt, C., & Gemuenden, H. G. (2006). Learning from users for radical innovation. *International Journal of Technology Management, 33*(1). doi:10.1504/IJTM.2006.008190

Lilien, G. L., Morrison, P. D., Searls, K., Sonnack, M., & Von Hippel, E. (2002). Performance assessment of the lead user idea-generation process for new product development. *Management Science, 48*(8), 1042–1059. doi:10.1287/mnsc.48.8.1042.171

Lusch, R. F. (2007). Marketing's evolving identify: Defining our future. *American Marketing Association, 26*(2).

Lüthje, C., & Herstatt, C. (2004). The lead user method: An outline of empirical findings and issues for future research. *R & D Management, 34*(5). doi:10.1111/j.1467-9310.2004.00362.x

Mattos, C. A., & Laurindo, F. J. B. (2008). The role of the web in improving customer input to the service/product development process: Brazilian cases. *Product: Management Development, 6*(1).

Moore, G. A. (1991). *Crossing the chasm: Marketing and selling high-tech products to mainstream customers.* New York, NY: Harper Business Essentials.

Morris, M., Bessant, J., & Barnes, J. (2006). Using learning networks to enable industrial development: Case studies from South Africa. *International Journal of Operations & Production Management, 26*(5), 532–557. doi:10.1108/01443570610659892

Muller, A., Hutchins, N., & Pinto, M. C. (2012). Applying open innovation where your company needs it most. *Strategy and Leadership, 40*(2). doi:10.1108/10878571211209332

Nalebuff, B., & Ayres, I. (2003). *Why not? How to use everyday ingenuity to solve problems big and small.* Boston, MA: Harvard Business School Press.

Nambisan, S. (2002). Designing virtual customer environments for new product development. *Academy of Management Review, 27*, 392–413.

Olson, E., & Bakke, G. (2001). Implementing the lead user method in a high technology firm: A longitudinal study of intentions versus actions. *Journal of Product Innovation Management, 18*(2), 388–395. doi:10.1016/S0737-6782(01)00111-4

Ong, M. (2009). *Fiat mio: Bringing crowdsourcing to the automotive industry.* Retrieved from http://www.headlightblog.com/2009/10/fiat-miobringing-crowd-sourcing-to-the-automotive-industry/

Piller, F. T., & Ihl, C. (2009). *Open innovation with customers.* Aachen, Germany: RWTH Aachen University.

Piller, F. T., & Walcher, D. (2006). Toolkits for idea competitions: A novel method to integrate users in new product development. *R & D Management, 36*(3), 307–318. doi:10.1111/j.1467-9310.2006.00432.x

Prandelli, E., Verona, G., & Raccagni, D. (2006). Diffusion of web-based product innovation. *California Management Review, 48*(4). doi:10.2307/41166363

Rossi, A. (2009). *A inovação aberta como fonte de geração de valor para as organizações.* Retrieved from http://www.fdc.org.br/pt/pesquisa/inovacao/Documents/artigos_blog/inovacao_aberta.pdf

Ryzhkova, N. (2009). *The contribution of the user innovation methods to open innovation.* Blekinge, Sweden: Blekinge Institute of Technology.

Santos, C. R., & Brasil, V. S. (2010). Envolvimento do consumidor em processos de desenvolvimento de produtos: um estudo qualitativo junto a empresas de bens de consumo. *Revista de Administração de Empresas, 50*(3).

Sawhney, M., & Prandelli, E. (2000). Communities of creation: Managing distributed innovation in turbulent markets. *California Management Review, 42,* 24–54. doi:10.2307/41166052

Sawhney, M., Verona, G., & Prandelli, E. (2005). Collaborating to create: The internet as a platform for customer engagement in product innovation. *Journal of Interactive Marketing, 19*(4). doi:10.1002/dir.20046

Shah, S. K., & Franke, N. (2003). How communities support innovative activities: An exploration of assistance and sharing among end-users. *Research Policy, 32,* 157–178. doi:10.1016/S0048-7333(02)00006-9

Shapiro, A. L. (2000). *The control revolution: How the internet is putting individuals in charge and changing the world we know.* New York, NY: Public Affairs.

Terwiesch, C., & Xu, Y. (2008). Innovation contests, open innovation, and multiagent problem solving. *Management Science, 54*(9), 1529–1543. doi:10.1287/mnsc.1080.0884

Tietz, R., Füller, J., & Herstatt, C. (2006). Signalling: An innovative approach to identify lead users in online communities . In Blecker, T., & Friedrich, G. (Eds.), *Customer Interaction and Customer Integration* (pp. 453–467). Berlin, Germany: GITO-Verlag.

Toubia, O., & Florès, L. (2007). Adaptive idea screening using consumers. *Marketing Science, 26*(3), 342–360. doi:10.1287/mksc.1070.0273

Van De Meer, H. (2007). Open innovation - The Dutch treat: Challenges in thinking in business models. *Creativity and Innovation Management, 6*(2), 192–202. doi:10.1111/j.1467-8691.2007.00433.x

Vanhaverbeke, W. (2006). The interorganisational context of open innovation. In H. Chesbrough, W. Vanhaverbeke, & J. West (Eds.), *Open Innovation: Researching a New Paradigm.* Oxford, UK: Oxford University Press.

Von Hippel, E. (1986). Lead users: A source of novel products concepts. *Management Science, 32*, 791–805. doi:10.1287/mnsc.32.7.791

Von Hippel, E. (1988). *The sources of innovation*. Oxford, UK: Oxford University Press.

Von Hippel, E. (1998). Economics of product development by users: The impact of 'sticky' local information. *Management Science, 44*(5), 629–644. doi:10.1287/mnsc.44.5.629

Von Hippel, E. (2002). *Horizontal innovation networks: By and for users*. MIT Sloan School of Management Working Paper, No. 4366-02. Cambridge, MA: MIT.

Von Hippel, E. (2005). *Democratizing innovation*. Cambridge, MA: MIT Press.

Von Hippel, E. (2007). Horizontal innovation networks: By and for users. *Industrial and Corporate Change, 16*(2), 293–315. doi:10.1093/icc/dtm005

Von Hippel, E., & Katz, R. (2002). Shifting innovation to users via toolkits. *Management Science, 48*(7), 821–833. doi:10.1287/mnsc.48.7.821.2817

Wentz, L. (2010). *At Fiat in Brazil, vehicle design is no longer by Fiat: Automaker is relying on consumers and social media for a 2010 concept car*. Retrieved from http://adage.com/results?endeca=1&return=endeca&search_offset=0& search_order_by=score&x=0&y=0&search_phrase=At+Fiat+in+Brazil%2C+Vehicle+Design+Is+No+Longer+By+Fiat

West, J., & Gallagher, S. (2006). Challenges of open innovation: The paradox of firm investment in open-source software. *R & D Management, 36*(3), 319–331. doi:10.1111/j.1467-9310.2006.00436.x

Yin, R. (2003). *Case study research: Design and methods*. London, UK: Sage.

Chapter 10
Facilitating the Egyptian Uprising:
A Case Study of Facebook and Egypt's April 6ᵗʰ Youth Movement

Mariam F. Alkazemi
University of Florida, USA

Brian J. Bowe
Michigan State University, USA

Robin Blom
Michigan State University, USA

EXECUTIVE SUMMARY

It has been suggested that social media offers important organizing tools for activists in countries where free expression is curtailed and news outlets are handcuffed by government censorship. The 2011 revolution in Egypt offers an opportunity to examine the extent to which social media fulfills the role that free journalism plays in more democratic societies. By analyzing messages posted in Arabic by activists from one of the largest Egyptian opposition groups, this study attempts to see what role Facebook played in the revolution. This chapter aims to fill a gap in scholarly understanding of the event while simultaneously contributing to the understanding of the importance of social media tools for activists and organizers. The results show that the organizers used Facebook largely to communicate a mixture of expressions of national pride, news events, and calls for mobilization on the ground to support their revolutionary efforts.

DOI: 10.4018/978-1-4666-2515-0.ch010

INTRODUCTION

It has been suggested that social media provide important organizing tools for activists in countries where free expression is curtailed and news outlets are handcuffed by government censorship. With technological gizmos, activists can bypass gatekeepers at news media organizations that are handcuffed by repressitarian governments (Bowe & Blom, 2010).

Despite general assertions that government controls are ineffective, threaten cultural differences, and hamper technological advances (Rodriguez & Spanik, 2003), Egypt has a long history of exerting repressive control over the Internet. In 2003, Egypt became the first state in the world to charge and imprison a blogger (Diebert & Rohozinski, 2008). The Committee to Protect Journalists (2009) placed Egypt at No. 10 on its list of the worst countries to be a blogger, citing government surveillance and open-ended detention of bloggers.

The continuous human rights violations inspired a variety of groups to stand up against the regime, such as Coptic Christians, feminists, Islamist-oriented intellectuals, university students, and labor activists (Blaydes, 2011). However, it was not until early 2011 when this coalition was able to unite a critical mass of protestors to take over main squares in Cairo and other prominent cities, which ultimately led to the ouster of President Hosni Mubarak. One way to understand and gauge the success of those mobilizing efforts is by examining what messages dissidents distributed among their online social networks.

The 2011 revolution in Egypt offers an opportunity to investigate the extent to which social media tools fulfill the role that journalism plays in more transparent societies, as some media coverage attributed a central role in the uprising to social media such as Facebook and Twitter. Those social media platforms were identified as among the most important protest tools available to Egyptians (Morillon & Julliard, 2010). For example, one *New York Times* reporter wrote that "the same Web tools that so many Americans use to keep up with college pals and post passing thoughts have a more noble role as well, as a scourge of despotism" (Shane, 2011, para. 3). Similarly, a *New Yorker* writer asserted that "Facebook and Twitter have undoubtedly accelerated the protests by spreading news that would otherwise have taken a long time to spread, by quickly connecting people who aren't generally able to connect in authoritarian countries, and by inflaming passions" (Thompson, 2011, para. 2).

One of the main opposition groups in the Egyptian uprising was the 6th of April Youth Movement. This movement, founded in 2008, has been noticed in part because of its ability to organize effectively via Facebook in the face of the government repression of such organizing, attracting some 70,000 group members in the run-up to a demonstration (Reese, 2009). The success of this Facebook group elevated the strike to an event of national significance, which Faris (2008) claimed, marked "the day when organizing tool met political reality to create elements that were strong enough to form storm clouds on the regime's horizon."

The role of social media in organizing the 2011 protests that led to the ouster of the Mubarak regime is important to study, and the 6th of April Youth Movement was one of the most prominent players in those protests. As Isherwood (2008) asserted, Internet organizing has transformed politics in Egypt "not by dramatically altering or revolutionizing politics, but rather by intensifying and speeding up trends that had already begun with satellite media and the opposition press" (p. 13).

Many commentators attributed the Egyptian protestors that led to the fall of Mubarak's regime to the Facebook activism of the 6th of April Youth Movement. However, many of these claims have not been critically examined through empirical research. This study uses a mixture of quantitative and qualitative content analysis of messages posted by the movement to investigate precisely what organizers were communicating with users during the height of the Egyptian uprising. By examining the nature of the messages posted in Arabic by the activists themselves to Facebook, this chapter aims to fill a gap in scholarly understanding of the event while simultaneously contributing to the understanding of the importance of social media tools for activists and organizers.

This chapter begins by providing a theoretical framework through which one may understand the impact of online media around the globe. The focus then shifts to Egypt, providing background information about the media freedoms and restrictions as well as the importance of online media in the Egyptian environment. Then, the chapter describes the 6th of April Youth Movement and their Facebook page, followed by an explanation of the importance of this organization's role in the Egyptian uprising. The following section describes and categorizes the message content of 661 Facebook posts analyzed for this chapter. The chapter ends by describing the findings and comparing them to the works of other mass communication scholars. The implications of such findings are located in the discussion section, and finally a conclusion is made about the role of social media on developing countries, especially pertaining to the Egyptian uprising which lead to the uprooting of the Mubarak regime.

BUREAUCRACIES FIGHTING FREE EXPRESSION ONLINE

Digital networks have created a situation where activists can spread more information more quickly and farther than before. Such changes have little impact on the actions of uncommitted groups, but they have had a large impact on how committed groups are able to organize (Gladwell & Shirky, 2011). As Duve (2003) noted, the

Web offers "a revolutionary technical infrastructure" that has transformed "not only forms of individual communication but also the way the news is distributed within countries and across borders" (p. 9). Where, in the past, dissenters had to smuggle film or photos out of the countries, nowadays those videos and pictures can instantly be put online with a world-wide audience in reach (Stanyer & Davidson, 2009).

Faris (2010) noted that social media networks make organizing cheaper and faster, therefore making it more feasible for groups to mobilize resources while they also help the spread of shared symbols and meanings. Thus, the Internet "has become the foremost frontier over which symbolic, financial, and cultural battles are fought" (Deuze, 2008, p. 27). The blogosphere provides a virtual deliberation space where the limits of free expression are tested when oppressive governments are "involved in a constantly evolving engagement with bloggers to define the boundaries of what can be said" (Abdel Dayem, 2009, p. 44).

Dictators stay in power when they create bureaucracies that oppress the masses, but where fraud and bribery are masked for outsiders (Luyendijk, 2007). In other words, they need to distort social reality (Scammell, 1988; Payne, 2008) and create a "façade democracy" where elections can be rigged and opposition forces can be threatened without backlashes (Faris, 2010, p. 4). Limitations on the freedom of expression are, therefore, put in place as a tool of attaining, preserving, or continuing power (Scammell, 1988). To do so successfully, authoritarians need to avoid the distribution of negative reports through mediated channels that can be reached by mass audiences, because such messages have sparked political and cultural change in the past.

Shirky (2010) illustrated this with the downfall of former Philippine president Joseph Estrada, who blamed a text messaging campaign by a few dissidents for organizing mass-scale protests. Another example was the ouster the Communist Party in Modova, in 2009. Even earlier, as Manzella (2000) explained, the Suharto regime in Indonesia was thrown out of power because activists were able to share news that was suppressed by official channels, and mobilize a mass-scale opposition, with the use of email lists.

Technological advances have often been associated with movements for social change — from the printing press' role in the Protestant Reformation to the use of fax machines to mobilize protestors in China's Tiananmen Square protests and the radio in Egypt (El Nashmi, et al., 2010).

The Internet has been the latest mediated platform that has had a profound effect on political landscapes around the globe, facilitating the exposure of human rights violations. Some dissidents have been able to notify the world on their blogs that they were going to be arrested as police or military officers were already standing on their doorsteps (Menon, 2000). An imprisoned American journalist used Twitter after being arrested for reporting on a demonstration (Simon, 2008). And, about a half million people have joined a Facebook page with photos of the battered face of Khaled Said, who was brutally killed by Egyptian police officers (Preston, 2011).

In countries where the government has tight control of mainstream news outlets, people can take over the watchdog role by distributing information online. A small group of concerned citizens in Georgia were able to "circumvent censorship" and even alarm international media (Idsvoog, 2008, p. 77). The successful dissemination of vital political information by bloggers and online journalist has been witnessed all over the planet: Kyrgyzstan (Kulikova & Perlmutter, 2007), Myanmar and Zimbabwe (Stanyer & Davidson, 2009, and Ukraine and Russia (Krasnoboka, 2002), among a variety of other nations with repressitarian governments (e.g., Endeshaw, 2004; Dashti, 2009). Thus, the Internet allows the rapid distribution of textual and visual information—domestically and internationally—in such a high speed that human right violations transform "from being an open secret to a public truth" (Shirky, 2010, p. 36).

Repressitarian regimes recognize that the World Wide Web functions as a revolutionary tool to spread rumors that can arouse increased hostility towards the elites in power. In countries, such as China and Iran, there are cybercop units patrolling the Internet in search of forbidden or other inappropriate messages (Endeshaw, 2004). Government officials can thwart dissent by blocking certain servers, domains, keywords, and IP addresses, and surveillance of individual Internet accounts. Citizens can also be arrested to stop them from posting information that regimes do not want to see shared among the population. More drastically, some countries block Internet access for almost all citizens (Hamdy, 2009; Deibert & Rohozinski, 2010).

Some tech-savvy protestors can utilize proxy websites and serves to avoid government interference, but most other bloggers are forced to censor themselves. The latter group needs to figure out what kind of information is considered tolerable by the government—with the ultimate possibility that officials eventually object and take action (Dayem, 2009, p. 44)

THE EGYPTIAN MEDIA ENVIRONMENT

In its 2010 report *Freedom on the Net*, the NGO Freedom House depicted a media landscape of broad connectivity that was subject to repression keyed to political events. According to the report, the Internet arrived in Egypt in 1993, with public access opened up in 1996. In 2002, the government introduced a program to give anyone with a telephone line access to the Internet. Egypt has long been considered a hostile environment with regard to free expression. Egypt's media environment is labeled "Partly Free" on the Press Freedom Index compiled by Freedom House. Even though the constitution guaranteed free expression, restrictions came via the

Emergency Law, Press Law, and penal code. The government owns all of the terrestrial television broadcasting outlets and controls the licensing of newspapers. Freedom House (2010) reported that at least five publications had their licenses revoked in 2009 (Freedom House, 2010).

As in other places in Northern Africa and the Middle East, the popular adoption of satellite television became a threat to regimes that wanted to control news messages. Because information was transmitted from outside the country, the old-fashioned censorship techniques of personal harassment did not work. Satellite television rapidly changed the media landscape in dictatorial states where governments did not fully outlaw the dishes. Egyptians were soon exposed to a much larger range of information sources than ever before (Lynch, 2006).

The changing mediascape was not limited to television. The Internet became another conduit for a surplus of information that the government was not able to control in its entirety. Thanks to an aggressive government promotion of the Internet use for economic reasons, the numbers of Egyptians accessing the Internet quadrupled in recent years, with 20 percent of the population going online in 2009 (Freedom House, 2010). Generally, the Internet was unfiltered, though some sites have been blocked. With some 16.6 million users, Egypt has one of the largest Internet penetration rates in Africa (Morillon & Julliard, 2010).

Regardless of government controls on expression, Egyptian computer users created a lively blogosphere (Freedom House, 2010) and used Internet media services as a platform for mobilization and dissension, becoming increasingly organized even in the face of government repression (Morillon & Julliard, 2010).

Yet, Egypt has been called one of the worst enemies of Internet freedom, where these draconian tactics were deployed by the now-ousted President Hosni Mubarak (Morillon & Julliard, 2010). In recent years, a number of bloggers were arrested for their online publications. Not only were they unable to distribute information for a while, afterward they became aware that self-censorship would be the only way to avoid additional jail time. "[T]heir detention is yet another example of the authorities' usual heavy-handed response to unknown manifestations of evolving new media platforms" (Hamdy, 2009, p. 99).

However, the surveillance on the Internet under Mubarak was less strict in comparison to printed newspapers. For instance, the government tolerated stories of the *Cyprus Times* and *Middle East Times* online, but censored the same stories for their print publications (El Nashmi, et al., 2010).

The Internet became a tool for protest movements that finally were able to fully exploit weaknesses in the censorship policies of the government during the final years of the Mubarak regime (Deibert, et al., 2010). Because bloggers had taken advantage of those opportunities, they had become important news sources for independent newspapers. As Faris (2010) explained, "Many bloggers consider themselves guardians of a kind of objectivity that they do not find in any of the newspapers or other media outlets in Egypt" (p. 63) and "blogs became sites of discussion and documentation—of the demonstrations themselves, and also of arrests" (p. 113). Thus, Egyptian human right activists were able to distribute information online to news outlets around the country that were not in full control of the regime. In addition, the bloggers then discussed the news stories, leading to shared conversations with fewer geographical and time barriers than before the rise of Egyptian blogs, around 2004.

Egypt has one of the most interconnected political blogging networks in the Arab world, with much room for dissent. It "is the one national grouping where we see evidence of the kind of large-scale political clustering found in the United States and other politically active blogospheres, such as Iran's" (Etling, et al., 2010, p. 1232).

El Nashmi et al. (2010) analyzed 250 discussions on the website *Egypt Sons* in 2006, and found that there was an extraordinary amount of criticism of President Mubarak. Especially for Islamists this website was an outlet to express their opposition to the regime.

Bloggers were able to organize mass-protests through online outlets. One example is a 2006 sit-in in Cairo's Tahrir Square, which also became the center of the protests five year later. Although the demonstration lasted a few days and participation was relatively high, the mobilizing efforts were not enough to topple the Mubarak government at the time. But with emails, blogs, Facebook, YouTube, and Twitter, other smaller protests were staged in the following years. This would eventually demonstrate the effectiveness of online organizing in Egypt (Fahmi, 2009).

The Egyptian government began a crackdown on bloggers in 2008. Prominent bloggers like Abdel Kareem Nabil Suleiman ("Kareem Amer"), Ahmed Abdel Fattah Mustafa, Tamer Mabrouk, and Wael Abbas were arrested and tried for crimes like "insulting the president," "attempting to undermine people's confidence in the armed forces," and illegal use of Internet connections (Morillon & Julliard, p. 15). "The regime appeared so threatened by this movement, and by the online organizers who formed its core, that they needed to crush it completely" (Faris, 2010, p. 125).

One of the most effective social media services to reach a large amount of people instantly is Facebook. As the third-most visited site in Egypt, Facebook "allows users to speak freely to one another and encourages them to form groups," which makes it "irresistible as a platform not only for social interaction but also for dissent," wrote *New York Times* reporter Samantha Shapiro (2009).

This development was not unnoticed by the Mubarak regime. Facebook was placed under surveillance in 2007, and the Egyptian Ministry of Interior used it to monitor and arrest activists (Morillon & Julliard 2010). Therefore, while activists were able to organize via Facebook, they still faced repercussions in the form of a "heavy-handed response" on the part of authorities, including arrests and detentions (Hamdy, 2009, p. 99).

FROM 6 APRIL, 2008, TO 25 JANUARY, 2011

The April 6 Youth Movement branched off from the Kefaya opposition group in 2008. It took its name from a 2008 textile strike in the city of Cairo, which was partially organized via Facebook (Morillon & Julliard, 2010). The organizers used new media tools such as Facebook, Twitter, and blogs (Ishani, 2011). One of the organizers had created a Facebook page to promote the strike, which reached more than 70,000 members within a few weeks (Preston, 2010). The movement was known for its technical know-how and was described as "a group of youth activists with a strong sense of Internet organizing and more than a little help from abroad" (Ishani, 2011, para. 2).

In 2009, planners began experimenting with online organizing techniques, including so-called "ghost servers" to confuse online monitoring systems in an attempt to stymie the close surveillance the regime kept on sites like Facebook (Ishani, 2011). On the one-year anniversary of that strike, activists called for a "Day of Anger," organized largely through SMS messaging (Morillon & Julliard 2010). The regime had come prepared this time, and the organizers had not galvanized public support like they had a year earlier. As a result, the movement's message did not resonate with a sufficient number of Egyptians to make a lasting difference—in part because there was a lack of on-the-ground organizing (Faris, 2010).

Moreover, the failed attempt to create another large-scale strike demonstrated some of the limitations of online organizing. As Gladwell (2010, para. 19) skeptically noted, "Facebook activism succeeds not by motivating people to make a real sacrifice, but by motivating them to do the things that people do when they are not motivated enough to make a real sacrifice." Thus, Facebook is perhaps better suited for the dissemination of information, rather than the motivation of actors (Faris, 2010). This is congruent with Shirky's (2008) argument that social tools help groups overcome the obstacles of locality of information and barriers to group reaction, and thus facilitate organization and collective action. This results in "larger, looser groups" that are able to "take on some kinds of coordinated action, such as protest movements and public media campaigns, that were previously reserved for formal organizations" (Shirky, 2010, p. 35).

The Egyptian opposition movements had to take a step back for a while, but suddenly generated much more traction in the first weeks of 2011 when a Tunisian revolt led to the ouster of President Zine El Abidine Ben Ali. This sudden power change in another Northern African country proved inspirational for Egyptian activists. A highly organized core of activists from six opposition groups meticulously planned a massive demonstration for January 25, in a way that would prevent riot police from stopping them, which marked the beginning of the 2011 revolt (Levinson & Coker, 2011).

The government tested the resistance of the protestors by thwarting online communication. Responding to threats of demonstrations on January 28, it simultaneously shut off Internet connectivity to four of its main ISPs. This move was unprecedented and affected institutions throughout Egypt, including ISPs, businesses, banks, Internet cafés, schools, and government offices—though the stock exchange remained open (Cowie, 2011; Gillmor, 2011; Johnson, 2011). That was an example of what the OpenNet Initiative referred to as just-in-time blocking, "a phenomenon in which access to information is denied during important political moments when the content may have the greatest potential impact such as elections, protests, or anniversaries of social unrest" (Crete-Nishihata & York, 2011, para. 6).

Facebook spokesman Andrew Noyes told the *New York Times* that the company saw its traffic from Egypt drop. "Although the turmoil in Egypt is a matter for the Egyptian people and their government to resolve, limiting Internet access for millions of people is a matter of concern for the global community," he said (Ritchel, 2011, para. 12). The *New York Times* attributed Egypt's Internet shutdown to regime fears that "the new arsenal of social networking helped accelerate Tunisia's revolution" (Shane, 2011, para. 2). In response, some protestors accessed the Internet via dial-up lines outside of Egypt (Gillmor, 2011). As of March 20, 2012, the Facebook page of the April 6 Youth Movement is followed by 326, 437 users.

Against this backdrop, it seems important to ask what kinds of messages the 6th of April Youth Movement disseminated to its followers. Were the messages intended to mobilize? Were they intended to explain the necessity for having large-scale protests?

EXAMINING THE ROLE OF FACEBOOK IN THE UPRISING

This chapter examines the Facebook page of the April 6th Youth Movement, describing the nature of the posts that were uploaded weeks before and after the so-called "Day of Rage" on January 25, 2011. This period coincided with a national holiday celebrating the police forces of Egypt and includes the resignation of Hosni Mubarak (Al Jazeera, 2011).

For the purposes of describing the types of messages that were used to facilitate the Egyptian uprising, all Facebook messages posted by the organizers on the group's "wall" were collected from January 17, 2011 through February 14. This timeframe was selected because it included messages preparing for the January 25 demonstrations as well as messages after the resignation of Mubarak and his regime. A total of 661 wall posts were collected and translated from Arabic into English by one of the authors.

The 661 posts examined on the page of the 6th of April Youth Movement were posted by the organization itself. These posts consisted of text, and sometimes even linked to traditional media, online audiovisual content, or images. Most often, these posts had a high number of individuals responding through the click of the "like" button, but also through a very active use of the comments feature. For the purposes of this study, only the text posted by the Facebook page administrators, the 6th of April Youth Movement, as status updates were examined.

After an initial examination of the posts, nine categories were created for coding. The categories included nationalistic or revolutionary slogans, mobilizing information, hard news, human interest news, national unity, rumors, the Egyptian's struggle, political demands, and criticism of the Egyptian government (see Table 1).

FINDINGS

A content analysis of 661 posts from the Facebook page of the 6th of April Youth Movement was conducted. Only messages posted by the Facebook page's administrators were examined in the content analysis. However, the average number of

Table 1. Descriptions of content categories

Categories	Descriptions
1. Mobilizing Information	Wall posts that specify a time, date, or location for protests with a tone of encouragement qualified for this category. In addition, this category included wall posts that encourage the interactivity features of online media.
2. National Unity	Wall posts that specify that more than one sector of Egyptian society in a tone that is conducive to unity and does not carry any undertone of division.
3. Hard News	Wall posts that provide specific news related to the developments of protesters over time and in various locations—including online.
4. Human Interest News	Wall posts that provide specific news related to the developments of protesters over time and in various locations—including virtual reality.
5. Political Demands	Wall posts that specify a political desire.
6. Rumors	Wall posts that provide any negative coverage of the protesters, and announcing information as false when necessary.
7. The Egyptian's Struggle	Wall posts that specify ways in which Egyptian people have suffered.
8. Criticism of the Government	Wall posts that contain any explicit expression of dissatisfaction of Egyptian authorities opposing protesters, including police, military, political parties, or individuals.
9. Nationalistic and Revolutionary Slogans	The text of wall posts that contain words, visuals, audio or any combination that depict a sense of glory of revolutions or Egyptian nationalism qualified for this category. This category also included posts with direct reference to other Arab countries and their reaction to the Arab spring.

comments per post was 252, which demonstrates that the group took advantage of the interactivity of online media. Some of the analyzed posts included links, images, or videos. For the purposes of this analysis, only the text of the 661 posts made by the administrators of the April 6th Youth Movement Facebook page were analyzed.

The content analysis resulted in a categorization of the posts. For the current study, 661 Facebook posts of the 6th of April Youth Movement posted between January 17, 2011 and February 14, 2011 were content analyzed. Of the 661 posts, 427 posts (64.6%) addressed nationalistic and revolutionary slogans. Many (30.9%) posts also released mobilizing information. The Facebook page revealed hard news in 195 posts (29.5%) and human interest news in 100 posts (15.1%). In addressing some of the rumors and negative coverage of the protests, the group uploaded 86 posts (13%). The Facebook page revealed criticisms of the Mubarak regime were present in 116 posts (17.5%), listed examples of the struggle of the Egyptian people in 72 posts (10.9%), and specified the political demands in 59 posts (8.9%). The Facebook posts of the 6th of April Youth Movement also called for national unity in 89 posts (13.5%). The categories were not mutually exclusive, and each wall post of the 6th of April Youth Movement fit into at least one of these categories. However, posts could contain information that made them fit into more than one category. Therefore, multiple categories could be selected for each post, providing a greater level of detail. One of the authors conducted the coding, while a second coder examined a random sub-sample of 216 messages (32% of total messages) to measure similarity amongst the two coders' analysis. Intercoder reliability was calculated for each variable using Kirppendorff's alpha. The coefficients for each variable were: Category 1,. 72.8; Category 2,. 64.7; Category 3,. 87.8; Category 4,. 73.5, Category 5,. 73.7; Category 6,. 94; Category 7,. 72.10; Category 8,. 83; Category 9,. 71.4. The average reliability for all variables was. 77 (see Table 2).

Table 2. Number of posts per category*

Category	Number of Posts
Nationalistic and Revolutionary Slogans	427 (64.6%)
Mobilizing Information	204 (30.9%)
Hard News	195 (29.5%)
Criticisms of the Government	116 (17.5%)
Human Interest News	100 (15.1%)
National Unity	89 (13.5%)
Rumors	86 (13%)
The Egyptian's Struggle	72 (10.9%)
Political Demands	59 (8.9%)

*Note: Wall posts could be coded for more than one category, so the percentages do not add up to 100.

Nationalistic and Revolutionary Slogans

The analysis of the messages shows that by far the most common category was the one expressing Egyptian patriotism or revolutionary pride (427 posts, 64.6%). These posts included nationalistic slogans or sentiments (like those used in the American, British, and French revolutions) that the protests would either end in death or freedom. Organizers asserted that ideas could not be killed. Some anecdotal posts were included, such as a man remembering his mother urging him to feed protestors when he was a boy.

The earliest posts in this category praised the efforts of those raising awareness. For example, one post presented the "wish that more people would support the cause." There were also depictions of the 2008 protests. One post commented that "on April 6th, 2008 we told everyone to stay home. On Jan. 25, 2011, we tell you to stay in the streets. The streets are ours, as is victory." Another post commented that the protesters "will be constructive and not destructive. Our voice will definitely bring about change." This post, which warned people not to be apathetic, encouraged attendance at the protests.

Once the protests began, the messages were more event-specific. For example: "Now we have arrived at Liberation Square. This is a sight that has never occurred before. Thank God!" Other posts celebrated the prospect of revolution across the Arab world. After Mubarak's resignation, the youth movement expressed a sense of duty to help "our Algerian brothers and the free people of Yemen" fight against their governmental regimes because "the Arab people in Tunisia began a path that Egypt has taken."

The posts in this category also include some information about the impact of some of the political uprisings happening across the Arab world. Some of them would thank Tunisia for sparking the flame of revolution in Egypt. One post had check marks by Tunisia and Egypt, and suggesting that the governmental regimes in Yemen and Algeria should also be overthrown. Some ridiculed rumors that blamed the United States, Israel, Hezbollah, Hamas, or Qatar for the revolution. Some posts made indirect attacks on Saudi Arabia by asking Mubarak to join Zeinalabidine Ben Ali in Jeddah. Some of the posts directly thanked Arab countries for the support of the protests. The major theme was that the posts acknowledged that their movement had global implications that would change the balance of power outside of Egypt.

Hard News

The next category was hard news, with 195 posts (29.5%). These posts described events as they happened—for example, the police damaging civilian cars or thousands of demonstrators marching across a specific landmark at the exact moment.

These posts would include information such as the confirmation that members of Mubarak's family were in London, the Ministry of Foreign Affairs was stormed, and certain metro stops were closed.

This category was most prevalent as the protests began and gained momentum. On Jan. 25, one post read, "there is news of a riot containing 1,000 protesters beginning in Liberation Square." Later in the afternoon, a post commented that "the protesters are the ones barricading the police in front of the police department in Dokki." In this way, the Facebook page served as a place for news updates, especially because the traditional state-controlled media was not to be trusted.

Some of the posts in this category critiqued ways that the traditional media covered the protests. This was most obvious on Jan. 26 when a link to the Al-Ahram newspaper was posted, along with a comment about "citizens exchanging chocolates and flowers with policemen" for the Jan. 25 day that commemorates the work of the police. Another post commented on how national broadcaster named Mahmood Saeed refused to appear on an Egyptian television program because he refused "to encourage lies against the protesters." In these ways, the Facebook posts were able to gauge the support for the protests among the traditional media.

Mobilizing Information

Another category (204 posts, 30.9%) included mobilizing information in the form of actual calls for support in a specific time and place or virtually. The posts in this section urged people to attend the protests. Some listed specific locations and times, while others offered encouragement and explained that newcomers were welcome at the Liberation Square. Some of these posts listed ways in which Egyptians suffered from the governing regime and explained that this is additional reason to protest. Some of these messages reminded people to bring donations of medical equipment, asked civilians to allow protestors to use their wireless Internet networks, or reminded civilians to protect their bodies from tear gas and other weapons.

Before the protests began, the posts in this category encouraged citizens to remain safe. "Please do not call any phone number at all, unless we formally announce it," one post read. The post stressed the importance of remaining responsible and aware, yet unafraid. After the protest, the posts continued.

A Jan. 26 post invited participants to join "us in the 'Million Misri' (Million Egyptians) protest after the Friday prayer on January 28th." On the same day, a post asked protesters to "take black paint to throw on police cars to obstruct their vision" as well as "a piece of cloth soaked in vinegar in case tear gas is used." Both these posts asked the Facebook page members to share this information with all their friends; however, only one of the posts mentioned that "the traditional media betrayed us, but you will not." This category of posts indicates the importance of the use of Facebook in the Egyptian uprising that resulted in the ousting of Mubarak.

This category also included posts with explicit calls for virtual support, such as direct requests to share the webpage. Others were less demanding and more inter-active, posting a revolutionary video and notifying all users that the creator of the video was available for dialogue via Facebook comments. Materials to make flyers for distribution in various cities were linked in some of the posts in this section. Ad-ditionally, there were posts to teach people how to bypass governmental censorship of Facebook and Twitter that non-Egyptians were encouraged to pass to Egyptians.

Some of the posts in this category revolved around expressing support for the protests. For example, one post noted the consolidation of three major Facebook pages in the Arab world "to support the dreams and legal rights of the Egyptian people." The support of Facebook pages of three musicians, Nazar Qebani, Abu Leef, and Ahlam Mosteghnemi, resulted in "708,641 Facebook members" having heard the news of Facebook protests on Jan. 25. This post demonstrates how some of the posts uploaded on the April 6th Youth Movement Facebook page were simply raising awareness of the ensuing protests.

When the Egyptian government recognized the use of social media as an orga-nizing tool, they attempted to deny access to these websites. Some posts addressed this by providing a link to proxy sites along with comments such as, "Please spread this information on some of the social media sites like Masrawi and YouTube as well as Web forums that are frequented by Egyptians. If Facebook gets blocked, you can connect to it by using software like Hot Spot Shield, which is linked, or Oprah and selecting the turbo option." Other messages encouraged virtual support in the protests by including "If you are not currently in Egypt, please send this program to your friends in Egypt." This suggests that the Facebook page of the April 6th Youth Movement was fundamentally used as an organizational tool for online activism.

Criticisms of Government

Criticisms of the Mubarak regime were the next highest variety of postings (17.5%). Some of these comments were very straightforward, suggesting Mubarak's regime had betrayed its people. There were criticisms of the Ministry of Foreign Affairs' assertion that the revolution in Tunis could not be replicated in Egypt. There were also links describing the investigation of the members of the police force that sided with protesters were included, with comments that asked why allegations of police officers torturing citizens were not investigated.

Before the Jan. 25 protest, there were criticisms of the Mubarak regime, but it is important to note that these condemnations were merely rhetorical and did not call for any specific action. For example, one anecdote criticized the Minister of Flight, who was accused of treating "officers of airspace control in the Cairo airport in a barbaric manner, as though they were his slaves." The poster humorously suggested that he would be appointed for a new position as the "Minister of Bad Behavior." This made-up position gives the reader an idea that the April 6th Youth Movement is not content, but also not ready to call for radical changes.

As the protests gained momentum, the nature of the posts became sharper and bolder. During the period in which Mubarak attempted to negotiate more democratic reforms, the Facebook page displayed messages that suggested that such compromise would be insufficient. "Democracy never came immediately after dictatorship," one post stated, expressing the need for "a transitional government, run by noble people with legal expertise." This post, uploaded on Feb. 3, even suggested specific individuals, formerly living abroad, who returned to support the transition to democracy. That post ended with a summary that the "dictator whom no one chose cannot suddenly volunteer to give us a democracy." It is evident that the posts that criticized Mubarak became more brazen with time and began to suggest which courses of action would hasten the goal of ending Mubarak's regime.

On Feb. 4, the protesters became increasingly confrontational and the Facebook posts by the movement demonstrated this. "There are over a million protesters in Alexandria, criticizing the Egyptian national television correspondent that said the protesters were in support of Mubarak," one post declared. The post continued, "Mubarak's regime will fall, as will the lying governmental television." This post sends a direct, clear message that anything except the demise of Mubarak's regime would no longer be tolerated.

Human-Interest News

Soft news posts were the next most common (15.1%). These posts included human-interest stories of employees stealing sugar because their salaries did not feed them. These posts also glorified the "heroes" who kept fighting despite attacks that included tear gas and water tanks. This section included stories of emotion, as it told anecdotes of a man describing how the protest changed his life as he stood in Liberation Square.

Before the protests, the posts in this category recalled instances in which Egyptians were involved with protests and resistance to the Mubarak regime. One post displayed a link to "rare footage from the April 6, 2008 protests," the comment stated that "the people of Mahala City were brave, and the police were afraid of attacking the masses." Similar posts displayed pictures of the 2008 protests, or told the tragic stories of those who were killed by the Mubarak regime.

Immediately after the Jan. 25, 2011, protest, the tone of the posts in these categories shifted. These posts presented stories of heroism in Liberation Square.

"People were buying food and water for other people," said one post. "Youth were exchanging ideas and debating with people they do not know. I found people giving vinegar and onions after the tear gas." Another post from the same day explained the story of a "brave men who used their bodies to stop the water tankers from attacking the protesters."

National Unity

Calls for national unity followed (13.5%). Posts in this section would describe the union of Christians and Muslims as Egyptian citizens, sometimes citing specific evidence for support such as the Egyptian Copts protecting the Muslims during the Friday prayers. Sometimes, it was more abstract by using names of Muslim and Christian Egyptians and calling them to protest. These posts praised the efforts of male and female citizens of Egypt, calling them all "knights" in one post. These posts even included Egyptian ex-patriots standing in solidarity with the protestors. Several of these posts even aimed at socioeconomic differences, explaining that nurses and construction workers would protest together, for example.

Some cultural knowledge is necessary to understand the Facebook posts that were created to encourage national unity of Egyptians. On Jan. 24, a Facebook post was uploaded with a comment that said, "I am Amir Botros, and I am going to protest to stand up for the rights of Sayed Bilal. I am Yousef Ahmed, and I am protesting to stand up for the rights of my sister Mariam Fekry." The name Botros is associated with Egypt's Christian community, and Bilal is associated with Muslims. Thus, a Copt was protesting to protect a Muslim. In the next line, it was a man saying that his reasons for protesting involved supporting women.

Another way the movement's Facebook page was able to unite different segments of Egyptian society was to remember those who emigrated from Egypt and their encouragement of the protests. Page administrators reminded participants that there are ties between those in Egypt and their family members who left in pursuit of better living conditions.

Rumors

The posts in the rumors category generally addressed the discrepancies between the opinions of people watching the protest from their homes and those participating in the protests (13%). The majority of these posts revolved around the theme of betrayal, including that of the media. In one instance, it was posted there were unknown individuals on television claiming to represent the 6th of April Youth Movement. In other posts, the protesters expressed that it was painful that citizens believing the lies of the pro-Mubarak media. One video in this section showed a sniper shooting protestors.

One tool the Egyptian government tried to employ against the protesters was misinforming the masses. This was seen when several reporters resigned by refusing to broadcast false information. One particular suspicion in the region regarded whether a foreign conspirator was involved somehow. The Facebook page of the April 6th Youth Movement responded sarcastically on Feb. 4 by posting comments such as, "The leadership of the Muslim Brotherhood, Hezbollah, the United States of America, Israel, Hammas, Qatar have safely arrived to the Liberation Square." The next day, a similar post went further to ridicule the suspicions by saying, "I saw with my own eyes Hassan Nasrallah distributing money to protestors that are standing by KFC. And Ahemedinejad was driving a truck and distributing stones by the Abdulmonem Reyadh Square. The Amir of Qatar was buying java beans from Alshabrawy restaurant near Alasaaf. They also discovered spies sent from the Genghis Khan and with them was a pigeon being grilled on coal." Such farce was employed in distancing fears associated with the protesters being foreign spies.

The Egyptians' Struggle

The grievances of the Egyptian people were the next most common posts (10.9%). Some of these posts were very direct, such as videos of the police torturing citizens or snipers shooting protesters. Others explained that Egypt was denying its citizens an education to conserve the status quo. Some of these expressed sorrow for citizens who committed suicide before the protests began. The majority of the posts in this category were posted before the protest and depicted anecdotal grievances used as reasons to support the revolution. For example, one post called it a "responsibility to go to El Mounera General Hospital right now to support the Egyptian citizen Abdo Abdel Hameed, who burnt himself because he was unable to get food stamps." A subsequent post about him commented, "You cannot fathom the extent of despair that makes someone end their life in this traumatic way. All Egyptians must have compassion for one another and stand in solidary. We forbid this poverty, class-disparity and lack of integrity." In this post, there is an actual list of issues that Egyptians want to eliminate by rising up against Mubarak's regime. It ends by declaring that such treatment by the government will no longer be tolerated.

Political Demands

The penultimate category was concrete political demands (8.9%). Some of these demands were made in a teasing tone, such as reminders that Mubarak's plane was waiting for him. Others had a very serious tone, explaining that the vice president must resign and that the people would not give Mubarak or any of his cabinet members six months to reform the government. Some posts asked those associated with the military to respect the Egyptian people. Some of these posts were made by the protesters to ask the remaining protesters to clean the Liberation Square, for instance.

In the past, it was very rare that an Egyptian would ask for President Mubarak to resign. Even in the Facebook page of the April 6th Youth Movement, it is clear that no one person wanted to take responsibility for a statement of such dire consequences. On Jan. 25, the group posted, "the people of Egypt want its regime to end." Such a statement is bold, but also broad enough that no one person would be held responsible for making it. However, as the protests picked up steam, this message was repeated more directly. On Feb. 2, the group posted, "We are not asking for anything more than the resignation of President, and this is our right!" This post, which began by indicating that it was responding to confusion about what political demands were being made, addressed the increased emotional environment. The post eventually stated, "We are non-violent, and what we want is our right as well as the right of those who were martyred." Thus, the Facebook posts adjusted to the rapidly changing political and social environment.

DISCUSSION

One of the defining characteristics of the 2011 Egyptian revolution that ended the long rule of President Hosni Mubarak was the emergence of a vibrant *vox populi*. Egyptian citizens wanted to be heard, and social media platforms like Facebook, Twitter, and YouTube were used as "electronic megaphones" to amplify the call for democratic reforms (Franklin, 2011, p. 17). This call—which first emerged in Tunisia some months earlier—echoed deep into the Arab world, resonating as far west as Morocco and as far east as Yemen. The current study shows how the April 6th Youth Movement utilized Facebook.

This content analysis of 661 Facebook posts revealed that organizers used Facebook largely to communicate a mixture of expressions of national pride, encouragement of protesters, news events, and calls for mobilization on the ground. While direct mobilizing information was not the primary use of the Facebook page, it was a significant component. The current study also shows that the Egyptian people were able to criticize the Mubarak regime through social media, unlike traditional media.

Furthermore, the mixture of information presented is similar to well-established notions of the role of journalism in society—to provide citizens with the information they need to be free and self-governing (Kovach & Rosenstiel, 2007). For example, the current study reveals that the organizers of the 6th of April Youth Movement announced the equivalent of hard news and human interest news on their Facebook page. The organizers also identified rumors that were circulating as false information, created a list of grievances of the Egyptian people, and announced political demands. This further bolsters the argument that social media can be used to bridge gaps in society that result from government repression of freedom of the press (Bowe & Blom, 2010).

The analysis of the April 6th Youth Movement's use of Facebook within the context of Egypt's media environment, which has long been considered incredibly hostile to bloggers and journalists who gave voice to political dissenters (Franklin, 2011; Freedom House, 2010; Committee to Protect Journalists, 2009). The meager press freedoms guaranteed in the Egyptian Constitution were not extended to bloggers, because they were not considered journalists (Hamdy, 2009). In fact, Egypt became the first state in the world to charge and imprison a blogger in 2003 (Diebert & Rohozinski, 2008). The Committee to Protect Journalists (2009) placed Egypt at No. 10 on its list of the worst countries to be a blogger, citing government surveillance and open-ended detention of bloggers.

The present study shows that such punishments did not stop protesters from expressing pride in both Egypt and revolutions across the Arab world. In fact, the analysis indicates that the 6th of April Youth Movement encouraged individuals in neighboring countries to stage similar revolts against existing regimes on their Facebook page. While it is clear that social media were used to mobilize protesters and posed a threat to Egyptian authorities, what this study is unable to determine is the degree to which the messages posted were received by the actual protestors. Just because a message is posted does not mean it is necessarily received. As Gladwell noted, "just because innovations in communications technology happen does not mean that they matter." Such innovations must solve actual communication problems (Gladwell & Shirky, 2011).

While many commentators are enthusiastic about the potential for social media to allow activists to organize, the experience of the Egyptian revolution shows there is reason for caution. During the height of the revolution, the government was largely able to shut down Internet access in the country. This unprecedented and extreme move had an impact upon institutions at every level of Egyptian society, including ISPs, businesses, banks, Internet cafés, schools, and government offices (Cowie, 2011; Gillmor, 2011; Johnson, 2011). This content analysis suggests that that online media possess true emancipatory potential, especially when the infrastructure of connectivity is owned by governments or large companies (Morozov, 2011; Gladwell & Shirky, 2011; Gladwell, 2010; Shirky, 2011, 2010).

In the immediate aftermath of Mubarak's ouster, all of the detained journalists tracked by the Committee to Protect Journalists were released, including blogger Karim Amer (Abdel Dayem, 2011). However, it remains to be seen whether Egypt will be able to make an enduring transition to a system in which freedom of expressed online as well as offline. As Starr (2003) insisted, "regulation of decentralized networks should be categorically opposed, on the grounds that it restricts the democratic freedoms exercised over those networks" (p. 95).

The current study does in fact reveal that the Facebook page of the April 6th Youth Movement was used to gather support for the protests in either a specific location or even virtually. Moreover, the Facebook posts illustrate the degree to which members of Egyptian society stood in solidarity, as national unity was prioritized. Yet, in September 2011, the Supreme Council of the Armed Forces, which replaced Mubarak, had begun taking measures to limit media freedom—including reinstating the security law that allowed for the prosecution of civilians and journalists in state security courts (Committee to Protect Journalists, 2011). Other speech-chilling steps included fining blogger Kareem Reda for launching a Facebook page urging a boycott of a natural gas company and handing down a three-year jail sentence to blogger Maikel Nabil Sanad for criticizing the military (Reporters without Borders, 2011). Prominent blogger Alaa Abd Al Fattah was also summoned for questioning by the military leaders after a protest turned violent (Mackey, 2011). Future researchers should continue to scrutinize the communications from organizations like the 6th of April Movement to see if there appears to be an increase or decrease in free expression.

Finally, this content analysis suggests that the successful use of online media in the Egyptian revolution impacted the Egyptian media environment, which was shaken by this revolution. Though the state-run media were deeply criticized during the revolution, a report published by *The Carnegie Endowment for International Peace* suggests that the economic structure of the Egyptian national press is functioning in such a way that makes it difficult to be emancipated from the corruption that was present during Mubarak's regime (Brown, 2011).

Brown (2011) predicted five developments that the Egyptian media will face after the revolution. First, the corruption of media officials may require time to be exposed and expelled. Second, employees may continue to agitate if their wages are not paid, or if the reforms take too long to be implemented. Third, the future membership in the organization that formerly mediated issues between the media and Mubarak's regime, the Journalists' Syndicate, will have to be more aggressive in tackling questions regarding the relationship between the media and government. Fourth, the election of a parliament should incorporate media reform legislation as well as an increase of salaries. Finally, the current national press will have to negotiate a new position in Egyptian society (Franklin, 2011). Despite the progress made by the revolutionaries and their use of social media, traditional legal reform is necessary in order to ensure any long-term impact on Egyptian society. The present analysis supports such reforms, as social media platforms can be utilized to push for such reforms in the absence of a healthy media environment.

In an interview, analyst Rik Ferguson of TrendMicro pointed out a larger implication of the Egypt government's ability to shut down Internet traffic. "What struck me most is that we've been extolling the virtues of the Internet for democracy and free speech, but an incident like this demonstrates how easy it is—particularly in a country where there's a high level of governmental control—to just switch this access off" (Johnson, 2011).

Another example of how susceptible Facebook can be to government control, the Tunisian government attempted to hack the passwords of all Tunisian Facebook users during that country's protest movement, which led to the ouster of longtime dictator Zine El Abidine Ben Ali. While the company discovered the security breach, it took five days for it to close the beach (Madrigal, 2011). These developments suggest a danger in placing too much faith in the democratizing effect of social media tools.

CONCLUSION

A content-analysis of 661 Facebook posts of the 6th of April Youth Movement revealed that Facebook was used as a mobilizing tool in the Egyptian revolution. Due to censorship that prevented the traditional media from criticizing the existing government, social media such as Facebook became a place for individual dissenters to express dissenting views and organize protests against the Mubarak regime. The messages posted between January 17, 2011 through February 14, 2011 communicated expressions of nationalistic and revolutionary slogans, hard news, human-interest news, mobilizing information, national unity, criticisms of the government, rumors, political demands, and the struggles of Egyptians.

SUMMARY

The Internet "has become the foremost frontier over which symbolic, financial, and cultural battles are fought" (Deuze, 2008, p. 27). Scholars and media commentators alike have suggested that social media offer important tools for young activists to employ for organizing in countries where free speech is curtailed and news media are subject to government censorship (Bowe, Blom, & Freedman, 2011; Bowe & Blom, 2010). The revolution in Egypt provides a useful case study to examine the extent to which social media tools can be effective for activists, as well as examples of the limitations of such use.

One way to understand the success of those mobilizing efforts is to examine what messages dissidents distributed among their networks. This chapter examined messages posted on Facebook in Arabic by one of the largest and most important Egyptian opposition groups—the 6th of April Youth Movement—to see what roles the site actually played during a key period in the revolution.

This chapter examined the Facebook page of the April 6th Youth Movement, describing the nature of the posts that were uploaded weeks before and after the so-called 'Day of Rage' on January 25, 2011. This period coincided with a national holiday celebrating the police forces of Egypt and includes the resignation of Hosni Mubarak (Al Jazeera, 2011). Organizers turned to Facebook for mobilizing information; to call for national unity; and to express nationalistic or revolutionary slogans. Other uses included disseminating news developments—issuing political demands, addressing rumors, airing the struggle of the Egyptian people, and criticizing government officials. In this way, social media fulfilled the role that journalism plays in democratic societies, becoming one of the most important protest tools in Egypt (Morillon & Julliard, 2010).

REFERENCES

Abdel Dayem, M. (2011). Courage in documenting Egypt's revolution. *Committee to Protect Journalists*. Retrieved from: http://www.cpj.org/blog/2011/02/journalists-courage-egypt-revolution.php

Al Jazeera. (2011). *Timeline: Egypt's revolution - Middle East - English*. Retrieved September 4, 2011, from http://english.aljazeera.net/news/middleeast/2011/01/201112515334871490.html

Black, J. (2008). Egypt's press: More free, still fettered. *Arab Media & Society, 2*.

Blaydes, L. (2011). *Elections and distributive politics in Mubarak's Egypt*. Cambridge, UK: Cambridge University Press. doi:10.1017/CBO9780511976469

Bowe, B. J., & Blom, R. (2010). Facilitating dissent: The ethical implications of political organizing via social media. *Politics, Culture and Socialization, 1*(4).

Bowe, B. J., Blom, R., & Freedman, E. (2012). Control and dissent: Online political organizing in repressitarian regimes. In *Human Rights and Information Communication Technologies: Trends and Consequences of Use*. Hershey, PA: IGI Global.

Brown, N. (2011). *Can the colossus be salvaged? Egypt's state-owned press in a post-revolutionary environment - Carnegie endowment for international peace*. Retrieved from http://carnegieendowment.org/2011/08/22/can-colossus-be-salvaged-egypt-s-state-owned-press-in-post-revolutionary-environment/4uah# Committee to Protect Journalists. (2009). *10 worst countries to be a blogger*. Retrieved from http://www.cpj.org/reports/2009/04/10-worst-countries-to-be-a-blogger.php

Cowie, J. (2011). Egypt leaves the internet. *Renesys*. [Blog]. Retrieved from http://www.renesys.com/blog/2011/01/egypt-leaves-the-internet.shtml

Crete-Nishihata, M., & York, J. C. (2011). Egypt's internet blackout: Extreme example of just-in-time blocking. *OpenNet Initiative*. Retrieved from http://opennet.net/blog/2011/01/egypt%E2%80%99s-internet-blackout-extreme-example-just-time-blocking

Dashti, A. A. (2009). The role of online journalism in political disputes in Kuwait. *Journal of Arab and Muslim Research*, *2*, 91–112. doi:10.1386/jammr.2.1and2.91/1

Dayem, M. A. (2009, Summer). Attempting to silence Iran's weblogistan. *Nieman Reports*, 42-44.

Deibert, R., & Rohozinski, R. (2008). Good for liberty, bad for security? Global civil society and the securitization of the internet. In Deibert, R., Palfrey, J., Rohozinski, R., & Zittrain, J. (Eds.), *Access Denied: The Practice and Policy of Global Internet Filtering*. Cambridge, MA: MIT Press.

Deibert, R., & Rohozinski, R. (2010). Control and subversion in Russian cyberspace. In Deibert, R., Palfrey, J., Rohozinski, R., & Zittrain, J. (Eds.), *Access Controlled: The Shaping of Power, Rights, and Rule in Cyberspace* (pp. 15–34). Cambridge, MA: MIT Press.

Deuze, M. (2008). Corporate appropriation of participatory culture. In Carpentier, N. (Ed.), *Participation and Media Production: Critical Reflections on Content Creation* (pp. 27–40). Newcastle upon Tyne, UK: Cambridge Scholars Publishers.

Duve, F. (2003). Preface. In Hardy, C., & Moller, C. (Eds.), *Spreading the Word on the Internet*. Vienna, Austria: Organization for Security and Co-Operation in Europe.

El Nashmi, E., Cleary, J., Molleda, J.-C., & McAdams, M. (2010). Internet political discussions in the Arab world: A look at online forums from Kuwait, Saudi Arabia, Egypt and Jordan. *International Communication Gazette*, *72*, 719–738. doi:10.1177/1748048510380810

Endeshaw, A. (2004). Internet regulation in China: The never-ending cat and mouse game. *Information & Communications Technology Law*, *13*, 41–57. doi:10.1080/1360083042000190634

Etling, B., Kelly, J., Faris, R., & Palfrey, J. (2010). Mapping the Arabic blogosphere: Politics and dissent online. *New Media & Society*, *12*, 1225–1243. doi:10.1177/1461444810385096

Fahmi, W. S. (2009). Bloggers' street movement and the right of the city (re)claiming Cairo's real and virtual "spaces of freedom". *Environment and Urbanization, 21,* 89–107. doi:10.1177/0956247809103006

Faris, D. (2010). *Revolutions without revolutionaries? Social media networks and regime response in Egypt.* (Unpublished Dissertation). Philadelphia, PA: University of Pennsylvania.

Franklin, S. (2011). Sunrise on the Nile. *Columbia Journalism Review, 49*(6), 17.

Freedom House. (2009). *Freedom on the net.* Retrieved from http://www.freedomhouse.org/template.cfm?page=383&report=79

Freedom House. (2010). *Freedom of the press 2010.* Retrieved from http://www.freedomhouse.org/template.cfm?page=533

Gillmor, D. (2011). Egypt's communications kill switch. *Salon.* Retrieved from http://www.salon.com/technology/dan_gillmor/2011/01/28/egypt_kill_switch

Gladwell, M. (2010, October 4). Small change: Why the revolution will not be tweeted. *New Yorker.* Retrieved from http://www.newyorker.com/reporting/2010/10/04/101004fa_fact_gladwell#ixzz1HuHZ927E

Gladwell, M., & Shirky, C. (2011, March/April). From innovation to revolution: Do social media make protests possible? *Foreign Affairs.* Retrieved from http://www.foreignaffairs.com/node/67189&cid=soc-tumblr-from_innovation_to_revolution-012511

Hamdy, N. (2008). Building capabilities of Egyptian journalist in preparation for media in transition. *Journal of Arab and Muslim Media Research, 1,* 215–243. doi:10.1386/jammr.1.3.215_1

Hamdy, N. (2009). Arab citizen journalism in action: Challenging mainstream media, authorities and media laws. *Westminster Papers in Communication and Culture, 6,* 92–112.

Idsvoog, K. (2008, Spring). Circumventing censorship with technology. *Nieman Reports,* 77-79.

Ishani, M. (2011, February 7). The hopeful network. *Foreign Policy.* Retrieved from http://www.foreignpolicy.com/articles/2011/02/07/the_hopeful_network

Isherwood, T. (2008, September). *A new direction or more of the same? Political blogging in Egypt.* Cairo, Egypt: Arab Media & Society.

Johnson, B. (2011). How Egypt switched off the internet. *GigaOm*. Retrieved from http://gigaom.com/2011/01/28/how-egypt-switched-off-the-internet/

Kovach, B., & Rosenstiel, T. (2007). *The elements of journalism*. New York, NY: Three Rivers Press.

Krasnoboka, N. (2002). Real journalism goes underground: The internet underground. *Gazette, 64*, 479–499. doi:10.1177/17480485020640050701

Kulikova, S. V., & Perlmutter, D. D. (2007). Blogging down the dictator? The Kyrgyz revolution and Samizdat websites. *International Communication Gazette, 69*, 29–50. doi:10.1177/1748048507072777

Levinson, C., & Coker, M. (2011, February 11). The secret rally that sparked an uprising. *Wall Street Journal*. Retrieved from http://online.wsj.com/article/SB100 01424052748704132204576135882356532702.html

Lynch, M. (2006). *Voices of the new Arab public: Iraq, Al-Jazeera, and Middle East politics today*. New York, NY: Columbia University Press.

Mackey, R. (2011, October 25). Egyptian activists summoned by military prosecutor. *New York Times*. Retrieved October 31, 2011, from http://thelede.blogs.nytimes.com/2011/10/25/after-call-from-obama-egypt-postpones-interrogation-of-activist-bloggers

Madrigal, A. (2011, January 24). The inside story of how Facebook responded to Tunisian hacks. *The Atlantic*. Retrieved from http://www.theatlantic.com/technology/archive/2011/01/the-inside-story-of-how-facebook-responded-to-tunisian-hacks/70044/

Manzella, J. C. (2000). Negotiating the news: Indonesian press culture and power during the political crises of 1997-8. *Journalism, 1*, 305–328. doi:10.1177/146488490000100303

Menon, K. (2000, September). Controlling the internet: Censorship online in China. *Quill Magazine, 82*.

Morillon, L., & Julliard, J. (2010). Enemies of the internet: Web 2.0 versus control 2.0. *Reporters without Borders*. Retrieved from http://www.rsf.org/ennemis.html

Payne, G. A. (2008). The exile of dissidence: Restrictions on the right to communicate in democracies. *Global Media Journal, 7*.

Preston, J. (2011, February 6). Movement began with outrage and a Facebook page that gave it an outlet. *New York Times*, p. A10.

Reese, A. (2009, Spring). Framing April 6: Discursive dominance in the Egyptian print media. *Arab Media & Society*.

Reporters without Borders. (2011, September 10). *Is the supreme council a new predator of press freedom?* Retrieved from http://en.rsf.org/egypt-is-the-supreme-council-a-new-10-09-2011,40962.html

Ritchel, M. (2011). Egypt cuts off most internet and cell phone service. *New York Times*. Retrieved from http://www.nytimes.com/2011/01/29/technology/internet/29cutoff.html?_r=3&adxnnl=1&adxnnlx=1300476961-GCNnGx7aXhmEfr4YKW121g

Rodriguez, F., & Spanik, K. (2003). Introduction. In Hardy, C., & Moller, C. (Eds.), *Spreading the Word on the Internet*. Vienna, Austria: Organization for Security and Co-Operation in Europe.

Scammell, M. (1988). Censorship and its history – A personal view. In Boyle, K. (Ed.), *Article 19 World Report 1988: Information, Freedom, and Censorship*. New York, NY: Times Books.

Shane, S. (2011, January 29). Spotlight again falls on web tools and change. *New York Times*. Retrieved from http://www.nytimes.com/2011/01/30/weekinreview/30shane.html?_r=2

Shapiro, S. M. (2009, January 22). Revolution, Facebook-style. *New York Times*. Retrieved from http://www.nytimes.com/2009/01/25/magazine/25bloggers-t.html

Shirky, C. (2010, January/February). The political power of social media: Technology, the public sphere, and political change. *Foreign Affairs*, 28–41.

Stanyer, J., & Davidson, S. (2009). *The internet and the visibility of oppression in non-democratic states: The online exposure of human rights violations and the other repressive acts*. Paper presented at the Annual Meeting of the International Communication Association. Chicago, IL.

Starr, S. (2003). Putting freedom back on the agenda. In Hardy, C., & Moller, C. (Eds.), *Spreading the Word on the Internet*. Vienna, Austria: Organization for Security and Co-Operation in Europe.

Thompson, N. (2011, January 27). Is Twitter helping in Egypt? *New Yorker*. Retrieved from http://www.newyorker.com/online/blogs/newsdesk/2011/01/is-twitter-helping-in-egypt.html#ixzz1HuIn9WZt

ADDITIONAL READING

Abdel Dayem, M. (2011, February 11). Courage in documenting Egypt's revolution. *Committee to Protect Journalists*. Retrieved from http://www.cpj.org/blog/2011/02/journalists-courage-egypt-revolution.php

Bowe, B. J., & Blom, R. (2010). Facilitating dissent: the ethical implications of political organizing via social media. *Politics, Culture & Socialization, 1*(4).

Bowe, B. J., Blom, R., & Freedman, E. (2012). Negotiating boundaries between control and dissent: Free speech, business and repressitarian governments. In Lannon, J. (Ed.), *Human Rights and Information Communication Technologies: Trends and Consequences of Use*. Hershey, PA: IGI Global.

Castells, M. (1997). An introduction to the information age. *City, 7*, 6–16. doi:10.1080/13604819708900050

Deibert, R. (2008). *Access denied: The practice and policy of global Internet filtering*. Cambridge, MA: MIT Press. doi:10.1109/TPC.2009.2032378

Howard, P. (2010). *The digital origins of dictatorship and democracy: Information technology and political Islam*. Oxford, UK: Oxford University Press. doi:10.1093/acprof:oso/9780199736416.001.0001

Khamis, S., & Vaughn, K. (2011). Cyberactivism in the Egyptian revolution: How civic engagement and citizen journalism tilted the balance. *Arab Media & Society, 13*. Retrieved from http://www.arabmediasociety.com/?article=769

Morillon, L., & Julliard, J. (2010). Enemies of the internet: Web 2.0 versus control 2.0. *Reporters without Borders*. Retrieved from http://www.rsf.org/ennemis.html

Morozov, E. (2011). *The net delusion: How not to liberate the world*. New York, NY: Public Affairs.

Shapiro, S. M. (2009, January 22). Revolution, Facebook-style. *New York Times*. Retrieved from http://www.nytimes.com/2009/01/25/magazine/25bloggers-t.htm

Shirky, C. (2011). *Cognitive surplus: How technology makes consumers into collaborators*. New York, NY: Penguin Books.

Wickham, C. (2002). *Mobilizing Islam: Religion, activism, and political change in Egypt*. New York, NY: Columbia University Press.

Chapter 11
Technological Support for Online Communities Focusing on Music Creation:
Adopting Collaboration, Flexibility, and Multiculturality from Brazilian Creativity Styles

Marcelo S. Pimenta
Federal University of Rio Grande do Sul (UFRGS), Brazil

Damián Keller
Federal University of Acre (UFAC), Brazil

Evandro M. Miletto
Federal Institute of Rio Grande do Sul (IFRS), Brazil

Luciano V. Flores
Federal University of Rio Grande do Sul (UFRGS), Brazil

Guilherme G. Testa
Federal University of Rio Grande do Sul (UFRGS), Brazil

EXECUTIVE SUMMARY

People have always found music significant in their lives, whether for enjoyment in listening, performing, or creating. However, music making in modern life tends to be restricted to the domain of the professional artists, instrumentalists, and singers. Since the advent of Web 2.0 and Rich Internet Applications, the authors' research group has been investigating the use of Web-based technology to support novice-oriented computer-based musical activities.

DOI: 10.4018/978-1-4666-2515-0.ch011

The main motivation of their work is the belief that no previous musical knowledge should be required for participating in creative musical activities. Consequently, any ordinary user—non-musician or novice—may enhance his creativity through engagement, entertainment, and self-expression. The goal of this chapter is to propose several concepts that emerged during their research concerning novice-oriented cooperative music creation and musical knowledge sharing (a sophisticated activity distinct from the common and well-known music sharing for listening). The authors also discuss key characteristics of Brazilian culture and the creativity styles that inspired their work. They illustrate their perspective by showing how concepts implemented and derived from cases investigated in Brazil represent a comprehensive context for embracing cooperation, flexibility, cross-cultural diversity and creativity. The resulting communityware has music as its intrinsic motivation.

INTRODUCTION

Art and music are basic human functions: Humankind has a burning desire to create as strong as the desire to communicate. People have always found listening, performing, or creating music significant in their lives, whether for enjoyment or for social cohesion. Music has immense value for our society—this is particularly true for developing countries like Brazil, South Africa, or India. However, on a more practical note, music making in modern life tends to be left in the hands of the professional artists, musicians, and singers.

Music creation is considered as mostly a solitary activity performed by musicians. However, given that music has also served as a natural motivation for community formation, new modalities have been created through the use of technology. One example of convergence of social activities and music making is the field of "Networked Music"—subject of a special issue of the Organised Sound Journal (Schedel & Young, 2005). Network music allows people to explore the implications of interconnecting their computers for musical purposes. Because networked music works result from the convergence of social and technological aspects of Internet, this area has attracted the interest of the music technology community. The existing applications—as described in a survey by Barbosa (2003)—have evolved towards sophisticated projects and concepts including, for example, real-time distance performance systems, and various systems for multi-user interaction and collaboration.

Rich Internet Applications such as YouTube (Google, 2009), MySpace (Media, 2009), and Flickr (Yahoo, 2009) have turned the passive user into an active producer of content, bringing into the picture new purposes, like engagement, entertainment and self-expression. Considering music as a social activity for sharing musical experiences (Gurevich, 2006; Miletto, et al., 2011; Keller, et al., 2011), by investigating social ways of music creation by novices, new modalities are created beyond music listening and sharing. The main motivation of our work is the belief that no previous musical knowledge should be required for participating in musically creative activities. Obviously, providing support for non-musicians or for musicians are not the same thing (Miletto, et al., 2007). Musician-oriented systems usually include full and complex information, concepts, and interface functionalities that are part of the "musician's world" and usually not understood by ordinary users.

During the last few years, our research group has been investigating the use of computing technology to support novice-oriented computer-based musical activities. The development of this support has followed an interdisciplinary approach, and involves a multidisciplinary team of experts in Computer Music, Human-Computer Interaction (HCI), Computer Supported Cooperative Work (CSCW), pointing toward a new field defined as Ubiquitous Music (Keller, et al., 2011b).

The goal of this chapter is to present and discuss some concepts that emerged during our research work—focused on Brazilian cases—concerning novice-oriented cooperative music creation and musical knowledge sharing (a sophisticated activity, which is distinct from the common and well-known music sharing for listening). We also discuss features of Brazilian culture and creativity styles adopted as inspirations for our work. We illustrate our point by showing how these concepts—implemented by support mechanisms—represent a comprehensive context to embrace cooperation, flexibility, cross-cultural diversity, and creativity in online communityware having music as its intrinsic motivation.

BRAZILIAN CULTURE AND BRAZILIAN CREATIVITY STYLE

Musical creation is a complex activity of artistic and creative nature, and is greatly influenced by specific contextual factors. In the particular case of Brazil, many factors of our cultural identity define unique relationships to creativity. This aspects were taken into account in CODES design and implementation.

We are inspired by concepts and ideas rooted in psychology with particular emphasis on human creativity. Creativity is a common term whose meaning is not always clear when applied to interdisciplinary initiatives. Research has pointed out creativity as a sociocultural and contextually embedded phenomenon (Fleith, 2011). As a consequence, the effects of cultural factors on the manifestation of creativity have been discussed worldwide (Amabile, 1996; Csikszentmihalyi, 1996; Lubart, 1999; Raina, 1993; Rudowicz, 2003; Simonton, 1994).

In the most general sense, culture is a term used by social field researchers to refer to a set of parameters that can be used to differentiate a social group significantly, such as nations, companies, and groups (Abou-Zeid, 2005). One of the most accepted definitions of culture is "the collective programming of the mind that distinguishes the members of one group or category of people from others" (Hofstede & Geert, 2005). Within a culture, a microculture is defined by influences such as geographical location (e.g. The South) or by ideological movement (e.g. Punk). Here we adopt the generic term "culture" both for culture and microculture. Cultural differences have been studied by anthropologists (e.g. Hofstede, Trompenaars, and Hall) to categorize culture according to different cultural dimensions (see for example Moran, et al., 2007; Reinecke, et al., 2010). Each culture defines how its people should approach and interact, thus the culture is influenced by many factors such as ethnicity, race, nationality, religion, or geography.

Since culture embraces all the (abstract and physical) human creative products it is important to investigate how culture drives creativity toward certain domains, improving the experience of creation sometimes in imaginative and idiosyncratic ways. Several studies (Fleith, 2011) suggest that creativity may be fostered or hindered by cultural characteristics such as socialization processes, beliefs, values, and traditions. Moreover, the socioeconomic status and historical roots of a nation can also influence the development of the creative activities. Thus, focusing specifically on Brazilian traits seems to be the most fruitful approach to understanding the social requirements for computer-assisted music making.

Brazil is the sixth largest country in the world, with one of largest economies among the developing countries. Brazil is the largest and only Portuguese speaking country in South America. It was colonized by Portugal from 1500 until 1822 when the country became independent. In the late 19th and early 20th centuries Italian, German, Spanish, Arab, and Japanese immigrants settled in Brazil and played an important role in its culture, creating a multicultural and multiethnic society. Brazilian culture is not, therefore, a homogeneous culture. Brazilians have adopted the notion that racial and cultural mixture defines their unique national identity. Indeed, Brazilian culture is a culture of a very diverse nature. A variety of people from different parts of the world helped to build a unique culture, which boasts the largest multiracial democracy on our planet. The ethnic and cultural mixing that occurred in the colonial period among Native Americans, Portuguese, and Africans formed the bulk of Brazilian cultural traits.

Multiculturality in Brazil is directly related to co-existence of different views and tolerance of multiple perspectives. Hence, the complexity of Brazilian identity has long been a subject of debate. Brazil is a large laboratory of civilization, where First Nations, European and African races were allowed to merge freely, in an atmosphere of absence of legal restrictions on miscegenation. This community of people representing very diverse ethnic origins necessarily coexists with cultural diversity. This is one of the reasons that motivate Brazilian people to be flexible, accepting naturally the different perspectives coming with multiculturality. If we recognize the creative processes as being highly fuzzy, the development of culturally oriented cooperative mechanisms for creativity and innovation should be adaptive and flexible.

Another important cultural characteristic of Brazilian people is a high capacity for improvisation and brainstorm-oriented creation: combining and improving on other people's ideas, welcoming unusual ideas and withholding harsh criticism. These characteristics usually furnish good outcomes with little resources, so may provide an important skill for survival.

Creativity is usually viewed as a positive construct within the Brazilian culture. The success of Brazilian people in several creative domains such as music, visual arts, football, and design may point to specific expressions of a general trend. Brazilian creativity styles may be characterized by three factors: multiculturality, flexibility, and brainstorm-oriented creation. Such characteristics of Brazilian creativity styles are the inspirations for our work. More specifically, CODES design aims to provide support for computer-mediated music creation where multiculturality, flexibility, and cooperative brainstorm-oriented creation are essential attributes for fostering innovation, inspiration, or insight and relevance. The next section presents the basic characteristics of CODES environment and explains how CODES principles were inspired by Brazilian creativity styles.

THE CODES ENVIRONMENT

CODES is a Web-based environment designed to support Cooperative Music Prototyping (CMP), with special focus on music novices. Differently from YouTube, Flickr, and even MySpace, where people only publish their content, Web systems for experimenting with music should also provide ways to allow for contributions and experiments. For this reason, we consider CODES as a system for music creation, instead of a system just for publishing music. CODES offers a high level music representation and user interface features to foster easy direct manipulation (drag-and-drop) of icons representing sound patterns (predefined MP3 samples with 4 seconds of duration).

Using adequate support features, CODES users can create, edit, share and publish simple musical pieces—or Musical Prototypes (MPs)—in their group or on the Web. These shared MPs can be repeatedly tested, listened to, and modified by the partners, who cooperate on prototype refinement. Users can start a new MP by choosing the name and the musical style they want. The selection of a musical style allows CODES to filter the sound patterns offered to the user. However, since all styles are available from the sound library, mixing sound patterns from different styles within the same musical prototype is still possible.

Edition in CODES includes actions like "drag-and-drop" sound patterns from the sound library to the editing area, "move," "organize," "delete," "expand" the duration, and "collapse" to listen to the final result. When sharing a musical proto-type, the "owner" user can invite CODES users to use a search engine or may send explicit invitations via e-mail to non-members asking them for cooperation. When someone accepts such an invitation, the user becomes a prototype partner and can edit the MP like the owner does.

The prototypical nature of CODES is designed and built to provide a novice-oriented perspective. At any time users can listen to the musical prototype and link arguments to their decisions. Thus, all prototype partners can discuss and change ideas about each step of the prototype refinement, in order to understand each other's decisions. When someone considers that the resulting sounds are good, a "publication request" can be triggered and the group may discuss and deliberate about the publication of this musical prototype in the CODES home page. This activity is called musical prototype publishing. As an alternative to publishing their music, users may export their musical prototype, and share it at will. Thus, a novice may experiment with music by combining, listening and rearranging pre-defined sound patterns to create simple musical pieces—the MPs. Furthermore, CODES users may cooperate with partners in a cyclical and collaborative process of prototype creation—called Cooperative Music Prototyping (CMP) through customized aware-ness, argumentation, and negotiation mechanisms until a final consensual prototype stage is reached.

Awareness Mechanisms in CODES

Through CODES, ordinary users may have the opportunity to be the actors of their own musical experiences. Using CODES anyone can draft, test, modify, and listen to Ps. These actions can be done both by the first authors and their partners that cooperate in the refinement of the MP. This implies a focus not only on community management (i.e., discovering, building, or maintaining virtual communities) but also on experimenting and participating in specific design practices using a suitable interaction vocabulary. This process suggests the existence of noteworthy distinct kinds of cooperation activities. Systems aiming to provide effective support for these different activities have to meet specific requirements. Awareness and conflict resolution are already considered critical issues in general CSCW systems. However, mechanisms existing in other systems need some adaptation to take into account the idiosyncrasies of the CMP context. The ultimate goal is to provide actual coop-eration, social knowledge construction, argumentation, and negotiation among the actors of the MP design activities. This type of cooperation is supported by a set of mechanisms borrowed from the Software Engineering and HCI areas and specially adapted for CODES, namely awareness, music prototyping rationale, authorship, version control, and conflict resolution (Pimenta, et al., 2011).

Design and Development of CODES

The design and development of CODES adopted a user-centered and incremental approach, taking into consideration social aspects such as the characteristics of the users, contexts, purpose, minimal technology requirements, and the nature of its possible influence on the novice user. The development team worked on three versions until a balance between a usable interface and a viable user experience to accomplish the musical and cooperative tasks was reached. Previous versions tried to use purely Web standard recommendations (W3C, 2012) with MIDI file support to play music samples. However, the results of the first experiments revealed interaction metaphors and a minimal sound quality as important requirements for lay people experimenting with music on the Web.

CODES is based on the classical client-server architecture for Web applications (see Figure 1). A previous version of CODES was based on a Java Web-application development framework but issues related to performance and usability showed the need of searching for a more suitable solution, and led to the redesign of the initial architecture. In the current version of CODES special attention was given to aspects related to interaction flexibility and usability since one of the main goals is to implement an adequate support for manipulation of complex musical information, cooperative activities and group awareness, to provide an effective interaction of the users with each other and with the environment itself. Thus, in the client-side, CODES uses scripts embedded within standard HTML.

Figure 1. CODES current architecture

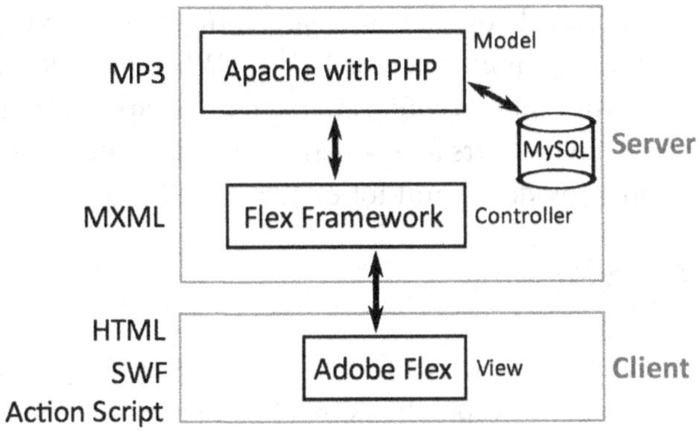

On the server side, CODES implements the Model-View-Controller (MVC). This model is used to separate the logic of the application in different parts with different responsibilities. In MVC, the "Model" part (Apache with PHP) connects the Web server with MySQL database, and represents all the information (the data) of the application; and the "Controller" part manages the communication of data and the business rules used to manipulate the data to and from the model. For this, CODES makes use of Adobe MXML (an XML-based language used to lay out user-interface components for Adobe Flex applications). This allowed the development stage to focus on the view part of this framework to deal with interface aspects. On the client-side the "View" part corresponds to elements of the user interface such as text, buttons, canvas, icons, checkbox items, and so forth; the GUI is made as simple as possible for running on a Web browser. The Adobe Flex a script language (ADOBE, 2009) was chosen to allow actions like drag-and-drop, use of sliders, scalable windows, and other facilities to manipulate the sound samples provided for this technology. The sound files used in CODES are small MP3 files, which can be quickly downloaded by the client-side ensuring a standard audio quality.

Related Work

The most representative systems found in the literature of collective musical creation or music experimentation on the Web concerned with musical experimentation by novices are: Daisyphone (Bryan-Kins, 2004), PitchWeb (Duckworth, 1999), Web-Drum (Burk, 2009), Public Sound Objects—PSOs (Barbosa, 2005), EduMusical system (Benini, et al., 2004), and JamSpace (Gurevich, 2006). A brief description of each system and a comparative analysis according to various criteria (categorized as technological and architectural, computer music related, HCI related, CSCW related) may be found at Miletto (2009). In summary, the main drawback of existing networked music systems comes from the lack of focus on effective cooperation—directly related to effective collaboration through techniques such as argumentation, authorship (allowing users to know their original contributions at anytime), interaction trace, awareness, group memory, and persistence. When these techniques are not adequately considered or explored within interaction design (taking into account real needs and tasks of the novice users for cooperative musical interactions), networked music systems do not provide support for effective novice usage.

Preliminary Assessments

The CODES environment is a testbed of our research. Being designed and developed to allow cooperative musical experimentation by novices to turn them creators of musical content, it needs to be tested and evaluated in real contexts with real users. Testing procedures have followed well-known subjective evaluation methods from the HCI field, targeting both qualitative and quantitative results. The users´ feedback was used as input for the redesign process. This assessment process revealed several requirements, showing the need for adopting a broad HCI approach to make CODES interaction design more efficient and effective for collaboration.

CODES assessment was made by users with different social profiles, ages, and skills.. Our goal was not only to get an overall (mainly subjective) feedback from users but to try out our proposals for non-technical cooperative design environments as well. Usability evaluation methods included Heuristic Evaluation (Nielsen, 1992, 1994a, 1994b) and User Testing (Rubin, 1994). The set of tasks was followed by a questionnaire with open and closed questions to be filled out.

A total of twenty-six individuals representative of the CODES target public (with ages ranging from 20 to 35 years, having no musical expertise, and using CODES for the first time) performed various musical tasks. These tasks were designed to simulate a scenario in which a novice user would learn how to interact, create, edit, and cooperate through a musical prototype. A cooperative scenario was composed by three different tasks at the MP editing level. The tasks included creation, edition, and sharing of CMP. Time taken to complete all the tasks ranged from 20 to 50 minutes.

User Testing (Rubin, 1994) was carried out in the presence of a facilitator (observer), a usability expert. He just read each task to the users, and took notes of any problems found and any verbal comments from them. The subjects were instructed to speak while the tasks were performed (Nielsen, 1992). Interaction and user comments were recorded using a video camera aimed at the computer screen.

After performing the tasks, users filled out a form with open and closed questions concerning the Nielsen's heuristics, such as visibility, contextualization, control and freedom, feedback, flexibility. The questionnaire featured items related to musical representation in CODES. The users would read the statements and answer questions by choosing the following options: "Totally Agree, Agree, Neutral, Disagree, and Totally Disagree."

The experiments were intended to be developed in a very restricted context. Despite this limitation, it has been possible to conclude that the system is intuitive and easy to use, making participants feel motivated to enhancing and sharing their musical experiences. Despite a few negative points, overall results were favorable and most of users (62%) indicated "totally agree" as positive answer.

CODES Principles Inspired by Brazilian Creativity Style

CODES design provides support for computer mediated music creation where multiculturality, flexibility, and cooperative brainstorm-oriented creation are essential attributes for originating (and subsequently developing) innovation and relevance. Using the technological support provided by CODES, novices are encouraged to create music. However, music creation demands flexibility and associative power. In this context, rigidity, or worry of failure are not welcome. All users should be capable of obtaining the joy of invention and the richness of variety.

CSCW concepts and tools have made more obvious the existence of a more connective, cooperative, and collective nature of creativity rather than the prevailing focus on the individual. The creative processes being highly fuzzy, the programming of cooperative tools for creativity and innovation should be adaptive and flexible.

Creativity models in music have been heavily influenced by general models of creativity such as Gardner (1993) and Wallas (1926). While some creativity models for music emphasize the cognitive dimensions of music creation (Webster, 2003; Chen, 2006; Collins, 2005), others consider its material dimension as an integral part of music creation (Bennett, 1976; Dingwall, 2008). In fact, to assess musical creativity is a very difficult task because social context, physical context, and personal factors shape the creative act and may determine the function and the dynamic of the creative processes involved (Keller, et al., 2011a). Given this complex scenario, to put into practice collaboration, flexibility and multiculturality, we have adopted two principles which have been confirmed by findings obtained during CODES development and usage: (a) Music creation by novices should be prototypical; and (b) Music creation by novices should be cooperative (Miletto, et al., 2011).

Within prototypical music creation, novices can draft an initial musical sketch (a simple MP) which can be tested, modified and listened to, applying a cyclical refinement process until a final stage is reached. In the music literature, "draft" is the term commonly applied to initial creative products. However, here the emphasis is on the cyclical prototyping process and not on the product itself. Consequently, in this chapter "prototype" and "draft" are equivalent. The prototyping process clearly resembles the incremental software development cycles adopted in the industry.. Since music creation can be considered a design activity, it seems natural and straightforward to adopt a prototypical process to model this activity.

In cooperative music creation, the refinement of an initial musical idea is a consequence of the collaboration of the author with her partners. Through the prototypical and cooperative nature of CODES, novices may thus have the opportunity to be, like experienced musicians, the actors of their own musical experiences. In this context, what matters is not necessarily the musical quality of the finished work, but giving the possibility of a creative experience to a larger community of participants. The members build a social network by explicit invitation to cooperate until a final consensual MP stage is reached.

In the next sections, we discuss the ideas behind the evolution of CODES. Social network services and online communities emerged as mechanisms where

music making always was the intrinsic motivation. CODES grew from an environment for supporting cooperative music creation towards communityware.

CODES AS COMMUNITYWARE: SUPPORTING SOCIAL NETWORK SERVICES AND ONLINE COMMUNITIES HAVING MUSIC AS INTRINSIC MOTIVATION

The goal of this section is to present and discuss several concepts developed by our research group concerning the support provided by CODES to an online community for cooperative music making. Our environment started out as a website that people could use to create their music interactively and cooperatively, but it has grown into a more general online community of people allowing to build an audience around music experimentation, music creation, (music) knowledge sharing, and entertainment.

In fact, Web 2.0 has turned the passive user into an active producer of content and shaper of the ultimate user experience, and the Web is becoming a rich and ideal means for social activities.

Now we are improving CODES in order to provide support for online communities involving people having music creation as their main common interest. Indeed, today's technology makes it easy for international and intercultural group members to brainstorm together remotely. The wide availability of Computer-Mediated Communication (CMC) technologies helps geographically dispersed group members to interact remotely and interculturally. We are convinced we can also provide technological support for creativity in musical activities adopting Brazilian Creative Styles for computer-aided music creation by novices. Within this context, users can merge freely their ideas, in an atmosphere of liberality and absence of legal restrictions, stimulating cooperation, cross-cultural dialog, flexibility, and creativity.

Our communityware has the potential to provide a basis for developing a number of learning processes and skills to help achieve some of the aims of music learning (e.g. listening, analyzing, interpreting, composing, for example). Existing musical environments make it difficult for anyone to create music without first developing basic music theory knowledge, music reading and writing skills. Within an online community, other users can provide feedback, and all participants can respond to this feedback and check their results. Novices learn by sharing and modifying others' artifacts and by accessing others' knowledge by means of argumentation and exchange of ideas with peers. By argumentation and interaction during the development of a music prototype, experienced users may promote music learning, positive interdependency, and collaborative learning by beginners.

In the next sections, we discuss concepts related to online communities, social networks, and the rationale behind evolution of CODES in order to become a communityware with users establishing relations based on common musical interests.

Social Network Services and Online Communities

With the advance of global computer networks like the Internet and mobile computing, the discussion of virtual communities (HCI, 2011) has become more active worldwide. People realized that the Internet and other network technologies could affect not just industries and economies but also our everyday life. The term virtualization denotes the phenomenon that increasing aspects of our lives take place online. Due to the variety of communication media, it is difficult to keep track of all people in one's personal social network. Therefore, it is necessary to support the management of social relationships.

According to Webster's Dictionary, the word community is defined as "a body of individuals organized into a unit or manifesting usually with awareness some unifying trait." Today the concept of community is based on the locality of human life and social interaction, where people share a space and possibly common goals.

While communicating with each other or providing and retrieving shared information, people constitute relationships to other people. Belonging to the same community implies influencing each other, either directly (e.g., via direct communication) or indirectly (e.g., via providing and retrieving public information). Thus, supporting virtual communities is strongly related to relationship management.

The combination of all these features has led to the creation of virtual communities (or technology-mediated communities) consisting of people who are not necessarily co-located and who rely on technology for most of their communication. Furthermore, these individuals work on interdependent tasks and share responsibility for the outcomes.

The most prominent (partly overlapping) purposes of virtual communities are listed below. A communityware is a collection of technologies/mechanisms providing support to these purposes, consequently helping people in developing their own virtual community:

a.   Sharing information,
b.   Knowledge management (not only addressing the management of explicit knowledge but also helping people to get together and find the right persons for the problem they are trying to solve),
c.   Supporting awareness (to know which people are around or to find other people sharing one's interests in order to initiate meetings "in real life"), and also

d.   Recommendation and matchmaking (due the huge amount of information stored, a recommender system analyze the user's preferences, public data, and sometimes even behaviour, and suggest interesting information [recommendation] or interesting persons [matchmaking]).

Sharing and exchanging information are common tasks in cooperative activities. Shared information may concern general knowledge and facts, or may register on-going or completed group work. Two main subclasses of shared information space systems can be distinguished. The first class includes hypertext systems like the World Wide Web. The second class contains systems supporting groups of people who share common interests or common goals ("communities"); often these systems are accessible via Web interfaces and incorporate hypertext features too. Communities using shared information spaces in the Internet as their primary communication media are often called virtual communities, or, synonymously, online communities. Central aspects of communities are that people voluntarily affiliate to a network and all participants benefit from the affiliation.

With respect to groups, we can distinguish between teams and communities. In general, according to Schlichter (1998), team members know each other and collaborate to achieve a common goal while community members have just common interests or preferences. The team is often formed through a management decision selecting team members according to their skills, competencies, and potential contributions to the specified team goal. Usually teams are tightly interacting groups with team interests dominating over the personal interests of the individual team members. Communities do not have a common goal and thus, the interaction between community members is usually loose. In most cases, they do not know each other and personal interests dominate over community interests.

Recently the term community has been used as a metaphor for the next stage of computing technologies, including the methodologies, mechanisms, and tools for creating, maintaining, and evolving social interaction in human societies. We believe there will be a dramatic shift in computing metaphors: from team to community metaphors. Given that the team metaphor has created research fields like groupware and CSCW we believe the community metaphor will generate new fields both in research and practice related to Social Networks, Online Communities, and communityware.

CODES: From Cooperative Activities to Online Communities

Social Networks Sites (SNS) and Online Communities are becoming hype on Internet these days. There are dozens of them, which try to aggregate groups of people with similar interests. As Boyd and Elisson (2007) define, SNS are "Web-based services that allow individuals to (1) construct a public or semi-public profile within a bounded system, (2) articulate a list of other users with whom they share a connection, and (3) view and traverse their list of connections and those made by others within the system."

CODES was conceived originally to be a CSCW system with a design based on cooperation and interaction concepts, so the evolution towards SNS and community-ware is straightforward. Even though support systems for both group types—teams and communities—have developed independently, both areas have something in common: the contact facilitation with unknown and known collaborators. While community support systems concentrated mostly on the building process, i.e. finding people with similar interests, CSCW focused on the collaboration process, i.e. the synchronization and exchange of information in the context of a specific team task. Like Schlichter (1998), we are convinced that awareness can be a common base for community support systems to improve contact building as well as for CSCW to maintain group work at a high performance level. Therefore, we need to address how we extend CODES from traditional CMP support and CSCW perspective towards online human community support.

CSCW tools have been developed for communication between isolated people, such as desktop electronic meeting systems. Though there is no standard definition of the term group, previous research and practice of groupware mainly addressed the collaborative work of already-organized people. A typical example features project members in the same company using workstations connected synchronously or asynchronously by local area networks. However, community computing is meant for more diverse and amorphous groups of people. Our goal is to support the process of organizing persons who are willing to share some level of mutual understanding and experiences. In other words, compared to current groupware studies, we focus on an earlier stage of collaboration: group formation from a wide variety of people.

Successful online communities motivate online participation. An online community provides people a place to come together using the Internet: it is always on and is a more accessible way to keep in touch with people who are geographically far or with those who have conflicting schedules.

Every online community has (sometimes implicit) rules that may specify how to participate and to engage with the community—from peripheral participation ("lurker") to explicitly recognized participation ("leader"). CSCW technologies can provide tools for supporting these roles. In the case of communities, these tools are used in combination, including text-based posts and chat rooms and forums that use voice, video, or avatars.

The community metaphor can create several different functions for encouraging social interaction in communities (Ishida, 1998):

1. Knowing each other;
2. Sharing preference and knowledge;
3. Generating consensus;
4. Supporting everyday life;
5. Assisting social events.

A virtual community is a social network of individuals who interact through specific media, potentially crossing geographical and political boundaries in order to pursue mutual interests or goals. One of the most pervasive types of virtual community include Social Networking Services (SNS), which consist of various online communities. Nowadays, there are lots of SNS with focus on music listening and sharing, rather than music creation. YouTube and Vimeo are video sites that feature musical contents. Some SNS, as Myspace, have a social character, merging social networks aspects with content distribution. Facebook includes several musical pages and bands profiles. Even Apple tried to foster a musical social network, known as Ping.

Traditionally, a SNS essentially consists of a representation of each user (often a profile), his/her social links, and a variety of additional services. CODES provides a distinct vision of a SNS having music as its intrinsic motivation, combining the traditional features (profiling, social links) to different and specific features related to CMP. Thus, CODES has three different levels of viewing and interaction:

a. **Level 1:** Public level, like an broadcasting channel, as Myspace, where posts are posted on to a "bulletin board" for everyone, without resorting to messaging users individually. Thus, people who do not know each other can check some data (personal information and prototypes) that the users select to publish, making this information available to any visitor;

b. **Level 2:** Restricted one-way level, as on Twitter or Google+, when users may subscribe to other users' posts—this is known as following and subscribers are known as followers. If a user follows someone, this is a non-mutual relationship, where who is being followed does not need to follow back. The follower can see someone else's timeline as an RSS feed and also access MPs and even modify it (if this option is allowed in the MP), but these modifications are just local and temporary. It is also possible to repost a post from another user, and share it with one's own followers;

c. **Level 3:** Partnership level, when two people follow each other, it establishes a collaborative relation, where they can, not only suggest, but also edit the prototypes together. In this case, they are named 'partners.'

CMP is an activity that involves people creating groups and working together on an MP as a shared workspace. In CODES, a cooperative musical prototype is initiated by someone that creates a new prototype, elaborates an initial contribution, and asks for the collaboration of other "partners" by sending explicit invitations.

Partners who accept the invitation can participate in the collaborative musical manipulation and refinement of the prototype. The group can publish the final or partial results of their CMP in the public spaces (level 1 above), in which interested users could discover it and follow (level 2 above) or join the collaboration as new partners (level 3 above).

In order to avoid undesired dependencies, inconsistencies and conflicts between contributions, preserving authorship among the several contributions of a community, CODES implements a particular layer-oriented version management mechanism. In this approach, each layer represents one partner's view, and the union of partners' contributions (a combination of layers) results in a cooperative MP version. Any partner can browse between the contributions, independently of the creator, keeping the creator's original ideas and authorship. It is also possible to edit another user's contribution, by issuing an explicit "modification request" to a partner. The interested reader can find more details in Pimenta et al. (2011).

CODES Social Features and User Interface Description

In our social networking services version of CODES, we choose to apply several well known HCI interface guidelines to create a dynamic and creative environment, providing SNS for the emergence of communities and enabling knowledge sharing by means of rich interaction and argumentation mechanisms associated with the MPs evolution. Several basic CODES features are similar to conventional features of Social Networking sites. Most often, individual users are encouraged to create profiles containing various information about themselves. To protect user privacy, social networks usually have controls that allow users to choose who can view their profile, contact them, add them to their list of contacts, and so on. Users can upload pictures of themselves to their profiles, post blog entries for others to read, search for users with similar interests, and compile and share lists of contacts. In addition, user profiles have a section dedicated to comments from friends and other members.

CMP is a simple cyclical process including the following activities: (a) MP creation, (b) MP edition, (c) MP sharing, and (d) MP publishing. Through a Music Prototyping Rationale (MPR) mechanism—based on the Design Rationale concept from HCI—each user may associate comments (i.e. an idea or an observation) and arguments (pro or cons) to any action on any MP. The arguments can be addressed to a specific partner or to the whole group. Due to the exploratory nature of CODES usage, MPR is one of its most important characteristics, allowing users to perceive and analyze group members' actions on music prototypes ("to understand WHAT my partners are doing") and the reasoning behind these actions ("to understand WHY my partners are doing it").

The CODES interface was designed to strike a balance between user interfaces that are so easy-to-use that they end up depleting their expressiveness, and others that are so complicated that they discourage beginners. The CODES user interface has three levels of interaction for different user profiles: (a) Public Level, (b) MP Editing Level, and (c) Sound Pattern Editing Level. The lowest level of CODES—sound pattern editing—is a kind of "piano roll" editor, having no social-oriented features. Therefore, we will only discuss the other two levels.

At the public level, anyone (including non-members) can access and explore musical prototypes, by searching and listening. Figure 2 shows a screenshot of the CODES Public Level. One of the goals at this level is to encourage the potential audience to become CODES members, and encourage members to publish their musical prototypes to foster the formation of a virtual community focusing on music.

Figure 2. Screenshot of the CODES public level

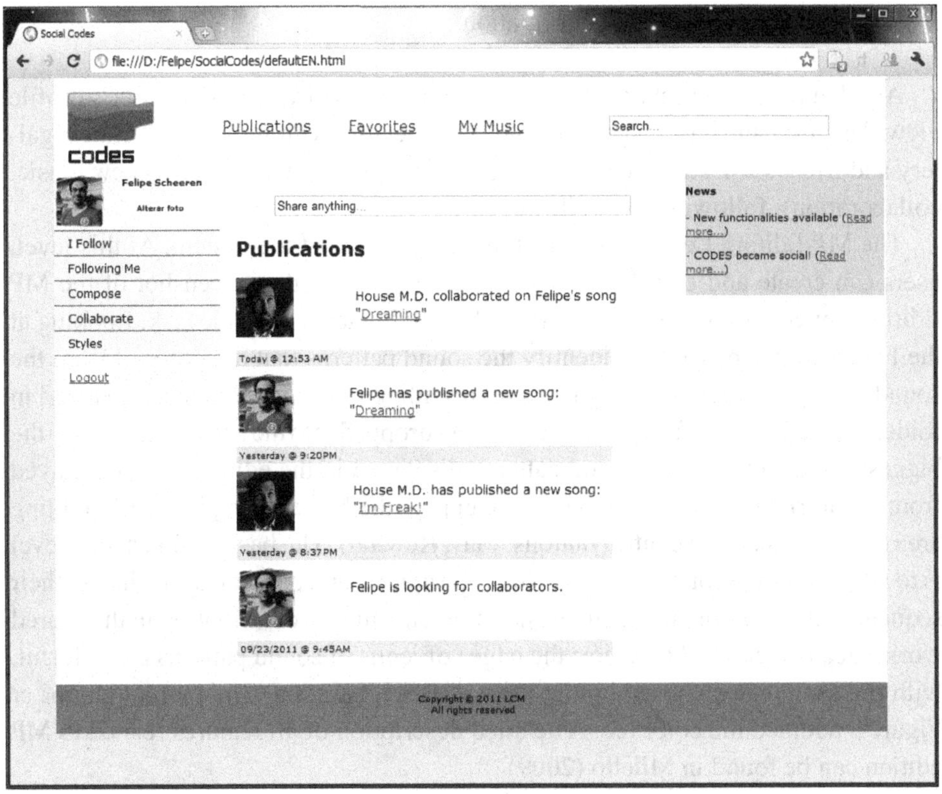

As depicted in Figure 2, the main page at the public level is divided into five areas:

- **Top Pane:** System logo, Publications (users' following updates), Favorites (users selection of people or songs who wants to follow in a closer way), My Music (user's own music approved to collaborate) and Search Field (to seek for users and compositions within a single box).
- **Left Pane:** User's name and picture, I Follow (who I choose to follow), Following me (who follows me), Compose (opens the CODES MP Editing Level interface), Collaborate (the user sees the MPs from people with mutual relation with the possibility to edit them), Styles (show musical styles, and, selecting one, it returns all the music whose owners tagged as belonging to that style) and logout.
- **Central Pane:** That is the place where the actions happen. All the things that you can choose in the other panes will appear on this one. Here, users will see their prototypes, following or follower lists, the search results, etc.
- **Right Pane:** Dedicated to the system use. It can be filled with, for example, system news, some hot topic (e.g., someone's prototype that became popular) or even advertising.
- **Bottom Pane:** Systems' information.

As it happens on Facebook, the user's main view is different of the user's profile view. The left pane has a bigger image of the person, with links for his music gallery and friends list. And the content pane shows new updates, such as new music, collaborations, followings, or followers.

The MP Editing Level is the most important level of the system. At this level, users can create and edit their MPs cooperatively (see the screenshot of the MP Editing Level in Figure 3). The edition of a MP in fact is a simple task. Looking at the Figure 3, it is possible to identify the sound patterns that are dragged from the sound library—a region having icons representing music instruments organized in folders named 'rock,' 'funk,' 'jazz,' etc.—and dropped into the MP editing area—the biggest region above. The sound patterns displayed in the editing area are played from left to right. At any time, the user can play the MP existing in the MP editing area (see the execution control buttons: Play, Rewind). The basic action at this level is to add or remove sound patterns within the editing area, as well as to change their sequence, size, combination, and position. Each author's contribution in the shared workspace is identified by color: the edges of icons of sound patterns are colorful, with the same color chosen by the user at the registration. The current author at Figure 3 adopted the color red. A detailed description of all features related to MP edition can be found in Miletto (2009).

Figure 3. Screenshot of the CODES MP editing level

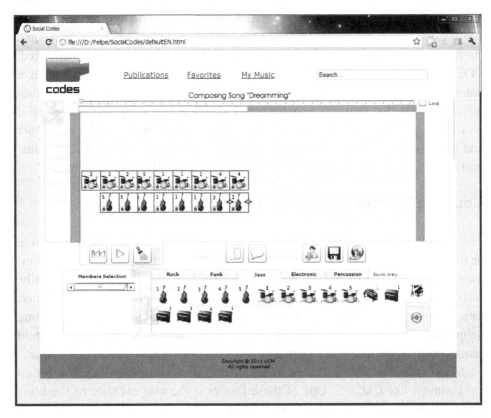

Every new MP is private, so without authorization no one is able to know about its existence. However, when a user goes into "My Music," she shows the MPs she has created and the MPs she is collaborating with (as a partner). At the preferences panel for each MP, the user can select the musical style of each composition (multiple tags are allowed), as well as one of the following distribution options:

- **Private:** No one but the owner will be able to edit/listen this MP.
- **Collaborative:** People will be able to listen and edit the parts of the MP that the owner sets as allowed to edit.
- **Public:** Everybody can listen. Collaborators can edit it and followers too.
- **Closed:** Everybody can listen, but only the author can edit.

Several difficulties were addressed in this work for bridging the gap between groups of novice users and the possibility of creating online communities for making music over the Web. One of the main challenges comprised the combination of cooperation-oriented mechanisms (for effective collaboration in a CMP) with community-oriented mechanisms (for effective community management). We are currently working to improve the experience of creating music prototypes through cooperation in CODES. At this point, our group is focusing on ways to increase and stimulate the cooperation and interaction among users. As previously mentioned, CODES has great potential to become communityware because of its cooperative nature. As part of the effort to encourage cooperation, we are investing on a recommender system that suggests possible relationships between users to create music prototypes together. Thus, this is an incentive for users to interact with each other and to expand their social relations in the virtual environment. We discuss some preliminary ideas about recommendations in CODES in the next section.

Coupling Recommendations to CODES

Traditionally, people rely on word of mouth when looking for reliable information or for good products. To support this process within a virtual music making community, the adoption of recommendation features may be a necessary. Basically, recommendation features include an analysis of the users' preferences and behaviors, to suggest interesting information (in CODES, regarding MPs) or interesting people (matchmaking). The amount of information stored in shared information spaces (such as the universe of partners and MPs in CODES) is often very large.

Many aspects should be taken into account in a recommender system for an environment like CODES. One of these factors is the musical taste of the users involved. When a user invites others to make contributions for a music prototype, she expects that his musical ideas will be understood, assimilated and respected. Consequently, the others' contributions will be made in accordance with her original concept, allowing the MP to converge toward a positive result. Therefore, an important challenge to develop a recommendation system in CODES is to evaluate and classify the users' musical tastes.

To determine and quantify a musical-taste measure, various sources of information on the users must be analyzed and taken into consideration. CODES allows the creation of MPs based on various musical styles predefined within the sound library. With this information, collected from the tracks that comprise each MP, it is possible to determine an approximation of the user's favourite musical styles: a proximity measure. This approach by itself may not be sufficient to assign a musical profile for a given user. However, it is a good starting point to be used in profiling musical preferences.

Another important aspect to spot similarities among user tastes is the user's personal data. A thorough profile of the user increases the certainty about her particular taste. Three basic aspects can be considered to ensure thorough information: (1)

selections of favorite musical styles; (2) decisions about the types of contributions that she is willing to accept from other users; and (3) the types of contributions she provides to other users. In an environment like CODES, recommender systems are a powerful tool for promoting the engagement and interaction among participants. A good level of knowledge of the users′ musical tastes and behaviors can help in the process of recommending possible forms of cooperation among users. This support leads to an improvement in the musical experience of the people involved.

Limitations of CODES

Some factors not scrutinized in this project may affect the general outcome of the music prototyping process and can be considered as limitations of this research. One of them is related to reliability and scalability issues. Nowadays, it is unknown how the system behaves under the stated conditions for a specified period of time as well as its capacity to handle a growing amount of work.

In addition, it must be stated that the lack of wide evaluation (currently, as a public tool in a unrestricted membership context) of CODES and its target public could indeed reveal new results and other requirements. Specifically, aspects related to server size, bandwidth, response time, performance, and security must be investigated in further experiments.

This research has not chosen the synchronous communication and interaction paradigm for two main reasons. On the one hand, this approach demands implementing complex structures to control concurrent access. On the other hand, the nature of the musical activity itself in which musical ideas can occur at anytime implies that the participants do not need to be online at the same time. Since the system can asynchronously store and retrieve all the sound pieces and actions performed by the users, synchronous interaction would forfeat an important aspect of the creativity process.

Other interface issues specifically related to computer music concepts—such as equalization, tempo manipulation (capacity to setup the speed at which music is played), duration of the sound patterns (currently fixed as four-second MP3 files), integration of the sound pattern editing level with other formats such as Music XML. Obviously, addressing these issues could bring new perspectives to experimentation regarding the capacity for manipulating musical information by novice users.

The Future of CODES

Since CODES usage is a melting pot of ideas on creativity, we are continuously planning additional features in order to improve the system, for example:

- The use of "folksonomy" (social tagging) as a method of collaboratively allowing the users to create their own tags for categorizing the content of the sound library;
- The possibility of users uploading their own musical samples, such as MP3 files, to the CODES sound library for further use in shared musical prototypes; another interesting possibility is to allow users to record samples of music through playing or singing on their personal mobile devices (this line of investigation would be related to the concept of ubiquitous music discussed above);
- The implementation of a specific mechanism to allow users to transmit their tentative musical ideas or drafts (called preliminarily "sonic argumentation");
- The development of a mechanism to write comments directly in the editing area with the purpose of adding lyrics;
- The use of the MIDI, MusicXML and other standard formats, to allow to import and export files from/to other systems, targeting in particular music notation editors and sequencers;
- The adoption of a common or public license to manage the creative products for members and others to build upon and to share. Note that all musical material produced in CODES is free to use and share, except in the case of commercial purposes.

CONCLUSION

This chapter presented several new applications and concepts resulting from our effort to provide effective support for novices in music creation. The concepts include cooperation, flexibility, cross-cultural diversity, and creativity in technologically-based network environments for music, with particular emphasis on CODES. The design approach employed in CODES is inspired by traits of Brazilian culture and creativity styles. We described how CODES adopts collaboration, flexibility, and multiculturality and how these concepts emerge from Brazilian creativity styles. We presented preliminary outcomes of this methodological approach and indicated new directions of applied research based on existing literature and on the experience we gathered through the development of CODES. Therefore, this chapter constitutes a excursion into a territory which includes many other possible perspectives and paths to be explored.

A characteristic of Brazilian people—common to people from other developing countries—is the combination of skills and traits like cooperation, flexibility, cross-cultural diversity, creating a highly creative context. For Brazilians, it is usual to combine and improve on other people's ideas, to welcome unusual ideas and to withhold rough criticism, usually yielding creative outcomes with little resources. With the available technologies allowing cultures and cultural expressions to interact, it is likely that this creative potential will become stronger. Keeping in mind this collaborative and flexible atmosphere inspired by Brazilian culture, CODES was designed for supporting dynamic and prototypical music creation processes and the formation and evolution of online communities. The main objective of this development effort has been to stimulate creativity among novices (non-musicians).

CODES as an environment for Cooperative Music Prototyping and as communityware shows that Web-based networked music environments can offer more than "consumer" possibilities for music making. Since adequate concepts and mechanisms are integrated within a single environment, novice users not only create music prototypes, they cooperate effectively becoming the creators of their own music and participating as active members of an online musical community.

One of CODES foundations is to consider that music creation by novices is about people having fun and entertainment (and maybe also learning), rather than following rules set by the designers of the software. However, CODES is not just about supporting novice people: features built for novices may help everyone interested in music making on the Web. CODES is open and accessible to all of us, from ordinary users to musicians. Rather than sharing and listening to ready-made works, CODES provides support and creates opportunities for creativity by allowing co-development and collaboration among people to generate original and custom-tailored music prototypes.

The importance of inventiveness and creativity in promoting economic development is well recognized. Under the new conditions of the digital economy, the sources of wealth are increasingly found in intellectual, as opposed to physical, capital. However, it is important to put in place technological support that enables developing countries to preserve their intellectual property heritage, including in music, art, and medicine, to ensure that this potential wealth is protected from unfair use, as well as to receive the benefits of its exchange within a global economy. Our work is a humble contribution to this end.

ACKNOWLEDGMENT

The authors are grateful to CAPES and CNPq (Brazil) for grants and fellowships, and express their thanks to UFRGS, IFRS, and UFAC for the continuous support.

REFERENCES

Abou-Zeid, E. (2005). A culturally aware model of inter-organizational knowledge transfer. *Knowledge Management Research & Practice, 3*, 146–155. doi:10.1057/palgrave.kmrp.8500064

Amabile, T. A. (1996). *Creativity in context*. Boulder, CO: Westview Press.

Barbosa, A. (2003). Displaced soundscapes: A survey of network systems for music and sonic art creation. *Leonardo Music Journal, 13*, 53–59. doi:10.1162/096112104322750791

Barbosa, A. (2005). Public sound objects: A shared environment for networked music practice on the web. *Organised Sound, 10*(3), 233–242. doi:10.1017/S135577180500097X

Benini, M., Fichemann, I. K., Zuffo, M. K., de Deus Lopes, R., & Batista, L. (Eds.). (2004). Musical: A case of interface usability for children. In *Proceedings of CELDA*, (pp. 319–326). CELDA.

Bennett, S. (1976). The process of musical creation: Interview with eight composers. *Journal of Research in Music Education, 24*, 3–13. doi:10.2307/3345061

Boyd, D. M., & Ellison, N. B. (2007). Social network sites: Definition, history, and scholarship. *Journal of Computer-Mediated Communication, 13*(1). Retrieved from http://jcmc.indiana.edu/vol13/issue1/boyd.ellison.html doi:10.1111/j.1083-6101.2007.00393.x

Bryan-Kinns, N., & Healey, P. G. T. (2004). Daisyphone: Support for remote music collaboration. In *Proceedings of the 2004 Conference on New Interfaces for Musical Expression*, (pp. 27-30). Singapore, Singapore: National University of Singapore.

Burk, P. (2012). *WebDrum*. Retrieved March 02, 2012, from http://www.transjam.com/webdrum/webdrum.html

Chen, C. W. (2006). The creative process of computer-assisted composition and multimedia composition: Visual images and music. (Doctor of Philosophy Thesis). Royal Melbourne Institute of Technology. Melbourne, Australia.

Collins, D. (2005). A synthesis process model of creative thinking in music composition. *Psychology of Music, 33*(2), 193–216. doi:10.1177/0305735605050651

Csikszentmihalyi, M. (1996). *Creativity*. New York, NY: HarperCollins.

Dingwall, C. (2008). Rational and intuitive approaches to music composition: The impact of individual differences in thinking/learning styles on compositional processes. (Bachelor of Music Dissertation Thesis). University of Sydney. Sydney, Australia.

Duckworth, W. (1999). Making music on the web. *Leonardo Music Journal, 1*(9), 13–17. doi:10.1162/096112199750316749

Fleith, D. S. (1999). *The effects of a creativity training program on creative abilities and self-concept in monolingual and bilingual elementary classrooms*. (Unpublished Doctoral Dissertation). University of Connecticut. Storrs, CT.

Fleith, D. S. (2011). Creativity in the Brazilian culture. *Online Readings in Psychology and Culture, 4*. Retrieved September 15, 2011, from http://scholarworks.gvsu.edu/orpc/vol4/iss3/3

Gardner, H. (1993). *Creating minds*. New York, NY: BasicBooks.

Google. (2009). Youtube. Retrieved July 02, 2011, from http://www.youtube.com/

Gurevich, M. (2006). Jamspace: Designing a collaborative networked music space for novices. In *Proceedings of NIME*, (pp. 118–123). NIME.

Hartmann, M. I. (2006). *Software architectures for the cooperative music prototyping environment CODES: Study and implementation*. Rio Grande do Sul, Brazil: Federal University of Rio Grande do Sul.

HCI. (2011). *Proceedings of the* 14th International Conference on Human-Computer Interaction. Retrieved August 22, 2011, from http://www.hcii2011.org/index.php?module=webpage&id=47

Hofstede, G. (2005). *Cultures and organizations: Software of the mind* (2nd ed.). New York, NY: McGraw-Hill.

Ishida, T. (1998). *Community computing: Collaboration over global information networks*. New York, NY: John Wiley and Sons.

Keller, D., Flores, L. V., Pimenta, M. S., Capasso, A., & Tinajero, P. (2011b). Convergent trends toward ubiquitous music. *Journal of New Music Research, 40*(3), 265–276. doi:10.1080/09298215.2011.594514

Keller, D., Lima, M. H., Pimenta, M. S., & Queiroz, M. (2011a). Assessing musical creativity: Material, procedural, and contextual dimensions. In *Proceedings of the 21st Congress of the Brazilian National Association of Research and Post-Graduation in Music (ANPPOM)*. Uberlândia, Brazil: ANPPOM. Retrieved from http://www. anppom.com.br/congressos_anteriores.php

Lubart, T. I. (1999). Creativity across cultures. In Sternberg, R. J. (Ed.), *Handbook of Creativity* (pp. 339–350). Cambridge, UK: Cambridge University Press.

Media, F. I. (2009). Myspace. Retrieved July 02, 2011 from http://www.myspace.com/

Miletto, E. M. (2009). CODES: An interactive novice-oriented web-based environment for cooperative musical prototyping. (PhD Thesis). Federal University of Rio Grande do Sul. Rio Grande do Sul, Brazil. Retrieved from https://www.lume.ufrgs. br/bitstream/handle/10183/22815/000740701.pdf?sequence=1

Miletto, E. M., Flores, L. V., Pimenta, M. S., Rutily, J., & Santagada, L. (2007). Interfaces for musical activities and interfaces for musicians are not the same: The case for codes, a web-based environment for cooperative music prototyping. In *Proceedings of the 9th International Conference on Multimodal Interfaces*, (pp. 201-207). New York, NY: ACM Press.

Miletto, E. M., Pimenta, M. S., Bouchet, F., Sansonnet, J.-P., & Keller, D. (2011). Principles for music creation by novices in networked music environments. *Journal of New Music Research, 40*(3). doi:10.1080/09298215.2011.603832

Moran, R. T., Harris, P. R., & Moran, S. V. (2007). *Managing cultural differences – Global leadership strategies for the 21st century* (7th ed.). London, UK: Elsevier.

Nielsen, J. (1992). *Evaluating the thinking-aloud technique for use by computer scientists*. Norwood, NJ: Ablex Publishing Corp.

Nielsen, J. (1994a). Enhancing the explanatory power of usability heuristics. In *Proceedings of CHI*, (pp. 152-158). New York, NY: ACM Press.

Nielsen, J. (1994b). Enhancing the explanatory power of usability heuristics. In *Proceedings of CHI*, (p. 210). New York, NY: ACM Press.

Pimenta, M. S., Miletto, E., & Flores, L. (2011). Cooperative mechanisms for networked music. *Future Generation Computer Systems, 27*(1), 100–108. doi:10.1016/j. future.2010.03.005

Raina, M. K. (1993). Ethnocentric confines in creativity research. In Isaksen, S. G., Murdock, M. C., Firestien, R. L., & Treffinger, D. J. (Eds.), *Understanding and Recognizing Creativity: The Emergence of a Discipline* (pp. 435–453). Norwood, NJ: Ablex.

Reinecke, K., Bernstein, A., & Schenkel, S. (2010). Modeling a user's culture. In *The Handbook of Research in Culturally-Aware Information Technology: Perspectives and Models*. Hershey, PA: IGI Global. doi:10.4018/978-1-61520-883-8.ch011

Rubin, J. (1994). *Handbook of usability testing: How to plan, design, and conduct effective tests*. New York, NY: Wiley.

Rudowicz, E. (2003). Creativity and culture: A two-way interaction. *Scandinavian Journal of Educational Research, 47*, 273–290. doi:10.1080/00313830308602

Schlichter, J., Koch, M., & Xu, C. (1998). Awareness - The common link between groupware and community support systems. In *Proceedings of CCSS*, (pp. 78-94). Berlin, Germany: Springer-Verlag.

Simonton, D. K. (1994). *Greatness*. New York, NY: The Guilford Press.

Torres, C. V., & Dessen, M. A. (2008). Brazilian culture, family, and its ethnic-cultural variety. *Arizona Journal of Hispanic Cultural Studies, 12*, 41–62.

W3C. (2012). Web standards. Retrieved February 10, 2012 from http://www.w3.org/standards/

Wallas, G. (1926). *The art of thought*. New York, NY: Harcourt Brace and World.

Webster, P. (2003). Asking music students to reflect on their creative work: Encouraging the revision process. In Yip, L. C. R., Leung, C. C., & Lau, W. T. (Eds.), *Curriculum Innovation in Music* (pp. 16–27). Hong Kong, China: The Hong Kong Institute of Education. doi:10.1080/1461380032000126337

Yahoo. (2009). Flickr. Retrieved July 02, 2011 from http://www.flickr.com

ADDITIONAL READING

Blanchard, E. G., & Mizoguchi, R. (2008). Designing culturally-aware tutoring systems: Towards an upper ontology of culture. Paper presented at the 1st Workshop on Culturally-Aware Tutoring Systems (CATS 2008). Montréal, Canada.

Dormann, C., & Chisalita, C. (2002). Cultural values in web site design. Paper presented at the European Conference on Cognitive Ergonomics. London, UK.

Hickey, M. (2003). Creative thinking in the context of music composition. In Hickey, M. (Ed.), *Why and How to Teach Music Composition: A New Horizon for Music Education* (pp. 31–53). Reston, VA: MENC.

Hofstede, G. (2001). *Culture's consequences: Comparing values, behaviors, institutions, and organizations across nations* (2nd ed.). Thousand Oaks, CA: SAGE Publications.

Hofstede, G. (2005). *Cultures and organizations: Software of the mind* (2nd ed.). New York, NY: McGraw-Hill.

Ishida, T. (1998). *Community computing and support systems: Social interaction in networked communities*. Berlin, Germany: Springer-Verlag.

Kaufman, J. C., & Sternberg, R. J. (Eds.). (2010). *The Cambridge handbook of creativity*. Cambridge, UK: Cambridge University Press. doi:10.1017/CBO9780511763205

Khaslavsky, J. (1998). Integrating culture into interface design. In *Proceedings of ACM CHI*, (pp. 365-366). ACM Press.

Lubart, T. I. (2010). Cross-cultural perspectives on creativity. In Kaufman, J. C., & Sternberg, R. J. (Eds.), *The Cambridge Handbook of Creativity* (pp. 265–278). Cambridge, UK: Cambridge University Press. doi:10.1017/CBO9780511763205.017

Luff, P., & Jirotka, M. (1998). Interactional resources for the support of collaborative activities: Common problems in the design of technologies to support groups and communities. [Berlin, Germany: Springer-Verlag.]. *Proceedings of CCSS, 1998*, 249–267.

Marcus, A. (2002). Dare we define user-interface design? *Interaction, 9*, 19–24. doi:10.1145/566981.566992

Marcus, A. (2006). Cross-cultural user-experience design. *Lecture Notes in Computer Science, 4045*, 16–24. doi:10.1007/11783183_4

Marcus, A., & Gould, E. W. (2000). Cultural dimensions and global web user-interface design: What? So what? Now what? In *Proceedings of Sixth Conference on Human Factors and the Web*. Austin, TX: ACM.

Miletto, E. M., Pimenta, M. S., & Vicari, R. M. (2005). Using codes: Cooperative music prototyping and educational perspectives. In *Proceedings of the International Computer Music Conference*, (vol. 1, pp. 387–390). Tampere, Finland: International Computer Music Association.

Recabarren, M., & Nussbaum, M. (2010). Exploring the feasibility of web form adaptation to users' cultural dimension scores. *User Modeling and User-Adapted Interaction, 20*, 87–108. doi:10.1007/s11257-010-9071-7

Reinecke, K., & Bernstein, A. (2007). Culturally adaptive software: Moving beyond internationalization. In *Proceedings of the 2ⁿᵈ International Conference on Usability and Internationalization (UI-HCII 2007)*, (pp. 201-210). Berlin, Germany: Springer-Verlag.

Reinecke, K., & Bernstein, A. (2011). Improving performance, perceived usability, and aesthetics with culturally adaptive user interfaces. *ACM Transactions on Computer-Human Interaction, 18*(2). doi:10.1145/1970378.1970382

Renzulli, J. S. (2002). Expanding the concept of giftedness to include co-cognitive traits and to promote social capital. *Phi Delta Kappan, 84*, 57–58.

Schedel, M., & Young, J. P. (2005). Editorial. *Organised Sound, 10*(3), 181–183. doi:10.1017/S1355771805000919

Shah, J. J., Vargas-Hernandez, N., & Smith, S. M. (2003). Metrics for measuring ideation effectiveness. *Design Studies, 24*, 111–134. doi:10.1016/S0142-694X(02)00034-0

Smith, A., & Yetim, F. (2004). Global human–computer systems: Cultural determinants of usability. *Interacting with Computers*, 16.

Starko, A. J. (1995). *Creativity in the classroom*. White Plains, NY: Longman.

Sternberg, R. J. (1986). A triarchic theory of intellectual giftedness. In Sternberg, R. J., & Davidson, J. E. (Eds.), *Conception of Giftedness* (pp. 223–243). Cambridge, UK: Cambridge University Press.

Torrance, E. P. (1990). *Torrance tests of creative thinking*. Bensenville, IL: Scholastic Testing Service.

Urban, K. K., & Jellen, H. G. (1996). *Test for creative thinking – Drawing production manual*. Frankfurt, Germany: Swets Test Services.

Vatrapu, R., & Pérez-Quiñones, M. A. (2006). Culture and usability evaluation: The effects of culture in structure interviews. *Journal of Usability Studies, 1*(4), 156–170.

Wang, H. C., Fussell, S. F., & Setlock, L. D. (2009). Cultural difference and adaptation of communication styles in computer-mediated group brainstorming. In *Proceedings of the 27th International Conference on Human Factors in Computing Systems*, (pp. 669–678). New York, NY: ACM Press.

Young, P. A. (2011). The significance of the culture based model in designing culturally aware tutoring systems. *AI & Society, 26*(1), 35–47. doi:10.1007/s00146-010-0282-6

Zaharias, P. (2008). Cross-cultural differences in perceptions of e–leaning usability: An empirical investigation. *International Journal of Technology and Human Interaction, 4*(3). doi:10.4018/jthi.2008070101

KEY TERMS AND DEFINITIONS

Cooperative Music Prototyping: Cooperative process of collective creation of Musical Prototypes, where partners cooperate not only by means of explicit conversation and explicit actions on a shared object space (formed by multiple versions of Musical prototypes), but also by interpreting the messages and actions of other partners.

Communityware: A collection of technologies/mechanisms supporting people in developing their own community, allowing to increase mutual knowledge (to know what others know) and mutual activities (to do what others do).

Creativitity: The experience of thinking, reacting, working in an imaginative and idiosyncratic way, which is characterized by a high degree of innovation and originality, divergent thinking and risk taking.

Music Creation: Creation of simple musical pieces (drafts, Musical Prototypes); an informal and experimental process distinct from the serious process called music composition, an activity carried out by composers.

Musical Prototypes: Simple musical pieces made by novices (non-musicians), drafts.

Networked Music: Area of Computer Music whose goal is to explore music practice situations where traditional aural and visual connections between participants are augmented, mediated or replaced by computer-controlled connections.

Novice: A music beginner, a person who lacks musical knowledge or who is learning the rudiments of music; novices are not necessarily children but anyone without a musical training, someone who is not expected to have any previous musical knowledge or who does not have enough knowledge to be classified as an amateur or a musician.

Online Communities: Communities using shared information spaces in the Internet as their primary communication media.

Chapter 12
Using Social Media Technology to Improve Collaboration:
A Case Study of Micro-Blogging Adoption in a South African Financial Services Company

Garron Stevenson
University of Cape Town, South Africa

Jean-Paul Van Belle
University of Cape Town, South Africa

EXECUTIVE SUMMARY

This chapter examines the use and adoption of micro-blogging within a large South African financial services company. This is done by means of a case study, which draws on three sources of data: user demographics, messages posted, and a survey focused on adoption and usage. The research objective was to evaluate enterprise micro-blogging's effectiveness as a collaboration tool, which enables informal communication among staff working in project teams. The analysis used a technology acceptance model as the theoretical framework but a more descriptive approach was used to investigate the actual use patterns as well as the barriers and benefits experienced by the users. Even though distinct barriers to adoption were uncovered, by focusing on creating the right groups within the tool and increasing management contributions potential users of micro-blogging platforms, these barriers can be reduced.

DOI: 10.4018/978-1-4666-2515-0.ch012

INTRODUCTION

In the long history of humankind (and animal kind, too) those who learned to collaborate and improvise most effectively have prevailed. - Charles Darwin

As companies become globalised, they become more dependent on networking technology to allow staff, partners, and clients to interact. The ability to work collaboratively is a core part of successful organisations and it is the trust between staff members, which forms the basis for effective collaboration (Handy, 1995). The awareness of an individual team member of his/her activities in the context of the activities of other team members can improve the collaboration between members of diverse teams (Dourish & Bellotti, 1992). This chapter will show that Web 2.0 technologies can increase the level of awareness between team members.

The success of social media platforms such as Facebook and Twitter in the public space has led to companies experimenting with similar technologies in the corporate space. This study examines the use of Yammer as a corporate social media platform. Launched by David Sacks (the founder of Geni, the genealogy site) in September 2008, Yammer is a corporate social network service. Unlike Twitter, which is used for broadcasting messages to the public, Yammer is used for private communication within organisations or between organisational members and pre-designated groups, making it an example of enterprise social software (Böhringer & Richter, 2009). Enabling staff to share interests and common values is vital for encouraging effective collaboration and knowledge sharing (Klein, 1998). In addition, collaboration and knowledge sharing are essential in an organisation, whether between members of the general staff population, or between specific team members.

Micro-blogs are a new arrival within the corporate software landscape (Riemer, Altenhofen, & Richter, 2011). The increasing popularity of similar tools such as Twitter within the public space has not yet seen the same rapid uptake through the implementation of collaboration tools within the software portfolios of companies. Yammer is a Web-based platform, which offers micro-blogging functionality to enterprise users in the form of closed groups of users. The groups are managed by only allowing users with a specific company's email address to sign up. In addition to standard micro-blogging features like posting messages, addressing messages and following people, Yammer also allows for threaded conversations, groups and file attachments (Riemer & Richter, 2010). These features make Yammer more useful for organisational use when compared to a micro-blogging platform like Twitter. Evidence shows that informal communication helps encourage trust and collaboration (Zhao & Rosson, 2009). However, it is not clear whether there is a corollary benefit to micro-blogging.

This study attempts to evaluate the role micro-blogging can play in increasing collaboration and trust among staff in a corporate environment situated in a developing country. Through a user survey and message classification, it is shown that the nature of the use of social media, specifically micro-blogging, within organisations improves and/or facilitates informal communication. It also demonstrates that corporate micro-blogging differs from public platforms in that, whilst the latter are more focused on the user, corporate micro-blogging focuses on shared work tasks and news; it is less about individual behaviour and activity (Riemer & Richter, 2011). Finally, this study uses the Technology Acceptance Model (TAM) constructs to evaluate how adoption within the organisation occurred (Davies, 1989). However, it is important to note that this research does not aim to demonstrate that the use of micro-blogging in an organisational context will result in improved organisational or team performance.

This chapter is organised as follows. The next section sketches the academic background for the case study by looking at how the enterprises have adopted Web 2.0, the importance of informal collaboration to the enterprise, the characteristics and benefits of micro-blogging, and research into enterprise micro-blogging. This is followed by a brief discussion on our research methodology. The subsequent sections discuss the findings of the message analysis and the user survey, respectively. The user survey looks not only at the usage, perceived usefulness, and ease of use, but also at the personal and team-related benefits as well as at the inhibitors. Two of these inhibitors, namely the relevance and management involvement, are explored in some more detail. The conclusion summarizes the findings but also highlights some of the limitations of the research.

BACKGROUND

Web 2.0 and the Enterprise

The rise in the use of Web 2.0 technologies within enterprises to facilitate communication has become known as Enterprise 2.0 (Böhringer & Richter, 2009). Web 1.0 was defined by its linked but static content. Web 2.0 is defined by the networked, participative, and collaborative nature of its applications and platforms (OReilly, 2007). The value of applications and services within the Web 2.0 space increases as more users and nodes are added to the network. The popularity of such sites and technologies is leading to increasing pressure to adopt said technologies within a corporate environment. These technologies are inherently collaborative and designed to enable sharing of information between multiple users (McAfee, 2006). Micro-blogging is a specific form of Web 2.0 technology where short (typically under

200 characters) messages are shared between members within a community. This encourages a less formal knowledge sharing between team and community members where groups interact based on shared interests or projects (McFedries, 2007).

The success of social media in general in the personal space has led businesses to consider the use of similar technologies within the business environment. Micro-blogging provides a lightweight and easy tool for staff to post brief updates about their daily activities and thoughts, and may help support knowledge sharing and communication in corporations. As micro-blogging is a new technology, which has not yet received wide adoption within companies, the benefits and risks of adoption are not yet clear. The role which micro-blogging should play within organisations is not clear either (Zhang, Qu, Cody, & Wu, 2010). This chapter evaluates micro-blogging within a corporate context in order to examine the current state of tools, which support more informal collaboration between virtual teams. By evaluating the existing landscape of similar collaborative tools and the nascent literature on micro-blogging within organisations, the proposed technical report will look for opportunities where companies can leverage micro-blogging to improve collaboration between virtual teams and virtual team members.

This section provides a broad conceptual overview of collaboration, the importance of informal and social communication amongst team members, virtual teams, and appropriate collaboration technologies with a view to establishing how to create greater cohesion and collaboration between team members. To this end, the rise of virtual communication in the modern networked economy and the impact this has on how people work together is evaluated along with the value of informal communication.

From this broad overview, the focus shifts to a narrower inspection of the benefits of improved collaboration and how individuals can make use of social media technologies, specifically micro-blogging. The nature, characteristics, benefits, and issues related to micro-blogging will be evaluated. Whilst there is some research on micro-blogging, there is relatively little peer-reviewed research on micro-blogging in the corporate setting.

A key thread that connects the topics covered in this review is the nature of virtual relationships. Companies now operate globally either through their own international divisions or with international partners. The nature of the work these organisations and the people working for them produce has also shifted from that of physical production to service and knowledge related work. Electronic channels need to be used effectively in order to compensate for the lack of richness provided by face-to-face communication. While email is by far the most common tool for communication and collaboration within virtual teams, the most successful teams and projects consist of people that make use of a combination of channels such as email and collaborative portals (Kayworth & Leidner, 2000). Care needs to be taken when selecting extra communications channels as they do not necessarily improve communication and may decrease the quality of collaboration between team members (Walvoord, Redden, Elliott, & Coovert, 2008).

Collaboration and the Value of Informal Communication

The need for collaboration within organisations has increased as the virtual nature of work has increased. The issues that face knowledge workers are less about the knowledge itself and more about the people who hold the skills and organisational knowledge. It is therefore more about whom than about what (Nardi, Whittaker, & Schwarz, 2000).

In order to increase the level of interaction between workers in a virtual environment, it is important to increase the level of informal communication. Therefore, the value of a collaboration network is measured by the strength of the ties within the network (Levin & Cross, 2004). Weak ties are connections within social networks that are not reinforced by organisational structures and teams. The traditional structures of organisations and teams tend to create closed and "siloed" communities based on function, which inhibit informal sharing within an organisation (Granovetter, 1983). Thus, the weak ties have an important role to play in introducing organically formed and valuable collaborative networks.

Informal communication creates "water cooler" conversations between team members. This informal communication process improves the cultural connectedness between team members and employees. Informal communication is equally, if not more, important within virtual teams as it provides a method for sharing workplace culture and increasing the feeling of connection between team members (Levin & Cross, 2004).

In order to compensate for the lack of face-to-face communication, many corporates are experimenting with collaborative Web 2.0 technologies such as blogs and social media sites (DiMicco, et al., 2008). Informal communication is seen as having both relational and personal benefits. Relational benefits relate to the perception of other team members, the establishment of common ground and the feeling of connectedness between team members (Zhao & Rosson, 2009). The personal benefits relate to the amount of valuable information team members can gain by participating in a specific social network (Zhao & Rosson, 2009). The greater the uncertainty surrounding a task, the more virtual teams rely on informal communication to manage their interaction (Abel, 1990). Informal communication also serves to address the four areas of awareness of team information (Gutwin & Greenberg, 2002):

- **Informal Awareness:** Where knowledge is shared about the action or intentions of team members (e.g. "I'm having trouble with this Java code").

- **Social Awareness:** Where the emotional context of team members' actions are shared (e.g. "I'm feeling positive about the new development manager").
- **Group-Structural Awareness:** Where the nature and structure of teams are communicated (e.g. "I'm going to submit the weekly review document from now on").
- **Workspace Awareness:** Where shared tasks are discussed (e.g. "The latest version on the business case is on the file server").

In addressing the four factors above, it is highly likely that virtual teams could experience greater collaboration and awareness should their communication be channeled through an appropriate medium.

What is Micro-Blogging?

Micro-blogging is a term, which describes the act of people sharing brief text updates about their work and social life (McFedries, 2007). This allows people to share their thoughts and activities in a quick and informal manner, which increases their social presence within the social networks they use. The popularity of micro-blogging is related to the minimal investment in time and effort that is required to contribute (McFedries, 2007).

A core concept of micro-blogging is that of "following" and "followers." Users may choose to "follow" other users. This means that they will automatically see posts made by users they follow. Similarly any posts a user makes will be seen by their "followers."

Micro-blogging combines the following characteristics:

- **Brevity:** Messages are short. In the case of Twitter, they are much like Short-Message-Service (SMS) messages and under 150 characters. This requires less from users who contribute, making them more likely to post without needing to allocate the time and effort required for longer posts.
- **Pervasive Access:** Most micro-blogging platforms allow for mobile and Web access, making updates easy for users even if they are away from their corporate network.
- **Broadcast Nature:** Posts made by users are broadcast to their followers, which increases the interaction between team members (Zhao & Rosson, 2009).

As Twitter is the most widely used example of micro-blogging in the public space, existing studies have focused on the use of Twitter. Typically, similar studies involve identifying different classes of Twitter users and their behaviours, geographic growth patterns, and the current size of the network. The classification of users show that they can be broadly categorised as information sources (also known as hubs), who are followed by many due to their valuable or important posts; information seekers, who post rarely but mainly follow others; and friends, who follow and post to peers, colleagues or family (Java, Song, Finin, & Tseng, 2009). The main types of information shared can also be categorised into four categories: daily chatter, conversations, sharing information/URLs, and reporting news (Java, et al., 2009).

Benefits of Micro-Blogging

Micro-blogging allows for a more personal presence in the digital sphere, one that is less formal than other digital channels (Zhao & Rosson, 2009). The quick and easy aspect of micro-blogging increases the likelihood of contributions from users as they can contribute without having to make large investments in time and energy. The improved ease of use makes people more likely to contribute to formal and informal discussions than traditional blogs and other channels such as forums and wikis. There is value in understanding the way people interact with micro-blogging in the workplace in order to understand how to make use of the technologies to improve the collaboration and cohesion, which exists within virtual teams.

Enterprise Micro-Blogging

The phenomenon known as Enterprise Micro-Blogging (or EMB) deals with the application of micro-blogging tools in the corporate environment, ostensibly to build stronger informal bonds and information sharing between members of (often virtual) teams. To date, hardly any research has been conducted on enterprise micro-blogging (Riemer, et al., 2011), and it is not yet clear if micro-blogging technologies can be used to improve collaboration between virtual teams; however, the rise of micro-blogging in the public social space as well as the adoption of earlier technologies such as forums suggests that they should not be ignored in the corporate arena.

Little peer-reviewed, published research on enterprise micro-blogging is currently available. A relatively early study attempted to model the adoption of EMB using a number of variables from traditional technology adoption models by means of four focus groups in a German context (Günther, Riehle, Krasnova, & Schöndienst, 2009). Two later studies focussed on an exploratory approach by looking mainly at the nature of the messages and collaborations using a case study approach. The first of these was the study in a large US-based multinational by (Zhang, et al., 2010), which is used as a baseline since it involved the largest number of messages and users. Two subsequent case study-based research reports have been released, one in US-based IBM (Ehrlich & Shami, 2010) with 34 users, and the other in an unidentified German company (Riemer, et al., 2011). As far as the authors could determine, *no* research has been conducted on enterprise micro-blogging in organisations located in developing or emerging countries.

Measuring and Analysing Enterprise Micro-Blogging

Zhang *et al.* (2010) published a study of the corporate usage of Yammer, a micro-blogging tool which is aimed at corporates and, unlike the public nature of Twitter, is designed for closed networks and user groups. They classified micro-blogging messages using the general characteristics as well as the message genre. The general message attributes includes message length and the ability to tag and group messages. The message genre can be seen to fall into one of the following categories (Zhang, et al., 2010):

- *"Me" messages constitute 16% of the use of Yammer. These messages are focused on the specific behaviour and interests of the person posting them.*
- *"Conversation Seeking" messages constitute 25% of usage. These messages are aimed at creating conversations around issues, which impact on the message poster.*
- *"Share news or new found" messages constitute 37% of the messages posted and are aimed at sharing links to information which the poster finds relevant to her and the team within which she operates.*
- *"About Yammer" messages constitute 21% of the posted messages and focus on the shared experience of using the micro-blogging tool.*
- *Other messages which are not easily categorised make up 1% of the postings.*

(Zhang, et al., 2010)

Zhang *et al.* (2010) continue to characterise users based on how they view the micro-blogging tool, using the following categories:

- **Demographics and Organisational Positioning:** Where does the user work within the organisation? Is there greater adoption amongst IT staff or Marketing staff?
- **Usage Statistics and Post Frequency:** What is the rate of adoption? How many users have signed up? How frequently do users post? Do users continue to post over time?
- **Perceived Usefulness, Value, and Benefits:** How do users get value from micro-blogging? How does it benefit their interaction with other team members?

- **The "Noise-to-Value Ratio" Paradoxes:** What is the ideal combination of relevant data and message frequency? Too few messages and nothing is relevant to the user. How to filter out valuable messages from the noise? Indeed, the feared high noise-to-value ratio may well be a key reason why corporates have been hesitant to introduce enterprise micro-blogging (Riemer, et al., 2011).

Current Issues and Investigation Areas for Micro-Blogging

Zhang *et al.* (2010) found that the key benefits of micro-blogging were to be found in users being aware of the work patterns of others and in making connections with other team members. Accordingly, this supports increased social awareness (Gutwin, et al., 2002) and weak-ties (Granovetter, 1983). Zhang *et al.* (2010) found that Yammer failed to demonstrate significant increases in social awareness and ties due to its predominant usage as a communication medium for external news items and information. They go on to suggest that the implementation of micro-blogging within organisations should take this into account and attempt to encourage greater sharing of personal experiences and information (Zhang, et al., 2010). One benefit that micro-blogging can support is the creation of groups that share specific interests or expertise. This sharing can cross national and cultural boundaries (Zhang, et al., 2010).

The key challenge for effective micro-blogging adoption involves the ability of users to filter valuable information from the large number of posts to the network. Yammer helps to minimise this concern by providing more extensive filtering capabilities such as groups, which extend its feature set beyond consumer technologies such as Twitter. Another key concern with Yammer is the fact that it is hosted outside the corporate network, "in the cloud." Zhang *et al.* (2010) suggest that regardless of security and privacy implementation, many users remain cautious about sharing corporate information on sites that, though private, are hosted outside of company networks.

Key Findings from the Literature

In summary, there is scant research on micro-blogging in a corporate context. There are, however, a number of comparable Web 2.0 studies which can shed light on the potential nature and value of micro-blogging and how it can contribute to more effective collaboration within teams. The short-messages and informal nature of Instant Messaging (IM) technologies can be compared to micro-blogging, as can the threaded discussions of forums. Similarly, blogs and forums provide a less formal method of interaction for staff and team members. Web 2.0 technologies allow for rich interaction and effective learning due to their inherently networked nature. Learning from the contributions of peers is a key element of the value provided by Web 2.0 solutions (Ullrich, et al., 2008).

Virtual teams, like any project teams, need effective means to communicate. There are very specific nuances to these communication needs in virtual teams that require attention, hence the focus of this review. A number of Web 2.0 technologies are effective media for formal and informal communication between project team members, and appear to increase social awareness and cohesion between teams. The issues seem to lie in the adoption and ongoing contribution of these technologies. According to the literature, sharing more personal information would increase team cohesion and collaboration. But the study by Zhang *et al.* (2010) seems to indicate that people within the corporate arena are not necessarily trusting of the platform or how the information stored inside the platform is managed or made accessible.

To engender improved trust in and greater adoption of micro-blogging, further investigation needs to be done in order understand the reasons for user adoption through specific technical implementation rules, such as hosting the platform within the corporate network instead of in the cloud. Adoption may also be improved through the greater use of traditional channels such as email in order to encourage and promote user adoption through education and internal marketing of the service. There would also appear to be value in understanding the types of conversations that occur within specific categories of users. Understanding the nature of specific user-groups and their needs can assist with formulating models for adoption within groups that show lower rates of adoption and usage of micro-blogging.

The next section deals with the methodology, which was used to address the research question: whether micro-blogging is an effective and appropriate social media technology for corporates to improve and/or facilitate collaboration between team members.

RESEARCH METHODOLOGY

The primary research took the form of a case study within a single organisation, evaluating the adoption of a single micro-blogging technology. In the light of the paucity of research in this area, the research was exploratory in nature.

The research was based on the assumption that micro-blogging will increase the level of collaboration within an organisation. The research evaluated both the effectiveness of the micro-blogging platform, considered how the platform is adopted and explored ways in which adoption can be increased. In order to achieve this, analysis of the usage of the platform as well as activities that occur outside of, but are influenced by, the platform were measured.

The focus of the research questions was to elicit and evaluate three key aspects:

1. The benefits experienced through the use of micro-blogging within an organisation.
2. The adoption patterns that occur.
3. The types of messages shared within a corporate micro-blogging environment and what these say about the nature of the communication within these networks.

The research was done through the evaluation of data within the scope of a single micro-blogging platform, Yammer, which was adopted within a financial services IT department. The nature of the relationships between team members and the nature of the information being shared and discussed was evaluated against frameworks for team collaboration. The platform in question was implemented on 31 July 2009 (the date of first sign-on), and the research into the adoption and usage was from the date of first adoption until 1 August 2010.

Data collection was done through the evaluation of information available within the micro-blogging platform (message analysis) and through a survey questionnaire. Although there were a total of 411 users signed up on the Yammer platform as of 29 June 2010, only 326 registered users had valid email addresses. In view of the relatively small number of users, a census approach was taken and the link to the questionnaire was sent to *all* users with a valid email address. From this sample population, 35 completed surveys plus 29 partially completed surveys were received resulting in a 19.6% response rate to the invitation email. The demographics of both the sample population and the respondents are described in more detail below under the heading of "User Demographics."

The instrument was based on the one used in the study by Zhang *et al.* (2010). However, additional questions were added to empirically measure the level of informal communication within the user group, as well as to measure elements of the Technology Acceptance Model (Davis, 1989). The survey was structured to elicit responses related to demographics, usefulness, adoption, and benefits. A copy of the survey is attached in the appendix. The survey responses were anonymous and no link was drawn between actual users and their responses.

All message threads from the company feed within the Yammer platform were systematically sampled—totaling 641 messages, and manually coded into the following classifications: team awareness and message content. The focus of the message classification scheme is on establishing how effective Yammer is at creating team awareness and evaluating how it differs from public micro-blogging platforms such as Twitter. In both cases, the nature of the messages should indicate how well the platform supports informal communication within a corporate environment.

MESSAGE ANALYSIS

The sample of 641 messages was gathered by "following" all users on the network and collecting all the messages visible within the Yammer website. Only primary messages and the initial responses were captured. The messages were analysed based on two perspectives: team awareness and message content.

Team awareness was investigated using the four categories of awareness of team information (Gutwin, et al., 1996). The aim is to evaluate the areas in which the use of Yammer improves informal awareness between staff. The four categories are:

- **Informal Awareness:** Messages concerning actions and intentions.
- **Social Awareness:** Messages relating to emotional context.
- **Group Structural Awareness:** Team-related messages.
- **Workspace Awareness:** Messages about shared tasks.

The message content evaluation was broadly based on the types from Zhang *et al.* (2010), as well as from DiMicco (2008) and Namaan (Naaman, Boase, & Lai, 2010). The focus was on evaluating the types of messages within the micro-blogging network and looking for the contribution they might make to increasing collaboration amongst the users of Yammer. Message content was classified using the following categories: information sharing; company sharing; about me; about others; opinions; and questions.

Of a total of 641 messages analysed, 200 (31.2%) were related to team awareness. These can be further broken down into the following categories (shown in Table 1).

A large percentage of the messages were not specifically team related. They were focused on the sharing of information. This information was predominantly news and links e.g. "Dilbert for today is peculiarly familiar..." (http://dilbert.com/strips/comic/2010-05-08/). This is mirrored in the study of Yammer by Zhang et al where, for instance, a full 37% of messages were the links and information (Zhang, et al., 2010). This is supported by the survey results where the most positive responses regarding the use of Yammer involve sharing with colleagues and getting a sense of what colleagues are thinking, feeling and doing.

Table 1. Team awareness messages

Type of Group Awareness Message	# Messages	% Messages
Informal Awareness: Actions and Intentions	36	18%
Social Awareness: Emotional Context	52	26%
Group Structural Awareness: Team Related	84	42%
Workspace Awareness: Shared Tasks	28	14%

Table 2. Study comparison

Message Classification	Zhang (2010)	This Study
Sharing	37%	46%
Me	16%	17%
Conversation	25%	32%
Yammer	21%	0%
Other	1%	5%

In previous studies, the analysis of the types of messages posted was used to compare Yammer to public micro-blogging platforms like Twitter and to other corporate collaboration platforms such as intranets. The following categories were simplified from the questions used in Zhang et al. (2010): Information Sharing, Company Sharing, About Me, About Others, Opinions, and Questions.

In both studies, the majority of messages were related to sharing, 37% for the Zhang study and 46% in this case study. Overall, there was a similarity between the results of the studies. The key difference is that the participants in this study did not appear to have any discussions relating to the Yammer platform itself. Apart from that, the relative importance of the classifications is similar (see Table 2).

A more recent study (Riemer & Richter, 2011) published after our analysis was concluded suggests different, more detailed categories, based on genre analysis. Their top six categories are: record information, ask questions, share information, coordination, discuss or clarify, provide update and future research. These are subdivided further into 18 micro-genres. Future researchers may wish to use the latter taxonomy.

SURVEY RESULTS

From the sample population of 326 users, 35 completed surveys plus 29 partially completed surveys were received, resulting in a 19.6% response rate to the invitation email. Because the survey responses were anonymous with no link between actual users and their responses it was not possible to draw any correlations between responses and behaviour, e.g. "positive respondents post more messages."

User Demographics

The case study examined a financial service company head office with 4000 employees. Yammer was initially launched in the IT department. There was no formal adoption

Table 3. Yammer user base characteristics

	Population Characteristics (n = 411)	Number	%
Gender	Male	197	47.9%
	Female	214	52.1%
Activity Level	Zero Posts	13	3.2%
	Single Posts	264	64.2%
	Double Posts	45	10.9%
	High Posts	89	21.7%

drive; it was left to grow organically. The vast majority (38) were based in the Cape Town head office although two responses were received from Johannesburg and one from the India office. In the end, 411 users signed up for Yammer. The Yammer user base was fairly equally split according to gender with 214 out of 411 users (52%) being female (Table 3).

A full 78% of the users were "low posters" having made two or fewer posts to the platform and then either stopped using Yammer or simply observed: 13 users posted zero, 264 users a single and 45 only two posts. The top 10 users accounted for 64.52% of the 3619 total posts. This sort of contribution level is to be expected and was found by Zhang et al. in their study where a similar percentage of users were "low posters": a full 61% made *no* postings and a further 29% between 1 and 10 posts; 7% posted 10 to 50 and less than 3% made more than 50 posts (Zhang, et al., 2010).

This also mirrors social media adoption trends and other studies (Krishnamurthy, Gill, & Arlitt, 2008). It is common for social media platforms to have a large percentage of users that simply consume information and do not contribute to the content or discussion at all (DiMicco, et al., 2008).

Most respondents (74.4%) were Generation X i.e. aged 30-45. This is representative of the demographics of the company: 20.5% identified themselves as Baby Boomers (45+) and only one respondent as a Gen-Y (<29).

An initial email was sent out to the IT community, leading 64% of the respondents to participate. This then spread to other areas through conversations and referrals (accounting for 26% of respondents' adoption). Clearly, a formal drive from management would have improved adoption as can be seen in further responses, which indicate that increased management involvement would have encouraged adoption.

Initial Adoption

Most usage was through the Yammer.com website, with the least used access channel being mobile phones. This contrasts with Facebook mobile adoption where 150

Figure 1. Usage trends

How often do you read Yammer posts?

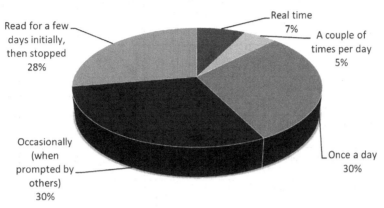

million of the 500 million users access the platform using mobile devices, and are twice as active as users who don't (Facebook, 2010) (see Figure 1).

Perceived Usefulness and Perceived Ease of Use

In order to understand the adoption of a new technology such as micro-blogging, some of the research questions within the survey were focused on the Perceived Usefulness and Perceived Ease of Use. These measures have been shown in the past to impact on the adoption of technology based solutions (Davis, 1989).

Table 4 summarizes the results.

The results for Perceived Usefulness indicate that the benefits of Yammer usage are far from clear within the sample group, with the greatest element in all categories being "undecided." Interestingly, this lack of agreement on the perceived usefulness was also the case in the study by Zhang *et al.* where, although the spread was wider, the median response was also neutral (26% of respondents). Only 30% of respondents agreed or agreed strongly, whereas 43% disagreed (Zhang, et al., 2010).

Most respondents found Yammer easy to use and users were able to complete most tasks they wanted to. There is some uncertainty amongst respondents when asked about their ability to make use of all the features within Yammer. There were only two groups created within Yammer during the adoption period studied. The first was amongst IT developers and the second amongst a team focused on Corporate Social Investment (CSI) initiatives. This contrasts with the study by Zhang et al where 26 groups were created and this was used as a reason for the lack of adoption in their study of hash tags and other similar usage conventions in public micro-blogging

Table 4. Perceived usefulness and ease of use of yammer

Perceived Usefulness	Agree Strongly	Agree	Neutral/ Undecided	Disagree	Disagree Strongly
Using Yammer in my job would increase my productivity	0.0%	15.0%	52.5%	20.0%	12.5%
Using Yammer would make it easier to do my job.	0.0%	15.0%	50.0%	22.5%	12.5%
I would find Yammer useful in my job	0.0%	30.0%	35.0%	25.0%	10.0%
Perceived Ease Of Use					
Learning to use Yammer would be easy for me	25.0%	60.0%	7.5%	3.0%	2.5%
I would find it easy to use Yammer to do what I want to do	22.5%	42.5%	22.5%	10.0%	2.5%
It is easy to use all the options available within Yammer	17.5%	42.5%	30.0%	7.5%	2.5%

platforms like Twitter (Zhang, et al., 2010). Hash tags are used within Twitter to identify themes and topics, e.g. "I am posting about #topic" and to address specific users e.g. "@user thanks for the information." Only 3.74% of messages in this case study contained hash tags. This is to be expected given the lower usage of Twitter in the survey group when compared to other external social media platforms.

Personal Benefits

DiMicco *et al.* (2008) categorise personal benefits and motivations of using a social media platform like Yammer as caring, climbing, and campaigning. Caring involves connecting to others, climbing involves career advancement and campaigning relates to specific projects or tasks which need organisational support. A summarised version of the results appears in Table 5.

Table 5. Personal benefits

Personal benefit or motivation	Positive	Undecided	Negative
Find out what others are working on	52.5%	17.5%	30%
Reach out to ask questions	60%	15%	25%
Make my work more visible to others	46.2%	20.5%	33.3%
Find people who share similar interests	67.5%	12.5%	20%
Learn more about company news and events	47.5%	25%	27.5%
Learn about industry news and trends	62.5%	22.5%	15%

There seems to be a focus on interaction with others within the organisation and less of a focus on individual users promoting themselves. This is contrary to the use of Twitter where posts tend to be focused on personal activities. This tendency was also noted by Zhang *et al.* where they note: "Employees use Yammer more for publishing news about their groups or business units instead of news about themselves." However, the responses are far from clear with a large percentage of users choosing "undecided" or "negative." The least positive responses were for "Make my work more visible to others" and "Learn more about company news and events."

Team Related Benefits

Even within a single company, as in this case study, often thousands of people are spread across many floors of a large building in many different functional departments. This environment makes it difficult for ideas to be shared among different functional teams.

Various team related questions were asked to discover if people made use of the platform to communicate with people in their immediate teams or within the extended organisation. Table 6 summarises the survey results.

From the results of the survey, it is more likely that people connect with colleagues who are known than who are not. It is also more likely that connections are to people in their work location than not. Respondents are also more likely to connect with people within their business unit and more likely to connect with their peers. This is to be expected given the sample for the case study. The localised nature of the interaction may dilute the value of the network if one considers the view that a collaborative network's strength is based on the strength of the weak ties within the network.

Table 6. Connectedness

Connectedness	Often or Always	Sometimes	Rarely or Never
people in my work location	44.70%	28.90%	26.30%
people I know	27.50%	45%	27.50%
my peers	22.50%	45%	32.50%
people within my business unit	20.50%	38.50%	41%
people I don't know	17.50%	50%	32.50%
people in other business units	17.50%	57.50%	25%
people at different levels of the business hierarchy	17.50%	45%	37.50%
people in other offices and locations	10%	37.50%	52.50%

Table 7. Informal awareness

Team Awareness (n = 40)	Positive (of which % strongly)	Undecided	Negative (of which % strongly)
Informal...share what I'm working on with colleagues, e.g. "I'm having trouble with this Java code."	32.5% (0%)	25%	42.5% (15%)
Social...get a sense of how my colleagues are feeling about things, e.g. "I'm feeling positive about the new development manager."	45% (7.5%)	20%	35% (15%)
Group Structural...understand changes in team and project structures, e.g. "I'm going to submit the weekly report from now on."	10% (0%)	35%	55% (15%)
Workspace...better interaction where shared tasks are discussed, e.g. "The latest version of the business case is on the file server."	20% (2.5%)	30%	50% (15%)

Team Awareness

This links back to the virtual teams Informal Awareness classification. People gain benefit by being aware of their colleagues' feelings and intentions (see Table 7).

The most positive responses regarding the use of Yammer involve sharing with colleagues and getting a sense of what colleagues are feeling. The shared projects and task elements are not seen as something, which people would like to use Yammer for. This does fit with the main use of social media, which is to increase the level of informal communication. In this case "Informal" and "Social" are clearly more relevant than "Group Structural" and "Workspace."

Inhibitors to Adoption

If the use of a social platform such as Yammer is to succeed within organisations, the reasons for using the platform need to be understood, along with the associated drivers and inhibitors. One section of the survey measured some factors, which could influence adoption and growth.

Interestingly, 60% of respondents talked to (32.5%) or invited (27.5%) others onto Yammer. This is not surprising given that connecting personally with co-workers, advancing careers and promoting projects are seen as the primary objectives of using of a social platform (DiMicco, et al., 2008). Thus, it appears that the challenge is not getting people to join Yammer but to get people to contribute. This is not a phenomenon unique to this case study: a high percentage of non-contributing users is to be expected (Zhang, et al., 2010).

Table 8. Reasons for not posting on Yammer

Reason(s) for not posting on Yammer	Nr resp	%
Not enough time	15	45%
Just wanted to read and learn	15	45%
Still learning about Yammer and similar social networking tools	12	36%
Nothing to broadcast	12	36%
Not sure what is appropriate to share	12	36%
Shy about posting	9	27%
Have privacy concerns (personal level) on who sees my posts	5	15%
Have privacy concerns (company level) on who sees my posts	5	15%
No value to me	4	12%
Lack of management support	3	9%
Interface is difficult to use	1	3%
Wanted to remain anonymous	1	3%

The top reason for not contributing to Yammer appears to be a lack of time. Also rated highly is the lack of familiarity with social networking ("still learning" and "not sure what is appropriate"). These could be addressed by raising awareness and providing information (see Table 8).

Other key inhibitors relate to privacy concerns (personal, company or anonymity); these would appear to be a matter of both education (again) and organisational culture. The final two important inhibitors are explored in more detail below because these can potentially be managed by the organisation: finding (or posting) relevant information i.e. information of value to the group, and the involvement of management.

Finding Relevance

With only 12.5% of respondents claiming to often find relevant information on Yammer, clearly finding relevance is an issue. Most people in the case study claimed that the best way to increase the relevance of messages is to select the right people to follow. The survey results indicate that people were more likely to communicate with people they already know. This also implies that people are unlikely to connect outside of their immediate work circles and will not gain additional organisational knowledge—they do not know what they do not know. The use of Yammer's group feature could address this issue: groups can be organised by focus or interest area and thereby facilitate the finding and sharing of specific types of organisational knowledge (Zhang, et al., 2010). Proper education about how to use the groups

Table 9. What people find important on Yammer

How do you find what is important to you on Yammer?	Nr resp	%
I select people to follow	22	58%
I try to read everything	11	29%
I sign up for groups	9	24%
I want to limit my focus but I don't know how	4	11%
Other	4	11%

feature might address the relevance problem. Perhaps seeding the platform with appropriate corporate groups may help improve the ability of users to gain relevance (see Table 9).

Management Involvement

In the study, there was little senior management involvement in and promotion of Yammer in the organisation. Only 6 senior managers posted anything to the network and of those 6, only 2 posted more than 10 messages. The survey results indicate that while greater management approval is seen as important (13% agree strongly and 29% agree), there is no consensus on this (with 29% disagreeing). However, rather than actual management approval, it is the actual contribution and involvement by management that is viewed as an important factor for adoption by most users (with 20% strongly agreeing and a further 53% agreeing versus only 13% disagreeing).

This was also the conclusion of a study on the use of corporate social media in a large US technology company: "In short, it seems that managers' participation is a key motivator in getting people to start contributing to enterprise social media, while comments and a diverse readership are key in getting them to sustain their contributions" (Brzozowski, Sandholm, & Hogg, 2009).

General Adoption Comments

A number of the free form comments indicate a concern that Yammer was an IT focused social and collaboration platform. This concern has some truth: the system was initially set up by IT staff, and IT staff are also more likely to be aware of and use similar technologies such as Twitter. Again, a formalised implementation drive with a focus on creating relevant groups for people seems important in creating effective adoption patterns. Alternatively, the tool could be reengineered to tag or stream content according to interest. Some interesting comments were:

At the moment, it appears to be very much an IT communication tool with little business value.

There usually isn't much of interest (workwise) on Yammer.

Just a general lack of creating awareness and understanding of the value that Yammer adds/can add.

Not always sure about the confidentiality of the stuff I work on.

I went in a few times some time ago and since it seemed mostly IT related comments I stopped using it.

Perhaps more importantly, the key issue with the adoption of micro-blogging in the enterprise could well be the user's (lack of) prior experience with the micro-blogging platform. When asked about it, it came as no surprise that most of the participants were already familiar with Web 2.0 tools. However, only 37% of respondents used Twitter as opposed to almost everyone using Facebook (see Figure 2).

Perhaps this implies that social media tools in the corporate space should follow the Facebook model instead of the Twitter model since only a small number of employees appear to be convinced of, or familiar with, the benefits of micro-blogging in their personal life.

Figure 2. Social media adoption

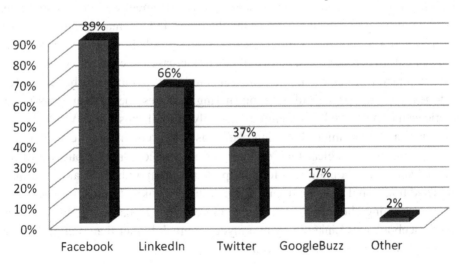

CONCLUSION

This case study analysed the use of Yammer within a closed corporate environment in order to evaluate its effectiveness in increasing collaboration between staff members. As Twitter has proven to be a valuable tool for informal communication in the public sphere, Yammer's value could potentially be of similar value in a closed corporate environment. This case study considered how Yammer is adopted as a new technology by measuring acceptance from both the usefulness and the ease of use perspectives.

Although Yammer was used fairly regularly by more than 40% of the people responding to the survey, more than half did not use it on a regular basis. This was reflected in the fairly low reported perceived usefulness. However, for those who did use it, the message analysis as well as the survey showed that the micro-blogging tool indeed fulfilled its role of allowing for informal sharing of information and knowledge, resulting in benefits at both the individual and the team levels. In addition, micro-blogging also fulfilled an important social function by raising team awareness in both the social and informal spaces. This finding appears to be in line with the findings of other studies, notably Zhang *et al.* (2010) and Ehrlich and Shami, (2010).

There were several issues that the surveyed respondents indicated regarding ease of use. Confusion about the benefits that the platform offers indicates some usability concerns with Yammer, especially its more advanced features. An example of this is the lack of an easy way for users to focus on groups, which provide interaction, collaboration, and sharing information. Training and communication regarding some more advanced skills as well as pre-populating groups are some of the ways corporates could look to improving adoption among staff. One important aspect which the survey revealed is that management involvement encourages adoption. This is not just endorsement but active involvement, and any management decision to implement Yammer or a similar micro-blogging tool should plan for personal management involvement and contributions to increase the chances of success.

In summary, it appears that micro-blogging indeed provides some benefits relating to team awareness and information sharing, but these benefits are clearly not experienced or perceived by *all* employees, only a small subsection. While the use of Yammer and other micro-blogging platforms could remain under consideration for corporate use, it is clear that Yammer and micro-blogging are but two of the potential social media platforms for enterprise adoption. Other social media platforms and traditional collaboration platforms such as wikis, forums, intranets, and instant messaging should be evaluated in more detail. In particular, the personal use of Facebook and LinkedIn by employees is much higher than that of Twitter, so perhaps this is a more fruitful avenue for exploration.

As indicated, there are some limitations with this case study. The number of Yammer users only accounted for a small fraction (about 1%) of the company staff contingent. This particular implementation and adoption was driven by the IT department and no formal communication and adoption process occurred. In addition, lacking a strongly established theoretical framework, a more in-depth exploration of the specific use motivations and benefits experienced by the different categories of users (especially the information sources and information seekers) would be very valuable. This would be best achieved through a qualitative research approach.

Future research can also investigate this or other micro-blogging platforms in other organisational contexts to see if organisation factors (such as size, culture, processes, management practices and styles, industry, etc.) or country contexts affect the findings. More case studies in this area may serve to generalize the findings.

REFERENCES

Barnes, S. J., & Böhringer, M. (2009). Continuance usage intention in microblogging services: The case of Twitter. *Information Systems Journal*, *2*(4), 1–13.

Böhringer, M., & Richter, A. (2009). Adopting enterprise 2.0: A case study on microblogging. In *Proceedings of the Ninth Conference Mensch und Computer,* (pp. 293-302). Oldenbourg.

Brzozowski, M. J., Sandholm, T., & Hogg, T. (2009). Effects of feedback and peer pressure on contributions to enterprise social media. In *Proceedings of the ACM 2009 International Conference on Supporting Group Work,* (pp. 61-70). ACM Press.

Davis, F. D. (1989). Perceived usefulness, perceived ease of use, and user acceptance of information technology. *Management Information Systems*, *13*(3), 319–340. doi:10.2307/249008

DiMicco, J., Millen, D. R., Geyer, W., Dugan, C., Brownholtz, B., & Muller, M. (2008). Motivations for social network at work. In *Proceedings of the ACM 2009 International Conference on Computer Supported Cooperative Work,* (pp. 711-720). ACM Press.

Dourish, P., & Bellotti, V. (1992). Awareness and coordination in shared workspaces. In *Proceedings of the 1992 ACM Conference on Computer-Supported Cooperative Work,* (pp. 107-114). New York, NY: ACM Press.

Ehrlich, K., & Shami, N. S. (2010). Microblogging inside and outside the workplace. In *Proceedings of the 4th International AAAI Conference on Weblogs and Social Media (ICWSM 2010)*. AAAI Publications.

Facebook. (2010). *Facebook mobile usage*. Retrieved from http://www.facebook. com/facebook?v=app_10531514314

Granovetter, M. (1983). The strength of weak ties: A network theory revisited. *Sociological Theory*, *1*, 201–233. doi:10.2307/202051

Günther, O., Riehle, D., Krasnova, H., & Schöndienst, V. (2009). Modeling microblogging adoption in the enterprise. In *Proceedings of the 15th Americas Conference on Information Systems (ACIS)*. ACIS.

Gutwin, C., & Greenberg, S. (2002). A descriptive framework of workspace awareness for real-time groupware. *Computer Supported Cooperative Work*, *11*(3-4), 441–446.

Handy, C. (1995). Trust and the virtual organization. *Harvard Business Review*, *73*(3), 40–50.

Java, A., Song, X., Finin, T., & Tseng, B. (2009). Why we Twitter: An analysis of a microblogging community. *Lecture Notes in Computer Science*, *5439*, 118–138. doi:10.1007/978-3-642-00528-2_7

Kayworth, T., & Leidner, D. (2000). The global virtual manager: a prescription for success. *European Management Journal*, *18*(2), 183–194. doi:10.1016/S0263-2373(99)00090-0

Klein, D. A. (1998). *The strategic management of intellectual capital*. Woburn, MA: Butterworth-Heinemann.

Levin, D. Z., & Cross, R. (2004). The strength of weak ties you can trust: The mediating role of trust in effective knowledge transfer. *Management Science*, *50*(11), 1477–1490. doi:10.1287/mnsc.1030.0136

McAfee, A. (2006). Enterprise 2.0: The dawn of emergent collaboration. *MIT Sloan Management Review*, *47*(3), 21–29.

McFedries, P. (2007). Technically speaking - Social networkers are all a-Twitter. *IEEE Spectrum*, *44*(10), 84. doi:10.1109/MSPEC.2007.4337670

Nardi, B. A., Whittaker, S., & Schwarz, H. (2000). *It's not what you know, it's who you know*. Retrieved from http://www.uic.edu/htbin/cgiwrap/bin/ojs/index.php/fm/article/viewArticle/741/650

OReilly. T. (2007). What is web 2.0: Design patterns and business models for the next generation of software. *Communications & Strategies*, *1*(17). Retrieved from http://ssrn.com/abstract=1008839

Riemer, K., Altenhofen, A., & Richter, A. (2011). What are you doing? Enterprise micro-blogging as context building. In *Proceedings of the 19th European Conference on Information Systems (ECIS)*. ECIS.

Riemer, K., & Richter, A. (2010). Tweet inside: Microblogging in a corporate context. In *Proceedings 23rd Bled eConference*. Bled eConference.

Ullrich, C., Borau, K., Luo, H., Tan, X., Shen, L., & Shen, R. (2008). Why web 2.0 is good for learning and for research: Principles and prototypes. In *Proceedings of the 17ᵗʰ International Conference on World Wide Web,* (pp. 705-714). ACM.

Walfoord, A. A. G., Redden, E. R., Elliott, L. R., & Coovert, M. D. (2008). Empowering followers in virtual teams: Guiding principles from theory and practice. *Computers in Human Behavior, 24*(5), 1884–1906. doi:10.1016/j.chb.2008.02.006

Zhang, J., Qu, Y., Cody, J., & Wu, Y. (2010). A case study of micro-blogging in the enterprise. In *Proceedings of the 28th International Conference on Human Factors in Computing Systems*, (pp. 123-132). New York, NY: ACM Press.

Zhao, D., & Rosson, M. B. (2009). How and why people Twitter. In *Proceedings of the ACM 2009 International Conference on Supporting Group Work*. New York, NY: ACM Press.

KEY TERMS AND DEFINITIONS

Enterprise Micro-Blogging (EMB): Enterprise Micro-blogging (sometimes abbreviated as EMB) is the use of micro-blogging in the corporate space instead of the usual social world. The aim is to improve the informal networking and information sharing between staff, often in their roles as members of a virtual team. EMB tools often allow additional features to be embedded in the messages such as (long) URLs or attachments. These tools also allow for additional security such as restricting membership to corporate employees.

Information Sources and Information Seekers: Micro-blogging users can be categorised according to the frequency of posts. A relatively small number of micro-bloggers act as hubs or information sources and are those who have a large number of followers, either because they post regularly or, sometimes, post more infrequently but their posts are considered to be of value, e.g. because they are in a senior position or possess in-depth knowledge. At the opposite end are the information seekers: users that post relatively rarely but follow a number of other users. Most micro-blogging users cannot easily be classified in either extreme and are known as 'friends,' i.e. they follow peers, colleagues, or family.

Micro-Blogging: Micro-blogging is a social networking tool whereby people share brief (typically less than 200 character long) text updates about their work and/ or personal life. So-called followers subscribe to the message stream as broadcast by particular users on a Web-based, often mobile device. The most popular software tool used for microblogging is Twitter, and the short messages are accordingly known as tweets.

Virtual Teams: Virtual teams can be categorised along two dimensions: the looseness of their structure and the degree of centralised control. Thus, virtual teams occupy a position in a continuum characterised by four exemplars: the pure, or very loosely coupled team without centralised control; transitional, where teams are constructed from multiple organisations and structures and move between different levels of virtual; hybrid, where teams are from multiple organisations, but follow a single method; and the least virtual option, where teams operate within a single organisation.

APPENDIX: THE SURVEY QUESTIONNAIRE

1. How did you first hear about Yammer?
   - ☐ From an email invitation
   - ☐ During a conversation with another user
   - ☐ From a specific event or meeting
   - ☐ Other: ....

2. How do you access Yammer?	Never	Rarely	Some-times	Very Often	Always
The website, www.yammer.com					
Automated email alerts					
Desktop applications					
Mobile phone application					

3. How often do you read Yammer posts?
   - ☐ Real time
   - ☐ Couple of times a day
   - ☐ Once a day
   - ☐ Occasionally (i.e. when prompted by others)
   - ☐ Read for a few days after joining, then stopped reading it

4. How do you think using Yammer will help you with your work?	Strongly Agree	Agree	Undecided	Disagree	Strongly Disagree
Using Yammer in my job will increase my productivity.					
Using Yammer would make it easier to do my job.					
I would find Yammer useful in my job.					

5. Yammer helps me to connect with…	Always	Very Often	Sometimes	Rarely	Never
…people I already know.					
…people I don't know.					
…people in my work location.					
…people in other offices and locations.					
…people in my business unit.					
…people in other business units.					
…my peers.					
…people at different levels of the business hierarchy.					

6. Yammer helps me…	Strongly Agree	Agree	Undecided	Disagree	Strongly Disagree
…find out what others are working on.					
…reach out to ask questions.					
…make my work more visible to others.					
…find people who share similar interests.					
…learn more about internal company news and events.					
…learn more about industry news and trends.					

Other | |

7. Yammer has already helped me to...	Strongly Agree	Agree	Undecided	Disagree	Strongly Disagree
...share what I'm working on with colleagues e.g. "I'm having trouble with this Java code."					
...get a sense of how my colleagues are feeling about things e.g. "I'm feeling positive about the new development manager."					
...understand changes in team and project structures e.g. "I'm going to submit the weekly review document from now on."					
...better interact where shared tasks are discussed e.g. "The latest version on the business case is on the file server."					

Other [   ]

8. How easy do you think Yammer is to use?	Strongly Agree	Agree	Undecided	Disagree	Strongly Disagree
Learning to use Yammer would be easy for me.					
I would find it easy to use Yammer to do what I want to do.					
It is easy to use all the options available within Yammer.					
How often do you find relevant information on Yammer?					

9. How often do you find relevant information on Yammer?
    ☐ Often
    ☐ Sometimes
    ☐ Seldom
    ☐ Never

10. If you have not posted things on Yammer, what are your reasons?
    ☐ Just wanted to read and learn
    ☐ Still learning about Yammer and similar social networking tools
    ☐ Shy about posting
    ☐ Not sure what is appropriate to share
    ☐ Have privacy concerns (personal level) on who sees my posts
    ☐ Have privacy concerns (company level) on who sees my posts
    ☐ Not enough time
    ☐ Wanted to remain anonymous
    ☐ Nothing to broadcast
    ☐ No value to me
    ☐ Interface is difficult to use
    ☐ Lack of management support
    ☐ Other [   ]

11. Have you told others about Yammer?
    ☐ Yes, I have invited others.
    ☐ Yes, I have talked to others.
    ☐ No.

12. If you have not posted things on Yammer, what are your reasons?
    ☐ I select people to follow
    ☐ I sign up for groups
    ☐ I try to read everything
    ☐ I want to limit my focus but I don't know how
    ☐ Other (please specify) [   ]

13. What would motivate you to make more use of Yammer?	Strongly Agree	Agree	Undecided	Disagree	Strongly Disagree
Training.					
Greater management approval.					
How management contributions and posts.					
More contributions and posts by colleagues.					
If I felt the system was more secure.					

Other [   ]

14. What generation are you part of?
    ☐ Baby Boomer (45 or above)
    ☐ Gen X (29-45)
    ☐ Gen Y (under 29)
    ☐ I would prefer not to answer.

15. Is there anything you'd like to add that wasn't covered in the survey?
    [   ]

16. What other social media do you use? (check all that apply)
    ☐ Facebook
    ☐ Twitter
    ☐ LinkedIn
    ☐ Google Buzz
    ☐ Foursquare
    ☐ Other [   ]

Chapter 13
Web 2.0 as a Foundation for Social Media Marketing:
Global Perspectives and the Local Case of Croatia

Vedran Podobnik
University of Zagreb, Croatia

Tomislav Grubisic
iSTUDIO, Croatia

Daniel Ackermann
iSTUDIO, Croatia

Ignac Lovrek
University of Zagreb, Croatia

EXECUTIVE SUMMARY

In the Web 1.0 era, users were passive consumers of a read-only Web. However, the emergence of Web 2.0 redefined the way people use information and communication services—users evolved into prosumers that actively participate and collaborate in the ecosystem of a read-write Web. Consequently, marketing is one among many areas affected by the advent of the Web 2.0 paradigm. Web 2.0 enabled the global proliferation of social networking, which is the foundation for Social Media Marketing. Social Media Marketing represents a novel Internet marketing paradigm based on spreading brand-related messages directly from one user to another. This is also the reason why Social Media Marketing is often referred to as the viral marketing. This chapter will describe: (1) how social networking became the most popular Web 2.0 service, and (2) how social networking revolutionized Internet marketing.

DOI: 10.4018/978-1-4666-2515-0.ch013

Both issues will be elaborated on two levels—the global and the Croatian level. The chapter will first present the evolution of social networking phenomenon which has fundamentally changed the way Internet users utilize Web services. During the first decade of 21st century, millions of people joined online communities and started using online social platforms, about 1.5 billion members of social networks globally in 2012. Furthermore, the chapter will describe how Internet marketing provided marketers with innovative marketing channels, which offer marketing campaign personalization, low-cost global access to consumers, and simple, cheap, and real-time marketing campaign tracking. Specifically, the chapter will focus on Social Media Marketing, the latest step in the Internet marketing evolution. The three most popular Social Media Marketing platforms (i.e., Facebook, Twitter, and Foursquare) will be described, and examples of successful marketing case studies in Croatia will be presented.

INTRODUCTION

We live in a networked society, being constantly surrounded by a very diverse set of networks. Communication networks enable us to interact in real time even when we are thousands of kilometers away. Computer networks provide us infrastructure to exchange information at superfast speeds. Electrical networks deliver us power to drive an opulent set of our household appliances. Television networks allow us to spend hours and hours sitting in a chair and not being bored. If we wanted to make this listing of various networks that strongly affect our everyday life complete, we would need to use the whole chapter just naming them. However, in 2012 a certain type of networks deserves a special attention. These are social networks—networks that connect us globally at an unprecedented scale by breaking the barrier of borders, languages, and cultures.

This chapter will focus on one specific part of value chain, which social networks have started to irretrievably change, regardless of the industry segment. Namely, the chapter will explain and demonstrate a potential of social networking to provide a novel medium for marketing. McKinsey and Company (Chui, et al., 2012) predicts a substantial value potential from using social technologies across value chain in major industry sectors (i.e., financial services, consumer packaged goods, professional services and advanced manufacturing) and social sector. Namely, they estimate that social technologies could create an additional value of $900 billion to $1.3 trillion annually across the four major industry segments mentioned. However, the highest potential for improving margins as well as the highest potential for improving productivity is identified in the "sales and marketing" part of the value chain. To be precise, for all studied major industry sectors McKinsey and Company predicted that utilization of *Social Media Marketing* (SMM) can result in "sales and marketing" margin increase of at least 1-2% and productivity boost of more than 20%. Moreover, McKinsey and Company estimates that every third consumer is influenced by social media. Furthermore, another consulting firm (Accenture, 2011), based on survey of more than 200 companies, found out that "nearly two-thirds of survey respondents considered social media an '*extremely important*' or '*very important*' channel through which to interact with consumers, prospects, partners and other stakeholders." Finally, the study from Forrester (Wasserman, 2012b) not only confirmed but also strengthened Accenture's conclusions by finding that marketers are "overwhelmingly aware that social is important—92% agree that social media has fundamentally changed how consumers engage with brands." Nevertheless, the same Forester's survey reveals that despite all of the hype about social media, only 49% of marketers fully integrated SMM into their brand-building strategy.

The presented surveys from leading consulting firms confirm the enormous potential of SMM and identify that companies just started or are about to start utilizing this new marketing tool. However, SMM is nascent and still defining its best practices and metrics. As a result, companies do not fully understand consequences of integrating SMM into their value chain and still search for best methods how to measure the SMM impact on their business processes. Zeisser perspicuously identified this immense challenge SMM faces today (Zeisser, 2010). "There is much hype about social networks and their potential impact on marketing," he says, "so many companies are diligently establishing presences on Facebook, Twitter, and other platforms. Yet the true value of social networks remains unclear, and while common wisdom suggests that they should be tremendous enablers and amplifiers of word of mouth, few companies have unlocked this potential." This chapter should be a small step towards understanding how to unlock a potential of SMM with the focus on emerging economies. Therefore, SMM will firstly be elaborated on a global level and afterwards successful examples specific for Croatia, a very good representative of European emerging economy, will be given.

BACKGROUND

In today's world, Social Network Services (SNS) have a global impact on a modern society. To set a scene, we will explain the factors that preceded the advent of a Web 2.0 and give details on how social networking became the most popular Web 2.0 service.

The Emergence of Web 2.0

The Internet emerged in the early 1970s, as a small network interconnecting just a few computers. As the Internet grew through the 1970s and 1980s, many people started to realize its potential. Nevertheless, the Internet did not experience real proliferation until the invention of the World Wide Web (WWW or simply Web 1.0), a service based on a client-server architecture and provisioned through the Internet infrastructure (Berners-Lee & Fischetti, 1999). Web 1.0, as an information medium that has enabled users to read and search interrelated information using computers connected to the Internet, has become the catalyst of the digital revolution in the 1990s and a global service that has touched almost every aspect of people's lives (Podobnik, Petric, Trzec, & Jezic, 2009).

Geared by technological (i.e., new trends in information and communication sector), societal (i.e., new lifestyle) and economic (i.e., new business and market trends) changes (Yoon, 2007) in the early 2000s, a Web 2.0 emerged. The Web 2.0, also known as the "Social Web," did not only allow the connection of information, but also linking people in the ad-hoc groups that can be assembled and disassembled according to the current need (Raman, 2009). While the focus of the Web 1.0 was *information*, in the Web 2.0 it is a *user*. Furthermore, the communication paradigm has also changed—the *client-server* architecture has been replaced by *peer network* nodes, where the same entity at the same time can produce and consume information (*prosumer* = producer + consumer) (Medman, 2006). The most significant implementations of Web 2.0 concept are wikis (e.g., Wikipedia, http://www.wikipedia.org), blogs (e.g., Mashable!, http://www.mashable.com), and social networks (e.g., Facebook, http://www.facebook.com).

The Global Proliferation of a Social Networking Phenomenon

Generally, a *network* can be defined as a set of nodes interconnected via links. Networks are built with a purpose of exchange and they can have various topologies. A *social network* is the specific implementation of a general network concept—the social network can be defined as a set of actors interconnected via relationships. Actors could be various—people, organizations, brands, etc. (Reid & Gray, 2007). Relationships could be various as well—acquaintance, familiar bond, dislike, etc. However, a notion of *common interest* is glue that always connects actors involved in a certain social network (Adamic & Adar, 2003). Social networks are based on *actor profiles* (Nosko, Wood, & Molema, 2010), while the creating principle could be twofold—*explicit* or *implicit*. In explicit social networks all connections between actors are direct result of intentional action of those actors, i.e., every social network user must initiate the connection with another user for them two to connect. Each user of the social network, therefore, consciously connects. Social relationships established by popular SNSs, such as Facebook, Twitter (http://twitter.com), and Foursquare (http://foursquare.com) are all based on *ego social networks*—every user is building his/her own social network by explicitly defining connections with other people. On the other hand, in an implicit social network (Yang, Zhou, Mao, Li, & Liu, 2010; Podobnik & Lovrek, 2010, 2011) all connections between users are result of a "third party" reasoning over user profiles. Mechanisms employed by the "third party" for the construction of the social network can be diverse, but have to be based on a calculation of users' profile similarity (Podobnik, Galetic, Trzec, & Jezic, 2010).

Social networks are well-developed area of study in social sciences, with a history longer than 50 years (Bojic, Lipic, & Podobnik, 2012). Everything has begun in 1960s with the Brown's identification of "a need for understanding complexities of collective human behavior at a level that is more objective and more scientific than the approach of psychology and sociology to the same problem" (Brown, 1965) and the Milgram's "small world experiment" which demonstrated the idea of "six degrees of separation" (Milgram, 1967; Travers & Milgram, 1969). However, it was not until the beginning of 2000s when social networks experienced a proliferation grounded on an advent of ICT-enabled (*Information and Communication Technology*) SNSs. This was a huge shift for people, who now became able to interconnect at a global scale in just few second and with just few mouse-clicks. Implementation of SNSs based on ICT infrastructure not only allowed people to map their social relationships from the real world to a virtual one, but also to build virtual communities with other people that share the same interests/activities. This is achieved through creating (semi-)public user profiles and defining a list of other user profiles (i.e., people) with whom they are associated. Although SNSs (Boyd & Ellison, 2007; Westland, 2010) less a decade ago represented only a drop in the sea of Web pages with different themes and purposes, today they are not only the most popular services based on ICT infrastructure, but also a truly global phenomenon which greatly affects the modern way of life.

In period between 2002 and 2006 a myriad of SNSs appeared on the scene, some of which have grown in the most popular SNSs—first started Friendster (http://www.friendster.com) (Rivlin, 2006), then MySpace (http://www.myspace.com) (Gillette, 2011) and LinkedIn (http://www.linkedin.com), followed by Facebook (Wan, Kumar, & Bukhari, 2008; Lampe, Ellison, & Steinfield, 2008) and Twitter (Kwak, Lee, Park, & Moon, 2010; Zeichick, 2009). Additionally, it is worth mentioning Gowalla (http://gowalla.com) and Foursquare, two location-based SNSs that were launched in 2007 and 2009, respectively. In mid-2011 Google launched its (latest, hopefully first successful) SNS called Google+ (http://plus.google.com). Google+ attracted 10 million users just 16 days after it has been launched (for comparison, Twitter needed 780 and Facebook needed 852 days to reach a user base of 10 million) (Butcher, 2011), 40 million users in four months time (Wasserman, 2011) and 170 million users in ten months time (Wasserman, 2012a). Although not yet an important SMM player, in mid-2012 Google acquired social media management platform Wildfire

(Indvik, 2012) what confirms that Google will be the next giant in the fight for its share of the fast-growing SMM market (Gartner predicts that SMM will with $8.8 million be the largest contributor to overall social media revenue projected to total $16.9 billion in 2012 [Gartner, 2012] while the social media revenue worldwide is expected to reach $34 billion by 2016 [Gupta, 2012]).

The first SNS which gathered over 100 million users was MySpace, which accomplished that in three years time (2003-2006). Meanwhile, in 2004, Facebook was founded (Facebook, 2012a) and started to develop very fast, becoming a threat to MySpace. Facebook grew to 100 million users in the year 2008, when it also overtook MySpace in the number of unique visitors (Mack, 2008). Since then, MySpace has been progressively losing its importance (in 2011 it had 30 million of users) while Facebook became the most important SNS with more than 950 million monthly active users (Facebook, 2012a) in mid-2012, thus reaching 42% of global Internet users (Internet World Stats, 2012). Facebook is currently not available in China so these numbers are even more impressive. Almost 60% of monthly active users (i.e., 550 million) use Facebook on a daily basis. Average user spends more than 50 minutes every day on Facebook, while Facebook gets more than 1 trillion page views every month. Facebook's additional strength is a huge mobile user base—in 2012 there are more than 550 million users which connect to Facebook through their mobile devices. In the 2010, although the real effects of Facebook's advent were yet to be seen, Mark Zuckerberg, Facebook's co-founder and CEO, was named TIME's 2010 Person of the Year (Grossman, 2010): "For connecting more than half a billion people and mapping the social relations among them, for creating a new system of exchanging information and for changing how we live our lives."

Other important SNS, Twitter, was founded in 2006 and has achieved 500 million registered users in mid-2012 (Semiocast, 2012). However, only 140 million users are active (i.e., they use Twitter at least once per a month) (Taylor, 2012). Twitter measures a popularity of a certain news in terms of Tweets Per Second (TPS). The TPS record is updated every few months, usually by events, which involve sports, entertainment, or Japan. The number one simultaneously tweeted event, by far, is the broadcast of the movie "Castle in the Sky" in Japan in December 2011. During one point in the TV broadcast, viewers joined forces sending tweets at the same time to symbolically help the movie's characters cast a spell. They sent 25,088 TPS (Hernandez, 2012). Castle in the Sky dethroned Beyonce's MTV Video Music Awards pregnancy disclosure followed by 8,868 TPS in August 2011 (Rao, 2011). However, the Beyonce MTV moment is currently only number six on the TPS list, having fallen behind four sports-related events. First, 80-yard touchdown pass by quarterback Tim Tebow in American football game overtime (Pittsburgh Steelers vs. Denver Broncos) in January 2012 resulted with 9,420 TPS and pushed Beyonce down the list. Afterwards, in February 2012 two Super Bowl moments took over the number two and three slots: Twitter reaction reached 12,233 TPS at the end of the game and 10,245 TPS during Madonna's halftime performance (for comparison, most-tweeted moment at the Super Bowl 2011 in February 2011 hit 4,064 TPS [Indvik, 2011]). Finally, in July 2012 most-tweeted moment at the European Football Championship 2012 Finals hit 15,538 TPS and took over the number two slot after Spain scored the second goal against Italy (Haberman, 2012). In terms of interesting past record events, the final game of the FIFA Women's World Cup in July 2011, between USA and Japan, had 7,196 TPS at the end of the game (Banks, 2011a) (the Women's World Cup Finals also far outpaces the Men's World Cup 2010's most-tweeted match—3,283 tweets were sent per second when Japan beat Denmark in June 2010 [Van Grove, 2011]). Furthermore, hard news such as word of Troy Davis' execution in September 2011 (7,671 TPS) and Steve Jobs' resignation in August 2011 (7,064 TPS) (Twitter, 2011), as well as Bin Laden's death in May 2011 (5,106 TPS) (Sutter, 2011; Larson, 2011) drew a significant peak. Finally, New Years Eve 2011 in Japan hit 6,939 TPS at its peak (Banks, 2011b), while on the day of the Japanese earthquake and Tsunami in March 2011 the Twitter usage reached 5,530 TPS (Taylor, 2011).

Third important SNS, Foursquare, was founded in 2009 and had achieved user base growth of 3400% in 2010 (Foursquare, 2011). In mid-2012, Foursquare has more than 20 million users and is still growing vehemently (Foursquare, 2012a). Foursquare is location-based SNS and as such exclusively aims at mobile users.

How Social Networking Became the Most Popular Web 2.0 Service

In 2010, social networking consumed up twice as much of our online time as any other activity (Ostrow, 2010). According to statistical data, SNSs accounted for 23% of time spent on the Web (43% rise from mid-2009 to mid-2010), while the next closest activity was online gaming, which made up 10% (10% rise from mid-2009 to mid-2010). The data also shows the degree to which social networking displaced other forms of communication, with e-mail as a percentage of online time dropping from 12% to 8% from mid-2009 to mid-2010. Instant messaging also saw a significant plunge in share, dropping from 5% to 4% from mid-2009 to mid-2010.

The pace with which new users have herded to SNSs has been amazing—SNS user penetration grew from only 8% of online adults in 2005 to 65% in 2011. Additionally, it is important to note that although SNSs are the most popular within young adults under age 30 (i.e., 83% of young Internet users are members of at least one social network), adults aged 65+ have seen the fastest rates of growth in recent years (Madden & Zickuhr, 2011). Only email and search engines are used more frequently than social networking tools (Purcell, 2011).

During the first decade of 21st century millions of people joined online communities and started using online social platforms, what led towards 1.5 billion members of social networks globally in 2012 (Chui, et al., 2012).

Social Networking in Croatia

Facebook has a little more than 1.5 million users from Croatia in mid-2012, what ranks Croatia 69 out of 213 countries listed (Socialbakers, 2012c). The growth rate of Croatian Facebook users in the first half of 2012 is only 1.5% what means that the period of rapid growth that started in 2007 is over now. The largest age group is 18-24 (31% of all Croatian users), followed by the users in the age of 25-34 (28% of all Croatian users). Distribution by gender is balanced—there are 51% male users and 49% female users in Croatia. Facebook is by far the most proliferated SNS in Croatia, with penetration of 34% compared to the country's population and 68% in relation to number of Internet users.

LinkedIn, business-related SNS, is the second most popular SNS in Croatia, gathering 180 thousand users in mid-2012, what ranks Croatia 46 out of 50 countries listed (Socialbakers, 2011d). However, the growth rate of Croatian LinkedIn users in the first half of 2012 is around 20% and the ratio *LinkedIn users* vs. *Facebook users* is roughly 1:8 (compared to average ratio of 1:3 among top-three countries with most LinkedIn users—USA, India, and UK), what means there is a lot of space for LinkedIn users' growth in Croatia. Twitter, Foursquare and Google+ attracted just several thousand active users in Croatia.

SOCIAL MEDIA MARKETING

Traditional marketing channels (Figure 1) include *radio and television, publications* such as *newspapers, magazines,* and *journals, telephones, postal mail, billboards,* and *face-to-face* message transfer. The main limitations of traditional marketing message channels are:

- **Non-Personalization:** i.e., all consumers are communicated with the same message promoting a certain product/service;
- **Untraceable (Local) Access to Users:** i.e., a marketing campaign usually reaches only local consumers; however businesses cannot know how many consumers really received their marketing messages because traditional marketing channels are unidirectional and non-interactive;

Figure 1. Traditional marketing channels

- **Infeasibility of Marketing Campaign Tracking:** i.e., tracking of marketing campaigns is not possible what makes very difficult to measure *Return-on-Investment* (ROI) for marketing campaigns.

Internet marketing (often referred as *online marketing* or *iMarketing*) is defined as a product/service promotion over the Internet infrastructure (Figure 2). Although other Internet services besides WWW can be utilized for Internet marketing (e.g., sending promotions via e-mail messages), the advent of Web 1.0 revolutionized not just Internet but Internet marketing as well.

Figure 2. Internet marketing channels

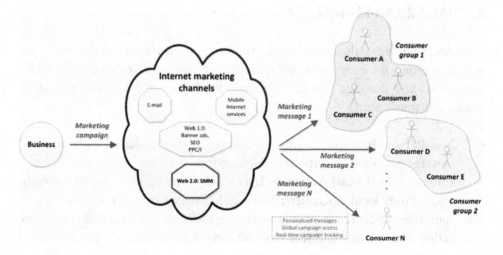

The Web 1.0 era enabled development of two Internet marketing paradigms (Jayamaha, 2011). The first paradigm, *Search Engine Optimization* (SEO) (Malaga, 2010), provides techniques to improve the visibility of a website in search engines via the unpaid (i.e., "organic" or "algorithmic") search results. The second paradigm, *Pay-Per-Click/Impression* (PPC/I) (Chen, Feng, & Whinston, 2010; Feng, Bhargava, & Pennock, 2007), enables websites to bid for advertising slots in the paid areas of search engines or affiliate sites. In the PPI model, which was used for marketing through traditional marketing channels as well, the advertiser is charged every time his/her ad is displayed. On the other hand, when PPC model is employed, advertiser pays only when a potential consumer clicks on his/her ad.

Internet marketing is one among many areas affected by an advent of the Web 2.0 paradigm. Web 2.0 enabled global proliferation of a social networking, which again is a foundation for Social Media Marketing. *Social Media Marketing* (SMM) represents a novel Internet marketing paradigm based on spreading brand-related messages directly from one user to another. This is the reasons why SMM is often referred as viral marketing as well.

Internet marketing, as a new tool in marketers' arsenal, has a number of advantages when compared to traditional marketing methods:

- **Inherent Personalization:** i.e., consumers often have their online profiles, what is especially true in Web 2.0 era where consumers posses very rich social network profiles (Nosko, Wood, & Molema, 2010);
- **Low-Cost Global Access to Consumers:** i.e., the ratio of total marketing campaign cost and number of reached users;
- **Simple, Cheap and Real-Time Tracking of Marketing Campaigns:** i.e., measurement of electronic actions such as ad clicks; or monitoring electronic traces such as identifying a location of the consumer who has clicked on the ad based on his/her IP (Internet Protocol) address.

However, Internet marketing is not a silver bullet solution for marketers and it has a number of limitations when compared to the traditional marketing methods as well:

- **Inability of Consumers to "Try Out" Tangible Product/Service before Buying:** e.g., "what is the actual scent of that new Chanel fragrance?" or "which size of this new Boss suit fits me best?";
- **Privacy Concerns:** e.g., "will someone exploit my personal information contained in my purchasing history from Amazon?";
- **Security Issues:** There are quite chances for fake deals which may end up with no product/service transaction (e.g., "will I actually get that camera I bought on eBay?") (Roca, Garcia, & Vega, 2009).

Table 1. A comparison of traditional and Internet marketing

	Traditional marketing	Internet marketing
Personalization of campaign messages	no	yes
Consumers can be clustered in groups with similar characteristics	no	yes
Consumer access	local	global, low-cost
Campaign tracking	not possible	simple, cheap and real-time tracking
Campaign interactivity	messages are unidirectional (i.e., from businesses towards consumers) and thus interactivity is not possible	messages can be two-directional and thus interactivity is possible
Users can "try out" products/services prior to buying	sometimes yes, sometimes not (it depends on the specific traditional marketing channel)	usually not (although some ICT services can be "tried out" during a trial period)
Consumer privacy	high	possibility for exploit of consumer personal information
Post-marketing transaction security	high	possibility for fake deals

Table 1 summarizes a comparison of presented differences between traditional and Internet marketing practices.

Social Media Marketing Based on Major Social Networking Services

We have already described a tremendous proliferation of SNSs during the last decade. Not just the flagship SNS service, Facebook, has been growing rapidly (Facebook, 2012b), but also new and innovative specialized SNSs, such as Foursquare, keep the pace. Simultaneously, brands search for media through which they can reach their consumers to communicate their messages with the lowest possible cost and the highest possible efficiency. As SNSs have been attracting more and more users, they became logical choice for a novel marketing medium. Few years ago, only brave and innovative brands had chosen SNSs for their marketing campaigns. Nevertheless, most of them achieved great results whereas now almost every larger brand has its own social media campaign.

Firstly, we will explain the possibilities of SMM through presenting social marketing strategies for three leading SNSs—Facebook, Twitter, and Foursquare. Afterwards, we will give an overview of Social Media Marketing in Croatia, with focus on two social media projects—Socialnumbers and Mediatoolkit.

The most important characteristic of social media is a social graph—a network of interconnected user profiles. Every user has its own profile and connects with other users, becomes a friend on Facebook and Foursquare or follows other users on Twitter. Additionally, apart from personal connections with friends and acquaintances, users connect with brands they interact in real life as well. For example, if one reads the New York Times, he/she connects with the profile of the New York Times on a certain social network to follow its updates. Furthermore, if a user is buying in the Walmart, he/she should be connected with the Walmart Facebook page and Twitter profile or if one drinks coffee in the Starbucks, he/she should be connected to Starbucks on Facebook, Twitter, and other SNSs as well. However, every SNS has it own differences from the SMM perspective. These differences will be elaborated further below.

Facebook

The most important element of brand promotion on the Facebook is that brand's Facebook page. Currently (i.e., year 2012) there exist two types of Facebook brand pages (Facebook, 2012c): *traditional Facebook brand page* and *new timeline-based Facebook brand page*.

Traditional Facebook brand pages (Figure 3) are usually organized in tabs, where every tab is much alike regular Web page (e.g., tab can contain pictures, videos or flash content). Tabs on Facebook pages can even integrate complex applications like e-commerce. Figure 3 shows an example of the Facebook page for a Croatian brand *Iskon* with the basic textual information tab selected (i.e., *Hot spot* tab).

Timeline-based Facebook brand pages (Figure 4) were introduced in late 2011 and they upgrade traditional Facebook brand pages with temporal dimension. Consequently, brand followers can browse for most important events in brand history (i.e., one can learn from Figure 4 that Croatian brand *Konzum* was founded before 1970 [see *timeline browser*], while more detailed brand messages are available by scrolling through the *timeline* part of the page). Furthermore, one can note that the brand Konzum currently has 132 thousand followers (i.e., see *application browser*) and that currently brand Konzum (i.e., one of sponsors of the Croatian team at London Olympic games) wishes good luck to Croatian athletes who participate in London Olympic games (i.e., see *brand cover*). Figure 4 shows how redesigned Facebook timeline-based brands pages serve as very convenient interactive channel for communicating both static brand info such as *brand main information, brand logo, brand contact,* and *brand history data,* as well as dynamic brand info such as *current marketing campaigns* (i.e., timeline status update in Figure 4—the announcement of Konzum

Figure 3. An example of the Facebook page for the Croatian brand "Iskon"

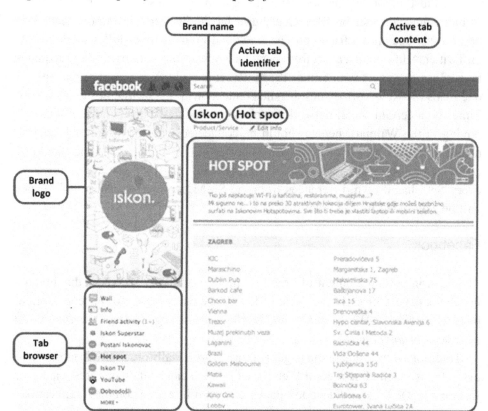

yacht sailing contest winners) or *current social responsibility activities* (i.e., cover photo in Figure 4—sponsorship of the Croatian team at London Olympic games).

A Facebook user can *like* certain brand's Facebook page and by doing so, he/she *follows* that brand. Administrators of Facebook pages have capability to post updates. These updates are then not visible just on the Facebook page of the brand whose page they administer, but can as well be visible on Facebook Walls of Facebook users connected to that brand. Update can be in form of short text, image, image gallery, question video, etc. Figure 5 presents example of a status update from the Facebook page of the *Museum of Modren Art (MoMA)*. Posting an update represents pushing a message to that brand's consumers. Now, it is no longer necessary for users to visit brand Web pages or portals to find news and other information connected with the brand they like, but information comes to consumers in the real-time. Such push-based CRM (*Customer Relationship Management*) enables consumers to find new information more quickly and in shorter time.

Figure 4. An example of the Facebook timeline page for the Croatian brand "Konzum"

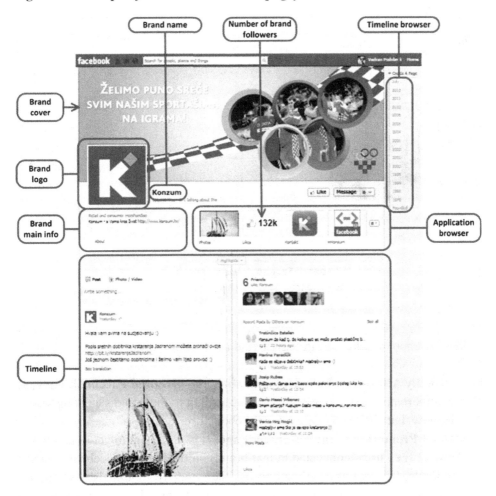

On the Facebook, there are a lot of status updates every minute and usually a user does not have time to read them all. To tackle that issue, Facebook introduced *EdgeRank* mechanism (Taylor, 2011; Walter, 2011). The EdgeRank is an index, which evaluates quality of every posted update on Facebook pages. Its purpose is to estimate which content to push to users and which content not to push. The EdgeRank considers that certain content is of high quality if content gets a lot of user interaction and feedback. This is the reason why it is important for brands to constantly improve Facebook interaction with their consumers, ask them questions, talk with them, etc. The EdgeRank is crucial for a success of social marketing on Facebook because it prevents spamming, which is the biggest challenge of every push-based CRM system.

Figure 5. An example of a status update on the Facebook page of the "Museum of Modern Art (MoMA)"

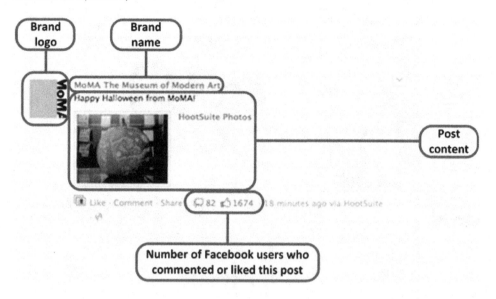

The Facebook marketing strategy should achieve the following:

1. **Visually Attractive, Easy-Recognizable, and Original Facebook Page:** It is important to make Facebook page according to the brand's existing visual identity, but with rich content for Facebook users;
2. **Good Promotion of the Facebook Page:** It is important to get as much followers (i.e., users connected to that brand) on the brand's Facebook page as possible. It is not same if a brand has thousand, 10 thousands or even 100 thousands followers. Larger user base enables the brand to communicate with a broader audience;
3. **Communication with Followers:** It is very important to communicate with brand followers in appropriate way. It is also important to achieve a lot of interaction and feedback from users because of the EdgeRank mechanism.

If these guidelines, which are generated from advices of experts that envisioned and managed hundreds of Croatian SMM campaigns, are followed, brands should get a large consumer audience to communicate with as well as an almost-free channel to broadcast its massages.

Apart from Facebook brands pages, branded Facebook applications, dynamic social applications on the Facebook platform, are also used to promote brand messages. Most common examples of branded Facebook applications are sweepstakes

Figure 6. An example of a branded Facebook application for a promotion of an insurance company

and contests where Facebook users play games with their Facebook friends with goal of getting a prize. Figure 6 shows an example of Facebook application where user has to park his/her car. Other cars on parking lot are his/her friends' cars and if he/she crashes one of those cars, friend who owns that car gets a message and virtual money to repair damage (from an insurance company). This witty branded Facebook application is used for a promotion of an insurance company in a very innovative manner.

Facebook ads (Facebook, 2012d) are the third most important promotion channel on the Facebook. Advertisements appear in the right-hand column of a Facebook page, as shown in Figure 7 on the example of the Facebook page of Mark Zuckerberg, the Facebook's founder.

Facebook ads can target users based on user profile information like:

- **Gender:** e.g., fragrance ad targets only female users;
- **Age:** e.g., clothes ad targets only teenagers;

Figure 7. Facebook ads are located in the right-hand column of a Facebook page

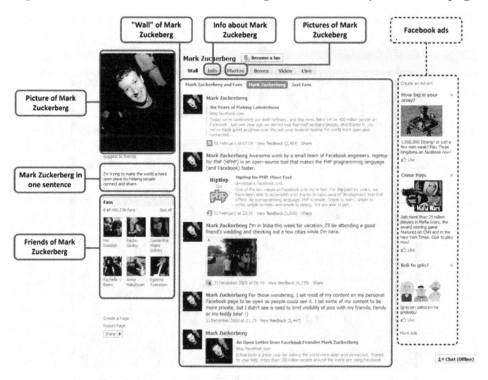

- **Location:** e.g., event ad targets only users currently located in Zagreb;
- **Interests:** e.g., concert ad targets only users which liked Facebook page of a band which performs on that concert;
- **Relationship Status:** e.g., divorce lawyer ad targets only married users.

Let us assume one more real-world situation—if a Croatian photographer wants to sell service of a wedding photography he/she can create Facebook ad, which will target engaged users located in Croatia and having between 25 to 35 years.

Facebook ads are charged for:

- The number of clicks the ad receives (i.e., Cost Per Click, CPC); or
- The number of impressions (i.e., views) of the ad (i.e., cost per thousand impressions, CPM).

The total amount that advertiser is charged will never exceed advertiser's daily or lifetime budget. Facebook selects the best ad to show based on the combination of the CPC or CPM and ad performance (the higher CPC/CPM value leads to the higher probability of ad display, assuming the ad performance is fixed). All Facebook ads compete with each other to show for each impression, regardless of their bid model (Facebook, 2012e). The minimum CPC is set to $0.01 and the minimum CPM is set to $0.02. The average CPC and CPM values depend on a country (the list with average CPC/CPM values is provided by Socialbakers (2012a)—e.g., in Croatia in mid-2012, the average CPC is $0.14 and the average CPM is $0.02, placing Croatia 170 out of 213 countries, what makes Facebook ads very cheap marketing medium in Croatia when compared to other countries). Russia is topping the list in mid-2012 with the average CPC of $1.55 and the average CPM of $0.22.

Facebook provided their guidelines for profiling brands on Facebook (Facebook, 2012f), as well as examples of success stories (Facebook, 2012g, 2012h).

Twitter

Twitter, SNS based on micro-blogging, offers brands to open their Twitter profiles (Twitter, 2012), which are similar to Facebook pages. Twitter profile can be branded via customisable background, as shown in Figure 8 on the example of McDonald's (i.e., one of the most valuable global brands) Twitter profile.

An administrator can post tweets (similar to status updates on a Facebook brand page). Tweets are short textual messages up to 140 characters. Every user can reply to tweets coming from a certain brand—in such a manner two-way communication is accomplished, as well as feedback to brand tweets is given.

Figure 8. An example of a Twitter brand profile for a top global brand "McDonald's"

The list of most popular Twitter brands (Socialbakers, 2012e) reveals that there are about 25 global brands with more than 1 million followers in mid-2012 (on the top of the list is the Brazilian brand *Claro Ronaldo* with 3.5 million followers). However, celebrities' profiles are much more popular on Twitter than brand profiles—the mid-2012 leader is the singer *Lady Gaga* with 28 million followers (Socialbakers, 2012f) and the most popular brand Claro Ronaldo is ranked 163. This shows there is a lot of potential for brands in using Twitter as their SMM channel, but they have to become more innovative to attract a larger base of followers.

Foursquare

Foursquare is a location based SNS with more than 1 million brands using it as a SMM channel (Foursquare, 2012b). The most important difference of this social network from Facebook and Twitter is that users do not exchange status updates and tweets about what are they doing and thinking, but they exchange information about their current location by checking into places. For example, if a user goes to a concert in the Sydney Opera, he/she checks in there and his/her Foursquare friends will know where he/she is. This is the reason why Foursquare offers different ways for brand marketing when compared to Facebook and Twitter.

The first Foursquare-based marketing mechanism, named *Foursquare Venues* (Foursquare, 2012b), targets brands with physical location (e.g., restaurants, cafes, hotels, stores). The Foursquare Venue represents a place where users can check in and get some reward for that action (this reward is referred to as the *Special*). There are various types of Specials, but the most popular are:

- **A Discount with Purchase:** e.g., when you check in a clothes store, you get $20 off for every $100 spent;
- **Something for Free:** e.g., when you check in a supermarket, you get a bag of chips for free if you buy a pack of beer;
- **Special Treatment:** e.g., when you check in a student canteen, you get access to the fast track service;
- **Reward for Loyal Customers:** e.g., when you check in the restaurant on your fifth visit, you get free drink.

Foursquare Venue mechanism provides a great promotion possibility for a brand because all of the user's Foursquare friends see that user's check ins. An example of a Foursquare Venue (i.e., check in at iSTUDIO's location) is shown in Figure 9(a), while one Foursquare Special (i.e., a $1.00 discount on best-selling CDs at Barnes & Noble) is presented in Figure 9(b).

Figure 9. (a) An example of a Foursquare Venue; (b) an example of a Foursquare Special

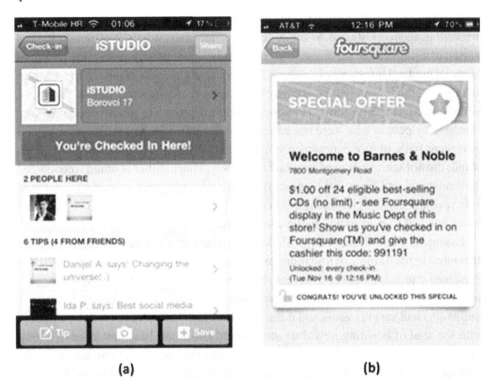

(a)   (b)

The second Foursquare-based marketing mechanism, named *Foursquare Brands* (Foursquare, 2012b), primarily targets brands without physical location (e.g., Coca Cola), but it can be used by brands with physical location as well. On Foursquare, users can connect with their friends but also with brands. Furthermore, brands can leave comments and suggestions (called tips) on various locations and users will get those comments when they check in at targeted locations. For example, the Iceland Tourist Board left entertaining (but also educational) comments on all popular tourist locations (This is Iceland, 2011). Consequently, when a tourist checks in at one of Iceland's airports he/she gets the following comment: *"This is an airport where most of my visitors land when they visit me in flying machines (Don't worry, it does not hurt when they land.). It is close to my Blue Lagoon, where many humans like to swim."*

Foursquare provided their guidelines for profiling brands on Foursquare (Foursquare, 2012c), as well as examples of success stories (Foursquare, 2012d).

Social Media Marketing in Croatia

Croatia follows global trends when referring to social media marketing. In 2009, marketing agencies started to apprehend the importance of social networks and started offering related services. In 2010, brands also started to realise the potential of social media. Unfortunately, during 2010 most of Croatian brands tried to implement social media campaigns on their own because of the perception of Facebook as a free-of-charge platform. However, as campaigns were mainly designed and managed by people who were not educated in the area of social media strategy and who were without any experience in implementation of social media campaigns, brands did not achieve desired results. Fortunately, a big number of brands recognized their mistake, and from 2011, most of Croatian brands have started to cooperate with specialized agencies, resulting in achieving a significant progress and gaining better level of ROI in social media campaigns.

Examples of four successful SMM campaigns in Croatia and the region are presented in the Table 2, while more examples are available via (iSTUDIO, 2012). Presented campaigns cover different industry sectors, ranging from health/beauty and media/news/publishing to food/beverages and telecom companies. Moreover, campaigns had various goals and durations (ranging from a short 15-day campaign with the goal of boosting new drug store brand consumer base and sales to a long half-year campaign with the goal of strengthening regional brand reputation for the leading water brand in Croatia). However, despite all differences among described campaigns they all resulted with great brand effects, what again confirms SMM as a very efficient marketing tool.

Socialnumbers

Socialnumbers (http://socialnumbers.com) is a portal offering rich statistical information about Facebook pages. It was launched in 2011 and first provided statistics only for Croatia and the neighboring countries. However, following initial success it rapidly proliferated across all relevant SMM markets and in mid-2012 Socialnumbers provide statistics for all European countries as well as 50 major countries outside the Europe. Information provided by Socialnumbers could be of interest to brand and community managers, marketing agencies, journalists, bloggers, academics, and all others interested in Facebook marketing. Socialnumbers gives an insight into:

- Ranked lists of Facebook brand pages by size and by quality;
- Specific graphs for every Facebook brand page showing trends regarding the number of followers, frequency of interactions and distribution of status updates;

Table 2. Examples of successful SMM campaigns in Croatia and the region

	Croatian brand "Bipa" (health/beauty)	Croatian brand "24sata" (media/news/ publishing)	Croatian brand "Jana" (food/beverages)	Croatian brand "Iskon" (telecom)
Facebook brands page link	http://www.facebook. com/bipa.hrvatska	http://www.facebook. com/ 24sata	http://www.face-book.com/ jana.water	http://www.facebook. com/ iskoninternet
Pre-campaign state	BIPA is a new drug store on a market, not so well known among wide audience. The competition is already stable and holds big percentage of the market.	24sata is a well-known media brand that wants to connect to people on a more personal level and get ahead of their competition.	Jana is the leading water brand in Croatia, known for its premium quality. After almost a decade of building the brand image and becoming recognized outside of Croatia Jana wants to conquer a larger number of markets.	Iskon is a broadband telecom company, in a market with a strong competition. Iskon's differentiation strategy is to be ahead of competition in innovation and creative marketing.
SMM campaign goals	• Have a memorable launch campaign • Gain large number of new followers to start building an engaged online community • Raise BIPA brand awareness • Raise sales	• Create a fun experience for April fool's day • Increase visits to the Web portal 24sata.hr • Connect people to the 24sata brand on a more personal level • Gain new Facebook followers	• Create a unique communication for every market where Jana is present • Increase the number of followers in selected countries • Increase brand awareness and strengthen brand reputation in every country	• Build a broader community on Facebook • Engage followers • Promotion of services
SMM campaign activities	• A welcome tab, that has communicated a special coupon with a 15% discount on the whole purchase for BIPA Facebook followers only, has been designed and implemented • Ads campaign was running along communicating the same message • High-level community management (answer every fan on every question) was set up from the start	• The application gave 24sata Facebook brand followers an option of generating funny articles about their friends – once brand followers generated a personal article about their friend they were offered to share it on their friend's Facebook wall, while the person who got the article opened it directly on 24sata.hr portal • The application was updated with new article templates after the initial campaign and still remains active while followers base grows	• Facebook communication becomes targeted by country: Croatia, Hungary, Slovenia, Serbia and others • A local social media agency is hired for community management in each country in the region • Special offers and activities are created for each country in the region: give-aways, ads, apps, tabs	• A special offer tab was created that enables Iskon Facebook followers to apply for Iskon services and receive a special 50% discount • Memory Application was created, a game in which players need to find matching pictures of Iskon's campaign characters and collect points; they can also challenge other players and collect game badges • Ads promoting the special offer for followers and the Memory contest were running simultaneously

continued on following page

Table 2. Continued

	Croatian brand "Bipa" (health/beauty)	Croatian brand "24sata" (media/news/ publishing)	Croatian brand "Jana" (food/beverages)	Croatian brand "Iskon" (telecom)
SMM campaign duration	15 days	30 days	6 months	45 days
SMM campaign results	• Many of the BIPA Facebook followers had their first buying experience with BIPA thanks to the campaign • 18,945 new followers • 11,000+ coupons downloaded • 150% bigger purchase per customer than average	• 17,000 new followers • Jump by one position up on the list of the most visited websites in Croatia • 34,998 users of funny articles application • 44,174 funny articles generated • Average feedback per shared funny article resulted in 114 actions (likes, comments, …)	• Targeted communication active in 5 regional countries • The number of followers increased up to 600% in each of the targeted countries • Interaction on the Jana Facebook brands page has increased by 300% compared to the previous, untargeted communication period	• 17,819 new followers • 1,578 clicks on the special offer tab • 6,741 players of the Memory application • 48,944 Memory games played • Every user spent 56 minutes on average playing Memory game

- Ranked list of the top status updates from Facebook brand pages;
- Ranked list of the top social media agencies;
- Ranked list of the most shared websites.

According to Socialnumbers, there have been almost 2,000 official Facebook pages in Croatia in mid-2012, what makes SMM very developed in Croatia when comparing with situation in the region (Austria [1,000 brands pages], Bosnia and Herzegovina [600 brands pages], Hungary [450 brands pages], Italy [700 brands pages], Montenegro [200 brands pages], Macedonia [650 brands pages], Serbia [110 brands pages], and Slovenia [1,700 brands pages]). The list of top ten most popular Facebook pages in Croatia in mid-2012 is the following:

1. **"Love Croatia, Croatian National Tourist board" (Travel/Leisure):** 775,000 followers;
2. **"24sata" (Media/News/Publishing):** 475,000 followers;
3. **"Put oko svijeta" (Travel/Leisure):** 395,000 followers;

4. **"Ok je OK!" (Media/News/Publishing):** 375,000 followers;
5. **"Index" (Media/News/Publishing):** 350,000 followers;
6. "Severina Vuckovic" (Musician/Band): 275,000 followers;
7. **"Vicevi" (Fun):** 250,000 followers;
8. **"Tportal Hr" (Media/News/Publishing):** 245,000 followers;
9. **"Jutarnji" (Media/News/Publishing):** 200,000 followers;
10. **"Dnevnik.hr" (Media/News/Publishing):** 195,000 followers.

Socialnumbers is the project run in cooperation of partners from different countries in order to offer opulent statistical information for each individual regional SMM market. The goal of Socialnumbers is not only to provide the statistics and business intelligence in community management but also to outline the best agencies and best cases in the area of social media. Figure 10 depicts a screenshot of the Socialnumbers website presenting graph for Facebook brand page of the Croatian retail and consumer merchandise brand Konzum showing trends regarding the number of Konzum's followers (please see Figure 4 for detailed explanation of the Konzum brand Facebook page).

Mediatoolkit

Mediatoolkit (http://mediatoolkit.com) (Youtube, 2012) is a Web service developed in Croatia that enables a real-time discovery, on a global scale, of the most popular and shared content originating from any website the user is interested in. Additionally,

Figure 10. A screenshot of the Socialnumbers website for the Croatian brand "Konzum"

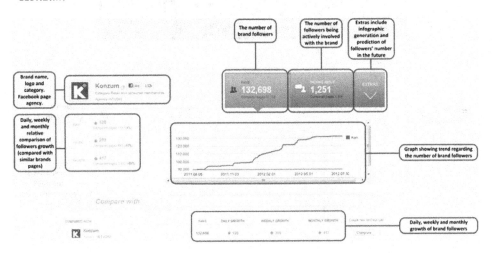

Mediatoolkit predicts which content will be popular in the near future. It is a fact that SNSs like Facebook, Twitter, LinkedIn, and others influence the consumption of news on the Web. What is being shared is being read, thus generating more and more traffic to websites that have share-friendly content. This is why there is a great need to know which content users will share with their friends.

When using Mediatoolkit, all a user has to do is to enter websites he/she is interested in (i.e., the user can enter any website, his/her own or the one that belongs to his/her competition). Next, Mediatoolkit analyzes each website and articles published on these sites to see how much users have shared observed articles on SNSs. Finally, as a result the user gets a list of the most shared (i.e., most popular) articles in real time.

During its calculations, Mediatoolkit pays a special attention to factors like total number of content shares. However, what is even more important for the final result are the rate of share growth and the time passed since the article has been published. Mediatoolkit analyzes these factors and uses the proprietary mathematical algorithms to rank each article. Once the system gathers all of described data, it can use mathematical algorithms again to identify growth patterns for each of websites. Now, using these recognized growth patterns, we can predict the popularity of each new article in the early stage after it has been published. Usually, it takes no longer than 10 minutes from the moment new article is published to identify how popular this article will be (see Figure 11).

Figure 11. A screenshot of the Mediatoolkit website

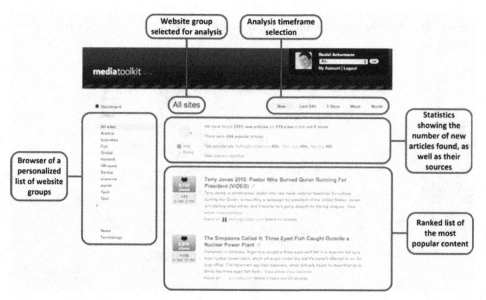

FUTURE RESEARCH DIRECTIONS

The Internet and SNSs are developing faster than ever. Every day we are witnesses of new social startups and innovative social services. We cannot even probably begin to imagine the possibilities that will be available in just five years from now. However, we can be sure that the evolution of SNSs in Croatia will follow the global trends. Currently, Facebook is the strongest SNS on the global level, as well as in Croatia. Facebook does not have only by far the largest user base, but also the most diverse demographics among SNSs in Croatia. These are the reasons, which make it hard to believe that Facebook will have real competitors in the next few years. It will remain the largest Croatian SNS and its user graph will be integrated in various kinds of applications. However, it will be interesting to follow the evolution of the latest Google's attempt in the SNS area—Google+, especially now after Google acquired social media management platform Wildfire in mid-2012. Not only Google+ has a tremendous growth in the number of users, but what is even more interesting from the SMM point of view, Google+ has introduced the new Pages feature in late 2011, enabling businesses, brands, and other entities represent themselves on Google+ (Google, 2011).

Facebook's strength is not only the number of its users, but also the fact that every user has its own virtual profile with real name, picture, information about him/her and links to his/her friends. This profile is not only available on Facebook anymore because more and more websites connect with Facebook over Facebook Connect for the ability to use Facebook profile on external websites. In our opinion, this trend will continue and we will encounter a lot of great integrations and Facebook-based mash-ups in the next several years. Nevertheless, Facebook alone will introduce lots of innovative services in the near future. Currently it tests Facebook credits, virtual currency for its users. With Facebook credits, a user can have virtual money and buy on the Web. Facebook's goal is to make Facebook credits available everywhere. Because of its huge user base, Facebook has great chance to achieve this goal. The other SNSs will also develop but less rapidly and in other directions. The best example is Foursquare, which is growing extremely fast and this trend will continue in next few years.

Given the dynamics of a superfast and ubiquitous Internet, a social media landscape defined by applications built on top of a Facebook platform and millions of connected devices, in the next few years we will see shifts in certain areas of media, such as television and radio. For example, Croatian national television station NovaTV already integrates user comments on interesting topics from Facebook in the program. Additionally, almost all radio stations in Croatia communicate with their listeners over the Facebook. Furthermore, friends and family, wherever they physically are, will exchange comments while watching the same show, will suggest other shows and even start onscreen video or voice calls. Social TV will be another element of personalization, one that combines the "me" with "my friends" (Bulkeley, 2010).

We envision the physical and digital worlds will become even more tightly connected. Today we are able to run in the park and track our progress online while sharing it with our friends or track our weight loss. Furthermore, we are able to shop in the large retail chains by smartphones, scanning bar codes with phone camera and ask Facebook friends for recommendations on certain products. Finally, group buying social sites, such as the biggest one named Kolektiva.hr (http://www.kolektiva.hr), revolutionized electronic commerce in Croatia and paved the way for introduction of mobile social shopping.

CONCLUSION

Social networking services not only represent a place where users spend hours and hours of their time every day, but also offer completely new ways of promotion, such as highly targeted and intensely personalized communication which is hard to achieve when using traditional media. A study (Swallow, 2011), which analysed behaviour of approximately 1500 consumers, strongly supports a claim that Facebook promotion has highly positive effects for brands. Namely, the study asserts that:

1. 56% of consumers said they are more likely to recommend a brand to a friend after becoming a follower on Facebook;
2. 51% of consumers said they are more likely to buy a product since becoming a follower on Facebook.

Facebook is the largest SNS and as such most attractive for most brands and marketers. Next strongest SNS is Twitter, but Twitter's attractiveness varies significantly from country to country. For example, in the US Twitter is very strong and attractive to marketers (there are 140 million registered Twitter users in the US [Semiocast, 2012]), whereas in Croatia Twitter has only several thousand users and as such is unattractive to mass marketing. Google+ was recently launched and the related statistics is still not known. Therefore, marketers will wait for some time to see the performance of Google+ and then choose whether to invest in their presence on Google+ or not to invest at all. Foursquare is the smallest in the set of major SNSs (20 million users only). Nevertheless, its growth is fast and it is inherently very different than other major SNSs, what makes it very attractive for smaller marketing campaigns (1 million brands are present on Foursquare).

The major advantage of Social Media Marketing is the fact that it provides almost-free message channel to consumers (e.g., Facebook or Twitter followers). For example, the brand connects with hundreds, thousands, or even millions of followers on Facebook (the most popular Facebook pages have tens of millions of followers—in mid-2012 Coca Cola leads the list with 48 millions of followers, Disney is the second with 38 million and Converse the third with 33 million [Socialbakers, 2011b]). Whatever the brand publishes, it will be forwarded to its followers free of charge. This way, the brand builds its own media channel for communication instead of buying it from marketing agencies through expensive marketing campaigns.

Another advantage of Social Media Marketing is a two-way as well as personalized and transparent communication. Not just most of traditional marketing approaches, but a huge portion of digital marketing as well, is based on a one-way communication. Brands send messages to readers or viewers without giving them a possibility of replying with a feedback. On the other hand, SNSs enable that every follower can reply to brand and give a feedback. For example, if the consumer's favourite retail chain posts a promotion scheduled for the next week, the consumer (which is as well that brand follower on social networks) can reply and ask questions (e.g., what products will be included), praise or express dissatisfaction. This way, the brand is getting valuable feedback, but also consumers are provided with transparent communication channel. If brand posts an announcement about a new product and other followers react positive about it, the consumer can choose to buy it. On the other hand, if brand posts an announcement about a new product and other followers complain, perhaps it is not a good idea for the consumer to buy that product.

REFERENCES

Accenture. (2011). *Making social media pay: Rethinking social media's potential to bolster B2B interactions, customer loyalty, revenues and brand reputation*. Accenture Report. New York, NY: Accenture.

Adamic, L. A., & Adar, E. (2003). Friends and neighbors on the web. *Social Networking, 25*(3), 211–230. doi:10.1016/S0378-8733(03)00009-1

Banks, E. (2011a). *World cup final sets two Twitter records*. Retrieved October 29, 2011, from http://edition.cnn.com/2011/TECH/social.media/07/18/world.cup.twitter.record.mashable/index.html

Banks, E. (2011b). *New year's tweets set new record*. Retrieved October 29, 2011, from http://mashable.com/2011/01/06/new-years-twitter-record

Berners-Lee, T., & Fischetti, M. (1999). *Weaving the web*. New York, NY: Harper.

Bojic, I., Lipic, T., & Podobnik, V. (2012). Bio-inspired clustering and data diffusion in machine social networks. In Abraham, A. (Ed.), *Computational Social Networks: Mining and Visualization* (pp. 51–79). London, UK: Springer Verlag. doi:10.1007/978-1-4471-4054-2_3

Boyd, D., & Ellison, N. (2007). Social network sites: Definition, history, and scholarship. *Journal of Computer-Mediated Communication, 13*(1), 210–230. doi:10.1111/j.1083-6101.2007.00393.x

Brown, R. (1965). *Social psychology*. New York, NY: Free Press.

Bulkeley, W. M. (2010). *TR10: Social TV*. Retrieved November 8, 2011, from http://www.technologyreview.com/communications/25084

Butcher, M. (2011). *Graph: How long it took Facebook, Twitter and Google+ to reach 10 million users*. Retrieved November 8, 2011, from http://eu.techcrunch.com/2011/07/22/graph-how-long-it-took-facebook-twitter-and-google-to-reach-10-million-users

Chen, J., Feng, J., & Whinston, A. B. (2010). Keyword auctions, unit-price contracts, and the role of commitment. *Production and Operations Management, 19*(3), 305–321. doi:10.1111/j.1937-5956.2009.01093.x

Chui, M., Manyika, J., Bughin, J., Dobbs, R., Roxburgh, C., & Sarazzin, H. (2012). *The social economy: Unlocking the value and productivity through social technologies. McKinsey Global Institute Report*. New York, NY: McKinsey Global Institute.

Facebook. (2012a). *Facebook key facts*. Retrieved August 1, 2012, from http://newsroom.fb.com/content/default.aspx?NewsAreaId=22

Facebook. (2012b). *Facebook timeline*. Retrieved August 1, 2012, from http://newsroom.fb.com/content/default.aspx?NewsAreaId=20

Facebook. (2012c). *Facebook for business*. Retrieved August 1, 2012, from https://www.facebook.com/business/pages

Facebook. (2012d). *Promote your business with ads and sponsored stories*. Retrieved August 1, 2012, from https://www.facebook.com/business/pages/#!/business/ads

Facebook. (2012e). *Ads: Campaign cost and budgeting*. Retrieved August 1, 2012, from https://www.facebook.com/help/?page=864

Facebook. (2012f). *Advertise on Facebook*. Retrieved August 1, 2012, from https://www.facebook.com/advertising

Facebook. (2012g). *State bicycle: Building a strong customer base*. Retrieved August 1, 2012, from https://www.facebook.com/advertising/success-stories/state-bicycle

Facebook. (2012h). *Luxury link: Building a strong customer base*. Retrieved August 1, 2012, from https://www.facebook.com/advertising/success-stories/luxury-link

Feng, J., Bhargava, H. K., & Pennock, D. M. (2007). Implementing sponsored search in web search engines: Computational evaluation of alternative mechanisms. *INFORMS Journal on Computing, 19*(1), 137–148. doi:10.1287/ijoc.1050.0135

Foursquare. (2011). *So we grew 3400% last year*. Retrieved October 29, 2011, from http://blog.foursquare.com/2011/01/24/2010infographic

Foursquare. (2012a). *About Foursquare*. Retrieved August 1, 2012, from https://foursquare.com/about

Foursquare. (2012b). *Foursquare for business*. Retrieved August 1, 2012, from https://foursquare.com/business

Foursquare. (2012c). *Foursquare merchant platform*. Retrieved August 1, 2012, from https://foursquare.com/business/merchants

Foursquare. (2012d). *Case studies*. Retrieved August 1, 2012, from https://foursquare.com/business/brands/casestudies

Gillette, F. (2011). *The rise and inglorious fall of Myspace*. Retrieved October 30, 2011, from http://www.businessweek.com/magazine/content/11_27/b4235053917570.htm

Google. (2011). *Google+ pages: Connect with all the things you care about*. Retrieved November 8, 2011, from http://googleblog.blogspot.com/2011/11/google-pages-connect-with-all-things.html

Grossman, L. (2010). *TIME's 2010 person of the year*. Retrieved October 30, 2011, from http://www.time.com/time/specials/packages/article/0,28804,2036683_2037183,00.html

Haberman, S. (2012). *Euro 2012 goal smashes tweets-per-second sports record*. Retrieved August 1, 2012, from http://mashable.com/2012/07/02/euro-2012-tweet-record

Hernandez, B. A. (2012). *The top 15 tweets-per-second records*. Retrieved August 1, 2012, from http://mashable.com/2012/02/06/tweets-per-second-records-twitter

Indvik, L. (2011). *Twitter set new tweets per second record during super bowl*. Retrieved October 29, 2011, from http://mashable.com/2011/02/09/twitter-super-bowl-tweets

Indvik, L. (2012). *Google acquires social media management platform wildfire*. Retrieved August 1, 2012, from http://mashable.com/2012/07/31/google-acquires-wildfire

Internet World Stats. (2012). *World internet users and population stats*. Retrieved August 1, 2012, from http://www.internetworldstats.com/stats.htm

iSTUDIO. (2012). *Our work – Featured projects*. Retrieved August 1, 2012, from http://www.istudio.hr/ourwork

Jayamaha, P. (2011). *Internet marketing – How, when, where?* Retrieved October 28, 2011, from http://print.dailymirror.lk/business/127-local/38977.html

Kwak, H., Lee, C., Park, H., & Moon, S. (2010). What is Twitter, a social network or a news media? In *Proceedings of the 19th International Conference on World Wide Web*, (pp. 591-600). New York, NY: ACM.

Lampe, C., Ellison, N. B., & Steinfield, C. (2008). Changes in use and perception of Facebook. In *Proceedings of the 2008 ACM Conference on Computer Supported Cooperative Work*, (pp. 721-730). New York, NY: ACM.

Larson, D. (2011). *Twitter stats & graphics on Osama bin Laden's death*. Retrieved October 29, 2011, from http://blog.tweetsmarter.com/twitter-stats/all-time-twitter-record-for-bin-ladens-death%E2%80%94graphics-and-links

Mack, G. (2008). *Facebook overtakes Myspace*. Retrieved November 8, 2011, from http://blog.alexa.com/2008/05/facebook-overtakes-myspace_07.html

Madden, M., & Zickuhr, K. (2011). *Pew internet report: 65% of online adults use social networking sites*. Retrieved October 28, 2011, from http://pewinternet.org/~/media//Files/Reports/2011/PIP-SNS-Update-2011.pdf

Malaga, R. A. (2010). Search engine optimization - Black and white hat approaches. *Advances in Computers*, *78*, 1–39. doi:10.1016/S0065-2458(10)78001-3

Medman, N. (2006). Doing your own thing on the net. *Ericsson Business Review*, *1*, 48–53.

Milgram, S. (1967). The small-world problem. *Psychology Today*, *1*(1), 61–67.

Nosko, A., Wood, E., & Molema, S. (2010). All about me - Disclosure in online social networking profiles - The case of Facebook. *Computers in Human Behavior*, *26*(3), 406–418. doi:10.1016/j.chb.2009.11.012

Ostrow, A. (2010). *Social networking dominates our time spent online*. Retrieved October 28, 2011, from http://mashable.com/2010/08/02/stats-time-spent-online

Podobnik, V., Galetic, V., Trzec, K., & Jezic, G. (2010). Group-oriented service provisioning in next generation network. In Srinivasan, D., & Jain, L. C. (Eds.), *Innovations in Multi-Agent Systems and Applications* (pp. 277–298). Berlin, Germany: Springer-Verlag. doi:10.1007/978-3-642-14435-6_10

Podobnik, V., & Lovrek, I. (2010). Telco agent: Enabler of paradigm shift towards customer-managed relationship. *Lecture Notes in Computer Science, 6276*, 251–260. doi:10.1007/978-3-642-15387-7_29

Podobnik, V., & Lovrek, I. (2011). An agent-based platform for ad-hoc social networking. *Lecture Notes in Computer Science, 6682*, 74–83. doi:10.1007/978-3-642-22000-5_9

Podobnik, V., Petric, A., Trzec, K., & Jezic, G. (2009). Software agents in new generation networks: Towards the automation of telecom processes. In Jain, L. C., & Nguyen, N. T. (Eds.), *Knowledge Processing and Decision Making in Agent-Based Systems* (pp. 71–99). Berlin, Germany: Springer-Verlag. doi:10.1007/978-3-540-88049-3_4

Purcell, K. (2011). *Pew internet report: Search and email still top the list of most popular online activities.* Retrieved October 28, 2011, from http://www.pewinternet.org/~/media//Files/Reports/2011/PIP_Search-and-Email.pdf

Raman, T. V. (2009). Toward 2W, beyond web 2.0. *Communications of the ACM, 52*(2), 52–59. doi:10.1145/1461928.1461945

Rao, L. (2011). *Beyonce pregnancy news at MTV VMAs births new Twitter record of 8,868 tweets per second.* Retrieved October 29, 2011, from http://techcrunch.com/2011/08/29/beyonce-pregnancy-news-at-the-mtv-vmas-births-new-twitter-record-with-8868-tweets-per-second

Reid, M., & Gray, C. (2007). Online social networks, virtual communities, enterprises, and information professionals. *Searcher, 15*(7), 32–51.

Rivlin, G. (2006). *How Friendster lost chance for a jackpot.* Retrieved October 29, 2011, from http://www.nytimes.com/2006/10/15/business/worldbusiness/15iht-friend.3160940.html

Roca, J. C., Garcia, J. J., & Vega, J. J. (2009). The importance of perceived trust, security and privacy in online trading systems. *Information Management & Computer Security, 17*(2), 96–113. doi:10.1108/09685220910963983

Semiocast. (2012). *Twitter reaches half a billion accounts.* Retrieved August 1, 2012, from http://semiocast.com/publications/2012_07_30_Twitter_reaches_half_a_billion_accounts_140m_in_the_US

Socialbakers. (2012a). *Advertising on Facebook*. Retrieved August 1, 2012, from http://www.socialbakers.com/facebook-advertising

Socialbakers. (2012b). *Facebook brands statistics*. Retrieved August 1, 2012, from http://www.socialbakers.com/facebook-pages/brands

Socialbakers. (2012c). *Facebook statistics by country*. Retrieved August 1, 2012, from http://www.socialbakers.com/facebook-statistics

Socialbakers. (2012d). *LinkedIn statistics by country*. Retrieved August 1, 2012, from http://www.socialbakers.com/linkedin-statistics

Socialbakers. (2012e). *Twitter statistics: Brands*. Retrieved August 1, 2012, from http://www.socialbakers.com/twitter/group/brands/page-1

Socialbakers. (2012f). *Twitter statistics: Overall*. Retrieved August 1, 2012, from http://www.socialbakers.com/twitter

Sutter, J. D. (2011). *Bin Laden's death sets Twitter record*. Retrieved October 29, 2011, from http://articles.cnn.com/2011-05-02/tech/bin.laden.twitter.record_1_twitter-users-tweets-facebook-friends?_s=PM:TECH

Swallow, E. (2011). *How consumers interact with brands on Facebook*. Retrieved October 30, 2011, from http://mashable.com/2011/09/12/consumers-interact-facebook

Taylor, C. (2011). *Twitter users react to massive quake, tsunami in Japan*. Retrieved October 29, 2011, from http://mashable.com/2011/03/11/japan-tsunami

Taylor, C. (2012). *Does Twitter have half a billion users?* Retrieved August 1, 2012, from http://mashable.com/2012/07/30/twitter-users-500-million

Taylor, D. (2011). *Everything you need to know about Facebook's EdgeRank*. Retrieved October 30, 2011, from http://thenextweb.com/socialmedia/2011/05/09/everything-you-need-to-know-about-facebook%e2%80%99s-edgerank

This is Iceland. (2011). *Iceland wants to be your friend on Foursquare*. Retrieved October 29, 2011, from http://aboutfoursquare.com/iceland-wants-to-be-your-friend-on-foursquare

Travers, J., & Milgram, S. (1969). An experimental study of the small world problem. *Sociometry, 32*(4), 425–443. doi:10.2307/2786545

Twitter. (2011). *#Yearinreview: Tweets per second*. Retrieved August 1, 2012, from http://blog.twitter.com/2011/12/yearinreview-tweets-per-second.html

Twitter. (2012). *Twitter for business*. Retrieved October 30, 2011, from http://business.twitter.com

Van Grove, J. (2011). *Twitter sets new record: 3,283 tweets per second.* Retrieved October 29, 2011, from http://mashable.com/2010/06/25/tps-record

Walter, E. (2011). *10 tips for posting on your brand's Facebook page.* Retrieved October 30, 2011, from http://mashable.com/2011/03/22/tips-brand-facebook-page

Wan, Y., Kumar, V., & Bukhari, A. (2008). Will the overseas expansion of Facebook succeed? *IEEE Internet Computing, 12*(3), 69–73. doi:10.1109/MIC.2008.70

Wasserman, T. (2011). *Google+ has 40 million users, says Larry Page.* Retrieved October 30, 2011, from http://mashable.com/2011/10/13/google-plus-40-million

Wasserman, T. (2012a). *Is Google+ the no. 3 social network? Depends how you measure it.* Retrieved May 25, 2012, from http://mashable.com/2012/04/11/google-plus-number-three

Wasserman, T. (2012b). *Only 49% of marketers have integrated social into brand building.* Retrieved May 25, 2012, from http://mashable.com/2012/05/07/49-percent-marketers-social-brand-building

Westland, J. C. (2010). Critical mass and willingness to pay for social networks. *Electronic Commerce Research and Applications, 9*(1), 6–19. doi:10.1016/j.elerap.2009.05.003

Yang, Q., Zhou, Z.-H., Mao, W., Li, W., & Liu, N. N. (2010). Social Learning. *IEEE Intelligent Systems, 25*(4), 9–11. doi:10.1109/MIS.2010.103

Yoon, J.-L. (2007). Telco 2.0: A new role and business model. *IEEE Communications Magazine, 45*(1), 10–12. doi:10.1109/MCOM.2007.284530

Youtube. (2012). *Media toolkit – Animated infographic.* Retrieved August 1, 2012, from http://www.youtube.com/watch?v=oXefMNfHVow

Zeichick, A. (2009). A-twitter over Twitter. *netWorker, 13*(1), 5–7. doi:10.1145/1516035.1516037

Zeisser, M. (2010, July). Unlocking the elusive potential of social networks. *The McKinsey Quarterly.*

ADDITIONAL READING

Aaker, J., & Smith, A. (2010). *The dragonfly effect: Quick, effective, and powerful ways to use social media to drive social change.* San Francisco, CA: Jossey-Bass.

Belavic, R., Basuga, M., Podobnik, V., Petric, A., & Lovrek, I. (2010). Agent-based social networking for mobile users. *International Journal of Intelligent Information and Database Systems*, *4*(6), 599–628. doi:10.1504/IJIIDS.2010.036895

Blanchard, O. (2011). *Social media ROI: Managing and measuring social media efforts in your organization*. Boston, MA: Pearson Education.

Bodnar, K. (2010). *The ultimate glossary: 101 social media marketing terms explained*. Retrieved October 30, 2011, from http://blog.hubspot.com/blog/tabid/6307/bid/6126/The-Ultimate-Glossary-101-Social-Media-Marketing-Terms-Explained.aspx

Carter, B. (2010). *Facebook advertising vs. Google AdWords*. Retrieved October 30, 2011, from http://www.searchenginejournal.com/facebook-advertising-vs-google-adwords

Chi, E. (2008). The social web: Research and opportunities. *IEEE Computer*, *41*(9), 88–91. doi:10.1109/MC.2008.401

Cialdini, R. B. (1993). *Influence: The psychology of persuasion*. New York, NY: Morrow.

Donath, J., & Boyd, D. (2004). Public displays of connection. *BT Technology Journal*, *22*(4), 71–82. doi:10.1023/B:BTTJ.0000047585.06264.cc

Evans, D. (2008). *Social media marketing: An hour a day*. Indianapolis, IN: Wiley Publishing.

Facebook. (2011f). *Facebook adverts*. Retrieved October 30, 2011, from https://www.facebook.com/advertising

Gartner. (2012). *Gartner says worldwide social media revenue forecast to reach $16.9 billion in 2012*. Retrieved August 1, 2012, from http://www.gartner.com/it/page.jsp?id=2092217

Godes, D., & Mayzlin, D. (2009). Firm-created word-of-mouth communication: Evidence from a field test. *Marketing Science*, *28*(4), 721–739. doi:10.1287/mksc.1080.0444

Gossieaux, F., & Moran, E. (2010). *The hyper-social organization: Eclipse your competition by leveraging social media*. New York, NY: McGraw-Hill.

Gupta, N. (2012). *Forecast: Social media revenue, worldwide, 2011-2016*. Retrieved August 1, 2012, from http://www.gartner.com/id=2061016

Iyengar, R., Van den Bulte, C., Eichert, J., West, B., & Valente, T. W. (2011). How social networks and opinion leaders affect the adoption of new products. *GfK Marketing Intelligence Review*, *3*(1), 17–25.

Iyengar, R., Van den Bulte, C., & Valente, T. W. (2011). Opinion leadership and social contagion in new product diffusion. *Marketing Science, 30*(2), 195–212. doi:10.1287/mksc.1100.0566

Katona, Z., Zubcsek, P., & Sarvary, M. (2011). Network effects and personal influences: Diffusion of an online social network. *JMR, Journal of Marketing Research, 48*(3), 425–443. doi:10.1509/jmkr.48.3.425

O'Neill, N. (2010). *The Facebook marketing dictionary.* Retrieved October 30, 2011, from http://www.allfacebook.com/facebook-marketing-dictionary

Pagedata. (2011). *PageData: Independent, accurate page metrics and trends from inside network.* Retrieved October 29, 2011, from http://pagedata.appdata.com

Parise, S., Guinan, P. J., & Weinberg, B. D. (2008). *The secrets of marketing in a web 2.0 world.* Retrieved October 30, 2011, from http://online.wsj.com/article/SB122884677205091919.html

Podobnik, V. (2010). *Multi-agent system for telecommunication service provisioning based on user profiles.* (Unpublished Doctoral Dissertation). University of Zagreb. Zagreb, Croatia.

Podobnik, V., & Lovrek, I. (2011). Transforming social networking from a service to a platform: A case study of ad-hoc social networking. In *Proceedings of the 13th International Conference on Electronic Commerce.* Liverpool, UK: ACM.

Podobnik, V., Striga, D., Jandras, A., & Lovrek, I. (2012). How to calculate trust between social network users? In *Proceedings of the 20th International Conference on Software, Telecommunications and Computer Networks.* IEEE Press.

Sambolec, I., Rukavina, I., & Podobnik, V. (2011). RecoMMobile: A spatiotemporal recommender system for mobile users. In *Proceedings of the 19th International Conference on Software, Telecommunications and Computer Networks,* (pp. 1-7). IEEE Press.

Solis, B. (2010). *Engage, revised and updated: The complete guide for brands and businesses to build, cultivate, and measure success in the new web.* Hoboken, NJ: John Wiley & Sons.

Van den Bulte, C., & Lilien, G. L. (2001). Medical innovation revisited: Social contagion versus marketing effort. *American Journal of Sociology, 106*(5), 1409–1435. doi:10.1086/320819

Van den Bulte, C., & Wuyts, S. (2007). *Social networks and marketing.* Cambridge, MA: Marketing Science Institute.

Vitak, J., Ellison, N. B., & Steinfield, C. (2011). The ties that bond: Re-examining the relationship between Facebook use and bonding social capital. In *Proceedings of the 2011 44th Hawaii International Conference on System Sciences*, (pp. 1-10). Washington, DC: IEEE Computer Society.

Watts, D. J., & Dodds, P. S. (2007). Influentials, networks, and public opinion formation. *The Journal of Consumer Research, 34*(4), 441–458. doi:10.1086/518527

Weaver, A., & Morrison, B. (2008). Social networking. *IEEE Computer, 41*(2), 97–100. doi:10.1109/MC.2008.61

Weimann, G. (1994). *The influentials: People who influence people*. Albany, NY: State University of New York Press.

Weinberg, T. (2009). *The new community rules: Marketing on the social web*. Sebastopol, CA: O'Reilly Media.

Weiser, M. (1991). The computer for the 21st century. *Scientific American, 265*(3), 94–104. doi:10.1038/scientificamerican0991-94

Weiser, M. (1994). The world is not a desktop. *Interactions (New York, N.Y.), 1*(1), 7–8. doi:10.1145/174800.174801

Wilson, C., Boe, B., Sala, A., Puttaswamy, K. P., & Zhao, B. Y. (2009). User interactions in social networks and their implications. In *Proceedings of the 4th ACM European Conference on Computer Systems*. New York, NY: ACM.

Yao, S., & Mela, C. F. (2011). A dynamic model of sponsored search advertising. *Marketing Science, 30*(3), 447–468. doi:10.1287/mksc.1100.0626

KEY TERMS AND DEFINITIONS

Facebook: The largest and the most influential global social networking service.

Social Media Marketing: An Internet marketing paradigm based on spreading brand-related messages directly from one social network user to another.

Social Network: A set of actors (e.g., people, organizations, brands) interconnected via relationships (e.g., acquaintance, familiar bond, dislike).

Social Networking Service: An information and communication service focused on building, managing, and utilizing social networks.

Viral Marketing: A marketing paradigm that utilizes pre-existing social network to increase brand awareness or to achieve other marketing objectives (e.g., high product sales or broad consumer base) through self-replicating viral process, analogous to the spread of viruses.

Web 2.0 as a Foundation for Social Media Marketing

Web 1.0: An information and communication service based on client-server architecture, enabling users to read and search interrelated information using computers connected to the Internet. The user in the Web 1.0 era is a passive consumer of a read-only Web.

Web 2.0: An information and communication service enabling not only the connection of information, but also linking people in the ad-hoc groups that can be assembled and disassembled according to the current need. The user in the Web 2.0 era is a prosumer, one who actively participates and collaborates in the ecosystem of a read-write Web.

Chapter 14
Virtual Collaborative Learning:
Opportunities and Challenges of Web 2.0–Based E-Learning Arrangements for Developing Countries

Wissam Tawileh
Technische Universität Dresden, Germany

Helena Bukvova
Technische Universität Dresden, Germany

Eric Schoop
Technische Universität Dresden, Germany

EXECUTIVE SUMMARY

New technologies are used increasingly to enhance people's lives in many fields, and education is a very important sector that can benefit from technological development. The idea of using technology to facilitate and enhance learning, known as electronic learning, has led to the development of a wide range of applications and implementations worldwide. Electronic learning can offer new opportunities for developing countries by increasing access to education and improving learning outcomes. This chapter presents Virtual Collaborative Learning (VCL) as a modern technology-enhanced team-learning arrangement based on a constructivist learning paradigm.

DOI: 10.4018/978-1-4666-2515-0.ch014

By utilizing Web 2.0 tools to empower and enhance classical e-Learning methods, VCL reaches far beyond classical Web-Based Training. Opportunities and challenges of VCL for developing countries will be discussed based on a long European teaching and research experience.

INTRODUCTION

The introduction of Internet has had a considerable impact of many aspects of our society, altering processes and approaches in public, private, and corporate settings. The uses of Internet range from information retrieval to social functions (Long & Baecker, 1997). Besides supporting and enhancing existing approaches, the use of Internet has facilitated new approaches in many different fields, creating 'e-Forms' such as e-Business, e-Commerce, e-Government, or e-Health. In this chapter, we will discuss a technology-enhanced approach from the area of education, known as electronic learning, i.e. e-Learning. Among the alleged benefits of e-Learning—in comparison to traditional learning practices where physical presence of teachers and learners in the same classroom environment is essential (Rumble, 2001)—are an access to a wider audience, an easier access to learning resources, and a time and space independence.

The emergence of Web 2.0 introduced new participation tools and communication channels for Internet users who were thus empowered to become real content creators and developers on the Web (Murugesan, 2007). Internet users can now actively create and share useful content, and easily participate in synchronous and asynchronous discussions and dialogs. In educational setting, modern Web-based participation tools offer teachers the ability to support collaboration in interactive learning environments they always needed (Jonassen, Peck, & Wilson, 1999).

In addition to traditional e-Learning and Web-based teaching practices, Computer-Supported Collaborative Learning (CSCL) further utilizes Information and Communication Technologies (ICT) and recently Web 2.0 features for an effective and efficient delivery of learning content in a modern, attractive, interactive, and learner-centered form. In this chapter, we will introduce and discuss a particular CSCL-arrangement called Virtual Collaborative Learning (VCL). The aim of VCL is to support both individual and collective learning processes and enable learners to develop their own knowledge and share it by interacting with teachers/tutors and other learners using modern communication and collaboration tools. While practicing this, new competencies in social media, teamwork, decision-making, and intercultural awareness can also be gained and developed (Schoop, Bukvova, & Gilge, 2006).

Developing countries have a considerable potential to benefit from e-Learning applications and use modern Web 2.0 features to improve local education practices and programs. This chapter offers an introduction to the state of the art and best practices of CSCL in higher education, in particular the VCL arrangement, based on the long research and teaching experience at the Chair of Business Informatics, especially Information Management, of the Technische Universität Dresden in Germany. The benefit opportunities and implementation challenges of VCL deployments will also be discussed, taking into consideration the special needs and limitations in development contexts.

In the Background section, we will review basic concepts to understand VCL and blended learning and the use of Web 2.0 applications to enrich the learning experience in virtual classroom environments. The practical implementation of these concepts in higher education will be explained with the help of three examples and the systematic approach of VCL-centered blended learning arrangements will be presented based on the experience with application in European settings.

The later part will discuss the potential of Web 2.0 to enhance learning experiences in developing countries through VCL and blended learning. The expected challenges and limitations of these practices will also be foreseen based on difficulties faced in previous studies and on frontier to technology and e-Learning in developing countries.

Recommendations will be then proposed to unlock the explored potential of Web 2.0 and VCL for education in developing countries, and to overcome possible limitations and boundaries, followed by a summary of future research requirements and intentions. A conclusion wraps-up the chapter highlighting the key findings and suggestions.

BACKGROUND

As education plays an essential role for development (World Bank, 2012), it is important to explore and consider new development opportunities in this sector and adopt new strategies to overcome learning difficulties and limitations. E-Learning applications have been implemented in many countries, also in developing regions, to enhance learning processes and improve educational impact (Gulati, 2008). In addition to locally gained experience, developing countries can benefit from international know-how and make use of applied best practices in using ICT to enhance local learning settings and support the overall national development.

The utilization of the Internet enables classical, computer-based e-Learning applications to reach a wider range of participants and enrich traditional learning practices. Web-Based Training (WBT) is an example of successful e-Learning applications that use the Web to "…create well-designed, learner-centered, interactive, engaging and facilitated learning environments" (Khan, 2001, p. 5). The emergence of Web 2.0 changed the way people use the Internet and encouraged them with new participation tools to be active content creators and knowledge contributors instead of a passive audience. In education, online interaction became a core element of modern e-Learning practices, where learners and teachers actively participate in collaborative knowledge construction and knowledge sharing processes. The new e-Learning approach "Online Collaborative Learning" continues to evolve based on the pedagogical success of traditional "Collaborative Learning" methodologies (Roberts, 2004).

This section characterizes the concepts of Web 2.0 and Collaborative Learning and introduces, based on the correlation between both concepts, Virtual Collaborative Learning as a modern technology-enhanced learning approach. It emphasizes the use of Web 2.0 tools to facilitate Virtual Collaborative Learning and provides practical examples of implementing VCL and Web 2.0 in higher education. An innovative, learner-centered collaborative blended-learning arrangement is then presented, illustrating a systematic approach to implement VCL in formal higher education based on Web 2.0 applications.

The Web 2.0

The 'Web 2.0' has neither a clear borderline nor a unique definition. The term was coined in 2004 during a brainstorming session at O'Reilly Media, discussing the future of the Web after the dot-com bubble's bursting in 2001. The collapse was a turning point for the Web that changed the understanding of Web-based business. Companies that survived the collapse had something in common: they started to see the Web as platform to deliver (Web) services. Their approach has changed from packaged Web-based applications and software tools towards principles and practices that qualitatively enhance users' experience on the Web, no matter which client computer or operating system they are using (O'Reilly, 2005).

The Web 2.0 addresses all Internet users not as a passive audience, but encourages their active participation in content creation and information sharing through collaborative tools and services. It represents a paradigm shift from interaction of users with the Web to interaction of users through the Web and enables people to decide what is important on and for *their own* Web (Gillmor, 2006).

Users of Web 2.0 create and edit their encyclopedia, share their photos and videos, tag and comment others photos and videos, subscribe to dynamic news feeds of their choice and interest, publish their thoughts and rapidly broadcast ideas online, rank and recommend downloaded media files, build virtual communities of friends and colleagues, and are nonetheless targeted with customized offers from modern advertisers on the user-centered Web. Wikipedia, Flickr, YouTube, RSS Feeds, Blogs, Twitter, Napster, and Facebook are just few examples of Web 2.0 services that make this personalized experience possible, largely independently from the type and version of hardware and software the user's side.

Focusing on the social interaction between users that is enabled by the Web 2.0, Selwyn and Grant (2009) highlight 'Social Software,' a central Web 2.0 feature, as an equivalent concept as it "…encompasses all types of internet applications that support interaction between and within groups." (p. 79). We will emphasis on this feature and the proposed definition for the purpose of this chapter.

Collaborative Learning

'Collaborative Learning' as a pedagogical methodology has its roots back in the eighteenth century, when George Jardine, professor of logic and philosophy at the University of Glasgow, realized that the university class does not meet his students' needs anymore. Jardine started a reform in higher education at his time by changing the content and teaching method of his logic and philosophy class to match the changes that were taking place in the society. Young students needed more freedom in the classroom and had to be prepared for the professional life in a democratic society. Jardine founded a peer-review method to assess students' writings and involved the students in the review process. The group work required for the peer-review tasks created a respectful social environment that could benefit both weak and strong students. Thus, essential elements of modern collaborative learning theories were already addressed in Jardine's class tow hundred years ago (Gaillet, 1994).

Learning as a "socially transmitted and situated process" (Klauser, Schoop, Wirth, Jungmann, & Gersdorf, 2004, p. 7) takes place in a learning environment where human interaction is the mediator of knowledge exchange between learners and teachers and among learners themselves. In these learning environments, learners participate in groups, whose members interact on multiple levels to meet their information needs. The interaction pyramid proposed by Bair (1989) describes four levels of interaction intensity that can be used to understand learner's experience in collaborative learning (see Figure 1).

The characteristics of each level—Informing, Coordinating, Collaborating, and Cooperating—differ in the way communication partners interact and the purpose of their interaction. At the informing level, the participants access information to satisfy individual goals. Each user looks for useful information individually and they may be no direct communication between the participants. At the coordinating level, the participants follow individual goals that are a part of a greater common interest, thus requiring a more intensive, often direct interaction. An intensive human interaction is required at the collaborating level where multiple people par-

Figure 1. Bair's human interaction levels (cf. Bair, 1989, p. 209)

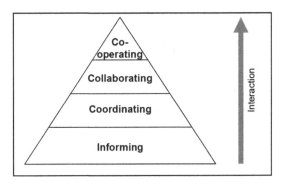

ticipate in the same process to achieve a common goal as a team, although their subtasks are individually assigned and their achievements individually evaluated. The highest level of human interaction should be reached while cooperating on a common goal as a team of which a common output will be evaluated as a whole.

Although there is no clear differentiation between collaborative and cooperative learning in the literature and many researchers use both terms synonymously (Johnson & Johnson, 1996), Slavin (2000) assumes that collaborative learning concentrates on solving ill-structured problems in groups as a goal where cooperative learning concentrates on the cooperation itself as a target-oriented collective action.

Based on applied experiences with post-graduate courses, Balázs (2003) defines collaborative learning in higher education as "the learner-centered common working on ill-structured academic tasks in self-organized small groups, in which learners are together responsible for the success of the entire group."

According to Balázs and Schoop (2004), special characteristics of collaborative learning are essential for successful interaction and cooperation inside groups. The absence of these characteristics threatens the group function and drives learners to dismiss the teamwork and form pseudo groups of which members meet each other but compete in their work (Johnson & Johnson, 1999). The important characteristics of collaborative learning are summarized in the following and illustrated in Figure 2.

Collaborative-learning settings belong to formal learning arrangements with given learning objectives and resources focusing on self-organized groups. Learners as group members share the responsibility for the whole group. They try to reach a common goal together and share the results of their teamwork, while periodically splitting into smaller groups or individual roles, thus parallelizing processes and increasing team productivity. To reach their common goal and synchronize separately achieved results successfully, learners, besides their individual role-based tasks, have to participate actively in the group and frequently interact with other group members. The group should internally find a consensus that is accepted and

Figure 2. Characteristics of collaborative learning (Balázs & Schoop, 2004, p. 5)

understood by all members to solve the given problem. As the problems are often ill-structured, they require a strong coordination and organization inside the group to be collectively solved. In the collaborative environment, learners have to share available, potentially limited resources in their group work. Negotiations for resource planning and exchange foster the social relationship inside the group. The strong social relationship increases personal trust and shapes a group identity, which enables transparent communication and successful cooperation in the team.

Multiple studies show that students' cooperation in collaborative learning environments enhances learners' performance, their learning processes, and outcomes (Johnson & Johnson, 1996). Sipusic et al. (1999) highlight the following important benefits of collaborative learning:

1. Enhancing information acquisition by offering learners more time to think and ask questions,
2. Learners can enhance their knowledge and ideas with feedback from other group members,
3. The need to elaborate knowledge to others increases the use of conceptual learning content,
4. Encouraging the helping behavior enhances the learning by all group members, and
5. More attention in motivate learning environments increases learners' knowledge acceptance.

Collaborative learning encourages learners' interaction and supports individual and group knowledge construction needed for long-lasting learning impact (Jonassen, 1996). Switzer (2004) identifies the positive influence of social negotiation on knowledge construction as a key issue in designing constructivist learning environments, and points out that collaboration facilitates learning in constructivist classes. Following a constructivist learning approach, students should learn to collect new information and use of their existing knowledge in a way that makes sense to them to recognize and solve problems in a learner-centered environment where the teacher plays the role of a facilitator rather than a person in charge (Sprague & Dede, 1999).

Virtual Collaborative Learning

Augmenting classical learning environments with modern technologies can convert individual teacher-centered processes to a learner-centered social interactive experience, which consequently improves the acceptance of learning content and activities among students and increases the impact and capacities of teaching practices. In this section we will review the history of using computers to implement collaborative learning methodologies and introduce the innovative computer-supported learning concept called 'Virtual Collaborative Learning (VCL)' that integrates modern ICT, especially Web 2.0 applications, in a classical educational system.

Computer-Mediated Communication (CMC) describes the act of human interaction using connected computers as a medium to exchange information. E-Mail is an example of this communication method. Educational institutes introduced a variety of CMC systems to enhance learning processes. These systems offered faster and more frequent interaction between learners and teachers in addition to time and location flexibility by enabling participants to communicate and remotely access learning resources at any time. The hope to foster cooperation and collaboration between learners using CMC faced, however, multiple restrictions, which encouraged researchers to discuss pedagogical designs that implement CMC technologies in collaborative learning scenarios (Paulus, 2005).

The benefits of collaborative learning for education were traditionally discussed and assumed for classical classroom environments, while CMC was usually used to enhance the communication in traditional learning setups. The argument that CMC technologies can support collaborative learning processes started a new research discipline that aims to combine collaborative learning theory and the theory of using CMC to enhance group learning (Brandon & Hollingshead, 1999).

The workshop held in San Diego in the year 1983 on the topic "joint problem solving and microcomputers" featured the role of computers as a medium for individuals' interaction in a group to collectively solve a common problem. The use of computers to empower collaborative learning was then highlighted in 1989 when the term "Computer-Supported Collaborative Learning (CSCL)" was first internationally used on a workshop in Italy. The focus on interaction between learners in CSCL environments required computers to offer the communication media for active collaboration rather than giving instructions to students (e.g. in computer-aided teaching or intelligent feedback agents) (Stahl, Koschmann, & Suthers, 2006).

Since then, research and implementation of CSCL in different settings and at multiple educational levels continued internationally. A review of the numerous impact evaluation studies conducted in the last years supports the claims that CSCL methods can improve the overall quality of learning. Some of the alleged positive effects of CSCL methods are: skills improvement, positive impact on atmosphere, positive attitude towards learning, acceptance to deal with more difficult problems, effective group dynamics and increased students' performance (Lehtinen, Hakkarainen, Lipponen, Rahikainen, & Muukkonen, 1999).

Based on her experience and research on using CMC to enhance collaborative learning, Hiltz (1988) coined the term 'Virtual Classroom' as a learning environment that supports group learning more effectively and more interactively than classical classroom environments. This innovative concept emphasizes on the role of technology as an interaction facilitator in learning groups and a creator of more accessible, flexible, and adaptive learning "spaces." Collaborative learning in virtual classrooms might form the future of e-Learning environments and is already being researched, developed, implemented, and evaluated at multiple educational institutes.

Rapidly evolving ICT enables the conception and construction of more flexible, interactive, attractive, and user-friendly collaborative learning settings especially using the Web as a communication channel. The educational potential of active participation rather than passive reception learning is considerable (Davies & Merchant, 2009). The wide range of interactive participation tools introduced by Web 2.0 applications can offer learners and teachers an enjoyable, more social and effective educational experience at their own pace independently from location and time, this is the 'Virtual Collaborative Learning (VCL)' experience.

In addition to the previously mentioned benefits of collaborative learning, the main didactical objective of VCL is to allow students to acquire additional competencies in the following four fields (Schoop, et al., 2006):

- Improved professional competence by active knowledge sharing in heterogeneous groups,
- Improved team competence by deliberately following roles and scenarios, the interaction and communication following certain rules and standards,
- Improved media competence by having to rely upon Internet technologies, and to cover up with its pros and cons while achieving tight project schedules, and
- Improved intercultural awareness by collaborating in internationally mixed teams with students and tutors who have different cultural and academic backgrounds.

Blended Learning

Learning processes take place in deliberately designed situations influenced by different parameters and limitations like time, place, content, methods, media, and form of communication. These situations form learning environments (or learning arrangements) (Lang & Pätzold, 2002). Classical learning environments can be enriched with Virtual Collaborative Learning using ICT. The didactically reasonable combination of classical classroom learning processes and virtual classroom online learning processes is called 'blended learning' (Seufert & Mayr, 2002). The blended learning concept follows the moderate constructivist learning approach that emphasizes on the importance of face-to-face instructor-led teaching in formal learning with the need for constructive activities that enable students to build their own understanding (Perkins, 1991).

To describe learning arrangements in a blended learning environment, learning scenarios can be structured according to three dimensions: time, location, and actors (see Figure 3):

- **Time-Based Dimension:** Indicates the learning process timing (synchronous or asynchronous),
- **Physical Dimension:** Locates where the learning process takes place (real or virtual),
- **Personal Dimension:** Describes the learners (an individual or a group).

Based on the variation in these parameters, eight different combinations that describe the most usual occurrences of traditional and virtual learning processes in blended learning environments can be identified. These combinations are according to Schoop et al. (2006, p. 145):

Figure 3. Blended learning environment: a combination of different dimensions (Schoop, et al., 2006, p. 145)

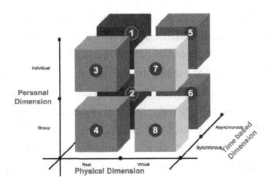

1. Asynchronous individual learning process in a real classroom (e.g. reading a text-book),
2. Asynchronous team learning process in a real classroom (e.g. blackboard communication, business games),
3. Synchronous individual learning process in a real classroom (e.g. traditional classroom lecture),
4. Synchronous team learning process in a real classroom (e.g. business case exercises in small teams),
5. Asynchronous individual learning process in a virtual classroom (e.g. self guided individual online learning – Web-based training),
6. Asynchronous team learning process in a virtual classroom (e.g. virtual collaborative learning using discussion forums, email, Weblogs, or wikiwebs),
7. Synchronous individual learning process in a virtual classroom (e.g. tele-lecture in an open distant learning environment), and
8. Synchronous team learning process in a virtual classroom (e.g. chat, audio conference, or video conference).

Virtual Collaborative Learning and Web 2.0

To enable asynchronous and synchronous team learning processes in virtual classroom, Virtual Collaborative Learning implements ICT to overcome time and location limitations and facilitate collaborative educational group work. This main role of ICT as an enabling infrastructure in a Virtual Collaborative Learning course should be clear to teachers and learners. They should not pay more attention to new technical tools than the original learning objectives or over spend course's time on trying to solve technical problems of the learning environment. The development of participants' media competence can occur while using online collaboration tools and should not replace the course subject.

Suitable collaboration tools and applications for a VCL environment need a careful selection and combination to easily facilitate learners' participation. Misunderstanding of the ICT role, selecting nonintuitive tools, and frequent technical problems may cause learners' frustration and rapid drop-off in the VCL course. When learners face repeated technical difficulties in virtual learning settings, they will become distracted by the ICT from the actual learning task (Schulmeister, 2001). If a complicated tool is needed for the learning environment, instructors can occasionally give short guidance and help learners to overcome technical problems without influencing the constructivist learning method. Learners should be able to freely construct their own knowledge once they learn how to use the tool (Switzer, 2004).

Modern Web 2.0 interactive applications can be effectively used to encourage collaboration in virtual learning settings by enabling learners to work in virtual teams

Figure 4. VCL supporting tools (cf. Balázs & Schoop, 2004, p. 19)

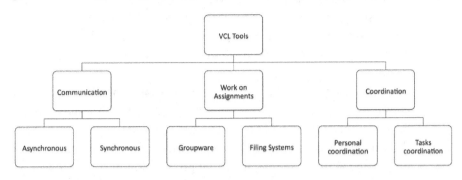

and accomplish a common learning task. The increasing use of Web 2.0 applications among students offers them essential technical knowledge that can be applied in the virtual collaborative learning activities. Selecting proper Web 2.0 collaboration tools reduces the risk of technical complications and encourages learners to actively use modern tools and concepts they might be familiar with to construct new knowledge.

To explain how Web 2.0 applications can support collaboration in VCL and which tools can be efficiently implemented, the required technical functions in the virtual classroom environment need to be identified. According to Balázs and Schoop (2004), ICT should be implemented in virtual collaborative learning environments to: facilitate communication, enable virtual work on assignments, and simplify coordination activities. Figure 4 categorizes the tools needed to support group work in VCL.

In addition to traditional Internet-based communication tools, Web 2.0 offers collaborative applications and services that can fulfill the mentioned requirements. The characteristics of the required tools are summarized here with some applications examples:

- **Communication:**
  - **Asynchronous Communication Tools:** These offer structured, documented, and long-lasting group discussions. Discussion forums and blogs are two easy-to-use example applications.
  - **Synchronous Communication Tools:** Real-time discussions and virtual group meetings are usually required for instant communication and urgent decisions. This can be done through text and voice/video chat or video conferencing sessions.
- **Work on Assignments:**
  - **Groupware:** A group of learners can collaborate on an editable structured Web page with a documented collaboration history. Wikis are a popular application for this task.

- ○ **Filing Systems:** The emerging cloud computing technology offers continuously extending storage spaces on the Web where documents can be hosted and accessed from multiple places and synchronized with different computer platforms. Web 2.0 file hosting services are an example.
- **Coordination:**
  - ○ **Personal Coordination:** Group structures and member identity increase learners' awareness of their relationship to the group and their responsibility for its success. Social networks are a Web 2.0 example that enables learners to create profiles with information about own interests and skills, assemble in virtual groups, administer members, and coordinate information distribution in the group.
  - ○ **Tasks Coordination:** Project management plays an important role for success in virtual group learning. Defining subtasks and milestones, allocating responsible members and keeping deadlines can be supported through Web 2.0 project management tools. Online calendars and Web-based scheduling tools simplify the coordination of online meetings or chat sessions and enable members to easily follow group appointments.

There is currently a long list of available Web 2.0 applications that can be used to facilitate students' participation and collaboration in VCL classes. Many of these applications are offered as free services and some services are so popular that almost every student might have already used one or more of them. Carefully selected and combined Web 2.0 tools in VCL courses can offer learners an enjoyable, user-friendly, and effective learning experience with affordable technical knowledge.

CSCL Practical Implementations

Different settings of CSCL have been implemented in multiple educational institutions at different educational levels. In the following, we present three examples of implementing VCL in higher education. The first example used internet-based video-conferencing to enhance an already existing classical higher educational collaborative learning environment. In the latter two examples, Web 2.0 applications were used to facilitate virtual collaboration in higher educational classes.

- **Face-to-Face vs. Virtual Collaborative Learning:** Sipusic et al. (1999) experimented with the use of online video communication to enhance a video-based face-to-face collaborative learning environment called 'Tutored Video Instruction' that was invented at Stanford University in the 1970s. In this face-to-face collaborative learning setup, a small group of students, led by a facilitator, played a prerecorded videotape of a previous lecture, and paused to discuss content, make notes, and ask questions. Students used verbal and non-verbal communication to collaborate in the face-to-face environment. To enable non-verbal communication in a similar virtual setup, a video-based virtual collaborative learning system called 'Distributed Tutored Video Instruction' was developed and tested. Video-conferencing enabled geographically distributed students to participate in the collaborative learning process through rich audiovisual discussions without losing the non-verbal communication sense. Later on, the system was enhanced with a collaborative note-taking tool that enabled students to make chronological notes in real-time while watching the tape and discussing content online. The facilitator could periodically publish the documented notes as a Webpage. This two years experiment showed that collaborative learning could benefit from ICT to enable remote students' participation. Although some technical problems faced the virtual collaborative learning setup, which was attributed to limited Internet bandwidth at the time, the performance of the participants in the virtual setting was equivalent to their peers in face-to-face environment.

- **Wikis for Academic Writing and Collaborative Learning:** Wheeler and Wheeler (2009) used a wiki as a collaborative writing platform improve the academic writing quality of 35 undergraduate and postgraduate students. The study observed collaborative writing as a social practice where students avoided offending their peers and showed a significant awareness development of properly citing information sources. Participants valued the chance to discuss their thoughts about the course on a public forum and were cautious about external audience reading their writing. Most of participated students enhanced their writing while creating or editing publically accessible wiki pages. They enjoyed using the wiki in the course and noticed an enhancement in their academic writing skills. Some of them started their own blog after the course, while others reported using the wiki content for their essays. A similar study was recently conducted at the Chair of Business Informatics, especially Information Management at the Technische Universität Dresden, which implemented a wiki in a formal higher educational course to encourage self-organized, collaborative writing on a given seminar topic (Kalb, Kummer, & Schoop, 2011).

- **Web 2.0 Applications in an e-Business Course:** Alaraj (2012) recently introduced a set of popular Web 2.0 applications to the e-Business course at Bethlehem University in Palestine. In this student-centered course, the traditional textbook was completely replaced by up-to-date online references recommended by the students themselves and the educator who played more a facilitator role. Students were asked to use Twitter for micro-blogging (i.e. creating short blog entries with up to 160 characters) on topics related to the course and the subject. A dedicated hashtag (the hash # symbol used on twitter to mark keywords and categorize tweets) was created to aggregate course-related tweets. A common blog enabled students to post and tag entries for their essays. Students were encouraged to start their professional social network on LinkedIn and link their tweets to their accounts using feeds. Common presentation slides and spreadsheets were created using Google Docs and short videos related to the topic were embedded from YouTube for the presentation session that was dated on a Google Calendar. Participants of this course successfully used Google AdWords in 'Google Online Marketing Challenge.' They collaboratively created plans and reports of their marketing campaigns using the university's wiki. The evaluation of this course showed the effectiveness of Web 2.0 applications in facilitating students' communication within groups and with the outside world. The interaction with Web 2.0 applications encouraged knowledge construction and improved professional skills such as writing.

These examples illustrate how ICT in particular Web 2.0 applications, can be practically used to enhance learning processes in higher education. Similar practical implementations are being conducted since the introduction of the Internet in higher educational institutions. Some implementations are intentionally designed to facilitate collaborative learning in virtual environments, while other experiments just tried to increase efficiency and attractiveness of classical learning courses using ICT capabilities. In the following section, we introduce a further CSCL arrangement, developed and tested in higher education at European institutions.

Virtual Collaborative Learning and Blended Learning in Formal Higher Education

In 2001, the VCL arrangement enabling group learning in virtual environments was developed at the Chair of Business Informatics, especially Information Management, at the Technische Universität Dresden, Germany. Since then, it has been applied in formal education, both locally and with international partner institutions. To date, the VCL arrangement has been applied 38 times in different learning scenarios. The arrangement was used 24 times in higher education settings and 18 times with students from international institutions, such as universities from Latvia, Lithuania, Russia, Turkey, China, Finland, and most recently Palestine. The arrangement has been evaluated after each application, focusing on improving different aspects of the learning and teaching experience of the participants and tutors. The VCL research thus follows the action research method (O'Brien, 2001), oriented on the design-based approach (Wang & Hannafin, 2005).

Figure 5. Model of a blended learning environment (Schoop, Bukvova, & Lieske, 2009, p. 16)

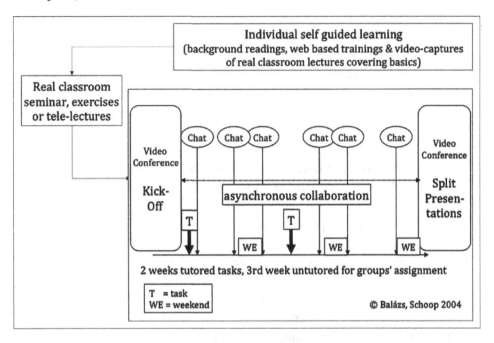

To reach a significant enhancement of learning efficiency, local and international virtual classroom projects are being conducted within a conceptual framework for planning, designing, preparing, operating, and evaluating VCL projects under continuous moderation and reflection by trained teletutors. In this systematic and controlled approach, VCL is far more than just an open learning community (Schoop, Michel, Miluniec, Kriksciuniene, & Brundzaite, 2005). Figure 5 illustrates this blended learning arrangement with a sample time plan for learning assignments.

At the Chair of Business Informatics, especially Information Management, Virtual Collaborative Learning is being implemented as a core element of a blended learning arrangement that includes a combination of local real classroom lectures, individual readings, online learning, and local on-site seminars, and a common (international) VCL project (Schoop, Gilge, & Bukvova, 2007). These blended learning arrangements deliver standard credit points (e.g. ECTS credits and grades) based on group assignments, presentations, and individual role-specific activities for every participant to be used in his or her local study course.

Students construct new knowledge by individually working on (online) learning materials, gathering in small (interdisciplinary/international) learning teams, collaborating with team members in real and virtual classroom environments to solve an ill-structured case/scenario, and using social software to document their collaboration in both environments. This learner-centered, tutored learning process aims to achieve the best learning results by: integrating interaction between learners and teachers and among learners themselves, considering interdisciplinary approaches, stressing professional and methodical responsibilities, developing soft skills, and taking place at the highest interaction level (Schoop, Bukvova, & Lieske, 2009).

To address the four human interaction levels defined by Bair (see Figure 1) in the learning process, the developed and implemented blended learning arrangement consists of four phases:

1. **Information Phase [Informing]:** Students obtain organizational information and guidelines and get introduced to the blended learning concept and the software tools will be used in the course.
2. **Self-Guided Learning Phase [Coordinating]:** Students work individually on provided online learning materials and recommended related readings. They can use an online forum for communication and organizational coordination.
3. **Workshop [Cooperating]:** Students work in small, self-organized groups on a common solution for a complex problem and present their ideas in a face-to-face learning environment.
4. **VCL Session [Collaborating]:** In this phase, students collaborate in a virtual classroom environment to solve an ill-structured task and document their findings.

The design of the presented VCL-based blended learning arrangement and its implementation in higher educational courses have been discussed and presented on an international level (Gersch, Lehr, & Weber, 2011; Bukvova, Lehr, Lieske, Weber, & Schoop, 2010; Schoop, et al., 2009). A recent implementation of this arrangement used social media both as a learning style and meanwhile as learning content (Wolff, Riedel, Jödiscke, Schoop, & Sonntag, 2011). The course aimed to familiarize students with social media applications and their integration in the enterprise's communication strategy while learning in a Web 2.0 based VCL setting so that students get familiar with concepts and tools of social media communication on one hand and the implementation of social media to enhance corporate processes on the other hand. All this occurs in a constructivist blended learning settings, where participants use these concepts to collaboratively solve a problem-based case study.

From the experience presented in this section of implementing VCL-based blended learning arrangements in different scenarios of formal higher education, both locally and in cooperation with international partner institutions, we recognize the reasonable potential for VCL in higher education which can be summed up, according to Balázs and Schoop (2004), as follows:

- More time for students to think about their ideas, state their questions and write their answers;
- Time flexibility by enabling groups to coordinate synchronous communication by themselves and students to plan their workload individually; the asynchronous communication between group members allows them to work on assignments at their own pace at the time they find suitable;
- Location flexibility as group members can 'meet' and work together virtually even when they are geographically separated;
- More concentration on the learning assignment through intensive target-oriented virtual communication;
- Freedom of work and opinion expression as students write their contributions in the group without restrictions and influence of dominant members;
- Active learning by constructing new knowledge and using previous knowledge to solve an ill-structured problem in a group through mutual discussions that tighten the gained knowledge;
- Continuous mentoring while students write their contributions in asynchronous communication environments; direct feedback from teachers and group members allow writers to enhance their contributions which increases the learning impact;
- Archiving of contributions and communications which documents the decision making process followed to solve the learning problem in addition to the documentation of the final solution;
- Supporting group work with virtual participation possibilities, especially for geographically distributed members; this enables the learning group to consider different perspectives on solving the problem; learners with accessibility limitations can also participate in this group learning; and
- Development of social competence that is important for both collaborative learning and for daily life; VCL participants take the responsibility for the overall group work results, learn how to build social relationships and experience how to communicate and express their ideas in a group.

VIRTUAL COLLABORATIVE LEARNING
FOR DEVELOPING COUNTRIES

After reviewing the enhancement potential for learning processes by fostering collaborative learning in student groups and the role of ICT in facilitating collaborative learning in virtual classroom settings, it is important to explore the chances of developing countries to benefit from VCL in enhancing local learning and teaching practices and the challenges these countries might face while implementing this innovative learning concept. In the following sections, we discuss the potential and challenges and identify important aspects that should be considered when planning VCL projects in development contexts.

Potential of Virtual Collaborative Learning for Developing Countries

As mentioned before, VCL enables learners to acquire professional and interpersonal skills that are important for study and professional life. Moreover, integrating VCL in the traditional learning environments can significantly enhance the learning process. Developing countries can benefit from the potential of VCL to expand learning programs, develop classical educational environments, and support the overall national development. Modern ICT can be used to overcome obstacles to educational development and to offer better education for a wider sector of the local community. A considerable potential of VCL for education in developing countries lies in addressing the following important issues:

- **Access to Education:** Integrating ICT in education can offer learners from community groups with limited access to educational resources a chance to participate in modern learning programs (Gulati, 2008). Where distance learning is a classical application of technology-supported education that crosses geographical boundaries, VCL can enhance the learning impact by increasing the acceptance and motivation of teachers and learners toward technology-supported learning programs in social, interactive, flexible, and more transparent learning environments. Inhabitants of rural areas and disabled learners can work in groups with their peers in urban educational institutes and enjoy the virtual classroom experience without physical constrains. VCL can offer better access not only to learning materials, but also to learning groups, mentors, and educational atmospheres.
- **Cost Efficiency:** Traditional distance learning programs are a solution when educational institutes are concerned about economic issues (Khan, 2005). VCL can furthermore enhance the cost efficiency by: (1) replacing face-to-

face meetings with virtual meetings instead of eliminating them and losing their collaborative impact, thus saving costs, (2) enabling tutors to intensively and efficiently mentor students in distributed learning groups from their own place, and (3) optimizing learning efforts and communication workload with flexible and effective time planning for teachers and learners.

- **Gender Equity:** VCL not only offers female learners in developing countries access to educational resources, but also enables them to actively participate in group discussions and interact with teachers and other learners in a comfortable environment with less domination of male peers. VCL should offer the opportunity for females who prefer online education courses, because they can better express themselves and highly value teacher's support and interaction (Anderson & Haddad, 2005). Although women often learn better through interactions in groups (Kwapong, 2007), they may face troubles in some developing communities in attending classical classroom courses or interacting with male peers because of traditional, cultural, or religious restrictions (Azaiza, 2011). In addition to flexibility in group assembly, VCL can offer a certain amount of anonymity for female participants to freely collaborate in the group. Another considerable advantage of VCL are the opportunities for female teachers to virtually work as teletutors even when they would be otherwise prevented from going to work due to home and family responsibilities.
- **Employability:** The previously mentioned main didactical objective of VCL is to develop professional, teamwork, new media, and intercultural competencies, which can increase employability chances for learners. The problem-based learning scenarios prepare students for professional life with relevant knowledge and important skills (Schoop, et al., 2007). Furthermore, VCL can also increases employability chances for women in developing countries through location and time flexibility as mentioned before.
- **Capacity Building:** As Virtual Collaborative Learning arrangements are based on modern ICT, it is important to qualify teachers to effectively use online communication and collaboration tools in the virtual learning environment. Teachers have to identify how ICT can help in reaching collaborative less authoritative learning approach (Beauchamp & Kennewell, 2008), and this is what they will experience while planning and implementing their VCL settings. The improvement of ICT skills at teachers and learners sides is important in the era of knowledge economy (Mnyanyi, Bakari, & Mbwette, 2011).

It has to be considered that developing countries differ in multiple aspects like education development level, language, population, and culture (Gulati, 2008). The mentioned potential of VCL may vary from one development context to another depending on the respective needs and resources. Nevertheless, it is worthwhile to consider the advantages of well-designed complex blended learning arrangements including VCL projects to enhance the learning experience and support the national development in these countries.

Virtual Collaborative Learning Challenges in Development Contexts

VCL utilizes ICT to enable collective knowledge construction through collaborative solution development of ill-structured complicated authentic problems in groups. A successful implementation of VCL requires a comprehensive situation and needs' assessment before planning and executing VCL courses to assure the significant acceptance and fruitful use of the collaborative learning platform by all participants.

Balázs and Schoop (2004) advice to integrate VCL in a blended learning arrangement only when it offers reasonable advantages to other learning forms to avoid failure and disappointment at both learners' and teachers' side. VCL should be used to facilitate collaborative learning in groups of geographically separated learners when the following conditions are fulfilled:

1. Learning objectives require active collaboration to solve complicated ill-structured problems,
2. Most learners have sufficient technical knowledge (prerequisites) to deal with online communication and collaboration tools used in the VCL course, and
3. The heterogeneity of the learning groups is not so high that it leads to problems in communication and understanding.

On the other hand, the main benefit of VCL for geographically non-separated learners is when the development of their communication and media competence is desired besides the development of social competence. However, the time and effort required to implement VCL should be affordable, and the didactical objective should be worthwhile. If these requirements are not present in a particular learning setting, other, probably more efficient, alternative group learning methods should be considered.

The implementation of Virtual Collaborative Learning may face obstacles because of its dependence on the virtual space on the Web. Characteristics of collaborative learning (Figure 2) are influenced by specifications of the virtual classroom environment in VCL. The following factors make collaborative learning on the Internet more difficult than in on-site settings (Balázs & Schoop, 2004):

- **Communication:** Troubles in communication arise as the distance between communication partners increases. The Internet enables individuals from far away (not only in time and space, but also in culture) to communicate with each other and allow difficulties to occur in the different types of virtual communication. *Textual communication* cannot involve all human senses; it requires more time to send a text message than speaking it out. The sender is not able to deliver the semantic of the message through non-verbal or meta-communication (e.g. gesture) in a textually shortened illustration. This causes a certain amount of information loss and allows misunderstanding between communication partners. In contrast, *Audio communication* enables meta-communication but also affects other message aspects and prevents parallel conversations between multiple communication partners. *Video communication* often has low image quality and is usually used in one-way transmission to optimize the connection bandwidth, which affects important communication elements.

- **Time Management:** Textual synchronous and asynchronous communication in virtual learning environments demands more time and concentration than face-to-face communication, which can be tiring for participants with limited typing skills. The typical VCL nature of continuous activity can also lead to work overload and frustration. VCL learners have to divide their time adequately and find balance between possible and required information needs to efficiently plan their work to solve the problem.

- **Social Relationships:** Successful collaborative learning requires active participation of learners to build their collaborative group where deep social commitment is essential. Cultural differences and communication difficulties might lead to misunderstandings in the group and negatively affect the collaboration between members. Group-specific rules and standards help members to build mutual trust in the virtual environment.

- **New Roles:** VCL is a learner-centered and learner-guided learning approach, where learners have the initiative and hold the responsibility for collaboration in the group. They organize the group work and manage their time to solve the learning problem with a minimal or no external guidance. Teachers merely play the role of tutors who facilitate the collaboration and solve conflicts in the group. They answer learners' questions and give them hints about information search without defining solutions and conditions. The time and location flexibilities and the work freedom offered by VCL can be challenging learners who are not familiar with self-organized learning and might thus reduce their achievement.

In addition to difficulties caused by the environment specifications of Virtual Collaborative Learning, developing countries may face further challenges when planning and implementing VCL in local educational systems. The following main obstacles to effectively initiate technology-supported learning programs in development contexts apply also for the introduction of VCL:

- **Technology and Infrastructure:** In order to use Web 2.0 collaboration and communication tools, VCL implementations need stable high-speed Internet connections for institutes, teachers, and learners. Developing countries face problems with the availability and costs of Internet bandwidth (Venter, 2003). Computer network infrastructure is also required for a virtual classroom with collaborative functions. Technologies used for education in developed countries are mostly not compatible with the needs and contexts of developing countries (Mnyanyi, et al., 2011). Even when suitable technology is available in development countries, it is unaffordable in many cases (Baggaley & Belawati, 2010).
- **Teachers and Tutors:** The challenge for teachers to use ICT in their daily work exists both in developed and development countries (Marshall & Ruohonen, 1998). Dealing with modern Web 2.0 technologies is even more challenging for teachers who are used to adopt ICT for authoritative teaching approaches (Beauchamp & Kennewell, 2008). Teachers and tutors may require further training, both regarding the use of tools and applications as well as their changed role in the classroom.
- **Integration Know-How:** The lack of knowledge in how to plan ICT and how to implement infrastructure at the educational decision making level in developing countries is an important reason why the adoption of these technologies in the classical learning processes is often opposed by the decision maker (Ruohonen, Mavengere, Nleya, & Deodhar, 2011).

It is important to point out, that developing countries differ in availability and costs of technology, educational systems and experiences and educational staff qualification. However, the limitations mentioned here have generally to be considered when designing and planning VCL projects in development regions.

Solutions and Recommendations

The potential for developing countries to enhance learning processes in local educational systems and address several national development issues is present. The implementation of VCL as a core of a blended-learning arrangement enables teachers and students to collaboratively construct and exchange knowledge. However, this approach should only be introduced when active collaboration is required to solve a complex unstructured learning problem and when the majority of participants possess enough experience with modern technologies used in the learning environment. Limited heterogeneity in the groups enables multiple perspectives and prevents problems in understanding or tolerating other opinions.

The special characteristics of collaborative learning in the virtual classroom can positively influence the common learning process by: (1) using the right communication style for each assignment or working phase, (2) helping learners to divide the work and manage their time and distinguish between relevant and non-relevant information to stay motivated, (3) fostering trust between group members and preventing communication and collaboration problems by defining and distributing group-specific standards and rules, and (4) allowing students to freely express their minds and guide the solution finding process themselves without detailed instructions from tutors who have to create, through thorough mentoring, a learning atmosphere where students willingly accept the learning responsibility.

Although developing countries strive to enhance the infrastructure and continuously adopt and implement new technologies, clear strategies to enhance education processes with ICT should be developed and supported from local decision makers in the government, institutional management, and the industry as investing in modern ICT technologies for education offers benefits for all stakeholders. The use of Free and Open Source Software solutions for VCL in blended learning arrangements reduces the technology's total cost of ownership, avoids vendor lock-in, and helps to develop local technologies.

Educational institutions in developing countries need to consider ICT awareness when planning their human resources development. The integration of modern technologies in the learning process is a very important field where educational personnel (also administrative staff) have to enhance their knowledge. Technology-aware staff helps in successfully implementing new learning methods.

In addition to being aware of the technology's role in enhancing the learning processes, decision makers have to get familiar with how to plan and implement ICT projects in the educational sector. Developing countries can benefit from multiple international cooperation programs that offer an excellent opportunity for know-how transfer and practical knowledge exchange.

On the societal and economical level, the main goal of developing countries is to gradually enhance their participation in global business processes. This leads to a growing integration of its companies and institutions into worldwide value chains, which demands from the future employees' proficiency in ICT-based intercultural communication and interaction, as it can be provided by VCL projects on business case studies following the problem-based learning approach in authentic, situative settings.

FUTURE RESEARCH DIRECTIONS

Despite the plenty of already conducted research studies on the use of Web 2.0 for education, there is still a need for more theoretically driven empirical research in this field at different educational levels. Selwyn and Grant highlighted the need for more empirical data on "…what is actually taking place when social software technologies meet education," "…what social software is actually being used for in education settings," and "what is social software making possible that were not possible before" in education (2009, pp. 82-83).

Introducing a new learning paradigm in a development context needs, furthermore, thorough research and development efforts that should consider already available international knowledge and experience in this field. Multiple international Virtual Collaborative Learning projects have been already accomplished, where the participation of developing countries was, however, very limited.

The future of VCL research for developing countries starts by initiating pilot VCL projects locally and in cooperation with regional and international partners. Learners' and teachers' acceptance of the new learning method, cultural opportunities or limitations of implementing VCL, sustainability of modern learning programs, and the intercultural effect on the collaborative learning process are interesting research questions that can improve the VCL practices and adapt the concept to better fit in development contexts.

CONCLUSION

Virtual Collaborative Learning is an innovative learning approach that utilizes modern Web 2.0 communication and cooperation tools to enhance learning processes by fostering collaboration between learners. The collaborative group work to solve an ill-structured complex learning problem in a virtual classroom enables effective collective knowledge construction and sharing, offers flexibility in time and location, and encourages learners from different places to actively participate in the learning process. VCL enables learners to acquire professional, team, new media and intercultural competencies that help them to start their professional life in the era of a globally networked knowledge economy.

Developing countries have the chance to cope with modern educational methods and enhance local learning programs by integrating VCL in suitable blended learning arrangements that meet local needs and requirements. Education is essential for national development and new technologies help to bridge the educational divide between developing and developed regions.

The first analysis shows an existing potential for VCL in developing countries based on experiences collected in previous classical technology-supported projects. However, comprehensive research projects on implementing VCL in development contexts are necessary to identify the real potential, needs, and challenges of using this innovative concept to address development issues that could not be addressed by traditional and classical e-Learning educational approaches. Findings from these projects will lead to specific recommendations for a successful transfer of existing VCL experience in developed countries (i.e. Europe) to developing countries.

REFERENCES

Alaraj, N. (2012). Effects of using web 2.0 applications in the e-business course on Palestinian students' professional development skills. In S. A. Anwar (Ed.), *Proceedings of the 5th Conference on e-Learning Excellence in the Middle East 2011: Sustainable Innovation in Education [capacity-building, blended learning and beyond],* (pp. 147–154). Dubai, United Arab Emirates: IEEE.

Anderson, D. M., & Haddad, C. J. (2005). Gender, voice, and learning in online course environments. *Journal of Asynchronous Learning Networks, 9*(1), 3–14.

Azaiza, K. (2011). Effectiveness of distance education for women in the Arab world. In M. Youssef & S. A. Anwar (Eds.), *Proceedings of the 4th Conference on e-Learning Excellence in the Middle East 2011: In Search of New Paradigms for Re-Engineering Education,* (pp. 209–222). Dubai, United Arab Emirates: IEEE.

Baggaley, J., & Belawati, T. (2010). *Distance education technologies in Asia.* Thousand Oaks, CA: Sage.

Bair, J. H. (1989). Supporting cooperative work with computers: Addressing meeting mania. In *Proceedings of the Thirty-Fourth IEEE Computer Society International Conference: Intellectual Leverage, Digest of Papers,* (pp. 208–217). IEEE Press.

Balázs, I. E. (2003). Experiences with virtual collaborative learning in post-graduate courses. In F. Malpica & C. Tremante (Eds.), *Proceedings of International Conference on Education and Information Systems: Technologies and Applications (EISTA 2003).* Orlando, FL: EISTA.

Balázs, I. E., & Schoop, E. (2004). Erfahrungen mit virtual collaborative learning am lehrstuhl wirtschaftsinformatik insbesondere informationsmanagement an der Technischen Universität Dresden - Band 1: Virtual collaborative learning: Ziele, design, erfahrungen. In R. Bogaschewsky, U. Hoppe, F. Klauser, E. Schoop, & C. Weinhardt (Eds.), *IMPULS EC Research Report 7*. Osnabrück, Germany: Electronic Commerce.

Beauchamp, G., & Kennewell, S. (2008). The influence of ICT on the interactivity of teaching. *Education and Information Technologies*, *13*(4), 305–315. doi:10.1007/s10639-008-9071-y

Brandon, D. P., & Hollingshead, A. B. (1999). Collaborative learning and computer-supported groups. *Communication Education*, *48*, 109–126. doi:10.1080/03634529909379159

Bukvova, H., Lehr, C., Lieske, C., Weber, P., & Schoop, E. (2010). Gestaltung virtueller kollaborativer lernprozesse in internationalen settings. *Proceedings of the Multikonferenz Wirtschaftsinformatik*, *2010*, 1449–1460.

Davies, J. A., & Merchant, G. (2009). *Web 2.0 for schools: Learning and social participation*. New York, NY: Peter Lang.

Gaillet, L. L. (1994). An historical perspective on collaborative learning. *Journal of Advanced Composition*, *14*(1), 93–110.

Gersch, M., Lehr, C., & Weber, P. (2011). Virtual collaborative learning in international settings – The Virtual seminar "net economy". *Proceedings of INTED*, *2011*, 5078–5085.

Gillmor, D. (2006). *We the media: Grassroots journalism by the people, for the people*. New York, NY: O'Reilly Media, Inc.

Gulati, S. (2008). Technology-enhanced learning in developing nations: A review. *International Review of Research in Open and Distance Learning*, *9*(1).

Hiltz, S. R. (1988). Collaborative learning in a virtual classroom: Highlights of findings. In *Proceedings of the 1988 ACM Conference on Computer-Supported Cooperative Work*, (pp. 282–290). New York, NY: ACM Press.

Johnson, D. W., & Johnson, R. T. (1996). Cooperation and the use of technology. *Handbook of Research for Educational Communications and Technology*, *1*, 1017–1044.

Johnson, D. W., & Johnson, R. T. (1999). *Learning together and alone: Cooperative, competitive, and individualistic learning*. Reading, MA: Allyn & Bacon.

Jonassen, D. H. (1996). *Computers in the classroom: Mindtools for critical thinking.* Upper Saddle River, NJ: Prentice-Hall, Inc.

Jonassen, D. H., Peck, K. L., & Wilson, B. G. (1999). *Learning with technology: A constructivist perspective.* New York, NY: Merrill.

Kalb, H., Kummer, C., & Schoop, E. (2011). *Implementing the "wiki way" in a course in higher education.* Retrieved from http://www.slideshare.net/kummerufer/implementing-the-wiki-way-in-a-course-in-higher-education

Khan, A. W. (2005). *Distance education for development.* Paper presented at the 2005 ICDE International Conference on Open and Distance Education. New Delhi, India.

Khan, B. H. (Ed.). (2001). *Web-based training.* Englewood Cliffs, NJ: Educational Technology Publications.

Klauser, F., Schoop, E., Wirth, K., Jungmann, B., & Gersdorf, R. (2004). The construction of complex internet-based learning environments in the field of tension of pedagogical and technical rationality. In Bogaschewsky, R., Hoppe, U., Klauser, F., Schoop, E., & Weinhardt, C. (Eds.), *IMPULS EC Research Report 10.* Osnabrück, Germany: Electronic Commerce.

Kwapong, O. A. T. F. (2007). Widening access to tertiary education for women in Ghana through distance education. *Online Submission, 8,* 65–79.

Lang, M., & Pätzold, G. (2002). *Multimedia in der Aus- und Weiterbildung: Grundlagen und Fallstudien zum netzbasierten Lernen.* Köln, Germany: Deutscher Wirtschaftsdienst.

Lehtinen, E., Hakkarainen, K., Lipponen, L., Rahikainen, M., & Muukkonen, H. (1999). Computer supported collaborative learning: A review. *The JHGI Giesbers Reports on Education, 10.*

Long, B., & Baecker, R. (1997). A taxonomy of Internet communication tools. *Proceedings of WebNet, 97,* 1–5.

Marshall, G., & Ruohonen, M. (1998). *Capacity building for IT in education in developing countries.* New York, NY: Springer.

Mnyanyi, C. B. F., Bakari, J. K., & Mbwette, T. S. A. (2011). Technologically-enhanced open and distance learning for all in developing countries. In M. Youssef & S. A. Anwar (Eds.), *Proceedings of the 4th Conference on e-Learning Excellence in the Middle East 2011: In Search of New Paradigms for Re-Engineering Education,* (pp. 8–17). Dubai, United Arab Emirates: IEEE.

Murugesan, S. (2007). Understanding web 2.0. *IT Professional, 9*(4), 34–41. doi:10.1109/MITP.2007.78

O'Brien, R. (2001). Um exame da abordagem metodológica da pesquisa ação. [An overview of the methodological approach of action research] In Richardson, R. (Ed.), *Teoria e Prática da Pesquisa Ação* [Theory and Practice of Action Research]. João Pessoa, Brazil: Universidade Federal da Paraíba.

O'Reilly, T. (2005, September 30). *What is web 2.0? Design patterns and business models for the next generation of software.* Retrieved June 17, 2012, from http://www.oreilly.de/artikel/web20.html

Paulus, T. M. (2005). Collaboration or cooperation? Analyzing small group interactions in educational environments. In Roberts, T. S. (Ed.), *Computer-Supported Collaborative Learning in Higher Education* (pp. 100–124). Hershey, PA: IGI Global. doi:10.4018/978-1-59140-408-8.ch005

Perkins, D. N. (1991). What constructivism demands of the learner. *Educational Technology, 31*(9), 19–21.

Roberts, T. S. (2004). *Online collaborative learning: Theory and practice.* Hershey, PA: IGI Global.

Rumble, G. (2001). The costs and costing of networked learning. *Journal of Asynchronous Learning Networks, 5*(2), 75–96.

Ruohonen, M., Mavengere, N., Nleya, N., & Deodhar, S. (2011). The use of free, Libre and open source software (FLOSS) for African higher education advancement and development. In M. Youssef & S. A. Anwar (Eds.), *Proceedings of the 4th Conference on e-Learning Excellence in the Middle East 2011: In Search of New Paradigms for Re-Engineering Education,* (pp. 44–54). Dubai, United Arab Emirates: IEEE.

Schoop, E., Bukvova, H., & Gilge, S. (2006). Blended learning – The didactical framework for integrative qualification processes. In *Proceedings of Conference on Integrative Qualification in eGovernment,* (pp. 142–156). IEEE.

Schoop, E., Bukvova, H., & Lieske, C. (2009). Blended learning arrangements for higher education in the changing knowledge society. In *Proceedings of the International Conference on Current Issues in Management of Business and Society Development 2009,* (pp. 11–17). Riga, Latvia: University of Latvia.

Schoop, E., Gilge, S., & Bukvova, H. (2007). How to implement "eBologna"? Didactical and organisational issues of a mobile ERASMUS module network. In Blum, U., Eckstein, A., & Eckstein, A. (Eds.), *Wirtschaftsinformatik im Fokus der Modernen Wissensökonomik - Netzwerkökonomie und Electronic Business, Electronic Learning, Systementwicklung und Modellierung: Festschrift für Prof. Dr. Dr. h.c. Wolfgang Uhr* (pp. 169–192). Academic Press.

Schoop, E., Michel, K.-U., Miluniec, A., Kriksciuniene, D., & Brundzaite, R. (2005). *Virtual collaborative learning in higher education and its potentials for lifelong learning - An empirical approach*. Paper presented at the EDEN Annual Conference. Helsinki, Finland.

Schulmeister, R. (2001). *Virtuelle universität- Virtuelles lernen*. München, Germany: Oldenbourg Verlag. doi:10.1524/9783486598926

Selwyn, N., & Grant, L. (2009). Researching the realities of social software use – An introduction. *Learning, Media and Technology, 34*(2), 79–86. doi:10.1080/17439880902921907

Seufert, S., & Mayr, P. (2002). Blended learning, hybrides lernen. In *Fachlexikon e-le@rning: Wegweiser durch das e-Vokabular*. Bonn, Germany: managerSeminare Gerhard May GmbH.

Sipusic, M. J., Pannoni, R. L., Smith, R. B., Dutra, J., Gibbons, J. F., & Sutherland, W. R. (1999). *Virtual collaborative learning: A comparison between face-to-face tutored video instruction (TVI) and distributed tutored video instruction (DTVI)*. New York, NY: Sun Microsystems Laboratories, Inc.

Slavin, R. E. (2000). *Educational psychology: Theory and practice*. Boston, MA: Allyn & Bacon.

Sprague, D., & Dede, C. (1999). Constructivism in the classroom: If I teach this way, am I doing my job? *Learning and Leading with Technology, 27*(1), 6–9.

Stahl, G., Koschmann, T., & Suthers, D. (2006). Computer-supported collaborative learning: An historical perspective. In *Cambridge Handbook of the Learning Sciences* (pp. 409–426). Cambridge, UK: Cambridge University Press.

Switzer, J. S. (2004). Teaching computer-mediated visual communication to a large section: A constructivist approach. *Innovative Higher Education, 29*(2), 89–101. doi:10.1023/B:IHIE.0000048792.40295.08

Venter, G. (2003). *Optimising internet bandwidth in developing country higher education*. Retrieved from http://www.inasp.info/file/dcc5f088365bd20a8e-80215bc98dec19/research-optimising-internet-bandwidth.html

Wang, F., & Hannafin, M. (2005). Design-based research and technology-enhanced learning environments. *Educational Technology Research and Development*, *53*(4), 5–23. doi:10.1007/BF02504682

Wheeler, S., & Wheeler, D. (2009). Using wikis to promote quality learning in teacher training. *Learning, Media and Technology*, *34*(1), 1–10. doi:10.1080/17439880902759851

Wolff, R., Riedel, J., Jödiscke, C., Schoop, E., & Sonntag, R. (2011). Social media communication: Social media used both as a learning content and as a learning style. In *Proceedings of the IADIS International Conference on e-Learning*, (pp. 41–45). Rome, Italy: IADIS.

World Bank. (2012). Education and development. *The World Bank - Education - Education and Development*. Retrieved November 24, 2011, from http://go.worldbank.org/F5K8Y429G0

KEY TERMS AND DEFINITIONS

Blended Learning: Is a combination of classical and virtual classroom environments.

CMC: Computer-Mediated Communication is information exchange using connected computers.

CSCL: Computer Supported Collaborative Learning uses ICT to facilitate learners' collaboration.

Social Software: Is (Web-based) computer mediated communication and collaboration services.

VCL: Virtual Collaborative Learning is collaborative learning in virtual classroom environment.

Web 2.0: Is the user-centered Web that encourages users' active contribution.

Wiki: Is a network-based collaborative structured writing software.

Chapter 15
The Use of Web 2.0 Technologies by Students from Developed and Developing Countries:
A New Zealand Case Study

Nuddy Pillay
Manukau Institute of Technology, New Zealand

EXECUTIVE SUMMARY

Web 2.0 technologies have not had the impact many perceived they would in many higher learning institutions in both developing and developed countries. Its potentiality has hardly been realised. Great strides have been made in designing and using Web 2.0 technologies to help students learn in the cognitive (mental), behavioural (psychomotor), and affective (feeling) domains. The major challenge is the application of Web 2.0 technologies to the conative (will) domain, which relates to an individual's intrinsic motivation to achieve goals. Students' participation in the Web 2.0 learning environment is influenced by their cultural background, language proficiency, communication style, socio-economic and technological circumstances, learning styles, and prior knowledge. This chapter explores the participation from various groups of students from developed and developing countries. These students are located in learning environments within a tertiary institute, which are facilitated by Web 2.0 technologies. It observes that the students' learning and successful participation in the Web 2.0 environment largely depends on the state of student's conative domain and the interface between their cultural background and learning preference.

DOI: 10.4018/978-1-4666-2515-0.ch015

INTRODUCTION

The first generation Web or Web 1.0 is viewed as an educational and communication resource (Cormode & Krishnamurthy, 2008) similar to traditional classroom resources (Greenhow, et al., 2009). Web 1.0 is predominantly read-only and has conventionally been seen as a source of information like a book or a means of representing information like a poster or a means of communicating information like a visiting speaker to provide authenticity to classroom learning. Most users browse, read, and gather information from a common entry point (Greenhow, et al., 2009). Web 2.0 characterises a shift from read-only to a read and write phase and more recently to a participatory (Anderson, 2007) and interactive phase. This has dramatically changed the way *users* engage and interact with computers, especially online technologies. Users are now construed as participants, collaborators and distributors in the business of creating and sharing knowledge (Pillay, 2007) both in the formal and informal spheres of their everyday activities (Lankshear & Knobel, 2006). The wider social ramifications of Web 2.0 have a bearing on the organisation and delivery of higher education. According to Sife *et al.* (2007), the pedagogical and socio-economic forces that have driven tertiary institutions to adopt and incorporate Web 2.0 technologies in teaching and learning include greater information access; greater communication; synchronous and asynchronous learning; increased co-operation and collaboration; cost-effectiveness and pedagogical improvement. However, Sife *et al.* (2007) also observe that the overall impact of these technologies is limited compared to what its original significance was anticipated to be, in meeting students' learning needs in tertiary institutions both in developed and developing countries.

It is accepted that the first wave of Web 2.0 has over-promised and under delivered (Kruse, 2004). Research conducted by Snow and Farr (1987), Kolbe (1989), and Reeves (2004), indicate a shift. This shift is away from designing and deploying Web 2.0 technologies to help people learn in the cognitive, behavioural, and affective domains to a focus on the conative domain. Conation refers to the connection of knowledge and affect to behaviour and is associated with the issue of *why* (Huitt, 1999). It is the personal will, the intention and striving to make choices with the purpose of achieving a goal (Jasinki, 2004). It is closely related to the concept of volition, which is the freedom to make choices about what to do. Huitt (1999) argues that conation is critical if an individual is to successfully engage in self-direction and self-regulation. This chapter explores this notion and proposes that cultural background, language proficiency, communication style, socio-economic and technological circumstances, learning styles, and prior knowledge impact upon an individual's conation, and this in turn has an effect on participation and engagement in a Web 2.0 learning environment.

This chapter discusses a case study in which Web 2.0 technologies were used in a course offered at an institution of higher learning in New Zealand which meets the needs of students from developed and developing countries. The objectives of this chapter are:

- To explore the implications of Web 2.0 for learning and teaching in higher education;
- To identify the challenges of applying these technologies in tertiary institutions in developing countries;
- To offer some recommendations to address these challenges.

To address these objectives the chapter is structured in the following way:

1. A conceptual background which overviews the theories and frameworks, upon which this study is based, is provided;
2. The case study is discussed by providing the background to the study and demographic details of the students;
3. An account of the unique institutional characteristics is presented;
4. An outline of the methodology used in the study is provided;
5. The results of the study are discussed;
6. Conclusions are then drawn and recommendations made;
7. Limitations of this study and avenues for further research are outlined
8. Key terms associated with study are defined;
9. A list of resources as additional reading is provided.

BACKGROUND

The Shift from Web 1.0 to Web 2.0 and the Implications for Learning and Teaching

While a plethora of views exist in relation to how the shift from Web 1.0 to Web 2.0 influences educational practices in higher education learning environments there is some commonality on the essential differences between Web 1.0 and Web 2.0. Cormode and Krishnamurthy (2008) argue that content creators were few in Web 1.0 with most users simply acting as consumers of content, while any participant can be a content creator in Web 2.0 and numerous technological aids have been designed to maximize the potential for content creation. They argue further that the autonomous nature of Web 2.0 is illustrated by creations of a large number of niche groups (collections of friends) who can exchange content of any kind (text, audio, and video) and tag, comment, and link to both intra-group and extra-group "pages." This theme of Web 1.0 being dissemination orientated and Web 2.0 being participatory and interactive is articulated by Anderson (2007), Eijkman (2008), Ruth and Houghton (2009), and Schroeder *et al.* (2010). The implications of this shift for learning and teaching will now be considered.

In higher education generally speaking, traditional online approaches to learning and teaching are typically based on teacher created learning materials (available through a learning management system (LMS)), fixed assessment deadlines, and assessment tasks designed and controlled by teachers. Lee and McLoughlin (2007) observe that with the advent of and growth in popularity of "Web 2.0" (O'Reilly, 2005) services and tools, the increased prevalence of User-Generated Content (UGC) has implications for learning environments in higher education, and is already influencing pedagogical choices and approaches (Williams & Jacobs, 2004). The affordances of Web 2.0 have made learner-centred education a reality, with tools like Web logs (blogs), wikis, media sharing applications, and social networking sites capable of supporting multiple communities of learning (Lee & McLoughlin, 2007). These tools facilitate and promote informal conversation, dialogue, collaborative content generation, and the sharing of information (Lee & McLoughlin, 2007), giving students access to a wide range of ideas to enable them to construct and share knowledge. Consequently, the traditional power relations between teacher (as all-knowing expert) and student (as learner) is constantly being challenged.

The Web 2.0 learning environment is viewed as a user-driven revolution (Lee & McLoughlin, 2007), with a discernible shift away from the production of Web content by traditional, "authoritative" sources (Anderson, 2007), towards content is that is generated by the users themselves. In academia, the users are students and they have at their disposal social software (Schroeder, et al., 2010) online spaces and skills to contribute ideas and publish their views, research, and interpretations online (Lee & McLoughlin, 2007). Consequently the Web 2.0 environment has reshaped the debate over both *what* we teach and *how* we teach it (Lee & McLoughlin, 2007).

In this chapter, a case study of using blogs as a learning tool will be presented. The term blog was initiated by Barger in 1997 (Paquet, 2003) and in its simplest form refers to a website consisting of the writer's opinions, personal diary entries, or links, called *posts*, arranged in reverse chronological order, in the format of an online journal. Most blogs also allow visitors to add a *comment* below a blog entry. This process of *posting* and *commenting* contributes to the nature of blogging (as an exchange of views) between a primary author and a group of secondary comment contributors, who communicate to an unlimited number of readers (Anderson, 2007).

A blog is typically made up of the following components:

- **Post Date:** Date and time the post was first published.
- **Category:** Category the post is labelled with.
- **Title:** Main title of the post.
- **Body:** Main content of the post.
- **Trackback:** Links back from other sites.
- **Comments:** Comments added by other readers.
- **Permalink:** The url of the full, individual article.
- **Footer:** Usually at the bottom of the post showing date/time, author, category, and statistics like number of views, comments, or trackbacks (Duffy & Bruns, 2006).

This authorship that blogs afford students is empowering and can have significant impact on the efficacy of their learning if it is supported by the institutional infrastructure and educational practices within them. Conole (2008) identifies a tension between the affordances of Web 2.0 and current educational practice. Conole (2008) opines that while the Web 2.0 environment is characterised by speed and immediacy; the ability to access large volumes of information with a mouse click, together with multiple communication channels and social networks seems contradictory to traditional notions of education; the need to reflect, to build cumulatively on existing knowledge and develop individual understanding over time. Conole (2008) argues further that a key characteristic of Web 2.0 is user participation—mash-ups, remixing, and co-construction are fundamental and widespread practices in Web 2.0. While there is more group-collaboration in the learning environment in recent years, students' are assessed largely by individual testing against a set of pre-defined criteria. The challenge which Conole (2008) identifies for Web 2.0 is even where there is learner-centred pedagogic practice current educational systems are not administrative processes and assessment practice are largely hierarchical differentiated educational structures. The question facing educational practitioners who are enthused by the affordances of Web 2.0 namely equity of participation and mutual negotiation is: will simply using Web 2.0 in learning environments be enough to bring about such changes or is something more needed (Conole, 2008)? From Conole's (2008) perspective there appears to be an irresolvable tension between current educational practice, which is essentially individualistic and objective, and the philosophies inherent in Web 2.0—namely social and subjective.

While considering the implications of Web 2.0 for learning and teaching we must be wary that we do not run the risk of hailing this new technological development as a driver for change in itself. Technological innovations—such as those of the industrial revolution—have often been linked to changes in human activity and wider society. However, such a technologically determinist position runs the risk of too strongly implying that technology development alone can create and drive change (Barnatt,

2008). The technological determinism—social agency debate is well documented (Adler, 2008). For the purposes of this chapter, a brief account of this debate will be presented with the intention of establishing the position taken here. Technological determinism has a range of positions or "harder" and "softer" variants (Adler, 2008). The distinction lies in how technology's causes and effects are viewed. In its assessments of technology's effects, proponents of "soft" technological determinism argue that technology is one important force amongst others, while proponents of "hard" technological determinism argue that technology is the main or the only significant driver (Adler, 2008). The antithetical view classified as human agency (Giddens, 1984) or the social constructivist view (e.g. Callon, 1986; Klein & Kleinman, 2002; Leonardi & Barley, 2010) argue that technology and technological implementation is not in itself responsible for change but instead change is driven by an ongoing stream of social action in which people respond to the technology's constraints and affordances, as well as to each other (Leornadi & Barley, 2010). Clearly the impact of Web 2.0 technologies in education generally, and teaching and learning in higher education specifically, cannot be ignored. Barnatt (2008) cites Poster who argued "the conquest of space and time by electronic media augurs more for institutions and for theory than a mere retuning of [existing] practices and ideas" (1992, p. 3) and Heim who suggests that some years ago interfacing with computers became "an ingredient in human knowing" and a "thread in the texture [of our] civilization" (1994, p. 60). Barnatt also makes reference to Turkle who suggested that whilst "for most of the last 50 years technology knew its place" and "seemed external," very recently computing and online technologies have become not just ubiquitous but also "highly intimate" in their facilitation of human relationships (2003, p. 42). In current social practice interfacing with information technology—and in particular engaging in interpersonal communications using Web 2.0 tools such as social networking sites—is a mainstream human activity (Barnatt, 2008). This activity has permeated all aspects of social life. Equally then the technology has been a driver of change but so to have been everyday social practices and skill sets as cultural (rather than technological) change drivers. Barnatt notes that:

Perhaps the greatest error being made by many in their analysis of Web 2.0 has been in labeling the phenomenon as a technological development. ...teenagers who spend hours every day on Facebook or MySpace have not become addicted to computers, but have instead embraced new and now dominant social norms, cultural expectations, and social skills, and that further it is these norms, expectations and skills that are the most significant part of Web 2.0's development. Web 2.0 involves technology. However, the changes with which it is associated are not about technology alone (Barnatt, 2008, p. 48).

It is Barnatt's (2008) position that this chapter favours since it acknowledges the crucial role that the social element plays in using technology. The interface between technology and social and cultural contexts is different in developed countries and developing countries. To contextualise the New Zealand case study in this chapter, a brief review of studies in developing countries will be presented.

Web 2.0 Technologies in Education in Developing Countries

While there is a wide range of research on Web 2.0 technologies in developed countries (Dimitrov, 2006; Duffy & Bruns, 2006; Anderson, 2007; Barnatt, 2008; Greenhow, 2009), there is not the same depth and range of research available for developing countries (Zakaria, et al., 2010). Developing country contexts have been typified by low living standards, high rates of population growth, low income per capita, and general economic and technological dependence on developed economies (Bakari, 2005). In the light of this reality, higher education is often seen as the route for students in these countries to gain entry into the competitive global economic market and improve their quality of life. The increasing need to rely on faster and reliable access to information and knowledge have also become crucial aspects. Consequently, recent developments in the education sector have seen a widespread recognition for the need to position eLearning in a broader context of the emerging knowledge economy (Kahiigi, et al., 2011). However, Garrison and Anderson (2007) point out that we are yet to fully experience the transformative effect of eLearning to support learning in developing countries. Kahiigi (2009) argues that there is an inherent assumption in developing countries that putting in place Information and Communication Technology (ICT) infrastructure and creating online courses equates to eLearning and thus leads to changes in the teaching and learning process. It is widely accepted (Zurita & Ryberg, 2005; Anderson, 2007; Barnatt, 2008; Greenhow, et al., 2009; Kahiigi, 2011) that changes in the mode of education delivery does not in itself translate into a positive development, nor a change or development in the teaching styles or teaching practices. Notwithstanding this, many higher education institutions in developing countries have adopted eLearning with the intention that it will improve the quality of teaching and learning; provide faster and improved access to learning materials; and to reduce the total cost of education as well as to enhance their academic profiles (Engelbrecht, 2003; cited in Kahiigi, et al., 2009). However, much of these efforts to enhance the learning environments in developing countries have been hampered by factors such as unreliable and inadequate ICT infrastructure and services, low levels of ICT literacy and experience, lack of effective teaching practice in their learning programmes and limited lecturer and management support to drive eLearning initiatives (Kahiigi, et al., 2009). As a result, eLearning has not yet fully penetrated the existing education systems in most developing countries.

While acknowledging these challenges for the use of eLearning in higher learning institutions, there are many notable examples of effective adoption and sustained use of technologies with desirable outcomes for students in developing countries. A selection of these studies, which are related to the themes of this chapter, will now be reviewed.

Zakaria *et al.* (2010) conducted research in Malaysia to establish whether studies conducted in developed countries like the USA, Australia and the UK can be generalised to developing countries. The aim of their study was to investigate Malaysian students' use of Information and Communication Technology (ICT) as well as Web 2.0 in classrooms. This study attempted to uncover the extent to which Malaysian students were using the technology in comparisons to other countries. Their study revealed the following key conclusions. Firstly, their results show that Malaysian students seem to feel more comfortable to approach friends or using search engines to obtain information rather than approaching their teachers. Therefore, teachers who expect their students to engage with them positively need to adopt unique strategies to achieve this. Secondly, their study concludes that common interaction activities are not entirely being replaced by Web 2.0 tools. Students' responses in their study show that traditional face-to-face meetings and the use of email for information exchange activities are still the preferred choice of students. Thirdly, they conclude that higher learning institutions may have overlooked the value of having social media phenomenon to be taken into classrooms. They argue further that the full potential of using Web 2.0 for learning can be hindered if learning institutions restrain access to selected tools or have major concerns with students publishing content in public domains. They recommend that student expectations; readiness of staff to implement Web 2.0 in classrooms and institutional policy on adopting external tools and issues on students posting external content in the public domain must be at the forefront of the eLearning agenda.

In another study, which reviews ICT infrastructure in developing countries with a case study from Iran, Omidinia *et al.* (2011) aim to analyse what Iran has achieved so far and what other steps need to be taken to make eLearning using Web 2.0 technologies a successful enterprise. They argue that in order for Iran to accrue the benefits of eLearning, innovative ways of delivering online content on the national backbone of ICT infrastructure need to be developed, instead of relying on expensive unreliable Internet. Omidinia *et al.* (2011) like Zakaria *et al.* (2010) focus on institutional policy and staff professional development issues. However, they also note that Iran lacks eLearning project implementation expertise both within academic institutions and the private sector. However, what is positive is the enthusiasm academic staff are showing towards the availability of open source software and technology for eLearning.

Generally speaking, Web 2.0 in Education in developing countries is specifically challenged by several context variables similar to the studies reviewed above. Nyirongo *et al.* (2009) conducted a study in Malawi and found that lack of equipment, knowledge and skills, involvement in decision making by academic staff members, infrastructure, technical, teaching and administrative support were hindering technology adoption in Education. Kistow (2009) who conducted a study in Trinidad and Tobago concurred with Nyirongo's (2009) conclusions. Sife *et al.* (2007) who focused on Tanzania presented similar conclusions. While it is dangerous generalising from these studies, it is evident that developing countries tend to face similar challenges in the adoption of technology particularly Web 2.0 in higher education.

Although New Zealand is categorised as a developed country its multi-cultural society and large immigrant population renders it a hotbed for educational research in the area of the extent to which Web 2.0 technologies are meeting the needs of the diversity encountered in classrooms.

Bearing the above discussion in mind the position taken here is that Web 2.0 is not about technology alone. While the technology will drive change in teaching and learning, it is the embedded social and cultural practices which take into account the affordances and constraints of Web 2.0 which will also, and perhaps equally, drive change in educational practice in both developed and developing countries. As educators involved in higher education, one of the challenges facing us is to leverage the most value from the generic tools and new practices and expectations of the Web 2.0 age. Web 2.0 technologies have enabled the shift from traditional teaching to participatory learning and recently to socially constructed learning. In traditional teaching or within the receptive view learning is mainly a process of acquiring chunks of information, typically delivered by a teacher (Sfard, 1998). The learner engages in this process intrapersonally. In the next stage, which is participatory, learning is viewed as a process of participating in various cultural practices and shared learning activities. The focus is on the process, that is, on learning to learn, and not so much on the outcomes or products (Lee & McLoughlin, 2007). The learner engages in this process interpersonally. In socially constructed learning or engaging in knowledge creation and sharing, learning means becoming part of a community, through creation and sharing of learning resources. In this process, learners are able to use the affordances of the Web 2.0 learning environment to move beyond participation to engage in creating knowledge actively by sharing ideas and co-creating learning resources.

Over the past few years the socially constructed view of learning described above, has been used in developing courses and applying this to the learning of groups of students within a tertiary institute in New Zealand. The application of this teaching approach to a particular group of students will now be outlined.

Cultural Background and Learning Styles

One of most popularly used frameworks for studying cultural background and communication is based on work conducted by Hofstede (1986). Hofstede developed a four-dimensional model of cultural differences, which distinguishes cultural behaviours that originate from different societies. The four dimensions he suggested were Power Distance (PD), individualism-collectivism, Uncertainty Avoidance (UA), and masculinity-femininity. Power distance refers to the degree to which people accept the unequal distribution of power and wealth in a society. In countries with high PD, individuals with high social status exert great power and influence (Gunawardena, et al., 2001). The Individual-Collectivist dimension refers to the tendency of members of a society to act as individuals or members of groups, and to which culture values individual versus collective achievement or well-being (Zhao, 2004). The Uncertainty-Avoidance dimension refers to the degree to which the individuals of a culture feel threatened by uncertain or unknown situations. Individuals from a culture with high UA are uneasy with unstructured ideas and situations (Hofstede, 1986). The fourth dimension Masculinity-Femininity refers to the degree to which the society prefers distinct gender roles (Hofstede, 1986). He further stated that challenges could arise when teachers and students come from different cultures. These challenges can occur due to differences in the social positions of teachers and students in the two societies, relevance of the curriculum within each of the societies, profiles of cognitive abilities between the populations of the two societies and expected teacher/student and student/student interactions (Hofstede, 1986). The Individual Collectivist dimension that Hofstede proposed will be examined in relation to the students in the case study discussed in this chapter.

Learning styles are often defined as 'characteristic cognitive, affective, and physiological behaviours that serve as relatively stable indicators of how learners perceive, interact with, and respond to the learning environment' (Ladd & Ruby, 1999, p. 363; cited in Heffernan, et al., 2010). The focus on identifying learning styles is crucial when a classroom has diverse learners from a range of cultural backgrounds to avoid a 'one size fits all' teaching style, which is inherently exclusionary and inhibits efficient and effective learning (Wynd & Bozman, 1996). The case of higher education classrooms in New Zealand is decidedly multi-cultural, multi-lingual, and multi-ethnic. While similarities exist between the different cultures the difference are often glossed over by the use of broad-brush labels. For example, the Ministry of Education in New Zealand (MOE) in statistical returns from tertiary institutes require figures about ethnic categories of students they (the MOE) classify as Pacific Island or Asian. New Zealand's population of Pacific Island peoples is a multi-ethnic, heterogeneous group comprising different languages and cultures. In education research reference is made to the term "Pasifika peoples" which is used to describe people living in New Zealand who have migrated from the Pacific Islands, or who identify with the Pacific Islands because of their ancestry or heritage (Gorinski & Fraser, 2006).

Pasifika peoples while they may appear similar are not homogenous. The terminology includes:

Those peoples who have been born in New Zealand or overseas. It is a collective terms used to refer to men, women and children who identify themselves with the islands and /or cultures of Samoa, Cook Islands, Tonga, Nuie, Tokelau, Fiji, Solomon Islands, Tuvalu and other Pasifika or mixed heritages. The term includes a variety of combinations of ethnicities, recent migrants or first, second, third, fourth and subsequent generations of New Zealand born Pasifika peoples (Gorinski & Fraser, 2006, p. 3).

A similar classification exists for the label Asian peoples. Asian peoples is a multi-ethnic, heterogeneous group comprising different languages and cultures. The term Asian is used to describe people living in New Zealand who have migrated from the Asian sub continent, or who identify with the Asian sub-continent because of their ancestry or heritage. Bearing this discussion in mind, the interface between cultural background and learning styles will be examined in relation to the way students classified themselves ethnically.

Culture and Conation

The interplay between culture and motivation to achieve and succeed out of free will has not been the focus of much research. For the purposes of this chapter, the individualism-collectivism dimension of culture will be explored in relation to the exercise of free will to achieve and perform. In Hofstede's (1986) terms, a society that emphasises the role of the individual is individualistic and the one emphasising the role of the group is collectivist (Dimitrov, 2006). Hofstede (1986) described individualism as a society in which "everybody is supposed to take care of himself/herself and his/her immediate family" (p. 48), versus collectivism where "people are born into extended families or clans who protected them in exchange for loyalty" (p. 48). The trend in the research literature is to assign individualism as a characteristic feature of English-speaking Western cultures such as the United States, Australia, Canada, and New Zealand, while collectivism is seen typical for Asian cultures (such as China, Japan, Korea, and Taiwan), Latin-American, African, Middle Eastern, Eastern (Dimitrov, 2006), and as well as the Pacific Islands (Samoa, Tonga, Niue, Fiji). Individualism is defined as valuing the self separately from the group, focusing on personal goals, and showing little emotional attachment to the group (Erez & Somech, 1996 cited in Dimitrov, 2006). Individualistic cultures are seen to be more open to the success and actualisation of the individual, while collectivist cultures work for the success of the family and the group (Dimitrov, 2006). Individualistic cultures are motivated by the self, while collectivistic cultures are motivated by the group. Collectivists, unlike individualists, define the self as an entity extending beyond the individual to include a particular group of others. The students in this study will be considered in terms of the cultural tendencies they exhibited as well as their conation.

THE CASE STUDY

Background to the Study

The study was conducted in an institute of higher learning, in South Auckland, New Zealand. The student population of this institution is very diverse in terms of age, ethnicity, and cultural background. One such student group was used as the sample for this study.

There is a strong emphasis placed on the success and retention of students at this institution and any strategy, which aims to improve success and retention rates, is generally given institutional support. All students are able to access course outlines, assessments and lecture notes for most courses using a Learning Management System (LMS) [*Blackboard v. 7*]. At the same time, lecturers are able to communicate with students using the email, discussion fora and the virtual classroom package which is bundled in the LMS. A positive e-learning culture existed among students and this was a sound foundation on which to base the use of blogs and blogging both as a tool for learning and assessment.

Methodology

The students who comprised the sample for this study were enrolled in a semester long, Level 4 (pre degree) Certificate in Communication Programme. There were five courses in this Programme, a writing course, a personal management course, an interpersonal communication course, a public communication course, and an e-Communication course. All courses were compulsory and students could enroll part time on any number of courses or full time on all courses. The students in this sample were full-time students enrolled in the e-Communication course. The researcher was the only course lecturer. The aims of this course were to introduce students to communication theory and processes in the context of technology (particularly electronic media) and to develop students' communication competencies

Table 1. Demographic details of students enrolled in course

Total number of students	35
Male	9
Female	26
School leavers (under 18 years of age)	10
19-25 year olds	10
26-34	6
35-44	5
45 and above	4
Ethnicity (NZ Ministry of Education category as disclosed by students)	
NZ European/ Pakeha	6
NZ Maori	7
Pacific Island	15
Asian	2
Indian	2
Other	3
International students	1
Students with disabilities	3

in this area through practical application. There were two, two hour teaching sessions each week for 17 weeks. Each teaching session of two hours duration was conducted in a computer laboratory with desktop computers. Table 1 indicates the student diversity prevalent in this cohort.

From initial observations in formulating this study, these diverse students could be broadly typified into three groups. The first group was "older" students who generally speaking, were very adept at oral communication and they were willing and able to share their ideas in face-to-face class discussion. The second group of "younger" students, generally speaking, were quieter during face-to-face discussion, yet performed as well as the first group in written tasks. The third group of students who were from "face-saving" cultures, irrespective of their age, also tended to avoid sharing their views publicly during small group discussion for fear of ridicule and possible embarrassment. Given these observations, the challenge faced was to create the classroom context in which students from each of these generalised groups were equally willing and able to share their ideas with others in the class. Duffy and Bruns (2006) argue that a digital literacy exists among students where flexible learning technologies need to be explored for collaborative and co-creative purposes. The blog was one such technology, which could enable collaborative content creation, formative evaluation of learner work and as importantly, individual as well as group reflection on learning experiences. Consequently, this study explored the use of the blog to facilitate student-student collaboration and communication and student-lecturer communication.

To gather data an online questionnaire adapted from Williams and Jacobs (2004) was used at the end of the course. For each question, students could comment on their responses if they chose to hence making the survey open-ended. Given that the researcher was the class lecturer, the use of the online questionnaire; ensured that the participants in the research were assured of confidentiality. They were also assured that their responses would have no impact whatsoever on their course results. The quantitative data was statistically analysed as shown in the tables in the results section and the qualitative data was analysed to established trends/patterns in student responses.

THE CONSTRUCTIVIST TEACHING AND LEARNING APPROACH USED IN THIS CASE STUDY

Seitzinger (2006) cites the following critical features as noted by Miers (2004):
   Constructivist learning should be:

- **Active and Manipulative:** Engaging students in interactions and explorations with learning materials and providing them opportunities for them to observe the results of their manipulations.
- **Constructive and Reflective:** Enabling student to integrate new ideas with prior knowledge to make meaning and enable learning through reflection
- **Intentional:** Providing opportunities for students to articulate their learning goals and monitor their progress in achieving them.
- **Authentic:** Challenging and real-world (or simulated) facilitating better understanding and learning to new situations.
- **Co-Operative, Collaborative, and Conversational:** Providing student's opportunities to interact with each other to clarify and share ideas, to seek assistance, to negotiate problems, and discuss solutions.

The Blog as a Constructivist Learning Tool

The blog was used as a constructivist-learning tool to engage the students typified into the three groups mentioned at the beginning of this case study. To do this effectively it was necessary to provide the students with some background to blogs and the blogging process as well as provide them the opportunity to gain the skills and knowledge to create their own blogs in a short space of time. For this to be efficient and effective, the process of creating, formatting, and uploading material to their blogs had to be automated and easy hence freeing students' attention to the actual task at hand. A student from a degree programme created a video presentation which provided the students in this course with a hands on user guide which allowed students to work "at their own pace in their own place" using blogging freeware (www.blogger.com) to learn about blogs and ultimately to create their own blogs.

Once students had created their own blogs using the video presentation, they had to construct their own profiles and then use their blog as an online learning journal in which they reflected on their perceptions of the learning materials and on their own learning process for a particular class topic. The process of knowledge creation and sharing was evidenced in student work by the way in which students learnt from their own observations and reflections and built on their knowledge, in response to comments by other students in the class.

Another requirement of the task was that students had to post their views on a topic, in this case, visual literacy. Thereafter they were required to read at least three posts of other students and comment on them. This task ensured that students had to do more than simply passively browse - which they were so used to when they "googled." They were put in a position where they had to consider someone else's views, formulate their own opinion about what they had read and then construct sentences to effectively articulate those opinions. Students were getting feedback on their ideas and opinions from their peers and this served to motivate them to both post and comment more. In this way, collaborative learning was taking place and a very closely knit community of practice was formed.

Results and Conclusions

The blog has a place in learning contexts where students have access to computers and the Internet and in which the teacher wants to encourage self-expression and creativity. Its linkages to other bloggers establish the same peer-group relationships found in non-virtual worlds (Huffaker, 2005). Its "underdetermined" design, where a system is engaging, yet intuitive and easy to learn (Cassell, 2002), makes it equitable for many age groups and both genders, and simple for teachers to implement. In the context in which it was used in this study, its strength was that it allowed students/bloggers to access their blogs and those of their peers anywhere at any time so that they were able to work "at their own place at their own pace." This created the opportunity for learning to continue outside the classroom and students engaged with each other in virtual space. Those students who were familiar with online social networking sites like Facebook, Myspace, and Bebo were more comfortable posting to their blogs than students who were not avid users of these sites. The former students moved seamlessly from the online social networking environment to the learning environment. In this study, the blog was both individualistic and collaborative. For example, students had a personal space to read and write alongside a shared space, where ideas were pooled, questions and issues were raised and answered. While journal writing conjures images of writers noting their thoughts in solitude, in this study it was found that blogs on the other hand facilitated the development of a community of students. Similar to the findings in this study, Seitzinger (2006) cites two instances to show how blogs create a community of students. In the first instance, Glogowski (2012), researching the use of blogs in primary education in Ontario, Canada, comments that when his students were deprived of blogs for a few weeks while he was transferring platforms, they suffered withdrawal symptoms:

This experience confirmed my belief that blogging is about creating communities... what they missed was situated writing, a cognitive activity situated within a specific space that fosters cognitive engagement. They missed interactions, interactions with texts and with each other through texts. (http://www.teachandlearn.ca/blog/2005/12/07/tools-interiorised/).

In the second instance Will Richardson (2012) responding to Glogowski's post notes:

... it's is striking to me how much different this level of concern is compared to all the paper content we've created in the past. It's all about the investment that we make in this, the idea that what we're writing has a legitimate audience. How different it must be for these students who want to stay connected to the people and the ideas that nurtured their learning. (http://Weblogg-ed.com/2006/caring-about-the-content/).

Similarly, in this study it was found that the students' blogs by their nature, afforded them the opportunity to construct their learning in a community and as a consequence they were more engaged with their learning and it had higher value with them. Put simply, they were the "owners" of their learning. Blogging, since it focused first on the individual and then the group or community, worked very well in this study. The class was divided into three groups—as explained earlier—with little sense of group belonging early in the semester and the lack of turn-taking and interpersonal communication skills was evident. The blogs students created provided a platform for individual expression and also reader commentary, critique and developing shared meaning in a non-threatening learning environment which reduced the effects of cultural difference and differing levels of face to face communication competence.

Tables 2 to 5 present the results of an online questionnaire open to all students who had been enrolled in the e-Communication course. There were 35 respondents,

Table 2. The blog as a medium for facilitating learning

Question 1: Do you think the class Blogs assisted you with your learning in this course	Score DC	%	Score DV	%
A. Strongly agree	10	63	4	21
B. Agree	5	31	10	53
C. Neither agree nor disagree	1	6	1	5
D. Disagree	0		2	11
E. Strongly disagree	0		1	5
F. No answer	0		1	

a response rate of 100%. Note that the 'no answer' response was removed from percentage calculations and these percentages may not add up to 100% as a result of rounding. All students in the class participated in the blogging activity.

For comparison between students from developed and developing countries students in this study were classified as New Zealanders or by cultural heritage associated with the Pacific Islands, Asia or India in relation to how they classified themselves ethnically in the categories of the MOE classification. Based on these responses the 35 students were then re-categorised as displaying characteristics of developed or developing countries as follows:

- **Developed Countries (DC):** 16 students (13 NZ born European/Pakeha and Maori; 3 students in the other category)
- **Developing countries (DV):** 19 students (15 "Pacific Island" students; 2 "Asian" students, and 2 "Indian" students)

Their responses will now be presented in these categories.

For both groups of students the class blogs proved useful in aiding their learning with 94% of the DC group either agreeing or strongly agreeing and 74% of the DV group either agreeing or strongly agreeing.

In response to the open-ended questions both sets of students felt that the blog allowed them the freedom to search for resources and share these out of lecture time. Some students felt that seeing other students views inspired them to write. One such comment was, "After reading other students blogs I felt confident I could do it too."

Interestingly, the two students who disagreed from the DV group felt that getting access to computers outside of class time hindered their learning.

The next set of questions related to the cultural background students identified with and their learning styles in relation to using blogs as a learning tool.

To establish the cultural identity of students without making assumptions three questions similar in nature to the one shown in Table 3 were asked.

The responses to this question and others in this set validated the claim that the majority of students who were identified in the DC group considered themselves individualist (75%) and the majority of students in the DV group identified themselves as collectivist (74%).

81% of students from the DC group indicated an individual learning preference and 79% of students from the DV group indicated a preference to learn in groups. This finding is consistent with other studies like, Erez and Somech, (1996) and Dimitrov, (2006).

The responses here indicate that students from the DC group felt that the class blogs suited their learning style preference with 69% agreeing or strongly agreeing. On the other hand, students from the DV group were of the view that the class blogs were less suited to their learning style preference with 37% disagreeing or strongly

Table 3. Students' cultural background (individualist or collectivist?)

Question 2. In your culture is the individual more important than the extended family/group/community or are they equally important?	Score DC	%	Score DV	%
A. The individual is more important	12	75	1	5
B. The extended family group/community is more important	1	6	14	74
C. The individual and the extended family/group/community are equally important	3	19	5	26

Table 4. Interface between learning style and cultural background

Question 3: In your culture, do people prefer to study and learn on their own or in groups?	Score DC	%	Score DV	%
A. On their own	13	81	2	11
B. In groups	1	6	15	79
C. No preference	2	13	2	11

Table 5. Blogs and learning style

Question 4: Do you believe that the class blogs were suited to the learning style preference in your culture?	Score DC	%	Score DV	%
A. Strongly agree	2	13	1	5
B. Agree	9	56	5	26
C. Neither agree nor disagree	3	3	5	26
D. Disagree	0		6	32
E. Strongly disagree	0		1	5
F. No answer	2		1	

disagreeing. In the open-ended answers students from this group supported their responses with comments like:

Before I put myself out there I would like to have a face to face discussion with my classmates just to check if I'm on the right track.

I like bouncing my ideas off others first before I write because I express myself in a small group better. On the blog everyone will see my work.

I didn't mind blogging but the class discussion really helped. I need both the face to face classes and the online blog to learn better.

In my culture we learn better from the teacher—he knows all the answers and can help us. I trust the teacher more than other students in the class.

These responses indicate that the students from the DV group have some reservations about working solely on their own and solely online. The need for face-to-face interaction should not be underestimated to support student learning. In addition, the response showing the value attached to the authority of the teacher in these cultures signals the need for cultural awareness on the part of the academic staff and institutions when using Web 2.0 technologies for learning. The expectation in power distant cultures is for teachers to set the tone and determine the direction of how students' learn (Olaniran, 2008). Without this, students from these cultures may experience role confusion, which could negatively impact on their learning.

General Student Feedback

Both groups DC and DV students were generally very positive about the use of blogs as one of the tools to help them learn better. They were clear that blogging was a useful way to engage them in the content and they enjoyed the "out of class interaction with their peers." The following comments reflect typical student responses. The responses are classified by group:

DC Group:

It was great to write what I wanted when I was in the mood to write. You can't always be at your best in class.

If it wasn't for marks I don't think I would have blogged- but when everyone was asking me if I read their blogs I read a few. ... it looked easy and then I started.

Reading other students' blogs was great because it gave me a better idea what to write. ..it gave me a kickstart.

I like the idea that I can say what I want without someone editing my words.

I enjoyed making comments on other students' blogs- it gave me a sense of power.

Noteworthy in these comments is the importance these students place on the extent to which blogging affords personal empowerment. For these students and others like them, blogs provide a virtual personal space (Glogoff, 2005) where they share their knowledge without censure and express their personal styles (Nardi, et al., 2004).

DV Group:

I thought I enjoyed speaking more than writing but once I got into it [blogging] it was great.

Once I saw other students making positive comments about my ideas I felt motivated and I wanted to write more.

While getting good comments from other students was nice It was great receiving good comments from my lecturer.

I enjoyed reading what other students had to write on my blog. It was like what I said mattered to them. It made me feel good!

These comments each indicate the need for further research in terms of culture, learning styles and using Web 2.0 technologies similar to the study by Olaniran (2009).

Blogging appealed to the students from the DC and DV groups for different reasons. The DV students found the blog appealing since their views were being evaluated by others and they got feedback from their peers. Interestingly, students from this group also offered criticism clearly showing caring and sensitivity to the feelings of the writer. Their feedback was relationship-orientated. On the other hand, students from the DC group found the blog appealing because they could write at their own pace at their own place. At the same time, their critique of their peers' writing was more task-orientated. It will be worthwhile to investigate whether associations exist between students' cultural background and motivation to maintain relationships or motivation to achieve assessment tasks.

Student Achievement and the Conative Domain

Student achievement in this course was improved as a result of them blogging. One concern was to establish what motivated them to engage in blogging to the extent they had done so that this could inform teaching strategies in other courses. This initiated an interest in the area of conation. Riggs provides the following conceptual definition of conation:

Conation can be thought of as "an internal engine" that drives the external tasks and desires. It is the interconnecting network of energy that transforms ideas into action. If we use an automobile metaphor, we might say that perception of reality will determine if the drive shaft (the work domain) is going to engage the engine (the brain), and the transmission (the heart of learning) to the total process. The drive shaft links "what I want to know" to "how I feel about the task" and subsequently "how I will ultimately respond to the task, the various situations in life, and the world in which I live" (Riggs, 2004, p. 2).

Riggs (2004) contends that arguments that as educators we cannot "make" students learn are misguided. He suggests that as educators we can awaken the elements of drive or free will through authentic and creative teaching. He argues that conative teachers create conative students. In the conative classroom performance is high and a climate of excellence is created and maintained through the development of mutual trust, respect, student potential, support, high expectations, a collaborative synergy, achievement, and happiness. In this learning environment, teachers are human resource developers and knowledge brokers, who utilize their skills to transform lives. A link that has been missing in our search for relevance in education is the link between conation and school achievement. An understanding of the crucial role the *will* to learn plays in sustainable school achievement and, ultimately, success in life, must receive our attention (Riggs, 2004).

The chart below illustrates the differences and the interconnectiveness of the relationships among the cognitive, affective, and conative domains (see Table 6).

While the students in this study showed that their will to succeed and their own intrinsic motivation ensured that they were successful, this is an avenue for further research.

Table 6. The relationship between the cognitive, affective, and conative domains

COGNITIVE (To Know)	AFFECTIVE (To Feel)	CONATIVE (To Have the Will)
I have to learn how the industrial revolution impacted rural areas.	I know I can research this topic and find the information I need.	I am having a difficult time finding what I need, but I will not give up!
Attributes	Attributes	Attributes
Knowing	Emotions	Will
Problem-Solving	Feelings	Persistence
Thinking Critically	Self-Perception	Wilfulness
Reflective Thinking	Self-Concept	Patience
Comprehending		Tenacity

RECOMMENDATIONS

Educational Cultural mismatch

The educational cultural mismatch between achievement requirements in educational institutions (individualistic in nature), and the cultural expectations of students (collectivistic in nature) and therefore collaborative, needs to be addressed to ensure that students feel culturally safe and catered for in their learning. If this is not the case then students are likely to exhibit behaviours and attitudes that are culturally appropriate in their home/community environment, but are incongruous with the institute's code of conduct (Garcia Coll & Magnuson, 2000).

Institutional Practices

Institutional practices impact upon student achievement. While students are willing and able to use Web 2.0 technologies in their learning, institutional practices are often traditional and assessment practices require them to engage in traditional tests, assignments, and examinations. Value has to be placed on the process of learning to the same extent that emphasis is placed on the product or outcome of learning. Students' work, as they craft their ideas and thinking in a collaborative online environment, needs to be given credit towards determining their achievement in a course. If this is not the case then the student cry of "is this for marks" will always precede their learning endeavour. This will have a negative impact on their conation.

The issue of student language competence in face-to-face classroom interaction as opposed to their language competence in the online environment needs to be addressed. Students' work in the online environment is often viewed with suspicion particularly if it is substantially better than their work in face-to-face classroom interaction. Institutional practices need to change to provide students who are not first language English speakers the opportunity to be assessed using a different medium other than in synchronous face-to-face settings. McNaughton's (2004) findings while researching school students is worthy of note here. McNaughton confirms earlier work by Wilkinson (1998) around factors contributing to the language divide between first and second language English speaking students. Wilkinson (1998) concluded that teachers' sensitivity to individual students' needs, teacher instructional practices, and school organisational practices were important factors influencing minority student achievement, not inability, family background, or a host of other explanations grounded in a monocultural deficit educational paradigm. A commitment to a multicultural institutional paradigm which is reflected both in teaching and assessment practices will work in the interest of all students but particularly for students who are from non-English speaking backgrounds. Using Web 2.0 technologies which are asynchronous for students from non-English speaking backgrounds is worth exploring in greater depth to reduce the overall impact of traditional institutional practices.

Socio-Cultural Deprivation

The low educational achievement of students who are not from the mainstream culture is often explained through the notion of socio-cultural deprivation. Proponents of this position argue that these students and their families do not have the social and cultural capital (Bourdieu, 1977) to perform in the modern education system and therefore their achievement is poor. This perspective is premised on the position that family resources, or their lack, are what creates educational disadvantage, rather than the education system (Gorinski & Fraser, 2006). In one study (Schoeffel & Meleisea, 1996; cited in Gorinski & Fraser, 2006) of Pacific Island families' attitudes to child training and discipline in Otara, South Auckland, found that many associated parenting skills were at odds with those of European New Zealanders. Schoeffel and Meleisea (1996) noted that such socialisation practices contributed to difficulties that children have with interactive teaching techniques. They suggested "that considerably more emphasis needs to be placed on developing the interactive learning abilities of Pacific Islands Polynesian children" (p. 134); that is, the children should conform to the institution. The notion of culturally and socially deficit students needs to be challenged by quality teaching which recognises and builds on students' prior experiences and knowledge. The collaborative spaces afforded by Web 2.0 technologies for students to create and co-create knowledge and share their ideas must be fully exploited so that students from other cultures outside of the mainstream culture, feel comfortable but more importantly have a greater opportunity to be successful in the higher education.

LIMITATIONS OF THIS STUDY

This study involved a small sample of students and evaluated the practice of blogging in the context of a single course. Consequently, the findings have limited generalisability.

This study was exploratory in nature, and while it drew some conclusions, the themes around culture and learning styles and conation and culture need far greater in-depth investigation.

Although New Zealand is categorised as a developed country its multi-cultural society and large immigrant population renders it a hotbed for educational research in the area of the extent to which Web 2.0 technologies are meeting the needs of the diversity encountered in classrooms. While the students in this study classified themselves as displaying the characteristics of peoples from developing countries a more definitive classification based on a wider range of criteria would have benefitted this study.

Finally, while attention was given in this study to learning styles of students based on individual and collectivist cultural dispositions, the other cultural elements were relatively ignored. One particular dimension the oral vs. written cultural traditions warranted closer scrutiny given that the Web 2.0 blogosphere is read/write and more tailored to the to the written traditions of individualistic cultures; whereas, collectivistic cultures foster a more oral tradition. Investigating other Web 2.0 technologies like podcasts and video conferencing would have shed more light on the dichotomy between the oral and written traditions in learning environments.

REFERENCES

Adler, P. S. (2008). Technological determinism. In Clegg, S., & Bailey, J. R. (Eds.), *International Encyclopedia of Organization Studies*. Thousand Oaks, CA: Sage Publications.

Anderson, P. (2007). *What is web 2.0? Ideas, technologies and implications for education*. Retrieved December 16, 2010, from http://www.jisc.ac.uk/media/documents/techwatch/tsw0701b.pdf

Barnatt, C. (2008). Higher education 2.0. *International Journal of Management Education*, 7(3), 47–56. doi:10.3794/ijme.73.250

Bourdieu, P. (1977). *Outline of a theory of practice*. Cambridge, UK: Cambridge University Press.

Callon, M. (1986). The sociology of an actor-network: The case of the electric vehicle. In Callon, M., Law, J., & Rip, A. (Eds.), *Mapping the Dynamics of Science and Technology* (pp. 19–34). London, UK: McMillan.

Conole, G. (2008). New schemas for mapping pedagogies and technologies. *Ariadne, 56*. Retrieved September 22, 2010 from http://www.ariadne.ac.uk/issue56/conole/

Cormode, G., & Krishnamurthy, B. (2008). Key differences between web 1.0 and web 2.0. *First Monday, 13*(6). Retrieved October 5, 2010, from http://www.uic.edu/htbin/cgiwrap/bin/ojs/index.php/fm/article/view/2125/1972

Dimitrov, D. (2006). Cultural differences in motivation for organizational learning and training. *International Journal Of Diversity In Organisations. Communities & Nations, 5*(4), 37–48.

Duffy, P., & Bruns, A. (2006). The use of blogs, wikis and RSS in education: A conversation of possibilities. In *Proceedings Online Learning and Teaching Conference 2006*, (pp. 31-38). Brisbane, Australia: IEEE. Retrieved September 11, 2008 from http://eprints.qut.edu.au

Eijkman, H. (2008). Web 2.0 as a non-foundational network-centric learning space. *Campus-Wide Information Systems, 25*(2), 93–104. doi:10.1108/10650740810866567

Erez, M., & Somech, A. (1996). Is group productivity loss the rule or the exception? Effects of culture and group-based motivation. *Academy of Management Journal, 39*(6), 1513–1537. doi:10.2307/257067

Garcia Coll, C., & Magnuson, K. (2000). Cultural differences as sources of developmental vulnerabilities and resources: A view from developmental research. In Meisels, S., & Shonkoff, J. (Eds.), *Handbook of Early Childhood Intervention* (pp. 94–111). Cambridge, UK: Cambridge University Press. doi:10.1017/CBO9780511529320.007

Giddens, A. (1984). *The constitution of society*. Berkeley, CA: University of California Press.

Glogoff, S. (2005). Instructional blogging: Promoting interactivity, student-centered learning, and peer input. *Innovate, 1*(5). Retrieved from http://www.innovateonline.info/pdf/vol1_issue5/Instructional_Blogging-__Promoting_Interactivity,_Student-Centered_Learning,_and_Peer_Input.pdf

Gorinski, R., & Fraser, C. (2006). *Literature review on the effective engagement of pasifika parents & communities in education*. Wellington, New Zealand: Ministry of Education.

Greenhow, C., Robelia, B., & Hughes, J. E. (2009). Learning, teaching, and scholarship in a digital age. *Educational Researcher, 38,* 246–259. doi:10.3102/0013189X09336671

Gunawardena, C. N., Nolla, A. C., Wilson, P. L., Lopez-Islas, J. R., Ramirez-Angel, N., & Megchun-Alpizar, R. M. (2001). A cross-cultural study of group process and development in online conferences. *Distance Education, 22*(1), 85–121. doi:10.1080/0158791010220106

Heffernan, T., Morrison, M., Basu, P., & Sweeney, A. (2010). Cultural differences, learning styles and transnational education. *Journal of Higher Education Policy and Management, 32*(1), 27–39. doi:10.1080/13600800903440535

Hofstede, G. (1986). Cultural differences in teaching and learning. *International Journal of Intercultural Relations, 10,* 301–320. doi:10.1016/0147-1767(86)90015-5

Huffaker, D. A., & Calvert, S. L. (2005). Gender, identity, and language use in teenage blogs. *Journal of Computer-Mediated Communication, 10*(2). Retrieved November 12 2008 from http://jcmc.indiana.edu/vol10/issue2/huffaker.html

Huitt, W. (1999). Conation as an important factor of mind. In *Educational Psychology: Interactive.* Valdosa, GA: Valdosa State University.

Jasinski, M. (2004). *EDUCHAOS: Go conative- Where there's a will you're away!* Retrieved March 15, 2010 from, http://learnscope.flexiblelearning.net.au/Learnscope/golearn.asp?Catewgory=11&DocumentId=6369

Kahiigi, E., Hansson, H., Danielson, M., Tusubira, F. F., & Vesisenaho, M. (2011). Collaborative elearning in a developing country: A university case study in Uganda. In *Proceedings of the European Conference on E-Learning,* (pp. 932-942). IEEE.

Kistow, B. (2009). E-learning at the Arthur Lok Jack graduate school of business: A survey of faculty members. *International Journal of Education and Development using Information and Communication Technology, 5*(4), 14-20.

Klein, H. K., & Kleinman, D. L. (2002). The social construction of technology: Structural considerations. *Science, Technology & Human Values, 27*(1), 28–52. doi:10.1177/016224390202700102

Kolbe, K. (1989). *Conative connection: Acting on instinct.* Beverly, MA: Kathy Kolbe.

Kruse, K. (2004). *The state of e-learning: Looking at history with the technology hypecycle.* Retrieved April 12, 2010, from http://www.e-learningguru.com/articles/art2.htm

Lankshear, C., & Knobel, M. (2006). *New literacies: Everyday practices and class-room learning* (2nd ed.). Maidenhead, UK: Open University Press.

Lee, M. J. W., & McLoughlin, C. (2007). Teaching and learning in the web 2.0 era: Empowering students through learner-generated content. *International Journal of Instructional Technology and Distance Learning, 4*(10), 21–34.

Leornardi, P. M., & Barley, S. R. (2010). What's under construction here? *The Academy of Management Annals, 4*(1), 1–51.

McNaughton, S. (2003). Profiling teaching and learning needs in beginning literacy instruction: The case of children in "low decile" schools in New Zealand. *Journal of Literacy Research.* Retrieved August 9, 2010, from http://www.findarticles.com/p/articles/mi_qa3785/is_200307/ai_n0201170/

Miers, J. (2004). *BELTS or braces? Technology school of the future*. Retrieved November 12 2007 from http://www.tsof.edu.au/research/Reports04/miers

Nardi, B. A., Schiano, D. J., Gumbrecht, M., & Swartz, L. (2004). Why we blog. *Communications of the ACM, 47*(12), 41–46. doi:10.1145/1035134.1035163

Nyirongo, N. K. (2009). *Technology adoption and integration: A descriptive study of a higher education institution in a developing nation*. (Unpublished Thesis PhD). Virginia Polytechnic Institute and State University. Blacksburg, VA. Retrieved from http://scholar.lib.vt.edu/theses/available/etd-04132009-095508/unrestricted/Nertha_etd_2009.pdf

O'Reilly, T. (2005). *What is web 2.0: Design patterns and business models for the next generation of software*. Retrieved December 15, 2006, from http://www.oreil-lynet.com/pub/a/oreilly/tim/news/2005/09/30/what-is-web-20.html

Olaniran, B. A. (2009). Culture, learning styles, and web 2.0. *Interactive Learning Environments, 17*(4), 261–271. doi:10.1080/10494820903195124

Omidinia, S., Masrom, M., & Selamat, H. (2011). Review of e-learning and ict infrastructure in developing countries (case study of Iran). *American Journal of Economics and Business Administration, 3*, 120–125. doi:10.3844/ajebasp.2011.120.125

Pillay, N. (2007). Search the y drive or simply ask Sally: Staff perceptions of knowledge creation in an organisation. *International Journal of Knowledge. Culture and Change Management, 5*(6), 77–86.

Reeves, T. C. (2004). *The will to fly: eLearning and the challenge of the conative domain.* Presentation of the e-Agenda International Round Table. Retrieved May 11 2011 from http;//www.Griffith.edu.au/text/conference/eagenda2004/ content rt speakers.html

Riggs, E. G. (2004). *Connecting with students'will to succeed: The power of conation*. Glenview, CA: Pearson Professional Development.

Ruth, A., & Houghton, L. (2009). The wiki way of learning. *Australasian Journal of Educational Technology, 25*(2), 135–152.

Schoeffel, P., Meleisea, M., David, R., Kalauni, R., Kalolo, K., & Kingi, P. (1996). Pacific islands Polynesian attitudes to child training and discipline in New Zealand: Some policy implications for social welfare and education. *Social Policy Journal of New Zealand: Te Puna Whakaaro, 6*, 134–147.

Schroeder, A., Minocha, S., & Schneider, C. (2010). The strengths, weaknesses, opportunities and threats of using social software in higher and further education teaching and learning. *Journal of Computer Assisted Learning, 26*, 159–174. doi:10.1111/j.1365-2729.2010.00347.x

Seitzinger, J. (2006). *Be constructive: blogs, podcasts, and wikis as constructivist learning tools*. Retrieved February 11, 2008 from http://www.elearningguild.com/pdf/2/073106des.pdf

Sfard, A. (1998). On two metaphors for learning and the dangers of choosing just one. *Educational Researcher, 27*(2), 4–13.

Sife, A. S., Lwoga, E. T., & Sanga, C. (2007). New technologies for teaching and learning: Challenges for higher learning institutions in developing countries. *International Journal of Education and Development using ICT, 3*(2), 57-67. Retrieved June 16, 2011 from http://ijedict.dec.uwi.edu/viewarticle.php?id=246

Snow, R. E., & Farr, M. J. (1987). Cognitive-conative-affective processes in aptitude, learning and instruction: An introduction. In Snow, R. E., & Farr, M. J. (Eds.), *Aptitude, Learning and Instruction* (p. 1010). Hoboken, NJ: Lawrence Erlbaum Associates.

Wilkinson, I. (1998). Dealing with diversity: Achievement gaps in reading literacy among New Zealand students. *Reading Research Quarterly, 33*, 144–167. doi:10.1598/RRQ.33.2.1

Williams, J. B., & Jacobs, J. (2004). Exploring the use of blogs as learning spaces in the higher education sector. *Australasian Journal of Educational Technology, 20*(2), 232-247. Retrieved October 2, 2007, from http://www.ascilite.org.au/ajet/ajet20/williams.html

Wynd, W. R., & Bozman, C. S. (1996). Student learning style: A segmentation strategy for higher education. *Journal of Education for Business, 71*(4), 232–235. doi:10.1080/08832323.1996.10116790

Zakaria, M. H., Watson, J., & Edwards, S. L. (2010). Investigating the use of web 2.0 technology by Malaysian students. *Multicultural Education & Technology Journal, 4*(1), 17–29. doi:10.1108/17504971011034700

Zurita, L., & Ryberg, T. (2005). Towards a collaborative approach of introducing e-learning in higher education institutions: How do university teachers conceive and react to transitions to e-learning. In *Proceedings WCCE 2005*. IFIP.

ADDITIONAL READING

Armstrong, J., & Franklin, T. (2008). *A review of current and developing international practice in the use of social networking (Web 2.0) in higher education*. Retrieved from http://www.franklinconsulting.co.uk/

Beach, R., Anson, C., Breuch, L. K., & Swiss, T. (2008). *Teaching writing using blogs, wikis, and other digital tools*. Norwood, MA: Christopher Gordon.

Bishop, R. (2003). Changing power relations in education: Kaupapa Māori messages for ʻmainstream' education in Aotearoa/New Zealand. *Comparative Education, 39*(2), 221–238. doi:10.1080/03050060302555

Bower, M. (2008). Affordance analysis - Matching learning tasks with learning technologies. *Educational Media International, 45*(1), 3–15. doi:10.1080/09523980701847115

Boyd, D. (2005). *Apophenia: Why web 2.0 matters: Preparing for glocalization*. Retrieved from http://www.zephoria.org/thoughts/archives /2005/09/05/why_web20_matte.html

Darwish, A., & Huber, D. (2003). Individualism vs collectivism in different cultures: A cross-cultural study. *Intercultural Education, 14*(1), 47–55. doi:10.1080/1467598032000044647

Ebner, M., Lienhardt, C., Rohs, M., & Meyer, I. (2010). Microblogs in higher education – A chance to facilitate informal and process oriented learning? *Computers and Education*. Retrieved from http://www.sciencedirect.com/science/article/B6V CJ4Y34W8F1/2/799ab0b1112d5696a251fca84be472c3

Eijkman, H., & Clarke, B. (2007). Towards a participatory learning and assessment culture in higher education: Leveraging social technologies to reframe our curricular practices. In *Proceedings of the International Conference on Information Communication Technologies in Education*. Heraklion, Crete: IEEE.

Ellison, N., & Wu, Y. (2008). Blogging in the classroom: A preliminary exploration of student attitudes andiImpact on comprehension'. *Journal of Educational Multimedia and Hypermedia, 17,* 99–122.

Exter, K. D., Rowe, S., Boyd, W., & Lloyd, D. (2012). Using web 2.0 technologies for collaborative learning in distance education—Case studies from an Australian university. *Future Internet, 4*(1), 216–237. doi:10.3390/fi4010216

Farmer, B., Yue, A., & Brooks, C. (2008). Using blogging for higher order learning in large cohort university teaching: A case study. *Australasian Journal of Educational Technology, 24*(2), 123–136.

Gibbs, G., & Simpson, C. (2004). Does your assessment support your students' learning? *Journal of Learning and Teaching in Higher Education, 1*(1), 3–31.

Herrington, J., Herrington, A., & Olney, I. (2012). Mobile learning in higher education: Authentic tasks, assessment and web 2.0. In T. Amiel & B. Wilson (Eds.), *Proceedings of World Conference on Educational Multimedia, Hypermedia and Telecommunications,* (pp. 1988-1993). Chesapeake, VA: AACE.

Higdon, J., & Topaz, C. (2009). Blogs and wikis as instructional tools. *College Teaching, 57,* 105–109. doi:10.3200/CTCH.57.2.105-110

Hofstede, G. (1984). *Culture's consequences.* Newbury Park, CA: Sage.

Kolbe, K. (1990). *The conative connection.* Reading, MA: Addison-Wesley.

Lwoga, E. (2012). Making learning and web 2.0 technologies work for higher learning institutions in Africa. *Campus-Wide Information Systems, 29*(2), 90–107. doi:10.1108/10650741211212359

Morrison, M., Sweeney, A., & Heffernan, T. (2003). Learning styles of on-campus and off-campus students: The challenge for marketing educators. *Journal of Marketing Education, 25,* 208–218. doi:10.1177/0273475303257520

O'Reilly, T. (2005a). *What is web 2.0: Design patterns and business models for the next generation of software.* Retrieved from http://www.oreillynet.com/pub/a/oreilly/tim/news/2005/09/30/what-is-web-20.html

Romiszowski, A. J. (2004). How's the e-learning baby? Factors leading to success or failure of an educational technology innovation. *Educational Technology, 44,* 5–27.

Samarawickrema, G., Benson, R., & Brack, C. (2010). Different spaces: Staff development for web 2.0. *Australasian Journal of Educational Technology, 26*(1), 44-49. Retrieved from http://www.ascilite.org.au/ajet/ajet26/samarawickrema.html

KEY TERMS AND DEFINITIONS

Conative Domain: An individual's intrinsic motivation to achieve goals.

Constructivist Learning Tools: Web- 2.0 technologies, which allow students to construct and reflect on their learning; to monitor their progress; to simulate real world situations in the classroom and to provide the opportunities for students to interact with each other to clarify, share ideas and seek assistance.

Educational Cultural Mismatch: The situation where the expectations of educational institutions are different from the cultural expectations of students.

Individualism-Collectivism Cultural Dimension: The orientation that people from different cultures have of placing their personal goals and needs above the needs of others in the group or community (individualistic) or before themselves (collectivistic).

Socially Constructed View of Learning: Students engage in knowledge creation and sharing and create and co-create learning resources.

Socio-Cultural Deprivation: The argument that students are ill-prepared for schooling and education because they lack social and cultural skills to be successful in education often referred to as the deficit model.

Technological Determinism-Social Agency Debate: This debate is around the issue of the role of technology in shaping society and driving social change the former position argues that technology is the main driver of change and the latter position argues that change happens since people act and respond to technology's benefits and constraints.

Chapter 16
Assessing E–Health in Africa:
Web 2.0 Applications

Alessia D'Andrea
IRPPS-CNR, Italy

Fernando Ferri
IRPPS-CNR, Italy

Patrizia Grifoni
IRPPS-CNR, Italy

EXECUTIVE SUMMARY

The aim of this chapter is to discuss the e-health readiness assessment in Africa by analysing the ICT usage and the different barriers for the implementation of e-health technologies. Moreover, the chapter analyses the e-health prospective by describing tree different e-health application areas: (1) electronic medical records, (2) telemedicine, and (3) e-commerce of health products.

INTRODUCTION

In Africa, healthcare services are primarily concentrated in urban areas while the greatest part of people resides in the rural areas, where health care services are often basic or inexistent. Consequently, a very high number of inhabitants of rural Africa does not have access to emergency health care services (Sanders & Chopra, 2006). Advances in Web 2.0 technologies are changing the way healthcare services are provided and the term "e-health" is broadly used to describe this evolution. There is

DOI: 10.4018/978-1-4666-2515-0.ch016

not a consensus on the definition e-Health concept. Eysenbach (2001) provides the following definition: "e-health is an emerging field in the intersection of medical informatics, public health and business, referring to health services and information delivered or enhanced through the Internet and related technologies." Marconi (2002) defines e-health as "the application of Internet and other related technologies in the healthcare industry to improve the access, efficiency, effectiveness, and quality of clinical and business processes utilized by healthcare organizations, practitioners, patients, and consumers in an effort to improve the health status of patients." A similar definition is given by Wyatt and Liu (2002) "e-health is the use of Internet technology by the public, health workers, and others to access health and lifestyle information, services and support; it encompasses telemedicine, telecare, etc." In Akeh et al. (2007), e-health is defined as "the ability to use Internet technology to provide health services and deliver care to individuals from geographically dispersed locations."

According to International Telecommunication Union (2008), the term e-health is extremely generic and can be referred to:

- Products, such as for example instruments for the monitoring blood pressure of patients in ambulatory;
- Systems such as for instance computer-assisted surgery systems, and services like: operating surgical and intensive care units, computer-assisted prescription services, contraindications and dosage levels and information services for patients and consumers.

Improving access to e-health services in developing countries and mainly in the African continent, has been receiving particular attention since the first World Telecommunication Development Conference (WTDC) in 1994. In 2005, the World Health Assembly recognized e-health as the way to achieve cost-effective and secure use of Web 2.0 technologies for health and urged its member states to consider drawing up long-term strategic plans for developing e-health services infrastructure. In 2008, the International Telecommunication Union (ITU) published a document (International Telecommunication Union, 2008) that represented guidelines for decision-makers in the health, telecommunications, and information technology sectors to develop e-health facilities and services in their countries. According to this document, e-health systems offer important benefits mainly in three different areas:

- **Productivity:** Cost reduction and avoidance, increased productivity, reduced duplication of tests/procedures and impacts on success of reform or change initiative.

- **Access:** A more easier access to health services in remote areas and reduction in wait-times for medical procedures.
- **Quality:** Reduction of mortality (specific causes), morbidity (clinical events, physiologic and metabolic measures), level of disability, functional status, symptom status, quality of life; privacy and security incidents and positive audit or operational review observations.

These benefits underline that today the use of the e-health technologies can be very important to improve the accurate delivery of care to African patients (Foster, et al., 2004; Bernstein & Goodman, 2004). However, their implementation in terms of adoption rate and acceptance still poses a big problem. Readiness assessment has been identified as an essential requirement for the success of E-Health in terms of adoption rate and/or acceptance. E-Health readiness assessment, is a pre-implementation evaluation method that represents an essential requirement prior to e-health implementation (Jennett, et al., 2003; Demiris, et al., 2004).

Starting from these considerations the aim of this chapter is to discuss the e-health readiness assessment in Africa by analysing the ICT usage and the different barriers for the implementation of e-health technologies that can refer to different sectors such as:

- **Political:** The political arena in Africa has an influence on the implementation of e-health technologies. This is due to a number of factors such as: political corruption, the lack of awareness and the insufficient knowledge of leaders and policy-makers of the benefits of the e-health technologies;
- **Economic:** All countries in the world today are living economic disadvantages due to the world financial crisis Africa being especially hit (Arieff, et al., 2008). This crisis has affected the financial resources at the disposal of the governments for necessary investments in e-health infrastructure and services. For this limited financial resources e-health projects have to compete with other projects in different sectors;
- **Socio-Cultural:** According to World Health Organization (2008), Africa is characterized by social and cultural influences such as: the "digital divide," the inadequacy of ICT infrastructure and e-health services and the limited ability and skills to use them, the stagnating political instability economic growth, and the lack of progress in life expectancy that impact on the implementation of the e-health technologies;
- **Technological:** According to International Telecommunication Union (2008), it is estimated that in Africa, only a small percentage of localities had telephone and Internet access. This situation renders the implementation of e-health technologies very difficult.

- **Legal:** This aspect refers to the violation of privacy and security related to the inappropriate health data exchange through the e-health technologies. Very little is known to people in Africa about these issues associated with certain e-health applications.

Moreover, the chapter analyses the e-health prospective by describing tree different e-health application areas: (1) electronic medical records, (2) telemedicine, and (3) e-commerce of health products.

The electronic medical records convert the current paper based documents into digital format, so that they are available electronically. They allow healthcare professionals access patients' data wherever they are in the country and potentially worldwide. Moreover, different healthcare professionals, with whom a patient interacts during his treatment, will share information and make better informed healthcare decisions. This has given rise to a total change. In fact, the process of accessing and collecting medical information has traditionally been paper-based. However, the paper-based system is inefficient for managing massive amounts of information that can affect the care of patients.

Telemedicine is the ability to provide interactive healthcare services by using Web 2.0 technologies; it allows physicians to visit patients with live over video for immediate care by capturing health data and video images for diagnosis and follow-up treatment at a later time.

Finally, with respect to the e-commerce of health products, many are the Web sites that offer the possibility to buy health products on-line but even if this allows to access 24 hours a day to drugs beyond national border and opportunities there are many problems with the quality of these products.

The chapter is organized as follow. Section 2 illustrated e-health initiatives and projects implemented in the African continent and some examples of readiness evaluation method. In section 3 the impacts that Web 2.0 technologies have in three different kinds of relationships (physician-physician; patient-patient and patient-physician) are described. Section 4 describes the ICT usage and the barriers to the development of e-health technologies in Africa. Section 5 describes three different e-health application areas are described. Finally section 6 concludes the chapter.

BACKGROUND

Africa is rich in natural resources and cultural heritages but at the same time it is very poor continent where diseases, such as AIDS and hepatitis represent a thorny problem. Aids and hepatitis pose the biggest threat by far, with an estimated seven million Africans expected to die from these diseases over the next 15 years. Based on the National Department of Health ante-natal survey (http://www.avert.org/south-africa-hiv-aids-statistics.htm) "the 30.2% of pregnant women (aged 15-49) were living with HIV in 2010. Until 1998 South Africa had one of the fastest expanding epidemics in the world, but since 2006 HIV prevalence among pregnant women has remained relatively stable."

Moreover, the healthcare sector in the rural areas, where there is the maximum density of ills, shows signs of remarkable problems in the quality of hospitals and the availability information, services and doctors. On the contrary, urban areas present highly specialised healthcare services. This situation fosters health divides because an increasing number of inhabitants of Africa do not have access to adequate healthcare services. E-Health can offer a set of innovative health solutions to promote behaviour change and provide a continuous medical assistance for all the people, independently to their location and social conditions. In particular, the accessibility to information and services represent the key element for a significant evolution. Advances and innovations in Information Technologies such as the Internet have paved the way to what we know or call e-Health.

The literature reports many e-Health studies and projects developed in Africa (Kifle, et al., 2006; Mbarika, 2004). There are a number of continental initiatives aimed at harnessing e-Health initiatives in Africa: the Pan African e-Network, the telemedicine Task Force, and many e-Health projects: the Telemedicine Network for Francophone African Countries (http://raft.hcuge.ch), the e-Portuguese Project (http://www.who.int/eportuguese/en), and the Pan-African e-Network Project (http://www.panafricanenetwork.com). One of the most important initiatives is the pilot assessment of e-Health/telemedicine commissioned by the World Health Organization (WHO) to determine the status of e-Health initiatives across the African continent (World Health Organization, 2010). WHO is the United Nations agency with a mandate in global public health. Its work is both legal (recommendations, resolutions, expert information, health standards, and regulations) and technical (action programmes, technical assistance upon request) in nature. In particular the WHO pilot assessment describes different the e-health projects developed in Africa and the research attempted to satisfy appropriate selection criteria in terms of project output. In Table 1 some of these projects containing results extracted from the WHO pilot assessment have been reported.

In most of these projects, the evaluation of the healthcare context take place in the post-implementation phase, which is, after e-health technologies are delivered (Makoul, et al., 2001; Poissant, et al., 2005; Chen, et al., 2006). However, even if post implementation evaluation is crucial for assessing the success and value of technologies (Alexander, 2007) the benefits of exploring the process use of evaluations have recently been argued (Forss, Renien, & Carlsson, 2007). As a type of pre-implementation evaluation method, the e-health readiness assessment represents

Table 1. Projects extracted from the WHO pilot assessment

Region and Country	Project Title	Project Results and Future Plans
North Africa		
Algeria	RAFT	**Results**: including Details of Courses and Participation in Teleconsultations, etc. at http://raft.hcuge.ch
Egypt	Swinfen Trust Teleconsultations	**Results:** wide variety of medical conditions treated in 40 developing countries (mainly not African) especially uncommon/complex problems, paediatric and other.
Southern and South Africa		
South Africa	Mindset Health Channel	**Results:** mass scale delivery of health education to both the general public and health care professionals.
Zambia	Support/Education for Zambian HCWs infected with HIV and/or caring for HIV/AIDS patients	**Results:** needs assessment performed, then focus on training, forming local support groups and monitoring progress.
West Africa		
Benin, Niger, and Rwanda	WHO programme to reduce deaths from Obstetric Complications	**Results:** Training of birth attendants and establishing subsequent trends in neonatal mortality.
Mali	Specialized distance pilot project	**Results:** project was found to be irrelevant due to different diagnostic resources and unsuccessful implementation training. Establishment of telegraphy network with Malienne Centre d'Imagerie connecting one district hospital.
East Africa		
Rwanda	Twubakane Decentralization and health project "Let's build together"	**Results:** anti malaria campaign, treating 155 000 households, reproductive health and child care services, strengthened health facility capacity, community based insurance, ownership of health services, entry point for other governance activities i.e. anti-corruption, fiscal and tax reforms.
Uganda	RAFT	**Results**: including Details of Courses and Participation in Teleconsultations, etc at http://raft.hcuge.ch.
Central Africa		
Central African Republic	Swinfen Trust Teleconsultations	**Results:** wide variety of medical conditions treated in 40 developing countries (mainly not African) especially uncommon/complex problems, paediatric and other.
Chad	Swinfen Trust Teleconsultations	**Results:** wide variety of medical conditions treated in 40 developing countries (mainly not African) especially uncommon/complex problems, paediatric and other.
Indian Ocean Islands		
Reunion	Paediatric cardiology teleconsultations	**Results:** as academic publications.
Madagascar	RAFT	**Results**: including Details of Courses and Participation in Teleconsultations, etc at http://raft.hcuge.ch.

a preventive action to individuate barriers during the implementation of e-health technologies. According to Brender (2006) during the readiness assessment the evaluation for E-Health technologies covers:

- **Relevance:** Assess whether the solution is entirely able to solve problems;
- **Problem Areas:** Identify the weakness in the solution;
- **Feasibility:** Analyse the resources needed to implement the solution;
- **Consistency:** Assess whether the solution is a coherent entity
- **Elements of Risk:** Assess any external conditions that will involve substantial risk.

Different studies in the literature provide examples of readiness assessment method. For instance, Campbell et al. (2001) developed a readiness framework by making semi-structured interviews to evaluate the video and computer components of telemedicine. Results individuate six themes:

- **Turf:** A threat to healthcare providers;
- **Efficacy:** Desire of healthcare providers to know e-health technologies in practice before investing in time and money;
- **Practice Context:** Barriers for the adopting of e-health technologies;
- **Apprehension:** As a human need to change;
- **Time to Learn:** Providers' need to take the time for learning e-health technologies;
- **Ownership:** Emotional involvement of healthcare providers.

Wickramasinghe *et al.* (2005) stated that there are three domains relevant to e-health readiness practitioner, organisation, and public. Their framework contains four main prerequisites:

- **ICT Architecture/Infrastructure:** Is an essential element for the implementation of E-Health initiatives;
- **Standardisation Policies, Protocols and Procedures:** Are key elements to enable far reaching coverage, a significant amount of document exchange and information flow;
- **User Access and Accessibility Policies and Infrastructure:** In particular in terms of: access to Internet services and access to e-services (Panagariya, 2000);
- **Governmental Regulation and Control:** In terms of: cost effectiveness, functionality, and ease of use.

Jennett *et al.* (2005) individuates six common factors within each type of readiness assessment:

- Core readiness identify need for along with an expressed dissatisfaction with existing service;
- Structural readiness defines adequate policies, human resources, training, funding, and appropriate equipment;
- Projection of benefits underlines the benefits that E-Health technologies could bring;
- Assessment of risk financial, privacy, security, etc.;
- Practitioners' awareness and education individuate the potential benefits and limitations of e-health technologies' adoptions;
- Intra-group and inter-group dynamics: define cooperation within or across the communities of interest.

In Overhage et al. (2005), descriptive statistics and subjective evaluation are used to explore seven important dimensions in creating e-health information exchange: clinical component, demonstration of community leadership and commitment, overall technical readiness, matching funds, plans for sustainable business model, use of r scalable and replicable tools, use of data standards. A scoring mechanism was not provided to determine readiness.

Although these frameworks were not tested a recent study by Khoja *et al.* (2007) aimed to test the reliability of E-Health readiness evaluation tools with four categories of measurements: scores of core-readiness, societal readiness, learning readiness/technological readiness, and policy readiness.

WEB 2.0 TECHNOLOGIES IN E-HEALTH SECTOR: PHYSICIANS AND PATIENTS' PERSPECTIVES

Internet is increasingly considered as one of the most promising enabling technologies that save costs, and increase safety. It is a popular resource for health information among patients and physicians. In the following sub-sections, the impacts that Web 2.0 technologies have in three different kinds of relationships (physician-physician; patient-patient and patient-physician) are described in detail.

The Physician-Physician Relationship

Since e-health's emergence, it has grown in use among physicians witch e-health use include: the access to Journals; searches for information on clinical protocols;

consultations with other specialists and searches for information related to specific patient problems (Casebeer, et al., 2002; Bennett, et al., 2004, 2005). The use of Web 2.0 technologies (such as Social Networks, Virtual communities, discussion forum, blog etc.) improves possibilities to maintain communication and collaboration among physicians. In a virtual space physicians aggregate observations from their daily practice and then challenge or collaborate each others' opinions, accelerating the emergence of trends and new insights on medications, treatments and devices (Ebner, et al., 2004). Web 2.0 technologies are essential requirements to ensure an effective and rapid communications among physicians, especially distant ones. Web 2.0 technology allows transmitting, extending, saving and managing knowledge shared among community members. The most common used Web 2.0 technologies are the asynchronous tools, such as: (1) discussion boards, that provide physicians with the ability to post and reply to messages in a common area, (2) whiteboard that allows physicians to brainstorm together, draw graphical objects into a shared window, etc., (3) video/audio conferencing, that allows making virtual face-to-face meeting, and sharing notepad, that provides community's members with the ability to create a document together (Malkary, 2005). Other functionalities concern the scheduling of common events and activities, the organization and retrieval of knowledge and the broadcast of shared documents to the Web. All these functionalities allow knowledge transfer between cross-border physicians. Web 2.0 technologies and in particular Social networks and Virtual communities emerge as one of the most authoritative and influential source of knowledge transfer between cross-border physicians. They have the aptitude to generate knowledge sharing among physicians, and facilitate the collaboration and exchange of ideas among them by preserving explicit as well as implicit (or tacit) knowledge created by the physician' relations. Community's explicit knowledge is stored in the community repository and includes any kind of information readily available to community's members, while tacit knowledge resides in minds of the community's members and, consequently, it is intangible.

Though technology cannot completely substitute face-to-face interactions, Web 2.0 applications can foster the growth of knowledge sharing among physicians. In this sense Web 2.0 applications will supplement, not supplant, traditional communities. Web 2.0 applications supplements traditional community in creating a more dynamic environment oriented to innovation and knowledge sharing. In healthcare sector Web 2.0 applications allow the enhancing of "meeting opportunities" among physicians. As consequence, emerge the increasing number of skills, competencies, and "knowledge profiles" of each physician involved into the Web 2.0 application. In this perspective, Web 2.0 applications amplify openness, interoperability, scalability, and extensibility of a traditional community. At the same time, this does not mean that Web 2.0 applications can completely substitute face-to-face interactions. On the contrary, face-to-face interactions are enabled and supported by electronic communications that try to make easier, more immediate, and less expensive the knowledge relations, amplifying their efficacy.

The Patient-Patient Relationship

Patients value the information they receive from e-health as much as, or almost as much as, information they receive from their doctors (Lewis & Behana, 2001). Patients' demands for information and services often increase after a diagnosis of a disease or during medical treatment. Patients may seek information to help them make sense of a diagnosis. Recent research on patients' information needs. Leimeister and Krcmar (2006) demonstrate a strong information interest in the following areas: 1) side effects; 2) explanation of disease and prognosis; 3) treatment options and explanations of therapy; 4) logistical issues (transportation, work, etc.); 5) lifestyle issues (exercise, diet, sexuality, smoking); 6) follow up/what happens after therapy finishes; 7) support or self help groups, alternative medicine.

Besides demands for information, there is a need to seek emotional support with other patients. Several studies have identified five, interrelated forms of emotional support common to face-to-face and virtual mutual aid groups. These kinds of emotional support help to reduce members' isolation; empathy; enhance self-esteem and sustain hope. For instance, people join Social Networks to experience a sense of community with others like themselves. To obtain this benefit, members must stay involved long enough to feel a sense of connection with other members. They are more likely to have this experience if they begin exchanging messages with other members. Researchers have found that when members write longer posts and ask questions, they are more likely to post again. There are various types of technologies used by patients to facilitate interactions within a Social Network. Some of these include:

- **E-mails:** The exchange of electronic messages between peers via e-mail is widespread. However, it is often a clumsy tool to be used to converse with other community members and it lacks security due to the high probability of deleting or misplacing mistakenly a document or a message.
- **Instant Messaging:** Exchanging messages simultaneously is a real-time approach used for immediate correspondence among individuals. Nevertheless, excessive instant messaging and/or many members participating in the same conversation can be annoying to users. In addition, it takes extra effort to save these conversations.
- **Newsgroup:** Represents a repository of messages posted by many users from different locations. It can be considered as a virtual space where physicians exchange ideas, discuss, communicate and even make friends (Roberts, 1998).

- **Web Conferencing:** Refers to synchronous (live) meetings, Web seminars, and applications sharing over the Web. In a Web conference, participants can see whatever is on the presenter's screen, and simultaneously share applications (ex: spread sheet) and discuss matters of common concern.
- **Blogs:** Is a cooperation environment that contains reverse chronologically order posts that are contained in a common Web page.
- **Wikis:** Provide an effective virtual forum that allows physicians to add content and also to edit content supporting collaborative writing, opening discussions, interaction and Web-authoring (Desilets, et al., 2005). They also provide an asynchronous platform for virtual community, and with their capacity to archive different page versions can act as repositories, thereby enabling effective knowledge management.

The Patient-Physician Relationship

The Internet's popularity as a health resource for patients is also impacting the patient-physician relationship. Web 2.0 technologies, in particular Social Networks, allow patients and physicians to share opinions and medical information every time. Social Networks offer to physicians an opportunity to improve the awareness of patient's health conditions and enhance their satisfaction.

They also give the opportunity to increase the involvement of patients in their treatments and improve access to health care information and communication possibilities between patients and physicians. Through the use of Social Networks, physicians have the possibility to communicate with patients continuously allowing to better collecting data. For patients with chronic illnesses, especially those in rural or outlying areas, consultation with an appropriate specialist can largely improve the quality and outcome of their healthcare. Social Networks can be used by doctors for example to send instant messages to patients reminding them when they need to take their medication. This enables to eliminate some administrative costs associated with hospitalisations (resulting from not taking the prescribed medication at the correct time).

There are many potential benefits for patients and physicians who communicate in Social Networks:

- Patients may feel more comfortable in addressing sensitive, complex or personal issues;
- Social Networks can solve problems related to large distances or patients' disability;
- Patients can influence physician prescribing decisions by presenting product information they find online.

However, it is important to understand the following aspects related to the communication between physicians and patients: (1) how the communication by Social Networks can be integrated with other communication approaches; (2) what are the patient and physician preferences in the use of Social Networks; (3) how to identify people that most likely can benefit from virtual communication.

A part from benefits Social Network does not have the capability to reproduce the traditional relationship because of the impossibility of the physical presence. In fact, medical practice includes complex processes as diagnosis, treatment, prognosis and these processes require the presence of the patient for several activities. In conclusion, we can observe that Social Networks can modify and integrate the traditional physician-patient relationship but, at the moment, cannot replace this relationship.

ICT USAGE AND BARRIERS FOR E-HEALTH IMPLEMENTATION IN AFRICA

The use of ICT has grown relatively rapidly in most urban areas of the African continent. However, the digital divide is still at its most extreme in rural areas, where the use of ICT is at early stage of development. According to the information and communication technologies in Africa—a status report (http://www.bellanet.org/partners/aisi/more/index.html) "most of the services and users are concentrated in the towns, while the majority of Africans are scattered in small communities spread-out across the vast rural areas. A very limited perfusion of the telecommunication networks into rural areas (often over 75% of the country's telephone lines are concentrated in the capital city) and irregular or non-existent electricity supplies are a common feature and a major barrier to use of ICTs." Moreover according to the Research ICT Africa 2011/2012 ICT access and usage survey (http://www.researchictafrica.net/home.php) "while in 2007/8 little access to the Internet on the continent with a large-scale absence of personal computers and smart phones and compounded by the high cost of connectivity, whether fixed or mobile, in 2011/2012 the mobile phone is the key entry point for Internet usage." The report underlines that while Uganda and Namibia demonstrate increased mobile Internet take up, in Ethiopia and Tanzania Internet remains negligible while South Africa is far behind countries where the regulator has enabled competition by enforcing cost-based mobile termination rates. The use of mobile technology in Uganda had an impact also on maternal mortality. The Rural Extended Services and Care for Ultimate Emergency Relief project made use mobile walkie-talkies and VHF radio to deliver health care to pregnant women. This resulted in timelier and increased patient referrals, as well as the delivery of health care to a larger number of pregnant women (Musoke, 2001).

The wider use of ICTs had more transparency and openness, through Kenya's Open Data initiative or the use of Facebook or Twitter to both inform international opinion and coordinate protests in the Arab Spring. This growing social dependence on ICTs developed new need in investing in ICT infrastructure.

However despite the use of ICT has grown relatively rapidly in many areas of the African continent, the development of e-health technology still presents numerous barriers that can be classified in five categories: political, economic, socio-cultural, technological and legal (as shown in Table 2).

Each Government can play an important role in encouraging investment in the development of the Internet and telecommunication infrastructures. However, in Africa governments adopt uncertain policies in the health sector (Okunade, 2005). Conflicting policies calls for a multi-partnership approach and a collective and participatory decision making-process. In Africa "few governments have develop roadmaps for e-health, but most are still lagging behind due to lack of vision, insufficient political will and corruption" (WHO, 2005). Moreover, there are also a lack of awareness and an insufficient knowledge of benefits that e-Health applications can have on health care sector by avoiding unnecessary or duplicate or diagnostic or therapeutic interventions, by improving communication between healthcare establishments and by widening access to health knowledge and evidence-based medicine.

It is also important to consider the limited financial resources at the disposal of the governments for Internet infrastructures. WBG (2005) reports that "there are a multitude of projects apart from e-health in this region, hence, e-health projects will have to compete with other projects for the limited resources." For example, Ericsson has announced that it is partnering with the Earth Institute at Columbia University to provide connectivity to the Millennium Villages project. This partnership is designed to bring Internet services in ten African countries.

However, it is necessary to take into account that socio-cultural factors too represent an obstacle for e-health tools and services diffusion. There are a lot of

Table 2. Barriers to e-health implementation in Africa

Political	- Political Corruption - Lack of awareness and the insufficient knowledge of benefits of e-health technologies
Economic	- Limited resources
Socio-cultural	- Digital divide - Lack of education
Technological	- Limited internet access
Legal	- Privacy and security

people that in Africa have difficulties in the availability and use Internet technology, based on gender, ethnic group belonging, and so on. Education appears to be very important for e-health diffusion, especially in the rural areas. An effective education will facilitate:

*   Communication between services and information providers and patients;
*   Patients' appreciation of e-health applications benefits.

Differences are also between women and men in ICT usage. Access to ICTs is low for women in the African continent is slow due to: low levels of literacy and education, lack of time, lack of materials, cost, safety opening times for public ICTs, socio-cultural expectations about women's roles and movement in public areas (Hafkin & Taggart, 2001).

With respect to Internet availability, while findings from various studies (Foster, Goodman, Osiakwan, and Bernstein) have reported significant progress in the diffusion of the Internet infrastructures in Africa, many African especially the inhabitants of rural areas, which represent the majority of the African population, have limited access to Internet. The number of African Internet users is somewhere between 1.5 to 2 million out of a continental population of 750 million (by Pierre Dandjinou SDNP/UNDP), and a great part of them are resident in South Africa. Moreover, Internet access tends to be concentrated in cities where users are in great part employees of corporations, universities, or private companies. Figure 1 shows the number of Internet users from 1996 to 2005 according to their activity.

Finally, there are legal barriers related to privacy and security issues. The implementation of e-health technology should be used with maintaining the privacy and security of patient's data but this aspect is not simple to control. In fact even if existing laws such as HIPPA's Privacy and Security Rules provide the necessary tools to have appropriate administrative and technical safeguards of patients information, it is often difficult or impossible to establish effective privacy and security protections during the transmission of data. For these reasons, it is important to incorporate appropriate privacy and security protections from the outset in the design of new e-health technologies.

E-HEALTH APPLICATION AREAS

The health sector needs many measures in order to ensure patient safety (Leonard, 2004). Internet is increasingly considered as one of the most promising enabling technologies that save costs, and increase safety. Internet applications present numerous benefits in health sector such as:

Figure 1. Number of internet users in Africa

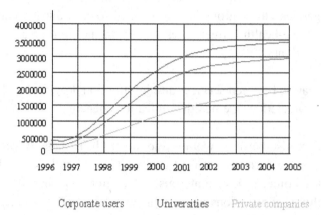

Corporate users   Universities   Private companies

- **Reduction of Patient Misidentification:** By reinforcing patient safety procedures.
- **Access to Patient Information:** The health status of the patient was obtained quickly from this information that is useful for physicians that do medical check-ups on patients. By using the Internet, physicians do not have to search through pages of information to find the most up to date information about the patients.

These benefits underline that today the use of the Internet in health sector can be very important to improve the accurate delivery of care to African patients. In the following sub-paragraphs we explore in particular tree different e-health application areas:

- Electronic Medical Records;
- Telemedicine;
- E-Commerce of Health Products.

In the following paragraphs these three areas are described in detail.

Electronic Medical Record

An electronic medical record is "a digitalized medical record." An electronic medical record system brings important benefits to the health system of Africa (Leonard, 2004). Such data collection can be performed with simple paper forms at the clinic level, but this approach tends to be difficult, time-consuming and may provide a little or no feedback to the staff collecting data. Clinicians can easily access previous records, and simple tools can be incorporated to warn of potential problems such as administration of incompatible drugs. Physicians can check on the outcomes of patients and perform epidemiological research studies. Networked electronic medical record systems allow these data can be entered from distant locations, and an effective patient management. The access to Web 2.0 communications tools allows staff to seek specialist advice from remote physicians.

Assessing resource requirements and preventing drug stock shortages, in opposite of the developed countries, can be a critical issue in the developing world. It requires an accurate knowledge of numbers of patients with particular requirements or types of disease and knowledge of drug stocks and supply. The electronic medical record can also be used to track patient outcomes, compliance with therapy and to record surgical procedures. Finally, electronic medical records can be used to rapidly produce aggregate reports, which should be more complete and accurate because physicians will more likely monitoring health of their own patients. Incorporating multiple functions into the same information system allows reuse of data and should help to justify the basic costs of set-up and technical support. The WHO asserts that a local development and adaptation of electronic medical record system in Africa is required.

However, despite the advantages the availability of electronic medical records implies disadvantages such as:

- Data mismanagement: inaccurate or incomplete;
- Data misuse: data used for other purposes adverse to the interests of the data subject (employment, insurance, commercial);
- Lack of transparency;
- Loss of freedom.

Health information collected in connection with e-health technology must be both secure and well managed. The implementation of e-health technology should be used with maintaining the privacy of patients. To understand this issue, it is noteworthy that the e-health technology, in a medical setting, is used only with the individual's consent. However, often, the consent to access the data is also used for non-medical uses. Each year, as a condition of applying for insurance, employment, and other objectives, millions of people are compelled to sign authorizations permitting access to their personal data for non medical purposes. These authorizations are nominally voluntary; people are not required to sign them, but if they do not, they will not be considered for specific benefits. In addition, for most of these authorizations, no limits are placed on the scope of the information disclosed and the extent of the authorization. However, existing laws provide the necessary tools to actively resist and prevent any unauthorized alteration of patient's records.

In particular, the HIPPA's Privacy and Security Rules state that doctors' practices must have appropriate administrative and technical safeguards to protect the privacy of confidential information. These safeguards convince people that the confidentiality and privacy of healthcare information, electronically collected, maintained, used, or transmitted is secure.

A report by the Federal Trade Commission on "Protecting consumer privacy in an era of rapid change" (http://europa.eu/rapid/pressReleasesAction.do?referen ce=IP/12/46&format=HTML) analyses the implications for consumer privacy of technological advances in the ICT domain.

According to the report "users are able to collect, store, manipulate and share vast amounts of consumer data for very little cost. These technological advances have led to an explosion of new business models that depend on capturing consumer data at a specific and individual level and over time." The report of the Business Sotware Alliance in February 2012 (http://portal.bsa.org/cloudscorecard2012/) states that there is a huge divide between developed and developing and countries in terms of adequate legislation for protection of personal health data. The report highlights that "even among developed countries there are conflicting data protection regulations which could hamper transfer of personal data across borders; an international approach is necessary to bring together the multiple data protection regimes and harmonize the business rules for providers and protection rules for the citizen."

The development and implementation of electronic medical record systems in Africa is the goal of numerous projects without data content or data exchange standards. This is producing the risk of creating a fragmented and chaotic information environment in which national data reporting and patient tracking would be severely impaired. WHO adds that in order to realize an efficient electronic medical record system in Africa that it is important to:

- Work with African Ministries of Health, the CDC, developers of electronic medical record systems used for Africa, and clinicians to establish basic standards to allow interoperability, patient tracking, and the possibility of national and cross national data mining.
- Work with African Ministries of Health on their Knowledge Management strategies with an emphasis on improving patient care and better use of data applied to decision making at all levels of the health system;
- Target investment in promising electronic medical record and clinical learning systems encouraging the transfer of promising technologies to other country settings.

Telemedicine

Telemedicine can be conceived as "provision of distance medical services using electronic communications." There are telemedicine applications in e-health (e.g., use of the Internet for teleconsulting between physicians). This could improve healthcare in Africa by allowing doctors to get healthcare and increase the availability of scarce specialists. Technology is an essential requirement to ensure an effective and rapid communications among physicians, especially if they are distant located. Web 2.0 technologies allow transmitting, extending, saving and managing knowledge shared among physicians. Tele-medicine tools enable the communication and sharing of medical information in electronic form, and thus facilitate access to remote expertise and knowledge. A physician located far from a reference center can consult her/his colleagues remotely in order to solve a difficult case, can follow a continuous distance learning course over the Internet to improve her/his knowledge, or access medical information from digital libraries. These tools can also be used to facilitate the information exchange between centers of medical expertise at national or international level (Fraser, et al., 2005).

There are various types of Web 2.0 technologies used by patients and physicians to from and facilitate interactions. Some of these tools include:

- **E-mails:** The exchange of electronic messages between peers via e-mail is widespread. However, it is often a clumsy tool to be used to converse with other community members and it lacks security due to the high probability of deleting or misplacing mistakenly a document or a message.
- **Instant Messaging:** Exchanging messages simultaneously is a real-time approach used for immediate correspondence among individuals (Ferguson, 1998). Nevertheless, excessive instant messaging and/or many members participating in the same conversation can be annoying to users. In addition, it takes extra effort to save these conversations.
- **Blogs:** Is a cooperation environment that contains reverse chronologically order posts that are contained in a common Web page.
- **Wikis:** Provide an effective virtual forum that allows physicians to add content and also to edit content supporting collaborative writing, opening discussions, interaction and Web-authoring.

This communication allows physicians to participate in continuous medical learning at a time and location convenient for them. Moreover, it provides real-time responses for critical cases. In real-time telemedicine, a telecommunications link allows instantaneous interaction. Videoconferencing is one of the most common forms of synchronous of telemedicine. Examples of real-time clinical telemedicine

Table 3. Importance and feasibility of telemedicine adoption in the Africa continent

IMPORTANCE	FEASIBILITY
There is a need for the provision of health care services, especially in rural areas.	The provision of healthcare services consumes a large portion of national budgets.
The modernization of internal communication in the hospitals represents the basis for the introduction of Telemedicine services.	The Internet is making access into Africa.
The maternity units could be connected by a Tele-medicine link to the maternity service in a regional hospital. This allows remote monitoring of the health of pregnant women.	Email has many advantages in rural areas: it is cheap, hardware and software requirements are simple, and the information does not have to be transmitted in real time.
Tourists would be encouraged to visit remote areas if there is a facility for Telemedicine.	The deployment of telecenters in rural areas could be useful to Telemedicine.

include: tele-audiology, tele-cardiology, tele-radiology, tele-rehabilitation, tele-dentistry, tele-neurology, etc.

The potential of telemedicine is particularly important for the African rural areas where specialists are rarely present and where distances and the quality of the transportation infrastructure hinder the physical movement of physicians and/or patients. However many of African countries cannot afford the very sophisticated Telemedicine solutions. Notwithstanding these obstacles, among many others, Telemedicine adoption is still important and feasible for most, if not all; African countries (Mbarika, 2004) (see Table 3).

E-Commerce of Health Products

The World Wide Web emerged in the last years as an interactive channel, owning all the characteristics to be utilised as a self-service. It permits real time answers to patients' requests, because it is an impressive source of health information, 24 hours available. Internet permits consumers to obtain extensive medical information helping them understand health treatment options. For these reasons, the use of Internet to buy health products is growing rapidly. Many people benefit from the convenience of this new tool. Drug sales over the World Wide Web can provide benefits to consumers. These benefits are many and include:

- Access to drugs beyond national border;
- Opportunities of shopping 24 hours a day; and a wide set of pharmaceutical products;
- Privacy for users who don't want to buy their medical products in a public place.

These benefits help to develop the health-market on Internet, where it is possible to identify consumers' preferences, tailoring the offer according to individual predilection in micro market area.

Several pharmacies on Internet allow the user to search drugs specifying a measure of convenience, safety, and privacy, offering detailed information on drug interactions, and utilizing the e-mail of customers to give information about orders. Frequently these pharmacies sell drugs with a lower cost than traditional pharmacies. Finally, the use of information and communication technology to transmit prescriptions from physicians to pharmacies can reduce errors in prescription.

Online shopping for health products offers many benefits for consumers, but it presents a number of serious risks too. In fact, consumers are now being threatened by the fraudulent Internet businesses that trade products illegally. In particular, trading medical products or buying some medical products from another country online may be illegal in some countries; therefore, before buying a product, it is necessary to understand if it is legal.

There are many reasons why health-products bought through the Internet could represent a danger for health. For example some health-products could be: fake; out of date; composed of dangerous ingredients; stored not correctly.

Moreover:

- **Efficacy May be Lacking:** The Internet use can produce difficulties to distinguish between products that meet the requirements of consumer' government and those that does not;
- **Instructions for use could be Inadequate:** This is a very significant risk, because medical products need to be accompanied by accurate instructions to be used properly;
- **Quality May be not Assured:** The product could contain dangerous ingredients;
- Health products sold through the Internet may circumvent the regulatory protection provided by authorities and governments for the health of citizens;
- Reimbursement could not be possible;
- Seeking health treatment through the Internet, can determine a waste of valuable resources because the treatments may not help;
- Products may not be allowed in the country of the consumer, moreover it is possible that health-products that are available only by prescription in one country are available without prescription in another one;
- Medicines with the same name may be different in different countries and countries may have different standards for the quality of medical products and their manufacture.

Internet is a valuable source of health information on several topics such as therapies, health-products, and medical organizations. When properly used, it allows quick and easy access to such information from online medical libraries, health associations, and government agencies.

However, the quality of health and medical product information on the Internet varies, and it is often difficult for the Internet users to identify the true source of the information and to determine whether it is reliable and complete. Since 1999, three initiatives described in James (2001) have highlighted the need for Africa to address e-Commerce as a priority area:

- **African Development Forum (ADF, 1999):** The theme was "The Challenge to Africa of Globalisation and the Information Age." Subsequently, papers were commissioned to tackle four priority themes: ICT Policies and Strategies; Electronic Commerce in Africa: "Opportunities for business and trade"; Youth and Learning: "Applications to support the educational process and meet the needs of Africa's youth"; and Health and ICTs: "Applications in support of the delivery of health care."
- **Pan African Initiative on e-Commerce:** The study set out to develop policy and strategy advice for African governments with regard to the steps necessary to stimulate an active and early African participation in e-Commerce.

The results of these initiatives underline that African governments need to act on their responsibility for creating an economic, legal, and regulatory environment that will enable and foster the growth of e-Commerce within their national economies. According to the WHO Policy Perspectives on Medicines, strong National Regulatory Authorities (NRAs) have to ensure that the manufacture and use of e-medicines are regulated effectively, to protect and promote public health. E-medicines regulation incorporates several reinforcing activities such as:

- Assessing and monitoring the efficacy, safety and quality of e-medicines;
- Surveillance of manufacturers, wholesalers and importers of e-medicines;
- Controlling advertising and promotion of e-medicines;
- Monitoring adverse reactions to e-medicines;
- Providing independent information on e-medicines to public.

Each government should develop and publicise a specific agenda, accompanied by a proposed timetable, for the actions that it will undertake to create an enabling environment for e-Commerce within its national economy.

CONCLUSION

The chapter discussed the e-health readiness assessment in Africa by analysing the ICT usage and the different barriers for the implementation of e-health technologies. In particular, political, economic, socio-cultural, technological, and legal barriers have been discussed.

The chapter also analysed the impacts that Web 2.0 technologies have in three different kinds of relationships (physician-physician; patient-patient and patient-physician).

With respect to the evolution of patient-physician communication Web 2.0 technologies have a relevant impact on the way in which patients and physician interact. They allow patients and physicians to share opinions, medical information and services every time and everywhere and offer to physicians an opportunity to improve the awareness of patient's health conditions and enhance their satisfaction.

Concerning the patient-patient relationship, the use of Web 2.0 technologies enables them to provide and receive information concerning treatments, health insurance, or particular medical problems. Information shared between users includes reports on how the disease had been contracted and how it affects daily life.

Regarding the relationships among physicians, Web 2.0 technologies allow them to participate in continuous medical education at a time and location convenient for them, along with useful communication. The use of Web 2.0 technologies improves possibilities to maintain communication and collaboration with colleagues investigating the same subjects. In a virtual space, physicians collect observations from their daily practice and collaborate with other physicians.

Finally, the chapter analysed the e-health prospective by describing tree different e-health application areas: (1) electronic medical records, (2) telemedicine, and (3) e-commerce of health products.

Electronic medical records bring important benefits to the health system of Africa:

- Such data collection can be performed with simple paper forms at the clinic level this allows to overcome potential problems such as administration of incompatible drugs;
- Clinicians can easily access previous records;
- Physicians can check on the outcomes of patients and perform epidemiological research studies;
- Tracking of patient outcomes, compliance with therapy and to record surgical procedures;
- Production of aggregate reports, which should be more complete and accurate because physicians can more likely monitoring health of their own patients.

However, security and privacy issues have to be considered; for this reason, it is important to incorporate appropriate privacy and security protections from the outset in the design of e-health technologies.

Tele-medicine enables the communication and sharing of medical information in electronic form, and thus facilitates access to remote expertise and knowledge. These tools can also be used to facilitate the information exchange between centers of medical expertise at national or international level.

Finally, with respect to the e-commerce of health products Internet is a valuable source of health information on several topics such as therapies, health-products, and medical organizations. When properly used, it allows quick and easy access to such information from online medical libraries, health associations, and government agencies. However, the quality of health and medical product information on the Internet varies, and it is often difficult for the Internet users to identify the true source of the information and to determine whether it is reliable and complete.

REFERENCES

Akeh, L., & Morfaw, Z. (2007). E-health Africa: Overcoming the barriers to its implementation: A case study of sub Sahara Africa. In *Proceedings of the Second Annual ICT4D Postgraduate Symposium (IX): e-Health and eGovernment.* IEEE.

Alexander, H. (2007). Health-service evaluations: Should we expect the results to change practice? *Evaluation, 9*(4), 405–414. doi:10.1177/1356389003094003

Arieff, A., Weiss, M. A., & Jones, V. C. (2008). *The global economic crisis: Impact on sub-Saharan Africa and global policy responses.* Washington, DC: Congressional Research Services.

Bennett, N. L., Casebeer, L. L., Kristofco, R., & Collins, B. C. (2005). Family physicians' information seeking behaviors: A survey comparison with other specialties. *BioMed Central Medical Informatics and Decision Making, 5,* 9. doi:10.1186/1472-6947-5-9

Bennett, N. L., Casebeer, L. L., Kristofco, R. E., & Strasser, S. M. (2004). Physicians' internet information-seeking behaviors. *The Journal of Continuing Education in the Health Professions, 24*(1), 31–38. doi:10.1002/chp.1340240106

Bernstein, A., & Goodman, S. E. (2005). Global diffusion of the internet IV. *The Internet in Togo, 15*(23), 371–392.

Botha, W. (2010). *Sustainable e-health business models in sub-Saharan Africa.* Unpublished.

Brender, J. (2006). *Evaluation methods for health informatics*. London, UK: Elsevier Inc.

Campbell, J. D., Harris, K. D., & Hodge, R. (2001). Introducing telemedicine technology to rural physicians and settings. *The Journal of Family Practice, 50*, 419–424.

Casebeer, L., Bennett, N., Kristofco, R., Carillo, A., & Centor, R. (2002). Physician internet medical information seeking and on-line continuing education use patterns. *The Journal of Continuing Education in the Health Professions, 22*(1), 33–42. doi:10.1002/chp.1340220105

Chen, X., Yamauchi, K., & Kato, K. (2006). Using the balanced scorecard to measure Chinese and Japanese hospital performance. *International Journal of Health Care Quality Assurance, 19*(4), 339–350. doi:10.1108/09526860610671391

Desilets, A., Paquet, S., & Vinson, N. (2005). *Are wikis usable?* Paper presented at the WikiSym 2005 Conference. San Diego, CA.

Ebner, W., Leimeister, J. M., & Krcmar, H. (2004). Trust in virtual healthcare communities: Design and implementation of trust-enabling functionalities. In *Proceedings of the Hawaii International Conference on System Sciences*. IEEE.

Eysenbach, G. (2001). What is e-health. *Journal of Medical Internet Research, 3*(2). doi:10.2196/jmir.3.2.e20

Ferguson, T. (1998). Digital doctoring-Opportunities and challenges in electronic patient-physician communication. *Journal of the American Medical Association, 280*(15), 1361–1362. doi:10.1001/jama.280.15.1361

Foster, W., Goodman, S. E., Osiakwan, E., & Bernstein, A. (2004). Global diffusion of the internet IV: The internet in Ghana. *Communications of the AIS, 13*(38), 654–681.

Fraser, H. S. F., Biondich, P., Moodley, D., Choi, S., & Szolovits, P. (2005). Implementing electronic medical record systems in developing countries. *Journal Informatics in Primary Care, 13*(2), 83–95.

Hafkin, N., & Taggart, N. (2001). *Gender, information technology and developing countries: An analytic study*. Washington, DC: WID Office USAID.

International Telecommunication Union. (2008). *DRAFT - Implementing e-health in developing countries guidance and principles ICT applications and cybersecurity division policies and strategies department*. New York, NY: ITU.

James, T. (2001). *Handbook for southern Africa*. Retrieved from http://link.wits. ac.za/papers/James-2001-Information-Policy-Handbook-Southern-Africa.pdf

Jennett, P. A., Gagnon, M. P., & Brandstadt, H. K. (2005). Preparing for success: Readiness models for rural telehealth. *Journal of Postgraduate Medicine, 51*(4), 279–285.

Khoja, S., Scott, R., Ishaq, A., & Mohsin, M. (2007). Testing reliability of ehealth readiness assessment tools for developing countries. *eHealth. International Journal (Toronto, Ont.), 3*(1).

Kifle, M., Mbarika, V. W. A., & Datta, P. (2006). Telemedicine in sub-Saharan Africa: The case of teleophthalmology and eye care in Ethiopia. *Journal of the American Society for Information Science and Technology, 57*(10), 1383–1393. doi:10.1002/asi.20448

Leimeister, J. M., & Krcmar, H. (2006). Designing and implementing virtual patient support communities: A German case study. In Murero, M., & Rice, R. E. (Eds.), *The Internet and Health Care: Theory, Research and Practice*. Mahwah, NJ: Lawrence Erlbaum Associates.

Leonard, K. (2004). The role of patients in designing health information systems: The case of applying simulation techniques to design an electronic patient record (EPR) interface. *Health Care Management Science, 7*, 275–284. doi:10.1007/s10729-004-7536-0

Lewis, D., & Behana, K. (2001). The internet as a resource for consumer healthcare. *Disease Management & Health Outcomes, 9*(5), 241–247. doi:10.2165/00115677-200109050-00001

Makoul, G., Curry, R. H., & Tang, P. C. (2001). The use of electronic medical records: Communication patterns in outpatient encounters. *Journal of the American Medical Informatics Association, 8*, 610–615. doi:10.1136/jamia.2001.0080610

Malkary, G. (2005). *Healthcare without bounds: Mobile computing for physicians*. Journal Mobile Computing for Physicians.

Marconi, J. (2002, May). E-health: Navigating the internet for health information healthcare. Advocacy White Paper. *Healthcare Information and Management Systems Society*.

Mbarika, V. (2004). TeleMedicine in Africa: A possible panacea for sub-Saharan Africa's medical nightmare. *Communications of the ACM, 47*(7), 21–24. doi:10.1145/1005817.1005838

Musoke, M. (2001). *Simple ICTs reduce maternal mortality in rural Uganda: A telemedicine case study*. Retrieved from http://www.medicusmundi.ch/mms/services/bulletin/bulletin200202/kap04/16musoke.html

Okunade, A. (2005). Analysis and implications of the determinants of healthcare expenditure in African countries. *Health Care Management Science, 8*, 267–276. doi:10.1007/s10729-005-4137-5

Overhage, J. M., Evans, L., & Marchibroda, J. (2005). Communities' readiness for health information exchange: The national landscape in 2004. *Journal of the American Medical Informatics Association, 12*, 107–112. doi:10.1197/jamia.M1680

Poissant, L., Pereira, J., & Tamblyn, R. (2005). The impact of electronic health records on time efficiency of physicians and nurses: A systematic review. *Journal of the American Medical Informatics Association, 12*(5), 505–516. doi:10.1197/jamia.M1700

Roberts, T. (1998). Are newsgroups virtual communities? In *Proceedings of the SIGCHI Conference on Human Factors in Computing Systems*, (pp. 360–367). ACM Press.

Sanders, D., & Chopra, M. (2006). Key challenges to achieving health for all in an inequitable society: The case of South Africa. *American Journal of Public Health, 96*(1), 73–78. doi:10.2105/AJPH.2005.062679

WHO. (2008). *Primary health care, now more than ever*. Geneva, Switzerland: WHO.

WHO. (2010). *An assessment of e-health projects and initiatives in Africa*. Geneva, Switzerland: WHO.

Wickramasinghe, N. S., Fadlalla, A. M. A., Geisler, E., & Schaffer, J. L. (2005). A framework for assessing e-health preparedness. *International Journal of Electronic Healthcare, 1*(3). doi:10.1504/IJEH.2005.006478

Wyatt, J. C., & Liu, J. L. Y. (2002). Basic concepts in medical informatics. *Journal of Epidemiology and Community Health, 56*, 808–812. doi:10.1136/jech.56.11.808

Compilation of References

ABC. (2011). *Facebook estrena el año con otro record*. Retrieved September 20, 2011, from http://www.abc.es/20110107/medios-redes/abci-facebook-600millones-usuarios-201101071119.html

Abdel Dayem, M. (2011). Courage in documenting Egypt's revolution. *Committee to Protect Journalists*. Retrieved from: http://www.cpj.org/blog/2011/02/journalists-courage-egypt-revolution.php

Abou-Zeid, E. (2005). A culturally aware model of inter-organizational knowledge transfer. *Knowledge Management Research & Practice*, *3*, 146–155. doi:10.1057/palgrave.kmrp.8500064

Accenture. (2011). *Making social media pay: Rethinking social media's potential to bolster B2B interactions, customer loyalty, revenues and brand reputation*. Accenture Report. New York, NY: Accenture.

Adamic, L. A., & Adar, E. (2003). Friends and neighbors on the web. *Social Networking*, *25*(3), 211–230. doi:10.1016/S0378-8733(03)00009-1

Adler, P. S. (2008). Technological determinism. In Clegg, S., & Bailey, J. R. (Eds.), *International Encyclopedia of Organization Studies*. Thousand Oaks, CA: Sage Publications.

Agopyan, V., & Lobo, R. (2007). O futuro do mestrado profissional. *Revista Brasileira de Pós-Graduação*, *4*(8), 293–302.

AIMC. (2011). *Navegantes en la Red. 13ª Encuesta a usuarios de Internet*. Retrieved June 20, 2011, from available in http://www.aimc.es

Ajzen, I. (1985). From intentions to actions: A theory of planned behavior. In Kuhl, J., & Beckmann, J. (Eds.), *Action Control: From Cognition to Behavior*. Berlin, Germany: Springer-Verlag. doi:10.1007/978-3-642-69746-3_2

Ajzen, I. (1991). The theory of planned behavior. *Organizational Behavior and Human Decision Processes*, *50*(2), 179–211. doi:10.1016/0749-5978(91)90020-T

Ajzen, I., & Fishbein, M. (1980). *Understanding attitudes and predicting social behavior*. Englewood Cliffs, NJ: Prentice-Hall.

Akeh, L., & Morfaw, Z. (2007). E-health Africa: Overcoming the barriers to its implementation: A case study of sub Sahara Africa. In *Proceedings of the Second Annual ICT4D Postgraduate Symposium (IX): e-Health and eGovernment*. IEEE.

Compilation of References

Al Jazeera. (2011). *Timeline: Egypt's revolution - Middle East - English.* Retrieved September 4, 2011, from http://english.aljazeera.net/news/middleeast/2011/01/201112515334871490.html

Alaraj, N. (2012). Effects of using web 2.0 applications in the e-business course on Palestinian students' professional development skills. In S. A. Anwar (Ed.), *Proceedings of the 5th Conference on e-Learning Excellence in the Middle East 2011: Sustainable Innovation in Education [capacity-building, blended learning and beyond]*, (pp. 147–154). Dubai, United Arab Emirates: IEEE.

Alby, T. (2007). *Web 2.0: Concepts, applications, technologies.* München, Germany: Hanser.

Alexander, C., Ishikawa, S., & Silverstein, M. (1977). *A pattern language: Towns, buildings, construction.* Oxford, UK: Oxford University Press.

Alexander, H. (2007). Health-service evaluations: Should we expect the results to change practice? *Evaluation, 9*(4), 405–414. doi:10.1177/1356389003094003

All Africa. (2010). *Visit to juba bar where old and new mix.* Retrieved from http://allafrica.com/stories/201010251086.html

Almeida, M. H. (2010). A pós-graduação no Brasil: Onde está e para onde poderia ir. In CAPES (Ed.), *Plano Nacional de Postgraduação (PNGP) 2010-2020,* (vol. 2, pp. 17-28). Rio de Janeiro, Brasilia: Academic Press.

Amabile, T. A. (1996). *Creativity in context.* Boulder, CO: Westview Press.

Ameinfo.com. (2007). 370 sat channels in arab world. *Ameinfo.com.* Retrieved August 5, 2011, from http://www.ameinfo.com/134225.html

Andersen, A., & Di Domenico, L. (1992). Diet vs. shape content of popular male and female magazines: A dose-response relationship to the incidence of eating disorders? *The International Journal of Eating Disorders, 11*(3), 283–287. doi:10.1002/1098-108X(199204)11:3<283::AID-EAT2260110313>3.0.CO;2-O

Anderson, P. (2007). *What is web 2.0? Ideas, technologies and implications for education.* London, UK: JISC Technology and Standards Watch. Retrieved from http://www.jisc.ac.uk/media/documents/techwatch/tsw0701b.pdf

Anderson, C. (2006). *The long tail: Why the future of business is selling less of more.* New York, NY: Hyperion.

Anderson, D. M., & Haddad, C. J. (2005). Gender, voice, and learning in online course environments. *Journal of Asynchronous Learning Networks, 9*(1), 3–14.

Anderson, J. A., & Meyer, T. P. (1975). Functionalism and the mass media. *Journal of Broadcasting, 19*(1), 11–22. doi:10.1080/08838157509363766

Anderson, R. E., & Dexter, S. (2005). School technology leadership: An empirical investigation of prevalence and effect. *Educational Administration Quarterly, 41*(1), 49–82. doi:10.1177/0013161X04269517

Andoni, L. (2011, February 11). The resurrection of pan-Arabism. *Al Jazeera English.* Retrieved September 10, 2011, from http://english.aljazeera.net/indepth/opinion/2011/02/201121115231647934.html

Angeles, L., & Gurstein, P. (2000). Planning for participatory capacity development: The challenges of participation and north-south partnership in capacity building projects. *Canadian Journal of Development Studies, 21*(1). doi:10.1080/02255189.2000.9669926

Antikainen, M., Mäkipää, M., & Ahonen, M. (2010). Motivating and supporting collaboration in open innovation. *European Journal of Innovation Management, 13*(1), 100–119. doi:10.1108/14601061011013258

Arab Advisor Group. (2010, June 8). News release. *Arab Advisor Group.* Retrieved August 15, 2011, from http://www.tegaranet.com/BAF/Arab%20Advisors%20press%20-%20FTA%20Satellite.pdf

Arieff, A., Weiss, M. A., & Jones, V. C. (2008). *The global economic crisis: Impact on sub-Saharan Africa and global policy responses.* Washington, DC: Congressional Research Services.

Ashley, H., Corbett, J., Jones, D., Garside, B., & Rambaldi, G. (2009). Change at hand: Web 2.0 for development. *Participatory Learning and Action, 59*(1), 8–20.

Augusto, M., & Coelho, F. (2009). Market orientation and new-to-the-world products: Exploring the moderating effects of innovativeness, competitive strength, and environmental forces. *Industrial Marketing Management, 38,* 94–108. doi:10.1016/j.indmarman.2007.09.007

Australian Government. (2011). *Engage getting on with government 2.0.* Retrieved from http://www.finance.gov.au/publications/gov20taskforcereport/chapter1.htm

Avgerou, C. (2010). Discourses on ICT and development. *Information Technologies & International Development, 6*(3), 1–18.

Axelrod, M., Brockman, S., Doumet, F., & Zahr, S. (2010). *E-commerce in Egypt.* Philadelphia, PA: Wharton School. Retrieved from http://knowledge.wharton.upenn.edu/arabic/article.cfm?articleid=1209

Azab, N. (2012). The role of the internet in shaping the political process in Egypt. *International Journal of E-Politics, 3*(2), 30–49. doi:10.4018/jep.2012040103

Azaiza, K. (2011). Effectiveness of distance education for women in the Arab world. In M. Youssef & S. A. Anwar (Eds.), *Proceedings of the 4th Conference on e-Learning Excellence in the Middle East 2011: In Search of New Paradigms for Re-Engineering Education,* (pp. 209–222). Dubai, United Arab Emirates: IEEE.

Babushkina, Y. (2011). Using web 2.0 for the information support of employees: The promise of web 2.0. *Journal of Scientific Information Processing, 38*(1).

Baggaley, J., & Belawati, T. (2010). *Distance education technologies in Asia.* Thousand Oaks, CA: Sage.

Bagozzi, R. P., & Burnkrant, R. E. (1985). Attitude organization and the attitude–behavior relationship: A reply to Dillon and Kumar. *Journal of Personality and Social Psychology, 49,* 1–16. doi:10.1037/0022-3514.49.1.47

Bahrain Center for Human Rights. (2012). Bahraini authorities block access to Google Earth and Google Video. *Bahrain Center for Human Rights.* Retrieved September 10, 2011, from http://www.bahrainrights.org/ref08080600

Bair, J. H. (1989). Supporting cooperative work with computers: Addressing meeting mania. In *Proceedings of the Thirty-Fourth IEEE Computer Society International Conference: Intellectual Leverage, Digest of Papers,* (pp. 208–217). IEEE Press.

Bakos, J. Y. (1991). A strategic analysis of electronic marketplaces. *Management Information Systems Quarterly, 15*(3), 295–310. doi:10.2307/249641

Compilation of References

Balázs, I. E. (2003). Experiences with virtual collaborative learning in post-graduate courses. In F. Malpica & C. Tremante (Eds.), *Proceedings of International Conference on Education and Information Systems: Technologies and Applications (EISTA 2003)*. Orlando, FL: EISTA.

Balázs, I. E., & Schoop, E. (2004). Erfahrungen mit virtual collaborative learning am lehrstuhl wirtschaftsinformatik insbesondere informationsmanagement an der Technischen Universität Dresden - Band 1: Virtual collaborative learning: Ziele, design, erfahrungen. In R. Bogaschewsky, U. Hoppe, F. Klauser, E. Schoop, & C. Weinhardt (Eds.), *IMPULS EC Research Report 7*. Osnabrück, Germany: Electronic Commerce.

Banks, E. (2011). *World cup final sets two Twitter records*. Retrieved October 29, 2011, from http://edition.cnn.com/2011/TECH/social.media/07/18/world.cup.twitter.record.mashable/index.html

Banks, E. (2011). *New year's tweets set new record*. Retrieved October 29, 2011, from http://mashable.com/2011/01/06/new-years-twitter-record

Barbosa, A. (2003). Displaced soundscapes: A survey of network systems for music and sonic art creation. *Leonardo Music Journal, 13*, 53–59. doi:10.1162/096112104322750791

Barbosa, A. (2005). Public sound objects: A shared environment for networked music practice on the web. *Organised Sound, 10*(3), 233–242. doi:10.1017/S135577180500097X

Barbosa, S., Gerhardt, M., & Kickul, J. (2007). The role of cognitive style and risk preference on entrepreneurial self-efficacy and entrepreneurial intentions. *Journal of Leadership & Organizational Studies, 13*(4), 86–104. doi:10.1177/10717919070130041001

Barnatt, C. (2008). Higher education 2.0. *International Journal of Management Education, 7*(3), 47–56. doi:10.3794/ijme.73.250

Barnes, S. J., & Böhringer, M. (2009). Continuance usage intention in microblogging services: The case of Twitter. *Information Systems Journal, 2*(4), 1–13.

Barnes, S., & Huff, S. L. (2003). Rising Sun: i-mode and the wireless internet. *Communications of the ACM, 46*(11), 79–84.

Baron, R., & Ensley, M. (2006). Opportunity recognition as the detection of meaningful patterns: Evidence from comparisons of novice and experienced entrepreneurs. *Management Science, 52*(9), 1331–1344. doi:10.1287/mnsc.1060.0538

Baron, S., Patterson, A., & Harris, K. (2006). Beyond technology acceptance: Understanding consumer practice. *International Journal of Service Industry Management, 17*(2), 111–135. doi:10.1108/09564230610656962

Barroca, L., Rapanotti, L., & Petre, M. (2010). *Developing research degrees online*. Paper presented at the ICERI (International Conference of Education, Reseach and Innovation). Rio de Janeiro, Brasilia.

Bauer, R. A. (1960). Consumer behavior as risk taking. In R. Hancock (Ed.), *Dynamic marketing for a changing world: Proceedings of 43rd Conference* (pp. 389-398). Chicago, IL: American Marketing Association.

Bauer, H. H., Barnes, S. J., Reichardt, T., & Neumann, M. M. (2005). Driving consumer acceptance of mobile marketing: A theoretical framework and empirical study. *Journal of Electronic Commerce Research, 6*(3), 181–191.

Baumgarten, J., & Chui, M. (2009). *E-government 2.0*. Retrieved from http://www.mckinseyquarterly.com/E-government_20_2408

Beauchamp, G., & Kennewell, S. (2008). The influence of ICT on the interactivity of teaching. *Education and Information Technologies*, *13*(4), 305–315. doi:10.1007/s10639-008-9071-y

Becherer, R., & Maurer, J. (1999). The proactive personality disposition and entrepreneurial behaviour among small company presidents. *Journal of Small Business Management*, *38*, 28–36.

Beer, D., & Burrows, R. (2007). Sociology and, of and in web 2.0: Some initial considerations. *Sociological Research Online*. Retrieved from http://www.socresonline.org.uk/12/5/17.html

Beer, D. (2008). Making friends with Jarvis Cocker: Music culture in the context of web 2.0. *Cultural Sociology*, *2*(2), 222–241. doi:10.1177/1749975508091034

Beetham, H., & Sharpe, R. (Eds.). (2007). *Rethinking pedagogy for a digital age*. Abingdon, UK: Routledge.

Benini, M., Fichemann, I. K., Zuffo, M. K., de Deus Lopes, R., & Batista, L. (Eds.). (2004). Musical: A case of interface usability for children. In *Proceedings of CELDA*, (pp. 319–326). CELDA.

Benmamoun, M., Kalliny, M. A., & Cropf, R. (2012). The Arab spring, MNEs, and virtual public spheres. *Multinational Business Review*, *20*(10), 26–43. doi:10.1108/15253831211217189

Bennett, N. L., Casebeer, L. L., Kristofco, R. E., & Strasser, S. M. (2004). Physicians' internet information-seeking behaviors. *The Journal of Continuing Education in the Health Professions*, *24*(1), 31–38. doi:10.1002/chp.1340240106

Bennett, N. L., Casebeer, L. L., Kristofco, R., & Collins, B. C. (2005). Family physicians' information seeking behaviors: A survey comparison with other specialties. *BioMed Central Medical Informatics and Decision Making*, *5*, 9. doi:10.1186/1472-6947-5-9

Bennett, R. C., & Cooper, R. G. (1981). Beyond the marketing concept. *Business Horizons*, *22*(3), 76–83. doi:10.1016/0007-6813(79)90088-0

Bennett, S. (1976). The process of musical creation: Interview with eight composers. *Journal of Research in Music Education*, *24*, 3–13. doi:10.2307/3345061

Bentley, C. M. (2008). Strategies to encourage local ownership of online collaboration technologies in West Africa. In N. Whitton & M. McPherson (Eds.), *ALT-C 2008: Rethinking the Digital Divide, the 15th Association for Learning Technology Conference*. Leeds, UK: ALT-C.

Bentley, C. M. (2009). *Using technology to enhance collaborative partnerships in West Africa: A project implementation by Canadian Crossroads International*. (Unpublished Master Internship Report). Concordia University. Montreal, Canada.

Bentley, C. M., & Labelle, P. (2008). A comparison of social tagging designs and user participation. In J. Greenberg & W. Klas (Eds.), *International Conference on Dublin Core and Metadata Applications: Metadata for Semantic and Social Applications,* (p. 205). Berlin, Germany: Universitätsverlag Göttingen.

Compilation of References

Berners-Lee, T., & Fischetti, M. (1999). *Weaving the web*. New York, NY: Harper.

Bernoff, J., & Li, C. (2008). Harnessing the power of the oh-so-social web. *MIT Sloan Management Review, 49*(3), 36–42.

Bernstein, A., & Goodman, S. E. (2005). Global diffusion of the internet IV. *The Internet in Togo, 15*(23), 371–392.

Bettelheim, B. (1986). *The informed heart*. Harmondsworth, UK: Penguin.

Biekart, K. (2008). Learning from Latin America: Recent trends in European NGO policymaking. In Bebbington, A., Hickey, S., & Mitlin, D. C. (Eds.), *Can NGOs make a Difference? The Challenge of Development Alternatives* (pp. 71–89). London, UK: Zed Books.

Bjerke, B., & Hultman, C. M. (2002). *Entrepreneurial marketing: The growth of small firms in the new economic era*. Cheltenham, UK: Edward Elgar.

Black, J. (2008). Egypt's press: More free, still fettered. *Arab Media & Society, 2*.

Blaydes, L. (2011). *Elections and distributive politics in Mubarak's Egypt*. Cambridge, UK: Cambridge University Press. doi:10.1017/CBO9780511976469

Blinn, N., Lindermann, N., & Nüttgens, M. (2009). Web 2.0 in SME networks - A design science approach considering multi-perspective requirements. In *Proceedings of the Fifteenth AMCIS*. San Francisco, CA: AMCIS.

Bof, A. M. (2004). Distance learning for teacher training in Brazil. *International Review of Research in Open and Distance Learning, 5*(1), 1–14.

Bohman, J., & Rehg, W. (1997). *Deliberative democracy: Essays on reason and politics*. Cambridge, MA: The MIT Press.

Böhringer, M., & Richter, A. (2009). Adopting enterprise 2.0: A case study on microblogging. In *Proceedings of the Ninth Conference Mensch und Computer*, (pp. 293-302). Oldenbourg.

Bojic, I., Lipic, T., & Podobnik, V. (2012). Bio-inspired clustering and data diffusion in machine social networks. In Abraham, A. (Ed.), *Computational Social Networks: Mining and Visualization* (pp. 51–79). London, UK: Springer Verlag. doi:10.1007/978-1-4471-4054-2_3

Boll, S. (2007). MultiTube: Where web 2.0 and multimedia could meet. *IEEE MultiMedia, 14*(1), 9–13. doi:10.1109/MMUL.2007.17

Bolton, B., & Thompson, J. (2004). *Entrepreneurs: Talent, temperament, technique* (2nd ed.). London, UK: Elsevier.

Bonabeau, E. (2009). Decisions 2.0: The power of collective intelligence. *MIT Sloan Management Review, 50*(2), 45–52.

Bonner, J. M., & Walker, O. C. Jr. (2004). Selecting influential business-to-business customers in new product development: Relational embeddedness and knowledge heterogeneity considerations. *Journal of Product Innovation Management, 21*(3), 55–69. doi:10.1111/j.0737-6782.2004.00067.x

Botha, W. (2010). *Sustainable e-health business models in sub-Saharan Africa*. Unpublished.

Boudreau, K., & Lakhani, K. R. (2009). How to manage outside innovation. *MIT Sloan Management Review, 50*(4).

Bourdieu, P. (1977). *Outline of a theory of practice*. Cambridge, UK: Cambridge University Press.

Bowe, B. J., & Blom, R. (2010). Facilitating dissent: The ethical implications of political organizing via social media. *Politics, Culture and Socialization, 1*(4).

Bowe, B. J., Blom, R., & Freedman, E. (2012). Control and dissent: Online political organizing in repressitarian regimes. In *Human Rights and Information Communication Technologies: Trends and Consequences of Use*. Hershey, PA: IGI Global.

Boyd, D. M., & Ellison, N. B. (2007). Social network sites: Definition, history, and scholarship. *Journal of Computer-Mediated Communication, 13*(1). Retrieved June 3, 2011, from http://jcmc.indiana.edu/vol13/issue1/boyd.ellison.html

Boyd, D. M., & Ellison, N. B. (2007). Social network sites: Definition, history, and scholarship. *Journal of Computer-Mediated Communication, 13*(1). Retrieved from http://jcmc.indiana.edu/vol13/issue1/boyd.ellison.htmldoi:10.1111/j.1083-6101.2007.00393.x

Brandon, D. P., & Hollingshead, A. B. (1999). Collaborative learning and computer-supported groups. *Communication Education, 48*, 109–126. doi:10.1080/03634529909379159

Braun, V., & Herstatt, C. (2008). The freedom-fighters: How incumbent corporations are attempting to control user-innovation. *International Journal of Innovation Management, 12*(3), 543–572. doi:10.1142/S1363919608002059

Brender, J. (2006). *Evaluation methods for health informatics*. London, UK: Elsevier Inc.

Bretschneider, U., Huber, M., Leimeister, J. M., & Krcmar, H. (2008). Community for innovations: Developing an integrated concept for open innovation. In *Proceedings of the IFIP 8.6 Conference*. Madrid, Spain: IFIP.

Brockhoff, K. (2003). Customers' perspectives of involvement in new product development. *International Journal of Technology Management, 26*(5/6), 464–481. doi:10.1504/IJTM.2003.003418

Bronfenbrenner, U. (1979). *The ecology of human development: Experiments by nature and design*. Cambridge, MA: Harvard University Press.

Brown, N. (2011). *Can the colossus be salvaged? Egypt's state-owned press in a post-revolutionary environment - Carnegie endowment for international peace*. Retrieved from http://carnegieendowment.org/2011/08/22/can-colossus-be-salvaged-egypt-s-state-owned-press-in-post-revolutionary-environment/4uah#

Brown, I. T. J. (2002). Individual and technological factors affecting perceived ease of use of web-based learning technologies in a developing country. *The Electronic Journal on Information Systems in Developing Countries, 9*(5), 1–15.

Brown, R. (1965). *Social psychology*. New York, NY: Free Press.

Bruns, A. (2008). *Blogs, Wikipedia, Second Life and beyond: From production to produsage*. New York, NY: Peter Lang.

Bryan-Kinns, N., & Healey, P. G. T. (2004). Daisyphone: Support for remote music collaboration. In *Proceedings of the 2004 Conference on New Interfaces for Musical Expression*, (pp. 27-30). Singapore, Singapore: National University of Singapore.

Compilation of References

Brzozowski, M. J., Sandholm, T., & Hogg, T. (2009). Effects of feedback and peer pressure on contributions to enterprise social media. In *Proceedings of the ACM 2009 International Conference on Supporting Group Work*, (pp. 61-70). ACM Press.

Buckner, E., & Kim, P. (2012). *A pedagogical paradigm shift: The Stanford mobile inquiry-based learning environment project (SMILE)*. Retrieved from http://elizabethbuckner.files.wordpress.com/2012/02/smile-concept-paper.pdf

Bughin, J. (2010). The future of user participation. *McKinsey Technology Initiative Perspectives, 3*.

Bughin, J. (2010). The power law of enterprise 2.0. In In-Lee (Ed.), Encyclopedia of E-Business Development and Management in the Global Economy. Hershey, PA: IGI Global.

Bughin, J., Hung Byers, A., & Chui, M. (2011, November). How social technologies are extending the organization. *The McKinsey Quarterly*.

Bughin, J., & Manyika, J. (2007, December). How businesses are using web 2.0: A McKinsey global survey. *The McKinsey Quarterly*.

Bughin, J., & Manyika, J. (2008). Bubble or paradigm change? Assessing the global diffusion of Enterprise 2.0. In Koohang, A., Harman, K., & Britz, J. (Eds.), *Knowledge Management-Research and Applications*. Hershey, PA: IGI Global.

Bukvova, H., Lehr, C., Lieske, C., Weber, P., & Schoop, E. (2010). Gestaltung virtueller kollaborativer lernprozesse in internationalen settings. [Göttingen, Germany: IEEE.]. *Proceedings of the Multikonferenz Wirtschaftsinformatik, 2010*, 1449–1460.

Bulkeley, W. M. (2010). *TR10: Social TV*. Retrieved November 8, 2011, from http://www.technologyreview.com/communications/25084

Burg, T. N., & Pircher, R. (2006). Social software in unternehmen. *Wissensmanagement, 8*, 26–28.

Burk, P. (2012). *WebDrum*. Retrieved March 02, 2012, from http://www.transjam.com/webdrum/webdrum.html

Burns, P. (2001). *Entrepreneurship and small business*. Hampshire, UK: Palgrave.

Busemann, K., & Christoph, G. (2009). Results of the ARD/ZDF online Study 2009 - Web 2.0: Popular communities among young users. *Media Perspectives, 7*, 356.

Busenitz. (1999). Entrepreneurial risk and strategic decision making: It's a matter of perspective. *Journal of Applied Behavioral Science, 35*(3), 325-340.

Buskens, I. (2011). The importance of intent: Reflecting on open development for women's empowerment. *Information Technologies & International Development, 7*(1), 71–76.

Butcher, M. (2011). *Graph: How long it took Facebook, Twitter and Google+ to reach 10 million users*. Retrieved November 8, 2011, from http://eu.techcrunch.com/2011/07/22/graph-how-long-it-took-facebook-twitter-and-google-to-reach-10-million-users

Bwalya, K. J., Du Plessis, T., & Rensleigh, C. (2011). Setting the foundations for e-democracy in Botswana: An exploratory study of intervention. In *Information Communication Technologies and the Virtual Public Sphere: Impact of Network Structures on Civil Society*. Hershey, PA: IGI Global. doi:10.4018/978-1-60960-159-1.ch012

Caby☐Guillet, L., Guesmi, S., & Maillard, A. (2009). Wiki professionnel et coopération en réseaux: Une étude explorative. *La Découverte – Réseaux, 154*, 195-227.

Callon, M. (1986). The sociology of an actor-network: The case of the electric vehicle. In Callon, M., Law, J., & Rip, A. (Eds.), *Mapping the Dynamics of Science and Technology* (pp. 19–34). London, UK: McMillan.

Campbell, J. D., Harris, K. D., & Hodge, R. (2001). Introducing telemedicine technology to rural physicians and settings. *The Journal of Family Practice, 50*, 419–424.

CAPES. (2010). *Ficha de avaliação do programa - Mestrado profissional.* Retrieved October 13, 2011, from http://www.fnmp. org.br/documentos/ficha-de-avaliacao-dos-mestrados-profissionais-2007-2009.pdf

Carbone, F., Contreras, J., Hernandez, J., & Gomez-Perez, J. (2012). Open innovation in an enterprise 3.0 framework- 3 case studies. *Expert Systems with Applications: An International Journal, 39*(10).

Casaló, L., Flavián, C., & Guinalíu, M. (2011). Antecedents and consequences of consumer participation in online communities: The case of the travel sector. *International Journal of Electronic Commerce, 15*(2), 137–167. doi:10.2753/JEC1086-4415150205

Casebeer, L., Bennett, N., Kristofco, R., Carillo, A., & Centor, R. (2002). Physician internet medical information seeking and on-line continuing education use patterns. *The Journal of Continuing Education in the Health Professions, 22*(1), 33–42. doi:10.1002/chp.1340220105

Casson, M., & Wadeson, N. (2006). The discovery of opportunities: Extending the economic theory of the entrepreneur. *Small Business Economics, 28*(4), 285–300. doi:10.1007/s11187-006-9037-7

Chaiken, S., & Stangor, C. (1987). Attitudes and attitude change. *Annual Review of Psychology, 38*, 575–630. doi:10.1146/annurev.ps.38.020187.003043

Chao, C. H., Wang, E., Shih, F., & Fan, Y. (2011). Understanding knowledge sharing in virtual communities. An integration of expectancy disconfirmation and justice theories. *Online Information Review, 35*(1), 134–153. doi:10.1108/14684521111113623

Chen, C. W. (2006). The creative process of computer-assisted composition and multimedia composition: Visual images and music. (Doctor of Philosophy Thesis). Royal Melbourne Institute of Technology. Melbourne, Australia.

Chen, J., Feng, J., & Whinston, A. B. (2010). Keyword auctions, unit-price contracts, and the role of commitment. *Production and Operations Management, 19*(3), 305–321. doi:10.1111/j.1937-5956.2009.01093.x

Chen, T. F. (2009). Building a platform of business model 2.0 to creating real business value with web 2.0 for web information services industry. *International Journal of Electronic Business Management, 7*(3), 168–180.

Chen, X., Yamauchi, K., & Kato, K. (2006). Using the balanced scorecard to measure Chinese and Japanese hospital performance. *International Journal of Health Care Quality Assurance, 19*(4), 339–350. doi:10.1108/09526860610671391

Cheong, J., & Park, M. C. (2005). Mobile Internet acceptance in Korea. *Internet Research, 15*(2), 125–140. doi:10.1108/10662240510590324

Chesbrough, H. W. (2003). The era of open innovation. *MIT Sloan Management Review, 44*(3), 35–41.

Chesbrough, H., & Crowther, A. K. (2006). Beyond high-tech: Early adopters of open innovation in other industries. *R & D Management, 36*(3), 229–236. doi:10.1111/j.1467-9310.2006.00428.x

Chiaroni, D., Chiesa, V., & Frattini, F. (2011). The open innovation journey: How firms dynamically implement the emerging innovation management paradigm. *Technovation, 31*, 34–43. doi:10.1016/j.technovation.2009.08.007

Choi, Y., Lévesque, M., & Shepherd, D. (2008). When should entrepreneurs expedite or delay opportunity exploitation? *Journal of Business Venturing, 23*(3), 333–355. doi:10.1016/j.jbusvent.2006.11.001

Choney, S. (2011, February 17). Bahrain Internet service starting to slow. *Technology on MSNBC*. Retrieved October 25, 2011, from http://technolog.msnbc.msn.com/_news/2011/02/17/6075162-bahrain-internet-service-starting-to-slow

Christensen, C. M. (1997). *The innovators dilemma: When new technologies cause great firms to fail*. Cambridge, MA: Harvard Business School Press.

Christensen, C. M., & Bower, J. L. (1996). Customer power, strategic investment, and the failure of leading firms. *Strategic Management Journal, 17*(3), 197–218. doi:10.1002/(SICI)1097-0266(199603)17:3<197::AID-SMJ804>3.0.CO;2-U

Christensen, J. F., Olesen, M. H., & Kjaer, J. S. (2005). The industrial dynamics of open innovation: Evidence from the transformation of consumer electronics. *Research Policy, 34*(10), 1533–1549. doi:10.1016/j.respol.2005.07.002

Chui, M., Miller, A., & Roberts, R. P. (2009). Six ways to make web 2.0 work. *McKinsey and Company*, 1-7.

Chui, M., & Bughin, J. (2010, December). The rise of the networked enterprise, web 2.0 finds its payday. *The McKinsey Quarterly*.

Chui, M., Manyika, J., Bughin, J., Dobbs, R., Roxburgh, C., & Sarazzin, H. (2012). *The social economy: Unlocking the value and productivity through social technologies. McKinsey Global Institute Report*. New York, NY: McKinsey Global Institute.

Citrin, A., Stern, D., Spangerberg, E., & Clark, M. (2003). Consumer need for tactile input. An Internet retailing challenge. *Journal of Business Research, 56*(11), 915–922. doi:10.1016/S0148-2963(01)00278-8

Clarke, R. (2008). Web 2.0 as syndication. *Journal of Theoretical and Applied Electronic Commerce Research, 3*(2), 30–43. doi:10.4067/S0718-18762008000100004

Clark, J. (1997). The state, popular participation and the voluntary sector. In Hulme, D., & Edwards, M. (Eds.), *NGOs, States and Donors: Too Close for Comfort (International Political Economy)*. Basingstoke, UK: Palgrave Macmillan. doi:10.1016/0305-750X(94)00147-Q

Clark, J. (2003). *Globalizing civic engagement: Civil society and transnational action*. London, UK: Earthscan.

Cogburn, D. (2004). Diversity matters, even at a distance: Evaluating the impact of computer-mediated communication on civil society participation in the world summit on the information society. *Information Technologies and International Development, 1*(3-4), 14–40. doi:10.1162/1544752043557404

Coleman, S., & Shane, P. (2011). *Connecting democracy: Online consultation and the flow of political communication*. Cambridge, MA: MIT Press.

Collins, D. (2005). A synthesis process model of creative thinking in music composition. *Psychology of Music, 33*(2), 193–216. doi:10.1177/0305735605050651

Comscore. (2011). *Mobile social networking audience grew 44 percent over past year in EU5*. Retrieved May 16, 2012, from http://www.comscore.com/Press_Events/Press_Releases/2011/11/Mobile_Social_Networking_Audience_Grew_44_Percent_Over_Past_Year_in_EU5

Conecta (2011). *6° observatorio de tendencias NOKIA: los jóvenes, los móviles y la tecnología.* Retrieved June 17, 2011, from http://www.conectarc.com/Articulos%20y%20Estudios/Highlights%206%BA%20Observatorio%20Final.pdf

Conole, G. (2008). New schemas for mapping pedagogies and technologies. *Ariadne, 56.* Retrieved September 22, 2010 from http://www.ariadne.ac.uk/issue56/conole/

Conole, G. (2010). *Learning design – Making practice explicit*. Paper presented at the ConnectEd 2010: 2nd International Conference on Design Education. Rio de Janeiro, Brasilia.

Conole, G. (2011). *Designing for learning in an open world*. Retrieved July 19, 2011, from http://cloudworks.ac.uk/cloudscape/view/2155

Conole, G., & Alevizou, P. (2010). *A review of the use of web 2.0 tools in higher education*. Retrieved October 13, 2011, from http://oro.open.ac.uk/23154/

Conole, G. (2009). Stepping over the edge: The implications of new technologies for education. In Lee, M. J. W., & McLoughlin, C. (Eds.), *Web 2.0-based e-learning: Applying social informatics for tertiary teaching*. Hershey, PA: IGI Global.

Constantinides, E. (2004). Influencing the online consumer's behaviour: The web experience. *Journal of Internet Research, 14*(2), 111–126. doi:10.1108/10662240410530835

Constantinides, E., & Fountain, S. (2008). Web 2.0: Conceptual foundations and marketing issues. *Journal of Direct. Data and Digital Marketing Practice, 9*(3), 231–244. doi:10.1057/palgrave.dddmp.4350098

Cooke, M., & Buckley, N. (2008). Web 2.0, social networks and the future of market research. *International Journal of Market Research, 50*, 267–292.

Cormode, G., & Krishnamurthy, B. (2008). Key differences between web 1.0 and web 2.0. *First Monday, 13*(6). Retrieved October 5, 2010, from http://www.uic.edu/htbin/cgiwrap/bin/ojs/index.php/fm/article/view/2125/1972

Costa, C. J. D., & Pimentel, N. M. (2009). The Brazilian open university system in the consolidation of the higher education distance learning offer in Brazil. *Educação Temática Digital, 10*(2), 71–90.

Council on Foreign Relations. (2011). *The new Arab revolt: What happened, what it means, and what comes next*. New York, NY: Council on Foreign Relations Press.

Cowie, J. (2011). Egypt leaves the internet. *Renesys*. [Blog]. Retrieved from http://www.renesys.com/blog/2011/01/egypt-leaves-the-internet.shtml

CPHC. (2004). *Towards benchmarking standards for taught masters degrees in computing*. London, UK: CPHC.

Crete-Nishihata, M., & York, J. C. (2011). Egypt's internet blackout: Extreme example of just-in-time blocking. *OpenNet Initiative*. Retrieved from http://opennet.net/blog/2011/01/egypt%E2%80%99s-internet-blackout-extreme-example-just-time-blocking

Crook, C. J. C., Fisher, T., Graber, R., Harrison, C., Lewin, C., et al. (2008). *Web 2.0 technologies for learning: the current landscape –Opportunities, challenges and tensions*. Retrieved September 12, 2011, from http://dera.ioe.ac.uk/1474/

Cropf, R., & Krummenacher, W. S. (Eds.). (2011). *Information communication technologies and the virtual public sphere: Impact of network structures on civil society*. Hershey, PA: IGI Global. doi:10.4018/978-1-60960-159-1

Crossroads International. (2006). *West African communications capacity building project*. Toronto, Canada: Gardner.

Csikszentmihalyi, M. (1996). *Creativity*. New York, NY: HarperCollins.

Cunningham, J., & Lischeron, J. (1991). Defining entrepreneurship. *Journal of Small Business Management, 29*(1), 45–61.

Cunningham, P., & Wilkins, J. A. (2009). A walk in the cloud. *Information Management Journal, 43*(1), 22–30.

Curtis, D., & Lawson, M. (2001). Exploring collaborative online learning. *Journal of Asynchronous Learning Networks, 5*(1), 21–34.

Czarniawska, B., & Wolff, R. (1991). Leaders, managers, entrepreneurs on and off the organizational stage. *Organization Studies, 12*(4), 529–546. doi:10.1177/017084069101200404

Dabarah, I. (2009, March 5). ...الإنترنت في ليبيا. الجميع يتمرّد على الحجب والرقابة مُستمرّة. *Elaph*. Retrieved September 10, 2011, from www.elaph.com/Web/Politics/2009/3/415948.htm

Daconta, M. (2003). *The semantic web: A guide to the future of XML, web services, and knowledge management*. New York, NY: John Wiley & Sons Inc.

Dada, D. (2006). e-Readiness for developing countries: Moving the focus from the environment to the users. *The Electronic Journal of Information Systems in Developing Countries, 27*(6), 1–14.

Dahan, E., & Hauser, Jr. (2002). The virtual customer. *Journal of Product Innovation Management, 19*, 332–353. doi:10.1016/S0737-6782(02)00151-0

Dahlander, L. (2006). *Managing beyond firm boundaries: Leveraging user innovation networks*. Gothenburg, Sweden: Chalmers University of Technology.

Dahl, R. (1971). *Polyarchy: Participation and opposition*. New Haven, CT: Yale University Press.

Dashti, A. A. (2009). The role of online journalism in political disputes in Kuwait. *Journal of Arab and Muslim Research, 2*, 91–112. doi:10.1386/jammr.2.1and2.91/1

Davies, J. A., & Merchant, G. (2009). *Web 2.0 for schools: Learning and social participation*. New York, NY: Peter Lang.

Davis, F. D. (1989). Perceived usefulness, perceived ease of use, and user acceptance of information technology. *Management Information Systems Quarterly, 13*(3), 319–340. doi:10.2307/249008

Davis, F. D., Bagozzi, R. P., & Warshaw, P. R. (1989). User acceptance of computer technology: A comparison of two theoretical models. *Management Science, 35*, 982–1003. doi:10.1287/mnsc.35.8.982

Dawes, S. S. (2002). The future of e-government. *Center for Technology in Government*. Retrieved August 13, 2012 from http://www.ctg.albany.edu/publications/reports/future_of_egov

Dayem, M. A. (2009, Summer). Attempting to silence Iran's weblogistan. *Nieman Reports*, 42-44.

De Saulles, M. (2008). Never too small to join the party. *Information World Review*. Retrieved from http://www.iwr.co.uk/informationworld-review/features/2225252/never-small-join-party

Dearden, A. (2008). User-centered design considered harmful1 (with apologies to Edsger Dijkstra, Niklaus Wirth, and Don Norman). *Information Technologies & International Development, 4*(3), 7–12. doi:10.1162/itid.2008.00013

Deibert, R., & Rohozinski, R. (2008). Good for liberty, bad for security? Global civil society and the securitization of the internet. In Deibert, R., Palfrey, J., Rohozinski, R., & Zittrain, J. (Eds.), *Access Denied: The Practice and Policy of Global Internet Filtering*. Cambridge, MA: MIT Press.

Deibert, R., & Rohozinski, R. (2010). Control and subversion in Russian cyberspace. In Deibert, R., Palfrey, J., Rohozinski, R., & Zittrain, J. (Eds.), *Access Controlled: The Shaping of Power, Rights, and Rule in Cyberspace* (pp. 15–34). Cambridge, MA: MIT Press.

Denning, P. (1992). Educating a new engineer. *Communications of the ACM, 32*(12), 83–97.

Deshpande, A., & Jadad, A. (2006). Web 2.0: Could it help move the health system into the 21st century. *Journal of Men's Health & Gender, 3*(4), 332–336. doi:10.1016/j.jmhg.2006.09.004

Desilets, A., Paquet, S., & Vinson, N. (2005). *Are wikis usable?* Paper presented at the WikiSym 2005 Conference. San Diego, CA.

Deuze, M. (2008). Corporate appropriation of participatory culture. In Carpentier, N. (Ed.), *Participation and Media Production: Critical Reflections on Content Creation* (pp. 27–40). Newcastle upon Tyne, UK: Cambridge Scholars Publishers.

Dholakia, R., & Uusitalo, O. (2002). Switching to electronic stores: Consumer characteristics and the perception of shopping benefits. *International Journal of Retail and Distribution Management, 30*(10), 459–469. doi:10.1108/09590550210445335

DiMicco, J., Millen, D. R., Geyer, W., Dugan, C., Brownholtz, B., & Muller, M. (2008). Motivations for social network at work. In *Proceedings of the ACM 2009 International Conference on Computer Supported Cooperative Work*, (pp. 711-720). ACM Press.

Dimitrov, D. (2006). Cultural differences in motivation for organizational learning and training. *International Journal Of Diversity In Organisations. Communities & Nations, 5*(4), 37–48.

Dingwall, C. (2008). Rational and intuitive approaches to music composition: The impact of individual differences in thinking/learning styles on compositional processes. (Bachelor of Music Dissertation Thesis). University of Sydney. Sydney, Australia.

Dogson, M., Gann, D., & Salter, A. (2006). The role of technology in the shift towards open innovation: The case of Procter & Gamble. *R & D Management, 36*(3), 333–346. doi:10.1111/j.1467-9310.2006.00429.x

Dourish, P., & Bellotti, V. (1992). Awareness and coordination in shared workspaces. In *Proceedings of the 1992 ACM Conference on Computer-Supported Cooperative Work,* (pp. 107-114). New York, NY: ACM Press.

Downes, S. (2009). Blogs in Learning. In Mishra, S. (Ed.), *STRIDE Handbook 8 - e-Learning* (pp. 88–91). New Delhi, India: Indira Gandhi National Open University.

Doyle, W., Fisher, R., & Young, J. (2002). Entrepreneurs: Relationships between cognitive style and entrepreneurial drive. *Journal of Small Business and Entrepreneurship, 16*(2), 2–20.

Duckworth, W. (1999). Making music on the web. *Leonardo Music Journal, 1*(9), 13–17. doi:10.1162/096112199750316749

Duffy, P., & Bruns, A. (2006). The use of blogs, wikis and RSS in education: A conversation of possibilities. In *Proceedings Online Learning and Teaching Conference 2006,* (pp. 31-38). Brisbane, Australia: IEEE. Retrieved September 11, 2008 from http://eprints.qut.edu.au

Duve, F. (2003). Preface. In Hardy, C., & Moller, C. (Eds.), *Spreading the Word on the Internet*. Vienna, Austria: Organization for Security and Co-Operation in Europe.

Eagly, A. H., & Chaiken, S. (1993). *The psychology of attitudes*. Fort Worth, TX: Harcourt Brace Jovanovich College Publishers.

Ebner, W., Leimeister, J. M., & Krcmar, H. (2004). Trust in virtual healthcare communities: Design and implementation of trust-enabling functionalities. In *Proceedings of the Hawaii International Conference on System Sciences*. IEEE.

Economic Intelligence Unit. (2007). *Collaboration- Transforming the way business works. Report from the EIU*. Cisco Systems.

Economic Times. (2012). *Zain and MTN target South Sudan as next mobile-money frontier*. Retrieved from http://articles.economictimes.indiatimes.com/2012-07-19/news/32747333_1_mobile-money-mobile-money-south-sudan

Ehrlich, K., & Shami, N. S. (2010). Microblogging inside and outside the workplace. In *Proceedings of the 4th International AAAI Conference on Weblogs and Social Media (ICWSM 2010)*. AAAI Publications.

Eid, G. (2012). *Libya: The internet in a conflict zone: The internet in the Arab world a new space of repression?* Retrieved September 10, 2011, from www.anhri.net/en/reports/net2004/libya.shtml

Eighmey, J. (1997). Profiling user responses to commercial web sites. *Journal of Advertising Research, 37*(May/June), 59–66.

Eighmey, J., & McCord, L. (1998). Adding value in the information age: Uses and gratifications of sites on the World Wide Web. *Journal of Business Research, 41*, 187–194. doi:10.1016/S0148-2963(97)00061-1

Eijkman, H. (2008). Web 2.0 as a non-foundational network-centric learning space. *Campus-Wide Information Systems, 25*(2), 93–104. doi:10.1108/10650740810866567

El Nashmi, E., Cleary, J., Molleda, J.-C., & McAdams, M. (2010). Internet political discussions in the Arab world: A look at online forums from Kuwait, Saudi Arabia, Egypt and Jordan. *International Communication Gazette, 72*, 719–738. doi:10.1177/1748048510380810

Elragal, A., & El-Telbany, O. (2012). Decision 2.0: An exploratory case study. [*th Hawaii International Conference on System Science.* IEEE Computer Society.]. *Proceedings of the, 2012*, 45.

E-Marketer.com. (2010). *Website.* Retrieved from http://www.emarketer.com/Article. aspx?R=1007506

Endeshaw, A. (2004). Internet regulation in China: The never-ending cat and mouse game. *Information & Communications Technology Law, 13*, 41–57. doi:10.1080/13600830420 00190634

Engeström, Y. (1987). *Learning by expanding: An activity theoretical approach to developmental research.* (F. Seeger, Trans.). Retrieved August 8, 2012, from http://lchc.ucsd.edu/MCA/Paper/Engestrom/expanding/toc.htm

Enkel, E., Gassmann, O., & Chesbrough, H. (2009). Open R&D and open innovation: Exploring the phenomenon. *R & D Management, 39*(4). doi:10.1111/j.1467-9310.2009.00570.x

Enkel, E., Kausch, C., & Gassmann, O. (2005). Managing the risk of customer integration. *European Management Journal, 23*(2), 203–213. doi:10.1016/j.emj.2005.02.005

Erez, M., & Somech, A. (1996). Is group productivity loss the rule or the exception? Effects of culture and group-based motivation. *Academy of Management Journal, 39*(6), 1513–1537. doi:10.2307/257067

Essoulami, S. (2006, January 7). The Arab press: Historical background. *AL-BAB.* Retrieved August 5, 2011, from http://www.al-bab.com/media/introduction.htm

Etling, B., Kelly, J., Faris, R., & Palfrey, J. (2010). Mapping the Arabic blogosphere: Politics and dissent online. *New Media & Society, 12*, 1225–1243. doi:10.1177/1461444810385096

European Commission. (2004). *Five-year assessment of the European Union research framework programmes 1999-2003.* Retrieved from http://ec.europa.eu/research/reports/2004/pdf/fya_en.pdf

Evans, M. (2010). *Exploring the use of twitter around the world.* Retrieved September 7, 2011, from http://blog.sysomos.com/2010/01/14/exploring-the-use-of-twitter-around-the-world/

Evans, P., & Wurster, T. (1999). *Blown to bits: How the new economics of information transforms strategy.* Boston, MA: Harvard Business School Press.

Ewers, J. (2006). Cyworld: Bigger than YouTube? *U.S. News & World Report.*

Eysenbach, G. (2001). What is e-health. *Journal of Medical Internet Research, 3*(2). doi:10.2196/jmir.3.2.e20

Facebook. (2010). *Facebook mobile usage.* Retrieved from http://www.facebook.com/facebook?v=app_10531514314

Facebook. (2011). Statistics. *Facebook.* Retrieved September 20, 2011, from http://www.facebook.com/press/info.php?statistics

Facebook. (2012). *Facebook key facts.* Retrieved August 1, 2012, from http://newsroom.fb.com/content/default.aspx?NewsAreaId=22

Compilation of References

Facebook. (2012). *Facebook timeline.* Retrieved August 1, 2012, from http://newsroom.fb.com/content/default.aspx?NewsAreaId=20

Facebook. (2012). *Facebook for business.* Retrieved August 1, 2012, from https://www.facebook.com/business/pages

Facebook. (2012). *Promote your business with ads and sponsored stories.* Retrieved August 1, 2012, from https://www.facebook.com/business/pages/#!/business/ads

Facebook. (2012). *Ads: Campaign cost and budgeting.* Retrieved August 1, 2012, from https://www.facebook.com/help/?page=864

Facebook. (2012). *Advertise on Facebook.* Retrieved August 1, 2012, from https://www.facebook.com/advertising

Facebook. (2012). *State bicycle: Building a strong customer base.* Retrieved August 1, 2012, from https://www.facebook.com/advertising/success-stories/state-bicycle

Facebook. (2012). *Luxury link: Building a strong customer base.* Retrieved August 1, 2012, from https://www.facebook.com/advertising/success-stories/luxury-link

Fahmi, W. S. (2009). Bloggers' street movement and the right of the city (re)claiming Cairo's real and virtual "spaces of freedom". *Environment and Urbanization, 21,* 89–107. doi:10.1177/0956247809103006

Fandy, M. (2007). *(Un)civil war of words: Media and politics in the Arab world.* Westport, CT: Academic Press.

Faris, D. (2010). *Revolutions without revolutionaries? Social media networks and regime response in Egypt.* (Unpublished Dissertation). Philadelphia, PA: University of Pennsylvania.

Feng, J., Bhargava, H. K., & Pennock, D. M. (2007). Implementing sponsored search in web search engines: Computational evaluation of alternative mechanisms. *INFORMS Journal on Computing, 19*(1), 137–148. doi:10.1287/ijoc.1050.0135

Ferguson, T. (1998). Digital doctoring-Opportunities and challenges in electronic patient-physician communication. *Journal of the American Medical Association, 280*(15), 1361–1362. doi:10.1001/jama.280.15.1361

Fishbein, M., & Ajzen, I. (1975). *Belief, attitude, intention and behavior: An introduction to theory and research.* New York, NY: Addison-Wesley.

Fitzgerald, R., Barrass, S., Campbell, J., Hinton, S., Ryan, Y., Whitelaw, M., et al. (2009). *Digital learning communities (DLC): Investigating the application of social software to support networked learning (CG6-36).* Retrieved October 14, 2011, from http://eprints.qut.edu.au/18476/

Fleith, D. S. (1999). *The effects of a creativity training program on creative abilities and self-concept in monolingual and bilingual elementary classrooms.* (Unpublished Doctoral Dissertation). University of Connecticut. Storrs, CT.

Fleith, D. S. (2011). Creativity in the Brazilian culture. *Online Readings in Psychology and Culture, 4.* Retrieved September 15, 2011, from http://scholarworks.gvsu.edu/orpc/vol4/iss3/3

Forrester Consulting. (2009). *Building the future of collaboration.* Retrieved from http://wwwimages.adobe.com/www.adobe.com/content/dam/Adobe/en/products/acrobat/pdfs/Building_The_Future_Of_Collaboration.pdf

Forrester, C. (2009, September/October). HDTV and the Mid-East. *International Broadcast Engineer*, 8-9.

Forshyte, S., & Shi, B. (2003). Consumer patronage and risk perceptions in Internet shopping. *Journal of Business Research*, *56*(11), 867–875. doi:10.1016/S0148-2963(01)00273-9

Foster, W., Goodman, S. E., Osiakwan, E., & Bernstein, A. (2004). Global diffusion of the internet IV: The internet in Ghana. *Communications of the AIS*, *13*(38), 654–681.

Foursquare. (2011). *So we grew 3400% last year*. Retrieved October 29, 2011, from http://blog.foursquare.com/2011/01/24/2010infographic

Foursquare. (2012). *About Foursquare*. Retrieved August 1, 2012, from https://foursquare.com/about

Foursquare. (2012). *Foursquare for business*. Retrieved August 1, 2012, from https://foursquare.com/business

Foursquare. (2012). *Foursquare merchant platform*. Retrieved August 1, 2012, from https://foursquare.com/business/merchants

Foursquare. (2012). *Case studies*. Retrieved August 1, 2012, from https://foursquare.com/business/brands/casestudies

Frana, P. (2004). Before the web there was gopher. *IEEE Annals of the History of Computing*, *26*(1), 20–41. doi:10.1109/MAHC.2004.1278848

Franke, N. (2009). How can users' creativity be implemented in new products and services? In *Proceedings of the European Conference on Innovation*. Lund, Sweden: Lund University.

Franke, N., & Schreier, M. (2002). Entrepreneurial opportunities with toolkits for user innovation and design. *International Journal on Media Management*, *4*(4), 225–234. doi:10.1080/14241270209390004

Franklin, S. (2011). Sunrise on the Nile. *Columbia Journalism Review*, *49*(6), 17.

Fraser, H. S. F., Biondich, P., Moodley, D., Choi, S., & Szolovits, P. (2005). Implementing electronic medical record systems in developing countries. *Journal Informatics in Primary Care*, *13*(2), 83–95.

Fredberg, T., Elmquist, M., & Ollila, S. (2008). *Managing open innovation – Present findings and future directions. VINNOVA Report VR 2008, n.02, VINNOVA*. Stockholm, Sweden: Swedish Governmental Agency for Innovation Systems.

Freedom House. (2009). *Freedom on the net*. Retrieved from http://www.freedomhouse.org/template.cfm?page=383&report=79

Freedom House. (2010). *Freedom of the press 2010*. Retrieved from http://www.freedomhouse.org/template.cfm?page=533

Freedom House. (2011). Worst of the worst 2011: The world's most repressive societies. *Freedom in the World 2011*. Retrieved September 10, 2011, from www.freedomhouse.org/uploads/special_report/101.pdf

Freitas, S. D. (2010). *Learning in immersive worlds: A review of game-based learning*. Retrieved from http://www.jisc.ac.uk/media/documents/programmes/elearninginnovation/gamingreport_v3.pdf

Friedman, T. (2007). *The world is flat: A brief history of the twenty-first century*. New York, NY: Picador.

Friman, J. (2010). *Consumer attitudes toward mobile advertising*. Unpublished doctoral dissertation, Department of Marketing and Management, School of Economics, Aalto University.

Fukuyama, F. (1999). *The great disruption: Human nature and the reconstitution of social order*. New York, NY: The Free Press.

Fullan, M. (2007). *The new meaning of educational change* (4th ed.). New York, NY: Teachers College Press.

Füller, J., & Matzler, K. (2007). Virtual product experience and customer participation – A chance for customer-centered, really new products. *Technovation*, *27*, 378–387. doi:10.1016/j.technovation.2006.09.005

Gaillet, L. L. (1994). An historical perspective on collaborative learning. *Journal of Advanced Composition*, *14*(1), 93–110.

Garcia Coll, C., & Magnuson, K. (2000). Cultural differences as sources of developmental vulnerabilities and resources: A view from developmental research. In Meisels, S., & Shonkoff, J. (Eds.), *Handbook of Early Childhood Intervention* (pp. 94–111). Cambridge, UK: Cambridge University Press. doi:10.1017/CBO9780511529320.007

Gardner, H. (1993). *Creating minds*. New York, NY: BasicBooks.

Garrison, D. R., Anderson, T., & Archer, W. (1999). Critical inquiry in a text-based environment: Computer conferencing in higher education. *The Internet and Higher Education*, *2*(2-3), 87–105. doi:10.1016/S1096-7516(00)00016-6

Garrison, D. R., & Arbaud, J. B. (2007). Researching the community of inquiry framework: Review, issues, and future directions. *The Internet and Higher Education*, *10*(3), 157–172. doi:10.1016/j.iheduc.2007.04.001

Gartner, W. (1989). Some suggestions for research on entrepreneurial traits and characteristics, entrepreneurship. *Theory into Practice*, *14*(1), 27–38.

Gaspoz, C. (2011). Prediction markets as web 2.0 tools for enterprise 2.0. In *Proceedings of the Seventeenth Americas Conference on Information Systems*. Detroit, MI: IEEE.

Gassmann, O. (2006). Opening up the innovation process: Towards an agenda. *R & D Management*, *36*(3), 223–228. doi:10.1111/j.1467-9310.2006.00437.x

Gates, C. (2007). Access control requirements for web 2.0 security and privacy. In *Proceedings of the IEEE Web, Web 2.0 Security and Privacy Workshop*. IEEE Press. Retrieved from http://w2spconf.com/2007/papers/paper-205-z_708.pdf

German, K. (2006, August 8). Two numbers on the same cell phone. *CNET Reviews*. Retrieved August 15, 2011, from http://reviews.cnet.com/4520-11282_7-6625917-1.html

Gersch, M., Lehr, C., & Weber, P. (2011). Virtual collaborative learning in international settings – The Virtual seminar "net economy". [INTED.]. *Proceedings of INTED*, *2011*, 5078–5085.

Ghanem, S., Kalliny, M., & Elghoul, S. (2010). The impact of technology on the Arab culture. In *Proceedings of the Academy of Marketing Science Cultural Perspectives in Marketing*. Academy of Marketing Science.

Ghannam, J. (2011). Social media in the Arab world: Leading up to the uprisings of 2011. *The Center for International Media Assistance.* Retrieved August 5, 2011, from http://cima.ned.org/sites/default/files/CIMA-Arab_Social_Media-Report_1.pdf

Giddens, A. (1984). *The constitution of society.* Berkeley, CA: University of California Press.

Gigler, B.-S., Custer, S., & Rahemtulla, H. (2011). *Realizing the vision of open government data.* Washington, DC: Open Development Technology Alliance.

Gillette, F. (2011). *The rise and inglorious fall of Myspace.* Retrieved October 30, 2011, from http://www.businessweek.com/magazine/content/11_27/b4235053917570.htm

Gillin, P. (2007). *The new influencers: A marketer's guide to the new social media.* San Francisco, CA: Quill Driver Books\Word Dancer Press.

Gillmor, D. (2011). Egypt's communications kill switch. *Salon.* Retrieved from http://www.salon.com/technology/dan_gillmor/2011/01/28/egypt_kill_switch

Gillmor, D. (2006). *We the media: Grassroots journalism by the people, for the people.* New York, NY: O'Reilly Media, Inc.

Gladwell, M. (2010). A small change: Why the revolution will not be tweeted. *The New Yorker.* Retrieved from http://www.newyorker.com/reporting/2010/10/04/101004fa_fact_gladwell?currentPage=all

Gladwell, M. (2010, October 4). Small change: Why the revolution will not be tweeted. *New Yorker.* Retrieved from http://www.newyorker.com/reporting/2010/10/04/101004fa_fact_gladwell#ixzz1HuHZ927E

Gladwell, M., & Shirky, C. (2011, March/April). From innovation to revolution: Do social media make protests possible? *Foreign Affairs.* Retrieved from http://www.foreignaffairs.com/node/67189&cid=soc-tumblr-from_innovation_to_revolution-012511

Gladwell, M. (2000). *The tipping point: How little things can make a big difference.* Boston, MA: Little Brown.

Glogoff, S. (2005). Instructional blogging: Promoting interactivity, student-centered learning, and peer input. *Innovate, 1*(5). Retrieved from http://www.innovateonline.info/pdf/vol1_issue5/Instructional_Blogging-_Promoting_Interactivity,_Student-Centered_Learning,_and_Peer_Input.pdf

Goetz, J., & Barger, C. (2008). Harnessing the media revolution to engage the youth market. *Journal of Integrated Marketing Communications.* Retrieved from http://jimc.medill.northwestern.edu/archives/2008/EngageYouthMarket.pdf

Google. (2009). Youtube. Retrieved July 02, 2011, from http://www.youtube.com/

Google. (2011). *Google+ pages: Connect with all the things you care about.* Retrieved November 8, 2011, from http://googleblog.blogspot.com/2011/11/google-pages-connect-with-all-things.html

Google. (2012). *Customer perspective on the rela benefits delivered by Google.* Google EVM Perspective Report. Google.

Gordon, F. T. (2002). *E-government – Introduction.* Retrieved from http://www.ercim.eu/publication/Ercim_News/enw48/intro.html

Gorinski, R., & Fraser, C. (2006). *Literature review on the effective engagement of pasifika parents & communities in education.* Wellington, New Zealand: Ministry of Education.

Grace, T. P. L. (2009). Wikis as a knowledge management tool. *Journal of Knowledge Management*, *13*(4), 64–74. doi:10.1108/13673270910971833

Granovetter, M. (1983). The strength of weak ties: A network theory revisited. *Sociological Theory*, *1*, 201–233. doi:10.2307/202051

Grant, I., & O'Donohoe, S. (2007). Why young consumers are not open to mobile marketing communication. *International Journal of Advertising*, *26*(2), 223–246.

Greenhow, C., Robelia, B., & Hughes, J. E. (2009). Learning, teaching, and scholarship in a digital age. *Educational Researcher*, *38*, 246–259. doi:10.3102/0013189X09336671

Grossman, L. (2010). *TIME's 2010 person of the year*. Retrieved October 30, 2011, from http://www.time.com/time/specials/packages/article/0,28804,2036683_2037183,00.html

Gruen, T. W., Osmonbekov, T., & Czaplewski, A. J. (2006). eWOM: The impact of customer-to-customer online know-how exchange on customer value and loyalty. *Journal of Business Research*, *59*, 449–456. doi:10.1016/j.jbusres.2005.10.004

Grunert, K. G., Jensen, B. B., Sonne, A. M., Brunsø, K., Byrne, D. V., & Clausen, C. (2008). User-oriented innovation in the food sector: Relevant streams of research and an agenda for future work. *Trends in Food Science & Technology*, *19*, 590–602. doi:10.1016/j.tifs.2008.03.008

Gulati, S. (2008). Technology-enhanced learning in developing nations: A review. *International Review of Research in Open and Distance Learning*, *9*(1).

Gunawardena, C. N., Nolla, A. C., Wilson, P. L., Lopez-Islas, J. R., Ramirez-Angel, N., & Megchun-Alpizar, R. M. (2001). A cross-cultural study of group process and development in online conferences. *Distance Education*, *22*(1), 85–121. doi:10.1080/0158791010220106

Günther, O., Riehle, D., Krasnova, H., & Schöndienst, V. (2009). Modeling microblogging adoption in the enterprise. In *Proceedings of the 15th Americas Conference on Information Systems (ACIS)*. ACIS.

Gurevich, M. (2006). Jamspace: Designing a collaborative networked music space for novices. In *Proceedings of NIME*, (pp. 118–123). NIME.

Gutwin, C., & Greenberg, S. (2002). A descriptive framework of workspace awareness for real-time groupware. *Computer Supported Cooperative Work*, *11*(3-4), 441–446.

Haberman, S. (2012). *Euro 2012 goal smashes tweets-per-second sports record*. Retrieved August 1, 2012, from http://mashable.com/2012/07/02/euro-2012-tweet-record

Habermas, J. (1991). *The structural transformation of the public sphere*. Cambridge, MA: The MIT Press.

Hacker, K. L., & Morgan, E. L. (2011). Issues of digital disempowerment and new media networking (NMN) in relation to e-government. In *Information Communication Technologies and the Virtual Public Sphere: Impact of Network Structures on Civil Society*. Hershey, PA: IGI Global. doi:10.4018/978-1-60960-159-1.ch005

Hafkin, N., & Taggart, N. (2001). *Gender, information technology and developing countries: An analytic study*. Washington, DC: WID Office USAID.

Ha, I., Yoon, Y., & Choi, M. (2007). Determinants of adoption of mobile games under mobile broadband wireless access environment. *Information & Management*, *44*, 276–286. doi:10.1016/j.im.2007.01.001

Hair, J. F., Anderson, R. E., Tatham, R. L., & Black, W. C. (1999). *Multivariate data analysis* (5th ed.). Englewood Cliffs, NJ: Prentice Hall.

Hamdy, N. (2008). Building capabilities of Egyptian journalist in preparation for media in transition. *Journal of Arab and Muslim Media Research*, *1*, 215–243. doi:10.1386/jammr.1.3.215_1

Hamdy, N. (2009). Arab citizen journalism in action: Challenging mainstream media, authorities and media laws. *Westminster Papers in Communication and Culture*, *6*, 92–112.

Handy, C. (1995). Trust and the virtual organization. *Harvard Business Review*, *73*(3), 40–50.

Harkins, A. M. (2008). Leapfrog principles and practices: Core components of education 3.0 and 4.0. *Futures Research Quarterly*, *24*(1), 19–32.

Hartmann, M. I. (2006). *Software architectures for the cooperative music prototyping environment CODES: Study and implementation*. Rio Grande do Sul, Brazil: Federal University of Rio Grande do Sul.

Hartung, C., Anokwa, Y., Brunette, W., & Lerer, A. (2010). Open data kit: Tools to build information services for developing regions. In *Proceedings of the International Conference on Information and Communication Technologies and Development - ICTD 2010*. London, UK: ICTD.

HCI. (2011). *Proceedings of the 14th International Conference on Human-Computer Interaction*. Retrieved August 22, 2011, from http://www.hcii2011.org/index.php?module=webpage&id=47

Heeks, R. (2001). Understanding e-governance for development. *Institute for Development Policy and Management*. Retrieved August 11, 2012 from http://unpan1.un.org/intradoc/groups/public/documents/NISPAcee/UNPAN015484.pdf

Heffernan, T., Morrison, M., Basu, P., & Sweeney, A. (2010). Cultural differences, learning styles and transnational education. *Journal of Higher Education Policy and Management*, *32*(1), 27–39. doi:10.1080/13600800903440535

Heim, M. (1993). *The metaphysics of virtual reality*. Oxford, UK: Oxford University Press.

Hennala, L., Parjanen, S., & Uotila, T. (2011). Challenges of multi-actor involvement in the public sector front-end innovation processes: Constructing an open innovation model for developing well-being services. *European Journal of Innovation Management*, *14*(3). doi:10.1108/14601061111148843

HEPI. (2010). *Postgraduate education in the United Kingdom*. Retrieved October 13, 2011, from http://www.hepi.ac.uk/466-1149/Postgraduate-Education-in-the-United-Kingdom.html

Hernandez, B. A. (2012). *The top 15 tweets-per-second records*. Retrieved August 1, 2012, from http://mashable.com/2012/02/06/tweets-per-second-records-twitter

Hill, C. (2011). *Global business today*. Boston, MA: Irwin/McGraw-Hill.

Hiltz, S. R. (1988). Collaborative learning in a virtual classroom: Highlights of findings. In *Proceedings of the 1988 ACM Conference on Computer-Supported Cooperative Work*, (pp. 282–290). New York, NY: ACM Press.

Hofstede, G. (1986). Cultural differences in teaching and learning. *International Journal of Intercultural Relations*, *10*, 301–320. doi:10.1016/0147-1767(86)90015-5

Hofstede, G. (2005). *Cultures and organizations: Software of the mind* (2nd ed.). New York, NY: McGraw-Hill.

Howe, J. (2009). *Crowdsourcing: Why the power of the crowd is driving the future of business*. New York, NY: Crown Business.

Hroub, K. (2009). *Internet freedom in the Arab world: Its impact, state controls, Islamisation and the overestimation of it all*. Retrieved September 10, 2011, from www.iemed.org/anuari/2009/aarticles/a267.pdf

Hsiao, J. (2010). Why internet users are willing to pay for social networking services? *Online Information Review*, *35*(5), 770–788. doi:10.1108/14684521111176499

Hsu, C. H., & Lu, H. P. (2004). Why do people play on-line games? An extended TAM with social influences and flow experience. *Information & Management*, *41*(7), 853–868. doi:10.1016/j.im.2003.08.014

Huffaker, D. A., & Calvert, S. L. (2005). Gender, identity, and language use in teenage blogs. *Journal of Computer-Mediated Communication, 10*(2). Retrieved November 12 2008 from http://jcmc.indiana.edu/vol10/issue2/huffaker.html

Huffington Post. (2010, November 24). *Facebook, Twitter and the search for peace in the Middle East*. Retrieved August 5, 2011, from http://www.huffingtonpost.com/arianna-huffington/facebook-twitter-and-the-_b_788378.html?ir=Technology

Huitt, W. (1999). Conation as an important factor of mind. In *Educational Psychology: Interactive*. Valdosa, GA: Valdosa State University.

Hung, C. L., Chou, J. C.-L., & Shu, K. Y. (2008). Searching for lead users in the context of web 2.0. In *Proceedings of the 2008 IEEE ICMIT*, (pp. 344-349). IEEE Press.

Idsvoog, K. (2008, Spring). Circumventing censorship with technology. *Nieman Reports*, 77-79.

Iivari, J. (2010). Varieties of user centredness: An analysis of four systems development methods. *Information Systems Journal*, *21*, 125–153. doi:10.1111/j.1365-2575.2010.00351.x

Im, I., Kim, Y., & Han, H. J. (2008). The effects of perceived risk and technology type on users' acceptance of technologies. *Information & Management*, *45*, 1–9. doi:10.1016/j.im.2007.03.005

Inauen, M., & Wicki, S. A. (2011). The impact of outside-in open innovation on innovation performance. *European Journal of Innovation Management*, *14*(4). doi:10.1108/14601061111174934

Indvik, L. (2011). *Twitter set new tweets per second record during super bowl*. Retrieved October 29, 2011, from http://mashable.com/2011/02/09/twitter-super-bowl-tweets

Indvik, L. (2012). *Google acquires social media management platform wildfire*. Retrieved August 1, 2012, from http://mashable.com/2012/07/31/google-acquires-wildfire

INEP. (2010). *Resumo técnico - Censo da Educação superior de 2009*. Retrieved October 17, 2011, from http://download.inep.gov.br/download/superior/censo/2009/resumo_tecnico2009.pdf

Insua, D. (2010). *E-democracy: A group decision and negotiation perspective*. Madrid, Spain: Springer.

International Telecommunication Union. (2008). *DRAFT - Implementing e-health in developing countries guidance and principles ICT applications and cybersecurity division policies and strategies department*. New York, NY: ITU.

Internet World Stats. (2011). *Internet usage in Asia*. Retrieved from http://www.internetworldstats.com/stats3.htm

Internet World Stats. (2011). *World stats usage and population statistics*. Retrieved August 5, 2010, from http://www.internetworldstats.com/stats19.htm

Internet World Stats. (2012). *Africa internet stats*. Retrieved from http://www.internetworldstats.com/africa.htm

Internet World Stats. (2012). *World internet users and population stats*. Retrieved August 1, 2012, from http://www.internetworldstats.com/stats.htm

Ishani, M. (2011, February 7). The hopeful network. *Foreign Policy*. Retrieved from http://www.foreignpolicy.com/articles/2011/02/07/the_hopeful_network

Isherwood, T. (2008, September). *A new direction or more of the same? Political blogging in Egypt*. Cairo, Egypt: Arab Media & Society.

Ishida, T. (1998). *Community computing: Collaboration over global information networks*. New York, NY: John Wiley and Sons.

iSTUDIO. (2012). *Our work – Featured projects*. Retrieved August 1, 2012, from http://www.istudio.hr/ourwork

ITU (International Telecommunication Union). (2011). *The world in 2011: ICT facts and figures*. Retrieved September 15, 2011, from http://www.itu.int/ITU-D/ict/material/FactsFigures2011.pdf

Jabbra, J. (1989). *Bureaucracy and development in the Arab world*. New York, NY: E. J. Brill. doi:10.1177/002190968902400101

Jakaria, Y. (2007). Studi pemetaan kemampuan teknologi informasi pendidikan dasar dan menengah di Indonesia. [Mapping of technology information in Indonesian basic and secondary education]. *Jurnal Pendidikan dan Kebudayaan, 66*(13), 488-506.

Jakarta Post. (2011, October 28). Internet users in Indonesia reaches 55 million people. *The Jakarta Post*. Retrieved from http://www.thejakartapost.com/news/2011/10/28/internet-users-indonesia-reaches-55-million-people.html

James, T. (2001). *Handbook for southern Africa*. Retrieved from http://link.wits.ac.za/papers/James-2001-Information-Policy-Handbook-Southern-Africa.pdf

Jankari, R. (2009, July 23). *Morocco's information technology market expands*. *Magharebia.com*. Retrieved September 10, 2011, from http://www.magharebia.com/cocoon/awi/xhtml1/en_GB/features/awi/features/2009/07/23/feature-03

Compilation of References

Jansen, A. (2005). *Assessing e-government progress– Why and what*. Retrieved August 12, 2012 from http://www.afin.uio.no/om_enheten/folk/ansatte/jansen.html

Janzik, L., & Herstatt, C. (2008). Innovation communities: Motivation and incentives for community members to contribute. In *Proceedings of the 2008 IEEE ICMIT*, (pp. 350-355). IEEE Press.

Jasinski, M. (2004). *EDUCHAOS: Go co-native- Where there's a will you're away!* Retrieved March 15, 2010 from, http://learnscope.flexiblelearning.net.au/Learnscope/golearn.asp?Catewgory=11&DocumentId=6369

Java, A., Song, X., & Finin, T. (2007). Why we Twitter: Understanding microblogging usage and communities. In *Proceedings of the Joint 9th WEBKDD and 1st SNA-KDD Workshop 2007*. San Jose, CA: WEBKDD.

Java, A., Song, X., Finin, T., & Tseng, B. (2009). Why we Twitter: An analysis of a microblogging community. *Lecture Notes in Computer Science, 5439*, 118–138. doi:10.1007/978-3-642-00528-2_7

Jayakhanthan, R., & Sundarajan, D. (2012). Enterprise crowdsourcing solution for software development in an outsourcing organization. In *Proceedings of the 11th International Conference on Current Trends in Web Engineering*. Springer-Verlag.

Jayamaha, P. (2011). *Internet marketing – How, when, where?* Retrieved October 28, 2011, from http://print.dailymirror.lk/business/127-local/38977.html

Jenkins, H. (2006). *Confronting the challenges of participatory culture: Media education for the 21st century*. Chicago, IL: MacArthur Foundation. Retrieved from http://www.digitallearning.macfound.org/atf/cf/%7B7E45C7E0-A3E0-4B89-AC9C-E807E1B0AE4E%7D/JENKINS_WHITE_PAPER.PDF

Jennett, P. A., Gagnon, M. P., & Brandstadt, H. K. (2005). Preparing for success: Readiness models for rural telehealth. *Journal of Postgraduate Medicine, 51*(4), 279–285.

Jhurree, V. (2005). Technology integration in education in developing countries: Guidelines to policy makers. *International Education Journal, 6*(4), 463–483.

Johnson, B. (2011). How Egypt switched off the internet. *GigaOm*. Retrieved from http://gigaom.com/2011/01/28/how-egypt-switched-off-the-internet/

Johnson, D. W., & Johnson, R. T. (1996). Cooperation and the use of technology. *Handbook of Research for Educational Communications and Technology, 1*, 1017–1044.

Johnson, D. W., & Johnson, R. T. (1999). *Learning together and alone: Cooperative, competitive, and individualistic learning*. Reading, MA: Allyn & Bacon.

Jonassen, D. H. (1996). *Computers in the classroom: Mindtools for critical thinking*. Upper Saddle River, NJ: Prentice-Hall, Inc.

Jonassen, D. H., Peck, K. L., & Wilson, B. G. (1999). *Learning with technology: A constructivist perspective*. New York, NY: Merrill.

Jonassen, D. H., & Rohrer-Murphy, L. (1999). Activity theory as a framework for designing constructivist learning environments. *Educational Technology Research and Development, 47*(1), 61–79. doi:10.1007/BF02299477

Jones, B. (2010). Entrepreneurial marketing and the web 2.0 interface. *Journal of Research in Marketing and Entrepreneurship, 12*(2), 143–152. doi:10.1108/14715201011090602

Jones, B., & Iredale, N. (2009). Entrepreneurship education and web 2.0. *Journal of Research in Marketing and Entrepreneurship, 11*(1), 66–77. doi:10.1108/14715200911014158

Junior, K. S. (2009). Distance education in Brazil: Paths, policies and perspective. *Educação Temática Digital, 10*(2), 16–36.

Kahiigi, E., Hansson, H., Danielson, M., Tusubira, F. F., & Vesisenaho, M. (2011). Collaborative elearning in a developing country: A university case study in Uganda. In *Proceedings of the European Conference on E-Learning*, (pp. 932-942). IEEE.

Kalb, H., Kummer, C., & Schoop, E. (2011). *Implementing the "wiki way" in a course in higher education*. Retrieved from http://www.slideshare.net/kummerufer/implementing-the-wiki-way-in-a-course-in-higher-education

Kamran, S. (2010). Mobile phone: Calling and texting patterns of college in Pakistan. *International Journal of Business and Management, 5*(4), 26–36.

Kaplan, A. (2012). If you love something, let it go mobile: Mobile marketing and mobile social media 4x4. *Business Horizons, 55*, 129–139. doi:10.1016/j.bushor.2011.10.009

Karger, D., & Quan, D. (2005). What would it mean to blog on the semantic web. *Web Semantics: Science. Services and Agents, 3*(2-3), 147–157. doi:10.1016/j.websem.2005.06.002

Karlekar, K. D., & Marchant, E. (2009). *Freedom of the press 2008: A global survey of media independence*. New York, NY: Freedom House.

Katz, E., Blumler, J. G., & Gurevitch, M. (1974). Utilization of mass communication by the individual. In Blumler, J. G., & Katz, E. (Eds.), *The uses of mass communication: Current perspective on gratifications research* (pp. 19–34). Beverly Hills, CA: Sage.

Kautz, K. (2010). Participatory design activities and agile software development. In J. Pries-Heje et al. (Eds.), *Human Benefit through the Diffusion Information Systems Design Science Research, IFIP AICT 318*, (303–316). Berlin, Germany: Springer.

Kayworth, T., & Leidner, D. (2000). The global virtual manager: a prescription for success. *European Management Journal, 18*(2), 183–194. doi:10.1016/S0263-2373(99)00090-0

Keegan, V. (2007, July 5). Amateurs can be good and bad news. *The Guardian*.

Keen, A. (2007). *The cult of the amateur: How today's internet is killing our culture*. New York, NY: Doubleday/Random House.

Keller, D., Lima, M. H., Pimenta, M. S., & Queiroz, M. (2011). Assessing musical creativity: Material, procedural, and contextual dimensions. In *Proceedings of the 21st Congress of the Brazilian National Association of Research and Post-Graduation in Music (ANPPOM)*. Uberlândia, Brazil: ANPPOM. Retrieved from http://www.anppom.com.br/congressos_anteriores.php

Keller, D., Flores, L. V., Pimenta, M. S., Capasso, A., & Tinajero, P. (2011). Convergent trends toward ubiquitous music. *Journal of New Music Research, 40*(3), 265–276. doi:10.1080/09298215.2011.594514

Keller, J. B., & Bichelmeyer, B. A. (2004). What happens when accountability meets technology integration. *TechTrends, 48,* 17–24. doi:10.1007/BF02763351

Khan, A. W. (2005). *Distance education for development*. Paper presented at the 2005 ICDE International Conference on Open and Distance Education. New Delhi, India.

Khan, B. H. (Ed.). (2001). *Web-based training*. Englewood Cliffs, NJ: Educational Technology Publications.

Khoja, S., Scott, R., Ishaq, A., & Mohsin, M. (2007). Testing reliability of ehealth readiness assessment tools for developing countries. *eHealth. International Journal (Toronto, Ont.), 3*(1).

Kifle, M., Mbarika, V. W. A., & Datta, P. (2006). Telemedicine in sub-Saharan Africa: The case of teleophthalmology and eye care in Ethiopia. *Journal of the American Society for Information Science and Technology, 57*(10), 1383–1393. doi:10.1002/asi.20448

Kim, P., Miranda, T., & Olaciregui, C. (2008). Pocket school: Exploring mobile technology as a sustainable literacy education option for underserved indigenous children in Latin America. *International Journal of Educational Development, 28*(4), 435–445. doi:10.1016/j.ijedudev.2007.11.002

Kim, T. (2008). *MEconomy*. New York, NY: Hanbit Media, Inc.

King, S. J. (2011). The constitutional monarchy option in Morocco and Bahrain. *Middle East Institute 2011*. Retrieved August 5, 2012, from http://www.mei.edu/sites/default/files/publications/King_0.pdf

Kistow, B. (2009). E-learning at the Arthur Lok Jack graduate school of business: A survey of faculty members. *International Journal of Education and Development using Information and Communication Technology, 5*(4), 14-20.

Klauser, F., Schoop, E., Wirth, K., Jungmann, B., & Gersdorf, R. (2004). The construction of complex internet-based learning environments in the field of tension of pedagogical and technical rationality. In Bogaschewsky, R., Hoppe, U., Klauser, F., Schoop, E., & Weinhardt, C. (Eds.), *IMPULS EC Research Report 10*. Osnabrück, Germany: Electronic Commerce.

Klein, D. A. (1998). *The strategic management of intellectual capital*. Woburn, MA: Butterworth-Heinemann.

Kleine, D. (2010). ICT4what? Using the choice framework to operationalise the capability approach to development. *Journal of International Development, 22,* 674–692. doi:10.1002/jid.1719

Klein, H. K., & Kleinman, D. L. (2002). The social construction of technology: Structural considerations. *Science, Technology & Human Values, 27*(1), 28–52. doi:10.1177/016224390202700102

Klososky, S. (2011). *Enterprise social technology: Harnessing the power*. New York, NY: GreenLeaf Book Group Press.

Ko, H., Cho, C.-H., & Roberts, S. M. (2005). Internet uses and gratifications: A structural equation model of interactive advertising. *Journal of Advertising, 34,* 57–70.

Kolbe, K. (1989). *Conative connection: Acting on instinct*. Beverly, MA: Kathy Kolbe.

Koranteng, J. (1997). Saudi ban on dishes doesn't stop viewing. *Advertising Age International, 16.*

Korten, D. C. (1990). *Getting to the 21st century: Voluntary action and the global agenda.* West Hartford, CT: Kumarian Press.

Kosalge, P., & Toole, O. (2010). Web 2.0 and business, ealy results on perception of web 2.0 and factors influencing its adoption. [AMCIS.]. *Proceedings of AMCIS, 2010,* 1–10.

Koushik, S., Birkinshaw, J., & Crainer, S. (2009). Using web 2.0 to create management 2.0. *Business strategy. RE:view, 20*(2), 20–23.

Kovach, B., & Rosenstiel, T. (2007). *The elements of journalism.* New York, NY: Three Rivers Press.

Kraidy, M. (2002). Arab satellite television between regionalization and globalization. *Global Media Journal, 1*(1). Retrieved August 5, 2011, from http://lass.calumet.purdue.edu/cca/gmj/fa02/gmj-fa02-kraidy.htm

Kraidy, M. (2010). *Reality television and Arab politics: Contention in public life.* Cambridge, UK: Cambridge University Press.

Kraidy, M., & Khalil, J. F. (2009). *Arab television industries.* Basingstoke, UK: Palgrave Macmillan.

Krasnoboka, N. (2002). Real journalism goes underground: The internet underground. *Gazette, 64,* 479–499. doi:10.1177/17480485020640050701

Krotz, F., & Eastman, S. T. (1999). Orientations toward television outside the home. *The Journal of Communication, 49*(1), 5–27. doi:10.1111/j.1460-2466.1999.tb02779.x

Kruse, K. (2004). *The state of e-learning: Looking at history with the technology hype-cycle.* Retrieved April 12, 2010, from http://www.e-learningguru.com/articles/art2.htm

Kulikova, S. V., & Perlmutter, D. D. (2007). Blogging down the dictator? The Kyrgyz revolution and Samizdat websites. *International Communication Gazette, 69,* 29–50. doi:10.1177/1748048507072777

Kuo, Y., & Yen, S. (2009). Towards an understanding of the behavioural intention to use 3G mobile value-added services. *Computers in Human Behavior, 25,* 103–110. doi:10.1016/j.chb.2008.07.007

Kwak, H., Lee, C., Park, H., & Moon, S. (2010). What is Twitter, a social network or a news media? In *Proceedings of the 19th International Conference on World Wide Web,* (pp. 591-600). New York, NY: ACM.

Kwapong, O. A. T. F. (2007). Widening access to tertiary education for women in Ghana through distance education. *Online Submission, 8,* 65–79.

Lai, L. S. L., & Turban, E. (2008). Groups formation and operations in the web 2.0 environment and social networks. *Group Decision and Negotiation, 17,* 387–402. doi:10.1007/s10726-008-9113-2

Lampe, C., Ellison, N. B., & Steinfield, C. (2008). Changes in use and perception of Facebook. In *Proceedings of the 2008 ACM Conference on Computer Supported Cooperative Work,* (pp. 721-730). New York, NY: ACM.

Lang, M., & Pätzold, G. (2002). *Multimedia in der Aus- und Weiterbildung: Grundlagen und Fallstudien zum netzbasierten Lernen.* Köln, Germany: Deutscher Wirtschaftsdienst.

Lankshear, C., & Knobel, M. (2006). *New literacies: Everyday practices and classroom learning* (2nd ed.). Maidenhead, UK: Open University Press.

Larson, D. (2011). *Twitter stats & graphics on Osama bin Laden's death.* Retrieved October 29, 2011, from http://blog.tweetsmarter.com/twitter-stats/all-time-twitter-record-for-bin-ladens-death%E2%80%94graphics-and-links

Laurie, M. (2011). *South Sudan launches electronic public finance management.* Retrieved from http://gbiportal.net/2011/07/08/south-sudan-launches-electronic-public-finance-management/

Laursen, K., & Salter, S. (2006). Open for innovation: The role of openness in explaining innovation performance among UK manufacturing firms. *Strategic Management Journal, 27,* 131–150. doi:10.1002/smj.507

Lave, J., & Wenger, E. (1991). *Situated learning: Legitimate peripheral participation.* Cambridge, UK: Cambridge University Press. doi:10.1017/CBO9780511815355

Lavine, H., Sweeney, D., & Wagner, S. H. (1999). Depicting women as sex objects in television advertising: Effects on body dissatisfaction. *Personality and Social Psychology Bulletin, 25*(8), 1049–1058. doi:10.1177/01461672992511012

Lazzarotti, V., & Manzini, R. (2009). Different modes of open innovation: A theoretical framework and an empirical study. *International Journal of Innovation Management, 13*(4), 615–636. doi:10.1142/S1363919609002443

Leadbeater, C., & Miller, P. (2004). *The pro-am revolution: How enthusiasts are changing our economy and society.* London, UK: Demos. Retrieved from http://www.demos.co.uk/publications/proameconomy/

Lee, E., Kwon, K., & Schumann, D. (2005). Segmenting the non-adopter category in the diffusion of internet banking. *International Journal of Bank Marketing, 23*(5), 414–437. doi:10.1108/02652320510612483

Lee, J., Park, D. H., & Han, I. (2008). The effect of negative online consumer reviews on product attitude: An information processing view. *Electronic Commerce Research and Applications, 7*(3), 341–352. doi:10.1016/j.elerap.2007.05.004

Lee, M. J. W., & McLoughlin, C. (2007). Teaching and learning in the web 2.0 era: Empowering students through learner-generated content. *International Journal of Instructional Technology and Distance Learning, 4*(10), 21–34.

Lee, S., DeWester, D., & Park, S. (2008). Web 2.0 and opportunities for small businesses. *Service Business, 2,* 335–345. doi:10.1007/s11628-008-0043-5

Lehtinen, E., Hakkarainen, K., Lipponen, L., Rahikainen, M., & Muukkonen, H. (1999). Computer supported collaborative learning: A review. *The JHGI Giesbers Reports on Education, 10.*

Leibhammer, J., & Weber, J. (2008). Enterprise 2.0: Analysis to state and prospects of the German economy. *BITKOM Federal Association for Information Technology.* Retrieved from http://www.bitkom.org/files/documents/BITKOM-Studie_Enterprise_2Punkt0.pdf

Leimeister, J. M., & Krcmar, H. (2006). Designing and implementing virtual patient support communities: A German case study. In Murero, M., & Rice, R. E. (Eds.), *The Internet and Health Care: Theory, Research and Practice*. Mahwah, NJ: Lawrence Erlbaum Associates.

Leonard, K. (2004). The role of patients in designing health information systems: The case of applying simulation techniques to design an electronic patient record (EPR) interface. *Health Care Management Science, 7*, 275–284. doi:10.1007/s10729-004-7536-0

Leornardi, P. M., & Barley, S. R. (2010). What's under construction here? *The Academy of Management Annals, 4*(1), 1–51.

Lettl, C. (2007). User involvement competence for radical innovation. *Journal of Engineering and Technology Management, 24*, 53–75. doi:10.1016/j.jengtecman.2007.01.004

Lettl, C., Herstatt, C., & Gemuenden, H. G. (2006). Learning from users for radical innovation. *International Journal of Technology Management, 33*(1). doi:10.1504/IJTM.2006.008190

Leung, L., & Wei, R. (1998). The gratifications of pager use: sociability, information-seeking, entertainment, usefulness and fashion and status. *Telematics and Informatics, 15*, 253–264. doi:10.1016/S0736-5853(98)00016-1

Leung, L., & Wei, R. (2000). More than just talk on the move: Uses and gratifications of the cellular phone. *Journalism & Mass Communication Quarterly, 77*(2), 308–320. doi:10.1177/107769900007700206

Levin, D. Z., & Cross, R. (2004). The strength of weak ties you can trust: The mediating role of trust in effective knowledge transfer. *Management Science, 50*(11), 1477–1490. doi:10.1287/mnsc.1030.0136

Levinson, C., & Coker, M. (2011, February 11). The secret rally that sparked an uprising. *Wall Street Journal*. Retrieved from http://online.wsj.com/article/SB10001424052748704132204576135882356532702.html

Levy, M. (2009). WEB 2.0 implications on knowledge management. *Journal of Knowledge Management, 13*(1), 120–134. doi:10.1108/13673270910931215

Levy, M., & Powell, P. (2005). *Strategies for growth in SMEs – The role of information and information systems*. Oxford, UK: Elsevier.

Lewis, D. (1998). Development NGOs and the challenge of partnership: Changing relations between north and south. *Social Policy and Administration, 32*(5), 501–512. doi:10.1111/1467-9515.00111

Lewis, D., & Behana, K. (2001). The internet as a resource for consumer healthcare. *Disease Management & Health Outcomes, 9*(5), 241–247. doi:10.2165/00115677-200109050-00001

Liao, C., Tsou, C., & Huang, M. (2007). Factors influencing the usage of 3G mobile services in Taiwan. *Online Information Review, 31*(6), 759–774. doi:10.1108/14684520710841757

Lilien, G. L., Morrison, P. D., Searls, K., Sonnack, M., & Von Hippel, E. (2002). Performance assessment of the lead user idea generation process for new product development. *Management Science, 48*(8), 1042–1059. doi:10.1287/mnsc.48.8.1042.171

Lim, C. P., & Hang, D. (2003). An activity theory approach to research of ICT integration in Singapore schools. *Computers & Education, 41*(1), 49–63. doi:10.1016/S0360-1315(03)00015-0

Lim, S., & Palacio-Marques, D. (2011). Culture and purpose of web 2.0 service adoption: A study in the USA, Korea and Spain. *The Service Industries Journal, 31*, 123–131. doi:10.1080/02642069.2010.485634

Litto, F. (2009). O retrato frente/verso da aprendizagem a distância no Brasil 2009. *Educação Temática e Digital, 10*(2), 108–122.

Litto, F., & Marthos, B. (Eds.). (2006). *Distance learning in Brazil: Best Practices 2006.* Rio de Janeiro, Brasilia: ABED.

Liu, C.-H., & Liu, H.-S. (2009). Increasing competitiveness of a firm and supply chain with web 2.0 initiatives. *International Journal of Electronic Business Management, 7*(4), 248–255.

London School of Economics Centre for Civil Society. (2004). *What is civil society?* Retrieved from http://www.lse.ac.uk/collections/CCS/what_is_civil_society.htm

Long, B., & Baecker, R. (1997). A taxonomy of Internet communication tools. *Proceedings of WebNet, 97*, 1–5.

Luarn, P., & Lin, H. (2005). Toward an understanding of the behavioral intention to use mobile banking. *Computers in Human Behavior, 21*(6), 873–891. doi:10.1016/j.chb.2004.03.003

Lubart, T. I. (1999). Creativity across cultures. In Sternberg, R. J. (Ed.), *Handbook of Creativity* (pp. 339–350). Cambridge, UK: Cambridge University Press.

Luck, E., & Mathews, S. (2010). What advertisers need to know about the iygeneration: An Australian perspective. *Journal of Promotion Management, 16*, 134–147. doi:10.1080/10496490903574559

Lueg, J. E., & Finney, R. Z. (2007). Interpersonal communication in the consumer socialization process: Scale development and validation. *Journal of Marketing Theory and Practice, 15*(1), 25–39. doi:10.2753/MTP1069-6679150102

Lusch, R. F. (2007). Marketing's evolving identify: Defining our future. *American Marketing Association, 26*(2).

Lüthje, C., & Herstatt, C. (2004). The lead user method: An outline of empirical findings and issues for future research. *R & D Management, 34*(5). doi:10.1111/j.1467-9310.2004.00362.x

Lu, Y., Tao, Z., & Wang, B. (2009). Exploring Chinese users' acceptance of instant messaging using the theory of planned behavior, the technology acceptance model and the flow theory. *Computers in Human Behavior, 25*, 29–39. doi:10.1016/j.chb.2008.06.002

Lynch, M. (2006). *Voices of the new Arab public: Iraq, Al-Jazeera, and Middle East politics today.* New York, NY: Columbia University Press.

Mack, G. (2008). *Facebook overtakes Myspace.* Retrieved November 8, 2011, from http://blog.alexa.com/2008/05/facebook-overtakes-myspace_07.html

Mackey, R. (2011, October 25). Egyptian activists summoned by military prosecutor. *New York Times.* Retrieved October 31, 2011, from http://thelede.blogs.nytimes.com/2011/10/25/after-call-from-obama-egypt-postpones-interrogation-of-activist-bloggers

Madden, M., & Zickuhr, K. (2011). *Pew internet report: 65% of online adults use social networking sites*. Retrieved October 28, 2011, from http://pewinternet.org/~/media//Files/Reports/2011/PIP-SNS-Update-2011.pdf

Madhavan, N. (2007). India gets more Net cool. *Hindustan Times*. Retrieved June 7, 2008, from http://www.hindustantimes.com/StoryPage/StoryPage.aspx?id=f2565bb8-663e-48c1-94eed99567577bdd

Madrigal, A. (2011, January 24). The inside story of how Facebook responded to Tunisian hacks. *The Atlantic*. Retrieved from http://www.theatlantic.com/technology/archive/2011/01/the-inside-story-of-how-facebook-responded-to-tunisian-hacks/70044/

Maina, W. (2009). Kenya: The state, donors and the politics of democratization. In van Rooy, A. (Ed.), *Civil Society and the Aid Industry* (pp. 134–167). London, UK: Earthscan Publications Ltd.

Makoul, G., Curry, R. H., & Tang, P. C. (2001). The use of electronic medical records: Communication patterns in outpatient encounters. *Journal of the American Medical Informatics Association*, 8, 610–615. doi:10.1136/jamia.2001.0080610

Malaga, R. A. (2010). Search engine optimization - Black and white hat approaches. *Advances in Computers*, 78, 1–39. doi:10.1016/S0065-2458(10)78001-3

Malkary, G. (2005). *Healthcare without bounds: Mobile computing for physicians*. Journal Mobile Computing for Physicians.

Manzella, J. C. (2000). Negotiating the news: Indonesian press culture and power during the political crises of 1997-8. *Journalism*, *1*, 305–328. doi:10.1177/146488490000100303

Marconi, J. (2002, May). E-health: Navigating the internet for health information healthcare. Advocacy White Paper. *Healthcare Information and Management Systems Society*.

Marshall, G., & Ruohonen, M. (1998). *Capacity building for IT in education in developing countries*. New York, NY: Springer.

Mashable Social Media. (2012). *Website*. Retrieved from http://mashable.com/2012/03/09/social-media-demographics/

Masurel, E., van Montfort, K., & Lentink, R. (2003). *SME: Innovation and the crucial role of the entrepreneur*. Amsterdam, The Netherlands: University of Amsterdam.

Mathwick, C. H., Malhotra, N., & Rigdon, E. (2002). The effect of dynamic retail experiences on experiential perceptions of value: An Internet and catalog comparison. *Journal of Retailing*, *78*(1), 51–60. doi:10.1016/S0022-4359(01)00066-5

Mattos, C. A., & Laurindo, F. J. B. (2008). The role of the web in improving customer input to the service/product development process: Brazilian cases. *Product: Management Development*, *6*(1).

Mawdsley, E., Townsend, J., Porter, G., & Oakley, P. (2002). *Knowledge, power and development agendas: NGOs north and south*. Oxford, UK: INTRAC.

Mbarika, V. (2004). TeleMedicine in Africa: A possible panacea for sub-Saharan Africa's medical nightmare. *Communications of the ACM*, *47*(7), 21–24. doi:10.1145/1005817.1005838

McAfee, A. P. (2009a, November). Shattering the myths about enterprise 2.0. *Harvard Business Review*. Retrieved from http://hbr.org/2009/11/shattering-the-myths-about-enterprise-20/ar/1

McAfee. (2010). *Web 2.0: A complex balancing act – The first global study on web 2.0 usage, risks and best practices.* Retrieved from http://www.mcafee.com/us/resources/reports/rp-first-global-study-web-2.0-usage.pdf

McAfee, A. (2006). Enterprise 2.0: The dawn of emergent collaboration. *MIT Sloan Management Review, 47*(3), 21–28.

McAfee, A. P. (2009). *Enterprise 2.0: New collaborative tools for your organization's toughest challenges.* Boston, MA: Harvard Business Review Publishing.

McFedries, P. (2007). Technically speaking - Social networkers are all a-Twitter. *IEEE Spectrum, 44*(10), 84. doi:10.1109/MSPEC.2007.4337670

McGowan, P. J., Wigand, R. T., & Betz, M. J. (Eds.). (1984). *Appropriate technology: Choice and development.* Durham, NC: Duke University Press.

McGuire, W. J. (1985). Attitudes and attitude change. In Lindzey, G., & Aronson, E. (Eds.), *Handbook of social psychology* (Vol. 19, pp. 233–346). New York, NY: Random House.

MCIT. (2012, April). *ICT indicators in brief – April 2012 – Monthly issue.* Retrieved from http://mcit.gov.eg/Upcont/Documents/Publications_2052012000_Eng.pdf

McKinsey. (2007). How business are using web 2.0: A McKinsey global survey. *The McKinsey Quarterly.* Retrieved from http://www.mckinseyquarterly.com/Marketing/How_businesses_are_using_Web_20_A_McKinsey_Global_Survey_1913_abstract

McKinsey. (2008). Building the web 2.0 enterprise: McKinsey global survey results. *The McKinsey Quarterly.* Retrieved from http://www.mckinseyquarterly.com

McLeod, D. (2006). QQ attracting eyeballs. *Financial Mail* (South Africa). Retrieved July 30, 2007, from LexisNexis.

McNaughton, S. (2003). Profiling teaching and learning needs in beginning literacy instruction: The case of children in "low decile" schools in New Zealand. *Journal of Literacy Research.* Retrieved August 9, 2010, from http://www.findarticles.com/p/articles/mi_qa3785/is_200307/ai_n0201170/

McQuail, D. (1995). *Mass communication theory.* Newbury Park, CA: Sage.

McTighe, K. (2011, May 11). Moroccan youth demands action, not words. *The New York Times.* Retrieved September 10, 2011, from http://www.nytimes.com/2011/05/12/world/middleeast/ 12iht-M12-MOROCCO-MOVEMENT.html?pagewanted=all

MEC. (2007). *Referencias de qualidade para educação superior a distância.* Retrieved October 13, 2011, from http://www.educacaoadistancia.blog.br/arquivos/REFERENCIAIS_DE_QUALIDADE_PARA_EDUCACAO_SUPERIOR_A_DISTANCIA.pdf

MEC. (2010). *Plano nacional de postgraduação (PNGP) 2011-2020.* Retrieved October 13, 2011, from http://www.capes.gov.br/sobre-a-capes/plano-nacional-de-pos-graduacao

Media, F. I. (2009). Myspace. Retrieved July 02, 2011 from http://www.myspace.com/

Medman, N. (2006). Doing your own thing on the net. *Ericsson Business Review, 1,* 48–53.

Mekay, E. (2011, February 23). One Libyan battle is fought in social and news media. *The New York Times.* Retrieved September 10, 2011, from http://www.nytimes.com/2011/02/24/world/middleeast/24iht-m24libya.html?_r=1

Menn, J. (2010, July 29). Virtually insecure. *Financial Times*, p. 9.

Menon, K. (2000, September). Controlling the internet: Censorship online in China. *Quill Magazine*, 82.

Mesgari, M., & Basselier, G. (2011). How online social networks create value for organizations: A resource based perspective. In *Proceedings of the Seventeenth Americas Conference on Information Systems*. Detroit, MI: IEEE.

Miers, J. (2004). *BELTS or braces? Technology school of the future*. Retrieved November 12 2007 from http://www.tsof.edu.au/research/Reports04/miers

Miletto, E. M. (2009). CODES: An interactive novice-oriented web-based environment for cooperative musical prototyping. (PhD Thesis). Federal University of Rio Grande do Sul. Rio Grande do Sul, Brazil. Retrieved from https://www.lume.ufrgs.br/bitstream/handle/10183/22815/000740701.pdf?sequence=1

Miletto, E. M., Flores, L. V., Pimenta, M. S., Rutily, J., & Santagada, L. (2007). Interfaces for musical activities and interfaces for musicians are not the same: The case for codes, a web-based environment for cooperative music prototyping. In *Proceedings of the 9th International Conference on Multimodal Interfaces*, (pp. 201-207). New York, NY: ACM Press.

Miletto, E. M., Pimenta, M. S., Bouchet, F., Sansonnet, J.-P., & Keller, D. (2011). Principles for music creation by novices in networked music environments. *Journal of New Music Research*, *40*(3). doi:10.1080/09298215.2011.603832

Milgram, S. (1967). The small-world problem. *Psychology Today*, *1*(1), 61–67.

Miller, M., Marks, A., & Decoulode, M. (2012). *Social software for business performance*. Retrieved from http://www.deloitte.com/assets/Dcom-UnitedStates/Local%20Assets/Documents/TMT_us_tmt/us_tmt_%20Social%20Software%20for%20Business_031011.pdf

Ministry of Education in Indonesia. (2011). *Panduan SchoolNet*. Jakarta, Indonesia: Ministry of Education in Indonesia.

Minocha, S. (2009). *A study of the effective use of social software by further and higher education in the UK to support student learning and teaching*. Retrieved October 21, 2011, from http://kn.open.ac.uk/public/workspace.cfm?wpid=8655

Minocha, S., & Kear, K. (2009). *Study of the effective use of social software to support student learning and engagement*. Retrieved October 13, 2011, from http://www.jisc.ac.uk/whatwedo/projects/socialsoftware08.aspx#downloads

Mnyanyi, C. B. F., Bakari, J. K., & Mbwette, T. S. A. (2011). Technologically-enhanced open and distance learning for all in developing countries. In M. Youssef & S. A. Anwar (Eds.), *Proceedings of the 4th Conference on e-Learning Excellence in the Middle East 2011: In Search of New Paradigms for Re-Engineering Education*, (pp. 8–17). Dubai, United Arab Emirates: IEEE.

Moore, G. A. (1991). *Crossing the chasm: Marketing and selling high-tech products to mainstream customers*. New York, NY: Harper Business Essentials.

Moor, J. (2003). *The second superpower rears its beautiful head*. Boston, MA: Harvard Law School.

Moran, J. M. (2009). The models and the evaluation of higher distance education in Brazil. *Educação Temática Digital, 10*(2), 54–70.

Moran, R. T., Harris, P. R., & Moran, S. V. (2007). *Managing cultural differences – Global leadership strategies for the 21st century* (7th ed.). London, UK: Elsevier.

Morillon, L., & Julliard, J. (2010). Enemies of the internet: Web 2.0 versus control 2.0. *Reporters without Borders*. Retrieved from http://www.rsf.org/ennemis.html

Moroccan Ministry of Industry, Trade, and New Technologies. (2010, June 21). *Digital Morocco 2013*. Retrieved September 10, 2011, from www.egov.ma/SiteCollectionDocuments/Morocco%20Digital.pdf

Morozov, E. (2009, June 17). Iran elections: A Twitter revolution? *The Washington Post*. Retrieved August 5, 2010, from http://www.washingtonpost.com/wp-dyn/content/discussion/2009/06/17/DI20090

Morris, M., Bessant, J., & Barnes, J. (2006). Using learning networks to enable industrial development: Case studies from South Africa. *International Journal of Operations & Production Management, 26*(5), 532–557. doi:10.1108/01443570610659892

Muk, A. (2007). Consumer's intentions to opt in to SMS advertising. *International Journal of Advertising, 26*(2), 177–198.

Muller, A., Hutchins, N., & Pinto, M. C. (2012). Applying open innovation where your company needs it most. *Strategy and Leadership, 40*(2). doi:10.1108/10878571211209332

Mumtaz, S. (2000). Factors affecting teachers' use of information and communications technology: A review of the literature. *Journal of Information Technology for Teacher Education, 9*, 319–341. doi:10.1080/14759390000200096

Murugesan, S. (2007). Understanding web 2.0. *IT Professional, 9*(4), 34–41. doi:10.1109/MITP.2007.78

Musoke, M. (2001). *Simple ICTs reduce maternal mortality in rural Uganda: A telemedicine case study*. Retrieved from http://www.medicusmundi.ch/mms/services/bulletin/bulletin200202/kap04/16musoke.html

Musser, J., O'Reilly, T., & O'Reilly Radar Team. (2006). Web 2.0 principles and best practices. In *O'Reilly Radar*, (p. 101). New York, NY: O'Reilly Media.

Mwanda, J. (2011). *New born South Sudan has ambitious goals*. Retrieved from http://globalgeopolitics.net/wordpress/2011/07/12/new-born-south-sudan-has-ambitious-goals/

Nalebuff, B., & Ayres, I. (2003). *Why not? How to use everyday ingenuity to solve problems big and small*. Boston, MA: Harvard Business School Press.

Nambisan, S. (2002). Designing virtual customer environments for new product development. *Academy of Management Review, 27*, 392–413.

Nardi, B. A., Schiano, D. J., & Gumbrecht, M. (2004). Blogging as social activity, or, would you let 900 million people read your diary? In *Proceedings of the 2004 ACM Conference on Computer Supported Cooperative Work*, (pp. 222-231). Chicago, IL: ACM Press.

Nardi, B. A., Whittaker, S., & Schwarz, H. (2000). *It's not what you know, it's who you know*. Retrieved from http://www.uic.edu/htbin/cgiwrap/bin/ojs/index.php/fm/article/viewArticle/741/650

Nardi, B. A., Schiano, D. J., Gumbrecht, M., & Swartz, L. (2004). Why we blog. *Communications of the ACM, 47*(12), 41–46. doi:10.1145/1035134.1035163

National Informatics Centre & UNESCO. (2005). *E-government tool-kit for developing countries*. New Delhi, India: National Informatics Centre and UNESCO.

Needle. (2010). Web 2.0 privacy and security issues won't go away. *IT Business Edge, eSecurity Planet: Internet Security for IT Pros*. Retrieved from http://www.esecurityplanet.com/trends/article.php/3878546/Web-20-Privacy-and-Security-Issues-Wont-Go-Away.htm

Negret, F. (2008). A identidade e a importância dos mestrados profissionais no Brasil e algumas considerações para a sua avaliação. *Revista Brasileira de Pós-Graduação, 5*(10), 217–225.

Netsize. (2011). *The Netsize Guide 2010: Mobile renaissance*. Retrieved September 13, 2011, from http://www.netsize.com/Ressources_Guide.htm

News, B. B. C. (2007, February 22). Egypt blogger jailed for 'insult'. *BBC News*. Retrieved August 5, 2011, from http://news.bbc.co.uk/2/hi/6385849.stm

News, B. B. C. (2011, June 27). Profile: Muammar Gaddafi. *BBC News*. Retrieved September 10, 2011, from http://www.bbc.co.uk/news/world-africa-12488278

Niblock, T. (2001). *Pariah states and sanctions in the Middle East: Iraq, Libya, Sudan*. Boulder, CO: Lynne Rienner Publishers.

Nie, N., & Lutz, E. (2000). Internet and society: A preliminary report. *Stanford University*. Retrieved August 5, 2011, from http://www.bsos.umd.edu/socy/alan/webuse/handouts/Nie%20and%20Erbring-Internet%20and%20Society%20a%20Preliminary%20Report.pdf

Nielsen, J. (1994). Enhancing the explanatory power of usability heuristics. In *Proceedings of CHI*, (pp. 152-158). New York, NY: ACM Press.

Nielsen. (2011). *Surging internet usage in Southeast Asia reshaping the media landscape*. Retrieved from http://blog.nielsen.com/nielsenwire/global/ surging-internet-usage-in-southeast-asia-reshaping-the-media-landscape/

Nielsen, J. (1992). *Evaluating the thinking-aloud technique for use by computer scientists*. Norwood, NJ: Ablex Publishing Corp.

Nieusma, D. (2004). Alternative design scholarship: Working toward appropriate design. *Design Issues, 20*(3), 13–24. doi:10.1162/0747936041423280

North, D. C. (2005). *Understanding the process of economic change*. Princeton, NJ: Princeton University Press.

Nosko, A., Wood, E., & Molema, S. (2010). All about me - Disclosure in online social networking profiles - The case of Facebook. *Computers in Human Behavior, 26*(3), 406–418. doi:10.1016/j.chb.2009.11.012

Nuh, M. (2010). *Rencana strategis kementrian pendidikan nasional*. Jakarta, Indonesia: Ministry of Education in Indonesia.

Nyirongo, N. K. (2009). *Technology adoption and integration: A descriptive study of a higher education institution in a developing nation.* (Unpublished Thesis PhD). Virginia Polytechnic Institute and State University. Blacksburg, VA. Retrieved from http://scholar.lib.vt.edu/theses/available/etd-04132009-095508/unrestricted/Nertha_etd_2009.pdf

Nysveen, H., Pedersen, P. E., & Thorbjornsen, H. (2005). Explaining intention to use mobile chat services: moderating effects of gender. *Journal of Consumer Marketing, 22*(5), 247–256. doi:10.1108/07363760510611671

Nysveen, H., Pedersen, P. E., & Thorbjornsen, H. (2005). Intentions to use mobile services: Antecedents and cross-service comparisons. *Academy of Marketing Science Journal, 33*(3), 330–346. doi:10.1177/0092070305276149

O'Brien, R. (2001). Um exame da abordagem metodológica da pesquisa ação. [An overview of the methodological approach of action research] In Richardson, R. (Ed.), *Teoria e Prática da Pesquisa Ação* [Theory and Practice of Action Research]. João Pessoa, Brazil: Universidade Federal da Paraíba.

O'Reilly, T. (2005). *What is web 2.0: Design patterns and business models for the next generation of software.* Retrieved December 15, 2006, from http://www.oreillynet.com/pub/a/oreilly/tim/news/2005/09/30/what-is-web-20.html

O'Reilly, T. (2005, September 30). *What is web 2.0? Design patterns and business models for the next generation of software.* Retrieved June 17, 2012, from http://www.oreilly.de/artikel/web20.html

Ocio Networks. (2011). *Estudio de hábitos de Internet 2010.* Retrieved September 27, 2011, from http://www.dataprix.com/files/Informacion,%20consumo%20de%20medios%20y%20redes%20sociales.pdf

OECD. (2007). *Participative web and user created content: Web 2.0, wikis and social networking.* Paris, France: OECD.

Okazaki, S., & Yague, M. J. (2012). Responses to an advergaming campaign on a mobile social networking site: An initial research report. *Computers in Human Behavior, 28,* 78–86. doi:10.1016/j.chb.2011.08.013

Oksman, V., & Raitiainen, T. (2001). *Perhaps it is a body part. How the mobile phone became an organic part of everyday lives of children and teenagers. Nodiska konferensen för medie-ock kommunikationfiorskning.* Island.

Okunade, A. (2005). Analysis and implications of the determinants of healthcare expenditure in African countries. *Health Care Management Science, 8,* 267–276. doi:10.1007/s10729-005-4137-5

Olaniran, B. A. (2009). Culture, learning styles, and web 2.0. *Interactive Learning Environments, 17*(4), 261–271. doi:10.1080/10494820903195124

Olson, E., & Bakke, G. (2001). Implementing the lead user method in a high technology firm: A longitudinal study of intentions versus actions. *Journal of Product Innovation Management, 18*(2), 388–395. doi:10.1016/S0737-6782(01)00111-4

Olwan, R. (2011, February 11). *UAE has highest mobile penetration in GCC.* Retrieved August 5, 2011, from http://www.olwan.org/index.php?option=com_content&view=article&id=80%3Auae-has-highest-mobile-penetration-in-gcc-&Itemid=210

Omidinia, S., Masrom, M., & Selamat, H. (2011). Review of e-learning and ict infrastructure in developing countries (case study of Iran). *American Journal of Economics and Business Administration*, *3*, 120–125. doi:10.3844/ajebasp.2011.120.125

Ong, M. (2009). *Fiat mio: Bringing crowdsourcing to the automotive industry*. Retrieved from http://www.headlightblog.com/2009/10/fiat-miobringing-crowdsourcing-to-the-automotive-industry/

Oosterlaken, I. (2009). Design for development: A capability approach. *Design Issues*, *25*(4), 91–102. doi:10.1162/desi.2009.25.4.91

Open Arab Internet. (2011). Facts and numbers. *Open Arab Internet*. Retrieved September 10, 2011, from http://old.openarab.net/en/node/1614

OpenNet Initiative. (2009, August 6). Morocco | OpenNet initiative. *OpenNet Initiative*. Retrieved September 10, 2011, from http://opennet.net/research/profiles/morocco

Ostergaard, S., & Hvass, M. (2008). eGovernment 2.0 – How can government benefit from web 2.0. *Journal of Systemics. Cybernetics and Informatics*, *6*(6), 13–18.

Ostrow, A. (2010). *Social networking dominates our time spent online*. Retrieved October 28, 2011, from http://mashable.com/2010/08/02/stats-time-spent-online

Overhage, J. M., Evans, L., & Marchibroda, J. (2005). Communities' readiness for health information exchange: The national landscape in 2004. *Journal of the American Medical Informatics Association*, *12*, 107–112. doi:10.1197/jamia.M1680

Özcan, Y. Z., & Kocak, A. (2003). A need or a status symbol? Uses of cellular telephone in Turkey. *European Journal of Communication*, *18*(2), 241–254. doi:10.1177/0267323103018002004

Ozok, A. A., & Wei, J. (2010). An empirical comparison of consumer usability preferences in online shopping using stationary and mobile devices: Results from a college student population. *Electronic Commerce Research*, *10*(2), 111–137. doi:10.1007/s10660-010-9048-y

Palmer, M. (2010, May 13). European officials call changes to Facebook settings 'unacceptable'. *Financial Times*, p. 17.

Parameswaran, M., & Whinston, A. (2007). Research issues in social computing. *Journal of the Association for Information Systems*, *8*(6), 336–350.

Parise, S., & Guinan, P. (2008). Marketing using web 2.0. In *Proceedings of the 41st Hawaii International Conference on System Sciences*. IEEE Press.

Parker, B., & Plank, R. (2000). A uses and gratifications perspective on the Internet: As a new information source. *American Business Review*, *18*(June), 43–49.

Paulus, T. M. (2005). Collaboration or cooperation? Analyzing small group interactions in educational environments. In Roberts, T. S. (Ed.), *Computer-Supported Collaborative Learning in Higher Education* (pp. 100–124). Hershey, PA: IGI Global. doi:10.4018/978-1-59140-408-8.ch005

Payne, G. A. (2008). The exile of dissidence: Restrictions on the right to communicate in democracies. *Global Media Journal*, *7*.

Pelgrum, W. (2001). Obstacles to the integration of ICT in education: Results from a worldwide educational assessment. *Computers & Education, 37,* 163–178. doi:10.1016/S0360-1315(01)00045-8

Pélissié du Rausas, M., Manyika, J., Hazan, E., Bughin, J., Chui, M., & Said, R. (2011). *Internet matters: The net's sweeping impact on growth, jobs, and prosperity.* McKinsey Global Institute.

Peris, M., Sperling, A., Blinn, N., Nüttgens, M., & Gehrke, N. (2011). Participatory design of web 2.0 applications in SME networks. In *Proceedings of the 24th Bled eConference eFuture: Creating Solutions for the Individual, Organisations and Society.* Bled, Slovenia: IEEE.

Perkins, D. N. (1991). What constructivism demands of the learner. *Educational Technology, 31*(9), 19–21.

Perraton, H., & Charlotte, C. (2001). Applying new technologies and cost-effective delivery system in basic education. *UNESCO.* Retrieved from http://www.unesco.org/education/wef/en-docs/findings/technofinal.pdf

Perthes, V. (2004). *Arab elites: Negotiating the politics of change.* Boulder, CO: Lynne Rienner Publishers.

Pew Research Center. (2012). *The future of money: Smartphone swiping in the mobile age.* Retrieved May 17, 2012, from http://www.pewinternet.org/~/media//Files/Reports/2012/PIP_Future_of_Money.pdf

Pillay, N. (2007). Search the y drive or simply ask Sally: Staff perceptions of knowledge creation in an organisation. *International Journal of Knowledge. Culture and Change Management, 5*(6), 77–86.

Piller, F. T., & Ihl, C. (2009). *Open innovation with customers.* Aachen, Germany: RWTH Aachen University.

Piller, F. T., & Walcher, D. (2006). Toolkits for idea competitions: A novel method to integrate users in new product development. *R & D Management, 36*(3), 307–318. doi:10.1111/j.1467-9310.2006.00432.x

Pimenta, M. S., Miletto, E., & Flores, L. (2011). Cooperative mechanisms for networked music. *Future Generation Computer Systems, 27*(1), 100–108. doi:10.1016/j.future.2010.03.005

Pitula, K., & Dysart-Gale, D. (2010). Expanding the boundaries of HCI: A case study in requirements engineering for ICT4D. *Information Technologies & International Development, 6*(1), 78–93.

Pleil, T. (2006). *Social software in editorial marketing.* Retrieved from http://thomaspleil.files.wordpress.com/2006/09/pleil-medien-2-0.pdf

Podobnik, V., Galetic, V., Trzec, K., & Jezic, G. (2010). Group-oriented service provisioning in next generation network. In Srinivasan, D., & Jain, L. C. (Eds.), *Innovations in Multi-Agent Systems and Applications* (pp. 277–298). Berlin, Germany: Springer-Verlag. doi:10.1007/978-3-642-14435-6_10

Podobnik, V., & Lovrek, I. (2010). Telco agent: Enabler of paradigm shift towards customer-managed relationship. *Lecture Notes in Computer Science, 6276,* 251–260. doi:10.1007/978-3-642-15387-7_29

Podobnik, V., & Lovrek, I. (2011). An agent-based platform for ad-hoc social networking. *Lecture Notes in Computer Science, 6682,* 74–83. doi:10.1007/978-3-642-22000-5_9

Podobnik, V., Petric, A., Trzec, K., & Jezic, G. (2009). Software agents in new generation networks: Towards the automation of telecom processes. In Jain, L. C., & Nguyen, N. T. (Eds.), *Knowledge Processing and Decision Making in Agent-Based Systems* (pp. 71–99). Berlin, Germany: Springer-Verlag. doi:10.1007/978-3-540-88049-3_4

Poissant, L., Pereira, J., & Tamblyn, R. (2005). The impact of electronic health records on time efficiency of physicians and nurses: A systematic review. *Journal of the American Medical Informatics Association, 12*(5), 505–516. doi:10.1197/jamia.M1700

Porter, M. (2001). Strategy and the internet. *Harvard Business Review*. Retrieved from http://hbswk.hbs.edu/item/2165.html

Porto, S. C. S., & Berge, Z. L. (2008). Distance education and corporate training in Brazil: Regulations and interrelationships. *International Review of Research in Open and Distance Learning, 9*(2).

Prahalad, C. K., & Ramaswarmy, V. (2000). Co-opting customer competence. *Harvard Business Review, 78*(1), 79–87.

Prandelli, E., Verona, G., & Raccagni, D. (2006). Diffusion of web-based product innovation. *California Management Review, 48*(4). doi:10.2307/41166363

Press Reference. (2011). *Morocco press, media, TV, radio, newspapers*. Retrieved September 10, 2011, from http://www.press-reference.com/Ma-No/Morocco.html

Preston, J. (2011, February 6). Movement began with outrage and a Facebook page that gave it an outlet. *New York Times*, p. A10.

Purcell, K. (2011). *Pew internet report: Search and email still top the list of most popular online activities*. Retrieved October 28, 2011, from http://www.pewinternet.org/~/media//Files/Reports/2011/PIP_Search-and-Email.pdf

QAA. (2000). *Subject benchmark computing*. Retrieved October 13, 2011, from http://www.qaa.ac.uk/Publications/Information-AndGuidance/Documents/computing07.pdf

QAA. (2008). *The framework for higher education qualifications in England, Wales and Northern Ireland*. Retrieved October 13, 2011, from http://www.qaa.ac.uk/Publications/InformationAndGuidance/Documents/FHEQ08.pdf

QAA. (2009). *An introduction to QAA*. Retrieved October 14, 2011, from http://www.qaa.ac.uk/Publications/InformationAndGuidance/Documents/IntroQAA.pdf

QAA. (2011). *Subject benchmark statement masters degrees in computing*. Retrieved October 13, 2011, from http://www.qaa.ac.uk/Publications/CircularLetters/Documents/QAA386_Computing.pdf

Raabe, A. (2007). *Social software in unternehmen: Wikis and weblogs for knowledge management and communication*. Saarbrücken, Germany: VDM Verlag.

Raaflaub, A. K., Ober, J., & Wallace, R. W. (2008). *Origins of democracy in ancient Greece*. Los Angeles, CA: University of California Press.

Rafaeli, S. (1986). The electronic bulletin board. A computer-driven mass-medium. *Computers and the Social Sciences, 2*, 123–131. doi:10.1177/089443938600200302

Raina, M. K. (1993). Ethnocentric confines in creativity research. In Isaksen, S. G., Murdock, M. C., Firestien, R. L., & Treffinger, D. J. (Eds.), *Understanding and Recognizing Creativity: The Emergence of a Discipline* (pp. 435–453). Norwood, NJ: Ablex.

Raman, T. V. (2009). Toward 2W, beyond web 2.0. *Communications of the ACM, 52*(2), 52–59. doi:10.1145/1461928.1461945

Raman, V. V. (2011). Habermas, networks and virtual public spheres: A blended deliberative model from developing countries. In *Information Communication Technologies and the Virtual Public Sphere: Impact of Network Structures on Civil Society.* Hershey, PA: IGI Global. doi:10.4018/978-1-60960-159-1.ch004

Rao, L. (2011). *Beyonce pregnancy news at MTV VMAs births new Twitter record of 8,868 tweets per second.* Retrieved October 29, 2011, from http://techcrunch.com/2011/08/29/beyonce-pregnancy-news-at-the-mtv-vmas-births-new-twitter-record-with-8868-tweets-per-second

Rao, M. (2011). *Mobile Africa report 2011: Regional hubs of excellence and innovation.* Retrieved August 8, 2012, from http://www.mobilemonday.net/reports/MobileAfrica_2011.pdf

Rao, S., & Troshani, I. (2007). A conceptual framework and propositions for the acceptance of mobile services. *Journal of Theoretical and Applied Electronic Commerce Research, 2*(2), 61–73.

Rask, M. (2008). The reach and richness of Wikipedia: Is Wikipedia only for the rich countries. *First Monday, 13*(6).

Rauch, A., & Frese, M. (2007). Born to be an entrepreneur? Revisiting the personality approach to entrepreneurship. In Baum, J., Frese, M., & Baron, R. (Eds.), *The Psychology of Entrepreneurship: The Organizational Frontiers* (pp. 41–65). Mahwah, NJ: Lawrence Erlbaum Associates Publishers.

Reason, P., & Bradbury, H. (Eds.). (2007). *The SAGE handbook of action research.* London, UK: Sage.

Redmiles, D. (2002). Introduction to the special issue on activity theory and the practice of design. *Computer Supported Cooperative Work, 11*, 1–11. doi:10.1023/A:1015215726353

Reese, A. (2009, Spring). Framing April 6: Discursive dominance in the Egyptian print media. *Arab Media & Society.*

Reeves, T. C. (2004). *The will to fly: eLearning and the challenge of the conative domain.* Presentation of the e-Agenda International Round Table. Retrieved May 11 2011 from http://www.Griffith.edu.au/text/conference/eagenda2004/ content rt speakers.html

Reid, M., & Gray, C. (2007). Online social networks, virtual communities, enterprises, and information professionals. *Searcher, 15*(7), 32–51.

Reinecke, K., Bernstein, A., & Schenkel, S. (2010). Modeling a user's culture. In *The Handbook of Research in Culturally-Aware Information Technology: Perspectives and Models.* Hershey, PA: IGI Global. doi:10.4018/978-1-61520-883-8.ch011

Reporters without Borders. (2010, October 20). *Europe falls from its pedestal, no respite in the dictatorships: 2010 world press freedom index.* Retrieved September 10, 2011, from www.rsf.org/IMG/CLASSEMENT_2011/GB/C_GENERAL_GB.pdf

Reporters without Borders. (2011). Countries under surveillance: Bahraïn. *Reporters without Borders*. Retrieved September 10, 2011, from http://en.rsf.org/surveillance-bahrain,39748.html

Reporters without Borders. (2011, September 10). *Is the supreme council a new predator of press freedom?* Retrieved from http://en.rsf.org/egypt-is-the-supreme-council-a-new-10-09-2011,40962.html

Ribeiro, C. (2010). A universidade como disputa da reprodução social: Contribuição ao debate sobre os mestrados profissionais. *Revista Brasileira de Pós-Graduação, 7*(14), 433–450.

Riemer, K., & Richter, A. (2010). Tweet inside: Microblogging in a corporate context. In *Proceedings 23rd Bled eConference*. Bled eConference.

Riemer, K., Altenhofen, A., & Richter, A. (2011). What are you doing? Enterprise microblogging as context building. In *Proceedings of the 19th European Conference on Information Systems (ECIS)*. ECIS.

Riggs, E. G. (2004). *Connecting with students' will to succeed: The power of conation*. Glenview, CA: Pearson Professional Development.

Ritchel, M. (2011). Egypt cuts off most internet and cell phone service. *New York Times*. Retrieved from http://www.nytimes.com/2011/01/29/technology/internet/29cutoff.html?_r=3&adxnnl=1&adxnnlx=1300476961-GCNnGx7aXhmEfr4YKW121g

Rivlin, G. (2006). *How Friendster lost chance for a jackpot*. Retrieved October 29, 2011, from http://www.nytimes.com/2006/10/15/business/worldbusiness/15iht-friend.3160940.html

Roberts, T. (1998). Are newsgroups virtual communities? In *Proceedings of the SIGCHI Conference on Human Factors in Computing Systems*, (pp. 360–367). ACM Press.

Roberts, T. S. (2004). *Online collaborative learning: Theory and practice*. Hershey, PA: IGI Global.

Robinson, P., Stimpson, D., Huefner, J., & Hunt, H. (1991). An attitude approach to the prediction of entrepreneurship. *Entrepreneurship Theory & Practice, 15*(4), 13–30.

Roca, J. C., Garcia, J. J., & Vega, J. J. (2009). The importance of perceived trust, security and privacy in online trading systems. *Information Management & Computer Security, 17*(2), 96–113. doi:10.1108/09685220910963983

Rodriguez, G., & Knuth, R. (2000). *Critical issue: Providing professional development for effective technology use*. Retrieved September 7, 2011, http://www.ncrel.org/sdrs/areas/issues/methods/technlgy/te1000.htm

Rodriguez, F., & Spanik, K. (2003). Introduction. In Hardy, C., & Moller, C. (Eds.), *Spreading the Word on the Internet*. Vienna, Austria: Organization for Security and Co-Operation in Europe.

Romizowski, A. (2005). *A study of distance education public policy and practice in the higher education sectors of selected countries: Synthesis of key findings*. Johannesburg, South Africa: South African Council on Higher Education (CHE).

Rossi, A. (2009). *A inovação aberta como fonte de geração de valor para as organizações*. Retrieved from http://www.fdc.org.br/pt/pesquisa/inovacao/Documents/artigos_blog/inovacao_aberta.pdf

Compilation of References

Rothwell, W. (2012). *Encyclopedia of human resource management, critical and emerging issues in human resources*. San Francisco, CA: John Wiley & Sons.

Royo-Vela, M., & Casamassima, P. (2011). The influence of belonging to virtual brand communities on consumers' affective commitment, satisfaction and word-of-mouth advertising: The ZARA case. *Online Information Review, 35*(4), 517–542. doi:10.1108/14684521111161918

Roy, S. (2009). Internet uses and gratifications. A survey in the Indian context. *Computers in Human Behavior, 25*, 878–886. doi:10.1016/j.chb.2009.03.002

Rubin, A. M. (1979). Television use by children and adolescents. *Human Communication Research, 5*, 109–120. doi:10.1111/j.1468-2958.1979.tb00626.x

Rubin, A. M. (1984). Ritualized and instrumental television viewing. *The Journal of Communication, 34*(3), 67–77. doi:10.1111/j.1460-2466.1984.tb02174.x

Rubin, J. (1994). *Handbook of usability testing: How to plan, design, and conduct effective tests*. New York, NY: Wiley.

Rudowicz, E. (2003). Creativity and culture: A two-way interaction. *Scandinavian Journal of Educational Research, 47*, 273–290. doi:10.1080/00313830308602

Ruiz, C., Sanz, S., Broz, A., & Marchuet, D. (2009). Mobile Internet adoption by Spanish consumers. In Head, M., & Li, E. (Eds.), *Mobile and ubiquitous commerce: Advanced e-business methods* (pp. 221–236). Hershey, PA: IGI Global. doi:10.4018/978-1-60566-366-1.ch012

Ruiz, C., Sanz, S., & Tavera, J. F. (2010). A comparative study of mobile messaging services acceptance to participate in television programmes. *Journal of Service Management, 21*(1), 69–102. doi:10.1108/09564231011025128

Rumble, G. (2001). The costs and costing of networked learning. *Journal of Asynchronous Learning Networks, 5*(2), 75–96.

Ruohonen, M., Mavengere, N., Nleya, N., & Deodhar, S. (2011). The use of free, Libre and open source software (FLOSS) for African higher education advancement and development. In M. Youssef & S. A. Anwar (Eds.), *Proceedings of the 4th Conference on e-Learning Excellence in the Middle East 2011: In Search of New Paradigms for Re-Engineering Education,* (pp. 44–54). Dubai, United Arab Emirates: IEEE.

Ruth, A., & Houghton, L. (2009). The wiki way of learning. *Australasian Journal of Educational Technology, 25*(2), 135–152.

Ryzhkova, N. (2009). *The contribution of the user innovation methods to open innovation*. Blekinge, Sweden: Blekinge Institute of Technology.

Saadeghvaziri, F., & Hosseini, H. K. (2011). Mobile advertising: An investigation of factors creating positive attitude in Iranian customers. *African Journal of Business Management, 5*, 394–404.

Saadeghvaziri, F., & Seyedjavadain, S. (2011). Attitude toward advertising: Mobile advertising vs advertising-in-general. *European Journal of Economics. Finance and Administrative Sciences, 28*, 104–114.

Sadeghi, P., Kuzimsky, C., & Benyoucef, M. (2011). *Towards a readiness model for health 2.0.* Paper presented at MEDES Conference 11. San Francisco, CA.

Sadowsky, G. (Ed.). (2012). *Accelerating development using the web: Empowering poor and marginalized populations.* Retrieved August 8, 2012, from http://public.webfoundation.org/2012/02/wf_study.pdf

Sakr, N. (2001). *Satellite realms: Transnational television, globalization and the Middle East.* New York, NY: Tauris.

Sakr, N. (2007). *Arab media and political renewal community, legitimacy and public life.* London, UK: Tauris.

Salam, M., Steenkamp, A., & khoury, F. (2008). The evolution of small and medium enterprise in digital business ecosystem. In *Proceedings of the Information and Communication Technologies: From Theory to Applications, 2008.* Damascus, Syria: ICTTA.

Sambasivan, M., Abdul, M., & Yusop, Y. (2009). Impact of personal qualities and management skills of entrepreneurs on venture performance in Malaysia: Opportunity recognition skills as a mediating factor. *Technovation, 29*(11), 798–805. doi:10.1016/j.technovation.2009.04.002

Sánchez, A., & Álvaro, A. (2011). *Hábitos de uso de los adolescentes españoles y de América Latina.* Retrieved February 17, 2011, from http://ticsyformacion.com/2011/09/05/uso-de-las-redes-sociales-por-adolescentes-espanoles-y-latinoamericanos-socialmedia

Sanchez-Franco, M. J., Villarejo, A. F., & Martin, F. A. (2009). The moderating effect of gender on relationship quality and loyalty toward Internet service providers. *Information & Management, 46*(3), 196–202. doi:10.1016/j.im.2009.02.001

Sanders, D., & Chopra, M. (2006). Key challenges to achieving health for all in an inequitable society: The case of South Africa. *American Journal of Public Health, 96*(1), 73–78. doi:10.2105/AJPH.2005.062679

Santos, C. R., & Brasil, V. S. (2010). Envolvimento do consumidor em processos de desenvolvimento de produtos: um estudo qualitativo junto a empresas de bens de consumo. *Revista de Administração de Empresas, 50*(3).

Santos, A. I. (2011). *Open educational resources in Brazil: State-of-the art, challenges and prospects for development and innovation.* Moscow, Russia: UNESCO Institute for Information Technology in Education.

Sanz, S., Ruiz, C., Pérez, I., & Hernández, A. (2011). *Papel moderador del género en el análisis de la lealtad a webs turísticas que ofrecen alojamiento.* Paper presented at the Marketing Trends Conference, Paris.

Sawhney, M., & Prandelli, E. (2000). Communities of creation: Managing distributed innovation in turbulent markets. *California Management Review, 42*, 24–54. doi:10.2307/41166052

Sawhney, M., Verona, G., & Prandelli, E. (2005). Collaborating to create: The internet as a platform for customer engagement in product innovation. *Journal of Interactive Marketing, 19*(4). doi:10.1002/dir.20046

Scammell, M. (1988). Censorship and its history – A personal view. In Boyle, K. (Ed.), *Article 19 World Report 1988: Information, Freedom, and Censorship.* New York, NY: Times Books.

Scarff, A. (2006). Advanced knowledge sharing with Intranet 2.0. *Knowledge Management Review, 9*(4).

Scharl, A., Dickinger, A., & Murphy, J. (2005). Diffusion and success factors of mobile marketing. *Electronic Commerce Research and Applications*, *4*(2), 159–173. doi:10.1016/j.elerap.2004.10.006

Schemm, P. (2012). *Morocco: Islamist justice and development party leads government*. Retrieved August 18, 2012 from http://www.huffingtonpost.com/2012/01/03/morocco-islamist-justice-and-development_n_1181086.html

Schlichter, J., Koch, M., & Xu, C. (1998). Awareness - The common link between groupware and community support systems. In *Proceedings of CCSS*, (pp. 78-94). Berlin, Germany: Springer-Verlag.

Schneckenberg, D. (2009). Web 2.0 and the empowerment of the knowledge worker. *Journal of Knowledge Management*, *13*(6), 509–520. doi:10.1108/13673270910997150

Schoeffel, P., Meleisea, M., David, R., Kalauni, R., Kalolo, K., & Kingi, P. (1996). Pacific islands Polynesian attitudes to child training and discipline in New Zealand: Some policy implications for social welfare and education. *Social Policy Journal of New Zealand: Te Puna Whakaaro*, *6*, 134–147.

Schoop, E., Bukvova, H., & Gilge, S. (2006). Blended learning – The didactical framework for integrative qualification processes. In *Proceedings of Conference on Integrative Qualification in eGovernment*, (pp. 142–156). IEEE.

Schoop, E., Bukvova, H., & Lieske, C. (2009). Blended learning arrangements for higher education in the changing knowledge society. In *Proceedings of the International Conference on Current Issues in Management of Business and Society Development 2009*, (pp. 11–17). Riga, Latvia: University of Latvia.

Schoop, E., Michel, K.-U., Miluniec, A., Kriksciuniene, D., & Brundzaite, R. (2005). *Virtual collaborative learning in higher education and its potentials for lifelong learning - An empirical approach*. Paper presented at the EDEN Annual Conference. Helsinki, Finland.

Schoop, E., Gilge, S., & Bukvova, H. (2007). How to implement "eBologna"? Didactical and organisational issues of a mobile ERASMUS module network. In Blum, U., Eckstein, A., & Eckstein, A. (Eds.), *Wirtschaftsinformatik im Fokus der Modernen Wissensökonomik - Netzwerkökonomie und Electronic Business, Electronic Learning, Systementwicklung und Modellierung: Festschrift für Prof. Dr. Dr. h.c. Wolfgang Uhr* (pp. 169–192). Academic Press.

Schout, L. (2011). Foss and civil society organisations (CSO): Why civil society is not embracing FOSS. *i4donline.net*. Retrieved September 23, 2011, from http://www.i4donline.net/oct04/civil.asp

Schroeder, A., Minocha, S., & Schneider, C. (2010). The strengths, weaknesses, opportunities and threats of using social software in higher and further education teaching and learning. *Journal of Computer Assisted Learning*, *26*, 159–174. doi:10.1111/j.1365-2729.2010.00347.x

Schroeder, A., Minocha, S., & Schneider, C. (2010). Social software in higher education: The diversity of applications and their contributions to student's learning experiences. *Communications of the Association for Information Systems*, *26*(1), 547–564.

Schroeder, A., Minocha, S., & Schneider, C. (2010). The strengths, weaknesses, opportunities and threats of using social software in higher and further education teaching and learning. *Journal of Computer Assisted Learning*, *26*(3), 159–174. doi:10.1111/j.1365-2729.2010.00347.x

Schulmeister, R. (2001). *Virtuelle universität-Virtuelles lernen*. München, Germany: Oldenbourg Verlag. doi:10.1524/9783486598926

Schumacher, E. F. (1973). *Small is beautiful: Economics as if people mattered*. New York, NY: Harper & Row.

Schumpeter, J. (1947). The creative response in economic history. *The Journal of Economic History*, 7(2), 149–159.

Secretariat, S. E. A. M. E. O. (2010). *Report: Status of ICT integration in education in Southeast Asian countries*. Retrieved from http://www.seameo.org/images/stories/Publications/Project_Reports/SEAMEO_ICT-Integration-Education2010.pdf

Seffah, A., & Grogono, P. (2002). *Learner-centered software engineering education: From resources to skills and pedagogical patterns*. Paper presented at the 15th Conference on Software Engineering Education and Training (CSEE&T 2002). Rio de Janeiro, Brasilia.

Seitzinger, J. (2006). *Be constructive: blogs, podcasts, and wikis as constructivist learning tools*. Retrieved February 11, 2008 from http://www.elearningguild.com/pdf/2/073106des.pdf

Selwyn, N., & Grant, L. (2009). Researching the realities of social software use – An introduction. *Learning, Media and Technology*, 34(2), 79–86. doi:10.1080/17439880902921907

Semiocast. (2012). *Twitter reaches half a billion accounts*. Retrieved August 1, 2012, from http://semiocast.com/publications/2012_07_30_Twitter_reaches_half_a_billion_accounts_140m_in_the_US

Sen, A. (2001). *Development as freedom*. Oxford, UK: Oxford University Press.

Seufert, S., & Mayr, P. (2002). Blended learning, hybrides lernen. In *Fachlexikon e-le@rning: Wegweiser durch das e-Vokabular*. Bonn, Germany: managerSeminare Gerhard May GmbH.

Sfard, A. (1998). On two metaphors for learning and the dangers of choosing just one. *Educational Researcher*, 27(2), 4–13.

Shah, S. K., & Franke, N. (2003). How communities support innovative activities: An exploration of assistance and sharing among end□users. *Research Policy*, 32, 157–178. doi:10.1016/S0048-7333(02)00006-9

Shane, S. (2011, January 29). Spotlight again falls on web tools and change. *New York Times*. Retrieved from http://www.nytimes.com/2011/01/30/weekinreview/30shane.html?_r=2

Shang, S., Li, E., Wu, Y., & Hou, O. (2011). Understanding web 2.0 service models: A knowledge creating perspective. *Information & Management*, 48, 178–184. doi:10.1016/j.im.2011.01.005

Shapiro, S. M. (2009, January 22). Revolution, Facebook-style. *New York Times*. Retrieved from http://www.nytimes.com/2009/01/25/magazine/25bloggers-t.html

Shapiro, A. L. (2000). *The control revolution: How the internet is putting individuals in charge and changing the world we know*. New York, NY: Public Affairs.

Shen, A., Lee, M., Cheung, C., & Chen, H. (2010). Gender differences in intentional social action: We-intention to engage in social network-facilitated team collaboration. *Journal of Information Technology*, 25(2), 152–169. doi:10.1057/jit.2010.12

Shin, D. (2010). Analysis of online social networks: a cross- national study. *Online Information Review*, *34*(3), 473–495. doi:10.1108/14684521011054080

Shirkey, C. (2003). *Power laws, weblogs, and inequality, networks, economics, and culture mailing list*. Retrieved from http://www.shirky.com/writings/powerlaw_weblog.html

Shirky, C. (2010, January/February). The political power of social media: Technology, the public sphere, and political change. *Foreign Affairs*, 28–41.

Sife, A. S., Lwoga, E. T., & Sanga, C. (2007). New technologies for teaching and learning: Challenges for higher learning institutions in developing countries. *International Journal of Education and Development using ICT, 3*(2), 57-67. Retrieved June 16, 2011 from http://ijedict.dec.uwi.edu/viewarticle.php?id=246

Simonton, D. K. (1994). *Greatness*. New York, NY: The Guilford Press.

Sipusic, M. J., Pannoni, R. L., Smith, R. B., Dutra, J., Gibbons, J. F., & Sutherland, W. R. (1999). *Virtual collaborative learning: A comparison between face-to-face tutored video instruction (TVI) and distributed tutored video instruction (DTVI)*. New York, NY: Sun Microsystems Laboratories, Inc.

Skog, B. (2002). Mobiles and the Norwegian teen: Identity, gender and class. In Katz, J. E., & Aakhus, M. (Eds.), *Perpetual contact*. New York, NY: Cambridge University Press.

Slavin, R. E. (2000). *Educational psychology: Theory and practice*. Boston, MA: Allyn & Bacon.

Smith, M., & Elder, L. (2010). Open ICT ecosystems transforming the developing world. *Information Technologies & International Development*, *6*(1), 65–71.

Snee, H. (2008). Web 2.0 as a social science research tool. *The British Library*. Retrieved from www.bl.uk/reshelp/bldept/socsci/socint/web2/web2.pdf

Snow, R. E., & Farr, M. J. (1987). Cognitive-conative-affective processes in aptitude, learning and instruction: An introduction. In Snow, R. E., & Farr, M. J. (Eds.), *Aptitude, Learning and Instruction* (p. 1010). Hoboken, NJ: Lawrence Erlbaum Associates.

Social Bakers. (2011). *Facebook statistics by country*. Retrieved September 8, 2011, http://www.socialbakers.com/facebook-statistics/

Socialbakers (2011). *Facebook adoption high, ad rates low in Spain*. Retrieved February 5, 2012, from http://www.emarketer.com/Article.aspx?R=1009047&ecid=a65060336 75d47f881651943c21c5ed4

Socialbakers. (2011). Morocco Facebook statistics, penetration, demography. *Socialbakers*. Retrieved September 10, 2011, from http://www.socialbakers.com/facebook-statistics/morocco

Socialbakers. (2011). Egypt Facebook statistics, penetration, demography. *Socialbakers*. Retrieved September 10, 2011, from http://www.socialbakers.com/facebook-statistics/egypt

Socialbakers. (2012). *Advertising on Facebook*. Retrieved August 1, 2012, from http://www.socialbakers.com/facebook-advertising

Socialbakers. (2012). *Facebook brands statistics*. Retrieved August 1, 2012, from http://www.socialbakers.com/facebook-pages/brands

Socialbakers. (2012). *Facebook statistics by country*. Retrieved August 1, 2012, from http://www.socialbakers.com/facebook-statistics

Socialbakers. (2012). *LinkedIn statistics by country*. Retrieved August 1, 2012, from http://www.socialbakers.com/linkedin-statistics

Socialbakers. (2012). *Twitter statistics: Brands*. Retrieved August 1, 2012, from http://www.socialbakers.com/twitter/group/brands/page-1

Socialbakers. (2012). *Twitter statistics: Overall*. Retrieved August 1, 2012, from http://www.socialbakers.com/twitter

Soderlund, M., & Rosegren, S. (2007). Receiving word-of-mouth from the service customer. An emotion-based effectiveness assessment. *Journal of Retailing and Consumer Services*, *14*, 123–136. doi:10.1016/j.jretconser.2006.10.001

So, H.-J., Seow, P., & Looi, C. K. (2009). Location matters: Leveraging knowledge building with mobile devices and Web 2.0 technology. *Interactive Learning Environments*, *17*(4), 367–382. doi:10.1080/10494820903195389

Sommer, L. H. (2010). Educação a distância: Problemas, perspectivas e possibilidades. *Em Aberto*, *23*(84), 1–15.

Sommer, L. H. (2010). Formação inicial de professores a distância: Questões para debate. *Em Aberto*, *23*(84), 17–30.

Soroa-Koury, S., & Yang, K. (2010). Factors affecting consumers' responses to mobile advertising. *Telematics and Informatics*, *27*(1), 103–113. doi:10.1016/j.tele.2009.06.001

SpannerWorks. (2007). *What is social media*. Retrieved from www.spannerworks.com/ebooks

Spink, P. (1997). A formação acadêmica e a ciência: Ampliando o debate sobre o mestrado profissional. *Revista de Administração Contemporânea*, *1*(3), 163–169. doi:10.1590/S1415-65551997000300009

Sprague, D., & Dede, C. (1999). Constructivism in the classroom: If I teach this way, am I doing my job? *Learning and Leading with Technology*, *27*(1), 6–9.

Stafford, T., Stafford, M., & Schkade, L. (2004). Determining uses and gratifications for the Internet. *Decision Sciences*, *35*(2), 259–288. doi:10.1111/j.00117315.2004.02524.x

Stahl, G., Koschmann, T., & Suthers, D. (2006). Computer-supported collaborative learning: An historical perspective. In *Cambridge Handbook of the Learning Sciences* (pp. 409–426). Cambridge, UK: Cambridge University Press.

Stanyer, J., & Davidson, S. (2009). *The internet and the visibility of oppression in non-democratic states: The online exposure of human rights violations and the other repressive acts*. Paper presented at the Annual Meeting of the International Communication Association. Chicago, IL.

Starr, S. (2003). Putting freedom back on the agenda. In Hardy, C., & Moller, C. (Eds.), *Spreading the Word on the Internet*. Vienna, Austria: Organization for Security and Co-Operation in Europe.

Stobbe, A. (2010). *Enterprise 2.0: How companies are tapping the benefits of web 2.0*. Berlin, Germany: Deutsche Bank Research.

Street, C. T., & Cameron, A. F. (2007). External relationships and the small business: A review of small business alliance and network research. *Journal of Small Business Management*, *45*(2), 239–266.

Sutter, J. D. (2011). *Bin Laden's death sets Twitter record*. Retrieved October 29, 2011, from http://articles.cnn.com/2011-05-02/tech/bin.laden.twitter.record_1_twitter-users-tweets-facebook-friends?_s=PM:TECH

Swallow, E. (2011). *How consumers interact with brands on Facebook*. Retrieved October 30, 2011, from http://mashable.com/2011/09/12/consumers-interact-facebook

Swan, K., Van't Hooft, M., Kratcoski, A., & Unger, D. (2005). Uses and effects of mobile computing devices in K-8 classrooms. *Journal of Research on Technology in Education*, *38*(1), 99–112.

Switzer, J. S. (2004). Teaching computer-mediated visual communication to a large section: A constructivist approach. *Innovative Higher Education*, *29*(2), 89–101. doi:10.1023/B:IHIE.0000048792.40295.08

Tao, G., Sultan, F., & Rohm, A. J. (2010). Factors influencing Chinese youth consumers' acceptance of mobile marketing. *Journal of Consumer Marketing*, *27*(7), 574–583. doi:10.1108/07363761011086326

Tapscott, D., & Williams, A. D. (2006). *Wikinomics: How mass collaboration changes everything*. London, UK: Portfolio Hardcover.

Taqiyyah, B. (2009). Jaringan oracle thinkquest masuk ke 7000 sekolah di jabar. *Kompas*. Retrieved September 13, 2011, http://tekno.kompas.com/read/2009/06/26/20490652/Jaringan.Oracle.ThinkQuest.Masuk.ke.7000.Sekolah.di.Jabar

Taylor, C. (2011). *Twitter users react to massive quake, tsunami in Japan*. Retrieved October 29, 2011, from http://mashable.com/2011/03/11/japan-tsunami

Taylor, C. (2012). *Does Twitter have half a billion users?* Retrieved August 1, 2012, from http://mashable.com/2012/07/30/twitter-users-500-million

Taylor, D. (2011). *Everything you need to know about Facebook's EdgeRank*. Retrieved October 30, 2011, from http://thenextweb.com/socialmedia/2011/05/09/everything-you-need-to-know-about-facebook%e2%80%99s-edgerank

Terwiesch, C., & Xu, Y. (2008). Innovation contests, open innovation, and multiagent problem solving. *Management Science*, *54*(9), 1529–1543. doi:10.1287/mnsc.1080.0884

ThinkQuest. (2011). *Winners 2011 ThinkQuest projects event*. Retrieved October 1, 2011, from http://www.thinkquest.org/library/winners/2011_projects.html

This is Iceland. (2011). *Iceland wants to be your friend on Foursquare*. Retrieved October 29, 2011, from http://aboutfoursquare.com/iceland-wants-to-be-your-friend-on-foursquare

Thomas, J. B., Peters, C. O., & Tolson, H. (2007). An exploratory investigation of the virtual community myspace.com: What are consumers saying about fashion? *Journal of Fashion Marketing and Management*, *11*(4), 587–603. doi:10.1108/13612020710824625

Thompson, N. (2011, January 27). Is Twitter helping in Egypt? *New Yorker*. Retrieved from http://www.newyorker.com/online/blogs/newsdesk/2011/01/is-twitter-helping-in-egypt.html#ixzz1HuIn9WZt

Thompson, M. (2008). ICT and development studies: Towards development 2.0. *Journal of International Development*, *20*, 821–835. doi:10.1002/jid.1498

Thorne, J. (2009, August 6). Moroccan dissent alive on Twitter. *The National*. Retrieved September 10, 2011, from http://www.thenational.ae/news/worldwide/africa/moroccan-dissent-alive-on-twitter

Thornton, P., & Houser, C. (2005). Using mobile phones in English education in Japan. *Journal of Computer Assisted Learning, 21*(3), 217–228. doi:10.1111/j.1365-2729.2005.00129.x

Tietz, R., Füller, J., & Herstatt, C. (2006). Signalling: An innovative approach to identify lead users in online communities. In Blecker, T., & Friedrich, G. (Eds.), *Customer Interaction and Customer Integration* (pp. 453–467). Berlin, Germany: GITO-Verlag.

TNS. (2011). *Mobile life 2011.* Retrieved October 3, 2011, from http://www.tnsglobal.com/research/key-insight-reports/D030D5468903455DA353587691807B5C.aspx

Toffler, A. (1984). *The third wave.* New York, NY: Bantam.

Tondeur, J., van Keer, H., van Braak, J., & Valcke, M. (2008). ICT integration in the classroom: Challenging the potential of a school policy. *Computers & Education, 51*(1), 212–223. doi:10.1016/j.compedu.2007.05.003

Torres, C. V., & Dessen, M. A. (2008). Brazilian culture, family, and its ethnic-cultural variety. *Arizona Journal of Hispanic Cultural Studies, 12*, 41–62.

Toubia, O., & Florès, L. (2007). Adaptive idea screening using consumers. *Marketing Science, 26*(3), 342–360. doi:10.1287/mksc.1070.0273

Trading Media. (2010). *The evolution of mobile phones in Saudi Arabia (present & future).* Retrieved August 5, 2010, from http://bayazidt.wordpress.com/com-546-papers/the-evolution-of-mobile-phones-in-saudi-arabia-present-future/

Travers, J., & Milgram, S. (1969). An experimental study of the small world problem. *Sociometry, 32*(4), 425–443. doi:10.2307/2786545

Trentmann, F. (2006). *The making of the consumer: Knowledge, power and identity in the modern world.* Oxford, UK: Berg.

Trust Metrics. (2011). *Online advertising, blogging, and social networking growing in the Arab world.* Retrieved August 5, 2010, from http://trustmetrics.com/blog/2011/04/online-advertising-blogging-and-social-networking-growing-in-the-arab-world/

Tryhorn, C. (2009, March 2). Mobile phone use passes milestone as UN report reveals global growth. *The Guardian.* Retrieved August 5, 2011, from http://www.guardian.co.uk/technology/2009/mar/03/mobile-phones1

Tsang, M. M., Ho, S. C., & Liang, T. P. (2004). Consumer attitudes toward mobile advertising: An empirical study. *International Journal of Electronic Commerce, 8*(3), 65–78.

Twitter. (2011). *#Yearinreview: Tweets per second.* Retrieved August 1, 2012, from http://blog.twitter.com/2011/12/yearinreview-tweets-per-second.html

Twitter. (2011). *Twitter is the best way to discover what's new in your world.* Retrieved August 5, 2010, from http://twitter.com/about

Twitter. (2012). *Twitter for business.* Retrieved October 30, 2011, from http://business.twitter.com

Ullrich, C., Borau, K., Luo, H., Tan, X., Shen, L., & Shen, R. (2008). Why web 2.0 is good for learning and for research: Principles and prototypes. In *Proceedings of the 17th International Conference on World Wide Web,* (pp. 705-714). ACM.

Compilation of References

Unesco Bangkok. (2004). *School networking: Lessons learned*. Retrieved from http://unesdoc.unesco.org/images/0013/001377/137741e.pdf

UNESCO. (2011). *Guidelines for open educational resources (OER) in higher education*. Retrieved from http://www.col.org/PublicationDocuments/Guidelines_OER_HE.pdf

United Nations. (2010). *E-government survey 2010 leveraging e-government at a time of financial and economic crisis*. Retrieved from http://www2.unpan.org/egovkb/global_reports/10report.htm

United Nations. (2011). *World economic situation and prospects 2011*. Retrieved from http://www.un.org/en/development/desa/policy/wesp/wesp_current/2011wesp_prerelease1.pdf

United Nations. (2012) *E-government survey 2012, e-government for the people*. Retrieved from http://unpan1.un.org/intradoc/groups/public/documents/un/unpan048065.pdf

Unwin, T. (Ed.). (2009). *ICT4D: Information and communication technology for development*. Cambridge, UK: Cambridge University Press.

Urban, G. (2003). *Customer advocacy: Is it for you?* Cambridge, UK: MIT Sloan School of Management.

val Relsen, M. (2012). *The lion's teeth - THE 'prehistory' of social watch*. Retrieved August 8, 2012 from http://www.socialwatch.org/node/79

Van De Meer, H. (2007). Open innovation - The Dutch treat: Challenges in thinking in business models. *Creativity and Innovation Management, 6*(2), 192–202. doi:10.1111/j.1467-8691.2007.00433.x

Van dijk, J., & Nieborg, N. (2009). Wikinomics and its discontents: A critical analysis of Web 2.0 business manifestos. *New Media & Society, 11*(4), 855–874.

Van Grove, J. (2011). *Twitter sets new record: 3,283 tweets per second*. Retrieved October 29, 2011, from http://mashable.com/2010/06/25/tps-record

van Reijswoud, V. (2009). Appropriate ICT as a tool to increase effectiveness in ICT4D: Theoretical considerations and illustrating cases. *The Electronic Journal of Information Systems in Developing Countries, 38*(9), 1–18.

van Reijswoud, V., & de Jager, A. (2008). *Free and open source software for development: Exploring expectations, achievements and the future*. Monza, Italy: Polimetrica.

van Rooy, A. (2000). Good news! You may be out of a job reflections on the past and future 50 years for northern NGOs. *Development in Practice, 10*(3), 300–318. doi:10.1080/09614520050116479

Vandewalle, D. J. (2008). *Libya since 1969: Qadhafi's revolution revisited*. New York, NY: Palgrave Macmillan.

Vanhaverbeke, W. (2006). The interorganisational context of open innovation. In H. Chesbrough, W. Vanhaverbeke, & J. West (Eds.), *Open Innovation: Researching a New Paradigm*. Oxford, UK: Oxford University Press.

Vargo, S. L., & Lusch, R. F. (2004). Evolving to a new dominant logic for marketing. *Journal of Marketing, 68*(1), 1–17. doi:10.1509/jmkg.68.1.1.24036

Vargo, S. L., Maglio, P. P., & Akaka, M. A. (2008). On value and value co-creation: A service systems and service logic perspective. *European Management Journal, 26*(3), 145–152. doi:10.1016/j.emj.2008.04.003

Venkatesh, V., Morris, M. G., Davis, G. B., & Davis, F. D. (2003). User acceptance of information technology: Toward a unified view. *Management Information Systems Quarterly, 27*(3), 425–478.

Venter, G. (2003). *Optimising internet bandwidth in developing country higher education.* Retrieved from http://www.inasp.info/file/dcc5f088365bd20a8e80215bc98dec19/research-optimising-internet-bandwidth.html

Vernooy, R. (2010). *Collaborative learning in practice: Examples from natural resource management in Asia.* Ottawa, Canada: International Development Research Centre. doi:10.1017/UPO9788175968639

Von Hippel, E. (2002). *Horizontal innovation networks: By and for users.* MIT Sloan School of Management Working Paper, No. 4366-02. Cambridge, MA: MIT.

Von Hippel, E. (1986). Lead users: A source of novel products concepts. *Management Science, 32,* 791–805. doi:10.1287/mnsc.32.7.791

Von Hippel, E. (1988). *The sources of innovation.* Oxford, UK: Oxford University Press.

Von Hippel, E. (1998). Economics of product development by users: The impact of 'sticky' local information. *Management Science, 44*(5), 629–644. doi:10.1287/mnsc.44.5.629

Von Hippel, E. (2005). *Democratizing innovation.* Cambridge, MA: MIT Press.

Von Hippel, E. (2007). Horizontal innovation networks: By and for users. *Industrial and Corporate Change, 16*(2), 293–315. doi:10.1093/icc/dtm005

Von Hippel, E., & Katz, R. (2002). Shifting innovation to users via toolkits. *Management Science, 48*(7), 821–833. doi:10.1287/mnsc.48.7.821.2817

Vygotsky, L. (1978). *Mind in society: The development of higher psychological processes.* Boston, MA: Harvard University Press.

W3C. (2012). Web standards. Retrieved February 10, 2012 from http://www.w3.org/standards/

Waldt, D., Rebbello, T. M., & Brown, W. J. (2009). Attitude of young consumers toward SMS advertising. *African Journal of Business Management, 3,* 444–452.

Walfoord, A. A. G., Redden, E. R., Elliott, L. R., & Coovert, M. D. (2008). Empowering followers in virtual teams: Guiding principles from theory and practice. *Computers in Human Behavior, 24*(5), 1884–1906. doi:10.1016/j.chb.2008.02.006

Walker, P. (2010, May 15). Facebook loses friends as privacy campaign grows. *The Guardian,* p. 7.

Wallas, G. (1926). *The art of thought.* New York, NY: Harcourt Brace and World.

Walsham, G. (2002). Cross-cultural software production and use: A structurational analysis. *Management Information Systems Quarterly, 26*(4), 359–380. doi:10.2307/4132313

Walter, E. (2011). *10 tips for posting on your brand's Facebook page.* Retrieved October 30, 2011, from http://mashable.com/2011/03/22/tips-brand-facebook-page

Wang, F., & Hannafin, M. (2005). Design-based research and technology-enhanced learning environments. *Educational Technology Research and Development, 53*(4), 5–23. doi:10.1007/BF02504682

Wang, S., Moon, S., Kwon, K., Evans, C., & Stefanone, M. (2010). Face off: Implications of visual cues on initiating friendship of Facebook. *Computers in Human Behavior, 26*(2), 226–234. doi:10.1016/j.chb.2009.10.001

Compilation of References

Wan, Y., Kumar, V., & Bukhari, A. (2008). Will the overseas expansion of Facebook succeed? *IEEE Internet Computing, 12*(3), 69–73. doi:10.1109/MIC.2008.70

Wasserman, T. (2011). *Google+ has 40 million users, says Larry Page.* Retrieved October 30, 2011, from http://mashable.com/2011/10/13/google-plus-40-million

Wasserman, T. (2012). *Is Google+ the no. 3 social network? Depends how you measure it.* Retrieved May 25, 2012, from http://mashable.com/2012/04/11/google-plus-number-three

Wasserman, T. (2012). *Only 49% of marketers have integrated social into brand building.* Retrieved May 25, 2012, from http://mashable.com/2012/05/07/49-percent-marketers-social-brand-building

Watson, R. T., Pitt, L. F., Berthon, P., & Zinkhan, G. M. (2002). U-Commerce: Expanding the universe of marketing. *Journal of the Academy of Marketing Science, 30*(4), 333–347. doi:10.1177/009207002236909

Webster, P. (2003). Asking music students to reflect on their creative work: Encouraging the revision process. In Yip, L. C. R., Leung, C. C., & Lau, W. T. (Eds.), *Curriculum Innovation in Music* (pp. 16–27). Hong Kong, China: The Hong Kong Institute of Education. doi:10.1080/1461380032000126337

Weinberg, B., Parise, S., & Guinan, P. J. (2007). Multichannel marketing: mindset and program development. *Business Horizons, 50*(5), 385–394. doi:10.1016/j.bushor.2007.04.002

Wei, R., Xiaoming, H., & Pan, J. (2010). Examining user behavioural response to SMS ads: Implications for the evolution of the mobile phone as a bona-fide medium. *Telematics and Informatics, 27*, 32–41. doi:10.1016/j.tele.2009.03.005

Weiss, H. M., & Cropanzano, R. (1996). Affective events theory: A theoretical discussion of the structure, causes and consequences of affective experiences at work. In Staw, B. M., & Cummings, L. L. (Eds.), *Research in organizational behavior* (pp. 1–74). Greenwich, CT: JAI Press.

Weller, M. (2011). *The digital scholar: How technology is transforming scholarly practice.* Basingstoke, UK: Bloomsbury Academic. doi:10.5040/9781849666275

Wenger, E. (1998). *Communities of practice: Learning, meaning, and identity.* Cambridge, UK: Cambridge University Press.

Wentz, L. (2010). *At Fiat in Brazil, vehicle design is no longer by Fiat: Automaker is relying on consumers and social media for a 2010 concept car.* Retrieved from http://adage.com/results?endeca=1&return=endeca&search_offset=0&search_order_by=score&x=0&y=0&search_phrase=At+Fiat+in+Brazil%2C+Vehicle+Design+Is+No+Longer+By+Fiat

West, J., & Gallagher, S. (2006). Challenges of open innovation: The paradox of firm investment in open-source software. *R & D Management, 36*(3), 319–331. doi:10.1111/j.1467-9310.2006.00436.x

Westland, J. C. (2010). Critical mass and willingness to pay for social networks. *Electronic Commerce Research and Applications, 9*(1), 6–19. doi:10.1016/j.elerap.2009.05.003

Wheeler, D. (2004). *The internet in the Arab world: Digital divides and cultural connections.* Retrieved August 5, 2010, from http://www.riifs.org/guest/lecture_text/Internet_n_arab-world_all_txt.htm

Wheeler, S., & Wheeler, D. (2009). Using wikis to promote quality learning in teacher training. *Learning, Media and Technology, 34*(1), 1–10. doi:10.1080/17439880902759851

WHO. (2008). *Primary health care, now more than ever*. Geneva, Switzerland: WHO.

WHO. (2010). *An assessment of e-health projects and initiatives in Africa*. Geneva, Switzerland: WHO.

Wickramasinghe, N. S., Fadlalla, A. M. A., Geisler, E., & Schaffer, J. L. (2005). A framework for assessing e-health preparedness. *International Journal of Electronic Healthcare*, *1*(3). doi:10.1504/IJEH.2005.006478

Wilkinson, I. (1998). Dealing with diversity: Achievement gaps in reading literacy among New Zealand students. *Reading Research Quarterly*, *33*, 144–167. doi:10.1598/RRQ.33.2.1

Williams, J. B., & Jacobs, J. (2004). Exploring the use of blogs as learning spaces in the higher education sector. *Australasian Journal of Educational Technology*, *20*(2), 232-247. Retrieved October 2, 2007, from http://www.ascilite.org.au/ajet/ajet20/williams.html

Williamson, O. (2002). the theory of the firm as governance structure: from choice to contract. *The Journal of Economic Perspectives*, *16*(3), 171–195. doi:10.1257/089533002760278776

Wilson, A. N. (2007, June 8). The internet is destroying the world as we know it. *Daily Mail Online*.

Wolff, R., Riedel, J., Jödiscke, C., Schoop, E., & Sonntag, R. (2011). Social media communication: Social media used both as a learning content and as a learning style. In *Proceedings of the IADIS International Conference on e-Learning*, (pp. 41–45). Rome, Italy: IADIS.

World Bank. (2012). Education and development. *The World Bank - Education - Education and Development*. Retrieved November 24, 2011, from http://go.worldbank.org/F5K8Y429G0

World Bank. (2012). *Poverty headcount ratio at $2 a day (PPP) (% of population)*. Retrieved August 8, 2012, from http://data.worldbank.org/indicator/SI.POV.2DAY

Wright, N., & Hinson, T. (2008). How blogs and social media are changing public relations and the way it is practiced. *The Public Relations Journal*, *2*(2).

Wyatt, J. C., & Liu, J. L. Y. (2002). Basic concepts in medical informatics. *Journal of Epidemiology and Community Health*, *56*, 808–812. doi:10.1136/jech.56.11.808

Wynd, W. R., & Bozman, C. S. (1996). Student learning style: A segmentation strategy for higher education. *Journal of Education for Business*, *71*(4), 232–235. doi:10.1080/08832323.1996.10116790

Xu, H., Oh, L. B., & Teo, H. H. (2009). Perceived effectiveness of text vs. multimedia location-based advertising messaging. *International Journal of Mobile Communications*, *7*(2), 154–177. doi:10.1504/IJMC.2009.022440

Yahoo. (2009). Flickr. Retrieved July 02, 2011 from http://www.flickr.com

Yang, K., & Lee, H. J. (2010). Gender differences in using mobile data services: Utilitarian and hedonic value approaches. *Journal of Research in Interactive Marketing*, *4*(2), 142–156. doi:10.1108/17505931011051678

Yang, Q., Zhou, Z.-H., Mao, W., Li, W., & Liu, N. N. (2010). Social Learning. *IEEE Intelligent Systems*, *25*(4), 9–11. doi:10.1109/MIS.2010.103

Yayehyirad, K. (2006). *E-government in Africa – Prospects, challenges and practices*. Retrieved from http://people.itu.int/~kitaw/egov/paper/E-Government_in_Africa.pdf

Compilation of References

Yel, M. (2008). *Ministry of telecommunications & postal service - Telecommunications policy*. Retrieved from http://www.motps.goss.org/index.php?option=com_content&view=article&id=54&Itemid=56&lang=en

Yin, R. (2003). *Case study research: Design and methods*. London, UK: Sage.

Yoon, J.-L. (2007). Telco 2.0: A new role and business model. *IEEE Communications Magazine, 45*(1), 10–12. doi:10.1109/MCOM.2007.284530

Yourdon, E. (2006). Creating business value with web 2.0. *Cutter IT Journal, 19*(10), 3–5.

Youtube. (2012). *Media toolkit – Animated infographic*. Retrieved August 1, 2012, from http://www.youtube.com/watch?v=oXefMNfHVow

Yuen, A. H. K., Law, N., & Wong, K. C. (2003). ICT implementation and school leadership: Case studies of ICT integration in teaching and learning. *Journal of Educational Administration, 41*, 158–170. doi:10.1108/09578230310464666

Zain Group & Telefonaktiebolaget LM Ericsson. (2009). *Economic impact of mobile communications in Sudan report*. Khartoum, Sudan: Zain Group.

Zakaria, M. H., Watson, J., & Edwards, S. L. (2010). Investigating the use of web 2.0 technology by Malaysian students. *Multicultural Education & Technology Journal, 4*(1), 17–29. doi:10.1108/17504971011034700

Zeichick, A. (2009). A-twitter over Twitter. *netWorker, 13*(1), 5–7. doi:10.1145/1516035.1516037

Zeiller, M., & Schauer, B. (2011). *Adoption, motivation and success factors for team collaboration in SME's, mimeographed*. Burgenland, Austria: University of Applied Science.

Zeisser, M. (2010, July). Unlocking the elusive potential of social networks. *The McKinsey Quarterly*.

Zenith Media. (2010). *Panorama de medios en España 2009*. Madrid, Spain: Zenith Optimedia Group.

Zenith Media. (2011). *Móviles y publicidad. Percepciones, usos y tendencias*. Madrid, Spain: Zenith Optimedia Group.

Zhang, J., Qu, Y., Cody, J., & Wu, Y. (2010). A case study of micro-blogging in the enterprise. In *Proceedings of the 28th International Conference on Human Factors in Computing Systems*, (pp. 123-132). New York, NY: ACM Press.

Zhao, D., & Rosson, M. B. (2009). How and why people Twitter. In *Proceedings of the ACM 2009 International Conference on Supporting Group Work*. New York, NY: ACM Press.

Zhao, Y., & Frank, K. A. (2003). Factors affecting technology uses in schools: An ecological perspective. *American Educational Research Journal, 40*(4), 803–840. doi:10.3102/00028312040004807

Zurita, L., & Ryberg, T. (2005). Towards a collaborative approach of introducing e-learning in higher education institutions: How do university teachers conceive and react to transitions to e-learning. In *Proceedings WCCE 2005*. IFIP.

About the Contributors

Nahed Azab is an IT Consultant and Professor. She plays an active role in planning and updating the curriculum, compiling and editing the material and course work, and teaching a number of IT undergraduate and postgraduate courses at the American University in Cairo and the Regional Information Technology Institute. In particular, Dr. Azab focuses on Electronic Commerce, Electronic Marketing, and Management Information Systems. She obtained her PhD from the School of Engineering and Information Sciences – Middlesex University, London (July 2010). Dr. Azab obtained her MSc. in Business Information Technology, School of Computing Sciences – Middlesex University, London (July 2002). Her career path encompassed software programming, analysis and design, computer center management, software instruction, and general IT consultancy with public and private entities such as the Ministry of State for Administrative Development and McKinsey and Company. Dr. Azab is a committee member in several journals, books, and conferences. She also presented a number of academic papers in journals, books, and conferences.

* * *

Daniel Ackermann has received M.Eng. from Faculty of Electrical Engineering and Computing, University of Zagreb in 2010. In 2009, he co-founded (with Tomislav Grubisic) iSTUDIO, the first Croatian full-service social media marketing agency. In a few years iSTUDIO became the leading CEE social media marketing agency and is now expanding internationally to the rest of Europe. At the beginning of 2011, iSTUDIO launched the mediatoolkit.com project. Mediatoolkit uses publicly available social interaction information and indicates most interesting content on the Internet at the specific moment. At the end of 2011 another project was launched—socialnumbers.com is an analytics portal for Facebook pages. At the beginning of 2012, the latest iSTUDIO project, called socialpuzzle.com, was launched. Socialpuzzle offers generic products for Facebook brands pages improvements. Daniel's main interests are new media, digital marketing, business development, and entrepreneurship.

Mariam F. Alkazemi is a Doctoral Student at the University of Florida's College of Communications and Journalism. She has taught a course dealing with international journalism titled "World Communications System" and a course relating media and culture called "Mass Media and You." Fluent in the Arabic and English languages, her research examines portrayals of Muslims in the American media and applies mass communications theories to the Arab and Muslim worlds. Alkazemi's writing has been published in *Peace through People: 50 Years of Global Citizenship*, a book that explains the history of the Washington, DC, non-profit diplomacy organization, Sister Cities International. Her contributions were acknowledged by Pulitzer prize-winning journalist Laura Sessions Stepp in her book, *Unhooked: How Young Women Pursue Sex, Delay Love, and Lose at Both.* Alkazemi earned a B.A. (Journalism) from George Washington University and M.A. degrees (Advertising, Public Relations) from Michigan State University.

Leonor Barroca is a Senior Lecturer in Computing at the Open University (UK), with a PhD in Computing from Southampton University, and an MSc in Computing from the University of Oxford. She has chaired the production and presentation of several distance education postgraduate modules, and co-chaired the development of a Virtual MPhil in Computing. She has experience of international collaborations in research and teaching and is currently director of a partnership in Botswana. Her research is in the Software Engineering area where she has published in international conferences and journals and been a member of international conferences programme committees; she has recently been carrying out research in the area of research skills development at a distance, and design in postgraduate distance education.

Mamoun Benmamoun is an Assistant Professor of International Business at the John Cook School of Business (JCSB) at Saint Louis University. He received his Ph.D. in Public Policy Analysis and Administration from Saint Louis University with research emphasize in international trade policy. He earned an MBA with emphasis in international business and finance, and a Bachelor degree in Applied Statistics. He teaches undergraduate and graduate courses in International Business. Prior to joining JCSB's faculty, he was a Research Associate with the Boeing Institute of International Business.

Caitlin Bentley is completing her PhD at the ICT4D Research Centre at Royal Holloway, University of London. Her topic explores the role of technology in mediating relationships between donors and CSOs. Caitlin is particularly interested in how technology can improve learning and accountability processes in development. She is also currently working for the Mapping for Results Programme at the World Bank, contributing to research on open development. Caitlin has worked as a knowledge officer, social media strategist, Web developer, and development project coordinator for organisations in Canada and abroad. In her career, she has worked closely with Civil Society Organizations (CSO) in several African countries on a range of technology capacity building projects. Caitlin holds a Bachelor of Arts in Computer Science from McGill University and a Master of Arts in Educational Technology from Concordia University, Canada.

Robin Blom is a Doctoral Student in the Media and Information Studies program at Michigan State University. He has served as a teaching and research assistant for the School of Journalism, and has been a fellow in the Interdisciplinary and Inquiry Teaching (IIT) program. He has earned his Bachelor's degree at the Hogeschool van Utrecht, The Netherlands (Journalism, 2004), and a Master's degree at Point Park University, Pittsburgh, PA (Journalism and Mass Communication, 2007). He also attended San Francisco State University and the State University of New York, New Paltz, as an exchange student. Robin has been a reporter for several national and regional newspapers in The Netherlands and the United States, and has written extensively about local politics, alcohol and drug addiction, and prosecution of drug dealers, among a variety of other topics.

Brian J. Bowe is a veteran journalist, author, and educator whose work examines the interplay of journalism and culture. His research probes media framing and agenda setting, the use of social media in political organizing, and news coverage of Muslims. Bowe is a fourth-year Ph.D. student in Michigan State University's Media and Information Studies program. In 2010, he co-produced the award-winning short documentary *The Death of an Imam*. He will spend 2012-13 teaching and conducting research in France as a Graduate Fellow at CELSA – Université Paris-Sorbonne. He was previously a Visiting Assistant Professor of Journalism at Grand Valley State University. Bowe has written extensively about music and has published books about The Ramones, The Clash, and Judas Priest and co-edited the anthology *CREEM: America's Only Rock 'n' Roll Magazine.* Bowe earned a B.A. (Journalism) and a M.S. (Communications) at Grand Valley State University.

Jacques Bughin, Ph.D, is Director of McKinsey and Company. Since joining in 1992, he has worked on more than 600 projects, mostly in Telecom, Media, and Technology. Dr. Bughin has worked for various companies in the domain of the Internet. This includes a strategic analysis of the search market; deployment of e-commerce including social media features optimization; and OTT video strategy for a major audio-visual group. He is a frequent speaker at worldwide conferences (such as NAB, Midem, INMA, ITU, the Internet Society, etc.) and has both Master degree and Ph.D. in Economics with summa cum laude He has published many business articles, quoted in the *Financial Times, Forbes,* and *Newsweek.* His McKinsey Quarterly articles, include: "Black-Scholes meets Seinfeld," "Home is Where the Network Is," "Reversing the Digital Slide," "A New Way to Measure World of Mouth," "How Companies Can Make the Most of User Generated Content," "The Next Step In Open Innovation," "How Companies are Marketing On-Line," "Building the Web 2.0 Enterprise," "Clouds, Big Data, And Smart Assets: 10 Tech-Enabled Trends To Watch," "How Poor Metrics Undermine Digital Marketing." He has published about 50 articles in leading international academic journals such as *Management Science, the Review of Economics and Statistics, the Journal of Industrial Economics,* and *the Journal of the European Economic Association.* He has co-authored a book titled *Managing Media Companies: Harnessing Creativity* (with A. Aris), Wiley, 2010 (two editions). He is a fellow of the Aspen Institute as well as of the ECAREQ, a think-thank on economic policy in Belgium; and a fellow of the Applied Economics of the KUL University, he co-leads the McKinsey Advisory Board on Media Management at INSEAD.

Helena Bukvova is a Lecturer and Researcher at the Technische Universität Dresden. She holds a Doctoral degree in Business Economics, especially information systems. She has extensive experience with the implementation of virtual collaborative learning in higher education practice. She is interested in research on e-collaboration both in education and in corporate settings. She has carried out research in the areas of Web 2.0 and Social Software, Digital Identity, and Self-Presentation.

Robert A. Cropf is Chair of the Department of Public Policy Studies at Saint Louis University and Professor of Public Policy. Some recent publications include "The Prospects for eGovernment and eGovernance in Zambia," co-authored with Joshua Nyirenda, "Creating an Accelerated Joint BA-MPA Degree Program for Adult Learners," co-authored with Jennifer Giancola, and "E-Government in Saudi Arabia: Between Promise and Reality," co-authored with Maher Al-Fakhri et al. His textbook, *Public Administration in the 21ˢᵗ Century* was published by Pearson-Longman in 2007. Two other books of his were published in 2011: *The Public Administration Casebook* (co-edited with Jennifer Giancola), by Pearson-Longman, and *Information Communication Technology and Virtual Public Spheres* (co-edited with Scott Krummenacher) published by IGI Global. His research interests include urban government and politics, eGovernment and eGovernance, public administration pedagogical theory, and local public finance issues.

Alessia D'Andrea received the M.S. degree in Communication Science at the University of Rome "La Sapienza," Italy in 2006 and the Ph.D. degree in Multimedia Communication from the University of Udine in 2011. She is currently a young researcher with the Institute of Research on Population and Social Policies of the National Research Council of Italy in Rome. She is mainly interested in Communication Science, Social Networks, Virtual Communities, Human-Machine-Interaction, Health Studies, and Risk Management. She is author of more than 20 papers on international conferences and international books. She was reviewer of some papers for the *Multimedia Tools and APplications (MTAP) Journal* and for the *Handbook E-Novation for Competitive Advantage in Collaborative Globalization: Technologies for Emerging E-Business Strategies.*

Fernando Ferri received the degree in Electronic Engineering in 1990 and the Ph.D. in Medical Informatics at the University of Rome "La Sapienza" in 1993. He is Senior Researcher of the National Research Council of Italy since 2001. He was Researcher from 1990 to 2001. He was Contract Professor from 1993 to 2000 of "Sistemi di Elaborazione" at the University of Macerata. He is author of more than 160 papers on international journals, books, and conferences. He has coordinated and participated in several national and international research projects. He has organized several international events such as scientific conferences and workshops and special issues as guest editor on international journals. He is member of some program committees of international workshops and conferences, and member of the editorial board of some international journals. His main research areas of interest are: social informatics, social computing, social networks, data and knowledge bases, human-machine interaction, user-machine natural interaction, multimodal interaction, Web 2.0 and Web 3.0, Internet of the future, user modelling, visual interaction, sketch-based interfaces, geographic information systems, risk management, and medical informatics.

Luciano V. Flores is a Ph.D. Student in Computer Science at the Federal University of Rio Grande do Sul (UFRGS), Brazil. He is member of the Computer Music Group (LCM) at UFRGS, and member and co-founder of the Ubiquitous Music Group (G-Ubimus). His areas of interest are human-computer interaction, computer music, mobile music, ubiquitous music, and computers in education.

Itana Maria de Souza Gimenes is a Full Professor of Software Engineering at the Universidade Estadual de Maringá, Paraná, Brazil. She did post-doctoral research at The Open University, UK, in 2011, which focused on learning design applied to software engineering. She also did post-doctoral research at the School of Computer Science, University of Waterloo, ON, Canada, in 2005, which focused on software product lines. She has a PhD in Computer Science from the University of York, Department of Computer Science, UK (1992). She was the President of the Brazilian Computer Society (SBC) Committee of Software Engineering (CEES) in

2007-2008 and 1998-1999. She is currently a member of the National Institute for Safety Critical Embedded System, a strategic project of CNPq coordinated by the ICMC/USP. Current research interests include: software product line, component-based development, workflow management systems and business process management, and software engineering education.

Jose Alcides Gobbo Jr. obtained his Bachelor degree in Economics (São Paulo State University – UNESP, 1995), Masters in Production Engineering (Methodist University of Piracicaba – UNIMEP, 1999), and PhD in Business Administration, with emphasis in operations management (Fundação Getúlio Vargas – FGV, 2004). He was Visiting Researcher in the Department of Packaging Logistics, University of Lund, Sweden (2008-2010). Currently, he is Associate Professor at Faculty of Engineering (FEB), São Paulo State University – UNESP, where he coordinates the Graduate Program in Production Engineering. Dr. Gobbo is ad-hoc advisor of research agencies and journals in the subject area. His interest's lies in the field of operations management, with emphasis on the following subjects: innovation, innovation networks, logistics and packaging, business networks, supply chain management, and operations strategy.

Patrizia Grifoni received the degree in Electronic Engineering in 1990 at the University of Rome "La Sapienza." She is Researcher at the Institute of Research on Population and Social Policies of the National Research Council of Italy since 1990. She has been contract Professor from 1993 to 2000 of "Image processing" at the University of Macerata. She is author of more than 130 papers on international journals, books, and conferences. She is leading and participating in several national and international research projects. She has experience in organizing several international scientific workshops and special issues as guest editor on international journals. She is member of some program committees of international workshops and conferences, and member of the editorial board of some international journals. Her main research areas of interest are: social informatics, social computing, social networks, human-machine interaction, multimodal interaction, sketch-based interfaces, multimedia applications, user modeling, data and knowledge bases, geographic information systems, risk management, Web 2.0 and Web 3.0, Internet of the future, GIS, social networks.

Tomislav Grubisic is an Internet Entrepreneur and a Co-Founder of iSTUDIO, the leading CEE social media digital agency. Tomislav was part of numerous projects in important Croatian Internet company mojPosao before he started iSTUDIO in 2009 with Daniel Ackermann. Tomislav always combined his passion for Internet products that enable people to work more easily and fascination with analytics and big data. He works on iSTUDIO's projects socialnumbers.com (social analytics tool), mediatoolkit.com (media analytics tool), and socialpuzzle (Facebook generic applications). He is interested in software development, product creation, company organization, and entrepreneurship.

Joan E. Hughes is an Associate Professor of Learning Technologies in the College of Education at The University of Texas at Austin. Her research examines preservice and inservice teachers' development of technological knowledge and practice of technology integration in content areas (see http://www.techedges.org). She currently leads a longitudinal study of laptop computing in preservice teacher education. She also generates case studies of school technology integration and is conducting an ethnography of high school iPad immersion, both by examining the intersections of technology leadership, teacher knowledge, and technology use among students in and out of school. Her recent publications are in *Educational Researcher*, *Educational Technology*, and *American Journal of Distance Education*. Dr. Hughes has 18 years of educational experience across elementary, middle school, and university levels. She earned her Ph.D. in Educational Psychology at Michigan State University.

Morris Kalliny is currently an Assistant Professor of Marketing at Saint Louis University. Dr. Kalliny earned a Ph.D. in International Business and Marketing from The University of Texas – Pan American. Prior to joining Saint Louis University, he served as the Business Program Director at Missouri University of Science and Technology. Professor Kalliny has written extensively about the Arab culture with a particular focus on advertising and media. Dr. Kalliny's research has appeared in many scholarly journals such as the *Journal of Advertising Research*, the *Journal of Global Marketing*, the *Multinational Business Review*, the *Journal of Marketing Communications*, the *Journal of Current Issues and Research in Advertising*, *Journal of Promotion Management*, *International Journal of Cross Cultural Management*, and many more.

Damián Keller (DMA, Stanford University, 2004; MFA, Simon Fraser University, 1999) teaches Music and Computing at the Federal University of Acre (UFAC), Brazil. Member and Co-Founder of the Ubiquitous Music Group (g-ubimus), his research focuses on everyday creativity, software design, and ecocomposition within the context of ubiquitous music making. His work at the Amazon Center for Music Research – NAP (2003) has been acknowledged by the CNPq with a research productivity grant (2008-2012).

Nermin Khalifa holds a PhD degree in Engineering and Information Science (2010) from Middlesex University, London, UK. Nermin has been specialised in e-buiness, e-commerce application, and supply chain management. She has experience in ERP systems as a SAP-certified business associate. She is working as Assistant Professor in Business Information System, AAST, Egypt, since 2000. She has a good record of teaching MIS and e-Commerce majors. She has many publications in the field of e-commerce, e-supply chain, enterprise resource planning, system dynamic and simulation, RFID, and global supply chain. These publications have been published in international conferences, well-known journals, and book chapters. Dr. Nermin has a good record of reviewing activities in international conferences, journals, and book chapters, such as *Journal of Supply Chain Management*, International Conferences on Operations and Supply Chain Management, IBIMA Conferences, IADIS Conferences.

Ignac Lovrek is with the Faculty of Electrical Engineering and Computing of the University of Zagreb, where he works as a Professor at the Department of Tele-communications. He authored and co-authored over one hundred papers published in books, journals, and conference proceedings. His research interests include electronic services market, software agent theory and applications in communication networks and information services, call and service modelling and processing, and soft technologies for telecommunications. He is a member of IEEE, ACM, GI – Special Interest Group on Petri Nets, and KES International.

Sergio Ricardo Mazini obtained his Bachelor degree in Information Systems (FATEB, 1996), Post Graduate in Analysis, Development and Project Management Systems (UNILINS, 2000), and he is Master in Production Engineering (São Paulo State University – UNESP, 2011). He is a Professor of Business Administration and Information Systems courses. He acts, also, as a Consultant and Systems Analyst at Orion Management Solutions. He has experience in business consulting, business management, development of information systems, innovation management, knowledge management, and enterprise portals.

Evandro Manara Miletto is an Associate Professor at the Federal Institute of Education, Science, and Technology of Rio Grande do Sul (IFRS), Porto Alegre Campus, Brazil. He is member of the Computer Music Group (LCM) at UFRGS. Prof. Miletto received his Master's and PhD degrees in Computer Science at the Federal University of Rio Grande do Sul (UFRGS), in 2005 and 2009, respectively. Since 2002, he has conducted multidisciplinary research on topics such as computer music, HCI, and CSCW. He is a member of the technical committee of Brazilian

Symposium on Computer Music (SBCM) as well as the Brazilian Symposium on Computers in Education (SBIE). His research is currently based on networked music, and focuses on novice users.

Agus Mutohar is a graduate (M.A.) of Learning Technologies at the University of Texas at Austin where he studied, after receiving a prestigious scholarship from Ford Foundation International Fellowship Program. His research focuses on technology integration in primary and secondary education in Indonesia and the use of new media in Indonesian education. He has presented at international conferences such as SITE (Society for Information Technology and Teacher Education) on a variety of topics related to technology integration, particularly in Indonesian context.

José Martí-Pareño (PhD, Polytechnic University of Valencia, Spain) is Associate Professor in the Department of Business, Faculty of Social Sciences, Universidad Europea de Madrid. His main research areas include marketing communications, mobile marketing, and new advertising formats, such as branded content and advergaming. His research has been published in refereed journals such as *Journal of Brand Management*. He has authored and co-authored seven books including *Engagement Marketing* (Financial Times/Prentice Hall, 2008).

Nuddy Pillay lectures and researches in a range of topics in the communication and elearning areas and continues to ensure his students are advantaged by his knowledge of organisational communication and his skills in using it for the purpose of technology solutions. After a successful career in South Africa, where he served as Head of Department at a College of Education and then as Operations and Management Consultant for a national private education company, he moved to New Zealand. Nuddy Pillay's first professional post in New Zealand was as Director of a private tutoring company. After two years, Nuddy moved to Macleans College to lead the integration of technologies into classroom teaching. After winning the Computerworld Excellence Award in 2003, Nuddy moved to Manukau Institute of Technology to apply his knowledge and skills to prepare students to occupy their places in media rich organisations. Nuddy Pillay continues to progress his passion for effective communication using digital media in the workplace and in education.

Marcelo S. Pimenta is an Associate Professor at Institute of Informatics (INF), Federal University of Rio Grande do Sul (UFRGS), in Brazil. He is head of LCM, the INF-UFRGS Computer Music Laboratory. He received his PhD in Informatique at Université Toulouse 1, France, in 1997 and the Bachelor and Master's degree in Computer Science at UFRGS in 1988 and 1991, respectively. Since 1998, he is member of a multidisciplinary research group at UFRGS working with topics in human-computer interaction, software engineering, and computer music with emphasis in the integration of these areas. Member and Co-Founder of the Ubiquitous Music Group (g-ubimus), currently his research within the context of ubiquitous music making focuses on novice-oriented creativity tools, networked music, and interaction patterns for music environments.

Vedran Podobnik is an Assistant Professor at the Department of Telecommunications of the Faculty of Electrical Engineering and Computing, University of Zagreb. He received M.Eng. (2006, Electrical Engineering) and Ph.D. (2010, Computer Science) degrees from the Faculty of Electrical Engineering and Computing, University of Zagreb. He currently specializes in Technology Policy at the Judge Business School, University of Cambridge. His research interests include social technologies, multi-agent systems, electronic markets, context-aware services, and business process automation. He co-authored over 50 scientific and professional papers as book chapters and articles in encyclopedia, journals, and conference proceedings. He is a member of IEEE and KES International associations.

Carla Ruiz-Mafé (PhD, University of Valencia) is Associate Professor of Marketing at the University of Valencia. Her research interests include consumer behaviour, business-to-business marketing, and direct marketing. She is particularly interested in the study of online consumer behaviour. She has published papers in *Internet Research, Online Information Review, Industrial Management and Data Systems, The Services Industries Journal, Journal of Service Management, Journal of Air Transport Management*, and the best Spanish refereed journals. She has presented papers at several conferences organised by the European Marketing Academy.

Silvia Sanz-Blas (PhD in Business and Economics, Universitat de València, Spain) is Associate Professor in the Department of Marketing, Faculty of Economics, Universitat de València. Her primary research interests include communication, sales, e-commerce, interactive marketing, and consumer behavior, and it has been published in *Internet Research, Online Information Review, Journal of Electronic Commerce Research, Journal of Consumer Behavior, Journal of Consumer Marketing, Journal of Vacation Marketing,* and the best Spanish refereed journals. At the same time, she has presented numerous papers at AM, AMS, and EMAC Conferences.

Eric Schoop is head of the Chair of Business Informatics, especially Information Management, at the Faculty of Business Management and Economics, Technische Universität Dresden, Germany, since 1993. In 1983, he graduated as Diplom-Volkswirt in Heidelberg, in 1987 as Dr. rer. pol. in Bamberg, and in 1993 as Dr. rer. pol. habil. in Würzburg. Main topics in research, teaching, and related project work are blended learning, knowledge management and knowledge-based collaborations in the Enterprise 2.0. As former Dean of Study Affairs and current Head of the Business Informatics study program and eLearning Representative of the faculty, his activities in academic self-administration focus on quality assurance and improvement of higher education teaching and learning processes by means of complex blended learning and virtual classroom arrangements.

Garron Stevenson obtained his BCom (Hons) degree from the University of Cape Town. This research into corporate micro-blogging was part of his research project. He has a career history in Internet companies and now works as a Digital Architect driving digital marketing strategy at Sanlam, a leading South African financial services institution. Garron also volunteer lectures in eMarketing at TSiBA, a not-for profit business school.

Wissam Tawileh holds a Bachelor of Science in Engineering from Damascus University and a Master of Science in Information Management and Information Technology from the University of Hildesheim. He is a Research Fellow at the Chair of Business Informatics, especially Information Management of the Technische Universität Dresden in Germany and Manager of the case-study-based Virtual Collaborative Learning Project in the German federal state of Saxony "Fallstudienverbund" funded by the European Social Fund (ESF). In addition to modern e-learning concepts and applications, his main area of interest within the domain of Information and Communication Technologies for Development (ICT4D), is know-how transfer of using modern technologies to support educational and national development in developing countries. He published and presented multiple research papers and served as a technical program committee member in several international academic conferences.

Guilheme Gregianin Testa is graduated in Computer Science at the Federal University of Rio Grande do Sul (UFRGS), where he researched Software Engineering for Web. Currently, he is finishing his Master's at UFRGS with the support of the National Council for Scientific and Technological Development (CNPq), where conduct researches involving software engineering and computer music, focusing in recommender systems and social matching.

Dimitrios I Tseles is Professor of Automation Department of Technology Education Institute (TEI) of Piraeus, Athens. He has a B.Sc in Physics, M.Sc in Electronic Control, M.Sc in Electronics and Communication Systems, and a PhD in Control Systems. He is the Chair and Founder of the Annual eRA (International Scientific Conference for the Contribution of Information Technology to Science, Economy,

Society, and Education). He is the publisher of two scientific books (CAD/DAM and Data Acquisition Systems) for tertiary education, several books about technical subjects, and notebooks for postgraduate students. He has also published widely in international scientific journals. He has also presented and published in many scientific conferences. He has led many inter-institutional collaborations including with University of the West of Scotland (when it was University of Paisley).

Abel Usoro lectures in the School of Computing, University of the West of Scotland, UK. His current research interests are information systems, which include knowledge management, e-learning, and tourism. He has published book chapters, in refereed international conferences, and journals (such as *International Journal of Global Information Management* and *International Journal of Knowledge Management*). His academic work and research have taken him to countries in Africa, Europe, Asia, North and South America. He is Editor-in-Chief of *Computing and Information Systems Journal*, Associate Editor of *JEDMIFM*, and member of editorial boards of other international journals. He is a member of scientific committees of many international conferences and chairs one of them (Conference on Information Technology and Economic Development). He is also a member of the British Computing Society and the lead editor of *Leveraging Developing Economies with the Use of Information Technology* published by IGI Global.

Jean-Paul Van Belle is a Professor in the Department of Information Systems at the University of Cape Town. He has authored or co-authored about 20 books/chapters, 20 journal articles, and more than 80 peer-reviewed published conference papers. His key research area is the social and organisational adoption of emerging information technologies in a developing world context. The key technologies researched include e-commerce, m-commerce, e/m-government, open source software, social networking, and cloud computing.

Vasileios Yfantis holds a BA honors degree in Marketing from the Technological Education Institute of Athens and an MSc in Information Technology with Web Technology from the University of the West of Scotland. Mr. Yfantis is currently employed within the Greek Government in a position that is related to the use of ICT for the citizens' service. He has also been a freelance journalist for more than 15 years by contributing content to both electronic and printed media. As a researcher, he has presented conference papers in both Europe and Africa and is co-author of the book *Leveraging Developing Economies with the Use of Information Technology: Trends and Tools* (IGI Global). The main areas of his research interests feature information communications technology, e-tourism, digital divide in developing countries, e-government, and the digital entertainment industry.

Index